COMIC
BOOK
PRICE GUIDE
COMPANION

THE OFFICIAL

OVERSTREET

COMIC BOOK

PRICE GUIDE
COMPANION

By
ROBERT M. OVERSTREET

FIFTH EDITION

HOUSE OF COLLECTIBLES • NEW YORK

Important Notice. All of the information, including valuations, in this book has been compiled from the most reliable sources, and every effort has been made to eliminate errors and questionable data. Nevertheless, the possibility of error, in a work of such immense scope, always exists. The publisher will not be held responsible for losses which may occur in the purchase, sale, or other transaction of items because of information contained herein. Readers who feel they have discovered errors are invited to *write* and inform us, so they may be corrected in subsequent editions. Those seeking further information on the topics covered in this book are advised to refer to the complete line of *Official Price Guides* published by the House of Collectibles.

 This is a registered trademark of Random House, Inc.

© 1991 by Robert Overstreet

Cover artwork ™ and © 1991 by Marvel Entertainment Group, Inc. All rights reserved.

All rights reserved under International and Pan-American Copyright Conventions.

Published by: House of Collectibles
            201 East 50th Street
            New York, New York 10022

Distributed by Ballantine Books, a division of Random House, Inc., New York, and simultaneously in Canada by Random House of Canada Limited, Toronto.

Manufactured in the United States of America

Library of Congress Catalog Card Number: 88-647216

ISBN: 0-876-37868-8

Fifth edition: November 1991

10 9 8 7 6 5 4 3 2 1

TABLE OF
CONTENTS

ACKNOWLEDGMENTS

COMIC BOOKS

Larry Bigman (Frazetta-Williamson data); Glenn Bray (Kurtzman data); Gary Carter (DC data); J. B. Clifford Jr. (E. C. data); Gary Coddington (Superman data); Wilt Conine (Fawcett data); Al Dellinges (Kubert data); R. C. Holland and Ron Pussell (Seduction and Parade of Pleasure data); Grant Irwin (Quality data); Richard Kravitz (Kelly data); Phil Levine (giveaway data); Fred Nardelli (Frazetta data); Michelle Nolan (love comics); Mike Nolan (MLJ, Timely, Nedor data); George Olshevsky (Timely data); Richard Olson (LOA data); Scott Pell ('50s data); Greg Robertson (National data); Frank Scigliano (Little Lulu data); Gene Seger (Buck Rogers data); Rick Sloane (Archie data); David R. Smith, Archivist, Walt Disney Productions (Disney data); Mike Tiefenbacher, Jerry Sinkovec, and Richard Yudkin (Atlas and National data); Jim Vadeboncoeur Jr. (Williamson and Atlas data); Kim Weston (Disney and Barks data); and Andrew Zerbe and Gary Behymer (M. E. data).

My appreciation must also be extended to Ron Pussell, Bruce Hamilton, Steve Geppi, Jon Warren, James Payette, Joe Vereneault, Jay Maybruck, John Verzyl, Terry Stroud, Hugh O'Kennon, John Snyder, Walter Wang, Gary Carter and Gary Colabuono for pricing research; to Tom Inge for his "Chronology of the American Comic Book"; and to Mark Bagley for his outstanding cover art.

BIG LITTLE BOOKS

Special thanks is due Harry B. Thomas for his advice and guidance both in pricing and data presentation; to Bruce Hamilton for his decades of support and knowledge in this field, and to the following people who contributed much needed data for this edition: Mike Tickal, Alan J. Soprych Jr. and Jon Warren.

An Overview
to
Comic Book
Collecting

INTRODUCTION

Comic book values listed in this reference work were recorded from convention sales, dealers' lists, adzines, and by special contact with dealers and collectors from coast to coast. Prices paid for rare comics vary considerably from one locale to another. We have attempted to list a realistic average between the lowest and highest range observed. The reader should keep in mind that the prices listed only reflect the market just prior to publication. Any new trends that have developed since the preparation of this book would not be shown.

The values listed are reports, not estimates. Each new edition of the guide is actually an average report of sales that occurred during the year; not an estimate of what we feel the books will be bringing next year. Even though many prices listed will remain current throughout the year, the wise user of this book would keep abreast of current market trends to get the fullest potential out of his invested dollar.

All titles are listed as if they were one word, ignoring spaces, hyphens and apostrophes. Page counts listed will always include covers.

IMPORTANT. Prices listed in this book are in U. S. currency and are for your reference only. This book is not a dealer's price list, although some dealers may base their prices on the values listed. The true value of any comic book is what you are willing to pay. Prices listed herein are an indication of what collectors (not dealers) would probably pay. For one reason or another, these collectors might want certain books badly, or else need specific issues to complete their runs and so are willing to pay more. Dealers are not in a position to pay the full prices listed, but work on a percentage depending largely on the amount of investment required and the quality of material offered. Usually they will pay from 20 to 70 percent of the list price depending on how long it will take them to sell the collection after making the investment; the higher the demand and better the condition, the more the percentage. Most dealers are faced with expenses such as advertising, travel, telephone and mailing, plus convention costs. These costs all go in before the books are sold. The high demand books usually sell right away but there are many other titles that are difficult to sell due to low demand. Sometimes a dealer will have cost tied up in this type of material for several years before finally moving it. Remember, his position is that of handling, demand and overhead. Most dealers are victims of these economics.

Everyone connected with the publication of this book advocates the collecting of comic books for fun and pleasure, as well as for nostalgia, art, and cultural values. Second to this is investment, which, if wisely placed in the best quality books (condition and contents considered), will yield dividends over the long term.

GRADING COMIC BOOKS

Before a comic book's true value can be assessed, its condition or state of preservation must be determined. In most comic books, the better the condition, the more desirable the book. The scarcer first and/or origin issues in MINT condition will bring several times the price of the same book in POOR condition. The grading of a comic book is done by simply looking at the book and describing its condition, which may range from absolutely perfect newsstand condition (MINT) to extremely worn, dirty, and torn (POOR). Numerous variables influence the evaluation of a comic's condition and all must be considered in the final evaluation. More important characteristics include tears, missing pieces, wrinkles, stains, yellowing, brittleness, tape repairs, water marks, spine roll, writing, and cover lustre. The significance of each of these is described more fully in the grading scale definitions. Whenever in doubt, consult with a reputable dealer or experienced collector in your area. The following grading guide is given to aid the panelologist.

MINT (M): Absolutely perfect in every way, regardless of age. No printing defects are allowed. The cover has full original gloss, is crisp, cut square with sharp corners and shows no imperfections of any sort. Minute color fading is allowed. The cover and all pages are creamy white and fresh; the spine is tight, flat, and clean with no stress lines; not even the slightest blemish can be detected around staples, along spine and edges or at corners. Arrival dates pencilled on the cover are usually acceptable so long as they are very small. When the surface of the front and back covers is held to the light, not the slightest wear, indentations, wrinkles or defects of any kind can be observed. As comics must be truly perfect to be in this grade, they are obviously extremely scarce and seldom are offered for sale. Books prior to 1970 in this grade can and usually do bring above guide prices.

NEAR MINT (NM): Nearly perfect. Upon close inspection, one or possibly two very tiny imperfections can be found. Often these imperfections are noticed only when holding the surface of the front and back covers under bright light. Possibly a tiny (1/16 inch) color flake missing at a staple, corner or edge. Or, a tiny (1/16 inch) spine tear is permitted if no other defects are observed. No crease of any kind. Near perfect cover gloss retained. Not more than three very tiny stress lines along the spine may be present. Pages and covers should be creamy to white, not yellow or brown. No color touch-up, repair or restoration of any kind is allowed in this grade. No printing defects are allowed. This grade is also very rare in books prior to 1970.

VERY FINE (VF): An excellent copy with outstanding eye appeal. Sharp, bright, clean and glossy with supple pages. Slight wear beginning to show; possibly 5 or 6 tiny wrinkles or stress lines at staples or along spine where cover has been opened a few times; still clean and flat with 80 percent of cover gloss retained. Pages and covers can be yellowish/tannish (at the least) but not brown and will usually be creamy to white. 4 or 5 tiny color flakes are acceptable. One 1/4 inch corner crease on an otherwise exceptional copy is permitted. Very minor restoration or repair is not allowed in this grade unless it is specifically noted and described. Comics in this grade are normally the highest grade offered for sale and often books graded higher are misgraded VFs.

FINE (FN): An exceptional, above average copy that shows minor wear, but still relatively flat, clean and glossy with no subscription crease, writing on cover (except an arrival date), brown margins or tape repairs. Typical defects include: Light spine wear, minor surface wear, a light crease (1/4 inch in length), minor yellowing/tanning to interior pages. Still a bright copy with 50 percent cover gloss. A few stress lines around staples and along spine to be expected, but not more than 1/8 inch in length. One small edge chip or several tiny chips are allowed. One minor tear is allowed when on an otherwise FVF copy. Very minor spine roll allowed on an otherwise clean and uncreased copy.

VERY GOOD (VG): The average used comic book most commonly found. Significant wear is obvious with original printing lustre and gloss almost gone; some discoloration or fading, but not soiled. One or two minor markings on covers is permitted as is a minor spine roll. Lightly creased along spine or extremities; a subscription crease is allowed. Cover could have a minor tear or crease where a corner was folded under or a loose center fold. A minor chip or piece missing is allowed when noted. No chunks missing. Pages and inside covers may be brown but not brittle, but would usually be yellowish to creamy. One small tape repair permitted. Still enough eye appeal to be collectible.

GOOD (G): A heavily worn copy but complete. Creased, scuffed, not glossy and soiled. Although a copy in this grade could have white pages and covers, the accumulation of defects such as creases, tears or chips and general wear prevent the book from a higher classification.

FAIR (F): Very heavily read and soiled, but still complete. Damaged beyond collectibility for most collectors, bringing 30 to 50 percent of the Good price.

POOR (p): Damaged; heavily weathered; soiled; or otherwise unsuited for collection purposes. Possibly incomplete or coverless; pages may be missing, bringing 15 to 25 percent of the Good price.

COVERLESS (c): Coverless comics are usually hard to sell and in many cases are worthless.

IMPORTANT: Comics in all grades with fresh extra white pages usually bring more. Books with defects such as pages or panels missing, coupons cut, torn or taped covers and pages, brown or brittle pages, restapled, taped spines, pages or covers, watermarked, printing defects, rusted staples, stained, holed, or other imperfections that distract from the original beauty, are worth less than if free of these defects.

Many of the early strip reprint comics were printed in hardback with dust jackets. Books with dust jackets are worth more. The value can increase from 20 to 50 percent depending on the rarity of book. Usually, the earlier the book, the greater the percentage. Unless noted, prices listed are without dust jackets. The condition of the dust jacket should be graded independently of the book itself.

STORAGE OF
COMIC BOOKS

Acids left in comic book paper during manufacture are the primary cause of aging and yellowing. Improper storage can accelerate the aging process.

The importance of storage is proven when looking at the condition of books from large collections that have surfaced over the past few years. In some cases, an entire collection has brown or yellowed pages approaching brittleness. Collections of this type were probably stored in too much heat or moisture, or exposed to atmospheric pollution (sulfur dioxide) or light. On the other hand, other collections of considerable age (30 to 50 years) have emerged with snow white pages and little sign of aging. Thus we learn that proper storage is imperative to insure the long life of our comic book collections.

Store books in a dark, cool place with an ideal relative humidity of 50 percent and a temperature of 40 to 50 degrees or less. Air conditioning is recommended. Do not use regular cardboard boxes, since most contain harmful acids. Use acidfree boxes instead. Seal books in Mylar (Mylar is a registered trademark of the DuPont Company) or other suitable wrappings or bags and store them in the proper containers or cabinets, to protect them from heat, excessive dampness, ultraviolet light (use tungsten filament lights), polluted air, and dust.

Many collectors seal their books in plastic bags and store them in a cool dark room in cabinets or on shelving. Plastic bags should be changed every two to three years, since most contain harmful acids. Cedar chest storage is recommended, but the ideal method of storage is to stack your comics (preferably in Mylar bags) vertically in acid-free boxes. The boxes can be arranged on shelving for easy access. Storage boxes, plastic bags, backing boards, Mylar bags, archival supplies, etc., are available from dealers.

HOW TO START
COLLECTING

Most collectors of comic books begin by buying new issues in mint condition directly off the newsstand or from their local comic store. (Subscription copies are available from several mail-order services.) Each week new comics appear on the stands that are destined to become true collectors items. The trick is to locate a store that carries a complete line of comics. In several localities this may be difficult. Most panelologists frequent several magazine stands in order not to miss something they want. Even then, it pays to keep in close contact with collectors in other areas. Sooner or later, nearly every collector has to rely upon a friend in Fandom to obtain for him an item that is unavailable locally.

Before you buy any comic to add to your collection, you should carefully inspect its condition. Unlike stamps and coins, defective comics are generally not highly prized. The cover should be properly cut and printed. Remember that every blemish or sign of wear depreciates the beauty and value of your comics.

The serious panelologist usually purchases extra copies of popular titles. He may trade these multiples for items unavailable locally (for example, foreign comics), or he may store the multiples for resale at some future date. Such speculation is, of course, a gamble, but unless collecting trends change radically in the future, the value of certain comics in mint condition should appreciate greatly, as new generations of readers become interested in collecting.

COLLECTING
BACK ISSUES

In addition to current issues, most panelologists want to locate back issues. Some energetic collectors have had great success in running down large hoards of rare comics in their home towns. Occasionally, rare items can be located through agencies that collect old papers and magazines, such as the Salvation Army. The lucky collector can often buy these items for much less than their current market value. Placing advertisements in trade journals, newspapers, etc., can also produce good results. However, don't be discouraged if you are neither energetic nor lucky. Most panelologists build their collections slowly but systematically by placing mail orders with dealers and other collectors.

Comics of early vintage are extremely expensive if they are purchased through a regular dealer or collector, and unless you have unlimited funds to invest in your hobby, you will find it necessary to restrict your collecting in certain ways. However you define your collection, you should be careful to set your goals well within your means.

PROPER HANDLING OF
COMIC BOOKS

Before picking up an old, rare comic book, caution should be exercised to handle it properly. Old comic books are very fragile and can be easily damaged. Because of this, many dealers hesitate to let customers personally handle their rare comics. They would prefer to remove the comic from its bag and show it to the customer themselves. In this way, if the book is damaged, it would be the dealer's responsibility—not the customer's. Remember, the slightest crease or chip could render an otherwise Mint book to Near Mint or even Very Fine. The following steps are provided to aid the novice in the proper handling of comic books: 1. Remove the comic from its protective sleeve or bag very carefully. 2. Gently lay the comic (unopened) in the palm of your hand so that it will stay relatively flat and secure. 3. You can now leaf through the book by carefully rolling or flipping the pages with the thumb and forefinger of your other hand. Caution: Be sure the book always remains relatively flat or slightly rolled. Avoid creating stress points on the covers with your fingers and be particularly cautious in bending covers back too far on Mint books. 4. After examining the book, carefully insert it back into the bag or protective sleeve. Watch corners and edges for folds or tears as you replace the book.

TERMINOLOGY

Many of the following terms and abbreviations are used in the comic book market and are explained here:

a—Story art;**a(i)**—Story art inks; **a(p)**—Story art pencils; **a(r)**—Story art reprint.

B&W—Black and white art.

Bondage cover—Usually denotes a female in bondage.

c—Cover art; **c(i)**—Cover inks; **c(p)**—Cover pencils; **c(r)**—Cover reprint.

Cameo—When a character appears briefly in one or two panels.

Colorist—Artist that applies color to the pen and ink art.

Con—A Convention or public gathering of fans.

Cosmic Aeroplane—Refers to a large collection discovered by Cosmic Aeroplane Books.

Debut—The first time that a character appears anywhere.

Drug propaganda story—Where comic makes an editorial stand about drug abuse.

Drug use story—Shows the actual use of drugs: shooting, taking a trip, harmful effects, etc.

Fanzine—An amateur fan publication.

File Copy—A high grade comic originating from the publisher's file.

First app.—Same as debut.

Flashback—When a previous story is being recalled.

G. A.—Golden Age (1930s–1950s).

Headlight—Protruding breasts.

i—Art inks.

Infinity cover—Shows a scene that repeats itself to infinity.

Inker—Artist that does the inking.

Intro—Same as debut.

JLA—Justice League of America.

JSA—Justice Society of America.

Lamont Larson—Refers to a large high grade collection of comics. Many of the books have Lamont or Larson written on the cover.

Logo—The title of a strip or comic book as it appears on the cover or title page.

Mile High—Refers to a large NM-Mint collection of comics originating from Denver, Colorado (Edgar Church collection).

nd—No date.

nn—No number.

N. Y. Legis. Comm.—New York Legislative Committee to Study the Publication of Comics (1951).

Origin—When the story of the character's creation is given.

p—Art pencils.

Penciler—Artist that does the pencils.

POP—Parade of Pleasure, book about the censorship of comics.

Poughkeepsie—Refers to a large collection of Dell Comics' "file copies" believed to have originated from Poughkeepsie, NY.

R or r—Reprint.

Rare—10 to 20 copies estimated to exist.

Reprint comics—Comic books that contain newspaper strip reprints.

S. A.—Silver Age (1956–1969).

Scarce—20 to 100 copies estimated to exist.

Silver proof—A black & white actual size print on thick glossy paper given to the colorist to indicate colors to the engraver.

S&K—Simon and Kirby (artists).

SOTI—Seduction of the Innocent, book about the censorship of comics.

Splash panel—A large panel that usually appears at the front of a comic story.

Very rare—1 to 10 copies estimated to exist.

X-over—When one character crosses over into another's strip.

Zine—See Fanzine.

HOW TO SELL
YOUR COMICS

If you have a collection of comics for sale, large or small, the following steps should be taken. (1) Make a detailed list of the books for sale, being careful to grade them accurately, showing any noticeable defects; i.e., torn or missing pages, centerfolds, etc. (2) Decide whether to sell or trade wholesale to a dealer all in one lump or to go through the long laborious process of advertising and selling piece by piece to collectors. Both have their advantages and disadvantages.

In selling to dealers, you will get the best price by letting everything go at once—the good with the bad—all for one price. Simply select names either from ads in this book or from some of the adzines mentioned below. Send them your list and ask for bids. The bids received will vary depending on the demand, rarity and condition of the books you have. The more in demand, and better the condition, the higher the bids will be.

On the other hand, you could become a "dealer" and sell the books yourself. Order a copy of one or more of the adzines. Take note how most dealers lay out their ads. Type up your ad copy, carefully pricing each book (using the Guide as a reference). Send finished ad copy with payment to adzine editor to be run. You will find that certain books will sell at once while others will not sell at all. The ad will probably have to be retyped, remaining books repriced, and run again. Price books according to how fast you want them to move. If you try to get top dollar, expect a much longer period of time. Otherwise, the better deal you give the collector, the faster they will move. Remember, in being your own dealer, you will have overhead expenses in postage, mailing supplies and advertising cost. Some books might even be returned for refund due to misgrading, etc.

In selling all at once to a dealer, you get instant cash, immediate profit, and eliminate the long process of running several ads to dispose of the books; but if you have patience, and a small amount of business sense, you could realize more profit selling them directly to collectors yourself.

WHERE TO BUY
AND SELL

Most of the larger cities have comic specialty shops that buy and sell old comic books. *The Comics Buyers Guide*, a weekly tabloid, published by Krause Publications, 700 E. State St., Iola, WI 54997 and *The Comic Book Marketplace*, P. O. Box 180534, Coronado, CA 92178-0534 are the best sources for buying and selling. These publications are full of ads buying and selling comic books. Comic book conventions are now held the year round in most of the larger cities. These conventions are an excellent source for buying and selling comic books. If you are an inexperienced collector, be sure to compare prices before you buy. Never send large sums of cash through the mail. Send money orders or checks for your personal protection. Beware of bargains, as the items advertised sometimes do not exist, but are only a fraud to get your money.

Learn how to grade properly. You will find that dealers vary considerably in how they grade their comics. For your own protection, your first order to a dealer should consist of an inexpensive book as a test of his grading. This initial order will give you a clue as to how the dealer grades as well as the care he takes in packaging his orders and the promptness in which he gets the order to you.

DIRECTORY OF
COMIC AND
NOSTALGIA SHOPS

This is a current up-to-date list, but is not all-inclusive. We cannot assume any responsibility in your dealings with these shops. This list is provided for your information only. When planning your trips, it would be advisable to make appointments in advance.

ALABAMA:

Camelot Books
2201 Quintard Ave.
Anniston, AL 36201
PH:205-236-3474

Wizard's Comics & Cards
324 N. Court St.
Florence, AL 35630
PH:205-236-3474

Discount Comic Book Shop
1301 Noble St.
Anniston, AL 36201
PH:205-238-8373

Sincere Comics
3738 Airport Blvd.
Mobile, AL 36608
PH:205-342-2603

ARIZONA:

FantaCity
1600 McCulloch Blvd., Unit #4-1B
Lake Havasu City, AZ 86403
PH:602-680-4004

Atomic Comics
1318 West Southern #9
Mesa, AZ 85202
PH:602-649-0807

Ed Kalb–Buy + Sell
(Mail Order Only)
1353 S. Los Alamos
Mesa, AZ 85204

AAA Best Comics, Etc.
8336 N. Seventh St. Suite #B-C
Phoenix, AZ 85020
PH:602-997-4012

Lost Dutchman Comics
5805 N. 7th St.
Phoenix, AZ 85014
PH:602-263-5249

All About Books & Comics
517 E. Camelback
Phoenix, AZ 85012
PH:602-277-0757

All About Books & Comics West
4208 W. Dunlap
Phoenix, AZ 85051
PH:602-435-0410

All About Books & Comics III
4000 N. Scottsdale Rd. #102
Scottsdale, AZ 85251
PH:602-994-1812

Planet Comics
10219 N. Scottsdale Rd.
Scottsdale, AZ 85254
PH:602-991-1972

The ONE Book Shop
120-A East University Dr.
Tempe, AZ 85281
PH:602-967-3551

ARKANSAS:

Paperbacks Plus
2207 Rogers Ave.
Fort Smith, AR 72901
PH:501-785-5642

The Comic Book Store
9307 Treasure Hill
Little Rock, AR 72207
PH:501-227-9777

Pie-Eyes
5223 W. 65th St.
Little Rock, AR 72209
PH:501-568-1414

Collector's Edition Comics
5310 MacArthur Dr.
North Little Rock, AR 72118
PH:501-753-2586

TNT Collectors Hut
503 W. Hale Ave.
Osceola, AR 72370
PH:501-563-5760

CALIFORNIA:

Comic Heaven
24 W. Main St.

Alhambra, CA 91801
PH:818-289-3945

Comic Relief
2138 University Ave.
Berkeley, CA 94704
PH:415-843-5002

Comics & Comix, Inc.
2461 Telegraph Ave.
Berkeley, CA 94704
PH:415-845-4091

Fantasy Kingdom
1802 W. Olive Ave.
Burbank, CA 91506
PH:818-954-8432

Book Castle
200 N. San Fernando Blvd.
Burbank, CA 91502
PH:818-845-1563

Movie World
212 N. San Fernando Blvd.
Burbank, CA 91502
PH:818-846-0459

Crush Comics & Cards
2785 Castro Valley Blvd.
Castro Valley, CA 94546
PH:415-581-4779

Collectors Ink
932 W. 8th Ave.
Chico, CA 95926
PH:916-345-0958

New Age Comics
225 Main St.
Chico, CA 95928
PH:916-898-0550

Comics & Comix, Inc.
6135 Sunrise Blvd.
Citrus Heights, CA 95610
PH:916-969-0717

Superior Comics
1630 Superior Ave.
Costa Mesa, CA 92627
PH:714-631-3933

Graphitti Comics & Games
4325 Overland Ave.
Culver City, CA 90230
PH:213-559-2058

Comic Quest
24344 Muirlands Blvd.
El Toro, CA 92630
PH:714-951-9668

Comic Gallery
675 N. Broadway
Escondido, CA 92025
PH:619-745-5660

The Comic Castle
330 5th St.
Eureka, CA 95501
PH:707-444-2665

Comics & Comix, Inc
1350 Travis Blvd.
Fairfield, CA 94533
PH:707-427-1202

Adventureland Comics
106 N. Harbor Blvd.
Fullerton, CA 92632
PH:714-738-3698

Fantasy Illustrated
12553 Harbor Blvd.

Garden Grove, CA 92640
PH:714-537-0087

Geoffrey's Comics
15530 Crenshaw Blvd.
Gardena, CA 90249
PH:213-538-3198

Bud Plant Comic Art
P. O. Box 1689
Grass Valley, CA 95945
PH:916-273-2166

Comic Grapevine
22 W. Lodi Ave.
Lodi, CA 95240
PH:209-368-1096

The American Comic Book Co.
3972 Atlantic Ave.
Long Beach, CA 90807
PH:213-426-0393

Cheap Comics 2
7779 Melrose Ave.
Los Angeles, CA 90046
PH:213-655-9323

Golden Apple Comics
7711 Melrose Ave.
Los Angeles, CA 90046
PH:213-658-6047

Golden Apple Comics
8934 West Pico Blvd.
Los Angeles, CA 90034
PH:213-274-2008

Graphitti-Westwood—UCLA
960 Gayley Ave.
Los Angeles, CA 90024
PH:213-824-3656

Pacific Comic Exchange, Inc.
(By Appointment Only)
P. O. Box 34849
Los Angeles, CA 90034
PH:213-836-PCEI

**WonderWorld Comic Books +
Baseball Cards**
1579 El Camino
Millbrae, CA 94030
PH:415-871-2674

Comic Pendragon
73 N. Milpitas Blvd.
Milpitas, CA 95035
PH:408-942-6903

Bonanza Books & Comics
Roseburg Square Center
813 W. Roseburg Ave.
Modesto, CA 95350-5058
PH:209-529-0415

**Ninth Nebula:
The Comic Book Store**
11517 Burbank Blvd.
North Hollywood, CA 91601
PH:818-509-2901

Golden Apple Comics
8962 Reseda Blvd.
Northridge, CA 91324
PH:818-993-7804

Freedonia Funnyworks
350 S. Tustin Ave.
Orange, CA 92666
PH:714-639-5830

Desert Comics
406 N. Palm Canyon Dr.

Palm Springs, CA 92262
PH:619-325-5805

Comics & Comix, Inc.
405 California Ave.
Palo Alto, CA 94306
PH:415-328-8100

Lee's Comics
3783 El Camino Real
Palo Alto, CA 94306
PH:415-493-3957

Bud Plant Illustrated Books
c/o Jim Vadeboncoeur, Jr.
3809 Laguna Ave.
Palo Alto, CA 94306
PH:415-493-1191 (evenings,
weekends)

Galaxy Comics & Cards
1503 Aviation Blvd.
Redondo Beach, CA 90278
PH:213-374-7440

Comics & Comix, Inc.
921 K St.
Sacramento, CA 95814
PH:916-442-5142

Comic Gallery
4224 Balboa Ave.
San Diego, CA 92117
PH:619-483-4853

Comics & Comix, Inc.
650 Irving
San Francisco, CA 94122
PH:415-665-5888

Comics & Comix, Inc.
700 Lombard St.
San Francisco, CA 94133
PH:415-982-3511

Comics and DaKind
1643 Noriega St.
San Francisco, CA 94122
PH:415-753-9678

The Funny Papers
7253 Geary Blvd.
San Francisco, CA 94121
PH:415-752-1914

Gary's Corner Bookstore
1051 San Gabriel Blvd.
San Gabriel, CA 91776
PH:818-285-7575

Comics Pendragon I
1189 Branham Lane
San Jose, CA 95118
PH:408-265-3233

**Bob Sidebottom's Comic
Collector Shop**
73 E. San Fernando
San Jose, CA 95113
PH:408-287-2254

The Comic Shop
2164 E. 14th St.
San Leandro, CA 94577
PH:415-483-0205

Lee's Comics
2222 El Camino Real
San Mateo, CA 94003
PH:415-571-1489

**San Mateo Comic Books,
Baseball Cards, & Original Art**
106 South B St.
San Mateo, CA 94401
PH:415-344-1536

Brian's Books
2767 El Camino
Santa Clara, CA 95051
PH:408-985-7481

R & K Comics
3153 El Camino Real
Santa Clara, CA 95051
PH:408-554-6512

Atlantis Fantasyworld
610 F Cedar St.
Santa Cruz, CA 95060
PH:408-426-0158

Hi De Ho Comics & Fantasy
525 Santa Monica Blvd.
Santa Monica, CA 90401
PH:213-394-2820

Superior Comics
220 Pier Ave.
Santa Monica, CA 90405
PH:213-396-7005

Forbidden Planet
14513 Ventura Blvd.
Sherman Oaks, CA 91403
PH:818-995-0151

Superhero Universe VIII
Sycamore Plaza
2955-A5 Cochran St.
Simi Valley, CA 93065

PH:805-583-3027 &
800-252-9997

Cheap Comics-1
12123 Garfield Ave.
South Gate, CA 90280
PH:213-408-0900

Altered Images
12661 Beach Blvd.
Stanton, CA 90680
PH:714-373-9922

Grapevine Comics & Cards
9321-C N. Thornton Rd.
Stockton, CA 95209
PH:209-952-9303

Graphitti Studio City
12080 Ventura Pl., No. 3
Studio City, CA 91604
PH:818-980-4976

Superhero Universe IV
18722 Ventura Blvd.
Tarzana, CA 93156
PH:818-774-0969

Pantechnicon
1165 E. Thousand Oaks Blvd.
Thousand Oaks, CA 91360
PH:805-495-0299

J & K Comics and Toys
3535 Torrance Blvd., Suite 9
Torrance, CA 90503
PH:213-540-9685

Roleplayers
5933 Adobe Rd.

29 Palms, CA 92277
PH:619-367-6282

Hi De Ho Comics & Fantasy
64 Windward Ave.
Venice, CA 90291
PH:213-399-6206

Ralph's Comic Corner
2377 E. Main St.
Ventura, CA 93003
PH:805-653-2732

The Second Time Around
391 E. Main St.
Ventura, CA 93003
PH:805-643-3154

Graphitti-South Bay!
Airport/Marina Hotel (Rear)
8639 Lincoln Blvd., No. 102
Westchester, L. A., CA 90045
PH:213-641-8661

COLORADO:

Colorado Comic Book Co.
220 N. Tejon St.
Colorado Springs, CO 80903
PH:719-635-2516

Heroes & Dragons
The Citadel #2158
Colorado Springs, CO 80909
PH:719-550-9570

CONNECTICUT:

A Timeless Journey
402 Elm St.

Stamford, CT 06902
PH:203-353-1720

FLORIDA:

Phil's Comic Shoppe
7778 Wiles Rd.
Coral Springs, FL 33067
PH:305-752-4514

Cliff's Books
209 N. Woodland Blvd. (17-92)
De Land, FL 32720
PH:904-734-6963

Family Book Shop
1301 N Woodland Blvd.
De Land, FL 32720
PH:904-736-6501

Novel Ideas
804 West University Ave.
Gainesville, FL 32601
PH:904-374-8593

Novel Ideas
3206 S.W. 35th Blvd.
Butler Plaza
Gainesville, FL 32608
PH:904-377-2694

Comics U.S.A.
5883 Lake Worth Rd.
Greenacres City, FL 33463
PH:407-433-9111

Charlie's Comics & Games
1255 West 46th St. #26
Hialeah, FL 33012
PH:305-557-5994

**Mark's Comics/
Louie's Baseball Cards**
1678 B Ridgewood Ave.
Holly Hills, FL 32117
PH:904-676-7464

Adventure Into Comics
3863 Lake Emma Rd.
Lake Mary, FL 32746
PH:407-333-9353

Past—Present—Future Comics
6186 S. Congress Ave., Suite A4
Lantana, FL 33462
PH:407-433-3068

Phil's Comic Shoppe
614 S. State Rd. 7
Margate, FL 33068
PH:305-977-6947

Comic Warehouse, Inc.
1029 Airport Rd. N., #B-6
Naples, FL 33942
PH:813-643-1020

Tropic Comics South, Inc.
742 N.E. 167th St.
N. Miami Beach, FL 33162
PH:305-940-8700

Adventure Into Comics
841 Bennett Rd.
Orlando, FL 32803
PH:407-896-4047

Cartoon Museum
4300 S. Semoran, Suite 109
Orlando, FL 32822
PH:407-273-0141

Enterprise 1701
2814 Corrine Dr.
Orlando, FL 32803
PH:407-896-1701

**Past—Present—Future Comics
North**
4270 Northlake Blvd.
Palm Beach Gardens, FL 33410
PH:407-775-2141

Sincere Comics
3300 N. Pace Blvd.
Pensacola, FL 32505
PH:904-432-1352

Tropic Comics
313 S. State Rd. 7
Plantation, FL 33317
PH:305-587-8878

Comics U.S.A.
3231 N. Federal Hwy.
Pompano Beach, FL 33064
PH:305-942-1455

New England Comics
Northdale Court
15836 N. Dale Mabry Hwy.
Tampa, FL 33618
PH:813-264-1848

Tropic Comics North, Inc.
1018 21st St. (U.S. 1)
Vero Beach, FL 32960
PH:407-562-8501

GEORGIA:

Titan Games & Comics, Inc.
5439 Riverdale Rd.

College Park, GA 30349
PH:404-996-9129

Titan Games & Comics IV
2131 Pleasant Hill Rd.
Duluth, GA 30136
PH:404-497-0202

The Comic Company, Ltd.
3320 D Thompson Bridge Rd. NE
Gainesville, GA 30506
PH:404-536-4340

Showcase Collectibles
(By Appointment)
P. O. Box 921185
Norcross, GA 30092
PH:404-594-0074

Fischer's Book Store
6569 Riverdale Rd.
Riverdale, GA 30274
PH:404-997-7323

Titan Games & Comics III
2585 Spring Rd.
Smyrna, GA 30080
PH:404-433-8226

Titan Games & Comics II
3853C Lawrenceville Hwy.
Tucker, GA 30084
PH:404-491-8067

HAWAII:

Compleat Comics Company
1728 Kaahumanu Ave.
Wailuku, Maui, HI 96793
PH:808-242-5875

IDAHO:

King's Komix Kastle
1706 N. 18th St. (appointments)
Boise, ID 83702
PH:208-343-7142

King's Komix Kastle II
2560 Leadville (drop in)
Mail: 1706 N. 18th
Boise, ID 83702
PH:208-343-7055

**New Mythology Comics &
Science Fiction**
1725 Broadway
Boise, ID 83706
PH:208-344-6744

ILLINOIS:

Friendly Frank's Distribution
(Wholesale Only)
727 Factory Rd.
Addison, IL 60101

Friendly Frank's Comics
11941 S Cicero
Alsip, IL 60658
PH:312-371-6760

All-American Comic Shops 3
9118 Ogden Ave.
Brookfield, IL 60513
PH:708-387-9588

Moondog's Comicland
1231 W. Dundee Rd.
Plaza Verde

Buffalo Grove, IL 60090
PH:708-259-6060

AF Books
1856 Sibley Blvd.
Calumet City, IL 60409
PH:708-891-2260

All-American Comic Shops 6
6457 W. Archer Ave.
Chicago, IL 60638
PH:312-586-5090

Comics for Heroes
1702 W. Foster
Chicago, IL 60640
PH:312-769-4745

Larry's Comic Book Store
1219 W. Devon Ave.
Chicago, IL 60660
PH:312-274-1832

Larry Laws
(by appointment only)
(Call First)
831 Cornelia
Chicago, IL 60657
PH:312-477-9247

Mikes on Mars
(An All-American Affiliate 7)
1753 W. 69th St.
Chicago, IL 60637
PH:312-778-6990

Moondog's Comicland
2301 N. Clark St.
Chicago, IL 60614
PH:312-248-6060

Joe Sarno's Comic Kingdom
5941 W. Irving Park Rd.
Chicago, IL 60634
PH:312-545-2231

Yesterday
1143 W. Addison St.
Chicago, IL 60613
PH:312-248-8087

All-American Comic Shops 5
1701 N. Larkin Ave.
Hillcrest Shopping Center
Crest Hill, IL 60435
PH:815-744-2094

Moondog's Comicland
114 S. Waukegan Rd.
Deerbrook Mall
Deerfield, IL 60015
PH:708-272-6080

The Paper Escape
205 W. First St.
Dixon, IL 61021
PH:815-284-7567

Graham Crackers Comics
5228 S. Main St.
Downers Grove, IL 60515
PH:708-852-1810

GEM Comics
156 N. York Rd.
Elmhurst, IL 60126
PH:708-833-8787

All-American Comic Shops, Ltd.
3514 W. 95th St.
Evergreen Park, IL 60642
PH:708-425-7555

Galaxy of Books
Rt 137 & Sheridan
CNW Great Lakes Train Station
Great Lakes, IL 60064
PH:708-473-1099

Moondog's Comicland
139 W. Prospect Ave.
Mt. Prospect, IL 60056
PH:708-398-6060

Moondog's Comicland
Randhurst Shopping Center
Mt. Prospect, IL 60056
PH:708-577-8668

Graham Cracker Comics
5 E. Chicago Ave.
Naperville, IL 60540
PH:708-355-4310

All-American Comic Shops 2
14620 S. LaGrange Rd.
Orland Park, IL 60462
PH:708-460-5556

All-American Comic Shops 4
22305 S. Central Park Ave.
Park Forest, IL 60466
PH:708-748-2509

Tomorrow Is Yesterday
5600 N. 2nd St.
Rockford, IL 61111
PH:815-633-0330

Moondog's Comicland
1455 W. Schaumburg Rd.
Schaumburg Plaza
Schaumburg, IL 60194
PH:708-529-6060

Family Book
3123 S. Dirksen Pkwy
Springfield, IL 62703
PH:217-529-1709

Unicorn Comics & Cards
216 S. Villa Ave.
Villa Park, IL 60181
PH:708-279-5777

Kane's Comics & Collectibles
749 W. Dundee Rd.
Wheeling, IL 60090
PH:708-808-8877

Heroland Comics
6963 W. 11th St.
Worth, IL 60482
PH:708-448-2937

Galaxy of Books
1908 Sheridan Rd.
Zion, IL 60099
PH:708-872-3313

INDIANA:

**Pen Comics &
Entertainment Store**
501 Main St.
Beech Grove, IN 46107
PH:317-782-3450

Comics Cave
1089 North National Rd.
Columbus, IN 47201
PH:812-372-8430

The Bookstack
112 W. Lexington Ave.

Elkhart, IN 46516
PH:219-293-3815

The Book Broker
2127 S. Weinbach (Fairlawn Ctr.)
Evansville, IN 47714
PH:812-479-5647

Broadway Comics
2423 Broadway
Fort Wayne, IN 46807
PH:219-744-1456

Friendly Frank's Distr., Inc.
(Wholesale Only)
3990 Broadway
Gary, IN 46408
PH:219-884-5052

Friendly Frank's Comics
220 Main St.
Hobart, IN 46342
PH:219-942-6020

Blue Moon Comics & Games
8336 E. West 10th St.
Indianapolis, IN 46234
PH:317-271-1479

**Cartoon Carnival & Nostalgia
Emporium**
7311 U.S. 31 South
Indianapolis, IN 46227
PH:317-889-8899

**Comic Carnival & Nostalgia
Emporium**
6265 N. Carrollton Ave.
Indianapolis, IN 46220
PH:317-253-8882

**Comic Carnival & Nostalgia
Emporium**
5002 S. Madison Ave.
Indianapolis, IN 46227
PH:317-787-3773

**Comic Carnival & Nostalgia
Emporium**
982 N. Mitthoeffer Rd.
Indianapolis, IN 46229
PH:317-898-5010

**Comic Carnival & Nostalgia
Emporium**
3837 N. High School Rd.
Indianapolis, IN 46254
PH:317-293-4386

John's Comic Closet
4610 East 10th St.
Indianapolis, IN 46201
PH:317-357-6611

Galactic Greg's
1407 Lincolnway
Valparaiso, IN 46383
PH:219-464-0119

IOWA:

Mayhem Collectibles
2532 Lincoln Way
Ames, IA 50010
PH:515-292-3510

Oak Leaf Comics
5219 University Ave.
Cedar Falls, IA 50428
PH:319-277-1835

Comic World & Baseball Cards
1626 Central Ave.
Dubuque, IA 52001
PH:319-557-1897

Oak Leaf Comics
23 - 5th S.W.
Mason City, IA 50401
PH:515-424-0333

The Comiclogue
520 Elm St.
P.O. Box 65304 (mail only)
West Des Moines, IA 50265
PH:515-279-9006

KANSAS:

Kwality Books, Comics, & Games
1111 Massachusetts St.
Lawrence, KS 66044
PH:913-843-7239

Air Capital Comics & Games
954 S. Oliver
Wichita, KS 67218
PH:316-681-0219

Air Capital Comics & Games
601 N West St., Suite #202
Wichita, KS 67203
PH:316-942-6642

Prairie Dog Comics East
Oxford Square Mall
6100 E. 21st St., Suite 190
Wichita, KS 67208
PH:316-688-5576

Prairie Dog Comics West
Maple Ridge Mall
7130 W. Maple, Suite 240
Wichita, KS 67209
PH:316-942-3456

KENTUCKY:

Pac-Rat's, Inc.
1051 Bryant Way
Greenwood Station S/C
Bowling Green, KY 42103
PH:502-782-8092

Comic Book World
7130 Turfway Rd.
Florence, KY 41042
PH:606-371-9562

The Great Escape
2433 Bardstown Rd.
Louisville, KY 40205
PH:502-456-2216

LOUISIANA:

B.T. & W.D. Giles
P. O. Box 271
Keithville, LA 71047
PH:318-925-6654

Bookworm of N.O.E.
7011 Read Blvd.
New Orleans, LA 70127
PH:504-242-7608

MAINE:

Lippincott Books
624 Hammond St.
Bangor, ME 04401
PH:207-942-4398

Moonshadow Comics
357 Maine Mall Rd.
South Portland, ME 04106
PH:207-772-4605

Book Barn
U.S. Rt 1, P. O. Box 557
Wells, ME 04090
PH:207-646-4926

MARYLAND:

Universal Comics
5300 East Dr.
Arbutus, MD 21227
PH:301-242-4578

Comic Book Kingdom, Inc.
4307 Harford Rd.
Baltimore, MD 21214
PH:301-426-4529

Geppi's Comic World
7019 Security Blvd.
Hechinger's Square
at Security Mall
Baltimore, MD 21207
PH:301-298-1758

Geppi's Comic World
Upper Level, Light St. Pavillion
301 Light St.

Baltimore, MD 21202
PH:301-547-0910

Big Planet Comics
4865 Cordell Ave.
Bethesda, MD 20814
PH:301-654-6856

The Magic Page
7416 Laurel-Bowie Rd. (Rt. 197)
Bowie, MD 20715
PH:301-262-4735

Alternate Worlds
9924 York Rd.
Cockeysville, MD 21030
PH:301-667-0440

The Closet of Comics
7319 Baltimore Ave. (U.S. 1)
College Park, MD 20740
PH:301-699-0498

Comic Classics
203 E. Main St.
Frostburg, MD 21532
PH:301-689-1823

Comic Classics
365 Main St.
Laurel, MD 20707
PH:301-792-4744, 490-9811

Zenith Comics & Collectibles
18200 Georgia Ave.
Olney, MD 20832
PH:301-774-1345

The Closet of Comics
Calvert Village Shopping Center

Prince Frederick, MD 20678
PH:301-535-4731

Geppi's Comic World
8317 Fenton St.
Silver Spring, MD 20910
PH:301-588-2546

Barbarian Bookshop
11254 Triangle Lane
Wheaton, MD 20902
PH:301-946-4184

MASSACHUSETTS:

New England Comics
168 Harvard Ave.
Allston (Boston), MA 02134
PH:617-783-1848

Comically Speaking
1322 Mass. Ave.
Arlington, MA 02174
PH:617-643-XMEN

Bargain Books and Collectibles
247 So. Main St.
Attleboro, MA 02703
PH:508-226-1668

Superhero Universe III
41 West St.
Boston, MA 02111
PH:617-423-6676

New England Comics
748 Crescent St.
East Crossing Plaza
Brockton, MA 02402
PH:508-559-5068

New England Comics
316 Harvard St.
Brookline, MA 02146
PH:617-566-0115

Superhero Universe I
1105 Massachusetts Ave.
Cambridge, MA 02138
PH:617-354-5344

World of Fantasy
529 Broadway
Everett, MA 02149
PH:617-381-0411

That's Entertainment
387 Main St.
Fitchburg, MA 01420
PH:508-342-8607

Bop City Comics
80 Worcester Rd.
Marshalls Mall
Framingham, MA 01701
PH:508-872-2317

Ernie's Bookland
143 Central St. Downtown Lowell
Lowell, MA 01854
PH:508-453-0445

New England Comics
12A Pleasant St.
Malden, MA 02148
PH:617-322-2404

Buddy's
(Wholesale, Subscription
Service)
P. O. Box 4

Medford, MA 02155
PH:617-322-5731

New England Comics
732 Washington St.
Norwood, MA 02062
PH:617-769-4552

Imagine That Bookstore
58 Dalton Ave.
Pittsfield, MA 01201
PH:413-445-5934

New England Comics
11 Court St.
Plymouth, MA 02360
PH:508-746-8797

New England Comics
1350 Hancock St.
Quincy, MA 02169
PH:617-770-1848

Park Nostalgia
1242 Wilbur Ave.
Somerset, MA 02725
PH:508-673-0303

The Outer Limits
457 Moody St.
Waltham, MA 02154
PH:617-891-0444

Mayo Beach Bookstore
Kendrick Ave., Mayo Beach
Wellfleet, MA 02667
PH:508-349-3154

Fabulous Fiction Book Store
984 Main St.

Worcester, MA 01603
PH:508-754-8826

That's Entertainment
151 Chandler St.
Worcester, MA 01609
PH:508-755-4207

MICHIGAN:

Tom & Terry Comics
508 Layfayette Ave.
Bay City, MI 48708
PH:517-895-5525

Curious Book Shop
307 E Grand River Ave.
East Lansing, MI 48823
PH:517-332-0112

Amazing Book Store, Inc.
3718 Richfield Rd.
Flint, MI 48506
PH:313-736-3025

Argos Book Shop
1405 Robinson Rd. SE
Grand Rapids, MI 49506
PH:616-454-0111

Tardy's Collectors Corner, Inc.
2009 Eastern Ave. SE
Grand Rapids, MI 49507
PH:616-247-7828

Book Stop
1160 Chicago Dr. SW
Wyoming, MI 49509-1004
PH:616-245-0090

MINNESOTA:

Collector's Connection
21 East Superior St.
Duluth, MN 55802-2088
PH:218-722-9551

**College of Comic Book
Knowledge**
3151 Hennepin Ave. S.
Minneapolis, MN 55408
PH:612-822-2309

Midway Book & Comic
1579 University Ave.
St. Paul, MN 55104
PH:612-644-7605

MISSISSIPPI:

Diversions
1670K Pass Rd.
Biloxi, MS 39531
PH:601-374-6632

Star Store
4212 N. State St.
Jackson, MS 39206
PH:601-362-8001

Spanish Trail Books
1006 Thorn Ave.
Ocean Springs, MS 39564
PH:601-875-1144

MISSOURI:

B & R Comix Center
4747 Morganford
St. Louis, MO 63116
PH:314-353-4013

Mo's Comics and Stories
4530 Gravois
St. Louis, MO 63116
PH:314-353-9500

The Book Rack
300 W. Olive
Springfield, MO 65806
PH:417-865-4945

MONTANA:

The Book Exchange
2335 Brooks
Trempers Shopping Center
Missoula, MT 59801
PH:406-728-6342

NEBRASKA:

Star Realm
7305 South 85th St.
Omaha, NE 68128
PH:402-331-4844

NEVADA:

Fandom's Comicworld of Reno
2001 East Second St.
Reno, NV 89502
PH:702-786-6663

NEW HAMPSHIRE:

James F. Payette
P. O. Box 750
Bethlehem, NH 03574
PH:603-869-2097

NEW JERSEY:

A & S Comics & Cards III
67 South Washington Ave.
Bergenfield, NJ 07621
PH:201-384-2307

The Comic Zone
71 Rt. 73 & Day Ave.
Berlin, NJ 08009
PH:609-768-8186

Fantasy Factory Comics
Harbortowne Plaza
Tilton Rd. & Black Horse Pike
Cardiff, NJ 08232
PH:609-641-0025

Time Warp Comics & Games
584 Pompton Ave.
Cedar Grove, NJ 07009
PH:201-857-9788

Rainbow Comics
Laurel Hill Plaza
Clementon, NJ 08021
PH:609-627-1711

Steve's Comic Relief
1555 St. George Ave.
Colonia, NJ 07067
PH:908-382-3736

Steve's Comic Relief
24 Mill Run Plaza
Delran, NJ 08075
PH:609-461-1770

Ron's Gallery of Collectibles
2177 Woodbridge Ave.
Edison, NJ 08817
PH:201-985-9210

Collector's Center, Inc.
729 Edgar Rd.
Elizabeth, NJ 07202
PH:908-355-7942

Thunder Road Comics & Cards
Parkway Plaza
831 Parkway Ave.
Ewing Township, NJ 08618
PH:609-771-1055

Star Spangled Comics
353 Route 22
King George Plaza
Green Brook, NJ 08812
PH:908-356-8338

Dreamer's Comics
103 Church St.
Hackettstown, NJ 07840
PH:908-850-5255

Thunder Road Comics & Cards
3694 Nottingham Way
Hamilton Square, NJ 08690
PH:609-587-5353

Steve's Comic Relief
106 Clifton Ave.
Lakewood, NJ 08701
PH:908-363-3899

Steve's Comic Relief
156A Mercer Mall
Lawrenceville, NJ 08648
PH:609-452-7548

Comics Plus
1300 Highway 35
Middletown, NJ 07748
PH:908-706-0102

Comic Museum
434 Pine St.
Mount Holly, NJ 08060
PH:609-261-0996

A & S Comics & Cards I
7113 Bergenline Ave.
North Bergen, NJ 07047
PH:201-869-0280

Comicrypt
521 White Horse Pike
Oaklyn, NJ 08107
PH:609-858-3877

Sparkle City (appointment only)
P. O. Box 67
Sewell, NJ 08080
PH:609-881-1174

A & S Comics & Cards II
396 Cedar Lane
Teaneck, NJ 07666
PH:201-801-0500

Steve's Comic Relief
635 Bay Ave.
Toms River, NJ 08753
PH:908-244-5003

Mr. Collector
327 Union Blvd.
Totowa, NJ 07512
PH:201-595-0900

Comics Plus
Ocean Plaza
Hwy. 35 & Sunset Ave.
Wanamassa, NJ 07712
PH:908-922-3308

NEW MEXICO:

The Comic Warehouse
9617 Menaul Blvd. NE
Albuquerque, NM 87112
PH:505-293-3065

Captain Comic's Specialty Shop
109 W. 4th St.
Clovis, NM 88101
PH:505-769-1543

NEW YORK:

Earthworld Comics
327 Central Ave.
Albany, NY 12206
PH:518-465-5495

FantaCo Enterprises Inc.
21 Central Ave., Level Two
Albany, NY 12210
PH:518-463-3667

**FantaCo Archival Research
Center**
21 Central Ave., Sublevel One
Albany, NY 12210
PH:518-463-3667

FantaCo Comic Shop
21 Central Ave., Level 2
Albany, NY 12210
PH:518-463-1400

FantaCon Organization Offices
21 Central Ave., Level 3
Albany, NY 12210
PH:518-463-1400

FantaCo Publications
21 Central Ave., Level 3
Albany, NY 12210
PH:518-463-3667

**Official Night Of The Living
Dead Comic Headquarters**
21 Central Ave., Level 2
Albany, NY 12210
PH:518-463-3667

Long Island Comics
1670-D Sunrise Hwy.
Bay Shore, NY 11706
PH:516-665-4342

Fordham Comics
390 East Fordham Rd.
Bronx, NY 10458
PH:212-933-9245

Wow Comics
652 E. 233rd St.
Bronx, NY 10466
PH:212-231-0913

Wow Comics
642 Pelham Parkway S.
Bronx, NY 10462
PH:212-829-0461

Brain Damage Comics
1301 Prospect Ave.
Brooklyn, NY 11218
PH:718-438-1335

Memory Lane
1301 Prospect Ave.
Brooklyn, NY 11218
PH:718-438-1335

Pinocchio Comic Shop
1814 McDonald Ave. near Ave. P
Brooklyn, NY 11223
PH:718-645-2573

Dimension Comics
R#1 Box 204-A
Cold Spring, NY 10516
PH:914-265-2649

Comics for Collectors
211 West Water St.
Elmira, NY 14901
PH:607-732-2299

Comics For Collectors
148 The Commons
Ithaca, NY 14850
PH:607-272-3007

Long Beach Books, Inc.
17 E. Park Ave.
Long Beach, NY 11561
PH:516-432-2265 & 432-0063

Comics & Hobbies
156 Mamaroneck Ave.
Mamaroneck, NY 10543
PH:914-698-9473

Port Comics & Cards
3120 Rt. 112
Medford, NY 11763
PH:516-732-9143

Alex's MVP Comics & Cards
256 E. 89th St.
New York, NY 10128
PH:212-831-2273

Big Apple Comics
2489 Broadway (92-93 St.)
New York, NY 10025
PH:212-724-0085

Funny Business
656 Amsterdam Ave.
(Corner 92nd St.)
New York, NY 10025
PH:212-799-9477

Golden Age Express
2489 Broadway (92-93)
New York, NY 10025
PH:212-769-9570

Jim Hanley's Universe
At A&S Plaza, 6th Floor
901 Ave. of Americas (at 33rd)
New York, NY 10001
PH:212-268-7088

Metropolis Collectibles
(by appointment)
7 West 18th St.
New York, NY 10011
PH:212-627-9691

West Side Comics
107 West 86 St.
New York, NY 10024
PH:212-724-0432

L & S Comix
1379 Jerusalem Ave.
N. Merrick, NY 11566
PH:516-489-XMEN, 489-9311

Fantastic Planet
24 Oak St.
Plattsburgh, NY 12901
PH:518-563-2946

Iron Vic Comics
1 Raymond Ave.
Poughkeepsie, NY 12603
PH:914-473-8365

Alien World, Inc.
322 Sunrise Hwy.
Rockville Center, NY 11570
PH:516-536-8151

Amazing Comics
12 Gillette Ave.
Sayville, NY 11782
PH:516-567-8069

Electric City Comics
1704 Van Vranken Ave.
Schenectady, NY 12308
PH:518-377-1500

Jim Hanley's Universe
350 New Dorp Lane
Staten Island, NY 10306
PH:718-351-6299

Comic Book Heaven
48-14 Skillman Ave.
Sunnyside, Queens, NY 11104
PH:718-899-4175

Dream Days Comic Book Shop
312 South Clinton St.
Syracuse, NY 13202
PH:315-475-3995

Michael Sagert
P. O. Box 456, Downtown
Syracuse, NY 13201
PH:315-475-3995

Twilight Book & Game Emporium, Inc.
1401 North Salina St.
Syracuse, NY 13208
PH:315-471-3139

Aquilonia Comics
412 Fulton St.
Troy, NY 12180
PH:518-271-1069

Ravenswood, Inc.
263 Genesee St.
Utica, NY 13501
PH:315-735-3699

Iron Vic Comics II
420 Windsor Hwy.
Vail's Gate, NY 12584
PH:914-565-6525

Collector's Comics
3247 Sunrise Hwy.
Wantagh, NY 11793
PH:516-783-8700

The Dragon's Den
2614 Central Park Ave.
Yonkers, NY 10710
PH:914-793-4630

NORTH CAROLINA:

Super Giant Books & Comics
344 Merrimon Ave.
Asheville, NC 28801
PH:803-576-4990

Heroes Aren't Hard to Find
Corner Central Ave. & The Plaza

P. O. Box 9181
Charlotte, NC 28299
PH:704-375-7462

Heroes Aren't Hard to Find
(Mail Order Subscriptions & Wholesale)
P. O. Box 9181
Charlotte, NC 28299
PH:704-376-5766, 800-321-4370

Heroes Are Here
208 South Berkeley Blvd.
Goldsboro, NC 27530
PH:919-751-3131

Parts Unknown—The Comic Book Store
The Cotton Mill Square
801 Merritt Dr./Spring Garden St.
Greensboro, NC 27407
PH:919-294-0091

Heroes Are Here, Too
116 E. Fifth St.
Greenville, NC 27584
PH:919-757-0948

The Nostalgia Newsstand
919 Dickinson Ave.
Greenville, NC 27834
PH:919-758-6909

Tales Resold
3936 Atlantic Ave.
Raleigh, NC 27604
PH:919-878-8551

The Booktrader
121 Country Club Rd.

Rocky Mount, NC 27801
PH:919-443-3993

**Bargain Books, Comics, &
Music**
Main St.
Downtowner Office Bldg.
Sylva, NC
No Phone

Bargain Bookstore II
Delwood Rd.
Waynesville, NC 28786
PH:704-452-2539

Heroes Aren't Hard to Find
Silas Creek Crossing Shop. Ctr.
3234 Silas Creek Pkwy.
Winston-Salem, NC 27103
PH:919-765-4370

NORTH DAKOTA:

Collector's Corner
City Center Mall
Grand Forks, ND 58201
PH:701-772-2518

**Tom's Coin, Stamp, Gem,
Baseball, & Comic Shop**
#2 1st SW
Minot, ND 58701
PH:701-852-4522

OHIO:

Trade Those Tunes®
1320 Whipple NW
Meyers Lake Plaza

Canton, OH 44708
PH:216-477-5535

Comic Book World
4103 North Bend Rd.
Cincinnati, OH 45211
PH:513-661-6300

Collectors Warehouse Inc.
5437 Pearl Rd.
Cleveland, OH 44129
PH:216-842-2896

Dark Star II
1410 West Dorothy Lane
Dayton, OH 45409
PH:513-293-7307

Troll and Unicorn
5460 Brandt Pike
Huber Heights, OH 45424
PH:513-233-6535

Bookie Parlor
2778 Wilmington Pike
Kettering, OH 45419
PH:513-293-2243

**Don Parker's Records &
Comics**
122 W. Loveland Ave.
Loveland, OH 45140
PH:513-677-3140

Rich's Comic Shoppe
2441 N. Verity Pkwy.
Middletown, OH 45042
PH:513-424-1095

Monarch Cards & Comics
2620 Airport Hwy.

Toledo, OH 43609
PH:419-382-1451

Funnie Farm Bookstore
328 N. Dixie Dr.
Vandalia, OH 45377
PH:513-898-2794

Dark Star Books
231 Xenia Ave.
Yellow Springs, OH 45387
PH:513-767-9400

OKLAHOMA:

New World Comics & Games
2203 W. Main
Norman, OK 73069
PH:405-321-7445

Planet Comics #1
918 W. Main
Norman, OK 73069
PH:405-329-9695

New World Comics & Games
6219 N. Meridian Ave.
Oklahoma City, OK 73112
PH:405-721-7634

New World Comics & Games
4420 S.E. 44th St.
Oklahoma City, OK 73135
PH:405-677-2559

Planet Comics #2
2136 S.W. 74th
Oklahoma City, OK 73159
PH:405-682-9144

Comic Empire of Tulsa
3122 S. Mingo Rd.
Tulsa, OK 74146
PH:918-664-5808

Comics, Cards & Collectibles
4618 East 31st St.
Tulsa, OK 74135
PH:918-749-8500

Starbase 21
2130 S. Sheridan Rd.
Tulsa, OK 74129
PH:918-838-3388

Want List Comics
Box 701932 (appointment only)
Tulsa, OK 74170-1932
PH:918-299-0440

OREGON:

More Fun
102 Will Dodge Way
Ashland, OR 97520
PH:503-488-1978

Pegasus Books
4390 S.W. Lloyd
Beaverton, OR 97005
PH:503-643-4222

Emerald City Comics
770 E. 13th
Eugene, OR 97401
PH:503-345-2568

Nostalgia Collectibles
527 Williamette St.

Eugene, OR 97401
PH:503-484-9202

House of Fantasy
2005 E. Burnside
P. O. Box 472
Gresham, OR 97030
PH:503-661-1815

It Came From Outer Space
10812 S.E. Oak St.
Milwaukie, OR 97222
PH:503-786-0865

Pegasus Books
10902 SE Main
Milwaukie, OR 97222
PH:503-652-2752

It Came From Outer Space
Plaza 205 Ste. P
9738 SE Washington
Portland, OR 97216
PH:503-275-2701

Pegasus Books
1401 SE Division St.
Portland, OR 97214
PH:503-233-0768

Pegasus Books
5015 NE Sandy
Portland, OR 97218
PH:503-284-4693

PENNSYLVANIA:

Cap's Comic Cavalcade
1980 Catasauqua Rd.

Allentown, PA 18103
PH:215-264-5540

Cap's Comic Cavalcade
Tilghman Square
Shopping Center
Allentown, PA 18104
PH:215-395-0979

Dreamscape Comics
404 West Broad St.
Bethlehem, PA 18018
PH:215-867-1178

Dreamscape Comics
9 East Third St.
Bethlehem, PA 18015
PH:215-865-4636

Showcase Comics
839 W. Lancaster Ave.
Bryn Mawr, PA 19010
PH:215-527-6236

Time Tunnel Collectibles
1001 Castle Shannon Blvd.
Castle Shannon, PA 15234
PH:412-531-8833

Comic Universe
Bazaar of All Nations, Store 228
Clifton Heights, PA 19018
PH:215-259-9943

Dreamscape Comics
25th St. Shopping Center
Easton, PA 18042
PH:215-250-9818

Comic Universe
446 MacDade Blvd.

Folsom, PA 19033
PH:215-461-7960

Comic Universe
395 Lancaster Ave.
Frazer, PA 19355
PH:215-889-3320

Comics & Collectibles, Inc.
983 W. County Line Rd.
Rosemore Shopping Center
Hatboro, PA 19040
PH:215-675-8708

Golden Unicorn Comics
860 Alter St.
Hazleton, PA 18201
PH:717-455-4645

Ott's Trading Post
201 Allegheny St.
Hollidaysburg, PA 16648
PH:814-696-3494

Charlie's Collectors Corner
100-D West Second St.
Hummelstown, PA 17036
PH:717-566-7216

The Comic Store
Station Square,
28 McGovern Ave.
Lancaster, PA 17602
PH:717-397-8737

Steve's Comic Relief
4153 Woerner Ave.
Levittown, PA 19057
PH:215-945-7954

Fat Jack's Comicrypt I
2006 Sansom St.
Philadelphia, PA 19103
PH:215-963-0788

Fat Jack's Comicrypt II
7598 Haverford Ave.
Philadelphia, PA 19151
PH:215-473-6333

Fat Jack's Comicrypt III
5736 North 5th St.
Philadelphia, PA 19120
PH:215-924-8210

Sparkle City Comics
Philadelphia, PA
(Philly area by appointment)
PH:609-881-1174

Steve's Comic Relief
1244 Franklin Mills Circle
Philadelphia, PA 19154
PH:215-281-3730

Adventure in Comics
1368 Illinois Ave.
Pittsburgh, PA 15216
PH:412-531-5644

BEM: The Store
622 South Ave.
Pittsburgh, PA 15221
PH:412-243-2736

Eide's Entertainment
1111 Penn Ave.
Pittsburgh, PA 15222
PH:412-261-0900

The Comic Store –West
Northwest Plaza
915 Loucks Rd.
York, PA 17404

RHODE ISLAND:

Starship Excalibur
Lincoln Mall
Rt. 116 Washington Hwy.
Lincoln, RI 02864
PH:401-334-3883

The Annex
314 Broadway
Newport, RI 02840
PH:401-847-4607

Starship Excalibur
60 Washington St.
Providence, RI 02903
PH:401-273-8390

Starship Excalibur
834 Hope St.
Providence, RI 02906
PH:401-861-1177

Starship Excalibur
830-832 Post Rd., Warwick Plaza
Warwick, RI 02888
PH:401-941-8890

SOUTH CAROLINA:

Super Giant Comics & Records
Market Place/Cinema Center
3466 Clemson Blvd.
Anderson, SC 29621
PH:803-225-9024

Book Exchange
1219 Savannah Hwy.
Charleston, SC 29407
PH:803-556-5051

Heroes Aren't Hard to Find
1415-A Laurens Rd.
Greenville, SC 29607
PH:803-235-3488

**Grand Slam Baseball Cards
& Comics**
2349-41 Cherry Rd.
Rock Hill, SC 29732
PH:803-327-4414

Super Giant Comics
Wal-Mart Plaza
7500 Greenville Hwy.
Spartanburg, SC 29301
PH:803-576-4990

Haven For Heroes
1131 Dick Pond Rd.
Surfside Beach, SC
PH:803-238-9975

TENNESSEE:

Comics and Curios #1
3472 Brainerd Rd.
Chattanooga, TN 37411
PH:615-698-1710

Comics and Curios #2
629 Signal Mountain Rd.
Chattanooga, TN 37405
PH:615-266-4315

Collector's Choice
3405 Keith St., Shoney's Plaza

Cleveland, TN 37311
PH:615-472-6649

Gotham City Comics
2075 Exeter #10
Germantown, TN 38138
PH:901-757-9665

Comics and Curios #3
5131-B Hixson Pike
Hixson, TN

Collector's Choice
2104 Cumberland Ave.
Knoxville, TN 37916
PH:615-546-2665

Comics Universe
1869 Hwy. 45 By-Pass North
Jackson, TN 38305
PH:901-664-9131

Mountain Comics
1210 N. Roan St.
Johnson City, TN 37602
PH:615-929-8245

Mountain Comics
1451 E. Center St.
Kingsport, TN 37664
PH:615-245-0364

The Great Escape
Gallatin Rd. at Old Hickory Blvd.
Madison, TN 37115
PH:615-865-8052

Comics And Collectibles
4730 Poplar Ave. #2
Memphis, TN 38117
PH:901-683-7171

Memphis Comics & Records
665 So. Highland
Memphis, TN 38111
PH:901-452-1304

Collector's World
1511 East Main St.
Murfreesboro, TN 37130
PH:615-895-1120

Collector's World
5751 Nolensville Rd.
Nashville, TN 37211
PH:615-333-9458

The Great Escape
1925 Broadway
Nashville, TN 37203
PH:615-327-0646

Walt's Paperback Books
2604 Franklin Rd.
Nashville, TN 37204
PH:615-298-2506

TEXAS:

**Lone Star Comics Books
& Games**
511 East Abram St.
Arlington, TX 76010
PH:817-Metro 265-0491

**Lone Star Comics Books
& Games**
5721 W. I-20 at Green Oaks Blvd.
Arlington, TX 76016
PH:817-478-5405

Mighty Comics
(Mail Order)
P.O. Box 110194
Carrollton, TX 75011-0194
PH:214-245-3474 & 466-1359
TDD

Lone Star Comics Books
& Games
11661 Preston Forest Village
Dallas, TX 75230
PH:214-373-0934

Remember When
2431 Valwood Pkwy.
Dallas, TX 75234
PH:214-243-3439

Lone Star Comics Books
& Games
3014 West 7th St.
Fort Worth, TX 76107
PH:817-654-0333

B & D Trophy Shop
4404 N. Shepherd
Houston, TX 77018
PH:713-694-8436

Bedrock City Comic Co.
6521 Westheimer
Houston, TX 77057
PH:713-780-0675

Houston's Favorite Game &
Comic Emporium
2007 Southwest Freeway at
Shepherd

Houston, TX 77098
PH:713-520-8700

Nan's Games and Comics Too!
2011 Southwest Freeway (US 59
at Shepherd)
Houston, TX 77098-4805
PH:713-520-8700

Third Planet Books
2439 Bissonnet
Houston, TX 77005
PH:713-528-1067

Lone Star Comics, Books
& Games
807 Melbourne
Hurst, TX 76053
PH:817-595-4375

Lone Star Comics, Books
& Games
2550 N. Beltline Rd.
Irving, TX 75062
PH:214-659-0317

Lone Star Comics, Books
& Games
3600 Gus Thomasson, Suite 107
Mesquite, TX 75150
PH:214-681-2040

Lone Star Comics, Books
& Games
1900 Preston Rd. #345
Plano, TX 75093
PH:214-985-1953

Comics (& Records) Unlimited
6858 Ingram Rd.

San Antonio, TX 78238
PH:512-522-9063

Comics Unlimited
2359 Austin Hwy.
San Antonio, TX 78218
PH:512-653-6588

Comics Unlimited
226 Bitters Rd., Suite 102
San Antonio, TX 78216
PH:512-545-9063

Comics Unlimited
7101 Blanco Rd.
San Antonio, TX 78216
PH:512-340-0074

Heroes & Fantasies
#114 North Star Mall
San Antonio, TX 78216
PH:512-366-2273

UTAH:

The Bookshelf
2456 Washington Blvd.
Ogden, UT 84401
PH:801-621-4752

Comics Utah
1956 S. 1100 East
Salt Lake City, UT 84105
PH:801-487-5390

Comics Utah
2985 W. 3500 South
Salt Lake City, UT 84119
PH:801-966-8581

VERMONT:

Comics Outpost
27 Granite St.
Barre, VT 05641
PH:802-476-4553 or
800-564-4553 in state

Comics City, Inc.
6 No. Winooski Ave.
Burlington, VT 05401
PH:802-865-3828

Earth Prime Comics
154 Church St.
Burlington, VT 05401
PH:802-863-3666

VIRGINIA:

Capital Comics Center
Storyland, U.S.A.
2008 Mt. Vernon Ave.
Alexandria, VA 22301 (D.C. area)
PH:703-548-3466

Geppi's Crystal City Comics
1675 Crystal Square Arcade
Arlington, VA 22202
PH:703-521-4618

Mountain Comics
509 State St.
Bristol, VA 24201
PH:703-466-6337

Burke Centre Books
5741 Burke Centre Pkwy.
Burke, VA 22015
PH:703-250-5114

Fantasia Comics and Records
1419½ University Ave.
Charlottesville, VA 22903
PH:804-971-1029

Fantasia Comics and Records
1861 Seminole Trail (29 North)
Charlottesville, VA 22901
PH:804-974-7512

Trilogy Shop #3
3580-F Forest Haven Lane
Chesapeake, VA 23321
PH:804-483-4173

Hole in the Wall Books
905 West Broad St.
Falls Church, VA 22046
PH:703-536-2511

Marie's Books and Things
1701 Princess Anne St.
Fredericksburg, VA 22401
PH:703-373-5196

Franklin Farm Books
13320-I Franklin Farm Rd.
Herndon, VA 22071
PH:703-437-9530

Trilogy Shop #2
700 E. Little Creek Rd.
Norfolk, VA 23518
PH:804-587-2540

Trilogy Shop #5
3535 Airline Blvd.
Portsmouth, VA 23701

Dave's Comics
7019-F Three Chopt Rd.
Richmond, VA 23226
PH:804-282-1211

Nostalgia Plus
601 Willow Lawn Drive
Richmond, VA 23230
PH:804-282-5532

B & D Comic Shop
3514 Williamson Rd. N.W.
Roanoke, VA 24012
PH:703-563-4161

Trilogy Shop #1
5773 Princess Anne Rd.
Virginia Beach, VA 23462
PH:804-490-2205

Trilogy Shop #4
857 S. Lynnhaven Rd.
Virginia Beach, VA 23452
PH:804-468-0412

WASHINGTON:

Paperback Exchange Yardbirds
2100 N. National Ave. (upstairs)
Chehalis, WA 98532
PH:206-748-4792

Everett Comics & Cards
2934½ Colby Ave.
Everett, WA 98201
PH:206-252-8181

Olympic Cards & Comics
311 S. Sound Ctr.
Lacey, WA 98503
PH:206-459-7721

Paperback Exchange
909 Sleater Kinney
Lacey, WA 98503
PH:206-456-8170

The Comic Character Shop
Old Firehouse Antique Mall
110 Alaskan Way South
Seattle, WA 98104
PH:206-283-0532

Corner Comics
6565 N.E. 181st
Seattle, WA 98155
PH:206-486-XMEN

Corner Comics II
5226 University Way N.E.
Seattle, WA 98105
PH:206-525-9394

**Gemini Book Exchange and
Comic Center**
9614 16th Ave. S.W.
Seattle, WA 98106
PH:206-762-5543

Golden Age Collectables, Ltd.
1501 Pike Place Market
401 Lower Level
Seattle, WA 98101
PH:206-622-9799

Zanadu Comics
1923 3rd Ave.
Seattle, WA 98101
PH:206-443-1316

Zanadu Comics
4518 University Way N.E.

2nd Floor, Arcade Bldg.
Seattle, WA 98105
PH:206-632-0989

The Book Exchange
N. 6504 Division
Spokane, WA 99208
PH:509-489-2053

The Book Exchange
University City East
E. 10812 Sprague
Spokane, WA 99206
PH:509-928-4073

Lady Jayne's Comics & Books
5969 6th Ave.
Tacoma, WA 98406
PH:206-564-6168

Ron's Coin & Book Center II
Valley Mall
Union Gap, WA 98907
PH:509-575-1180

Pegasus Books
813 Grand Blvd.
Vancouver, WA 98661
PH:206-693-1240

Galaxy Comics
1720 5th St., Suite D
Wenatchee, WA 98801
PH:509-663-4330

Ron's Coin & Book Center
6 N. 3rd St.
Yakima, WA 98901
PH:509-248-1117

WEST VIRGINIA:

Cheryl's Comics & Toys
5216½ MacCorkle Ave. S.E.
Charleston, WV 25304
PH:304-925-7269

Comic World
613 West Lee St.
Charleston, WV 25302
PH:304-343-3874

Comic World
1204 4th Ave.
Huntington, WV 25701
PH:304-522-3923

**Triple Play Cards, Comics,
& Collectibles**
6A Bank St.
Nitro, WV 25143
PH:304-755-5529

Books & Things
2506 Pike St.
Parkersburg, WV 26101
PH:304-422-0666

**Triple Play Cards, Comics
& Collectibles**
335 4th Ave.
South Charleston, WV 25303
PH:304-744-2602

WISCONSIN:

Westfield's Comics, Etc.
17125E W. Bluemound Rd.
Loehmann's Plaza
Brookfield (Milwaukee), WI
53005-9998
PH:414-821-0242

River City Cards & Comics
512 Cass St.
La Crosse, WI 54601
PH:608-782-5540

Capital City Comics
1910 Monroe St.
Madison, WI 53711
PH:608-251-8445

Capital City Comics
6640 Odana Rd.
in Market Square
Madison, WI 53711
PH:608-833-6964

20th Century Books
108 King St.
Madison, WI 53703
PH:608-251-6226

Westfield's Comics, Etc.
Whitney Square Mall
676 S. Whitney Way
Madison, WI 53711
PH:608-277-1280

**The Westfield Company of
Wisconsin, Inc.**
(Comic Subscription Service)
8608 University Green
P. O. Box 470
Middleton, WI 53562
PH:608-836-1945

Capital City Comics
2565 North Downer St.
Milwaukee, WI 53210
PH:414-332-8199

CANADA:

ALBERTA:

Comic Legends–Head Office
#205, 908 17th Ave. S.W.
Calgary, Alberta, Can. T2T 0A3
PH:403-245-5884

Comic Legends
Bay #8, 10015 Oakfield Dr. SW
Calgary, Alberta, Can.
PH:403-251-5964

**Scorpio Comics, Books, &
Sports Cards**
7640 Fairmount Dr. SE
Calgary, Alberta, Can. T2H 0X8
PH:403-258-0035

Comic Legends
1275 3rd Ave., South
Lethbridge, Alberta, Can.
PH:403-327-8558

BRITISH COLUMBIA:

L.A. Comics & Books
371 Victoria St.
Kamloops, B.C., Can. V2C 2A3
PH:604-828-1995

Page After Page
1763 Harvey Ave.
Kelowna, B.C., Can. V1Y 6G4
PH:604-860-6554

Ted's Paperback & Comics
269 Leon Ave.
Kelowna, B.C., Can. V1Y 6J1
PH:604-763-1258

The Comic Guard Co.
190 East 11th Ave.
Prince Rupert, B.C.,
Can. V8J 4B9
PH:604-627-7106

Island Fantasy
#29 Market Square
560 Johnson St.
Victoria, B.C., Can. V8W 3C6
PH:604-381-1134

MANITOBA:

International Comic Book Co.
Calvin Slobodian
859 4th Ave.
Rivers, Man., Can. R0K 1X0
PH:204-328-7846

Collector's Slave
156 Imperial Ave.
Winnipeg, Man., Can. R2M 0K8
PH:204-237-4428

Comic Factory II
380 Donald St.
Winnipeg, Man., Can. R3B 2J2
PH:204-957-1978

Doug Sulipa's Comic World
374 Donald St.

Winnipeg, Man., Can. R3B 2J2
PH:204-943-3642

NOVA SCOTIA:

Members Only Comic Service
(Mail Order Service Only)
6257 Yale St.
Halifax, N.S., Can. B3L 1C9
PH:902-423-MOCS

ONTARIO:

Starlite Comics and Books
132 Westminster Drive South
Cambridge, Ont., Can. N3H 1S8
PH:519-653-6571

Lookin' For Heroes
93 Ontario St. S.
Kitchener, Ont., Can. N2G 1X5
PH:519-570-0873

QUEBEC:

Capitaine Quebec-Dollard
4305 Blvd. St. Jean
D.D.O., Que., Can. H9H 2A4
PH:514-620-1866

Capitaine Quebec-Snowdon
5108 Decarie
Montreal, Que., Can. H3X 2H9
PH:514-487-0970

Capitaine Quebec-Centre-Ville
1837 St. Catherine O.

Montreal, Que., Can. H3H 1M2
PH:514-939-9970

Cosmix
931 Decarie
Montreal, Que., Can. H4L 3M3
PH:514-744-9494

Multinational Comics/Cards
8918A Lajeunesse
Montreal, Que., Can. H2M 1R9
PH: 514-385-6273

Premiere Issue
27 'A' D'Auteuil
Quebec City (Vieux-Quebec)
Can. G1R 4B9
PH:418-692-3985

**Comix Plus (1,000,000 Comix
affil.)**
1475 McDonald
St. Laurent, Que., Can.
PH:514-334-0732

Capitaine Quebec-Verdun
4422 Wellington
Verdun, Que., Can. H4G 1W5
PH:514-768-1351

AUSTRALIA

Australian Comics Trader
P. O. Box 786
Penrith, NSW 2751, Australia
PH: (047) 36-2095

ENGLAND

Stateside Comics PLC
125 East Barnet Rd.
Barnet, London EN4 8RF,
England
PH:(01144) 81 449 5535

Adventure Into Comics
P. O. Box 606
London, England SE 24 9NP

COMIC BOOK
CONVENTIONS

As is the case with most other aspects of comic collecting, comic book conventions, or cons as they are referred to, were originally conceived as the comic book counterpart to science-fiction fandom conventions. There were many attempts to form successful national cons prior to the time of the first one that materialized, but they were all stillborn. It is interesting that after only three relatively organized years of existence, the first comic con was held. Of course, its magnitude was nowhere near as large as most established cons held today.

What is a comic con? As might be expected, there are comic books to be found at these gatherings. Dealers, collectors, fans, whatever they call themselves can be found trading, selling, and buying the adventures of their favorite characters for hours on end. Additionally, if at all possible, cons have guests of honor, usually professionals in the field of comic art, either writers, artists, or editors. The committees put together panels for the con attendees where the assembled pros talk about certain areas of comics, most of the time fielding questions from the assembled audience. At cons one can usually find displays of various and sundry things, usually original art. There might be radio listening rooms; there is most certainly a daily showing of different movies, usually science-fiction or horror type. Of course there is always the chance to get together with friends at cons and just talk about comics; one also has a good opportunity to make new friends who have similar interests and with whom one can correspond after the con.

It is difficult to describe accurately what goes on at a con. The best way to find out is to go to one or more if you can.

The addresses below are those currently available for conventions to be held in the upcoming year. Unfortunately, addresses for certain major conventions are unavailable as this list is being compiled. Once again, the best way to keep abreast of conventions is through the various adzines. Please remember when of conventions is through the various adzines. Please remember when writing for convention information to include a self-addressed, stamped envelope for reply. Most conventions are non-profit, so they appreciate the help. Here is the list:

COMIC BOOK CONVENTION
CALENDAR FOR 1992

AMERICON—March 1992, Florrie Chappell Gym, Georgia Southwestern College, Americus, GA. Contact Elwyn Hightower, GSW Box 813, Georgia Southwestern College, Americus, GA 31709.

ATLANTA FANTASY FAIR XVII—July 1992, Atlanta Hilton & Towers, Atlanta, GA. Info: Atlanta Fantasy Fair, 4175 Eliza Ct., Lithonia, GA 30058. PH: (404) 985-1230.

BIG-D SUPER COMIC & COLLECTIBLES SHOW (Formally CHILDHOOD TREASURES)—July 1992, Dallas Sheraton Park Central Hotel, Hwy 635 & Coit Rd. Write Don Maris, Box 111266 Arlington, TX 76007. (817) 261-8745

CAROLINA COMIC BOOK FAIR—For info contact New Dimension Comics, 2609 Central Ave., Charlotte, NC 28205. PH: (704) 372-4376.

CAROLINA CON X—Sept. 1992, Sponsored by The Carolina Pictorial Fiction Assn. Send SASE to Steve Harris, 100 E. Augusta Place, Greenville, SC 29605.

CENTRAL NEW JERSEY COMIC BOOK SHOW—Held monthly on Sundays at the Washington Twp. Volunteer Fire Dept., Rt. 130, Robbinsville. Contact Michael Chaudhuri of EMCEE Conventions, P.O. Box 151, Hightstown, NJ 08520. PH: (609) 448-7585.

CHICAGO—BASEBALL CARD & COMIC BOOK SHOW—Held monthly at University of Illinois at Chicago. For more info call Rich at (312) 733-2266.

CHICAGO COMICON—Larry Charet, 1219-A West Devon Ave., Chicago, IL 60660. PH: (312) 274-1832.

CREATION CON—249-04 Hillside Ave., Bellerose, N.Y. 11426. PH: (718) 343-0202. Holds major conventions in the following cities: Atlanta, Boston, Cincinnati, Cleveland, Detroit, London, Los Angeles, Philadelphia, Rochester, San Francisco, and Washington, D.C. Write or call for details.

CROWN POINT'S PREMIERE MONTHLY CARD AND COMIC SHOW—Crown Point, IN, Knights of Columbus, 700 Merrillville Rd. Contact Marilyn Hall, P.O. Box 507, Crown Point, IN. 46307. PH:(219) 663-8561.

DALLAS FANTASY FAIR—A Bulldog Prod. Convention. For info: Lary Lankford, P.O. Box 820488, Dallas, TX 75382. PH: (214) 349-3367.

DETROIT AREA COMIC BOOK/BASEBALL CARD SHOWS—Held every 2–3 weeks in Royal Oak and Livonia Mich., write: Michael Goldman, Suite 231, 19785 W. 12 Mile Rd., Southfield, MI 48076. PH: (313) 350-2633.

EL PASO FANTASY FESTIVAL—c/o Rita's Fantasy Shop, No. 34 Sunrise Center, El Paso, TX 79904. PH: (915) 757-1143. Late July-Early August.

GREAT EASTERN CONVENTIONS— 225 Everitts Road, Ringoes, NJ 08551, PH: (201) 788-6845. Holds cons in the following cities: Atlanta, Boston, Chicago, Los Angeles, New York and San Francisco.

HEROES CONVENTION '92—June 1992. H. Shelton Drum, P. O. Box 9181, Charlotte, NC 28299, PH: (704) 376-5766 or 1-800-321-4370.

ILLINOIS/INDIANA—Pinsky Baseball Card & Comic Book Supershow, c/o Louis Pinsky, P.O. Box 1072, Lombard, IL 60148-8072, PH: (708) 620-0865. Holds conventions in these cities: Illinois: Alsip, Carol Stream, Coun-tryside/LaGrange, Crystal Lake, Downers Grove, Elgin, Glen Ellyn/Lombard, Itasca, Oakbrook Terrace, Willowbrook/Hinsdale. Indiana: Merrillville.

ISLAND NOSTALGIA COMIC BOOK/BASEBALL CARD SHOWS— Hauppauge, N.Y. Holiday Inn off L.I.E. exit 55, 10a.m.–4p.m. 1740 Express Drive South, Hauppauge, N.Y., For more info call Dennis (516) 724-7422 or Day of Shows only (516) 234-3030, ext 450.

KANSAS CITY COMIC CONVENTION (Formally MO-KAN

COMICS FESTIVAL)—c/o Kansas City Comic Book Club, 734 North 78th St., Kansas City, KS 66112.

LONG ISLAND COMIC BOOK & COLLECTOR'S CONVENTION—Held monthly. Rockville Centre, Holiday Inn, 173 Sunrise Hwy, Long Island, NY. For info: Cosmic Comics & Books of Rockville Centre, 139 N. Park Ave., Rockville Centre, NY 11570. (516) 763-1133.

LOS ANGELES COMIC BOOK & SCIENCE FICTION CONVENTION— Held monthly. For information contact: Bruce Schwartz, 1802 West Olive Ave., Burbank, CA 91506. PH: (818) 954-8432.

MICHIANA COMICON—April, October 1992, South Bend, IN. Contact Jim Rossow, 53100 Poppy Rd., South Bend, IN 46628. PH: (219) 232-8129.

MOBI-CON 92—June 1992, The Days Inn (Airport & I-65), Mobile, AL 36608. For more info: Mobi-Con, P.O. Box 161257, Mobile, AL 36608.

MOTOR CITY COMIC CON—Dearborn, MI. Held March & Oct. 1992 at the Dearborn Civic Center, 15801 Michigan Ave. Contact Michael Goldman, Suite 231, 19785 W. 12 Mile Rd., Southfield, MI 48076. PH: (313) 350-2633.

NOSTALIGA CON—Held in Elizabeth, NJ, Lyndhurst, NJ, Hempstead, NY. Contact George Downes, G.A. Corp., Box 572, Nutley, NJ 07110. PH: (201) 661-3358.

THE ORIGINAL LONG ISLAND MONTHLY COMIC BOOK & BASEBALL CARD SHOW—Held 1st Sunday each month at the Coliseum Motor Inn, 1650 Hempstead Turnpike, East Meadow, Long Island, NY. Contact: Perry Albert, P.O. Box 66, Fredonia, NY 14063. PH: (716) 672-2913.

ORLANDO CON—Sept. 1992, International Inn, Orlando, FL. Info: Jim Ivey, 4300 S. Semoran, Suite 109, Orlando, FL 32822-2453. PH: (407) 273-0141.

SAN DIEGO COMIC-CON—Box 17066, San Diego, CA 92117. July 4th week, 1992, San Diego Convention Center.

THE SCENIC CITY COMICS & COLLECTIBLES FAIR—April 1992, Chattanooga at Eastgate Mall, Mark Derrick, 3244 Castle Ave., Chattanooga, TN 37412. PH: (615) 624-3704.

SEATTLE CENTER CON—Apr., July, Oct. 1992, Box 2043, Kirkland, WA, 98033. PH: (206) 822-5709 or 827-5129.

SEATTLE QUEST NORTHWEST—Seattle, WA. Write: Ron Church or Steve Sibra, P.O. Box 82676, Kenmore, WA 98028.

WESTERN NEW YORK COMIC BOOK BASEBALL CARD & COLLECTIBLES SHOW—Held monthly. Masonic Lodge, 321 E. Main St., Fredonia, NY. Contact: Perry Albert, P.O. Box 66, Fredonia, NY 14063. PH: (716) 672-2913.

A CHRONOLOGY OF
THE DEVELOPMENT
OF THE AMERICAN
COMIC BOOK

By M. Thomas Inge

Precursors: The facsimile newspaper strip reprint collections constitute the earliest "comic books." The first of these was a collection of Richard Outcault's **Yellow Kid** from the Hearst **New York American** in March 1897. Commercial and promotional reprint collections, usually in cardboard covers, appeared through the 1920s and featured such newspaper strips as **Mutt and Jeff, Foxy Grandpa, Buster Brown,** and **Barney Google.** During 1922 a reprint magazine, **Comic Monthly,** appeared with each issue devoted to a separate strip, and from 1929 to 1930 George Delacorte published 36 issues of **The Funnies** in tabloid format with original comic pages in color, becoming the first four-color comic newsstand publication.

1933: The Ledger syndicate published a small broadside of their Sunday comics on 7" by 9" plates. Employees of Eastern Color Printing Company in New York, sales manager Harry I. Wildenberg and salesman Max C. Gaines, saw it and figured that two such plates would fit a tabloid page, which would produce a book about 7½" x 10" when folded. Thus, 10,000 copies of **Funnies on Parade,** containing 32 pages of Sunday newspaper reprints, was published for Proctor and Gamble to be given away as premiums. Some of the strips included were: **Joe Palooka, Mutt and Jeff, Hairbreadth Harry,** and **Reg'lar Fellas.** M. C. Gaines was very impressed with this book and convinced Eastern Color that he could sell a lot of them to such big advertisers as Milk-O-Malt, Wheatena, Kinney Shoe Stores, and others to be used as premiums and radio giveaways. So, Eastern Color printed **Famous Funnies: A Carnival of Comics,** and then **Century of Comics,** both as before, containing Sunday newspaper reprints. Mr. Gaines sold these books in quantities of 100,000 to 250,000.

1934: The giveaway comics were so successful that Mr. Gaines believed that youngsters would buy comic books for ten cents like the "Big Little Books" coming out at that time. So, early in 1934, Eastern Color ran off 35,000 copies of **Famous Funnies, Series 1,** 64 pages of reprints for Dell Publishing Company to be sold for ten cents in chain stores. Since it sold out promptly on the stands, Eastern Color, in May 1934, issued **Famous Funnies** No. 1 (dated July 1934) which became, with issue No. 2 in July, the first monthly comic magazine. The title continued for over 20 years through 218 issues, reaching a circulation peak of over 400,000 copies a month. At the same time, Mr. Gaines went to the sponsors of Percy Crosby's **Skippy,** who was on the radio, and convinced them to put out a Skippy book, advertise it on the air, and give away a free copy to anyone who bought a tube of Phillip's toothpaste. Thus 500,000 copies of **Skippy's Own Book of Comics** was run off and distributed through drug stores everywhere. This was the first four-color comic book of reprints devoted to a single character.

1935: Major Malcolm Wheeler-Nicholson's National Periodical Publications issued in February a tabloid-sized comic publication called **New Fun,** which became **More Fun** after the sixth issue and converted to the normal comic book size after issue eight. **More Fun** was the first comic book of a standard size to publish original material and continued publication until 1949. **Mickey Mouse Magazine** began in the summer, to become **Walt Disney's Comics and Stories** in 1940, and combined original material with reprinted newspaper strips in most issues.

1936: In the wake of the success of **Famous Funnies,** other publishers, in conjunction with the major newspaper strip syndicates, inaugurated more reprint comic books: **Popular Comics** (News-Tribune, February), **Tip Top Comics** (United Features, April), **King Comics** (King Features, April), and **The Funnies** (new series, NEA, October). Four issues of **Wow Comics,** from David McKay and Henle Publications, appeared, edited by S. M. Iger and including early art by Will Eisner, Bob Kane, and Alex Raymond. The first non-reprint comic book devoted to a single theme was **Detective Picture Stories** issued in December by The Comics Magazine Company.

1937: The second single-theme title, **Western Picture Stories,** came in February from The Comics Magazine Company, and the third was **Detective Comics,** an offshoot of **More Fun,** which began in

March to be published to the present. The book's initials, "D.C.," have long served to refer to National Periodical Publications, which was purchased from Major Nicholson by Harry Donenfeld late this year.

1938: "DC" copped a lion's share of the comic book market with the publication of **Action Comics** No. 1 in June which contained the first appearance of Superman by writer Jerry Siegel and artist Joe Shuster, a discovery of Max C. Gaines. The "man of steel" inaugurated the "Golden Era" in comic book history. Fiction House, a pulp publisher, entered the comic book field in September with **Jumbo Comics**, featuring Sheena, Queen of the Jungle, and appearing in oversized format for the first eight issues.

1939: The continued success of "DC" was assured in May with the publication of **Detective Comics** No. 27 containing the first episode of Batman by artist Bob Kane and writer Bill Finger. **Superman Comics** appeared in the summer. Also, during the summer, a black and white premium comic titled **Motion Picture Funnies Weekly** was published to be given away at motion picture theatres. The plan was to issue it weekly and to have continued stories so that the kids would come back week after week not to miss an episode. Four issues were planned but only one came out. This book contains the first appearance and origin of the Sub-Mariner by Bill Everett (8 pages) which was later reprinted in **Marvel Comics.** In November, the first issue of **Marvel Comics** came out, featuring the Human Torch by Carl Burgos and the Sub-Mariner reprint with color added.

1940: The April issue of **Detective Comics** No. 38 introduced Robin the Boy Wonder as a sidekick to Batman, thus establishing the "Dynamic Duo" and a major precedent for later costume heroes who would also have boy companions. **Batman Comics** began in the spring. Over 60 different comic book titles were being issued, including **Whiz Comics** begun in February by Fawcett Publications. A creation of writer Bill Parker and artist C. C. Beck, **Whiz's** Captain Marvel was the only superhero ever to surpass Superman in comic book sales. Drawing on their own popular pulp magazine heroes, Street and Smith Publications introduced **Shadow Comics** in March and **Doc Savage Comics** in May. A second trend was established with the summer appearance of the first issue of **All-Star Comics,** which brought several superheroes together in one story and in its third issue that winter would announce the establishment of the Justice Society of America.

1941: Wonder Woman was introduced in the spring issue of **All-Star Comics** No. 8, the creation of psychologist William Moulton Marston and artist Harry Peter. **Captain Marvel Adventures** began this year. By the end of 1941, over 160 titles were being published, including **Captain America** by Jack Kirby and Joe Simon, **Police Comics** with Jack Cole's Plastic Man and later Will Eisner's Spirit, **Military Comics** with Blackhawk by Eisner and Charles Cuidera, **Daredevil Comics** with the original character by Charles Biro, **Air Fighters** with Airboy also by Biro, and **Looney Tunes & Merrie Melodies** with Porky Pig, Bugs Bunny, and Elmer Fudd, reportedly created by Bob Clampett for the Leon Schlesinger Productions animated films and drawn for the comics by Chase Craig. Also, Albert Kanter's Gilberton Company initiated the **Classics Illustrated** series with **The Three Musketeers.**

1942: Crime Does Not Pay by editor Charles Biro and publisher Lev Gleason, devoted to factual accounts of criminals' lives, began a different trend in realistic crime stories. **Wonder Woman** appeared in the summer. John Goldwater's character Archie, drawn by Bob Montana, first published in **Pep Comics,** was given his own magazine, **Archie Comics,** which has remained popular over 40 years. The first issue of **Animal Comics** contained Walt Kelly's "Albert Takes the Cake," featuring the new character of Pogo. In mid-1942, the undated Dell Four Color title, No. 9, **Donald Duck Finds Pirate Gold,** appeared with art by Carl Barks and Jack Hannah. Barks, also featured in **Walt Disney's Comics and Stories**, remained the most popular delineator of Donald Duck and later introduced his greatest creation, Uncle Scrooge, in **Christmas on Bear Mountain** (Dell Four Color No. 178). The fantasy work of George Carlson appeared in the first issue of **Jingle Jangle Comics,** one of the most imaginative titles for children ever to be published.

1945: The first issue of **Real Screen Comics** introduced the Fox and the Crow by James F. Davis, and John Stanley began drawing the **Little Lulu** comic book based on a popular feature in the **Saturday Evening Post** by Marjorie Henderson Buell from 1935 to 1944. Bill Woggon's **Katy Keene** appears in issue No. 5 of **Wilbur Comics** to be followed by appearances in **Laugh, Pep, Suzie** and her own comic book in 1950. The popularity of Dick Briefer's satiric version of the Frankenstein monster, originally drawn for **Prize Comics** in 1941, led to the publication of **Frankenstein** by Prize publications.

1950: The son of Max C. Gaines, William M. Gaines, who earlier had inherited his father's firm Educational Comics (later Entertaining Comics), began publication of a series of well-written and masterfully drawn titles which would establish a "New Trend" in comics magazines: **Crypt of Terror** (later **Tales from the Crypt**, April), **The**

Vault of Horror (April), **The Haunt of Fear** (May), **Weird Science** (May), **Weird Fantasy** (May), **Crime SuspenStories** (October), and **Two-Fisted Tales** (November), the latter stunningly edited by Harvey Kurtzman.

1952: In October "E.C." published the first number of **Mad** under Kurtzman's creative editorship, thus establishing a style of humor which would inspire other publications and powerfully influence the underground comic book movement of the 1960s.

1953: All Fawcett titles featuring Captain Marvel were ceased after many years of litigation in the courts during which National Periodical Publications claimed that the superhero was an infringement on the copyrighted Superman.

1954: The appearance of Fredric Wertham's book **Seduction of the Innocent** in the spring was the culmination of a continuing war against comic books fought by those who believed they corrupted youth and debased culture. The U. S. Senate Subcommittee on Juvenile Delinquency investigated comic books and in response the major publishers banded together in October to create the Comics Code Authority and adopted, in their own words," "the most stringent code in existence for any communications media." Before the Code took effect, more than 1,000,000,000 issues of comic books were being sold annually.

1955: In an effort to avoid the Code, "E.C." launched a "New Direction" series of titles, such as **Impact, Valor, Aces High, Extra, M.D.,** and **Psychoanalysis,** none of which lasted beyond the year. **Mad** was changed into a larger magazine format with issue No. 24 in July to escape the Comics Code entirely, and "E.C." closed down its line of comic books altogether.

1956: Beginning with the Flash in **Showcase** No. 4, Julius Schwartz began a popular revival of "DC" superheroes which would lead to the "Silver Age" in comic book history.

1957: Atlas reduced the number of titles published by two-thirds, with **Journey into Mystery** and **Strange Tales** surviving, while other publishers did the same or went out of business. Atlas would survive as a part of the Marvel Comics Group.

1960: After several efforts at new satire magazines (**Trump** and **Humbug**), Harvey Kurtzman, no longer with Gaines, issued in August the first number of another abortive effort, **Help!**, where the early work of underground cartoonists Jay Lynch, Skip Williamson, Gilbert Shelton, and Robert Crumb appeared.

1961: Stan Lee edited in November the first **Fantastic Four,**

featuring Mr. Fantastic, the Human Torch, the Thing, and the Invisible Girl, and inaugurated an enormously popular line of titles from Marvel Comics featuring a more contemporary style of superhero.

1962: Lee introduced **The Amazing Spider-Man** in August, with art by Steve Ditko, **The Hulk** in May and **Thor** in August, the last two produced by Dick Ayers and Jack Kirby.

1963: Marvel's **The X-Men,** with art by Jack Kirby, began a successful run in November, but the title would experience a revival and have an even more popular reception in the 1980s.

1965: James Warren issued **Creepy,** a larger black and white comic book, outside Comics Code's control, which emulated the "E.C." horror comic line. Warren's **Eerie** began in September and **Vampirella** in September 1969.

1967: Robert Crumb's **Zap** No. 1 appeared, the first popular underground comic book to achieve wide popularity, although the undergrounds had begun in 1962 with **Adventures of Jesus** by Foolbert Sturgeon (Frank Stack) and 1964 with **God Nose** by Jack Jackson.

1970: Editor Roy Thomas at Marvel begins **Conan the Barbarian** based on fiction by Robert E. Howard with art by Barry Smith, and Neal Adams began to draw for "DC" a series of **Green Lantern/Green Arrow** stories which would deal with relevant social issues such as racism, urban poverty, and drugs.

1972: The Swamp Thing by Berni Wrightson begins in November from "DC".

1973: In February, "DC" revived the original Captain Marvel with new art by C. C. Beck and reprints in the first issue of **Shazam** and in October **The Shadow** with scripts by Denny O'Neil and art by Mike Kaluta.

1974: "DC" began publication in the spring of a series of oversized facsimile reprints of the most valued comic books of the past under the general title of "Famous First Editions," beginning with a reprint of **Action** No. 1 and including afterwards **Detective Comics** No. 27, **Sensation Comics** No. 1, **Whiz Comics** No. 2, **Batman** No. 1, **Wonder Woman** No. 1, **All-Star Comics** No. 3, **Flash Comics** No. 1, and **Superman** No. 1. Mike Friedrich, an independent publisher, released **StarReach** with work by Jim Starlin, Neal Adams, and Dick Giordano, with ownership of the characters and stories invested in the creators themselves.

1975: In the first collaborative effort between the two major comic book publishers of the previous decade, Marvel and "DC" produced together an oversized comic book version of MGM's **Marvelous**

Wizard of Oz in the fall, and then the following year in an unprecedented crossover produced **Superman vs. the Amazing Spider-Man**, written by Gerry Conway, drawn by Ross Andru, and inked by Dick Giordano.

1976: Frank Brunner's **Howard the Duck,** who had appeared earlier in Marvel's **Fear** and **Man-Thing,** was given his own book in January, which because of distribution problems became an overnight collector's item. After decades of litigation, Jerry Siegel and Joe Shuster were given financial recompense and recognition by National Periodical Publications for their creation of Superman, after several friends of the team made a public issue of the case.

1977: Stan Lee's **Spider-Man** was given a second birth, fifteen years after his first, through a highly successful newspaper comic strip, which began syndication on January 3 with art by John Romita. This invasion of the comic strip by comic book characters continued with the appearance on June 6 of Marvel's **Howard the Duck**, with story by Steve Gerber and visuals by Gene Colan. In an unusually successful collaborative effort, Marvel began publication of the comic book adaptation of the George Lucas film **Star Wars,** with script by Roy Thomas and art by Howard Chaykin, at least three months before the film was released nationally on May 25. The demand was so great that all six issues of **Star Wars** were reprinted at least seven times, and the installments were reprinted in two volumes of an oversized Marvel Special Edition and a single paperback volume for the book trade. Dave Sim, with an issue dated December, began self-publication of his **Cerebus the Aardvark,** the success of which would help establish the independent market for non-traditional black-and-white comics.

1978: In an effort to halt declining sales, Warner Communications drastically cut back on the number of "DC" titles and overhauled its distribution process in June. The interest of the visual media in comic book characters reached a new high with the Hulk, Spider-Man, and Doctor Strange, the subjects of television shows; with various projects begun to produce film versions of Flash Gordon, Dick Tracy, Popeye, Conan, The Phantom, and Buck Rogers; and with the movement reaching an outlandish peak of publicity with the release of **Superman** in December. Two significant applications of the comic book format to traditional fiction appeared this year: **A Contract with God and Other Tenement Stories** by Will Eisner and **The Silver Surfer** by Stan Lee and Jack Kirby. Eclipse Enterprises published Don McGregor and Paul Gulacy's **Sabre,** the first graphic album produced for the direct sales market, and initiated a policy of paying royalties and granting copyrights to comic book creators. Wendy and Richard Pini's **Elfquest,** a self-publishing project begun this year, eventually became so popular that it achieved bookstore distribution. The magazine **Heavy Metal** brought to American attention the avant garde comic book work of European artists.

1980: Publication of the November premier issue of **The New Teen Titans,** with art by George Perez and story by Marv Wolfman, brought back to widespread popularity a title originally published by "DC" in 1966.

1981: The distributor Pacific Comics began publishing titles for direct sales through comic shops with the inaugural issue of Jack Kirby's **Captain Victory and the Galactic Rangers** and offered royalties to artists and writers on the basis of sales. "DC" would do the same for regular newsstand comics in November (with payments retroactive to July 1981), and Marvel followed suit by the end of the year. The first issue of **Raw,** irregularly published by Art Spiegelman and Francoise Mouly, carried comic book art into new extremes of experimentation and innovation with work by European and American artists. With issue No. 158, Frank Miller began to write and draw Marvel's **Daredevil** and brought a vigorous style of violent action to comic book pages.

1982: The first slick format comic book in regular size appeared, **Marvel Fanfare No. 1,** with a March date. Fantagraphics Books began publication in July of **Love and Rockets** by Mario, Gilbert, and Jaime Hernandez and brought a new ethnic sensibility and sophistication in style and content to comic book narratives for adults.

1983: This year saw more comic book publishers, aside from Marvel and DC, issuing more titles than had existed in the past 40 years, most small independent publishers relying on direct sales, such as Americomics, Capital, Eagle, Eclipse, First, Pacific, and Red Circle, and with Archie, Charlton, and Whitman publishing on a limited scale. Frank Miller's mini-series **Ronin** demonstrated a striking use of swordplay and martial arts typical of Japanese comic book art, and Howard Chaykin's stylish but controversial **American Flagg** appeared with an October date on its first issue.

1984: A publishing, media, film, and merchandising phenomenon began with the first issue of **Teenage Mutant Ninja Turtles** from Mirage Studios by Kevin Eastman and Peter Laird.

1985: Ohio State University's Library of Communication and Graphic Arts hosted the first major exhibition devoted to the comic book May 19 through August 2. In what was billed as an irreversible decision, the silver age superheroine Supergirl was killed in the seventh (October) issue of **Crisis on Infinite Earths,** a limited series intended to reorganize and simplify the DC universe on the occasion of the publisher's 50th anniversary.

1986: In recognition of its twenty-fifth anniversary, Marvel began publication of several new ongoing titles comprising Marvel's "New Universe," a self-contained fictional world. DC attracted extensive publicity and media coverage with its revisions of the character of **Superman** by John Byrne and of **Batman** in the **Dark Knight** series by Frank Miller. **Watchmen,** a limited-series graphic novel by Alan Moore and artist Dave Gibbons, began publication with a September issue from DC and Marvel's **The 'Nam,** written by Vietnam veteran Doug Murray and penciled by Michael Golden, began with its December issue. DC issued guidelines in December for labelling their titles as either for mature readers or for readers of all ages; in response, many artists and writers publicly objected or threatened to resign.

1987: Art Spiegelman's **Maus: A Survivor's Tale** was nominated for the National Book Critics Circle Award in biography, the first comic book to be so honored. A celebration of Superman's fiftieth birthday began with the opening of an exhibition on his history at the Smithsonian's Museum of American History in Washington, DC, in June and a symposium on "The Superhero in America" in October.

1988: Superman's birthday celebration continued with a public party in New York and a CBS television special in February, a cover story in **Time** magazine in March (the first comic book character to appear on the cover), and an international exposition in Cleveland in June. With issue number 601 for May 24, **Action Comics** became the first modern weekly comic book, which ceased publication after 42 issues with the December 13 number. In August, DC initiated a new policy of allowing creators of new characters to retain ownership of them rather than rely solely on work-for-hire.

1989: The fiftieth anniversary of Batman was marked by the release of the film **Batman,** starring Michael Keaton as Bruce Wayne and Jack Nicholson as the Joker; it grossed more money in the weekend it opened than any other motion picture in film history to that time.

1990: The publication of a new **Classics Illustrated** series began in January from Berkley/First with adaptations of Poe's **The Raven and Other Poems** by Gahan Wilson, Dickens' **Great Expectations** by Rick Geary, Carroll's **Through the Looking Glass** by Kyle Baker, and Melville's **Moby Dick** by Bill Sienkiewicz, with extensive media attention. The adaptation of characters to film continued with the most successful in terms of popularity and box-office receipts being **Teenage Mutant Ninja Turtles** and Warren Beatty's **Dick Tracy.** In November, the engagement of Clark Kent and Lois Lane was announced in **Superman** No. 50 which brought public fanfare about the planned marriage.

Note: A special word of thanks is due Gerard Jones for his suggestions and contributions to the above chronology.

HOW TO USE
THIS BOOK

The author of this book has included a selection of key titles covering a variety of subjects that are mostly collected. The comic book titles are listed alphabetically for easy reference. All key issues and important contents are pointed out and priced in three grades—good, fine and near mint.

Most comic books listed are priced in groups: 11-20, 21-30, 31-50, etc. The prices listed in the right hand column are for each single comic book in that grouping.

The prices shown represent the current range, but since prices do change constantly, the values in this book should be used as a guide only.

A general selection of titles is represented here, so for more detailed information please consult *The Official Overstreet Comic Book Price Guide*, master guide.

Comic Book
Listings

A

ABBOTT AND COSTELLO (. . . Comics)
Feb, 1948-No. 40, Sept, 1956 (Mort Drucker art in most issues)
St. John Publishing Co.

	Good	Fine	N-Mint
1	24.00	73.00	170.00
2	12.00	36.00	84.00
3-9 (#8, 8/49; #9, 2/50)	7.00	21.00	50.00
10-Son of Sinbad story by Kubert (new)	13.00	40.00	90.00
11,13-20 (#11, 10/50; #13, 8/51; #15, 12/52)	4.50	14.00	32.00
12-Movie issue	6.00	18.00	42.00
21-30: 28 r-#8. 30-Painted-c	4.00	12.00	28.00
31-40: #33, 38-r	3.00	9.00	21.00
3D #1 (11/53)-Infinity-c	20.00	60.00	140.00

ACE COMICS
April, 1937-No. 151, Oct-Nov, 1949
David McKay Publications

	Good	Fine	N-Mint
1-Jungle Jim by Alex Raymond, Blondie, Ripley's Believe It Or Not, Krazy Kat begin	165.00	415.00	1000.00
2	53.00	160.00	370.00
3-5	37.00	110.00	260.00
6-10	27.00	81.00	190.00
11-The Phantom begins (In brown costume, 2/38)	34.00	100.00	235.00
12-20	20.00	60.00	140.00
21-25,27-30	16.50	50.00	115.00
26-Origin Prince Valiant (begins series?)	46.00	140.00	325.00
31-40: 37-Krazy Kat ends	12.00	36.00	84.00
41-60	10.00	30.00	70.00
61-64,66-76-(7/43; last 68 pgs.)	8.50	25.50	60.00
65-(8/42; Flag-c)	9.00	27.00	63.00
77-84 (3/44; all 60 pgs.)	7.00	21.00	50.00
85-99 (52 pgs.)	6.00	18.00	42.00
100 (7/45; last 52 pgs.)	7.00	21.00	50.00
101-134: 128-11/47; Brick Bradford begins. 134-Last Prince Valiant (All 36 pgs.)	5.00	15.00	35.00
135-151: 135-6/48; Lone Ranger begins	4.00	12.00	28.00

Action Comics #13, © DC Comics

ACTION COMICS (. . . Weekly No. 601-642)
6/38-No. 583, 9/86; No. 584, 1/87-Present
National Periodical Publ./Detective Comics/DC Comics

	Good	Fine	VF-NM
1-Origin & 1st app. Superman	6,600.00	16,500.00	36,000.00
(Issues 1-10 are all scarce to rare)			

	Good	Fine	N-Mint
1(1976,1983)-Giveaway; paper cover, 16 pgs. in color; reprints complete			
Superman story from #1 ('38)	.70	2.00	4.00
1(1987 Nestle Quik giveaway; 1988, 50 cent-c)		.25	.50
2	835.00	2100.00	5000.00
3 (Scarce)	670.00	1675.00	4000.00
4	450.00	1125.00	2700.00
5 (Rare)	535.00	1340.00	3200.00
6-1st Jimmy Olsen (called office boy)	450.00	1125.00	2700.00
7,10-Superman covers	585.00	1460.00	3500.00
8,9	385.00	960.00	2300.00
11,12,14: 14-Clip Carson begins, ends #41	200.00	500.00	1200.00
13-Superman cover; last Scoop Scanlon	292.00	730.00	1750.00

	Good	Fine	N-Mint
15-Superman cover	292.00	730.00	1750.00
16	165.00	410.00	980.00
17-Superman cover; last Marco Polo	220.00	550.00	1320.00
18-Origin 3 Aces; 1st X-Ray Vision?	155.00	385.00	925.00
19-Superman covers begin	200.00	500.00	1200.00
20-'S' left off Superman's chest; Clark Kent works at 'Daily Star'			
	185.00	460.00	1100.00
21,22,24,25: 24-Kent at Daily Planet. 25-Last app. Gargantua T. Potts, Tex Thompson's sidekick	115.00	290.00	700.00
23-1st app. Luthor (w/red hair) & Black Pirate; Black Pirate by Moldoff; 1st mention of The Daily Planet (4/40)	168.00	415.00	1000.00
26-30	90.00	225.00	540.00
31,32: 32-1st Krypto Ray Gun in Superman	68.00	170.00	410.00
33-Origin Mr. America	80.00	200.00	480.00
34-40: 37-Origin Congo Bill. 40-Intro/1st app. Star Spangled Kid & Stripesy			
	68.00	170.00	410.00
41	63.00	158.00	380.00
42-1st app./origin Vigilante; Bob Daley becomes Fat Man; origin Mr. America's magic flying carpet	92.00	230.00	550.00
43-46,48-50: 44-Fat Man's I.D. revealed to Mr. America. 45-1st app. Stuff			
	63.00	158.00	380.00
47-1st Luthor cover in Action Comics	75.00	188.00	450.00
51-1st app. The Prankster	58.00	146.00	350.00
52-Fat Man & Mr. America become the Ameri-commandos; origin Vigilante retold			
	63.00	158.00	380.00
53-60: 56-Last Fat Man. 59-Kubert Vigilante begins?, ends #70. 60-First app. Lois Lane as Superwoman	47.00	115.00	280.00
61-63,65-70: 63-Last 3 Aces	42.00	105.00	255.00
64-Intro Toyman	47.00	115.00	280.00
71-79: 74-Last Mr. America	37.00	92.00	220.00
80-2nd app. & 1st Mr. Mxyztplk-c (1/45)	60.00	150.00	360.00
81-90: 83-Intro Hocus & Pocus	37.00	92.00	220.00
91-99: 93-X-Mas-c. 99-1st small logo (7/46)	32.00	81.00	195.00
100	75.00	188.00	450.00
101-Nuclear explosion-c	43.00	108.00	260.00
102-120: 105,117-X-Mas-c	33.00	83.00	200.00
121-126,128-140: 135,136,138-Zatara by Kubert	32.00	80.00	190.00
127-Vigilante by Kubert; Tommy Tomorrow begins			
	43.00	110.00	260.00
141-157,159-161: 156-Lois Lane as Super Woman. 160-Last 52 pgs.			
	32.00	80.00	190.00

	Good	Fine	N-Mint
158-Origin Superman	40.00	100.00	240.00
162-180: 168,176-Used in **POP**, pg. 90	20.00	60.00	140.00
181-201: 191-Intro. Janu in Congo Bill. 198-Last Vigilante. 201-Last pre-code			
issue	19.00	57.00	132.00
202-220	16.00	48.00	110.00
221-240: 224-1st Golden Gorilla story	12.50	37.50	88.00
241,243-251: 248-Congo Bill becomes Congorilla. 251-Last Tommy Tomorrow			
	9.30	28.00	66.00
242-Origin & 1st app. Braniac (7/58); 1st mention of Shrunken City of Kandor			
	63.00	190.00	440.00
252-Origin & 1st app. Supergirl (5/59); Re-intro Metallo (see Superboy #49 for 1st			
app.)	68.00	205.00	480.00
253-2nd app. Supergirl	11.85	35.50	83.00
254-1st meeting of Bizarro & Superman	14.00	43.00	100.00
255-1st Bizarro Lois & both Bizarros leave Earth to make Bizarro World			
	10.30	31.00	72.00
256-261: 259-Red Kryptonite used. 261-1st X-Kryptonite which gave Streaky his			
powers; last Congorilla in Action; origin & 1st app. Streaky The Super Cat			
	6.30	19.00	44.00
262,264-266,268-270	4.70	14.00	33.00
263-Origin Bizarro World	5.70	17.00	40.00
267(8/60)-3rd Legion app; 1st app. Chameleon Boy, Colossal Boy, & Invisible Kid			
	34.00	102.00	242.00
271-275,277-282: Last 10 cent issue	4.30	13.00	31.00
276(5/61)-6th Legion app; 1st app. Braniac 5, Phantom Girl, Triplicate Girl,			
Bouncing Boy, Sun Boy, & Shrinking Violet; Supergirl joins Legion			
	12.50	37.50	88.00
283(12/61)-Legion of Super-Villains app.	5.70	17.00	40.00
284(1/62)-Mon-el app.	5.70	17.00	40.00
285(2/62)-12th Legion app; Braniac 5 cameo; Supergirl's existence revealed to			
world	5.70	17.00	40.00
286-290: 286-Legion of Super Villains app. 287-14th Legion app. (cameo). 288-			
Mon-el app.; r-origin Supergirl. 289-16th Legion app. (Adult); Lightning Man			
& Saturn Woman's marriage 1st revealed. 290-17th Legion app; Phantom			
Girl app.	2.85	8.50	20.00
291,292,294-299: 292-2nd app. Superhorse (see Adv. 293). 297-Mon- el app; 298-			
Legion app.	1.85	5.50	13.00
293-Origin Comet (Superhorse)	4.30	13.00	30.00
300	2.15	6.50	15.00
301-303,305-308,310-320: 306-Braniac 5, Mon-el app. 307-Saturn Girl app. 314-			
r-origin Supergirl; J.L.A. x-over. 317-Death of Nor-Kan of Kandor. 319-			

	Good	Fine	N-Mint
Shrinking Violet app.	1.15	3.50	7.00
304-Origin & 1st app. Black Flame	1.15	3.50	7.00
309-Legion app.	1.15	3.50	8.00
321-333,335-340: 336-Origin Akvar(Flamebird). 340-Origin, 1st app. Parasite			
	.85	2.50	5.00
334-Giant G-20; origin Supergirl, Streaky, Superhorse & Legion (all-r)			
	1.70	5.00	12.00
341-346,348-359	.70	2.00	4.00
347,360-Giant Supergirl G-33,G-45; 347-Origin Comet-r. 360-Legion-r; r-origin Supergirl	1.15	3.50	8.00
361-372,374-380: 365-Legion app. 370-New facts about Superman's origin. 376-Last Supergirl in Action. 377-Legion begins	.35	1.00	2.00
373-Giant Supergirl G-57; Legion-r	1.00	3.00	6.00
381-402: 392-Last Legion in Action. Saturn Girl gets new costume.			
393-402-All Superman issues	.25	.75	1.50
403-413: All 52 pg. issues; 411-Origin Eclipso-(r). 413-Metamorpho begins, ends #418	.25	.75	1.50
414-424: 419-Intro. Human Target. 421-Intro Capt. Strong; Green Arrow begins. 422,423-Origin Human Target	.25	.75	1.50
425-Neal Adams-a; The Atom begins	.35	1.00	2.00
426-436,438,439,442,444-450	.25	.75	1.50
437,443-100 pg. giants	.35	1.00	2.00
440-1st Grell-a on Green Arrow	.70	2.00	4.00
441-Grell-a on Green Arrow continues	.40	1.25	2.50
451-499: 454-Last Atom. 458-Last Green Arrow. 487-1st app. Microwave Man; origin Atom retold. 488-Earth II Superman & Lois Lane wed	.25	.75	1.50
500-($1.00, 68 pgs.)-Infinity-c; Superman life story; shows Legion statues in museum	.60	1.20	
501-551,554-582: 511-514-New Airwave. 513-The Atom begins. 517- Aquaman begins; ends #541. 521-1st app. The Vixen. 532-New Teen Titans cameo. 535,536-Omega Men app.; 536-New Teen Titans cameo. 544-(Mando paper, 68pgs.)-Origins New Luthor & Brainiac; Omega Men cameo. 546-J.L.A. & New Teen Titans app. 551-Starfire becomes Red-Star	.50	1.00	
552,553-Animal Man-c & app. (2/84 & 3/84)	2.00	6.00	12.00
583-Alan Moore scripts	2.00	6.00	12.00
584-Byrne-a begins; New Teen Titans app.	.25	.75	1.50
585-597,599: 586-Legends x-over		.50	1.00
598-1st app. Checkmate	.50	1.50	3.00
600-($2.50, 84 pgs., 5/88)	.70	2.00	4.00

	Good	Fine	N-Mint
601-642-Weekly issues ($1.50, 52 pgs.); 601-Re-intro The Secret Six. 611-614: Catwoman (new costume in #611). 613-618: Nightwing			
	.25	.75	1.50
643-Superman & monthly issues begin again; Perez-c/a/scripts begin; Cover swipe Superman #1	.25	.75	1.50
644-649,651-661,663-670: 654-Part 3 of Batman storyline. 655-Free extra 8 pgs. 660-Death of Lex Luthor		.50	1.00
650-($1.50, 52 pgs.)-Lobo cameo (last panel)	.25	.75	1.50
662-Clark Kent tells Lois he's Superman; continued in Superman #53			
	.35	1.05	2.50
667-($1.75-c,52 pgs.)	.25	.75	1.80
Annual 1 (10/87)-Art Adams-c/a(p)	1.00	3.00	6.00
Annual 2 (7/89, $1.75, 68 pgs.)-Perez-c/a(i)	.35	1.00	2.00

ADVANCED DUNGEONS & DRAGONS
Dec, 1988-Present ($1.25, color) (Newsstand #1 is Holiday, 1988-89)
DC Comics

	Good	Fine	N-Mint
1-Based on TSR role playing game	1.70	5.00	10.00
2	1.15	3.50	7.00
3	.75	2.25	4.50
4-10: Later issues $1.50 cover	.40	1.25	2.50
11-15	.30	.85	1.70
16-24	.25	.75	1.50
24-35: 24-Begin $1.75-c	.30	.90	1.80
Annual 1 (1990, $3.95, 68 pgs.)	.70	2.00	4.00

ADVENTURE COMICS (Formerly New Adventure)
(. . . Presents Dial H For Hero #479-490)
No. 32, 11/38-No. 490, 2/82; No. 491, 9/82-No. 503, 9/83
National Periodical Publications/DC Comics

	Good	Fine	N-Mint
32-Anchors Aweigh (ends #52), Barry O'Neil (ends #60, not in #33), Captain Desmo (ends #47), Dale Daring (ends #47), Federal Men (ends #70), The Golden Dragon (ends #36), Rusty & His Pals (ends #52) by Bob Kane, Todd Hunter (ends #38) and Tom Brent (ends #39) begin	108.00	270.00	650.00
33-38	63.00	160.00	380.00
39(1/39)-Jack Wood begins, ends #42: 1st mention of Marijuana in comics			
	70.00	175.00	420.00

Adventure Comics #270, © DC Comics

	Good	Fine	VF-NM
40-(Rare, 7/39, on stands 6/10/39)-The Sandman begins; believed to be 1st conceived story (see N.Y. World's Fair '39 for 1st published app.); Socko Strong begins, ends #54 | 800.00 | 2000.00 | 4800.00 |

	Good	Fine	N-Mint
41	167.00	417.00	1000.00

42,44,46,47: All Sandman covers. 47-Steve Conrad Adventurer begins, ends #76

	125.00	312.00	750.00
43,45	112.00	280.00	675.00

	Good	Fine	VF-NM
48-Intro. & 1st app. The Hourman by Bernard Baily | 750.00 | 1875.00 | 4500.00 |

	Good	Fine	N-Mint
49,50: 50-Cotton Carver by Jack Lehti begins, ends #59? | 107.00 | 265.00 | 640.00 |

51-60: 53-1st app. Jimmy "Minuteman" Martin & the Minutemen of America in Hourman; ends #78. 58-Paul Kirk Manhunter egins (1st app.), ends #72

	100.00	250.00	600.00

	Good	Fine	VF-NM
61-1st app. Starman by Jack Burnley	417.00	1040.00	2500.00

	Good	Fine	N-Mint
62-65,67,68,70: 67-Origin The Mist. 70-Last Federal Men			
	87.00	215.00	520.00
66-Origin/1st app. Shining Knight	117.00	290.00	700.00
69-1st app. Sandy the Golden Boy (Sandman's sidekick) by Bob Kane; Sandman dons new costume	108.00	270.00	650.00
71-Jimmy Martin becomes costume aide to the Hourman; 1st app. Hourman's Miracle Ray machine	87.00	215.00	520.00

	Good	Fine	VF-NM
72-1st Simon & Kirby Sandman	368.00	915.00	2200.00
73-(Scarce)-Origin Manhunter by Simon & Kirby; begin new series			
	400.00	1000.00	2400.00

	Good	Fine	N-Mint
74-80: 74-Thorndyke replaces Jimmy, Hourman's assistant. 77-Origin Genius Jones; Mist story. 80-Last Simon & Kirby Manhunter & Burnley Starman			
	108.00	270.00	650.00
81-90: 83-Last Hourman. 84-Mike Gibbs begins, ends #102			
	70.00	175.00	420.00
91-Last Simon & Kirby Sandman	60.00	150.00	360.00
92-99,101,102: 92-Last Manhunter. 102-Last Starman, Sandman, & Genius Jones. Most-S&K-c	46.00	115.00	275.00
100	75.00	185.00	450.00
103-Aquaman, Green Arrow, Johnny Quick, Superboy begin; 1st small logo (4/46)			
	183.00	460.00	1100.00
104	58.00	145.00	350.00
105-110	48.00	120.00	290.00
111-120: 113-X-Mas-c	42.00	105.00	250.00
121-126,128-130: 128-1st meeting Superboy & Lois Lane			
	33.00	85.00	200.00
127-Brief origin Shining Knight retold	38.00	95.00	225.00
131-141,143-149: 132-Shining Knight 1st return to King Arthur time; origin aide Sir Butch	29.00	73.00	175.00
142-Origin Shining Knight & Johnny Quick retold			
	33.00	85.00	200.00
150,151,153,155,157,159,161,163-All have 6 pg. Shining Knight stories by Frank Frazetta. 159-Origin Johnny Quick	43.00	110.00	260.00
152,154,156,158,160,162,164-169: 166-Last Shining Knight. 168-Last 52 pgs.			
	23.00	70.00	160.00
170-180	21.00	62.00	145.00

	Good	Fine	N-Mint
181-199: 189-B&W and color illo in **POP**	19.00	56.00	130.00
200	26.00	78.00	180.00
201-209: 207-Last Johnny Quick (not in 205). 209-Last Pre-code issue; origin Speedy	19.00	57.00	130.00
210-1st app. Krypto (Superdog)	157.00	470.00	1100.00
211-220: 214,220-Krypto app.	16.00	48.00	110.00
221-246: 237-1st Intergalactic Vigilante Squadron (Legion tryout)	13.50	41.00	95.00
247(4/58)-1st Legion of Super Heroes app.; 1st app. Cosmic Boy, Lightning Boy (later Lightning Lad in #267), & Saturn Girl (origin)	246.00	738.00	1725.00
248-252,254,255: All Kirby Green Arrow. 255-Intro. Red Kryptonite in Superboy (used in #252 but with no effect)	8.50	25.50	60.00
253-1st meeting of Superboy & Robin; Green Arrow by Kirby	11.00	32.50	75.00
256-Origin Green Arrow by Kirby	34.00	102.00	235.00
257-259	8.50	25.50	60.00
260-1st Silver Age origin Aquaman	28.00	86.00	200.00
261-266,268,270: 262-Origin Speedy in Green Arrow. 270-Congorilla begins, ends #281,283	6.50	19.50	45.00
267(12/59)-2nd Legion of Super Heroes; Lightning Boy now called Lightning Lad; new costumes for Legion	61.00	183.00	425.00
269-Intro. Aqualad; last Green Arrow (not in #206)	11.50	34.00	80.00
271-Origin Luthor	16.00	48.00	110.00
272-274,277-280: 279-Intro White Kryptonite in Superboy. 280-1st meeting Superboy-Lori Lemaris	4.50	14.00	32.00
275-Origin Superman-Batman team retold (see World's Finest #94)	8.50	25.50	60.00
276-(9/60) Re-intro Metallo (3rd app?); story similar to Superboy #49	4.50	14.00	32.00
281,284,287-289: 281-Last Congorilla. 284-Last Aquaman in Adv. 287, 288-Intro. Dev-Em, the Knave from Krypton. 287-1st Bizarro Perry White & J. Olsen. 289-Legion cameo (statues)	4.00	12.00	28.00
282(3/61)-5th Legion app; intro/origin Star Boy	10.00	30.00	70.00
283-Intro. The Phantom Zone	6.00	18.00	42.00
285-1st Bizarro World story (ends #299) in Adv. (See Action #255)	7.00	21.00	50.00
286-1st Bizarro Mxyzptlk	5.70	17.00	40.00
290 (11/61)-8th Legion app; origin Sunboy in Legion (last 10 cent issue)	9.30	28.00	65.00

	Good	Fine	N-Mint
291,292,295-298: 292-1st Bizarro Lana Lang & Lucy Lane. 295-1st Bizarro Titano			
	3.50	10.50	24.00
293(2/62)-13th Legion app; Mon-el & Legion Super Pets (1st app. & origin) app. (1st Superhorse). 1st Bizarro Luthor & Kandor			
	6.85	20.50	48.00
294-1st Bizarro M. Monroe, Pres. Kennedy	6.50	19.50	45.00
299-1st Gold Kryptonite (8/62)	3.60	11.00	25.00
300-Legion series begins; Mon-el leaves Phantom Zone (temporarily), joins Legion	30.00	90.00	210.00
301-Origin Bouncing Boy	9.30	28.00	65.00
302-305: 303-1st app. Matter Eater Lad. 304-Death of Lightning Lad in Legion			
	5.15	15.50	36.00
306-310: 306-Intro. Legion of Substitute Heroes. 307-1st app. Element Lad in Legion. 308-1st app. Lightning Lass in Legion	4.00	12.00	28.00
311-320: 312-Lightning Lad back in Legion. 315-Last new Superboy story; Colossal Boy app. 316-Origins & powers of Legion given. 317-Intro. Dream Girl in Legion; Lightning Lass becomes Light Lass; Hall of Fame series begins. 320-Dev-Em 2nd app.	2.85	8.50	20.00
321-Intro Time Trapper	2.15	6.50	15.00
322-330: 327-Intro Timber Wolf in Legion. 329-Intro Legion of Super Bizarros			
	1.85	5.50	13.00
331-340: 337-Chlorophyll Kid & Night Girl app. 340-Intro Computo in Legion			
	1.70	5.00	12.00
341-Triplicate Girl becomes Duo Damsel	1.15	3.50	8.00
342-345,347,350,351: 345-Last Hall of Fame; returns in 356,371. 351-1st app. White Witch	1.00	3.00	7.00
346,348,349: 346-1st app. Karate Kid, Princess Projectra, Ferro Lad, & Nemesis Kid. 348-Origin Sunboy; intro Dr. Regulus in Legion			
349-Intro Universo & Rond Vidar	1.15	3.50	8.00
352,354-360: 355-Insect Queen joins Legion (4/67)			
	1.00	3.00	6.00
353-Death of Ferro Lad in Legion	1.50	4.50	10.00
361-364,366,368-370: 369-Intro Mordru in Legion	.75	2.25	4.50
365,367,371,372: 365-Intro Shadow Lass; lists origins & powers of L.S.H. 367-New Legion headquarters. 371-Intro. Chemical King. 372-Timber Wolf & Chemical King join	.90	2.75	5.50
373,374,376-380: Last Legion in Adv.	.75	2.25	4.50
375-Intro Quantum Queen & The Wanderers	.90	2.75	5.50
381-389,391-400: 381-Supergirl begins. 399-Unpubbed G.A. Black Canary story. 400-New costume for Supergirl		.60	1.20
390-Giant Supergirl G-69	.70	2.00	4.00

	Good	Fine	N-Mint
401,402,404-410: 409-420-52pg. issues		.60	1.20
403-68pg. Giant G-81	.70	2.00	4.00
411,413: 413-Hawkman by Kubert; G.A. Robotman-r/Det. #178; Zatanna begins,			
ends #421		.40	.80
412-Reprints origin Animal Man/Str. Advs. #180	1.00	3.00	6.00
414-Reprints 2nd Animal Man/Stra. Advs. #184	.70	2.00	4.00
415,420-Animal Man reprints	.35	1.00	2.00
416-Giant DC-100 Pg. Super Spect. #10; GA-r		.60	1.20
417-Morrow Vigilante; Frazetta Shining Knight r-/Adv. #161; origin The			
Enchantress		.60	1.20
418,419,421-424: Last Supergirl in Adv.		.40	.80
425-New look, content change to adventure; Toth-a, origin Capt. Fear			
	.25	.75	1.50
426-458: 427-Last Vigilante. 435-Mike Grell's 1st comic work ('74).			
440-New Spectre origin. 457,458-Eclipso app.		.40	.80
459,460,463-466 ($1.00 size, 68 pgs.)		.45	.90
461,462: Death of Earth II Batman	.70	2.00	4.00
467-490: 467-Starman by Ditko, Plastic Man begin, end 478. 469,470-Origin			
Starman		.40	.80
491-499: 491-100 pg. Digest size begins. 493-Challengers of the Unknown begins			
by Tuska w/brief origin		.60	1.20
500-All Legion-r (Digest size, 148 pgs.)	.25	.80	1.60
501-503-G.A.-r		.60	1.20

ADVENTURES INTO THE UNKNOWN
Fall, 1948-No. 174, Aug, 1967 (No. 1-33: 52 pgs.)
American Comics Group

(1st continuous series horror comic; see Eerie #1)

1-Guardineer-a; adapt. of 'Castle of Otranto' by Horace Walpole			
	55.00	165.00	385.00
2	27.00	81.00	190.00
3-Feldstein-a, 9 pgs.	28.00	86.00	200.00
4,5	16.00	48.00	110.00
6-10	12.00	36.00	84.00
11-16,18-20: 13-Starr-a	8.50	25.50	60.00
17-Story similar to movie 'The Thing'	12.00	36.00	84.00
21-26,28-30	7.00	21.00	50.00
27-Williamson/Krenkel-a, 8 pgs.	14.00	42.00	100.00
31-50: 38-Atom bomb panels	5.00	15.00	35.00
51(1/54)-58 (3-D effect-c/stories)	11.50	34.00	80.00

	Good	Fine	N-Mint
59-3-D effect story only	7.00	21.00	50.00
60-Woodesque-a by Landau	4.00	12.00	28.00
61-Last pre-code issue (1-2/55)	3.50	10.50	24.00
62-70	2.65	8.00	18.00
71-90	1.70	5.00	12.00
91,96(#95 on inside),107,116-All contain Williamson-a			
	2.85	8.50	20.00
92-95,97-99,101-106,108-115,117-127	1.50	4.50	10.00
100	2.00	6.00	14.00
128-Williamson/Krenkel/Torres-a(r)/Forbidden Worlds #63; last 10 cent issue			
	1.70	5.00	12.00
129-150	1.15	3.50	8.00
151-153: 153-Magic Agent app.	.70	2.00	5.00
154-Nemesis series begins (origin), ends #170	1.15	3.50	8.00
155-167,169-174: 157-Magic Agent app.	.70	2.00	5.00
168-Ditko-a(p)	1.15	3.50	8.00

ADVENTURES OF DEAN MARTIN AND JERRY LEWIS, THE (The Adventures of Jerry Lewis No. 41 on)
July-Aug. 1952-No. 40, Oct. 1957
National Periodical Publications

	Good	Fine	N-Mint
1	41.00	122.00	285.00
2	20.00	60.00	140.00
3-10	11.00	32.00	75.00
11-19: Last pre-code (2/55)	5.70	17.00	40.00
20-30	4.30	13.00	30.00
31-40	3.15	9.50	22.00

ADVENTURES OF JERRY LEWIS, THE (Advs. of Dean Martin & Jerry Lewis No. 1-40)
No. 41, Nov, 1957-No. 124, May-June, 1971
National Periodical Publications

	Good	Fine	N-Mint
41-60	2.65	8.00	18.00
61-80: 68,74-Photo-c	2.00	6.00	14.00
81-91,93-96,98-100: 89-Bob Hope app.	1.15	3.50	8.00
92-Superman cameo	1.50	4.50	10.00
97-Batman/Robin x-over; Joker-c/story	2.65	8.00	18.00
101-104-Neal Adams-c/a; 102-Beatles app.	2.65	8.00	18.00
105-Superman x-over	1.50	4.50	10.00

	Good	Fine	N-Mint
106-111,113-116	.70	2.00	4.00
112-Flash x-over	1.50	4.50	10.00
117-Wonder Woman x-over	.85	2.50	5.00
118-124	.50	1.50	3.00

ADVENTURES OF SUPERMAN (Formerly Superman)
No. 424, Jan, 1987-Present
DC Comics

424	.35	1.00	2.00
425-449: 426-Legends x-over. 432-1st app. Jose Delgado who becomes Gang-buster in #434. 436-Byrne scripts begin. 436,437- Millennium x-over. 438-New Brainiac app. 440-Batman app.		.60	1.20
450-463,465-479,481-484: 457-Perez plots. 463-Superman/Flash race. 467-Part 2 of Batman story. 473-Hal Jordan, Guy Gardner x-over		.50	1.00
464-Lobo-c & app. predates Lobo #1	.25	.75	1.50
480-($1.75-c,52 pgs.)	.30	.90	1.80
Annual 1 (9/87)-Starlin-c	.25	.70	1.40
Annual 2 (1990, $2.00, 68 pgs.)-Byrne-c/a(i); Legion '90 (Lobo) app.	.25	.70	1.40

ADVENTURES OF THE FLY (The Fly, No. 2; Fly Man No. 32-39)
Aug, 1959-No. 30, Oct, 1964; No. 31, May, 1965
Archie Publications/Radio Comics

1-Shield app.; origin The Fly; S&K-c/a	40.00	120.00	276.00
2-Williamson, S&K, Powell-a	22.00	66.00	155.00
3-Origin retold; Davis, Powell-a	14.00	43.00	100.00
4-Neal Adams-a(p)(1 panel); S&K-c; Powell-a; Shield x-over	10.00	30.00	70.00
5-10: 7-Black Hood app. 8,9-Shield x-over. 9-1st app. Cat Girl. 10-Black Hood app.	6.00	18.00	42.00
11-13,15-20: 16-Last 10 cent issue. 20-Origin Fly Girl retold	3.50	10.50	24.00
14-Intro. & origin Fly Girl	5.15	15.50	36.00
21-30: 23-Jaguar cameo. 29-Black Hood cameo. 30-Comet x-over in Fly Girl	2.30	7.00	16.00
31-Black Hood, Shield, Comet app.	3.00	9.00	21.00

ADVENTURES OF THE JAGUAR, THE
Sept, 1961-No. 15, Nov, 1963
Archie Publications (Radio Comics)

	Good	Fine	N-Mint
1-Origin Jaguar (1st app?); by J. Rosenberger	11.70	35.00	82.00
2,3: 3-Last 10 cent issue	5.70	17.00	40.00
4,5-Catgirl app.	4.00	12.00	28.00
6-10: 6-Catgirl app.	3.15	9.50	22.00
11-15: 13,14-Catgirl, Black Hood app. in both	2.30	7.00	16.00

AIRBOY COMICS (Air Fighters Comics No. 1-22)
V2#11, Dec, 1945-V10#4, May, 1953 (No V3#3)
Hillman Periodicals

	Good	Fine	N-Mint
V2#11	30.00	90.00	210.00
12-Valkyrie app.	20.00	60.00	140.00
V3#1,2(no #3)	17.00	51.00	120.00
4-The Heap app. in Skywolf	14.00	43.00	100.00
5-8,10,11: 6-Valkyrie app.	12.00	36.00	85.00
9-Origin The Heap	14.00	43.00	100.00
12-Skywolf & Airboy x-over; Valkyrie app.	16.00	48.00	110.00
V4#1-Iron Lady app.	14.00	43.00	100.00
2,3,12: 2-Rackman begins	8.50	25.50	60.00
4-Simon & Kirby-c	10.00	30.00	70.00
5-11-All S&K-a	12.00	36.00	85.00
V5#1-9: 4-Infantino Heap. 5-Skull-c	6.00	18.00	42.00
10,11: 10-Origin The Heap	6.00	18.00	42.00
12-Krigstein-a(p)	8.00	24.00	55.00
V6#1-3,5-12: 6,8-Origin The Heap	6.00	18.00	42.00
4-Origin retold	7.00	21.00	50.00
V7#1-12: 7,8,10-Origin The Heap	6.00	18.00	42.00
V8#1-3,6-12	5.00	15.00	35.00
4-Krigstein-a	7.00	21.00	50.00
5(#100)	6.00	18.00	42.00
V9#1-12: 2-Valkyrie app. 7-One pg. Frazetta ad	5.00	15.00	35.00
V10#1-4	5.00	15.00	35.00

AIR FIGHTERS COMICS (Airboy Comics #23 (V2#11) on)
Nov, 1941; No. 2, Nov, 1942-V2#10, Fall, 1945
Hillman Periodicals

	Good	Fine	N-Mint
V1#1-(Produced by Funnies, Inc.); Black Commander only app.			
	100.00	300.00	700.00
2(11/42)-(Produced by Quality artists & Biro for Hillman); Origin Airboy &			

	Good	Fine	N-Mint
Iron Ace; Black Angel, Flying Dutchman & Skywolf begin; Fuje-a; Biro-c/a			
	150.00	450.00	1050.00
3-Origin The Heap & Skywolf	78.00	235.00	550.00
4	53.00	160.00	375.00
5,6	39.00	118.00	275.00
7-12	32.00	96.00	225.00
V2#1,3-9: 5-Flag-c; Fuje-a. 7-Valkyrie app.	28.50	86.00	200.00
2-Skywolf by Giunta; Flying Dutchman by Fuje; 1st meeting Valkyrie & Airboy (She worked for the Nazis in beginning)	36.00	107.00	250.00
10-Origin The Heap & Skywolf	36.00	107.00	250.00

All-American Comics #20, DC Comics

ALL-AMERICAN COMICS (. . . West. 103-126, . . . Men of War 127 on)
April, 1939-No. 102, Oct, 1948
National Periodical Publications/All-American

1-Hop Harrigan, Scribbly, Toonerville Folks, Ben Webster, Spot Savage, Mutt &
Jeff, Red White & Blue, Adv. in the Unknown, Tippie, Reg'lar Fellers,
Skippy, Bobby Thatcher, Mystery Men of Mars, Daiseybelle, & Wiley of

	Good	Fine	N-Mint
West Point begin	250.00	625.00	1500.00
2-Ripley's Believe It or Not begins, ends #24	92.00	230.00	550.00
3-5: 5-The American Way begins, ends #10	64.00	160.00	385.00

6,7: 6-Last Spot Savage; Popsicle Pete begins, ends #26, 28. 7-Last Bobby

	Good	Fine	N-Mint
Thatcher	50.00	150.00	300.00
8-The Ultra Man begins	83.00	208.00	500.00
9,10: 10-X-Mas-c	57.00	144.00	345.00

11-15: 12-Last Toonerville Folks. 15-Last Tippie & Reg'lar Fellars

	Good	Fine	VF-NM
	47.00	118.00	285.00

16-(Rare)-Origin/1st app. Green Lantern (7/40) & begin series; created by Martin

	Good	Fine	N-Mint
Nodell	2,165.00	5,420.00	13,000.00
17-(Scarce)-2nd Green Lantern	500.00	1250.00	3000.00
18-N.Y. World's Fair-c/story	350.00	875.00	2100.00

	Good	Fine	VF-NM

19-Origin/1st app. The Atom (10/40); Last Ultra Man

	Good	Fine	N-Mint
	400.00	1000.00	2400.00

20-Atom dons costume; Hunkle becomes Red Tornado; Rescue on Mars begins, ends #25; 1 pg. origin Green Lantern

	Good	Fine	N-Mint
	175.00	438.00	1050.00

21-23: 21-Last Wiley of West Point & Skippy. 23-Last Daiseybelle; 3 Idiots begin, end #82

	117.00	291.00	700.00

24-Sisty & Dinky become the Cyclone Kids; Ben Webster ends. Origin Dr. Mid-Nite & Sargon, The Sorcerer in text with app.

	Good	Fine	VF-NM
	125.00	312.00	750.00

25-Origin & 1st story app. Dr. Mid-Nite by Stan Asch; Hop Harrigan becomes Guardian Angel; last Adventure in the Unknown

	Good	Fine	N-Mint
	283.00	710.00	1700.00
26-Origin/1st story app. Sargon, the Sorcerer	142.00	354.00	850.00

27: #27-32 are misnumbered in indicia with correct No. appearing on cover. Intro. Doiby Dickles, Green Lantern's sidekick

	183.00	460.00	1100.00
28-Hop Harrigan gives up costumed I.D.	83.00	208.00	500.00
29,30	83.00	208.00	500.00
31-40: 35-Doiby learns Green Lantern's I.D.	62.00	154.00	370.00
41-50: 50-Sargon ends	54.00	135.00	325.00
51-60: 59-Scribbly & the Red Tornado ends	46.00	115.00	275.00
61-Origin/1st app. Solomon Grundy	158.00	395.00	950.00

	Good	Fine	N-Mint
62-70: 70-Kubert Sargon; intro Sargon's helper, Maximillian O'Leary			
	40.00	100.00	240.00
71-88,90-99: 71-Last Red White & Blue. 72-Black Pirate begins (not in #74-82); last Atom. 73-Winky, Blinky & Noddy begins, ends #82. 90-Origin Icicle. 99-Last Hop Harrigan	33.00	83.00	200.00
89-Origin Harlequin	42.00	105.00	250.00
100-1st app. Johnny Thunder by Alex Toth	67.00	167.00	400.00
101-Last Mutt & Jeff	53.00	135.00	320.00
102-Last Green Lantern, Black Pirate & Dr. Mid-Nite			
	67.00	165.00	400.00

ALL-AMERICAN MEN OF WAR (Previously All-American Western)
No. 127, Aug-Sept, 1952-No. 117, Sept-Oct, 1966
National Periodical Publications

	Good	Fine	N-Mint
127 (1952)	34.00	102.00	240.00
128 (1952)	21.50	65.00	150.00
2(12-1/'52-53)-5	19.00	58.00	135.00
6-10	11.50	34.00	80.00
11-18: Last precode (2/55)	10.00	30.00	70.00
19-28	8.00	24.00	55.00
29,30,32-Wood-a	8.70	26.00	61.00
31,33-40	5.70	17.00	39.00
41-50	4.00	12.00	28.00
51-56,58-70	2.85	8.50	20.00
57-1st Gunner & Sarge by Andru	4.00	12.00	28.00
71-80	1.60	4.80	11.00
81-100: 82-Johnny Cloud begins, ends #111,114,115			
	1.00	3.00	7.00
101-117: 112-Balloon Buster series begins, ends #114,116; 115-Johnny Cloud app.			
	.90	2.75	5.50

ALL-AMERICAN WESTERN (Formerly All-American Comics; Becomes
      All-American Men of War)
No. 103, Nov, 1948-No. 126, June-July, 1952 (103-121: 52 pgs.)
National Periodical Publications

103-Johnny Thunder & his horse Black Lightning continues by Toth, ends #126;
    Foley of The Fighting 5th, Minstrel Maverick, & Overland Coach begin;
    Captain Tootsie by Beck; mentioned in **Love and Death**

| | 26.00 | 77.00 | 180.00 |

	Good	Fine	N-Mint
104-Kubert-a	17.00	51.00	120.00
105,107-Kubert-a	14.00	43.00	100.00
106,108-110,112: 112-Kurtzman "Pot-Shot Pete," (1 pg.)			
	11.00	32.00	75.00
111,114-116-Kubert-a	11.50	34.00	80.00
113-Intro. Swift Deer, J. Thunder's new sidekick; classic Toth-c; Kubert-a			
	13.00	40.00	90.00
117-126: 121-Kubert-a	9.30	28.00	65.00

ALL-FLASH (. . . Quarterly No. 1-5)
Summer, 1941-No. 32, Dec-Jan, 1947-48
National Periodical Publications/All-American

	Good	Fine	VF-NM
1-Origin The Flash retold by E. Hibbard	400.00	1000.00	2400.00
	Good	Fine	N-Mint
2-Origin recap	125.00	312.00	750.00
3,4	83.00	210.00	500.00
5-Winky, Blinky & Noddy begins, ends #32	62.00	156.00	375.00
6-10	54.00	135.00	325.00
11-13: 12-Origin The Thinker. 13-The King app.			
	46.00	115.00	275.00
14-Green Lantern cameo	50.00	125.00	300.00
15-20: 18-Mutt & Jeff begins, ends #22	40.00	100.00	240.00
21-31	35.00	87.00	210.00
32-Origin The Fiddler; 1st Star Sapphire	42.00	105.00	250.00

ALL-SELECT COMICS (Blonde Phantom No. 12 on)
Fall, 1943-No. 11, Fall, 1946
Timely Comics (Daring Comics)

	Good	Fine	N-Mint
1-Capt. America, Human Torch, Sub-Mariner begin; Black Widow app.			
	229.00	573.00	1375.00
2-Red Skull app.	110.00	270.00	650.00
3-The Whizzer begins	67.00	167.00	400.00
4,5-Last Sub-Mariner	54.00	135.00	325.00
6-9: 6-The Destroyer app. 8-No Whizzer	46.00	115.00	275.00
10-The Destroyer & Sub-Mariner app.; last Capt. America & Human Torch issue			
	46.00	115.00	275.00
11-1st app. Blonde Phantom; Miss America app.; all Blonde Phantom-c by Shores			
	75.00	188.00	450.00

ALL STAR COMICS (All Star Western No. 58 on)
Summer, 1940-No. 57, Feb-Mar, 1951; No. 58, Jan-Feb, 1976 -
   No. 74, Sept-Oct, 1978
National Periodical Publ./All-American/DC Comics

	Good	Fine	VF-NM
1-The Flash (#1 by Harry Lampert), Hawkman (by Shelly), Hourman, The Sandman, The Spectre, Biff Bronson, Red White & Blue begin; Ultra Man's only app.	750.00	1875.00	4500.00
	Good	Fine	N-Mint
2-Green Lantern, Johnny Thunder begin	350.00	875.00	2100.00
	Good	Fine	VF-NM
3-Origin & 1st app. The Justice Society of America; Dr. Fate & The Atom begin; Red Tornado cameo; last Red White & Blue	1415.00	3540.00	8500.00
	Good	Fine	N-Mint
4	383.00	960.00	2300.00
5-1st app. Shiera Sanders as Hawkgirl	400.00	1000.00	2400.00
6-Johnny Thunder joins JSA	267.00	670.00	1600.00
7-Batman, Superman, Flash cameo; last Hourman; Doiby Dickles app.	267.00	670.00	1600.00
	Good	Fine	VF-NM
8-Origin & 1st app. Wonder Woman (added as 8 pgs. making book 76 pgs.; origin cont'd in Sensation #1); Dr. Fate dons new helmet; Dr.Mid-Nite, Hop Harrigan text stories & Starman begin; Shiera app.; Hop Harrigan JSA guest	533.00	1335.00	3200.00
	Good	Fine	N-Mint
9,10: 9-Shiera app. 10-Flash, Green Lantern cameo, Sandman new costume	208.00	520.00	1250.00
11,12: 11-Wonder Woman begins; Spectre cameo; Shiera app. 12-Wonder Woman becomes JSA Secretary	183.00	460.00	1100.00
13-15: Sandman w/Sandy in #14 & 15; 15-Origin Brain Wave; Shiera app.	175.00	438.00	1050.00
16-19: 19-Sandman w/Sandy	130.00	325.00	780.00
20-Dr. Fate & Sandman cameo	130.00	325.00	780.00
21-23: 21-Spectre & Atom cameo; Dr. Fate by Kubert; Dr. Fate, Sandman end. 22-Last Hop Harrigan; Flag-c. 23-Origin Psycho Pirate; last Spectre & Starman	113.00	285.00	680.00
24-Flash & Green Lantern cameo; Mr. Terrific only app.; Wildcat, JSA guest; Kubert Hawkman begins	113.00	285.00	680.00
25-27: 25-The Flash & Green Lantern start again. 27-Wildcat, JSA guest	104.00	260.00	625.00

	Good	Fine	N-Mint
28-32	87.00	220.00	525.00
33-Solomon Grundy, Hawkman, Doiby Dickles app.			
	175.00	440.00	1050.00
34,35-Johnny Thunder cameo in both	80.00	240.00	480.00
36-Batman & Superman JSA guests	175.00	525.00	1050.00
37-Johnny Thunder cameo; origin Injustice Society; last Kubert Hawkman			
	89.00	223.00	535.00
38-Black Canary begins; JSA Death issue	104.00	260.00	625.00
39,40: 39-Last Johnny Thunder	64.00	160.00	385.00
41-Black Canary joins JSA; Injustice Society app.	62.00	156.00	375.00
42-Atom & the Hawkman don new costumes	62.00	156.00	375.00
43-49,51-56: 55-Sci/Fi story	62.00	156.00	375.00
50-Frazetta art, 3 pgs.	71.00	177.00	425.00
57-Kubert-a, 6 pgs. (Scarce)	80.00	200.00	480.00
V12#58-74(1976-78)-Flash, Hawkman, Dr. Mid-Nite, Wildcat, Dr. Fate, Green Lantern, Star Spangled Kid, & Robin app.; intro Power Girl. 58-JSA app. 69-1st app. Huntress			
		.25	.50

ALL TOP COMICS
1945; No. 2, Sum, 1946-No. 18, Mar, 1949
Fox Features Synd./Green Publ./Norlen Mag.

1-Cosmo Cat & Flash Rabbit begin	11.00	32.00	75.00
2	5.30	16.00	38.00
3-7	4.00	12.00	28.00
8-Blue Beetle, Phantom Lady, & Rulah, Jungle Goddess begin (11/47); Kamen-c			
	64.00	193.00	450.00
9-Kamen-c	39.00	118.00	275.00
10-Kamen bondage-c	41.00	123.00	285.00
11-13,15-17: 15-No Blue Beetle	30.00	90.00	210.00
14-No Blue Beetle; used in **SOTI**, illo-"Corpses of colored people strung up by their wrists"	37.00	110.00	260.00
18-Dagar, Jo-Jo app; no Phantom Lady or Blue Beetle			
	24.00	73.00	170.00

ALL WESTERN WINNERS (Formerly All Winners; becomes Western Winners with No. 5; see Two-Gun Kid No. 5)
No. 2, Winter, 1948-49-No. 4, April, 1949
Marvel Comics(CDS)

2-Black Rider (Origin & 1st app.) & his horse Satan, Kid Colt & his horse Steel,

	Good	Fine	N-Mint
& Two-Gun Kid & his horse Cyclone begin	21.50	65.00	150.00
3-Anti-Wertham editorial	15.00	45.00	105.00
4-Black Rider I.D. revealed	15.00	45.00	105.00

ALL WINNERS COMICS (All Teen #20)

Summer, 1941-No. 19, Fall, 1946; No. 21, Winter, 1946-47 (no No. 20) (No. 21
    continued from Young Allies No. 20)
USA No. 1-7/WFP No. 10-19/YAl No. 21

	Good	Fine	VF-NM
1-The Angel & Black Marvel only app.; Capt. America by Simon & Kirby, Human Torch & Sub-Mariner begin	350.00	875.00	2100.00

	Good	Fine	N-Mint
2-The Destroyer & The Whizzer begin; Simon & Kirby Captain America	167.00	415.00	1000.00
3,4	129.00	323.00	775.00
5,6: 6-The Black Avenger only app.; no Whizzer story	88.00	220.00	525.00
7-10	71.00	177.00	425.00
11,13-18: 14-16-No Human Torch	46.00	115.00	275.00
12-Red Skull story; last Destroyer; no Whizzer story	50.00	125.00	300.00
19-(Scarce)-1st app. & origin All Winners Squad (Capt. America & Bucky, Human Torch & Toro, Sub-Mariner, Whizzer, & Miss America; r-in Fantasy Masterpieces #10	108.00	271.00	650.00
21-(Scarce)-All Winners Squad; bondage-c	100.00	250.00	600.00

(2nd Series-August, 1948, Marvel Comics (CDS))
(Becomes All Western Winners with No. 2)

	Good	Fine	N-Mint
1-The Blonde Phantom, Capt. America, Human Torch, & Sub-Mariner app.	88.00	220.00	525.00

ALPHA FLIGHT (See X-Men #120,121)

Aug, 1983-Present (#52-on are direct sale only)
Marvel Comics Group

	Good	Fine	N-Mint
1-Byrne-a begins (52pgs.)-Wolverine & Nightcrawler cameo	.85	2.50	5.00
2-Origin Marrina & Alpha Flight	.40	1.25	2.50
3-11: 3-Concludes origin Alpha Flight	.35	1.00	2.00
12-Double size; death of Guardian	.40	1.25	2.50
13-Wolverine app.	1.70	5.00	10.00

	Good	Fine	N-Mint
14-16: 16-Wolverine cameo	.25	.75	1.50
17-X-Men x-over; Wolverine cameo	.85	2.50	5.00
18-28: 25-Return of Guardian. 28-Last Byrne-a	.25	.75	1.50
29-32,35-49		.65	1.30
33,34: 33-X-Men (Wolverine) app. 34-Origin Wolverine			
	1.00	3.00	6.00
50-Double size	.25	.75	1.50
51-Jim Lee's first work at Marvel	1.40	4.25	8.50
52,53-Wolverine app. 53-Jim Lee-a	.75	2.25	4.50
54,63,64-No Jim Lee-a		.65	1.30
55-62-Jim Lee-a(p)	.50	1.50	3.00
65-74,76-86,91-99,101,102: 74-Wolverine, Spider-Man app.			
	.25	.75	1.50
75-Double size ($1.95, 52 pgs.)	.35	1.00	1.95
87-90-Wolverine 4 part story w/Jim Lee covers	.50	1.50	3.00
100-($2.50-c, 52 pgs.)-Avengers app.	.40	1.25	2.50
Annual 1 (9/86, $1.25)	.30	.90	1.80
Annual 2(12/87, $1.25)		.65	1.30

AMAZING FANTASY (Formerly Amazing Adult Fantasy #7-14)
No. 15, Aug, 1962 (Sept, 1962 shown in indicia)
Marvel Comics Group (AMI)

	Good	Fine	N-Mint
15-Origin & 1st app. of Spider-Man by Ditko; Kirby/Ditko-c			
	365.00	1460.00	3650.00

AMAZING-MAN COMICS
No. 5, Sept, 1939-No. 27, Feb, 1942
Centaur Publications

	Good	Fine	VF-NM
5(No.1)(Rare)-Origin/1st app. A-Man the Amazing Man by Bill Everett; The Cat-Man by Tarpe Mills (also #8), Mighty Man by Filchock, Minimidget & sidekick Ritty, & The Iron Skull by Burgos begins			
	800.00	2000.00	4800.00

	Good	Fine	N-Mint
6-Origin The Amazing Man retold; The Shark begins; Ivy Menace by Tarpe Mills app.			
	233.00	585.00	1400.00
7-Magician From Mars begins; ends #11	142.00	426.00	850.00
8-Cat-Man dresses as woman	86.00	257.00	600.00
9-Magician From Mars battles the 'Elemental Monster,' swiped into The Spectre			

	Good	Fine	N-Mint
in More Fun #54 & 55	84.00	252.00	590.00
10,11: 11-Zardi, the Eternal Man begins; ends #16; Amazing Man dons costume; last Everett issue	72.00	215.00	500.00
12,13	70.00	210.00	490.00
14-Reef Kinkaid, Rocke Wayburn (ends #20), & Dr. Hypno (ends #21) begin; no Zardi or Chuck Hardy	56.00	167.00	390.00
15,17-20: 15-Zardi returns; no Rocke Wayburn. 17-Dr. Hypno returns; no Zardi	43.00	130.00	300.00
16-Mighty Man's powers of super strength & ability to shrink & grow explained; Rocke Wayburn returns; no Dr. Hypno; Al Avison (a character) begins, ends #18 (a tribute to the famed artist)	46.00	137.00	320.00
21-Origin Dash Dartwell (drug-use story); origin & only app. T.N.T.	43.00	130.00	300.00
22-Dash Dartwell, the Human Meteor & The Voice app; last Iron Skull & The Shark; Silver Streak app.	43.00	130.00	300.00
23-Two Amazing Man stories; intro/origin Tommy the Amazing Kid; The Marksman only app.	46.00	137.00	320.00
24,27: 24-King of Darkness, Nightshade, & Blue Lady begin; end #26; 1st App. Super-Ann	43.00	130.00	300.00
25,26 (Scarce)-Meteor Martin by Wolverton in both; 26-Electric Ray app.	72.00	215.00	505.00

AMAZING SPIDER-MAN, THE (See Amazing Fantasy, Marvel Tales,
  Marvel Team-Up, Spectacular . . . , Spider-Man & Web of Spider-man)
March, 1963-Present
Marvel Comics Group

	Good	Fine	N-Mint
1-Retells origin by Steve Ditko; 1st Fantastic Four x-over; intro. John Jameson & The Chameleon; Kirby-c	355.00	1420.00	3550.00
1-Reprint from the Golden Record Comic set with record (still sealed)	9.50	28.50	66.00
	19.00	57.00	132.00
2-1st app. the Vulture & the Terrible Tinkerer	143.00	430.00	1000.00
3-Human Torch cameo; intro. & 1st app. Doc Octopus; Dr. Doom & Ant-Man app.	100.00	300.00	700.00
4-Origin & 1st app. The Sandman; Intro. Betty Brant & Liz Allen	71.00	213.00	500.00
5-Dr. Doom app.	66.00	198.00	460.00
6-1st app. Lizard	71.00	213.00	500.00
7,8,10: 8-Fantastic Four app. 10-1st app. Big Man & Enforcers	47.00	141.00	330.00

The Amazing Spider-Man #122, © Marvel Comics

9-1st app. Electro (origin)	51.00	153.00	360.00
11,12: 11-1st app. Bennett Brant	29.00	86.00	200.00
13-1st app. Mysterio	36.00	108.00	250.00
14-1st app. The Green Goblin; Hulk x-over	90.00	270.00	625.00
15-1st app. Kraven the Hunter	32.00	96.00	225.00
16,19: 16-1st Daredevil x-over.	23.00	70.00	160.00
17-2nd app. Green Goblin	43.00	130.00	300.00
18-1st app. Ned Leeds who later becomes Hobgoblin			
	25.00	75.00	175.00
20-Origin & 1st app. The Scorpion	22.00	66.00	155.00
21,22: 22-1st app. Princess Python	16.00	48.00	110.00
23-3rd app. The Green Goblin (c/story)	23.50	71.00	165.00
24	14.00	43.00	100.00
25-(6/65)-1st app. Mary Jane Watson (cameo; face not shown); 1st app. Spencer			
Smythe	17.00	51.00	120.00
26-4th app. The Green Goblin; 1st app. Crime Master; dies in #27			
	19.00	58.00	135.00
27-5th app. The Green Goblin	18.00	54.00	125.00
28-Origin & 1st app. Molten Man	18.50	56.00	130.00
29,30	13.50	41.00	95.00
31-38: 31-1st app. Harry Osborn, Gwen Stacy & Prof. Warren. 36-1st app. Looter.			
37-Intro. Norman Osborn. 38-Last Ditko issue			
	9.30	28.00	65.00

	Good	Fine	N-Mint
39-The Green Goblin-c/story; Green Goblin's I.D. revealed as Norman Osborn			
	11.00	32.00	75.00
40-Origin The Green Goblin (1st told origin)	14.00	43.00	100.00
41-1st app. Rhino	7.00	21.00	50.00
42-2nd app. Mary Jane Watson (cameo in last 2 panels); 1st time face is shown			
	7.85	23.50	55.00
43-49: 46-Intro. Shocker	5.70	17.00	40.00
50-1st app. Kingpin	21.00	63.00	145.00
51-2nd app. Kingpin	8.50	25.50	60.00
52-60: 52-1st app. Joe Robertson. 56-1st app. Capt. George Stacy. 59- 1st app. Brainwasher (alias Kingpin)	4.50	14.00	32.00
61-80: 67-1st app. Randy Robertson. 73-1st app. Silvermane. 78-1st app. Prowler			
	2.85	8.50	20.00
81-89,91-93,95,99: 83-1st app. Schemer & Vanessa (Kingpin's wife). 93-1st app. Arthur Stacy	2.30	7.00	16.00
90-Death of Capt. Stacey	3.00	9.00	21.00
94-Origin retold	4.50	14.00	32.00
96-98-Drug books not approved by CCA; Green Goblin storyline			
	5.00	15.00	35.00
100-Anniversary issue	11.50	34.00	80.00
101-1st app. Morbius the Living Vampire	3.15	9.50	22.00
102-Origin Morbius (52 pgs.)	3.70	11.00	26.00
103-118: 108-1st app. Sha-Shan. 110-1st app. Gibbon. 111-Kraven the Hunter app. 113-1st app. Hammerhead	2.00	6.00	14.00
119,120-Spider-Man vs. Hulk	2.65	8.00	18.00
121-Death of Gwen Stacy (r-/in Marv. Tales #98)	8.30	25.00	58.00
122-Death of The Green Goblin (r-/in Marvel Tales #99)			
	12.70	38.00	89.00
123-128: 124-1st app. Man Wolf, origin in #125	1.85	5.50	13.00
129-1st app. The Punisher (2/74)	36.00	108.00	250.00
130-133,138-160: 139-1st Grizzly. 143-1st Cyclone	1.50	4.50	10.00
134-Punisher cameo (7/74); 1st app. Tarantula	2.85	8.50	20.00
135-Punisher app. (8/74)	8.50	25.50	60.00
136-Reappearance of The Green Goblin (Harry Osborn)			
	2.85	8.50	20.00
137-Green Goblin-c/story (Harry Osborn)	1.70	5.00	12.00
161-Nightcrawler app. from X-Men; Punisher cameo			
	1.60	4.80	11.00
162-Punisher, Nightcrawler app.	3.15	9.50	22.00
163-173,181-190: 167-1st app. Will O' The Wisp. 171-Nova app. 181-Origin retold; gives life history of Spidey	.85	2.50	5.00

	Good	Fine	N-Mint
174,175-Punisher app.	2.30	7.00	16.00
176-180-Green Goblin app.	1.50	4.50	10.00
191-193,195-199,203-219: 196-Faked death of Aunt May. 203-2nd app. Dazzler. 210-1st app. Madame Web. 212-1st app. Hydro Man			
	.85	2.50	5.00
194-1st app. Black Cat	1.50	4.50	9.00
200-Giant origin issue	2.65	8.00	16.00
201,202-Punisher app.	3.60	11.00	22.00
220-237: 225-Foolkiller c-story (2/82) 226,227-Black Cat returns. 236-Tarantula dies. 235-Origin Will-'O-The-Wisp	.85	2.50	5.00
238-1st app. Hobgoblin; came with skin "Tatooz" decal			
	5.50	16.50	38.00
239-2nd app. Hobgoblin	2.85	8.50	20.00
240-248: 241-Origin The Vulture	.85	2.50	5.00
249-251: Hobgoblin app. 251-Last old costume	1.35	4.00	8.00
252-Spider-Man dons new costume (5/84); ties with Spectacular Spider-Man #90 for 1st new costume	1.85	5.50	11.00
253-1st app. The Rose	1.00	3.00	6.00
254	.70	2.00	4.00
255,263-274,278-280,282-283	.50	1.50	3.00
256-1st app. Puma	.60	1.75	3.50
257-261: Hobgoblin app. 259-Spidey back to old costume			
	1.35	4.00	8.00
262-Spider-Man unmasked	.85	2.50	5.00
275-277: Hobgoblin app. 275-Origin-r by Ditko ($1.25, double-size)			
	1.15	3.50	7.00
281-Hobgoblin battles Jack O'Lantern	1.00	3.00	7.00
284-Punisher cameo; Gang War story begins	1.30	4.00	8.00
285-Punisher app.	2.50	7.50	15.00
286-288: 288-Last Gang War	.85	2.50	5.00
289-(52 pgs.)-Hobgoblin's i.d. revealed as Ned Leeds			
	3.00	9.00	18.00
290-292	.70	2.00	4.00
293,294-Part 2 & 5 of Kraven story from Web of Spider-Man. 294-Death of Kraven	1.15	3.50	7.00
295-297	.85	2.50	5.00
298-Todd McFarlane-c/a begins; 1st Venom (cameo) not in costume			
	5.30	16.00	32.00
299-McFarlane-a; 1st app. Venom (cameo) in costume			
	2.65	8.00	16.00

	Good	Fine	N-Mint
300 ($1.50, 52 pgs.; 25th Anniversary)-Last black costume; 1st full Venom story			
	5.60	17.00	34.00
301-305: 301 ($1.00 issues begin). 304-1st bi-weekly issue			
	2.65	8.00	16.00
306-311,313-315: 306-Cover swipe from Action #1			
	2.00	6.00	12.00
312-Hobgoblin battles Green Goblin	2.50	7.50	15.00
316-323,325: 319-Bi-weekly begins again	1.15	3.50	7.00
324-Sabertooth app.; McFarlane cover only	2.15	6.50	13.00
326,327,329: 327-Cosmic Spidey continues from Spect. Spider-Man. (no McFarlane-c/a)	.35	1.00	2.00
328-Hulk x-over; last McFarlane issue	1.15	3.50	7.00
330,331-Punisher app.	.50	1.50	3.00
332-336,338-345: 341-Tarantula app.		.50	1.00
337-Hobgoblin app.	.30	.90	2.00
346,347-Venom app.	.25	.75	1.50
348,349,351-353	.25	.75	1.50
350-($1.50-c, 52 pgs.)	.25	.75	1.50
Annual 1 (1964)-Origin Spider-Man; 1st app. Sinister Six; Kraven the Hunter app.			
	24.00	72.00	170.00
Annual 2	10.00	30.00	70.00
Special 3	4.30	13.00	30.00
Special 4 (1967) Spidey battles Human Torch (New 41 pg. story)			
	5.50	16.50	33.00
Special 5-8 (12/71)	2.15	6.50	15.00
King Size 9 ('73)-Green Goblin app.	2.50	7.50	15.00
Annual 10(6/76)-Old Human Fly app.	1.00	3.00	6.00
Annual 11(9/77), 12(8/78)	1.00	3.00	6.00
Annual 13(11/79)-Byrne-a	1.15	3.50	7.00
Annual 14(12/80)-Miller-c/a(p), 40 pgs.	1.35	4.00	8.00
Annual 15(1981)-Miller-c/a(p); Punisher app.	3.35	10.00	20.00
Annual 16-20: 16(12/82)-Origin/1st app. new Capt. Marvel (female heroine). 17(12/83). 18 ('84). 19(11/85). 20(11/86)-Origin Iron Man of 2020			
	.85	2.50	5.00
Annual 21('87)-Special wedding issue	1.15	3.50	7.00
Annual 22('88, $1.75, 68 pgs.)-1st app. Speedball; Evolutionary War x-over			
	1.15	3.50	7.00
Annual 23 ('89, $2.00, 68 pgs.)-Atlantis Attacks; origin Spider-Man retold; She-Hulk app.; Byrne-c	.85	2.50	5.00
Annual 24 ('90, $2.00, 68 pgs.)-Ant-Man app.	.50	1.50	3.00
Annual 25 ('91, $2.00-c)	.30	.90	2.00

AMERICA'S BEST COMICS
Feb, 1942-No. 31, July, 1949
Nedor/Better/Standard Publications

	Good	Fine	N-Mint
1-The Woman in Red, Black Terror, Captain Future, Doc Strange, The Liberator, & Don Davis, Secret Ace begin	62.00	185.00	435.00
2-Origin The American Eagle; The Woman in Red ends	34.00	100.00	235.00
3-Pyroman begins	25.00	75.00	175.00
4	21.50	64.00	150.00
5-Last Captain Future (not in #4); Lone Eagle app.	18.50	56.00	130.00
6,7: 6-American Crusader app. 7-Hitler, Mussolini & Hirohito-c	16.50	49.00	115.00
8-Last Liberator	13.00	40.00	90.00
9-The Fighting Yank begins; The Ghost app.	13.00	40.00	90.00
10-14: 10-Flag-c. 14-American Eagle ends	11.50	34.00	80.00
15-20	11.00	32.00	75.00
21,22: 21-Infinity-c. 22-Capt. Future app.	9.30	28.00	65.00
23-Miss Masque begins; last Doc Strange	12.00	36.00	84.00
24-Miss Masque bondage-c	11.00	32.00	75.00
25-Last Fighting Yank; Sea Eagle app.	9.30	28.00	65.00
26-The Phantom Detective & The Silver Knight app.; Frazetta text illo & some panels in Miss Masque	12.00	36.00	84.00
27-31: 27,28-Commando Cubs. 27-Doc Strange. 28-Tuska Black Terror.			
29-Last Pyroman	9.30	28.00	65.00

ANIMAL COMICS
Dec-Jan, 1941-42-No. 30, Dec-Jan, 1947-48
Dell Publishing Co.

	Good	Fine	N-Mint
1-1st Pogo app. by Walt Kelly (Dan Noonan art in most issues)	86.00	257.00	600.00
2-Uncle Wiggily begins	36.00	107.00	250.00
3,5	25.00	75.00	175.00
4,6,7-No Pogo	14.00	42.00	100.00
8-10	17.00	51.00	120.00
11-15	11.00	32.00	75.00
16-20	7.00	21.00	50.00
21-30: 25-30-"Jigger" by John Stanley	5.00	15.00	35.00

ANIMAL MAN (Also see Action Comics #552, 553, DC Comics Presents,
    Secret Origins, Strange Advs. #180 & Wonder Woman #267)
Sept, 1988-Present ($1.25-$1.50, color)
DC Comics

	Good	Fine	N-Mint
1-Bolland c-1-32; Grant Morrison scripts begin	4.15	12.50	25.00
2	2.70	8.00	16.00
3,4	1.50	4.50	9.00
5-10: 6-Invasion tie-in	1.00	3.00	6.00
11-15	.85	2.50	5.00
16-20	.70	2.00	4.00
21-26: 24-Arkham Asylum story. 25-Inferior Five app. 26-Last Grant Morrison scripts; part photo-c	.50	1.50	3.00
27-38	.30	.90	1.80

ANNIE OAKLEY (Also see Two-Gun Kid & Wild Western)
Spring, 1948-No. 4, 11/48; No. 5, 6/55-No. 11, 6/56
Marvel/Atlas Comics(MPI No. 1-4/CDS No. 5 on)

1 (1st Series), '48)-Hedy Devine app.	18.50	56.00	130.00
2 (7/48, 52 pgs.)-Kurtzman-a, "Hey Look," 1 pg; Intro. Lana; Hedy Devine app; Captain Tootsie by Beck	13.00	40.00	90.00
3,4	10.00	30.00	70.00
5 (2nd Series)(1955)-Reinman-a	6.50	19.00	45.00
6-9: 6,8-Woodbridge-a. 9-Williamson-a (4 pgs.)	5.00	15.00	35.00
10,11: 11-Severin-c	4.30	13.00	30.00

ANNIE OAKLEY AND TAGG (TV)
1953-No. 18, Jan-Mar, 1959; July, 1965 (all photo-c)
Dell Publishing Co./Gold Key

4-Color 438 (#1)	8.50	25.50	60.00
4-Color 481,575	5.30	16.00	38.00
4(7-9/55)-10	4.30	13.00	30.00
11-18(1-3/59)	3.60	11.00	25.00
1(7/65-Gold Key)-Photo-c	3.00	9.00	21.00

ANTHRO (See Showcase #74)
July-Aug, 1968-No. 6, July-Aug, 1969
National Periodical Publications

	Good	Fine	N-Mint
1-Howie Post-a in all	2.15	6.50	15.00
2-6: 6-Wood-c/a (inks)	1.50	4.50	10.00

AQUAMAN (See Adventure, Brave & the Bold, Detective, Justice League of America, More Fun #73, Showcase #30, & World's Finest)
Jan-Feb, 1962-No. 56, Mar-Apr, 1971; No. 57, Aug-Sept, 1977 - No. 63, Aug-Sept, 1978
National Periodical Publications/DC Comics

1-Intro. Quisp	28.25	84.75	198.00
2	12.50	37.50	88.00
3-5	8.75	26.25	61.00
6-10	5.75	17.25	40.00
11-20: 11-1st app. Mera. 18-Aquaman weds Mera; JLA cameo	4.50	13.50	31.00
21-32,34-40: 23-Birth of Aquababy. 26-Huntress app.(3-4/66). 29-1st app. Ocean Master, Aquaman's step-brother	2.85	8.50	20.00
33-1st app. Aqua-Girl	3.00	9.00	22.00
41-47,49	1.25	3.75	9.00
48-Origin reprinted	1.50	4.50	10.00
50-52-Deadman by Neal Adams	1.85	5.50	13.00
53-56('71): 56-1st app. Crusader	.90	2.75	5.50
57('77)-63: 58-Origin retold	.55	1.65	3.30

AQUAMAN
Feb, 1986-No. 4, May, 1986 (Mini-series)
DC Comics

1-New costume	.85	2.50	5.00
2-4	.50	1.50	3.00
Special 1 ('88, $1.50, 52 pgs.)	.35	1.00	2.00

AQUAMAN
June, 1989-No. 5, Oct, 1989 ($1.00, mini-series)
DC Comics

1-5: Giffen plots/breakdowns; Swan-p		.50	1.00
Special 1 (Legend of . . . , $2.00, 1989, 52 pgs.)	.35	1.00	2.00

ARCHIE COMICS (Archie No. 158 on)(See Jackpot, Little . . . , & Pep)
(First Teen-age comic) (Radio show 1st aired 6/2/45, by NBC)
Winter, 1942-43-No. 19, 3-4/46; No. 20, 5-6/46-Present
MLJ Magazines #1-19/Archie Publ. #20 on

	Good	Fine	VF-NM
1 (Scarce)-Jughead, Veronica app.	367.00	920.00	2200.00
	Good	Fine	N-Mint
2	118.00	354.00	825.00
3 (60 pgs.)	86.00	260.00	600.00
4,5	59.00	178.00	415.00
6-10	41.00	122.00	285.00
11-20: 15,17,18-Dotty & Ditto by Woggon	25.00	75.00	175.00
21-30: 23-Betty & Veronica by Woggon	17.00	51.00	120.00
31-40	11.00	32.00	75.00
41-50	7.00	21.00	50.00
51-70 (1954): 51,65-70-Katy Keene app.	4.00	12.00	28.00
71-99: 72-74-Katy Keene app.	2.35	7.00	16.00
100	3.00	9.00	18.00
101-130 (1962)	1.15	3.50	8.00
131-160	.70	2.00	4.00
161-200	.40	1.25	2.50
201-240		.60	1.20
241-282		.50	1.00
283-Cover/story plugs "International Children's Appeal" which was a fraudulent charity, according to TV's 20/20 news program broadcast July 20, 1979			
		.60	1.25
284-388: 300-Anniversary issue		.50	1.00
Annual 1('50)-116 pgs. (Scarce)	86.00	257.00	600.00
Annual 2('51)	43.00	130.00	300.00
Annual 3('52)	25.00	75.00	175.00
Annual 4,5(1953-54)	18.00	54.00	125.00
Annual 6-10(1955-59)	10.00	30.00	70.00
Annual 11-15(1960-65)	4.30	13.00	30.00
Annual 16-20(1966-70)	1.50	4.50	10.00
Annual 21-26(1971-75)	.60	1.75	3.50
Annual Digest 27('75)-58('83-'90)(. . . Magazine #35 on)		.60	1.20

ARCHIE'S GIRLS, BETTY AND VERONICA
1950-No. 347, 1987
Archie Publications (Close-Up)

	Good	Fine	N-Mint
1	71.00	215.00	500.00
2	36.00	107.00	250.00
3-5	19.00	58.00	135.00
6-10: 10-2pg. Katy Keene app.	16.00	48.00	110.00
11-20: 11,13,14,17-19-Katy Keene app. 20-Debbie's Diary, 2 pgs.			
	10.00	30.00	70.00
21-30: 27-Katy Keene app.	8.00	24.00	56.00
31-50	5.30	16.00	38.00
51-74	3.50	10.50	24.00
75-Betty & Veronica sell souls to Devil	7.00	21.00	50.00
76-99	2.00	6.00	14.00
100	2.65	8.00	18.00
101-140: 118-Origin Superteen. 119-Last Superteen story			
	1.00	3.00	7.00
141-180	.50	1.50	3.00
181-220		.60	1.20
221-347: 300-Anniversary issue		.35	.70
Annual 1 (1953)	43.00	130.00	300.00
Annual 2 (1954)	20.00	60.00	140.00
Annual 3-5 ('55-'57)	14.00	43.00	100.00
Annual 6-8 ('58-'60)	10.00	30.00	70.00

ARCHIE'S PAL, JUGHEAD
1949-No. 126, Nov, 1965
Archie Publications

1 (1949)	69.00	205.00	480.00
2 (1950)	34.00	103.00	240.00
3-5	22.00	65.00	155.00
6-10: 7-Suzie app.	13.00	40.00	90.00
11-20	10.00	30.00	70.00
21-30: 23-25,28-30-Katy Keene app. 28-Debbie's Diary app.			
.	6.50	19.00	45.00
31-50	3.70	11.00	26.00
51-70	2.65	8.00	18.00
71-100	1.50	4.50	9.00
101-126	1.00	3.00	6.00
Annual 1 (1953)	32.00	96.00	225.00
Annual 2 (1954)	19.00	58.00	135.00
Annual 3-5 (1955-57)	13.00	40.00	90.00

	Good	Fine	N-Mint
Annual 6-8 (1958-60)	9.00	27.00	62.00

ASTONISHING (Formerly Marvel Boy No. 1, 2)
No. 3, April, 1951-No. 63, Aug, 1957
Marvel/Atlas Comics(20CC)

	Good	Fine	N-Mint
3-Marvel Boy continues	32.00	95.00	225.00
4-6-Last Marvel Boy; 4-Stan Lee app.	25.00	75.00	175.00
7-10	7.00	21.00	50.00
11,12,15,17,20	5.70	17.00	40.00
13,14,16,19-Krigstein-a	6.50	19.00	45.00
18-Jack The Ripper story	6.50	19.00	45.00
21,22,24	4.50	14.00	32.00
23-E.C. swipe-'The Hole In The Wall' from Vault Of Horror #16			
	5.70	17.00	40.00
25-Crandall-a	5.70	17.00	40.00
26-29: 29-Decapitation-c	4.00	12.00	28.00
30-Tentacled eyeball story	6.50	19.00	45.00
31-37-Last pre-code issue	3.50	10.50	24.00
38-43,46,48-52,56,58,59,61	2.65	8.00	18.00
44-Crandall swipe/Weird Fantasy #22	4.00	12.00	28.00
45,47-Krigstein-a	4.00	12.00	28.00
53,54: 53-Crandall, Ditko-a. 54-Torres-a	3.50	10.50	24.00
55-Crandall, Torres-a	4.00	12.00	28.00
57-Williamson/Krenkel-a (4 pgs.)	5.00	15.00	35.00
60-Williamson/Mayo-a (4 pgs.)	5.00	15.00	35.00
62-Torres, Powell -a	2.85	8.50	20.00
63-Last issue; Woodbridge-a	2.85	8.50	20.00

ASTONISHING TALES
Aug, 1970-No. 36, July, 1976 (#1-7: 15 cents; #8: 25 cents)
Marvel Comics Group

	Good	Fine	N-Mint
1-Ka-Zar by Kirby(p) & Dr. Doom by Wood begin; Kraven the Hunter-c/story			
	1.85	5.50	11.00
2-Kraven the Hunter-c/story; Kirby, Wood-a	1.25	3.75	7.50
3-6: Smith-p; Wood-a-#3,4. 5-Red Skull app.	1.65	5.00	9.75
7,8: 8-(52 pgs.)-Last Dr. Doom & Kirby-a	1.25	3.75	7.50
9-Lorna-r	.50	1.50	2.85
10-Barry Smith-a(p)	.60	1.80	4.00
11-Origin Ka-Zar & Zabu	.55	1.65	3.30

Astonishing Tales #26, © Marvel Comics

	Good	Fine	N-Mint
12-Man-Thing by Neal Adams (apps. #13 also)	.75	2.25	4.40
13-24: 20-Last Ka-Zar. 21-It! the Living Colossus begins, ends #24		.75	1.70
25-Deathlok the Demolisher begins (1st app.); Perez 1st work, 2pgs. (8/74)			
	6.50	19.50	40.00
26-28,30	3.00	9.00	18.00
29-Origin Guardians of the Galaxy	3.30	9.90	20.00
31-36: 36-Last Deathlok	2.00	6.00	12.00

ASTRO BOY (TV)
August, 1965 (12 cents)
Gold Key

1(10151-508)	18.50	56.00	130.00

ATOM, THE (. . . & the Hawkman #39 on) (See All-American, Brave & the Bold,
    Detective, Flash Comics #80, Showcase & World's Finest)
June-July, 1962-No. 38, Aug-Sept, 1968
National Periodical Publications

	Good	Fine	N-Mint
1-Intro Plant-Master; 1st app. Maya	62.00	185.00	430.00
2	21.00	62.00	145.00
3-1st Time Pool story; 1st app. Chronos (origin)	13.00	40.00	90.00
4,5: 4-Snapper Carr x-over	9.70	29.00	68.00
6-10: 7-Hawkman x-over (1st Atom & Hawkman team-up). 8-Justice League, Dr. Light app.	8.00	24.00	55.00
11-15	5.50	16.50	38.00
16-20: 19-Zatanna x-over	3.70	11.00	26.00
21-28,30	2.30	7.00	16.00
29-Golden Age Atom x-over (1st S.A. app.)	7.00	21.00	50.00
31-38: 31-Hawkman x-over. 36-G.A. Atom x-over. 37-Intro. Major Mynah; Hawkman cameo	2.30	7.00	16.00

ATOM & HAWKMAN, THE (Formerly The Atom)
No. 39, Oct-Nov, 1968-No. 45, Oct-Nov, 1969
National Periodical Publications

	Good	Fine	N-Mint
39-45: 43-1st app. Gentlemen Ghost, origin-44	1.75	5.25	12.00

AUTHENTIC POLICE CASES
2/48-No. 6, 11/48; No. 7, 5/50-No. 38, 3/55
St. John Publishing Co.

	Good	Fine	N-Mint
1-Hale the Magician by Tuska begins	13.00	40.00	90.00
2-Lady Satan, Johnny Rebel app.	9.00	27.00	62.00
3-Veiled Avenger app.; blood drainage story plus 2 Lucky Coyne stories; used in SOTI, illo. from Red Seal #16	19.00	56.00	130.00
4,5: 4-Masked Black Jack app. 5-Late 1930s Jack Cole-a(r); transvestism story	8.00	24.00	56.00
6-Matt Baker-c; used in SOTI, illo-"An invitation to learning," r-in Fugitives From Justice #3; Jack Cole-a; also used by the N.Y. Legis. Comm.	19.00	56.00	130.00
7,8,10-14: 7-Jack Cole-a; Matt Baker art begins #8; Vic Flint in #10-14	8.00	24.00	56.00
9-No Vic Flint	6.50	19.00	45.00
15-Drug-c/story; Vic Flint app.; Baker-c	8.00	24.00	56.00
16,18,20,21,23	4.00	12.00	28.00
17,19,22-Baker-c	4.30	13.00	30.00
24-28 (All 100 pages): 26-Transvestism	11.00	32.00	75.00
29,30	2.65	8.00	18.00
31,32,37-Baker-c	3.00	9.00	21.00

	Good	Fine	N-Mint
33-Transvestism; Baker-c	3.70	11.00	26.00
34-Drug-c by Baker	3.70	11.00	26.00
35-Baker-c/a(2)	3.50	10.50	24.00
36-Vic Flint strip-r; Baker-c	2.65	8.00	18.00
38-Baker-c/a	3.70	11.00	26.00

AVENGERS, THE (See Solo Avengers, Tales Of Suspense, West Coast
Avengers & X-Men Vs. . . .)
Sept, 1963-Present
Marvel Comics Group

1-Origin & 1st app. The Avengers (Thor, Iron Man, Hulk, Ant-Man, Wasp)

	Good	Fine	N-Mint
	125.00	375.00	875.00
2	46.00	138.00	325.00
3-1st Sub-Mariner x-over (outside the F.F.)	28.50	86.00	200.00

4-Revival of Captain America who joins the Avengers; 1st Silver Age app. of

	Good	Fine	N-Mint
Captain America (3/64)	66.00	198.00	460.00
4-Reprint from the Golden Record Comic set	7.00	21.00	50.00
With Record (still sealed)	14.00	43.00	100.00
5-Hulk leaves	18.00	54.00	125.00

6-10: 6-Intro The Masters of Evil. 8-Intro Kang. 9-Intro Wonder Man who dies in

	Good	Fine	N-Mint
same story.	14.00	43.00	100.00
11-Spider-Man-c & x-over	14.00	43.00	100.00

12-16: 15-Death of Zemo. 16-New Avengers line-up (Hawkeye, Quicksilver,
Scarlet Witch join; Thor, Iron Man, Giant-Man, Wasp leave.)

	Good	Fine	N-Mint
	9.30	28.00	65.00
17-19: 19-Intro. Swordsman; origin Hawkeye	6.50	19.00	45.00
20-22: Wood inks	4.50	14.00	32.00
23-30: 28-Giant-Man becomes Goliath	3.15	9.50	22.00
31-40	2.30	7.00	16.00

41-52,54-56: 48-Origin/1st app. new Black Knight. 52-Black Panther joins; 1st
app. The Grim Reaper. 54-1st app. new Masters of Evil

	Good	Fine	N-Mint
	1.60	4.80	11.00
53-X-Men app.	1.85	5.50	13.00
57-1st app. The Vision	4.50	14.00	32.00
58-Origin The Vision	3.50	10.50	24.00

59-67: 59-Intro. Yellowjacket. 60-Wasp & Yellowjacket wed. 63-Goliath becomes
Yellowjacket; Hawkeye becomes the new Goliath. 65-Last 12 cent issue.

	Good	Fine	N-Mint
66,67: B. Smith-a	1.85	5.50	13.00
68-70	1.45	4.40	8.80
71-1st app. The Invaders; Black Knight joins	1.50	4.50	10.00

	Good	Fine	N-Mint
72-82,84-86,88-91: 80-Intro. Red Wolf	1.30	3.85	7.70
83-Intro. The Liberators (Wasp, Valkyrie, Scarlet Witch, Medusa & the Black Widow)	1.45	4.40	8.80
87-Origin The Black Panther	1.55	4.65	11.00
92-Neal Adams-c	1.35	4.00	9.50
93-(52 pgs.)-Neal Adams-c/a	5.50	16.50	38.00
94-96-Neal Adams-c/a	3.50	10.50	24.00
97-G.A. Capt. America, Sub-Mariner, Human Torch, Patriot, Vision, Blazing Skull, Fin, Angel, & new Capt. Marvel x-over	1.40	4.20	10.00
98-Goliath becomes Hawkeye; Smith c/a(i)	2.65	8.00	18.00
99-Smith/Sutton-a	2.65	8.00	18.00
100-Smith-c/a; featuring everyone who was an Avenger	4.70	14.00	33.00
101-106,108,109: 101-Harlan Ellison scripts	1.10	3.30	6.60
107-Starlin-a(p)	1.25	3.75	9.00
110,111-X-Men app.	1.75	5.25	12.00
112-1st app. Mantis	1.45	4.40	8.80
113-120: 116-118-Defenders/Silver Surfer app.	.90	2.75	5.50
121-130: 123-Origin Mantis	.90	2.75	5.50
131-140: 136-Ploog-r/Amaz. Advs. #12	.75	2.20	4.40
141-149: 144-Origin & 1st app. Hellcat	.50	1.55	3.10
150-Kirby-a(r); new line-up: Capt. America, Scarlet Witch, Iron Man, Wasp, Yellowjacket, Vision & The Beast	.50	1.55	3.10
151-163: 151-Wonderman returns with new costume	.50	1.55	3.10
164-166-Byrne-a	.75	2.30	4.60
167-180	.45	1.30	2.60
181-191-Byrne-a. 181-New line-up: Capt. America, Scarlet Witch, Iron Man, Wasp, Vision, Beast & The Falcon. 183-Ms. Marvel joins. 185-Origin Quicksilver & Scarlet Witch	.40	1.30	2.60
192-202: Perez-a. 195-1st Taskmaster. 200-Double size; Ms. Marvel leaves	.35	1.00	2.00
203-213,215-262,264-271,273: 211-New line-up: Capt. America, Iron Man, Tigra, Thor, Wasp & Yellowjacket. 213-Yellowjacket leaves. 215,216-Silver Surfer app. 216-Tigra leaves. 217-Yellowjacket & Wasp return. 225-Hawkeye & She-Hulk join. 227-Capt. Marvel (female) joins; origins of Ant-Man, Wasp, Giant-Man, Goliath, Yellowjacket, & Avengers. 230-Yellowjacket quits. 231-Iron Man leaves. 232-Starfox (Eros) joins. 234-Origin Quicksilver, Scarlet Witch. 236-New logo. 238-Origin Blackout. 240-Spider-Woman revived. 250-($1.00, 52 pgs.)	.25	.75	1.50
214-Ghost Rider-c/story	.50	1.50	3.50

	Good	Fine	N-Mint
263-1st app. X-Factor (1/86)(story continues in Fantastic Four #286)			
	.70	2.00	4.00
272-Alpha Flight guest star	.35	1.00	2.00

274-299: 291-$1.00 issues begin. 297-Black Knight, She-Hulk & Thor resign. 298-
  Inferno tie-in .60 1.20

| 300 ($1.75, 68 pgs.)-Thor joins | .30 | .90 | 1.80 |

301-304,306-340: 302-Re-intro Quasar. 314-318-Spider-Man x-over.
  320-324-Alpha Flight app. (320-cameo) .50 1.00

| 305-Byrne scripts begin | .35 | 1.00 | 2.00 |

AVENGERS SPOTLIGHT (Formerly Solo Avengers #1-20)
No. 21, Aug, 1989-No. 40, Jan, 1991 (.75-$1.00, color)
Marvel Comics

| 21 (75 cents)-Byrne-c/a | | .50 | 1.00 |

22-40 ($1.00): 26-Acts of Vengeance story. 31-34-U.S. Agent series. 36-Heck-i. 37-
  Mortimer-i. 40-The Black Knight app. .50 1.00

AVENGERS WEST COAST (Formerly West Coast Avengers)
No. 48, Sept, 1989-Present ($1.00, color)
Marvel Comics

48,49: Byrne-c/a & scripts continue thru #57.		.55	1.10
50-Re-intro original Human Torch	.25	.75	1.50
51-76: 54-Cover swipe/F.F. #1. 57-Last Byrne-c/a		.50	1.00

B

BABY HUEY, THE BABY GIANT
9/56-#97, 10/71; #98, 10/72; #99, 10/80; #100, 10/90-Present
Harvey Publications

	Good	Fine	N-Mint
1-Infinity-c	22.00	65.00	150.00
2	11.00	32.00	75.00
3-Baby Huey takes anti-pep pills	6.50	19.00	45.00
4,5	4.35	13.00	30.00
6-10	2.15	6.50	15.00
11-20	1.35	4.00	9.00
21-40	1.00	3.00	7.00
41-60	.85	2.50	5.00
61-79(12/67)	.50	1.50	3.00
80(12/68)-95-All 68 pg. Giants	.70	2.00	4.00
96,97-Both 52 pg. Giants	.60	1.75	3.50
98-99: Regular size	.25	.75	1.50
100-102 ($1.00)		.50	1.00

BATGIRL SPECIAL (See Teen Titans #50)
1988 (One shot, color, $1.50, 52 pgs)
DC Comics

	Good	Fine	N-Mint
1	1.35	4.00	8.00

BATMAN (See Brave & the Bold, Detective, 80-Page Giants, The Joker, Justice League of America, Justice League Int., Legends of the Dark Knight, Shadow of the.., Star Spangled, 3-D Batman, Untold Legend of . . . , & World's Finest)
Spring, 1940-Present
National Periodical Publ./Detective Comics/DC Comics

	Good	Fine	VF-NM
1-Origin The Batman retold by Bob Kane; see Detective #33 for 1st origin; 1st app. Joker & The Cat (Catwoman); has Batman story without Robin originally planned for Detective #38. This book was created entirely from the inventory of Detective Comics	3,000.00	7,500.00	18,000.00

(Prices vary widely on this book)

	Good	Fine	N-Mint
2	760.00	1875.00	4500.00

Batman #11, © DC Comics

	Good	Fine	N-Mint
3-1st Catwoman in costume; 1st Puppetmaster app.			
	550.00	1250.00	3000.00
4	417.00	1040.00	2500.00
5-1st app. of the Batmobile with its bat-head front			
	308.00	770.00	1850.00
6-10: 8-Infinity-c	225.00	562.00	1350.00
11-Classic Joker-c (3rd Joker-c, 6-7/42)	250.00	620.00	1500.00
12-15: 13-Jerry Siegel, creator of Superman appears in a Batman story. 14-2nd			
Penguin-c (12-1/42-43)	183.00	460.00	1100.00

	Good	Fine	VF-NM
16-Intro Alfred (4-5/43)	258.00	645.00	1550.00

	Good	Fine	N-Mint
17-20: 18-Hitler, Hirohito, Mussolini-c	117.00	292.00	700.00
21,22,24,26,28-30: 22-1st Alfred solo	108.00	270.00	650.00
23-Joker-c/story	142.00	355.00	850.00
25-Only Joker/Penguin team-up	133.00	335.00	800.00
27-Christmas-c	108.00	270.00	650.00
31,32,34-36,38,39: 31-Infinity logo-c. 32-Origin Robin retold. 38- Penguin-c			
	67.00	167.00	400.00

	Good	Fine	N-Mint
33-Christmas-c	83.00	210.00	500.00
37,40,44-Joker-c/stories	92.00	230.00	550.00
41-43,45,46: 42-2nd Catwoman-c (8-9/47). 43-Penguin-c. 45-Christmas cover			
	58.00	146.00	350.00
47-1st detailed orign The Batman (6-7/48)	183.00	460.00	1100.00
48-1000 Secrets of Batcave; r-in #203	63.00	156.00	375.00
49-Joker-c/story; 1st Vicki Vale & Mad Hatter	92.00	230.00	550.00
50-Two-Face impostor app.	58.00	146.00	350.00
51,53,54,56-61: 57-Centerfold is a 1950 calendar. 58-Penguin-c. 161- Origin			
Batman Plane II	52.00	131.00	315.00
52,55-Joker-c/stories	71.00	178.00	425.00
62-Origin Catwoman; Catwoman-c	64.00	160.00	385.00
63-65,67-72,74-77,79,80: 65,69-Catwoman-c. 68-Two-Face app. 72-Last 52 pgs.			
74-Used in **POP**, Pg. 90	42.00	105.00	250.00
66,73-Joker-c/stories	56.00	140.00	335.00
78-(8-9/53)-Roh Kar, The Man Hunter from Mars story-the 1st lawman of Mars to			
come to Earth (green skinned)	52.00	130.00	310.00
81-89: 84-Catwoman-c; Two-Face app. 86-Intro Batmarine (Batman's submarine).			
89-Last Pre-Code issue	42.00	105.00	250.00
90,91,93-99: 97-2nd app. Bat-Hound	27.00	70.00	165.00
92-1st app. Bat-Hound	35.00	87.00	210.00
100	125.00	312.00	750.00
101-104,106-109	22.00	66.00	155.00
105-1st Batwoman in Batman	28.50	86.00	200.00
110-Joker story	28.00	84.00	195.00
111-120: 113-1st app. Fatman	16.00	48.00	110.00
121,122,124-126,128,130	13.00	40.00	90.00
123-Joker story; 2nd app. Bat-Hound	16.00	48.00	110.00
127-Joker story; Superman cameo	16.00	48.00	110.00
129-Origin Robin retold; bondage-c	13.50	41.00	95.00
131-135,137-139,141-143: Last 10 cent issue. 131-Intro 2nd Batman & Robin			
series. 133-1st Bat-Mite in Batman. 134-Origin The Dummy. 139-Intro old			
Bat-Girl	9.30	28.00	65.00
136-Joker-c/story	14.00	43.00	100.00
140,144-Joker stories	10.00	30.00	70.00
145,148-Joker-c/stories	11.50	34.00	80.00
146,147,149,150	7.00	21.00	50.00
151,153,154,156-158,160-162,164-170: 164-New Batmobile; New look &			
Mystery Analysts series begins	5.00	15.00	35.00
152-Joker story	5.70	17.00	40.00
155-1st S.A. app. The Penguin	13.00	40.00	90.00

	Good	Fine	N-Mint
159,163-Joker-c/stories	7.00	21.00	50.00
171-Riddler app.(5/65), 1st since 12/48	36.00	108.00	250.00
172-175,177,178,180,181,183,184: 181-Batman & Robin poster insert; intro. Poison Ivy	3.50	10.50	24.00
176-80-Pg. Giant G-17; Joker-c/story	4.50	14.00	32.00
179-2nd app. Silver Age Riddler	7.85	23.50	55.00
182,187-80 Pg. Giants G-24, G-30; Joker-c/stories	4.30	13.00	30.00
185-80 Pg. Giant G-27	3.70	11.00	26.00
186-Joker-c/story	2.65	8.00	18.00
188-192,194-197,199: 197-Early SA Catwoman app.	2.15	6.50	15.00
193-80-Pg. Giant G-37	2.30	7.00	16.00
198-80-Pg. Giant G-43; Joker story; Origin-r	2.85	8.50	20.00
200-Joker-story; retells origin of Batman & Robin	14.00	43.00	100.00
201-Joker story	2.30	7.00	16.00
202,204-207,209,210	1.50	4.50	9.00
203-80 Pg. Giant G-49; r/#48, 61, & Det. 185; Batcave Blueprints	1.70	5.00	12.00
208-80 Pg. Giant G-55; New origin Batman by Gil Kane	2.15	6.50	15.00
211,212,214-217: 216-Alfred given a new last name-"Pennyworth." (see Detective #96)	1.50	4.50	9.00
213-80-Pg. Giant G-61; origin Alfred, Joker(r/Det. 168), Clayface; new origin Robin	4.30	13.00	30.00
218-80-Pg. Giant G-67	1.70	5.00	12.00
219-Neal Adams-a	2.65	8.00	18.00
220,221,224-227,229-231	1.35	4.00	8.00
222-Beatles take-off	2.30	7.00	16.00
223,228,233-80-Pg. Giants G-73,G-79,G-85	1.70	5.00	10.00
232,237-N. Adams-a. 232-Intro/1st app. Ras Al Ghul. 237-G.A. Batman reprint/Det. #37; Wrightson/Ellison plots	2.85	8.50	20.00
234-1st S.A. app. Two-Face; N. Adams-a; 52 pg. issues begin, end #242	4.30	13.00	30.00
235,236,239-242: 239-XMas-c. 241-Reprint/#5	1.15	3.50	7.00
238-DC-8 100 pg. Super Spec.; unpubbed G.A. Atom, Sargon, Plastic Man stories; Doom Patrol origin-r; Batman, Legion, Aquaman-r; N. Adams-c	1.35	4.00	8.00
243-245-Neal Adams-a	2.15	6.50	15.00
246-250,252,253: 253-Shadow app.	1.15	3.50	7.00
251-N. Adams-c/a; Joker-c/story	4.30	13.00	30.00
254,256-259,261-All 100 pg. editions; part-r	1.35	4.00	8.00

	Good	Fine	N-Mint
255-N. Adams-c/a; tells of Bruce Wayne's father who wore bat costume & fought crime (100 pgs.)	1.70	5.00	12.00
260-Joker-c/story (100pgs.)	2.85	8.50	20.00
262-285,287-290,292,293,295-299: 262-68pgs. 266-Catwoman back to old costume	.70	2.00	4.00
286,291,294-Joker-c/stories	1.00	3.00	6.00
300-Double-size	1.00	3.00	6.00
301-320,322-352,354-356,358,360-365,367,369,370: 304-(44 pgs.). 311- Batgirl reteams w/Batman. 316-Robin returns. 323,324-Catman & Catwoman app. 332-Catwoman's 1st solo. 325-Death of Comm. Gordon. 345-New Dr. Death app. 361-1st app. Harvey Bullock	.70	2.00	4.00
321,353,359-Joker-c/stories	1.00	3.00	6.00
357-1st app. Jason Todd (3/83); see Det. 524	1.35	4.00	8.00
366-Jason Todd 1st in Robin costume; Joker-c/story	4.15	12.50	25.00
368-1st new Robin in costume (Jason Todd)	3.35	10.00	20.00
371-399,401-403: 386,387-Intro Black Mask (villain). 401-2nd app. Magpie	.50	1.50	3.00

(NOTE: *Most issues between 397 & 432 were reprinted in 1989 and sold in multi-packs. Some are not identified as reprints but have newer ads copyrighted after cover dates. 2nd and 3rd printings exist.*)

	Good	Fine	N-Mint
400 ($1.50, 64pgs.)-Dark Knight special; intro by Stephen King; Art Adams/Austin-a	3.00	9.00	18.00
404-Miller scripts begin (end 407); Year 1	1.70	5.00	10.00
405-407: 407-Year 1 ends (See Det. for Year 2)	1.00	3.00	6.00
408-410: New Origin Jason Todd (Robin)	1.00	3.00	6.00
411-416,421-425: 412-Origin/1st app. Mime. 415,416-Millennium tie-ins.			
416-Nightwing-c/story	.50	1.50	3.00
417-420: "Ten Nights of the Beast" storyline	1.50	5.50	13.00
426-($1.50, 52 pgs.)-"A Death In The Family" storyline begins, ends #429	2.50	8.00	18.50
427-"A Death in the Family" part II	1.50	4.50	11.00
428-Death of Robin (Jason Todd)	1.50	5.50	13.00
429-Joker-c/story; Superman app.	1.00	3.00	6.00
430-432	.30	.90	1.80
433-435-"Many Deaths of the Batman" story by John Byrne-c/scripts	.50	1.50	3.00
436-Year 3 begins (ends #439); origin original Robin retold by Nightwing (Dick Grayson)	.85	2.50	5.00
436-2nd print		.50	1.00
437-439: 437-Origin Robin continued	.50	1.50	3.00

	Good	Fine	N-Mint
440,441: "A Lonely Place of Dying" Parts 1 & 3; 440-1st app. Timothy Drake			
	.25	.70	1.40
442-1st app. New Robin (Timothy Drake)	.85	2.50	5.00
443-456,458-464: 445-447-Batman goes to Russia. 448,449-"The Penguin Affair" parts 1 & 3. 450,451-Joker-c/stories. 452-454-"Dark Knight Dark City" storyline		.60	1.20
457-Timothy Drake officially becomes Robin & dons new costume			
	1.35	4.00	8.00
457-2nd printing		.50	1.00
465-Robin rejoins Batman	.25	.75	1.50
466-474		.50	1.00
Annual 1(8-10/61)-Swan-c	28.50	86.00	200.00
Annual 2	12.00	36.00	85.00
Annual 3(Summer, '62)-Joker-c/story	13.50	41.00	95.00
Annual 4,5	5.70	17.00	40.00
Annual 6,7(7/64)	4.30	13.00	30.00
Annual 8(10/82)	.85	2.50	5.00
Annual 9(7/85), 10(8/86), 12('88, $1.50)	.55	1.65	3.30
Annual 11('87, $1.25)-Alan Moore scripts	.85	2.50	5.00
Annual 13('89, $1.75, 68 pgs.)-Gives history of Bruce Wayne, Dick Grayson, Jason Todd, Alfred, Comm. Gordon, Barbara Gordon (Batgirl) & Vicki Vale; Morrow-i	.35	1.10	2.20
Annual 14('90, $2.00, 68pgs.)-Origin Two-Face	.35	1.00	2.00
Annual 15('91, $2.00, 68pgs.)-Armageddon 2001	.35	1.00	2.00
Special 1(4/84)-Golden c/a(p)	.85	2.50	5.00

BATMAN FAMILY, THE
Sept-Oct, 1975-No. 20, Oct-Nov, 1978 (No.1-4, 17-on: 68 pages)
(Combined with Detective Comics with No. 481)
National Periodical Publications/DC Comics

	Good	Fine	N-Mint
1-Origin Batgirl-Robin team-up (The Dynamite Duo); reprints plus one new story begins; N. Adams-a(r)	.85	2.50	5.00
2-5: 3-Batgirl & Robin learn each's I.D.	.50	1.50	3.00
4	.50	2.00	4.00
6,9-Joker's daughter on cover	.50	2.00	4.00
7,8,10,14-16: 10-1st revival Batwoman	.50	1.50	3.00
11-13: Rogers-p. 11-New stories begin; Man-Bat begins	.85	2.50	5.00
17-($1.00 size)-Batman, Huntress begin	.50	1.50	3.00
18-20: Huntress by Staton in all. 20-Origin Ragman retold			
	.30	.90	1.75

BATMAN: SON OF THE DEMON
Sept, 1987 (80 pgs., hardcover, $14.95)
DC Comics

	Good	Fine	N-Mint
1-Hardcover	9.50	28.50	57.00
Limited signed & numbered hard-c (1,700)	14.00	42.00	85.00
Softcover w/new-c ($8.95)	2.30	7.00	14.00
Softcover, 2nd print (1989, $9.95)-4th print	1.55	4.65	9.50

BATMAN: THE CULT
1988-No. 4, Nov, 1988 ($3.50, color, deluxe mini-series)
DC Comics

1-Wrightson-a/painted-c in all	2.65	8.00	16.00
2	2.00	6.00	12.00
3,4	1.50	3.00	10.00

BATMAN: THE DARK KNIGHT RETURNS
March, 1986-No. 4, 1986
DC Comics

1-Miller story & a(p); set in the future	7.50	22.50	45.00
1-2nd printing	1.30	4.00	8.00
1-3rd printing	.55	1.65	3.50
2-Carrie Kelly becomes Robin (female)	4.15	12.45	25.00
2-2nd printing	.85	2.55	5.00
2-3rd printing	.50	1.50	3.00
3-Death of Joker	1.50	4.50	10.00
3-2nd printing	.55	1.65	3.50
4-Death of Alfred	1.15	3.50	7.00

BATMAN: THE KILLING JOKE
1988 ($3.50, 52pgs. color, deluxe, adults)
DC Comics

1-Bolland-c/a; Alan Moore scripts	4.30	13.00	26.00
1-2nd thru 8th printings	.85	2.50	5.00

BATMAN: THE OFFICIAL COMIC ADAPTATION OF THE WARNER BROS. MOTION PICTURE
1989 ($2.50, $4.95, 68 pgs.) (Movie adaptation)
DC Comics

	Good	Fine	N-Mint
1-Regular format ($2.50)-Ordway-c/a	.70	2.00	4.00
1-Prestige format ($4.95)-Diff.-c, same insides	1.00	3.00	6.00

BEVERLY HILLBILLIES (TV)
4-6/63-No. 18, 8/67; No. 19, 10/69; No. 20, 10/70; No. 21, Oct, 1971
Dell Publishing Co.

1-Photo c-1-3,5,8-14,17-21	7.00	21.00	50.00
2	3.50	10.50	24.00
3-10	2.65	8.00	18.00
11-21: 19-Reprints #1	2.15	6.50	15.00

BEWARE THE CREEPER (See Brave & the Bold, Flash & Showcase)
May-June, 1968-No. 6, March-April, 1969
National Periodical Publications

1-Ditko-a in all; c-1-5	3.60	11.00	25.00
2-6: 6-G. Kane-c	2.15	6.50	15.00

BILL BOYD WESTERN (Also see Hopalong Cassidy & Western Hero)
Feb, 1950-No. 23, June, 1952 (1-3,7,11,14-on: 36 pgs.) (Movie star)
Fawcett Publications

1-Bill Boyd & his horse Midnite begin; photo front/back-c			
	25.00	75.00	175.00
2-Painted-c	15.00	45.00	105.00
3-Photo-c begin, end #23; last photo back-c	13.50	41.00	95.00
4-6 (52 pgs.)	11.00	32.00	75.00
7,11 (36 pgs.)	8.50	25.50	60.00
8-10,12,13 (52 pgs.)	9.30	28.00	65.00
14-22	8.00	24.00	55.00
23-Last issue	8.50	25.50	60.00

BILLY THE KID ADVENTURE MAGAZINE
Oct, 1950-No. 30, 1955
Toby Press

1-Williamson/Frazetta, 4 pgs; photo-c	16.00	48.00	110.00
2-Photo-c	4.00	12.00	28.00
3-Williamson/Frazetta "The Claws of Death," 4 pgs. plus Williamson art			
	17.00	51.00	120.00

	Good	Fine	N-Mint
4,5,7,8,10: 7-Photo-c	2.65	8.00	18.00
6-Frazetta story assist on "Nightmare;" photo-c	7.00	21.00	50.00
9-Kurtzman Pot-Shot Pete; photo-c	6.00	18.00	42.00
11,12,15-20: 11-Photo-c	2.30	7.00	16.00
13-Kurtzman-r/John Wayne #12 (Genius)	2.65	8.00	18.00
14-Williamson/Frazetta; r-of #1, 2 pgs.	5.00	15.00	35.00
21,23-30	1.70	5.00	12.00
22-Williamson/Frazetta-r(1pg.)/#1; photo-c	1.85	8.00	18.00

BLACK CAT COMICS (. . . Western #16-19; . . . Mystery #30 on)
June-July, 1946-No. 29, June, 1951 (See Speed Comics #17)
Harvey Publications (Home Comics)

	Good	Fine	N-Mint
1-Kubert-a	28.00	86.00	200.00
2-Kubert-a	16.00	48.00	110.00
3,4: 4-The Red Demons begin (The Demon #4 & 5)	11.50	34.00	80.00
5,6-The Scarlet Arrow app. in ea. by Powell; S&K-a in both. 6-Origin Red Demon	14.00	43.00	100.00
7-Vagabond Prince by S&K plus 1 more story	14.00	43.00	100.00
8-S&K-a; Kerry Drake begins, ends #13	13.00	40.00	90.00
9-Origin Stuntman (r-/Stuntman #1)	16.00	48.00	110.00
10-20: 14,15,17-Mary Worth app. plus Invisible Scarlett O'Neil-#15,20,24	10.00	30.00	70.00
21-26	8.50	25.50	60.00
27-Used in **SOTI**, pg. 193; X-Mas-c; 2 pg. John Wayne story	10.00	30.00	70.00
28-Intro. Kit, Black Cat's new sidekick	10.00	30.00	70.00
29-Black Cat bondage-c; Black Cat stories	9.30	28.00	65.00

BLACK CAT MYSTERY (Formerly Black Cat; . . . Western Mystery #54; . . .
    Western #55,56; . . . Mystery #57; . . . Mystic #58-62; Black Cat #63-65)
No. 30, Aug, 1951-No. 65, April, 1963
Harvey Publications

	Good	Fine	N-Mint
30-Black Cat on cover only	8.00	24.00	55.00
31,32,34,37,38,40	5.00	15.00	35.00
33-Used in **POP**, pg. 89; electrocution-c	5.70	17.00	40.00
35-Atomic disaster cover/story	6.50	19.00	45.00
36,39-Used in **SOTI**: #36-Pgs. 270,271; #39-Pgs. 386-388	8.50	25.50	60.00

	Good	Fine	N-Mint
41-43	4.50	14.00	32.00
44-Eyes, ears, tongue cut out; Nostrand-a	5.30	16.00	38.00
45-Classic "Colorama" by Powell; Nostrand-a	9.30	28.00	65.00
46-49,51-Nostrand-a in all	6.00	18.00	42.00
50-Check-a; Warren Kremer?-c showing a man's face burning away			
	9.30	28.00	65.00
52,53 (r-#34 & 35)	3.70	11.00	26.00
54-Two Black Cat stories (2/55, last pre-code)	6.00	18.00	42.00
55,56-Black Cat app.	4.00	12.00	28.00
57(7/56)-Simon?-c	2.85	8.50	20.00
58-60-Kirby-a(4)	5.30	16.00	38.00
61-Nostrand-a; "Colorama" r-/45	4.30	13.00	30.00
62(3/58)-E.C. story swipe	3.15	9.50	22.00
63-Giant(10/62); Reprints; Black Cat app.; origin Black Kitten			
	4.50	14.00	32.00
64-Giant(1/63); Reprints; Black Cat app.	4.50	14.00	32.00
65-Giant(4/63); Reprints; Black Cat app.	4.50	14.00	32.00

BLACKHAWK (Uncle Sam #1-8; see Military & Modern Comics)
No. 9, Winter, 1944-No. 243, 10-11/68; No. 244, 1-2/76-No. 250,
12/77; No. 251, 10/82-No. 273, 11/84
Comic Magazines(Quality)No. 9-107(12/56); National Periodical Publ. No. 108
(1/57)-250; DC Comics No. 251 on

	Good	Fine	N-Mint
9 (1944)	115.00	345.00	800.00
10 (1946)	50.00	150.00	350.00
11-15: 14-Ward-a; 13,14-Fear app.	38.00	114.00	265.00
16-20: 20-Ward Blackhawk	32.00	95.00	225.00
21-30	24.00	72.00	165.00
31-40: 31-Chop Chop by Jack Cole	17.00	51.00	120.00
41-49,51-60	12.00	36.00	84.00
50-1st Killer Shark; origin in text	15.00	45.00	105.00
61-Used in **POP**, pg. 91	11.00	32.00	75.00
62-Used in **POP**, pg. 92 & color illo	11.00	32.00	75.00
63-65,67-70,72-80: 70-Return of Killer Shark. 75-Intro. Blackie the Hawk			
	10.00	30.00	70.00
66-B&W and color illos in **POP**	10.00	30.00	70.00
71-Origin retold; flying saucer-c; A-Bomb panels	13.00	40.00	90.00
81-86: Last pre-code (3/55)	9.30	28.00	65.00
87-92,94-99,101-107	6.50	19.00	45.00

	Good	Fine	N-Mint
93-Origin in text	8.00	24.00	56.00
100	8.50	25.50	60.00
108-Re-intro. Blackie, the Hawk, their mascot; not in #115			
	24.30	73.00	170.00
109-117	5.85	17.50	41.00
118-Frazetta r-/Jimmy Wakely #4 (3 pgs.)	7.50	22.50	52.00
119-130	3.00	9.00	21.00
131-163,165,166: 133-Intro. Lady Blackhawk. 143-Kurtzman r-/Jimmy Wakely			
#4. 166-Last 10 cent issue	2.15	6.50	15.00
164-Origin retold	2.30	7.00	16.00
167-180	1.15	3.50	8.00
181-190	1.00	3.00	6.00
191-197,199-202,204-210: Combat Diary series begins. 197-New look for			
Blackhawks	.70	2.00	4.00
198-Origin retold	1.00	3.00	6.00
203-Origin Chop Chop (12/64)	.85	2.50	5.00
211-243(1968): 228-Batman, Green Lantern, Superman, The Flash cameos. 230-			
Blackhawks become superheroes. 242-Return to old costumes			
	.70	2.00	4.00
244 ('76) -250: 250-Chuck dies	.35	1.00	2.00
251-264: 251-Origin retold; Black Knights return		.50	1.00
265-273 (75 cent cover price)		.50	1.00

BLACK RIDER (Formerly Western Winners)
No. 8, 3/50-No. 18, 1/52; No. 19, 11/53-No. 27, 3/55
Marvel/Atlas Comics(CDS No. 8-17/CPS No. 19 on)

	Good	Fine	N-Mint
8 (#1)-Black Rider & his horse Satan begin; 36 pgs; photo-c			
	20.00	60.00	140.00
9-52 pgs. begin, end #14	10.00	30.00	70.00
10-Origin Black Rider	12.00	36.00	85.00
11-14(Last 52 pgs.)	7.00	21.00	50.00
15-19: 19-Two-Gun Kid app.	6.50	19.50	45.00
20-Classic-c; Two-Gun Kid app.	7.00	21.00	50.00
21-26: 21-23-Two-Gun Kid app. 24,25-Arrowhead app. 26-Kid Colt app.			
	5.00	15.00	35.00
27-Last issue; last precode. Kid Colt app. The Spider (a villain) burns to death			
	5.30	16.00	38.00

BLACK TERROR (See America's Best & Exciting Comics)
Wint, 1942-43-No. 27, June, 1949
Better Publications/Standard

	Good	Fine	N-Mint
1-Black Terror, Crime Crusader begin	68.00	205.00	475.00
2	32.00	96.00	225.00
3	24.00	72.00	165.00
4,5	19.00	56.00	130.00
6-10: 7-The Ghost app.	14.00	43.00	100.00
11-20: 20-The Scarab app.	12.00	36.00	85.00
21-Miss Masque app.	13.00	40.00	90.00
22-Part Frazetta-a on one Black Terror story	13.50	41.00	95.00
23,25-27	11.50	34.00	80.00
24-1/4 pg. Frazetta-a	12.00	36.00	85.00

BLONDE PHANTOM (Formerly All-Select #1-11) (See Marvel Mystery)
No. 12, Winter, 1946-47-No. 22, March, 1949
Marvel Comics (MPC)

	Good	Fine	N-Mint
12-Miss America begins, ends #14	54.00	161.00	375.00
13-Sub-Mariner begins	36.00	107.00	250.00
14,15; 14-Male Bondage-c; Namora app. 15-Kurtzman's "Hey Look"			
	30.00	90.00	210.00
16-Captain America with Bucky app.; Kurtzman's "Hey Look"			
	39.00	118.00	275.00
17-22: 22-Anti-Wertham editorial	29.00	86.00	200.00

BLONDIE COMICS (See Ace Comics, King Comics & Magic Comics)
Spring, 1947-No. 163, Nov, 1965; No. 164, Aug, 1966-No. 175, Dec, 1967; No. 177,
    Feb, 1969-No. 222, Nov, 1976
David McKay #1-15/Harvey #16-163/King #164-175/Charlton #177 on

	Good	Fine	N-Mint
1	11.00	32.00	75.00
2	5.00	15.00	35.00
3-5	3.70	11.00	26.00
6-10	2.85	8.50	20.00
11-15	2.00	6.00	14.00
16-(3/50; 1st Harvey issue)	2.30	7.00	16.00
17-20	1.70	5.00	12.00
21-30	1.30	4.00	9.00
31-50	1.00	3.00	7.00
51-80	.85	2.60	6.00
81-124,126-130	.85	2.50	5.00
125 (80 pgs.)	1.00	3.00	7.00
131-136,138,139	.70	2.00	4.00

	Good	Fine	N-Mint
137,140-(80 pages)	.85	2.60	6.00
141-166(#148,155,157-159,161-163 are 68 pgs.)	.85	2.60	6.00
167-One pg. Williamson ad	.35	1.00	2.00
168-175,177-222 (no #176)	.25	.75	1.50

The Blue Beetle #14, © Fox Publications

BLUE BEETLE, THE (Also see All Top, & Mystery Men)
Winter, 1939-40-No. 60, Aug, 1950
Fox Publ. No. 1-11, 31-60; Holyoke No. 12-30.

	Good	Fine	N-Mint
1-Reprints from Mystery Men 1-5; Blue Beetle origin; Yarko the Great-r/from Wonder/Wonderworld 2-5 all by Eisner; Master Magician app.; (Blue Beetle in 4 different costumes)	158.00	400.00	950.00
2-K-51-r by Powell/Wonderworld 8,9	61.00	182.00	425.00
3-Simon-c	43.00	130.00	300.00
4-Marijuana drug mention story	30.00	90.00	210.00
5-Zanzibar The Magician by Tuska	25.00	75.00	175.00
6-Dynamite Thor begins; origin Blue Beetle	24.00	72.00	165.00
7,8-Dynamo app. in both. 8-Last Thor	22.00	65.00	150.00

	Good	Fine	N-Mint
9,10-The Blackbird & The Gorilla app. in both. 10-Bondage/hypo-c			
	19.00	58.00	135.00
11(2/42)-The Gladiator app.	19.00	58.00	135.00
12(6/42)-The Black Fury app.	19.00	58.00	135.00
13-V-Man begins, ends #18; Kubert-a	22.00	66.00	155.00
14,15-Kubert-a in both. 14-Intro. side-kick (c/text only), Sparky (called Spunky			
#17-19)	22.00	65.00	150.00
16-18	17.00	50.00	115.00
19-Kubert-a	19.00	58.00	135.00
20-Origin/1st app. Tiger Squadron; Arabian Nights begin			
	19.00	58.00	135.00
21-26: 24-Intro. & only app. The Halo. 26-General Patton story & photo			
	13.00	40.00	90.00
27-Tamaa, Jungle Prince app.	11.00	32.00	75.00
28-30(2/44)	9.30	28.00	65.00
31(6/44), 33-40: "The Threat from Saturn" serial in #34-38			
	7.00	21.00	50.00
32-Hitler-c	10.00	30.00	60.00
41-45	6.00	18.00	42.00
46-The Puppeteer app.	6.50	19.00	45.00
47-Kamen & Baker-a begin	38.00	115.00	265.00
48-50	30.00	90.00	210.00
51,53	27.00	81.00	190.00
52-Kamen bondage-c	38.00	115.00	265.00
54-Used in **SOTI**. Illo-"Children call these 'headlights' comics"			
	57.00	171.00	400.00
55,57(7/48)-Last Kamen issue	27.00	81.00	190.00
56-Used in **SOTI**, pg. 145	27.00	81.00	190.00
58(4/50)-60-No Kamen-a	4.50	14.00	32.00

BLUE BEETLE
V2#1, June, 1964-V2#5, Mar-Apr, 1965; V3#50, July, 1965-V3#54,
Feb-Mar, 1966; #1, June, 1967-#5, Nov, 1968
Charlton Comics

V2#1-Origin Dan Garrett-Blue Beetle	4.30	13.00	30.00
2-5, V3#50-54	2.85	8.50	20.00
1(1967)-Question series begins by Ditko	7.00	21.00	50.00
2-Origin Ted Kord-Blue Beetle; Dan Garrett x-over			
	2.65	8.00	18.00
3-5 (All Ditko-c/a in #1-5)	2.00	6.00	14.00

BLUE BOLT
June, 1940-No. 101 (V10No.2), Sept-Oct, 1949
Funnies, Inc. No. 1/Novelty Press/Premium Group of Comics

	Good	Fine	N-Mint
V1#1-Origin Blue Bolt by Joe Simon, Sub-Zero, White Rider & Super Horse, Dick Cole, Wonder Boy & Sgt. Spook	121.00	365.00	850.00
2-Simon-a	65.00	195.00	455.00
3-1 pg. Space Hawk by Wolverton; S&K-a	50.00	150.00	350.00
4,5-S&K-a in each; 5-Everett-a begins on Sub-Zero			
	46.00	140.00	325.00
6,8-10-S&K-a	41.00	125.00	290.00
7-S&K-c/a	43.00	130.00	300.00
11,12	19.00	58.00	135.00
V2#1-Origin Dick Cole & The Twister; Twister x-over in Dick Cole, Sub- Zero, & Blue Bolt. Origin Simba Karno who battles Dick Cole through V2#5 & becomes main supporting character V2#6 on; battle-c			
	13.00	40.00	90.00
2-Origin The Twister retold in text	10.00	30.00	70.00
3-5: 5-Intro. Freezum	8.00	24.00	56.00
6-Origin Sgt. Spook retold	7.00	21.00	50.00
7-12: 7-Lois Blake becomes Blue Bolt's costume aide; last Twister			
	5.70	17.00	40.00
V3#1-3	4.50	14.00	32.00
4-12: 4-Blue Bolt abandons costume	3.70	11.00	26.00
V4#1-Hitler, Tojo, Mussolini-c	4.50	14.00	32.00
V4#2-12: 3-Shows V4#3 on-c, V4#4 inside (9-10/43). 5-Infinity-c. 8-Last Sub-Zero	3.00	9.00	21.00
V5#1-8, V6#1-3,5-10, V7#1-12	2.00	6.00	14.00
V6#4-Racist cover	3.00	9.00	21.00
V8#1-6,8-12, V9#1-5,7,8	1.70	5.00	12.00
V8#7,V9#6,9-L. B. Cole-c	2.30	7.00	16.00
V10#1,2,(#100,101)-Last Dick Cole, Blue Bolt	2.00	6.00	14.00

BLUE RIBBON COMICS (. . . Mystery Comics No. 9-18)
Nov, 1939-No. 22, March, 1942 (1st MLJ series)
MLJ Magazines

1-Dan Hastings, Richy the Amazing Boy, Rang-A-Tang the Wonder Dog begin; Little Nemo app. (not by W. McCay); Jack Cole-a(3)			
	129.00	385.00	900.00
2-Bob Phantom, Silver Fox (both in #3), Rang-A-Tang Club & Cpl. Collins			

	Good	Fine	N-Mint
begin; Jack Cole-a	54.00	160.00	375.00
3-J. Cole-a	36.00	107.00	250.00
4-Doc Strong, The Green Falcon, & Hercules begin; origin & 1st app. The Fox & Ty-Gor, Son of the Tiger	41.00	122.00	285.00
5-8: 8-Last Hercules; 6,7-Biro, Meskin-a. 7-Fox app. on-c	25.00	75.00	175.00
9-(Scarce)-Origin & 1st app. Mr. Justice	107.00	320.00	750.00
10-13: 12-Last Doc Strong. 13-Inferno, the Flame Breather begins, ends #19; Devil-c	46.00	140.00	325.00
14,15,17,18: 15-Last Green Falcon	41.00	122.00	285.00
16-Origin & 1st app. Captain Flag	79.00	235.00	550.00
19-22: 20-Last Ty-Gor. 22-Origin Mr. Justice retold	36.00	107.00	250.00

BOB COLT (Movie star)
Nov, 1950-No. 10, May, 1952
Fawcett Publications

1-Bob Colt, his horse Buckskin & sidekick Pablo begin; photo front/ back-c begin			
	25.00	75.00	175.00
2	16.50	50.00	115.00
3-5	14.00	43.00	100.00
6-Flying Saucer story	12.00	36.00	85.00
7-10: 9-Last photo back-c	11.00	32.00	75.00

BOB STEELE WESTERN (Movie star)
Dec, 1950-No. 10, June, 1952
Fawcett Publications

1-Bob Steele & his horse Bullet begin; photo front/back-c begin			
	25.00	75.00	175.00
2	16.50	50.00	115.00
3-5: 4-Last photo back-c	14.00	43.00	100.00
6-10: 10-Last photo-c	11.00	32.00	75.00

BONANZA (TV)
June-Aug, 1960-No. 37, Aug, 1970 (All Photo-c)
Dell/Gold Key

| 4-Color 1110 (6-8/60) | 8.50 | 25.50 | 60.00 |
| 4-Color 1221,1283, & #01070-207, 01070-210 | 7.00 | 21.00 | 50.00 |

	Good	Fine	N-Mint
1(12/62-Gold Key)	7.00	21.00	50.00
2	4.00	12.00	28.00
3-10	3.00	9.00	21.00
11-20	2.30	7.00	16.00
21-37: 29-Reprints	1.50	4.50	10.00

BORIS KARLOFF TALES OF MYSTERY (TV) (. . . Thriller No. 1,2)
No. 3, April, 1963-No. 97, Feb, 1980
Gold Key

3-8,10-(Two #5's, 10/63,11/63)	1.30	4.00	9.00
9-Wood-a	1.70	5.00	12.00
11-Williamson-a, Orlando-a, 8 pgs.	1.70	5.00	12.00
12-Torres, McWilliams-a; Orlando-a(2)	1.15	3.50	8.00
13,14,16-20	.85	2.60	6.00
15-Crandall,Evans-a	1.00	3.00	7.00
21-Jeff Jones-a(3 pgs.) "The Screaming Skull"	1.00	3.00	7.00
22-30: 23-Reprint; photo-c	.70	2.00	4.00
31-50	.40	1.25	2.50
51-74: 74-Origin & 1st app. Taurus		.60	1.20
75-97: 80-86-(52 pages)		.40	.80

BORIS KARLOFF THRILLER (TV) (Becomes Boris Karloff Tales . . .)
Oct, 1962-No. 2, Jan, 1963 (80 pages)
Gold Key

1-Photo-c	3.00	9.00	24.00
2	2.75	8.25	22.00

BOY COMICS (Boy Illustories No. 43-108)(Stories by Charles Biro)
No. 3, April, 1942-No. 119, March, 1956
Lev Gleason Publications (Comic House)

3(No.1)-Origin Crimebuster, Bombshell & Young Robin Hood; Yankee Longago, Case 1001-1008, Swoop Storm, & Boy Movies begin; 1st app. Iron Jaw			
	112.00	335.00	780.00
4-Hitler, Tojo, Mussolini-c	49.00	145.00	340.00
5	39.00	118.00	275.00
6-Origin Iron Jaw; origin & death of Iron Jaw's son; Little Dynamite begins, ends #39	82.00	245.00	575.00
7,9: 7-Flag & Hitler, Tojo, Mussolini-c	32.00	95.00	225.00

	Good	Fine	N-Mint
8-Death of Iron Jaw	36.00	107.00	250.00
10-Return of Iron Jaw; classic Biro-c	46.00	140.00	325.00
11-14: 11-Classic Iron Jaw-c. 14-Iron Jaw-c	21.00	64.00	150.00
15-Death of Iron Jaw	26.00	77.00	180.00
16,18-20	14.00	43.00	100.00
17-Flag-c	16.00	48.00	110.00
21-26	9.30	28.00	65.00

27-29,31,32-(All 68 pages). 28-Yankee Longago ends. 32-Swoop Storm & Young

Robin Hood end	10.00	30.00	70.00
30-(68 pgs.)-Origin Crimebuster retold	12.00	36.00	85.00
33-40: 34-Crimebuster story(2); suicide-c/story	5.00	15.00	35.00
41-50	3.50	10.50	24.00
51-59: 57-Dilly Duncan begins, ends #71	2.30	7.00	16.00
60-Iron Jaw returns	3.00	9.00	21.00
61-Origin Crimebuster & Iron Jaw retold	4.00	12.00	28.00
62-Death of Iron Jaw explained	4.00	12.00	28.00
63-73: 73-Frazetta 1-pg. ad	2.00	6.00	14.00

74-88: 80-1st app. Rocky X of the Rocketeers; becomes "Rocky X" #101; Iron
Jaw, Sniffer & the Deadly Dozen begins, ends #118

	1.70	5.00	12.00
89-92-The Claw serial app. in all	2.15	6.50	15.00
93-Claw cameo; Check-a(Rocky X)	2.85	8.50	20.00
94-97,99	1.70	5.00	12.00
98-Rocky X by Sid Check	3.15	9.50	22.00
100	2.65	8.00	18.00

101-107,109,111,119: 111-Crimebuster becomes Chuck Chandler. 119-Last

Crimebuster	1.70	5.00	12.00
108,110,112-118-Kubert-a	2.65	8.00	18.00

BOY COMMANDOS (See Detective #64 & World's Finest Comics #8)
Winter, 1942-43-No. 36, Nov-Dec, 1949
National Periodical Publications

1-Origin Liberty Belle; The Sandman & The Newsboy Legion x-over in Boy

Commandos; S&K-a, 48 pgs.	175.00	438.00	1050.00
2-Last Liberty Belle; S&K-a, 46 pgs.	71.00	215.00	500.00
3-S&K-a, 45 pgs.	50.00	150.00	350.00
4,5	29.00	86.00	200.00
6-8,10: 6-S&K-a	21.00	62.00	145.00
9-No S&K-a	14.00	43.00	100.00
11-Infinity-c	14.00	43.00	100.00

	Good	Fine	N-Mint
12-16,18-20	11.50	34.00	80.00
17-Sci/fi-c/story	12.00	36.00	85.00
21,22,24,25: 22-Judy Canova x-over	8.50	25.50	60.00
23-S&K-c/a(all)	10.00	30.00	70.00
26-Flying Saucer story (3-4/48)-4th of this theme			
	9.30	28.00	65.00
27,28,30: 30-Cleveland Indians story	8.50	25.50	60.00
29-S&K story (1)	9.30	28.00	65.00
31-35: 32-Dale Evans app. on-c & story. 34-Intro. Wolf, their mascot			
	8.50	25.50	60.00
36-Intro The Atomobile c/sci-fi story	11.00	32.00	75.00

The Brave and the Bold #29, © DC Comics

BRAVE AND THE BOLD, THE
Aug-Sept, 1955-No. 200, July, 1983
National Periodical Publications/DC Comics

1-Viking Prince by Kubert, Silent Knight, Golden Gladiator begin

	93.00	279.00	650.00

	Good	Fine	N-Mint
2	42.00	126.00	295.00
3,4	25.00	73.00	170.00
5-Robin Hood begins	18.00	54.00	125.00
6-10: 6-Robin Hood by Kubert; Golden Gladiator last app.; Silent Knight; no			
Viking Prince	19.00	57.00	133.00
11-22: 22-Last Silent Knight	14.25	43.00	100.00
23-Viking Prince origin by Kubert	16.50	50.00	115.00
24-Last Viking Prince by Kubert	16.50	50.00	115.00
25-1st app. Suicide Squad	9.50	28.00	66.00
26,27-Suicide Squad	8.30	25.00	58.00
28-(2-3/60)-Justice League intro./1st app.; origin Snapper Carr			
	220.00	660.00	1530.00
29,30-Justice League	86.00	258.00	600.00
31-33-Cave Carson (#31 is 1st app.)	7.00	21.00	50.00
34-Origin/1st app. Silver-Age Hawkman & Byth by Kubert			
	43.00	130.00	300.00
35,36-Hawkman by Kubert; origin Shadow Thief #36			
	13.00	40.00	90.00
37-39-Suicide Squad. 38-Last 10 cent issue.	6.50	19.00	45.00
40,41-Cave Carson Inside Earth: #40 has Kubert art	6.50	19.00	45.00
42,44-Hawkman by Kubert	8.70	26.00	61.00
43-Origin Hawkman by Kubert retold	12.00	36.00	83.00
45-49-Strange Sports Stories by Infantino	1.70	5.00	12.00
50-The Green Arrow & Manhunter From Mars; team-ups begin			
	8.70	26.00	61.00
51-Aquaman & Hawkman	2.00	6.00	14.00
52-Sgt. Rock by Kubert, Haunted Tank, Johnny Cloud, & Mlle. Marie			
	2.00	6.00	14.00
53-Atom & The Flash by Toth	2.50	7.50	17.00
54-Kid Flash, Robin & Aqualad; 1st app./origin Teen Titans (6-7/64)			
	17.50	52.50	122.00
55-Metal Men & The Atom	1.05	3.15	7.50
56-The Flash & Manhunter From Mars	1.05	3.15	7.50
57-Origin & 1st app. Metamorpho (12-1/64-65)	8.30	25.00	58.00
58-Metamorpho by Fradon	1.85	5.50	13.00
59-Batman & Green Lantern; 1st Batman team-up in Brave and the Bold			
	4.85	14.50	34.00
60-Teen Titans (2nd app.)-1st app. new Wonder Girl (Donna Troy), who joins			
Titans (6-7/65)	6.00	18.00	42.00
61,62-Origin Starman & Black Canary by Anderson. 62-Huntress app.			
	1.60	4.80	11.00

	Good	Fine	N-Mint
63-Supergirl & Wonder Woman	1.10	3.25	6.50
64-Batman Versus Eclipso (see H.O.S. #61)	2.70	8.00	19.00
65-Flash & Doom Patrol	1.10	3.25	6.50
66-Metamorpho & Metal Men	1.10	3.25	6.50
67-Batman & The Flash by Infantino; Batman team-ups begin, end #200			
	1.25	3.75	8.50
68-Batman/Joker/Riddler/Penguin-c/story	2.50	7.50	17.00
69-78: Batman team-ups	1.25	3.75	8.50
79-Batman-Deadman by Neal Adams	2.70	8.00	19.00
80-Batman-Creeper; N. Adams-a	2.30	7.00	16.00
81-Batman-Flash; N. Adams-a	2.30	7.00	16.00
82-Batman-Aquaman; N. Adams-a; origin Ocean Master retold			
	2.30	7.00	16.00
83-Batman-Teen Titans; N. Adams-a	3.70	11.00	26.00
84-Batman(GA)-Sgt. Rock; N. Adams-a	2.50	7.50	17.00
85-Batman-Green Arrow; 1st new costume for Green Arrow by Neal Adams			
	2.50	7.50	17.00
86-Batman-Deadman; N. Adams-a	2.50	7.50	17.00
87-92: Batman team-ups	1.10	3.25	6.50
93-Batman-House of Mystery; N. Adams-a	2.30	7.00	16.00
94-Batman-Teen Titans	1.10	3.25	6.50
95-99: 97-Origin Deadman-r	.90	2.75	5.50
100-Batman-Green Lantern-Gr. Arrow-Black Canary-Robin; Deadman by N. Adams (52 pgs., 25 cents)			
	2.30	7.00	16.00
101-Batman-Metamorpho; Kubert Viking Prince	.60	1.75	3.50
102-Batman-Teen Titans; N. Adams-a(p)	.90	2.75	5.50
103-110: Batman team-ups	.60	1.75	3.50
111-Batman/Joker-c/story	1.25	3.75	8.50
112-117: All 100 pgs.; Batman team-ups	.75	2.25	4.50
118-Batman/Wildcat/Joker-c/story	.75	2.25	4.50
119-128,131-140: Batman team-ups	.40	1.25	2.50
129,130-Batman/Joker-c/stories	1.25	3.75	8.50
141-Batman vs. Joker-c/story	1.25	3.75	7.50
142-190,192-199: 143,144-(44 pgs.). 148-XMas-c. 149-Batman-Teen Titans. 150-Anniversary issue; Superman. 179-LSH. 182-Batman/Robin. 181-Hawk & Dove. 183-Riddler. 187-Metal Men. 196-Origin Ragman retold. 197-Earth II Batman & Catwoman marry	.35	1.15	2.25
191-Batman/Joker-c/story	.90	2.75	5.50
200-Double-sized (64 pgs.); printed on Mando paper; Earth One & Earth Two Batman team-up; Intro/1st app. Batman & The Outsiders			
	1.10	3.25	6.50

BRENDA STARR
No. 13, 9/47; No. 14, 3/48; V2No.3, 6/48-V2#12, 12/49
Four Star Comics Corp./Superior Comics Ltd.

	Good	Fine	N-Mint
V1#13-By Dale Messick	36.00	107.00	250.00
14-Kamen bondage-c	36.00	107.00	250.00
V2#3-Baker-a?	29.00	86.00	200.00
4-Used in **SOTI**, pg. 21; Kamen bondage-c	32.00	95.00	225.00
5-10	25.00	75.00	175.00
11,12 (Scarce)	30.00	90.00	210.00

BUCK JONES (Also see Crackajack Funnies & Master Comics #7)
No. 299, Oct, 1950-No. 850, Oct, 1957 (All Painted-c)
Dell Publishing Co.

	Good	Fine	N-Mint
4-Color 299(#1)-Buck Jones & his horse Silver-B begin; painted back-c begins,			
ends #5	10.00	30.00	70.00
2(4-6/51)	5.00	15.00	35.00
3-8(10-12/52)	3.70	11.00	26.00
4-Color 460,500,546,589	3.50	10.50	24.00
4-Color 652,733,850	2.30	7.00	16.00

BUCK ROGERS (Also see Famous Funnies)
Winter, 1940-41-No. 6, Sept, 1943
Famous Funnies

	Good	Fine	N-Mint
1-Sunday strip reprints by Rick Yager; begins with strip #190; Calkins-c			
	125.00	375.00	875.00
2 (7/41)-Calkins-c	75.00	225.00	525.00
3 (12/41), 4 (7/42)	61.00	182.00	425.00
5-Story continues with Famous Funnies No. 80; Buck Rogers, Sky Roads			
	54.00	161.00	375.00
6-Reprints of 1939 dailies; contains B.R. story "Crater of Doom" (2 pgs.) by			
Calkins not reprinted from Famous Funnies	54.00	161.00	375.00

BUCK ROGERS (. . . in the 25th Century No. 5 on) (TV)
Oct, 1964; No. 2, July, 1979-No. 16, May, 1982 (No #10)
Gold Key/Whitman No. 7 on

	Good	Fine	N-Mint
1(10128-410)-Painted-c; 12 cents	2.85	8.50	20.00
2(8/79)-Movie adaptation	.35	1.00	2.00

	Good	Fine	N-Mint
3-9,11-16: 3,4-Movie adaptation; 5-new stories		.50	1.00

BUGS BUNNY
1942-No. 245, 1983
Dell Publishing Co./Gold Key No. 86-218/Whitman No. 219 on

Large Feature Comic 8(1942)-(Rarely found in fine-mint condition)

	Good	Fine	N-Mint
	59.00	175.00	410.00
4-Color 33 ('43)	35.00	105.00	245.00
4-Color 51	20.00	60.00	140.00
4-Color 88	12.00	36.00	85.00
4-Color 123('46),142,164	7.00	21.00	50.00
4-Color 187,200,217,233	6.00	18.00	42.00
4-Color 250-Used in **SOTI**, pg. 309	6.00	18.00	42.00
4-Color 266,274,281,289,298('50)	4.50	14.00	32.00
4-Color 307,317(#1),327(#2),338,347,355,366,376,393			
	3.70	11.00	26.00
4-Color 407,420,432	2.65	8.00	18.00
28(12-1/52-53)-30	1.50	4.50	10.00
31-50	.85	2.60	6.00
51-85(7-9/62)	.75	2.25	5.00
86(10/62)-88-Bugs Bunny's Showtime-(80 pgs.)(25 cents)			
	2.25	6.75	18.00
89-100	.70	2.00	4.00
101-120	.40	1.25	2.50
121-140	.35	1.00	2.00
141-170		.60	1.20
171-228,230-245		.35	.70
229-Swipe of Barks story/WDC&S 223		.40	.80

BUGS BUNNY
June, 1990-No. 3, Aug, 1990 ($1.00, color, mini-series)
DC Comics

	Good	Fine	N-Mint
1-Daffy Duck, Elmer Fudd, others app.	.25	.75	1.50
2,3		.50	1.00

BULLETMAN (See Master Comics & Nickel Comics)
Sum, 1941-#12, 2/12/43; #14, Spr, 1946-#16, Fall, 1946 (nn 13)
Fawcett Publications

	Good	Fine	N-Mint
1	167.00	420.00	1000.00
2	76.00	230.00	535.00
3	54.00	160.00	375.00
4,5	46.00	140.00	325.00
6-10: 7-Ghost Stories as told by the night watchman of the cemetery begins;			
Eisnerish-a	39.00	118.00	275.00
11,12,14-16 (nn 13)	34.00	100.00	235.00

BULLWINKLE (TV) (. . . and Rocky No. 20 on) (Jay Ward)
3-5/62-#11, 4/74; #12, 6/76-#19, 3/78; #20, 4/79-#25, 2/80
Dell/Gold Key

4-Color 1270 (3-5/62)	8.50	25.50	60.00
01-090-209 (Dell, 7-9/62)	8.50	25.50	60.00
1(11/62, Gold Key)	5.70	17.00	40.00
2(2/63)	5.00	15.00	35.00
3(4/72)-11(4/74-Gold Key)	1.50	4.50	10.00
12(6/76)-reprints	.85	2.50	5.00
13(9/76), 14-new stories	1.00	3.00	7.00
15-25	.85	2.50	5.00
Mother Moose Nursery Pomes 01-530-207 (5-7/62-Dell)			
	5.70	17.00	40.00

BULLWINKLE (. . . & Rocky No. 2 on) (TV)
July, 1970-No. 7, July, 1971
Charlton Comics

1	1.70	5.00	12.00
2-7	1.15	3.50	8.00

C

CAPTAIN ACTION
Oct-Nov, 1968-No. 5, June-July, 1969 (Based on Ideal toy)
National Periodical Publications

	Good	Fine	N-Mint
1-Origin; Wood-a; Superman-c app.	3.60	11.00	25.00
2,3,5-Kane/Wood-a	2.50	7.50	17.00
4	1.85	5.50	13.00
. . . & Action Boy ('67)-Ideal Toy Co. giveaway	4.00	12.00	28.00

CAPTAIN AMERICA (Formerly Tales of Suspense #1-99; Captain America and
    the Falcon #134-223) (Also see The Avengers #4)
No. 100, April, 1968-Present
Marvel Comics Group

100-Flashback on Cap's revival with Avengers & Sub-Mariner

	Good	Fine	N-Mint
	31.00	93.00	220.00
101	8.00	24.00	55.00
102-108	4.70	14.00	33.00
109-Origin Capt. America	5.70	17.00	40.00
110,111,113-Steranko-c/a. 110-Rick becomes Cap's partner. 110-Hulk x-over. 111- Death of Steve Rogers. 113-Cap's funeral	6.30	19.00	44.00
112-Origin retold	2.50	7.50	17.00
114-116,118-120	1.85	5.50	13.00
117-1st app. The Falcon	2.15	6.50	15.00
121-140: 121-Retells origin. 133-The Falcon becomes Cap's partner; origin Modok. 137,138-Spider-Man x-over. 140-Origin Grey Gargoyle retold	1.15	3.50	8.00
141-171,176-179: 143-(52 pgs.). 155-Origin; redrawn with Falcon added. 164-1st app. Nightshade. 176-End of Capt. America	.85	2.50	5.00
172-175-X-Men x-over	1.50	4.50	10.00
180-Intro/origin of Nomad; Steve Rogers becomes Nomad	.85	2.50	5.00
181-Intro & origin of new Capt. America	.85	2.50	5.00
182,184-200: 186-True origin The Falcon	.70	2.00	4.00
183-Death of new Cap; Nomad becomes Cap.	.85	2.50	5.00
201-240,242-246: 233-Death of Sharon Carter. 235-Daredevil x-over; (7/79)-Miller involved? 244,245-Miller-c	.50	1.50	3.00
241-Punisher app.; Miller-c	7.85	23.50	55.00
247-255-Byrne-a. 255-Origin; Miller-c	.60	1.75	3.50

	Good	Fine	N-Mint
256-281,283-285,289-322,324-336: 265-Nick Fury app. 266-Spider-Man app. 267-1st app. Everyman. 269-1st Team America. 281-1950s Bucky returns. 284-Patriot (Jack Mace) app. 285-Death of Patriot. 298-Origin Red Skull			
	.35	1.00	2.00
282-1st app. new Nomad (Jack Monroe); Bucky becomes Nomad			
	.50	1.50	3.00
286-288-Deathlok app.	.50	1.50	3.00
323-1st app. Super Patriot	.70	2.00	4.00
327-Captain America battles Super Patriot	.50	1.50	3.00
328-Origin & 1st app. D-Man	.50	1.50	3.00
332-Old Cap resigns	1.70	5.00	10.00
333-Intro new Captain (Super Patriot)	1.15	3.50	7.00
334	.90	2.75	5.50
335-340: 339-Fall of the Mutants tie-in	.85	2.50	5.00
341-343,345-349	.30	.85	1.70
344-Double size, $1.50	.35	1.10	2.20
350-($1.75, 68 pgs.)-Return of Steve Rogers (original Cap) to original costume			
	.75	2.25	4.50
351-354: 351-Nick Fury app. 354-1st app. U.S. Agent (see Avengers West Coast)			
	.30	.85	1.70
355-382,384-390: 375-Daredevil app.		.50	1.00
383-($2.00, 68 pgs.)-50th anniversary issue; Red Skull story; Jim Lee-c(i)			
	.35	1.00	2.00
Special 1(1/71)	1.70	5.00	12.00
Special 2(1/72)-Colan-r/Not Brand Echh	1.30	4.00	9.00
Annual 3-7: 3(4/76), 4(1977, 52 pgs.)-Kirby-c/a, 5(1981, 52 pgs.), 6 (11/82, 52 pgs.), 7('83, 52 pgs.)	.40	1.25	2.50
Annual 8(9/86)-Wolverine featured	5.00	15.00	35.00
Annual 9(1990, $2.00, 68 pgs.)-Nomad back-up	.35	1.00	2.00
Annual 10(1991, $2.00, 68 pgs.)-Origin retold	.35	1.00	2.00

CAPTAIN AMERICA COMICS (See All Winners & Marvel Mystery)
Mar, 1941-No. 75, Jan, 1950; No. 76, 5/54-No. 78, 9/54
  (No. 74 & 75 titled Capt. America's Weird Tales)
Timely/Marvel Comics (TCI 1-20/CmPS 21-68/MjMC 69-75/Atlas Comics
  (PrPI 76-78)

	Good	Fine	VF-NM
1-Origin & 1st app. Captain America & Bucky by S&K; Hurricane, Tuk the Caveboy begin by S&K; Red Skull app. Hitler-c			
	2,335.00	5,835.00	14,000.00
(Prices vary widely on this book)			

	Good	Fine	N-Mint
2-S&K Hurricane; Tuk by Avison (Kirby splash)	600.00	1500.00	3600.00
3-Red Skull app; Stan Lee's 1st text	435.00	1085.00	2600.00
4-1st full page panel in comics	285.00	710.00	1700.00
5	267.00	665.00	1600.00
6-Origin Father Time; Tuk the Caveboy ends	217.00	540.00	1300.00
7-Red Skull app	217.00	540.00	1300.00
8-10-Last S&K issue, (S&K centerfold #6-10)	183.00	460.00	1100.00
11-Last Hurricane, Headline Hunter; Al Avison Captain America begins, ends #20			
	142.00	355.00	850.00
12-The Imp begins, ends #16; Last Father Time	139.00	350.00	835.00
13-Origin The Secret Stamp; classic-c	150.00	375.00	900.00
14,15	139.00	348.00	835.00
16-Red Skull unmasks Cap	158.00	395.00	950.00
17-The Fighting Fool only app.	125.00	312.00	750.00
18,19-Human Torch begins #19	108.00	270.00	650.00
20-Sub-Mariner app.; no Human Torch	108.00	270.00	650.00
21-25: 25-Cap drinks liquid opium	100.00	250.00	600.00
26-30: 27-Last Secret Stamp; last 68 pg. issue? 28-60 pg. issues begin?			
	89.00	223.00	535.00
31-36,38-40	80.00	200.00	480.00
37-Red Skull app.	87.00	217.00	520.00
41-47: 41-Last Jap War-c. 46-German Holocaust-c. 47-Last German War-c			
	67.00	167.00	400.00
48-58,60	63.00	156.00	375.00
59-Origin retold	90.00	225.00	540.00
61-Red Skull-c/story	80.00	200.00	480.00
62,64,65: 65-"Hey Look" by Kurtzman	63.00	156.00	375.00
63-Intro/origin Asbestos Lady	67.00	167.00	400.00
66-Bucky is shot; Golden Girl teams up with Captain America & learns his I.D.; origin Golden Girl	76.00	190.00	455.00
67-Captain America/Golden Girl team-up; Mxyztplk swipe; last Toro in Human Torch	63.00	156.00	375.00
68,70-Sub-Mariner/Namora, and Captain America/Golden Girl team-up in each. 70-Science fiction- c/story	63.00	156.00	375.00
69,71-73: 69-Human Torch/Sun Girl team-up. 71-Anti Wertham editorial; The Witness, Bucky app.	63.00	156.00	375.00
74-(Scarce)(1949)-Titled "C.A.'s Weird Tales;" Red Skull app.			
	98.00	245.00	585.00
75(2/50)-Titled "C.A.'s Weird Tales;" no C.A. app.; horror cover/ stories			
	66.00	165.00	395.00

	Good	Fine	N-Mint
76-78(1954): Human Torch/Toro stories	42.00	105.00	250.00

Captain Marvel #33, © Marvel Comics

CAPTAIN MARVEL (See Marvel Spotlight & Marvel Super-Heroes #12)
May, 1968-No. 19, Dec, 1969; No. 20, June, 1970-No. 21, Aug, 1970; No. 22,
    Sept, 1972-No. 62, May, 1979
Marvel Comics Group

	Good	Fine	N-Mint
1	10.00	30.00	70.00
2	2.85	8.50	20.00
3-5	1.70	5.00	12.00
6-11: 11-Smith/Trimpe-c; Death of Una	1.15	3.50	8.00
12-24: 17-New costume	1.00	3.00	6.00
25-Starlin-c/a; Thanos saga begins (cameo)	1.50	4.50	10.00
26-Starlin-c/a; 2nd app. Thanos	2.50	7.50	18.00
27-Starlin-c/a; 3rd app. Thanos	1.75	5.25	12.00
28-Starlin-c/a; 4th app. Thanos (saga ends #34)	1.25	3.75	9.00
29,30-32-Thanos cameos only.	1.15	3.50	8.00

	Good	Fine	N-Mint
33-1st origin Thanos; Capt. Marvel battles Thanos	1.50	4.50	10.00
34-Starlin c/a ends	1.00	3.00	6.00
35,37-62: 36-Origin recap; Starlin-a (3 pgs.). 39-Origin Watcher. 41,43- Wrightson			
part inks; #43-c(i)	.25	.75	1.50
36-reprints origin/1st app. Capt. Marvel from Marvel Super-Heroes #12			
	.40	1.20	3.00

CAPTAIN MARVEL ADVENTURES (See Special Edition Comics)
1941 (March)-No. 150, Nov, 1953 (#1 on stands 1/16/41)
Fawcett Publications

	Good	Fine	VF-NM
nn(#1)-Captain Marvel & Sivana by Jack Kirby. The cover was printed on unstable			
paper stock and is rarely found in Fine or Mint condition; blank inside-c			
	1334.00	3335.00	8000.00

(Prices vary widely on this book)

	Good	Fine	N-Mint
2-(Advertised as #3, which was counting Special Edition Comics as the real #1);			
Tuska-a	186.00	560.00	1300.00
3-Metallic silver-c	100.00	300.00	700.00
4-Three Lt. Marvels app.	71.00	215.00	500.00
5	57.00	171.00	400.00
6-10	45.00	135.00	315.00
11-15: 13-Two-pg. Capt. Marvel pin-up. 15-Comic cards on back-c begin, end #26			
	36.00	107.00	250.00
16,17: 17-Painted-c	32.00	95.00	225.00
18-Origin & 1st app. Mary Marvel & Marvel Family (12/11/42); painted-c; Mary			
Marvel by Marcus Swayze	46.00	140.00	325.00
19-Mary Marvel x-over; Christmas-c	30.00	90.00	210.00
20,21-With miniature comic attached to-c	86.00	260.00	600.00
20,21-Without miniature	26.00	77.00	180.00
22-Mr. Mind serial begins	43.00	130.00	300.00
23-25	24.00	73.00	170.00
26-30: 26-Flag-c	20.00	60.00	140.00
31-35: 35-Origin Radar	19.00	56.00	130.00
36-40: 37-Mary Marvel x-over	16.00	48.00	110.00
41-46: 42-Christmas-c. 43-Capt. Marvel 1st meets Uncle Marvel; Mary Batson			
cameo. 46-Mr. Mind serial ends	13.00	40.00	90.00
47-50	11.50	34.00	80.00
51-53,55-60: 52-Origin & 1st app. Sivana Jr.; Capt. Marvel Jr. x-over			
	10.00	30.00	70.00

	Good	Fine	N-Mint
54-Special oversize 68-pg. issue	11.00	32.00	75.00
61-The Cult of the Curse serial begins	11.50	34.00	80.00
62-66-Serial ends; Mary Marvel x-over in #65. 66-Atomic War-c			
	9.30	28.00	65.00
67-77,79: 69-Billy Batson's Christmas; Uncle Marvel, Mary Marvel, Capt. Marvel Jr. x-over. 71-Three Lt. Marvels app. 79-Origin Mr. Tawny			
	8.50	25.50	60.00
78-Origin Mr. Atom	10.00	30.00	70.00
80-Origin Capt. Marvel retold	15.00	45.00	105.00
81-84,86-90: 81,90-Mr. Atom app. 82-Infinity-c. 86-Mr. Tawny app.			
	8.00	24.00	55.00
85-Freedom Train issue	10.00	30.00	70.00
91-99: 96-Mr. Tawny app.	7.00	21.00	50.00
100-Origin retold	14.00	43.00	100.00
101-120: 116-Flying Saucer issue (1/51)	6.50	19.00	45.00
121-Origin retold	8.50	25.50	60.00
122-141,143-149: 138-Flying Saucer issue (11/52). 141-Pre-code horror story "The Hideous Head-Hunter"	6.50	19.00	45.00
142-Used in **POP**, pgs. 92,96	6.50	19.00	45.00
150-(Low distribution)	11.50	34.00	80.00

CAPTAIN MARVEL, JR. (See Marvel Family, Master & Whiz Comics)
Nov, 1942-No. 119, June, 1953 (nn 34)
Fawcett Publications

1-Origin Capt. Marvel Jr. retold (Whiz No. 25); Capt. Nazi app.			
	129.00	385.00	900.00
2-Vs. Capt. Nazi; origin Capt. Nippon	64.00	193.00	450.00
3,4	47.00	140.00	325.00
5-Vs. Capt. Nazi	36.00	107.00	250.00
6-10: 8-Vs. Capt. Nazi. 9-Flag-c. 10-Hitler-c	29.00	86.00	200.00
11,12,15-Capt. Nazi app.	24.00	72.00	165.00
13,14,16-20: 13-Hitler-c. 14-X-Mas-c. 16-Capt. Marvel & Sivana x-over. 19-Capt. Nazi & Capt. Nippon app.	18.00	54.00	125.00
21-30: 25-Flag-c	11.50	34.00	80.00
31-33,36-40: 37-Infinity-c	7.00	21.00	50.00
35-#34 on inside; cover shows origin of Sivana Jr. which is not on inside. Evidently the cover to #35 was printed out of sequence and bound with contents to #34	7.00	21.00	50.00
41-50	5.00	15.00	35.00
51-70: 53-Atomic Bomb-c/story	4.30	13.00	30.00

	Good	Fine	N-Mint
71-99,101-104: 104-Used in **POP**, pg. 89	3.60	11.00	25.00
100	4.30	13.00	30.00
105-114,116-119: 119-Electric chair-c	3.60	11.00	25.00
115-Injury to eye-c; Eyeball story w/injury-to-eye panels			
	5.70	17.00	40.00

CAPTAIN MIDNIGHT (Radio, films, TV) (See The Funnies & Popular)
Sept, 1942-No. 67, Fall, 1948 (#1-14: 68 pgs.)
Fawcett Publications

1-Origin Captain Midnight; Captain Marvel cameo on cover			
	125.00	315.00	750.00
2	50.00	150.00	350.00
3-5	36.00	107.00	250.00
6-10: 9-Raboy-c. 10-Raboy Flag-c	25.00	75.00	175.00
11-20: 11,17-Raboy-c	16.50	50.00	115.00
21-30	13.00	40.00	90.00
31-40	10.00	30.00	70.00
41-59,61-67: 54-Sci/fi theme begins?	7.00	21.00	50.00
60-Flying Saucer issue (2/48)-3rd of this theme; see Shadow Comics V7#10 & Boy Commandos #26	11.50	34.00	80.00

CASPER, THE FRIENDLY GHOST (Becomes Harvey Comics Hits No. 61
    (No. 6), and then continued with Harvey issue No. 7)
9/49-No. 3, 8/50; 9/50-No. 5, 5/51
St. John Publishing Co.

1(1949)-Origin & 1st app. Baby Huey	54.00	160.00	375.00
2,3	30.00	90.00	210.00
1(9/50)	37.00	110.00	260.00
2-5	24.00	70.00	165.00

CASPER, THE FRIENDLY GHOST (Paramount Picture Star . . .)
No. 7, Dec, 1952-No 70, July, 1958
Harvey Publications (Family Comics)

Note: No. 6 is Harvey Comics Hits No. 61 (10/52)

7-Baby Huey begins, ends #9	17.00	51.00	120.00
8-10: 10-Spooky begins(1st app.), ends #70?	8.50	25.50	60.00
11-19: 19-1st app. Nightmare (4/54)	5.70	17.00	40.00
20-Wendy the Witch begins (1st app., 5/54)	6.50	19.50	45.00

	Good	Fine	N-Mint
21-30: 24-Infinity-c	4.50	14.00	32.00
31-40	3.75	11.25	26.00
41-50	3.00	9.00	21.00
51-70	2.30	7.00	16.00

CAT, THE
Nov, 1972-No. 4, June, 1973
Marvel Comics Group

1-Origin The Cat; Mooney-a(i); Wood-c(i)/a(i)	1.15	3.50	8.00
2-4: 2-Mooney-a(i). 3-Everett inks. 4-Starlin/Weiss-a(p)			
	.85	2.60	6.00

CATMAN COMICS (Crash No. 1-5)
5/41-No. 17, 1/43; No. 18, 7/43-No. 22, 12/43; No. 23, 3/44-No. 26, 11/44; No. 27, 4/45-No. 30, 12/45; No. 31, 6/46-No. 32, 8/46
Holyoke Publishing Co./Continental Magazines V2#12, 7/44 on

1(V1#6)-Origin The Deacon & Sidekick Mickey, Dr. Diamond & Rag-Man; The Black Widow app.; The Catman by Chas. Quinlan & Blaze Baylor begin			
	71.00	215.00	500.00
2(V1#7)	34.00	100.00	235.00
3(V1#8), 4(V1#9): 3-The Pied Piper begins	27.00	80.00	185.00
5(V2#10)-Origin Kitten; The Hood begins (c-redated), 6,7(V2#11,12)			
	22.00	65.00	150.00
8(V2#13,3/42)-Origin Little Leaders; Volton by Kubert begins (his 1st comic book work)	29.00	88.00	205.00
9(V2#14)	19.00	58.00	135.00
10(V2#15)-Origin Blackout; Phantom Falcon begins			
	19.00	58.00	135.00
11(V3#1)-Kubert-a	19.00	58.00	135.00
12(V3#2)-15, 17, 18(V3#8, 7/43)	14.00	43.00	100.00
16 (V3#5)-Hitler, Tojo, Mussolini, Stalin-c	17.00	51.00	120.00
19 (V2#6)-Hitler, Tojo, Mussolini-c	17.00	51.00	120.00
20(V2#7)-23(V2#10, 3/44)	14.00	43.00	100.00
nn(V3#13, 5/44)-Rico-a; Schomburg bondage-c	13.00	40.00	90.00
nn(V2#12, 7/44)	13.00	40.00	90.00
nn(V3#1, 9/44)-Origin The Golden Archer; Leatherface app.			
	13.00	40.00	90.00
nn(V3#2, 11/44)-L. B. Cole-c	18.00	54.00	125.00
27-Origin Kitten retold; L. B. Cole Flag-c	19.00	58.00	135.00

	Good	Fine	N-Mint
28-Catman learns Kitten's I.D.; Dr. Macabre, Deacon app.; L. B. Cole-c/a			
	22.00	65.00	150.00
29-32-L. B. Cole-c; bondage-#30	18.00	54.00	125.00

CATWOMAN (Also see Action Comics Weekly #611-614 & Batman)
Feb, 1989-No. 4, May, 1989 ($1.50, mini-series, mature readers)
DC Comics

	Good	Fine	N-Mint
1	2.30	7.00	14.00
2	1.35	4.00	8.00
3,4: 3-Batman cameo. 4-Batman app.	.85	2.50	5.00

CEREBUS THE AARDVARK
Dec, 1977-Present ($1.70-$2.00, B&W)
Aardvark-Vanaheim

	Good	Fine	N-Mint
1-2000 print run; most copies poorly printed	40.00	125.00	250.00

Note: There is a counterfeit version known to exist. It can be distinguished from the original in the following ways: inside cover is glossy instead of flat; black background on the front cover is blotted or spotty.

	Good	Fine	N-Mint
2-Dave Sim art in all	18.30	55.00	110.00
3-Origin Red Sophia	14.50	43.50	88.00
4-Origin Elrod the Albino	10.00	30.00	60.00
5,6	8.30	25.00	50.00
7-10	5.30	16.00	32.00
11,12: 11-Origin Capt. Coachroach	6.00	18.00	36.00
13-15: 14-Origin Lord Julius	3.30	10.00	20.00
16-20	2.00	6.00	12.00
21-Scarcer	10.00	30.00	60.00
22-Low distribution; no cover price	3.00	9.00	18.00
23-30: 26-High Society storyline begins	1.70	5.00	10.00
31-Origin Moonroach	2.30	7.00	14.00
32-40	.90	2.70	5.40
41-50,52: 52-Cutey Bunny app.	.75	2.25	4.50
51-Not reprinted; Cutey Bunny app.	2.70	8.00	16.00
53-Intro. Wolveroach (cameo)	1.15	3.15	6.30
54-Wolveroach 1st full story	1.50	4.50	9.00
55,56-Wolveroach app.	1.05	3.15	6.30
57-60	.55	1.60	3.20
61,62: Flaming Carrot app.	.75	2.25	4.50
63-68	.60	1.80	3.60

	Good	Fine	N-Mint
69-75	.50	1.45	2.90
76-79	.45	1.35	2.70
80-150	.40	1.15	2.30

Challengers of the Unknown #16, © DC Comics

CHALLENGERS OF THE UNKNOWN (See Showcase #6, 7, 11, 12)
4-5/58-No. 77, 12-1/70-71; No. 78, 2/73-No. 80, 6-7/73;
No. 81, 6-7/77-No. 87, 6-7/78
National Periodical Publications/DC Comics

1-Kirby/Stein-a(2)	90.00	270.00	635.00
2-Kirby/Stein-a(2)	52.00	156.00	365.00
3-Kirby/Stein-a(2) 3	40.00	120.00	280.00
4-8-Kirby/Wood-a plus c-#8	33.00	100.00	230.00
9,10	16.50	50.00	115.00
11-15: 14-Origin Multi-Man	10.25	31.00	72.00
16-22: 18-Intro. Cosmo, the Challengers Spacepet. 22-Last 10 cent issue			
	8.00	24.00	55.00

	Good	Fine	N-Mint
23-30	4.25	12.75	30.00
31-Retells origin of the Challengers	3.50	10.50	24.00
32-40	2.00	6.00	14.00
41-60: 43-New look begins. 48-Doom Patrol app. 49-Intro. Challenger Corps. 51-Sea Devils app. 55-Death of Red Ryan. 60-Red Ryan returns			
	1.15	3.50	8.00
61-73,75-77: 64,65-Kirby origin-r, parts 1 & 2. 69-1st app. Corinna			
	.50	1.50	3.00
74-Deadman by Tuska/N. Adams	1.30	4.00	9.00
78-87: 82-Swamp Thing begins	.35	1.00	2.00

CHAMBER OF DARKNESS
Oct, 1969-No. 8, Dec, 1970
Marvel Comics Group

	Good	Fine	N-Mint
1-Buscema-a(p)	2.65	8.00	18.00
2-Neal Adams script	1.15	3.50	8.00
3-Smith, Buscema-a	1.30	4.00	9.00
4-A Conanesque tryout by Smith; reprinted in Conan #16			
	4.30	13.00	30.00
5,6,8: 5-H.P. Lovecraft adaptation	.70	2.00	4.00
7-Wrightson-c/a, 7pgs. (his 1st work at Marvel); Wrightson draws himself in 1st & last panels	1.70	5.00	12.00
1-(1/72; 25 cent Special)	1.00	3.00	6.00

CHAMPIONS, THE
October, 1975-No. 17, Jan, 1978
Marvel Comics Group

	Good	Fine	N-Mint
1-The Angel, Black Widow, Ghost Rider, Hercules, Ice Man (The Champions) begin with origin; Kane/Adkins-c; Venus x-over	1.50	4.50	10.00
2-10,16: 2,3-Venus x-over	.85	2.50	5.00
11-15,17-Byrne-a	1.00	3.00	6.00

CHECKMATE (See Action Comics #598)
April, 1988-No. 33, Jan, 1991 ($1.25)
DC Comics

	Good	Fine	N-Mint
1	.40	1.25	2.50
2	.30	.90	1.80
3-5	.25	.75	1.50

	Good	Fine	N-Mint
6-30: 13-30 are $1.50, new format		.65	1.30
31-33 ($2.00-c)	.35	1.00	2.00

CISCO KID, THE (TV)
July, 1950-No. 41, Oct-Dec, 1958
Dell Publishing Co.

	Good	Fine	N-Mint
4-Color 292(#1)-Cisco Kid, his horse Diablo, & sidekick Pancho & his horse Loco			
begin; painted-c begin	11.00	32.00	75.00
2(1/51)-5	5.00	15.00	35.00
6-10	4.30	13.00	30.00
11-20	3.15	9.50	22.00
21-36-Last painted-c	2.65	8.00	18.00
37-41: All photo-c	6.00	18.00	42.00

CLASSIC X-MEN (Becomes X-Men Classic #46 on)
Sept, 1986-No. 45, Mar, 1990 (#27 on: $1.25)
Marvel Comics Group

	Good	Fine	N-Mint
1-Begins-r of New X-Men	1.35	4.00	8.00
2-4	.85	2.50	5.00
5-9	.70	2.00	4.00
10-Sabretooth app.	1.15	3.50	7.00
11-15	.50	1.50	3.00
16,18-20	.40	1.25	2.50
17-Wolverine-c	1.00	3.00	6.00
21-25,27-30: 27-r/X-Men #121	.35	1.00	2.00
26-r/X-Men #120; Wolverine-c/app.	1.00	3.00	6.00
31-38,40-42,44,45: 35-r/X-Men #129	.30	.90	1.80
39-New Jim Lee-a (2nd on X-Men)	.85	2.50	5.00
43-Byrne-c/a(r); $1.75, double-size	.40	1.25	2.50

CLUE COMICS
Jan, 1943-No. 15(V2#3), May, 1947
Hillman Periodicals

	Good	Fine	N-Mint
1-Origin The Boy King, Nightmare, Micro-Face, Twilight, & Zippo			
	47.00	140.00	325.00
2	24.00	73.00	170.00
3	19.00	58.00	135.00
4	16.00	48.00	110.00

	Good	Fine	N-Mint
5	13.00	40.00	90.00
6,8,9: 8-Palais-c/a(2)	10.00	30.00	70.00
7-Classic torture-c	14.00	43.00	100.00
10-Origin The Gun Master	11.00	32.00	75.00
11	7.00	21.00	50.00
12-Origin Rackman; McWilliams-a, Guardineer-a(2)			
	10.00	30.00	70.00
V2#1-Nightro new origin; Iron Lady app.; Simon & Kirby-a			
	14.00	43.00	100.00
V2#2-S&K-a(2)-Bondage/torture-c; man attacks & kills people with electric iron.			
Infantino-a	14.00	43.00	100.00
V2#3-S&K-a(3)	14.00	43.00	100.00

COMIC CAVALCADE
Winter, 1942-43-No. 63, June-July, 1954
   (Contents change with No. 30, Dec-Jan, 1948-49 on)
All-American/National Periodical Publications

	Good	Fine	VF-NM
1-The Flash, Green Lantern, Wonder Woman, Wildcat, The Black Pirate by Moldoff (also #2), Ghost Patrol, and Red White & Blue begin; Scribbly app., Minute Movies	267.00	665.00	1600.00

	Good	Fine	N-Mint
2-Mutt & Jeff begin; last Ghost Patrol & Black Pirate; Minute Movies			
	125.00	312.00	750.00
3-Hop Harrigan & Sargon, the Sorcerer begin; The King app.			
	92.00	230.00	550.00
4,5: 4-The Gay Ghost, The King, Scribbly, & Red Tornado app. 5- Christmas-c			
	80.00	240.00	480.00
6-10: 7-Red Tornado & Black Pirate app.; last Scribbly. 9-X-mas-c			
	60.00	150.00	360.00
11,12,14-20: 12-Last Red White & Blue. 15-Johnny Peril begins, ends #29. 19-Christmas-c			
	49.00	123.00	295.00
13-Solomon Grundy app.; X-mas-c	83.00	210.00	500.00
21-23	49.00	123.00	295.00
24-Solomon Grundy x-over in Green Lantern	60.00	150.00	360.00
25-29: 25-Black Canary app.; X-mas-c. 26-28-Johnny Peril app. 28- Last Mutt & Jeff. 29-(10-11/48)-Last Flash, Wonder Woman, Green Lantern & Johnny Peril; Wonder Woman invents "Thinking Machine;" 1st computer in comics?			
	38.00	95.00	230.00

	Good	Fine	N-Mint
30-(12-1/48-49)-The Fox & the Crow, Dodo & the Frog & Nutsy Squirrel begin			
	23.00	70.00	160.00
31-35	10.00	30.00	70.00
36-49	8.00	24.00	55.00
50-62(Scarce)	10.00	30.00	70.00
63(Rare)	17.00	51.00	120.00

COMICS AND STORIES (See Walt Disney's . . .)

COMICS MAGAZINE, THE (. . . Funny Pages #3)(Funny Pages #6 on)
May, 1936-No. 5, Sept, 1936 (Paper covers)
Comics Magazine Co.

	Good	Fine	N-Mint
1-Dr. Mystic, The Occult Detective by Siegel & Shuster (1st episode continues in More Fun #14); 1pg. Kelly-a; Sheldon Mayer-a			
	225.00	562.00	1350.00
2-Federal Agent by Siegel & Shuster; 1pg. Kelly-a			
	96.00	290.00	675.00
3-5	82.00	245.00	575.00

CONAN, THE BARBARIAN (See Chamber of Darkness #4)
Oct, 1970-Present
Marvel Comics Group

	Good	Fine	N-Mint
1-Origin/1st app. Conan by Barry Smith; Kull app.			
	19.00	57.00	130.00
2	7.00	21.00	50.00
3-(low distribution in some areas)	11.50	34.00	80.00
4,5	5.70	17.00	40.00
6-10: 8-Hidden panel message, pg. 14. 10-52 pgs.; Black Knight-r; Kull story by Severin	3.60	11.00	25.00
11-13: 11-(52 pgs.). 12-Wrightson-c(i)	2.85	8.50	20.00
14,15-Elric app.	3.85	11.50	27.00
16,19,20: 16-Conan-r/Savage Tales #1	2.15	6.50	15.00
17,18-No Barry Smith-a	1.35	4.00	8.00
21,22: 22-has r-from #1	1.85	5.50	13.00
23-1st app. Red Sonja	2.50	7.50	17.00
24-1st full story Red Sonja; last Smith-a	2.50	7.50	17.00
25-John Buscema-c/a begins	1.35	4.00	8.00
26-30	.70	2.00	4.00
31-36,38-40	.40	1.25	2.50

	Good	Fine	N-Mint
37-Neal Adams-c/a	.85	2.50	5.00
41-43,46-49: 48-Origin retold	.30	.85	1.70
44,45-N. Adams-i(Crusty Bunkers). 45-Adams-c	.35	1.00	2.00
50-57,59,60: 59-Origin Belit	.30	.85	1.70
58-2nd Belit app. (see Giant-Size Conan #1)	.50	1.50	3.00
61-99: 68-Red Sonja story cont'd from Marvel Feature #7. 84-Intro. Zula. 85-Origin Zula. 87-R/Savage Sword of Conan #3 in color			
		.60	1.20
100-(52 pg. Giant)-Death of Belit	.40	1.25	2.50
101-114,116-193		.50	1.00
115-Double size		.60	1.20
194-199,201-249: 196-200,204,241,242-Red Sonja app. 232-Young Conan storyline begins; Conan is born		.50	1.00
200-Double size ($1.50)	.25	.75	1.50
250-($1.50, 52 pgs.)	.25	.75	1.50

COO COO COMICS (. . . the Bird Brain No. 57 on)
Oct, 1942-No. 62, April, 1952
Nedor Publ. Co./Standard (Animated Cartoons)

	Good	Fine	N-Mint
1-Origin/1st app. Super Mouse & begin series (cloned from Superman)-The first funny animal super hero	11.50	34.00	80.00
2	5.00	15.00	35.00
3-10 (3/44)	3.15	9.50	22.00
11-33: 33-1pg. Ingels-a	2.30	7.00	16.00
34-40,43-46,48-50-Text illos by Frazetta in all	4.00	12.00	28.00
41-Frazetta-a(2)	8.50	25.50	60.00
42,47-Frazetta-a & text illos.	6.00	18.00	42.00
51-62: 56-Last Supermouse?	1.70	5.00	12.00

CRACKAJACK FUNNIES
June, 1938-No. 43, Jan, 1942
Dell Publishing Co.

	Good	Fine	N-Mint
1-Dan Dunn, Freckles, Myra North, Wash Tubbs, Apple Mary, The Nebbs, Don Winslow, Tom Mix, Buck Jones, Major Hoople, Clyde Beatty, Boots begin	91.00	272.00	635.00
2	43.00	130.00	300.00
3	29.00	88.00	205.00
4,5	24.00	72.00	165.00
6-8,10	19.00	56.00	130.00

	Good	Fine	N-Mint
9-(3/39)-Red Ryder strip-r begin by Harman; 1st app. in comics & 1st cover app.			
	27.00	80.00	185.00
11-14	17.00	51.00	120.00
15-Tarzan text feature begins by Burroughs (9/39); not in #26,35			
	19.00	56.00	130.00
16-24	13.00	40.00	90.00
25-The Owl begins; in new costume #26 by Frank Thomas			
	30.00	90.00	210.00
26-30: 28-Owl-c. 29-Ellery Queen begins	23.00	70.00	160.00
31-Owl covers begin	20.00	60.00	140.00
32-Origin Owl Girl	23.00	70.00	160.00
33-38: 36-Last Tarzan issue	16.00	48.00	110.00
39-Andy Panda begins (intro/1st app.)	17.00	51.00	120.00
40-43: 42-Last Owl cover	14.00	43.00	100.00

Crack Comics #9, © Quality Comics

CRACK COMICS (. . . Western No. 63 on)
May, 1940-No. 62, Sept, 1949
Quality Comics Group

	Good	Fine	N-Mint
1-Origin The Black Condor by Lou Fine, Madame Fatal, Red Torpedo, Rock Bradden & The Space Legion; The Clock, Alias the Spider, Wizard Wells, & Ned Brant begin; Powell-a; Note: Madame Fatal is a man dressed up as a woman			
	185.00	560.00	1300.00
2	90.00	270.00	630.00
3	66.00	200.00	465.00
4	57.00	171.00	400.00
5-10: 5-Molly The Model begins. 10-Tor, the Magic Master begins			
	45.00	135.00	315.00
11-20: 18-1st app. Spitfire?	39.00	118.00	275.00
21-24-Last Fine Black Condor	30.00	90.00	210.00
25,26	20.00	60.00	140.00
27-(1/43)-Intro & origin Captain Triumph by Alfred Andriola (Kerry Drake artist)			
	43.00	130.00	300.00
28-30	17.00	51.00	120.00
31-39: 31-Last Black Condor	10.00	30.00	70.00
40-46	7.00	21.00	50.00
47-57,59,60-Capt. Triumph by Crandall	8.00	24.00	56.00
58,61,62-Last Captain Triumph	6.00	18.00	42.00

CRACK WESTERN (Formerly Crack Comics)
No. 63, Nov, 1949-No. 84, May, 1953 (36 pgs., 63-68,74-on)
Quality Comics Group

	Good	Fine	N-Mint
63(#1)-Two-Gun Lil (origin & 1st app.)(ends #84), Arizona Ames, his horse Thunder (sidekick Spurs & his horse Calico), Frontier Marshal (ends #70), & Dead Canyon Days (ends #69) begin; Crandall-a	10.00	30.00	70.00
64,65-Crandall-a	8.00	24.00	56.00
66,68-Photo-c. 66-Arizona Ames becomes A. Raines (ends #84)			
	7.00	21.00	50.00
67-Randolph Scott photo-c; Crandall-a	8.50	25.50	60.00
69(52pgs.)-Crandall-a	7.00	21.00	50.00
70(52pgs.)-The Whip (origin & 1st app.) & his horse Diablo begin (ends #84); Crandall-a	7.00	21.00	50.00
71(52pgs.)-Frontier Marshal becomes Bob Allen F. Marshal (ends #84); Crandall-c/a	8.50	25.50	60.00
72(52pgs.)-Tim Holt photo-c	7.00	21.00	50.00
73(52pgs.)-Photo-c	5.00	15.00	35.00
74-76,78,79,81,83-Crandall-c	5.70	17.00	40.00
77,80,82	3.50	10.50	24.00
84-Crandall-c/a	8.00	24.00	55.00

CRASH COMICS (Catman Comics No. 6 on)
May, 1940-No. 5, Nov, 1940
Tem Publishing Co.

	Good	Fine	N-Mint
1-The Blue Streak, Strongman (origin), The Perfect Human, Shangra begin; Kirby-a	100.00	300.00	700.00
2-Simon & Kirby-a	50.00	150.00	350.00
3-Simon & Kirby-a	40.00	120.00	280.00
4-Origin & 1st app. The Catman; S&K-a	65.00	195.00	455.00
5-S&K-a	40.00	120.00	280.00

CRIME DOES NOT PAY (Formerly Silver Streak Comics No. 1-21)
No. 22, June, 1942-No. 147, July, 1955 (1st crime comic)
Comic House/Lev Gleason (Title inspired by film)

	Good	Fine	N-Mint
22 (23 on cover, 22 on indicia)-Origin The War Eagle & only app.; Chip Gardner begins; #22 was rebound in Complete Book of True Crime (Scarce)	90.00	270.00	630.00
23 (Scarce)	50.00	150.00	350.00
24-Intro. & 1st app. Mr. Crime (Scarce)	43.00	130.00	300.00
25-30	23.00	70.00	160.00
31-40	13.00	40.00	90.00
41-Origin & 1st app. Officer Common Sense	9.30	28.00	65.00
42-Electrocution-c	11.00	32.00	75.00
43-46,48-50: 44,45,50 are 68 pg. issues	7.00	21.00	50.00
47-Electric chair-c	11.00	32.00	75.00
51-62,65-70	4.00	12.00	28.00
63,64-Possible use in **SOTI**, pg. 306. #63-Contains Biro-Gleason's self censorship code of 12 listed restrictions (5/48)	4.00	12.00	28.00
71-99: 87-Chip Gardner begins, ends #99	2.65	8.00	18.00
100	3.00	9.00	21.00
101-104,107-110: 102-Chip Gardner app.	2.00	6.00	14.00
105-Used in **POP**, pg. 84	2.00	6.00	14.00
106,114-Frazetta, 1 pg.	2.00	6.00	14.00
111-Used in **POP**, pgs. 80 & 81; injury-to-eye story illo	1.70	5.00	12.00
112,113,115-130	1.30	4.00	9.00
131-140	1.15	3.50	8.00
141,142-Last pre-code issue; Kubert-a(1)	2.30	7.00	16.00
143,147-Kubert-a, one each	2.30	7.00	16.00
144-146	1.00	3.00	7.00

CRIME EXPOSED
June, 1948; Dec, 1950-No. 14, June, 1952
Marvel Comics (PPI)/Marvel Atlas Comics (PrPI)

	Good	Fine	N-Mint
1(6/48)	10.00	30.00	70.00
1(12/50)	6.00	18.00	42.00
2	3.60	11.00	25.00
3-11,14: 10-Used in **POP**, pg. 81	2.65	8.00	18.00
12-Krigstein & Robinson-a	3.00	9.00	21.00
13-Used in **POP**, pg. 81; Krigstein-a	3.50	10.50	24.00

CRIME PATROL
No. 7, Summer, 1948-No. 16, Feb-Mar, 1950
E. C. Comics

	Good	Fine	N-Mint
7-Intro. Captain Crime	35.00	105.00	245.00
8-14: 12-Ingels-a	30.00	90.00	210.00
15-Intro. of Crypt Keeper (inspired by Witches Tales radio show) & Crypt of Terror	82.00	245.00	575.00
16-2nd Crypt Keeper app.	68.00	205.00	475.00

CRIME SMASHERS
Oct, 1950-No. 15, Mar, 1953
Ribage Publishing Corp. (Trojan Magazines)

	Good	Fine	N-Mint
1-Used in **SOTI**, pg. 19,20, & illo-"A girl raped and murdered;" Sally the Sleuth begins	32.00	95.00	225.00
2-Kubert-c	16.00	48.00	110.00
3,4	12.00	36.00	84.00
5-Wood-a	19.00	56.00	130.00
6,8-11	10.00	30.00	70.00
7-Female heroin junkie story	11.00	32.00	75.00
12-Injury to eye panel; 1 pg. Frazetta-a	11.50	34.00	80.00
13-Used in **POP**, pgs. 79,80; 1 pg. Frazetta-a	10.00	30.00	70.00
14,15	10.00	30.00	70.00

CRIME SUSPENSTORIES (Formerly Vault of Horror No. 12-14)
No. 15, Oct-Nov, 1950-No. 27, Feb-Mar, 1955
E. C. Comics

15-Identical to #1 in content; #1 printed on outside front-c. #15 (formerly "The

	Good	Fine	N-Mint
Vault of Horror") printed and blackened out on inside front cover with Vol. 1, No. 1 printed over it	82.00	245.00	575.00
1	64.00	193.00	450.00
2	38.00	115.00	265.00
3-5	25.00	75.00	175.00
6-10	19.00	58.00	135.00
11,12,14,15	13.50	41.00	95.00
13,16-Williamson-a	17.00	50.00	115.00
17-Williamson/Frazetta-a, 6 pgs.	19.00	56.00	130.00
18,19: 19-Used in SOTI, pg. 235	11.50	34.00	80.00
20-Cover used in **SOTI**, illo-"Cover of a children's comic book"	15.00	45.00	105.00
21,25-27	8.50	25.50	60.00
22,23-Used in Senate investigation on juvenile delinquency. 22-Ax decapitation-c	12.00	36.00	85.00
24-`Food For Thought' similar to 'Cave In' in Amazing Detective Cases #13 ('52)	8.50	25.50	60.00

CRISIS ON INFINITE EARTHS
Apr, 1985-No. 12, Mar, 1986 (12 issue maxi-series)
DC Comics

	Good	Fine	N-Mint
1-1st DC app. Blue Beetle & Detective Karp from Charlton; Perez-c on all	.75	2.20	4.40
2	.55	1.65	3.30
3	.45	1.40	2.80
4-6: 6-Intro Charlton's Capt. Atom, Nightshade, Question, Judomaster, Peacemaker & Thunderbolt	.35	1.10	2.20
7-Double size; death of Supergirl	.75	2.20	4.40
8-Death of Flash	.90	2.75	5.50
9-11: 9-Intro. Charlton's Ghost. 10-Intro. Charlton's Banshee, Dr. Spectro, Image, Punch & Jewellee	.35	1.10	2.20
12-Dbl. size; deaths of Dove, Kole, Lori Lemaris, Sunburst, G.A. Robin & Huntress; Kid Flash becomes new Flash	.70	2.00	4.00

D

DAFFY (. . . Duck No. 18 on) (See Looney Tunes)
#457, 3/53-#30, 7-9/62; #31, 10-12/62-#145, 1983 (No #132,133)
Dell Publishing Co./Gold Key No. 31-127/Whitman No. 128 on

	Good	Fine	N-Mint
4-Color 457(#1)-Elmer Fudd x-overs begin	2.65	8.00	18.00
4-Color 536,615('55)	1.70	5.00	12.00
4(1-3/56)-11('57)	1.30	4.00	9.00
12-19(1958-59)	1.00	3.00	7.00
20-40(1960-64)	.70	2.00	4.00
41-60(1964-68)	.40	1.25	2.50
61-90(1969-73)-Road Runner in most		.60	1.20
91-131,134-145(1974-83)		.40	.80

DALE EVANS COMICS (Also see Queen of the West . . .)
Sept-Oct, 1948-No. 24, July-Aug, 1952 (No. 1-19: 52 pgs.)
National Periodical Publications

1-Dale Evans & her horse Buttermilk begin; Sierra Smith begins by Alex Toth		
	26.00	77.00	180.00
2-Alex Toth-a	17.00	50.00	115.00
3-11-Alex Toth-a	13.50	41.00	95.00
12-24	7.00	21.00	50.00

DAMAGE CONTROL
5/89-#4, 8/89; V2#1, 12/89-#4, 2/90 ($1.00, color, both mini-series)
Marvel Comics

1-3		.50	1.00
4-Wolverine app.	.25	.75	1.50
V2#1,3		.60	1.20
2,4-Punisher app.	.30	.90	1.80

DANIEL BOONE (TV)
Jan, 1965-No. 15, Apr, 1969
Gold Key

1	1.70	5.00	12.00
2-5	.85	2.60	6.00
6-15: 4,6-Fess Parker photo-c	.70	2.00	4.00

Daredevil #158, © Marvel Comics

DAREDEVIL (. . . & the Black Widow #92-107 on-c only)
April, 1964-Present
Marvel Comics Group

	Good	Fine	N-Mint
1-Origin & 1st app. Daredevil; r-/in Marvel Super Heroes #1, 1966. Death of Battling Murdock; intro Foggy Nelson & Karen Page			
	103.00	310.00	720.00
2-Fantastic Four cameo	38.00	114.00	265.00
3-Origin & 1st app. The Owl	23.00	70.00	160.00
4,5: 5-New Costume; Wood-a begins	13.50	41.00	95.00
6,8-10: 8-Origin/1st app. Stilt-Man	10.00	30.00	70.00
7-Dons new red costume & battles Sub-Mariner	12.00	36.00	85.00
11-15: 12-Romita's 1st work at Marvel. 13-Facts about Ka-Zar's origin; Kirby-a			
	6.50	19.00	45.00
16,17-Spider-Man x-over	7.85	23.50	55.00
18-20: 18-Origin & 1st app. Gladiator	5.00	15.00	35.00
21-30: 24-Ka-Zar app.	3.15	9.50	22.00
31-40	2.30	7.00	18.00

	Good	Fine	N-Mint
41-49: 41-Death Mike Murdock. 43-Vs. Capt. America			
	1.70	5.00	12.00
50-53: 50-52-Smith-a. 53-Origin retold	2.00	6.00	14.00
54-56,58-60	1.15	3.50	8.00
57-Reveals I.D. to Karen Page	1.30	4.00	9.00
61-99: 62-1st app. Nighthawk. 81-Oversize issue; Black Widow begins			
	1.00	3.00	7.00
100-Origin retold	2.15	6.50	15.00
101-106,108-113,115-120	.85	2.50	5.00
107-Starlin-c	1.00	3.00	6.00
114-1st app. Deathstalker	1.15	3.50	7.00
121-130,133-137: 124-1st app. Copperhead; Black Widow leaves. 126-1st New Torpedo	.50	1.50	3.00
131-Origin Bullseye (1st app. in Nick Fury #15)	2.50	7.50	18.00
132-Bullseye app.	.70	2.00	4.00
138-Ghost Rider-c/story; Byrne-a	1.30	4.00	9.00
139-157: 142-Nova cameo. 148-30 & 35 cent issues exist. 150-1st app. Paladin. 151-Reveals I.D. to Heather Glenn. 155-Black Widow returns. 156-1960s Daredevil app.	.50	1.50	3.00
158-Frank Miller art begins (5/79); origin/death of Deathstalker (See Spect. Spider-Man for Miller's 1st D.D.)	5.70	17.00	40.00
159	2.65	8.00	18.00
160,161	1.50	4.50	9.00
162-Ditko-a, no Miller-a	.40	1.25	2.50
163,164: 163-Hulk cameo. 164-Origin	1.35	4.00	8.00
165-167,170	1.00	3.00	6.00
168-Origin/1st app. Elektra	2.85	8.50	20.00
169-Elektra app.	1.35	4.00	8.00
171-175: 174,175-Elektra app.	.70	2.00	4.00
176-180-Elektra app. 179-Anti-smoking issue mentioned in the Congressional Record	.50	1.50	3.00
181-Double size; death of Elektra; Punisher cameo out of costume			
	1.50	4.50	9.00
182-184-Punisher app. by Miller	2.00	6.00	12.00
185-191: 187-New Black Widow. 189-Death of Stick. 190-Double size; Elektra returns, part origin. 191-Last Miller Daredevil	.25	.75	1.50
192-195,197-210: 208-Harlan Ellison scripts		.60	1.20
196-Wolverine app.	1.50	4.50	10.00
211-225: 219-Miller scripts		.50	1.00
226-Frank Miller plots begin	.25	.75	1.50
227-Miller scripts begin	.70	2.00	4.00

	Good	Fine	N-Mint
228-233-Last Miller scripts	.35	1.00	2.00
234-237,239,240,242-247		.50	1.00
238-Mutant Massacre; Sabretooth app.	.70	2.00	4.00
241-Todd McFarlane-a(p)	.50	1.50	3.00
248,249-Wolverine app.	1.00	3.00	6.00
250,251,253,258		.50	1.00
252-Double size, 52 pgs. Fall of the Mutants	.40	1.25	2.50
254-Origin & 1st app. Typhoid Mary	1.70	5.00	10.00
255-2nd app. Typhoid Mary	1.00	3.00	6.00
256-3rd app. Typhoid Mary	.85	2.50	5.00
257-Punisher app.	4.15	12.50	25.00
259,260-Typhoid Mary app. 260-Double size	.50	1.50	3.00
261-291,294-298: 272-Intro Shotgun (villain). 282-Silver Surfer app. (cameo in #281). 283-Capt. America app.		.50	1.00
292,293-Punisher app.		.60	1.20
Special 1(9/67, 25 cents, 68 pgs.)-new art	2.15	6.50	15.00
Special 2,3: 2(2/71, 25 cents, 52 pgs.)-Entire book has Powell/Wood-r; Wood-c. 3(1/72)-reprints	1.15	3.50	8.00
Annual 4(10/76)	.70	2.00	4.00
Annual 4(#5)('89, $2.00, 68 pgs.)-Atlantis Attacks	.40	1.25	2.50
Annual 6(1990, $2.00, 68 pgs.)-Sutton-a	.35	1.00	2.00
Annual 7(1991, $2.00, 68 pgs.)	.35	1.00	2.00

DAREDEVIL COMICS (See Silver Streak Comics)
July, 1941-No. 134, Sept, 1956 (Charles Biro stories)
Lev Gleason Publications (Funnies, Inc. No. 1)

	Good	Fine	VF-NM
1-No. 1 titled "Daredevil Battles Hitler;" The Silver Streak, Lance Hale, Cloud Curtis, Dickey Dean, Pirate Prince team up w/Daredevil and battle Hitler; Daredevil battles the Claw; Origin of Hitler feature story. Hitler photo app. on-c	335.00	835.00	2000.00

	Good	Fine	N-Mint
2-London, Pat Patriot, Nightro, Real American No. 1, Dickie Dean, Pirate Prince, & Times Square begin; intro. & only app. The Pioneer, Champion of America	143.00	430.00	1000.00
3-Origin of 13	85.00	260.00	600.00
4	71.00	215.00	500.00
5-Intro. Sniffer & Jinx; Ghost vs. Claw begins by Bob Wood, ends #20	65.00	195.00	450.00
6-(#7 on indicia)	54.00	160.00	375.00

	Good	Fine	N-Mint
7-10: 8-Nightro ends	45.00	140.00	325.00
11-London, Pat Patriot end; bondage/torture-c	41.00	125.00	290.00
12-Origin of The Claw; Scoop Scuttle by Wolverton begins (2-4 pgs.), ends #22, not in #21	63.00	190.00	440.00
13-Intro. of Little Wise Guys	63.00	190.00	440.00
14	32.00	95.00	225.00
15-Death of Meatball	48.00	145.00	335.00
16,17	29.00	85.00	200.00
18-New origin of Daredevil-Not same as Silver Streak #6	63.00	190.00	440.00
19,20	25.00	75.00	175.00
21-Reprints cover of Silver Streak #6(on inside) plus intro. of The Claw from Silver Streak #1	38.00	115.00	265.00
22-30	16.00	48.00	110.00
31-Death of The Claw	29.00	85.00	200.00
32-37: 35-Two Daredevil stories begin, end #68 (35-40 are 64 pgs.)	11.00	32.00	75.00
38-Origin Daredevil retold from #18	22.00	65.00	150.00
39,40	11.00	32.00	75.00
41-50: 42-Intro. Kilroy in Daredevil	7.00	21.00	50.00
51-69-Last Daredevil issue (12/50)	5.00	15.00	35.00
70-Little Wise Guys take over book; McWilliams-a; Hot Rock Flanagan begins, ends #80	2.85	8.50	20.00
71-79,81: 79-Daredevil returns	2.15	6.50	15.00
80-Daredevil x-over	2.30	7.00	16.00
82,90-One page Frazetta ad in both	2.30	7.00	16.00
83-89,91-99,101-134	1.70	5.00	12.00
100	3.00	9.00	21.00

DARING COMICS (Formerly Daring Mystery)
No. 9, Fall, 1944-No. 12, Fall, 1945
Timely Comics (HPC)

9-Human Torch & Sub-Mariner begin	41.00	122.00	285.00
10-The Angel only app.	35.00	105.00	245.00
11,12-The Destroyer app.	35.00	105.00	245.00

DARING MYSTERY COMICS (Comedy Comics No. 9 on; title changed to
Daring Comics with No. 9)
1/40-No. 5, 6/40; No. 6, 9/40; No. 7, 4/41-No. 8, 1/42
Timely Comics (TPI 1-6/TCI 7,8)

	Good	Fine	VF-NM
1-Origin The Fiery Mask by Joe Simon; Monako, Prince of Magic, John Steele, Soldier of Fortune, Doc Doyle begin; Flash Foster & Barney Mullen, Sea Rover only app.	670.00	1670.00	4000.00

	Good	Fine	N-Mint
2-(Rare)-Origin The Phantom Bullet & only app.; The Laughing Mask & Mr. E only app.; Trojak the Tiger Man begins, ends #6; Zephyr Jones & K-4 & His Sky Devils app., also #4	335.00	835.00	2000.00
3-The Phantom Reporter, Dale of FBI, Breeze Barton, Captain Strong & Marvex the Super-Robot only app.; The Purple Mask begins	235.00	585.00	1400.00
4-Last Purple Mask; Whirlwind Carter begins; Dan Gorman, G-Man app.	150.00	375.00	900.00
5-The Falcon begins; The Fiery Mask, Little Hercules app. by Sagendorf in the Segar style; bondage-c	150.00	375.00	900.00
6-Origin & only app. Marvel Boy by S&K; Flying Flame, Dynaman, & Stuporman only app.; The Fiery Mask by S&K; S&K-c	191.00	480.00	1150.00
7-Origin The Blue Diamond, Captain Daring by S&K, The Fin by Everett, The Challenger, The Silver Scorpion & The Thunderer by Burgos; Mr. Millions app.	170.00	415.00	1000.00
8-Origin Citizen V; Last Fin, Silver Scorpion, Capt. Daring by Borth, Blue Diamond & The Thunderer; S&K-c; Rudy the Robot only app.	140.00	355.00	850.00

DARKHAWK
Mar, 1991-Present ($1.00, color)
Marvel Comics

1-Origin/1st app. Darkhawk; Hobgoblin cameo	.40	1.25	2.50
2,3-Spider-Man & Hobgoblin app.	.25	.75	1.50
4-10		.50	1.00

DARK SHADOWS (TV)
March, 1969-No. 35, Feb, 1976 (Photo-c: 2-7)
Gold Key

1(30039-903)-With pull-out poster (25 cents)	14.00	43.00	100.00
1-Without poster	7.00	21.00	50.00
2	6.50	19.00	45.00
3-With pull-out poster	8.50	25.50	60.00
3-Without poster	5.70	17.00	40.00

	Good	Fine	N-Mint
4-7: Last photo-c	5.70	17.00	40.00
8-10	4.00	12.00	28.00
11-20	3.00	9.00	21.00
21-35: 30-last painted-c	2.15	6.50	15.00
Story Digest 1 (6/70)-Photo-c	3.60	11.00	25.00

DATE WITH JUDY, A (Radio/TV, and 1948 movie)
Oct-Nov, 1947-No. 79, Oct-Nov, 1960 (No. 1-25: 52 pgs.)
National Periodical Publications

	Good	Fine	N-Mint
1-Teenage	13.00	40.00	90.00
2	6.50	19.00	45.00
3-10	4.50	14.00	32.00
11-20	2.85	8.50	20.00
21-40	2.15	6.50	15.00
41-45: 45-Last pre-code (2-3/55)	1.70	5.00	12.00
46-79: 79-Drucker-c/a	1.30	4.00	9.00

DC COMICS PRESENTS
July-Aug, 1978-No. 97, Sept, 1986 (Superman team-ups in all)
DC Comics

	Good	Fine	N-Mint
1-12,14-25: 19-Batgirl	.25	.75	1.50
13-Legion of Super Heroes (also in #43 & 80)	.40	1.25	2.50
26-(10/80)-Green Lantern; intro Cyborg, Starfire, Raven, New Teen Titans; Starlin-c/a; Sargon the Sorcerer back-up; 16 pg. preview of the New Teen Titans	1.15	3.50	7.00
27-40,42-71,73-76,79-84,86-97: 31,58-Robin. 35-Man-Bat. 52-Doom Patrol. 82-Adam Strange. 83-Batman & Outsiders. 86-88-Crisis x-over. 88-Creeper	.25	.75	1.50
41-Superman/Joker-c/story	.50	1.50	3.00
72-Joker/Phantom Stranger-c/story	.50	1.50	3.00
77,78-Animal Man app. (77-cover app. also)	1.00	3.00	6.00
85-Swamp Thing; Alan Moore scripts	.50	1.50	3.00
Annual 1-4: 1(9/82)-G.A. Superman. 2(7/83)-Intro/origin Superwoman. 3(9/84)-Shazam. 4(10/85)-Superwoman		.60	1.20

DEATHLOK (Also see Astonishing Tales #25)
July, 1990-No. 4, Oct, 1990 ($3.95, limited series, 52 pgs.)
Marvel Comics

	Good	Fine	N-Mint
1-Guice-a(p)	1.15	3.50	7.00
2-4: 2-Guice-a(p). 3,4-Denys Cowan-a, c-4	.85	2.50	5.00

DEATHLOK
July, 1991-Present ($1.75, color)
Marvel Comics

1-Silver ink cover	.35	1.00	2.00
2-4	.30	.90	1.80

DEATHSTROKE: THE TERMINATOR (See New Teen Titans #2)
Aug., 1991-Present ($1.75, color)
DC Comics

1	.35	1.00	2.00
2-4	.30	.90	1.80

DEFENDERS, THE (Also see Marvel Feature; The New . . . #140-on)
Aug, 1972-No. 152, Feb, 1986
Marvel Comics Group

1-The Hulk, Doctor Strange, & Sub-Mariner begin	4.30	13.00	30.00
2-9: 4-Valkyrie joins. 9,10-Avengers app.	1.30	4.00	9.00
10-Thor battles Hulk	1.60	4.80	11.00
11-25: 15,16-Magneto & Brotherhood of Evil Mutants app. from X-Men			
	.70	2.00	4.00
26-29-Guardians of the Galaxy app.	1.15	3.50	7.00
30-50: 31,32-Origin Nighthawk. 35-Intro. New Red Guardian. 44-Hellcat joins. 45-			
Dr. Strange leaves	.50	1.50	3.00
51-72: 53-1st app. Lunatik in cameo(Lobo lookalike). 55-Origin Red Guardian;			
Lunatik cameo. 56-1st full Lunatik story. 61-Lunatik & Spider-Man app. 70-73-			
Lunatik (origin #71) .	35	1.00	2.00
73-75-Foolkiller II app. (Greg Salinger). 74-Nighthawk resigns			
	.70	2.00	4.00
76-95,97-151: 77-Origin Omega. 78-Original Defenders return thru #101. 100-			
Double size. 104-The Beast joins. 106-Death of Nighthawk. 125-Double size;			
1st app. Mad Dog; intro. new Defenders. 129-New Mutants cameo. 150-Dbl.			
size; origin Cloud	.25	.75	1.50
96-Ghost Rider app.	.40	1.25	2.50
152-Double size; ties in with X-Factor & Secret Wars II			
	.35	1.00	2.00

	Good	Fine	N-Mint
Annual 1 (11/76, 52 pgs.)-All new-a	.50	1.50	3.00

DEMON, THE (See Detective Comics No. 482-485)
Aug-Sept, 1972-V3#16, Jan, 1974
National Periodical Publications

1-Origin; Kirby-c/a in 1-16	1.15	3.50	8.00
2-16	.70	2.00	4.00

DENNIS THE MENACE
8/53-#14, 1/56; #15, 3/56-#31, 11/58; #32, 1/59-#166, 11/79
Standard Comics/Pines No.15-31/Hallden (Fawcett) No.32 on

	Good	Fine	N-Mint
1-1st app. Mr. & Mrs. Wilson, Ruff & Dennis' mom & dad; Wiseman-a, written by Fred Toole-most issues	23.00	70.00	160.00
2	11.50	34.00	80.00
3-10	6.50	19.00	45.00
11-20	4.00	12.00	28.00
21-30: 22-1st app. Margaret w/blonde hair	2.15	6.50	15.00
31-40: 31-1st app. Joey	1.50	4.50	10.00
41-60	1.00	3.00	7.00
61-90	.70	2.00	4.00
91-166	.30	1.00	2.00

DETECTIVE COMICS
March, 1937-Present
National Periodical Publications/DC Comics

	Good	Fine	VF-NM
1-(Scarce)-Slam Bradley & Spy by Siegel & Shuster, Speed Saunders by Guardineer, Flat Foot Flannigan by Gustavson, Cosmo, the Phantom of Disguise, Buck Marshall, Bruce Nelson begin; Chin Lung-c from 'Claws of the Red Dragon' serial; Flessel-c (1st?)	2165.00	5400.00	13,000.00

(Estimated up to 35 total copies exist, 1 in NM/Mint)

	Good	Fine	VF-NM
2 (Rare)	670.00	1670.00	4000.00
3 (Rare)	535.00	1335.00	3200.00

	Good	Fine	N-Mint
4,5: 5-Larry Steele begins	300.00	750.00	1800.00
6,7,9,10	192.00	480.00	1150.00
8-Mister Chang-c	250.00	625.00	1500.00
11-17,19: 17-1st app. Fu Manchu in Det.	167.00	420.00	1000.00
18-Fu Manchu-c	225.00	560.00	1350.00

Detective Comics #109, © DC Comics

	Good	Fine	N-Mint
20-The Crimson Avenger begins (1st app.)	250.00	625.00	1500.00
21,23-25	120.00	300.00	725.00
22-1st Crimson Avenger-c (12/38)	175.00	440.00	1050.00
26	138.00	345.00	825.00

	Good	Fine	VF-NM
27-The Batman & Commissioner Gordon begin (1st app.) by Bob Kane (5/39);			
Batman-c (1st)	6,800.00	17,000.00	37,000.00

(Prices vary widely on this book)

	Good	Fine	N-Mint
27 (1984)-Oreo Cookies giveaway (32 pgs., paper-c, r-/Det. 27, 38 & Batman No.			
1 (1st Joker)	1.15	3.50	7.00
28	870.00	2200.00	5200.00

	Good	Fine	VF-NM
29-Batman-c; Doctor Death app.	915.00	2300.00	5500.00

	Good	Fine	N-Mint
30,32: 30-Dr. Death app. 32-Batman uses gun	380.00	950.00	2300.00

	Good	Fine	VF-NM
31-Classic Batman-c; 1st Julie Madison, Bat Plane (Bat-Gyro) & Batarang			
	915.00	2300.00	5500.00

	Good	Fine	VF-NM
33-Origin The Batman; Batman gunholster-c	1200.00	3000.00	7200.00

	Good	Fine	N-Mint
34-Steve Malone begins; 2nd Crimson Avenger-c	335.00	835.00	2000.00
35-Batman-c begin; hypo-c	500.00	1250.00	3000.00

36,37: 36-Origin Hugo Strange. 37-Cliff Crosby begins; last Batman solo story

	370.00	915.00	2200.00

	Good	Fine	VF-NM
38-Origin/1st app. Robin the Boy Wonder (4/40)	1300.00	3250.00	7800.00

	Good	Fine	N-Mint
39	315.00	790.00	1900.00

40-Origin & 1st app. Clay Face (Basil Karlo); 1st Joker cover app. (6/40)

	315.00	790.00	1900.00
41-Robin's 1st solo	200.00	500.00	1200.00
42-44: 44-Crimson Avenger-new costume	150.00	375.00	900.00
45-1st Joker story in Det. (3rd app.)	225.00	560.00	1350.00

46-50: 48-1st time car called Batmobile; Gotham City 1st mention. 49-Last Clay

Face	135.00	340.00	810.00

51-57,59: 59-Last Steve Malone; 2nd Penguin; Wing becomes Crimson Avenger's

aide	108.00	270.00	650.00
58-1st Penguin app.; last Speed Saunders	200.00	500.00	1200.00
60-Intro. Air Wave	117.00	290.00	700.00
61,63: 63-Last Cliff Crosby; 1st app. Mr. Baffle	100.00	250.00	600.00
62-Joker-c/story (2nd Joker-c, 4/42)	138.00	345.00	825.00

64-Origin & 1st app. Boy Commandos by Simon & Kirby (6/42); Joker app.

	267.00	665.00	1600.00
65-Boy Commandos-c	132.00	335.00	800.00
66-Origin & 1st app. Two-Face	183.00	460.00	1100.00
67,70: 67-1st Penguin-c (9/42)	87.00	215.00	520.00
68-Two-Face-c/story	92.00	230.00	550.00
69-Joker-c/story	117.00	290.00	700.00
71-Joker-c/story	105.00	260.00	625.00

72-75: 73-Scarecrow-c/story. 74-1st Tweedledum & Tweedledee; S&K-a

	80.00	200.00	480.00

76-Newsboy Legion & The Sandman x-over in Boy Commandos; S&K-a; Joker-

c/story	121.00	302.00	725.00
77-79: All S&K-a	80.00	200.00	480.00
80-Two-Face app.; S&K-a	83.00	210.00	500.00

81,82,84,86-90: 81-1st Cavalier app. 89-Last Crimson Avenger

	71.00	178.00	425.00

83-1st "Skinny" Alfred; last S&K Boy Commandos? Most issues #84 on signed

S&K are not by them	80.00	200.00	480.00

	Good	Fine	N-Mint
85-Joker-c/story; Last Spy	93.00	235.00	560.00
91,102-Joker-c/story	87.00	215.00	520.00
92-99: 96-Alfred's last name 'Beagle' revealed, later changed to 'Pennyworth'-214.			
99-Penguin-c	64.00	160.00	385.00
100 (6/45)	96.00	240.00	575.00
101,103-108,110-113,115-117,119,120: 114-1st small logo (8/46). 120- Penguin-c			
	58.00	145.00	350.00
109,114,118-Joker-c/stories	80.00	200.00	480.00
121-123,125-127,129,130: 122-1st Catwoman-c (4/47). 126-Penguin-c			
	56.00	140.00	335.00
124,128-Joker-c/stories	73.00	185.00	440.00
131-136,139: 137-Last Air Wave	48.00	120.00	285.00
137-Joker-c/story	64.00	160.00	385.00
138-Origin Robotman (See Star Spangled No. 7, 1st app.); series ends No. 202			
	83.00	210.00	500.00
140-The Riddler-c/story (1st app., 10/48)	150.00	375.00	900.00
141,143-148,150: 150-Last Boy Commandos	48.00	120.00	285.00
142-2nd Riddler-c/story	75.00	190.00	450.00
149-Joker-c/story	63.00	155.00	375.00
151-Origin & 1st app. Pow Wow Smith	50.00	125.00	300.00
152,154,155,157-160: 152-Last Slam Bradley	48.00	120.00	285.00
153-1st Roy Raymond app.; origin The Human Fly	50.00	125.00	300.00
156(2/50)-The new classic Batmobile	58.00	145.00	350.00
161-167,169-176: Last 52 pgs.	50.00	125.00	300.00
168-Origin the Joker	183.00	460.00	1100.00
177-189,191-199,201-204,206-212,214-216: 185-Secret of Batman's utility belt. 187-Two-Face app. 202-Last Robotman & Pow Wow Smith. 216-Last pre-code			
(2/55)	33.00	84.00	200.00
190-Origin Batman retold	50.00	125.00	300.00
200	48.00	120.00	285.00
205-Origin Batcave	50.00	125.00	300.00
213-Origin Mirror Man	46.00	115.00	275.00
217-224	32.00	80.00	190.00
225-(11/55)-1st app. Martian Manhunter-John Jones, later changed to J'onn J'onzz; also see Batman #78	193.00	580.00	1350.00
226-Origin Martian Manhunter continued	48.00	144.00	340.00
227-229	30.00	90.00	210.00
230-1st app. Mad Hatter	36.00	108.00	250.00
231-Origin Martian Manhunter retold	23.00	70.00	160.00
232,234,236-240	20.00	60.00	140.00

	Good	Fine	N-Mint
233-Origin & 1st app. Batwoman	61.00	183.00	425.00
235-Origin Batman & his costume	30.00	90.00	210.00
241-260: 246-Intro. Diane Meade, J. Jones' girl. 257-Intro. & 1st app. Whirly Bats			
	15.00	45.00	105.00
261-264,266,268-270: 261-1st app. Dr. Double X. 262-Origin Jackal			
	11.50	34.00	80.00
265-Batman's origin retold with new facts	16.50	50.00	115.00
267-Origin & 1st app. Bat-Mite	12.00	36.00	85.00
271,272,274-280: 276-2nd Bat-Mite	9.00	27.00	62.00
273-J'onn J'onzz I.D. revealed for 1st time	10.00	30.00	70.00
281-297: 287-Origin J'onn J'onzz retold. 292-Last Roy Raymond. 293-Aquaman begins, ends #300. 297-Last 10 cent issue (11/61)			
	6.50	19.00	45.00
298-1st modern Clayface (Matt Hagen)	11.50	34.00	80.00
299-326,329,330: 311-Intro. Zook in John Jones; 1st app. Catman. 322- Bat-Girl's 1st app. in Det. 326-Last J'onn J'onzz, story cont'd in H.O.M. #143; intro. Idol-Head of Diabolu	3.60	11.00	25.00
327-Elongated Man begins, ends #383; 1st new look Batman with new costume			
	4.00	12.00	28.00
328-Death of Alfred	6.50	19.00	45.00
331,333-340,342-358,360-364,366-368,370: 345-Intro Block Buster. 351- Elongated Man new costume. 355-Zatanna x-over in Elongated Man. 356-Alfred brought back in Batman	2.15	6.50	15.00
332,341,365-Joker-c/stories	3.15	9.50	22.00
359-Intro/origin new Batgirl	3.15	9.50	22.00
369-Neal Adams-a	3.50	10.50	24.00
371-386,389,390	1.50	4.50	10.00
387-R/1st Batman story from #27; Joker-c	3.15	9.50	22.00
388-Joker-c/story	2.30	7.00	16.00
391-394,396,398,399,401,403,405,406,409: 392-1st app. Jason Bard. 401-2nd Batgirl/Robin team-up	1.35	4.00	8.00
395,397,402,404,407,408,410-Neal Adams-a	2.00	6.00	14.00
400-Origin & 1st app. Man-Bat; 1st Batgirl/Robin team-up; Neal Adams-a			
	2.85	8.50	20.00
411-420: 414-52 pgs. begin, end #424. 418-Creeper x-over			
	1.35	4.00	8.00
421-436: 424-Last Batgirl; 1st She-Bat. 426-436-Elongated Man app. 428,434-Hawkman begins, ends #467	1.15	3.50	7.00
437-New Manhunter begins by Simonson, ends #443			
	1.70	5.00	10.00
438-443 (All 100 pgs.): 439-Origin Manhunter. 440-G.A. Manhunter, Hawkman,			

	Good	Fine	N-Mint

Dollman, Gr. Lantern; Toth-a. 441-G.A. Plastic Man, Batman, Ibis-r. 442-G.A. Newsboy Legion, Bl. Canary, Elongated Man, Dr. Fate-r. 443-Origin The Creeper-r; death of Manhunter; G.A. Green Lantern, Spectre-r. 444-G.A. Kid Eternity-r. 445-G.A. Dr. Midnite-r

	Good	Fine	N-Mint
	1.50	4.50	9.00
444, 445-100 pg issues	1.35	4.00	8.00
446-465,469,470,480: 457-Origin retold & updated. 480-(44 pgs.)			
	1.00	3.00	6.00
466-468,471-474,478,479-Rogers-a; 478-1st app. 3rd Clayface (Preston Payne). 479-(44 pgs.)	1.70	5.00	10.00
475,476-Joker-c/stories; Rogers-a	3.00	9.00	18.00
477-Neal Adams-a(r); Rogers-a, 3pgs.	2.00	6.00	12.00
481-(Combined with Batman Family, 12/78-1/79)(Begin $1.00, 68 pg. issues, ends #495); 481-495-Batgirl, Robin solo stories	1.50	4.50	9.00
482-Starlin/Russell, Golden-a; The Demon begins (origin-r), ends #485 (by Ditko #483-485)	1.00	3.00	6.00
483-40th Anniversary issue; origin retold; Newton Batman begins			
	1.15	3.50	7.00
484-499,501-503,505-523: 484-Origin Robin. 485-Death of Batwoman. 487-The Odd Man by Ditko. 489-Robin/Batgirl team-up. 490-Black Lightning begins. 491(492 on inside). 519-Last Batgirl. 521-Green Arrow series begins. 523-Solomon Grundy	.70	2.00	4.00
500-($1.50)-Batman/Deadman team-up	1.35	4.00	8.00
504-Joker-c/story	1.15	3.50	7.00
524-2nd app. Jason Todd (cameo)(3/83)	.85	2.50	5.00
525-3rd app. Jason Todd (See Batman #357)	.70	2.00	4.00
526-Batman's 500th app. in Detective Comics·(68 pgs., $1.50); contains 55 pg. Joker story	2.00	6.00	12.00
527-531,533,534,536-568,571: 542-Jason Todd quits as Robin (becomes Robin again #547). 549,550-Alan Moore scripts(Gr. Arrow). 554-1st new Black Canary. 566-Batman villains profiled. 567-Harlan Ellison scripts	.50	1.50	3.00
532,569,570-Joker-c/stories	1.00	3.00	6.00
535-Intro new Robin (Jason Todd)-1st appeared in Batman			
	1.00	3.00	6.00
572 (60 pgs., $1.25)-50th Anniversary of Det.	.70	2.00	4.00
573	.50	1.50	3.00
574-Origin Batman & Jason Todd retold	.85	2.50	5.00
575-Year 2 begins, ends #578	2.50	7.50	15.00
576-578: McFarlane-c/a	2.00	6.00	12.00

579-597,601-610: 579-New bat wing logo. 589-595-(52 pgs.)-Each contain free 16

	Good	Fine	N-Mint
pg. Batman stories. 604-607-Mudpack storyline; 604, 607-Contain Batman mini-posters. 610-Faked death of Penguin	.25	.75	1.50
598-($2.95, 84 pgs.)-"Blind Justice" storyline begins by Batman movie writer Sam Hamm, ends #600	1.70	5.00	10.00
599	1.35	2.00	4.00
600-($2.95, 84 pgs.)-50th Anniversary of Batman in Det.; 1 pg. N. Adams pin-up, among other artists	1.00	3.00	6.00
611-626,628-640: 615-"The Penguin Affair" part 2 (See Batman #448, 449). 617-Joker-c/story	.50	1.00
627-($2.95, 84 pgs.)-Batman's 600th app. in Det.; reprints 1st story/#27 plus 3 versions (2 new) of same story	.55	1.60	3.20
Annual 1(1988, $1.50)	.85	2.50	5.00
Annual 2(1989, $2.00, 68 pgs.)	.70	2.00	4.00
Annual 3(1990, $2.00, 68 pgs.)	.35	1.00	2.00

DICK TRACY (. . . Monthly #1-24; also see Popular & Super Comics)
Jan, 1948-No. 24, Dec, 1949
Dell Publishing Co.

	Good	Fine	N-Mint
1-('34-r)	40.00	120.00	280.00
2,3	22.00	65.00	150.00
4-10	19.00	56.00	130.00
11-18: 13-Bondage-c	14.00	43.00	100.00
19-1st app. Sparkle Plenty, B.O. Plenty & Gravel Gertie in a 3-pg. strip not by Gould	16.00	48.00	110.00
20-1st app. Sam Catchem; c/a not by Gould	12.00	36.00	85.00
21-24-Only 2 pg. Gould-a in each	12.00	36.00	85.00

DICK TRACY (Cont'd from Dell series) (. . . Comics Monthly #25-140)
No. 25, Mar, 1950-No. 145, April, 1961
Harvey Publications

	Good	Fine	N-Mint
25	16.00	48.00	110.00
26-28,30: 28-Bondage-c	12.00	36.00	85.00
29-1st app. Gravel Gertie in a Gould-r	16.00	48.00	110.00
31,32,34,35,37-40: 40-Intro/origin 2-way wrist radio	11.00	32.00	75.00
33-"Measles the Teen-Age Dope Pusher"	12.00	36.00	85.00
36-1st app. B.O. Plenty in a Gould-r	12.00	36.00	85.00
41-50	9.30	28.00	65.00
51-56,58-80: 51-2 pgs Powell-a	8.50	25.50	60.00

	Good	Fine	N-Mint
57-1st app. Sam Catchem, Gould-r	11.00	32.00	75.00
81-99,101-140	6.50	19.00	45.00
100	7.00	21.00	50.00
141-145 (25 cents) (titled "Dick Tracy")	6.00	18.00	42.00

DISNEY'S DUCKTALES (TV)
Oct, 1988-No. 13, May, 1990 (1,2,9-11: $1.50; 3-8: 95 cents, color)
Gladstone Publishing

1-Barks-r	.60	1.75	3.50
2-11: 2,4-6,9-11-Barks-r. 7-Barks-r (1 pg.)	.35	1.00	2.00
12,13 ($1.95, 68 pgs.)-Barks-r; 12-r/F.C. #495	.35	1.10	2.20

DOCTOR STRANGE (Formerly Strange Tales #1-168)
No. 169, 6/68-No. 183, 11/69; 6/74-No. 81, 2/87
Marvel Comics Group

169(#1)-Origin; panel swipe/M.D. #1-c	9.70	29.00	68.00
170-183: 177-New costume	3.15	9.50	22.00
1(6/74)-Brunner-c/a	3.15	9.50	22.00
2	1.60	4.80	11.00
3-5	1.00	3.00	6.00
6-26: 21-Origin-r/Doctor Strange #169	.50	1.50	3.00
27-77,79-81: 56-Origin retold		.60	1.20
78-New costume	.35	1.00	2.00
Annual 1 (1976)-New Russell-a	.50	1.50	3.00

DOCTOR STRANGE/GHOST RIDER SPECIAL
Apr, 1991 ($1.50, color)
Marvel Comics

1-Same cover/contents as Dr. Strange S.S. #28	.70	2.00	4.00

DOCTOR STRANGE, SORCERER SUPREME
Nov, 1988-Present (Mando paper, $1.25-1.50, direct sales only)
Marvel Comics

1 ($1.25)	.85	2.50	5.00
2-10,12-14,16-27,29,30,32-35 ($1.50): 3-New Defenders app. 5-Guice-c/a begins			
26-Werewolf by Night app.	.25	.75	1.50
11-Hobgoblin app.	.35	1.00	2.00

	Good	Fine	N-Mint
15-Unauthorized Amy Grant photo-c	1.00	3.00	6.00
28-Ghost Rider app.; has same cover and contents as Dr. Strange/Ghost Rider			
Special #1	.70	2.00	4.00
31-Infinity Gauntlet x-over	.35	1.00	2.00

DOLL MAN (Also see Feature Comics #27)
Fall, 1941-No. 7, Fall, '43; No. 8, Spring, '46-No. 47, Oct, 1953
Quality Comics Group

	Good	Fine	N-Mint
1-Dollman (by Cassone) & Justin Wright begin	107.00	320.00	750.00
2-The Dragon begins; Crandall-a(5)	55.00	165.00	385.00
3,4	40.00	120.00	280.00
5-Crandall-a	29.00	86.00	200.00
6,7(1943)	21.00	62.00	145.00
8(1946)-1st app. Torchy by Bill Ward	23.00	70.00	160.00
9	18.00	54.00	125.00
10-20	14.00	43.00	100.00
21-30	12.00	36.00	85.00
31-36,38,40: Jeb Rivers app. #32-34	10.00	30.00	75.00
37-Origin Dollgirl; Dollgirl bondage-c	13.00	40.00	90.00
39-"Narcotics . . . the Death Drug"-c-/story	10.00	30.00	70.00
41-47	7.00	21.00	50.00

DONALD DUCK (Walt Disney's . . . #262 on; see Disney's Ducktales, Mickey & Donald, & Walt Disney's Comics & Stories)
1940-#84, 9-11/62; #85, 12/62-#245, 1984; #246, 10/86-#279, 5/90
Dell Publishing Co./Gold Key No. 85-216/Whitman No. 217-245/
    Gladstone Publishing No. 246 on

	Good	Fine	VF-NM
4-Color 4(1940)-Daily 1939 strip-r by Al Taliaferro			
	357.00	1070.00	2500.00

	Good	Fine	N-Mint
Large Feature Comic 16(1/41?)-1940 Sunday strips-r in B&W			
	170.00	515.00	1200.00

Large Feature Comic 20('41)-Comic Paint Book, r-single panels from Large Feature #16 at top of each page to color; daily strip-r across bottom of each page

	230.00	685.00	1600.00

	Good	Fine	VF-NM

4-Color 9('42)-"Finds Pirate Gold;"-64 pgs. by Carl Barks & Jack Hannah (pgs. 1,2,5,12-40 are by Barks, his 1st comic book work; © 8/17/42)

	370.00	1115.00	2800.00

	Good	Fine	VF-NM
4-Color 29(9/43)-"Mummy's Ring" by Carl Barks; reprinted in Donald Duck Adventures #14	243.00	730.00	1850.00

(Prices vary widely on all above books)

	Good	Fine	N-Mint
4-Color 62(1/45)-"Frozen Gold;" 52 pgs. by Carl Barks; reprinted in Donald Duck Adventures #4	120.00	360.00	910.00
4-Color 108(1946)-"Terror of the River;" 52 pgs. by Carl Barks	90.00	270.00	680.00
4-Color 147(5/47)-in "Volcano Valley" by Carl Barks	60.00	180.00	455.00
4-Color 159(8/47)-in "The Ghost of the Grotto;" 52 pgs. by Carl Barks; reprinted in Donald Duck Adventures #9	54.00	160.00	410.00
4-Color 178(12/47)-1st Uncle Scrooge by Barks	64.00	192.00	485.00
4-Color 189(6/48)-by Carl Barks; reprinted in Donald Duck Adventures #19	54.00	160.00	410.00
4-Color 199(10/48)-by Carl Barks; mentioned in **Love and Death**	54.00	160.00	410.00
4-Color 203(12/48)-by Barks	36.00	108.00	270.00
4-Color 223(4/49)-by Barks; reprinted in Donald Duck Adventures #3	50.00	150.00	380.00
4-Color 238(8/49), 256(12/49)-by Barks	27.00	81.00	205.00
4-Color 263(2/50)-Two Barks stories; r-in Donald Duck #278	27.00	81.00	205.00
4-Color 275(5/50), 282(7/50), 291(9/50), 300(11/50)-All by Carl Barks; 291 reprinted in Donald Duck Advs. #16	25.00	75.00	190.00
4-Color 308(1/51), 318(3/51)-by Barks; 318-reprinted in Donald Duck Adventures #2,19	21.00	63.00	160.00
4-Color 328(5/51)-by Carl Barks	23.00	70.00	175.00
4-Color 339(7-8/51), 379-not by Barks	4.35	13.00	30.00
4-Color 348(9-10/51), 356,394-Barks-c only	6.50	19.00	45.00
4-Color 367(1-2/52)-by Barks	20.00	60.00	150.00
4-Color 408(7-8/52), 422(9-10/52)-All by Carl Barks	20.00	60.00	150.00
26(11-12/52)-In "Trick or Treat" by Carl Barks	22.00	65.00	165.00
27-30-Barks-c only	4.30	13.00	30.00
31-40	2.65	8.00	18.00
41-44,47-50	2.00	6.00	14.00
45-Barks-a, 6 pgs.	7.00	21.00	55.00
46-"Secret of Hondorica" by Barks, 24 pgs.; reprinted in Donald Duck #98 & 154	8.00	24.00	60.00
51-Barks, 1/2 pg.	1.70	5.00	12.00

	Good	Fine	N-Mint
52-"Lost Peg-Leg Mine" by Barks, 10 pgs.	6.50	19.50	50.00
53,55-59	1.60	4.80	11.00
54-"Forbidden Valley" by Barks, 26 pgs.	7.50	22.00	58.00
60-"Donald Duck & the Titanic Ants" by Barks, 20 pgs. plus 6 more pages			
	6.50	19.50	50.00
61-67,69,70	1.30	4.00	9.00
68-Barks-a, 5 pgs.	3.75	11.25	26.00
71-Barks-r, 1/2 pg.	1.50	4.50	10.00
72-78,80,82-97,99,100: 96-Donald Duck Album	1.15	3.50	8.00
79,81-Barks-a, 1pg.	1.50	4.50	10.00
98-Reprints #46 (Barks)	2.15	6.50	15.00
101-133: 102-Super Goof. 112-1st Moby Duck	.85	2.50	6.00
134-Barks-r/#52 & WDC&S 194	1.00	3.00	7.00
135-Barks-r/WDC&S 198, 19 pgs.	.70	2.00	5.00
136-153,155,156,158	.50	1.50	3.00
154-Barks-r(#46)	.70	2.00	5.00
157,159,160,164: 157-Barks-r(#45). 159-Reprints/WDC&S #192 (10 pgs.).			
160-Barks-r(#26). 164-Barks-r(#79)	.40	1.25	2.50
161-163,165-170	.25	.75	1.50
171-173,175-187,189-191		.60	1.20
174,188: 174-R/4-Color #394. 188-Barks-r/#68	.35	1.00	2.00
192-Barks-r(40 pgs.) from Donald Duck #60 & WDC&S #226,234 (52 pgs.)			
	.40	1.25	2.50
193-200,202-207,209-211,213-218: 217 has 216 on-c			
		.50	1.00
201,208,212: 201-Barks-r/Christmas Parade #26, 16 pgs. 208-Barks-r/ #60 (6 pgs.).			
212-Barks-r/WDC&S #130	.35	1.00	2.00
219-Barks-r/WDC&S #106,107, 10 pgs. ea.		.60	1.20
220-227,231-245		.35	.70
228-230: 228-Barks-r/F.C. #275. 229-Barks-r/F.C. #282. 230-Barks-r/ #52 &			
WDC&S #194	.25	.75	1.50
246-(1st Gladstone issue)-Barks-r/FC #422	1.50	4.50	9.00
247-249: 248-Barks-r/DD #54. 249-Barks-r/DD #26			
	.70	2.00	4.00
250-($1.50, 68 pgs.)-Barks-r/4-Color #9	2.50	7.50	15.00
251-256: 251-Barks-r/45 Firestone. 254-Barks-r/FC #328. 256-Barks-r/ FC #147			
	.50	1.50	3.00
257-($1.50, 52 pgs.)-Barks-r/Vac. Parade #1	.70	2.00	4.00
258-260	.40	1.25	2.50
261-277: 261-Barks-r/FC #300. 275-Kelly-r/FC #92	.25	.75	1.50
278-($1.95, 68 pgs.)-Rosa-a; Barks-r/FC #263	.40	1.25	2.50

	Good	Fine	N-Mint
279-($1.95, 68 pgs.)-Rosa-c; Barks-r/MOC #4	.40	1.25	2.50

DONALD DUCK ADVENTURES (Walt Disney's . . . #4 on)
Nov, 1987-No. 20, Apr, 1990
Gladstone Publishing

	Good	Fine	N-Mint
1	.55	1.65	3.30
2-r/F.C. #308	.35	1.10	2.20
3,4,6,7,9-11,13,15-18: 3-r/F.C. #223. 4-r/F.C. #62. 9-r/F.C. #159. 16-r/F.C. #291; Rosa-c. 18-r/F.C. #318; Rosa-c	.30	.85	1.70
5,8-Don Rosa-a	.35	1.10	2.20
12 ($1.50, 52pgs)-Rosa-c/a w/Barks poster	.35	1.10	2.20
14-r/F.C. #29, "Mummy's Ring"	.40	1.25	2.50
19 ($1.95, 68 pgs.)-Barks-r/F.C. #199	.35	1.00	2.00
20 ($1.95, 68 pgs.)-Barks-r/F.C. #189 & cover-r	.35	1.00	2.00

DON WINSLOW OF THE NAVY (Movie, radio, TV) (See Crackajack Funnies
   & Popular Comics)
2/43-#64, 12/48; #65, 1/51-#69, 9/51; #70, 3/55-#73, 9/55
Fawcett Publications/Charlton No. 70 on

	Good	Fine	N-Mint
1-(68 pgs.)-Captain Marvel on cover	47.00	140.00	325.00
2	23.00	70.00	160.00
3	16.00	48.00	110.00
4-6: 6-Flag-c	12.00	36.00	84.00
7-10: 8-Last 68 pg. issue?	8.50	25.50	60.00
11-20	5.70	17.00	40.00
21-40	4.00	12.00	28.00
41-63	2.85	8.50	20.00
64(12/48)-Matt Baker-a	3.15	9.50	22.00
65(1/51)-69(9/51): All photo-c. 65-Flying Saucer attack	4.00	12.00	28.00
70(3/55)-73: 70-73 r-/#26,58 & 59	2.65	8.00	18.00

DOOM PATROL, THE (My Greatest Adv. No. 1-85; see Showcase)
No. 86, 3/64-No. 121, 9-10/68; No. 122, 2/73-No. 124, 6-7/73
National Periodical Publications

	Good	Fine	N-Mint
86-1 pg. origin	7.00	21.00	50.00
87-99: 88-Origin The Chief. 91-Intro. Mento. 99-Intro. Beast Boy who later became the Changeling in the New Teen Titans	5.00	15.00	35.00

The Doom Patrol #19, © DC Comics

	Good	Fine	N-Mint
100-Origin Beast Boy; Robot-Maniac series begins	6.50	19.50	46.00
101-110: 102-Challengers/Unknown app. 105-Robot-Maniac series ends. 106- Negative Man begins (origin)	2.85	8.50	20.00
111-120	2.30	7.00	16.00
121-Death of Doom Patrol; Orlando-c	7.00	21.00	50.00
122-124(reprints)	.35	1.00	2.00

DOOM PATROL
Oct, 1987-Present (New format, direct sale, $1.50 #19 on)
DC Comics

	Good	Fine	N-Mint
1	.35	1.00	2.00
2-18: 3-1st app. Lodestone. 4-1st app. Karma. 8,15,16-Art Adams-c(i). 18- Invasion		.50	1.00
19-New format & Grant Morrison scripts begin	3.35	10.00	20.00
20-25	1.70	5.00	10.00
26-30: 29-Superman app.	1.00	3.00	6.00
31-40: 39-Preview of World Without End	.40	1.25	2.50

	Good	Fine	N-Mint
41-49	.25	.75	1.50
50 ($2.50, 52 pgs.)	.40	1.25	2.50
. . . And Suicide Squad Special 1($1.50,3/88)	.25	.75	1.50
Annual 1 ('88, $1.50)	.25	.75	1.50

DRAGONLANCE
Dec, 1988-Present ($1.25-$1.50, color, Mando paper)
DC Comics

1-Based on TSR game	1.00	3.00	6.00
2	.70	2.00	4.00
3-5	.60	1.75	3.50
6-10: 6-Begin $1.50-c	.50	1.50	3.00
11-15	.35	1.00	2.00
16-34: 25-Begin $1.75-c	.30	.90	1.80
Annual 1 (1990, $2.95, 68 pgs.)	.50	1.50	3.00

DURANGO KID, THE
Oct-Nov, 1949-No. 41, Oct-Nov, 1955 (All 36 pgs.)
Magazine Enterprises

1-Charles Starrett photo-c; Durango Kid & his horse Raider begin; Dan Brand &
   Tipi (origin) begin by Frazetta & continue through #16

	Good	Fine	N-Mint
	39.00	118.00	275.00
2 (Starrett photo-c)	25.00	75.00	175.00
3-5 (All-Starrett photo-c)	21.50	64.00	150.00
6-10: 7-Atomic weapon-c/story	11.00	32.00	75.00
11-16-Last Frazetta issue	8.00	24.00	55.00
17-Origin Durango Kid	10.00	30.00	70.00
18-Fred Meagher-a on Dan Brand begins	5.50	16.50	38.00
19-30: 19-Guardineer-c/a(3) begin, end #41. 23-Intro. The Red Scorpion			
	5.50	16.50	38.00
31-Red Scorpion returns	4.50	14.00	32.00
32-41-Bolle/Frazetta-a (Dan Brand)	6.00	18.00	42.00

DYNAMO (Also see T.H.U.N.D.E.R. Agents)
Aug, 1966-No. 4, June, 1967 (25 cents)
Tower Comics

1-Crandall/Wood, Ditko/Wood-a; Weed series begins; NoMan & Lightning			
cameos; Wood-c/a	3.60	11.00	25.00
2-4: Wood-c/a in all	2.65	8.00	18.00

E

EERIE (Strange Worlds No. 18 on)
No. 1, Jan, 1947; No. 1, May-June, 1951-No. 17, Aug-Sept, 1954
Avon Periodicals

	Good	Fine	N-Mint
1(1947)-1st horror comic; Kubert, Fugitani-a; bondage-c			
	43.00	130.00	300.00
1(1951)-Reprints story/'47 No. 1	24.00	70.00	165.00
2-Wood-c/a; bondage-c	26.00	77.00	180.00
3-Wood-c; Kubert, Wood/Orlando-a	26.00	77.00	180.00
4,5-Wood-c	24.00	70.00	165.00
6,13,14	9.30	28.00	65.00
7-Wood/Orlando-c; Kubert-a	16.00	48.00	110.00
8-Kinstler-a; bondage-c; Phantom Witch Doctor story			
	9.30	28.00	65.00
9-Kubert-a; Check-c	11.00	32.00	75.00
10,11-Kinstler-a	8.50	25.50	60.00
12-Dracula story from novel, 25 pgs.	11.50	34.00	80.00
15-Reprints No. 1('51) minus-c(bondage)	5.70	17.00	40.00
16-Wood-a r-/No. 2	7.00	21.00	50.00
17-Wood/Orlando & Kubert-a; reprints #3 minus inside & outside Wood-c			
	9.30	28.00	65.00

80 PAGE GIANT (. . . Magazine No. 1-15) (25 cents)
8/64-No. 15, 10/65; No. 16, 11/65-No. 89, 7/71 (All reprints)
National Periodical Publications (#1-56: 84 pgs.; #57-89: 68 pages)

	Good	Fine	N-Mint
1-Superman Annual	11.00	44.00	88.00
2-Jimmy Olsen	5.70	17.00	40.00
3,4,6,7,9-11,13,14: 3-Lois Lane. 4-Flash-G.A.-r; Infantino-a			
	3.30	10.00	23.00
5-Batman; has Sunday newspaper strip; Catwoman-r; Batman's Life Story-r (25th anniversary special)	4.85	14.50	34.00
8-More Secret Origins-origins of JLA, Aquaman, Robin, Atom, & Superman; Infantino-a	12.00	36.00	83.00
12-Batman; has Sunday newspaper strip	3.30	11.50	27.00
15-Superman and Batman; Joker-c/story	4.85	14.50	34.00

ELEKTRA: ASSASSIN
Aug, 1986-No. 8, Mar, 1987 (Limited series)(Adults)
Epic Comics (Marvel)

	Good	Fine	N-Mint
1-Miller scripts in all	.90	2.75	5.50
2	.70	2.00	4.00
3-7	.50	1.50	3.00
8	.75	2.25	4.50

ELEKTRA SAGA, THE
Feb, 1984-No. 4, June, 1984 ($2.00, Baxter paper)
Marvel Comics Group

	Good	Fine	N-Mint
1-4-r/Daredevil 168-190; Miller-c/a	1.00	3.00	6.00

ELLERY QUEEN
May, 1949-No. 4, Nov, 1949
Superior Comics Ltd.

	Good	Fine	N-Mint
1-Kamen-c; L.B. Cole-a; r-in Haunted Thrills	22.00	65.00	150.00
2-4: 3-Drug use stories(2)	13.00	40.00	90.00

ELLERY QUEEN (TV)
13/52-No. 2, Summer/52 (Saunders painted covers)
Ziff-Davis Publishing Co.

	Good	Fine	N-Mint
1-Saunders-c	22.00	65.00	150.00
2-Saunders bondage, torture-c	19.00	56.00	130.00

EXCALIBUR (Also see Marvel Comics Presents #31)
1987; Oct, 1988-Present ($1.50, Baxter)($1.75 #24-31, 33 on)
Marvel Comics

	Good	Fine	N-Mint
Special Edition nn (The Sword is Drawn)(1987, $3.25)-This is the 1st Excalibur comic	2.00	6.00	12.00
Special Edition nn (2nd print, 10/88, $3.50)	1.00	3.00	6.00
Special Edition nn (3rd print, 12/89, 4.50)	.75	2.25	4.50
1($1.50)-X-Men spin-off; Nightcrawler, Shadowcat(Kitty Pryde), Capt. Britain, Phoenix & Meggan begin	1.50	4.50	9.00
2	1.00	3.00	6.00
3,4	.70	2.00	4.00
5-10	.50	1.50	3.00

	Good	Fine	N-Mint
11-15: 10,11-Rogers/Austin-a	.35	1.00	2.00
16-23,32: 19-Austin-i. 21-Intro Crusader X	.25	.75	1.50
24-31,33-44: 24-John Byrne app. in story. 27-B. Smith-a(p)			
	.30	.90	1.80
... Mojo Mayhem nn ($4.50, 12/89)-Art Adams/Austin-c/a			
	.85	2.50	5.00
... The Possession (7/91, $2.95-c)- ... Special on-c	.50	1.50	3.00

EXCITING COMICS
April, 1940-No. 69, Sept, 1949
Nedor/Better Publications/Standard Comics

	Good	Fine	N-Mint
1-Origin The Mask, Jim Hatfield, Sgt. Bill King, Dan Williams begin			
	68.00	205.00	475.00
2-The Sphinx begins; The Masked Rider app.	30.00	90.00	210.00
3	26.00	77.00	180.00
4	20.00	60.00	140.00
5	16.00	48.00	110.00
6-8	13.00	40.00	90.00
9-Origin/1st app. of The Black Terror & sidekick Tim, begin series			
	68.00	205.00	475.00
10-13	29.00	86.00	200.00
14-Last Sphinx, Dan Williams	19.00	58.00	135.00
15-The Liberator begins (origin)	24.00	71.00	165.00
16-20: 20-The Mask ends	13.00	40.00	90.00
21,23-30: 28-Crime Crusader begins, ends #58	12.00	36.00	85.00
22-Origin The Eaglet; The American Eagle begins	13.00	40.00	90.00
31-38: 35-Liberator ends, not in 31-33	11.50	34.00	80.00
39-Origin Kara, Jungle Princess	17.00	51.00	120.00
40-50: 42-The Scarab begins. 49-Last Kara, Jungle Princess. 50-Last American Eagle	14.00	43.00	100.00
51-Miss Masque begins	19.00	58.00	135.00
52-54: Miss Masque ends	14.00	43.00	100.00
55-Judy of the Jungle begins(origin), ends #69; 1 pg. Ingels-a			
	19.00	58.00	135.00
56-58: All airbrush-c	17.00	51.00	120.00
59-Frazetta art in Caniff style; signed Frank Frazeta (one t), 9 pgs.			
	21.50	64.00	150.00
60-66: 60-Rick Howard, the Mystery Rider begins. 66-Robinson/ Meskin-a			
	13.00	40.00	90.00
67-69	8.50	25.50	60.00

F

FAMOUS FUNNIES
1933-No. 218, July, 1955
Eastern Color

	Good	Fine	VF-NM
A Carnival of Comics (probably the second comic book), 36 pgs., no date given, no publisher, no number; contains strip reprints of The Bungle Family, Dixie Dugan, Hairbreadth Harry, Joe Palooka, Keeping Up With the Jones, Mutt & Jeff, Reg'lar Fellers, S'Matter Pop, Strange As It Seems, and others. This book was sold by M. C. Gaines to Wheatena, Milk-O-Malt, John Wanamaker, Kinney Shoe Stores, & others to be given away as premiums and radio giveaways (1933).			
	400.00	1000.00	2400.00
Series 1-(Very rare)(nd-early 1934)(68 pgs.) No publisher given (Eastern Color Printing Co.); sold in chain stores for 10 cents. 35,000 print run. Contains Sunday strip reprints of Mutt & Jeff, Reg'lar Fellers, Nipper, Hairbreadth Harry, Strange As It Seems, Joe Palooka, Dixie Dugan, The Nebbs, Keeping Up With the Jones, and others. Inside front and back covers and pages 1-16 of Famous Funnies Series 1, #s 49-64 reprinted from **Famous Funnies, A Carnival of Comics**, and most of pages 17-48 reprinted from **Funnies on Parade**. This was the first comic book sold.			
	835.00	2100.00	5000.00
No. 1 (Rare)(7/34-on stands 5/34)-Eastern Color Printing Co. First monthly newsstand comic book. Contains Sunday strip reprints of Toonerville Folks, Mutt & Jeff, Hairbreadth Harry, S'Matter Pop, Nipper, Dixie Dugan, The Bungle Family, Connie, Ben Webster, Tailspin Tommy, The Nebbs, Joe Palooka, & others.	670.00	1670.00	4000.00
2 (Rare)	167.00	415.00	1000.00
3-Buck Rogers Sunday strip reprints by Rick Yager begins, ends #218; not in #191-208; the number of the 1st strip reprinted is pg. 190, Series No. 1			
	235.00	585.00	1400.00
4	78.00	235.00	550.00
5	63.00	190.00	440.00
6-10	50.00	150.00	350.00

	Good	Fine	N-Mint
11,12,18-Four pgs. of Buck Rogers in each issue, completes stories in Buck Rogers #1 which lacks these pages; #18-Two pgs. of Buck Rogers reprinted in Daisy Comics #1	43.00	130.00	300.00
13-17,19,20: 14-Has two Buck Rogers panels missing. 17-1st Christmas-c on a newsstand comic	32.00	95.00	225.00
21,23-30: 27-War on Crime begins; part photo-c. 29-X-Mas-c			
	23.00	70.00	160.00

	Good	Fine	N-Mint

22-Four pgs. of Buck Rogers needed to complete stories in Buck Rogers #1
| | 25.00 | 75.00 | 175.00 |

31-34,36,37,39,40: 33-Careers of Baby Face Nelson & John Dillinger traced
| | 17.00 | 51.00 | 120.00 |

35-Two pgs. Buck Rogers omitted in Buck Rogers #2
| | 19.00 | 56.00 | 130.00 |

38-Full color portrait of Buck Rogers
| | 17.00 | 51.00 | 120.00 |

41-60: 41,53-X-Mas-c. 55-Last bottom panel, pg. 4 in Buck Rogers redrawn in
Buck Rogers #3
| | 12.00 | 36.00 | 85.00 |

61-64,66,67,69,70
| | 10.00 | 30.00 | 70.00 |

65,68-Two pgs. Kirby-a-"Lightnin & the Lone Rider"
| | 11.00 | 32.00 | 75.00 |

71,73,77-80: 80-Buck Rogers story continues from Buck Rogers #5
| | 8.50 | 25.50 | 60.00 |

72-Speed Spaulding begins by Marvin Bradley (artist), ends #88. This series was
written by Edwin Balmer & Philip Wylie and later appeared as film & book
"When Worlds Collide"
| | 9.30 | 28.00 | 65.00 |

74-76-Two pgs. Kirby-a in all
| | 8.00 | 24.00 | 55.00 |

81-Origin Invisible Scarlet O'Neil; strip begins #82, ends #167
| | 6.50 | 19.00 | 45.00 |

82-Buck Rogers-c
| | 8.00 | 24.00 | 55.00 |

83-87,90: 87 has last Buck Rogers full page-r. 90-Bondage-c
| | 6.50 | 19.00 | 45.00 |

88-Buck Rogers in "Moon's End" by Calkins, 2 pgs.(not reprints). Beginning with
#88, all Buck Rogers pages have rearranged panels
| | 7.00 | 21.00 | 50.00 |

89-Origin Fearless Flint, the Flint Man
| | 7.00 | 21.00 | 50.00 |

91-93,95,96,98-99,101-110: 105-Series 2 begins (Strip Page #1)
| | 5.00 | 15.00 | 35.00 |

94-Buck Rogers in "Solar Holocaust" by Calkins, 3 pgs.(not reprints)
| | 6.00 | 18.00 | 42.00 |

97-War Bond promotion, Buck Rogers by Calkins, 2 pgs.(not reprints)
| | 6.00 | 18.00 | 42.00 |

| 100 | 6.00 | 18.00 | 42.00 |
| 111-130 | 4.00 | 12.00 | 28.00 |

131-150: 137-Strip page No. 110 omitted
| | 2.85 | 8.50 | 20.00 |

| 151-162,164-168 | 2.30 | 7.00 | 16.00 |

163-St. Valentine's Day-c
| | 2.85 | 8.50 | 20.00 |

169,170-Two text illos. by Williamson, his 1st comic book work
| | 5.50 | 16.50 | 38.00 |

	Good	Fine	N-Mint
171-180: 171-Strip pgs. 227,229,230, Series 2 omitted. 172-Strip Pg. 232 omitted			
	2.30	7.00	16.00
181-190: Buck Rogers ends with start of strip pg. 302, Series 2			
	1.85	5.50	13.00
191-197,199,201,203,206-208: No Buck Rogers	1.60	4.70	11.00
198,202,205-One pg. Frazetta ads; no Buck Rogers	2.00	6.00	14.00
200-Frazetta 1 pg. ad	2.15	6.50	15.00
204-Used in POP, pgs. 79,99	2.15	6.50	15.00
209-Buck Rogers begins with strip pg. 480, Series 2; Frazetta-c			
	26.00	77.00	180.00
210-216: Frazetta-c. 211-Buck Rogers ads by Anderson begins, ends #217. #215-Contains B. Rogers strip pg. 515-518, series 2 followed by pgs. 179-181, Series 3	26.00	77.00	180.00
217,218-Buck Rogers ends with pg. 199, Series 3	2.30	7.00	16.00

FANTASTIC COMICS
Dec, 1939-No. 23, Nov, 1941
Fox Features Syndicate

	Good	Fine	N-Mint
1-Intro/Origin Samson; Stardust, The Super Wizard, Space Smith, Sub Saunders (by Kiefer), Capt. Kidd begin	130.00	390.00	915.00
2-Powell text illos	65.00	195.00	455.00
3-5: 3-Powell text illos	54.00	160.00	375.00
6-9: 6,7-Simon-c	43.00	130.00	300.00
10-Intro/origin David, Samson's aide	32.00	95.00	225.00
11-17,19,20,22: 16-Stardust ends	25.00	75.00	175.00
18-1st app. Black Fury & sidekick Chuck; ends #23			
	29.00	86.00	200.00
21,23: 21-The Banshee begins(origin); ends #23; Hitler-c. 23-Origin The Gladiator			
	29.00	86.00	200.00

FANTASTIC FOUR
Nov, 1961-Present
Marvel Comics Group

	Good	Fine	N-Mint
1-Origin/1st app. The Fantastic Four; origin The Mole Man (Marvel's 1st superhero group since the GA)	360.00	1440.00	3600.00
1-Golden Record Comic Set-r	11.00	32.00	75.00
with record (still sealed)	21.50	65.00	150.00
1-Reprint('91, $2.95-c)	.50	1.50	3.00
2-Vs. The Skrulls (last 10 cent issue)	136.00	408.00	950.00

Fantastic Four #72, © Marvel Comics

	Good	Fine	N-Mint
3-Fantastic Four don costumes & establish Headquarters; brief 1pg. origin; intro			
The Fantasticar	100.00	300.00	700.00
4-1st Silver Age Sub-Mariner app.	100.00	300.00	700.00
5-Origin & 1st app. Doctor Doom	107.00	321.00	750.00
6-Sub-Mariner, Dr. Doom team up; 1st Marvel villain team-up			
	72.00	216.00	500.00
7-10: 7-1st app. Kurrgo. 8-1st app. Puppet-Master & Alicia Masters			
	49.00	147.00	340.00
11-Origin The Impossible Man	33.00	100.00	230.00
12-Fantastic Four Vs. The Hulk (1st x-over)	37.00	111.00	260.00
13-Intro. The Watcher; 1st app. The Red Ghost	29.00	88.00	200.00
14-19: 16-1st Ant-Man x-over (7/63). 18-Origin The Super Skrull. 19-Intro. Rama-			
Tut	20.00	60.00	140.00
20-Origin The Molecule Man	21.50	65.00	150.00
21-1st Sgt. Fury x-over (11/63)	11.50	34.00	80.00
22-24,27: 27-1st Doctor Strange x-over (6/64)	11.00	32.00	75.00
25,26-The Thing vs. The Hulk. 26-1st Avengers x-over (5/64)			
	23.00	69.00	160.00

	Good	Fine	N-Mint
27-1st Dr. Strange x-over (6/64)	11.50	34.00	80.00
28-Early X-Men x-over	13.00	40.00	90.00
29,30: 30-Intro. Diablo	8.00	24.00	55.00

31-40: 31-Early Avengers x-over. 33-1st app. Attuma; part photo-c. 35-Intro/1st
    app. Dragon Man. 36-Intro/1st app. Madam Medusa & the Frightful Four
    (Sandman, Wizard, Paste Pot Pete). 39-Wood inks on Daredevil (early x-over)

	5.70	17.00	40.00

41-47: 41-43-Frightful Four app. 44-Intro. Gorgan. 45-Intro. The Inhumans

	4.00	12.00	28.00

48-Partial origin/1st app. Silver Surfer & Galactus(3/66); Galactus app. in last

panel (cameo); 1st of 3 part story	31.00	93.00	215.00
49-2nd app. Silver Surfer & Galactus	9.50	28.50	66.00
50-Silver Surfer battles Galactus	13.50	41.00	95.00
51,54: 54-Inhumans cameo	3.15	9.50	22.00
52-1st app. The Black Panther	4.30	13.00	30.00
53-Origin Black Panther	3.60	11.00	25.00
55-Thing battles Silver Surfer	5.00	15.00	35.00
56-60: Silver Surfer x-over. 59,60-Inhumans cameo	4.15	12.50	29.00
61-65,68-70: 61-Silver Surfer cameo	3.30	10.00	23.00
66,67-1st app. & origin Him (Warlock)	4.00	12.00	28.00
71,73,78-80	1.85	5.50	13.00
72,74-77: Silver Surfer app. in all	2.65	8.00	18.00

81-88: 81-Crystal joins & dons costume. 82,83-Inhumans app. 84-87- Dr. Doom

app. 88-Last 12 cent issue	1.60	4.80	11.00
89-99,101,102: 94-Intro. Agatha Harkness	1.30	4.00	9.00
100	5.50	16.50	39.00
103-111: 108-Last Kirby issue (not in #103-107)	1.15	3.50	8.00
112-Hulk Vs. Thing	2.85	8.50	20.00
113-115: 115-Last 15 cent issue	1.15	3.50	8.00
116-120: 116-(52 pgs.)	1.00	3.00	7.00
121-123-Silver Surfer x-over	1.30	4.00	9.00

124-127,129-149: 126-Origin F.F. retold; cover swipe of F.F. #1. 129-Intro.
    Thundra. 130-Sue leaves F.F. 131-Quicksilver app. 132-Medusa joins. 133-
    Thundra Vs. Thing. 142-Kirbyish-a by Buckler begins. 143-Dr. Doom app.

	.85	2.50	5.00
128-Four pg. insert of F.F. Friends & Fiends	1.00	3.00	6.00
150-Crystal & Quicksilver's wedding	1.00	3.00	6.00

151-154,158-160: 151-Origin Thundra. 159-Medusa leaves, Sue rejoins

	.70	2.00	4.00
155-157: Silver Surfer in all	.85	2.50	5.00

161-180: 164-The Crusader (old Marvel Boy) revived(origin #165). 176-Re-intro

	Good	Fine	N-Mint
Impossible Man; Marvel artists app.	.45	1.35	2.70
181-199: 190-191-Fantastic Four break up	.25	.80	1.60
200-Giant size; F.F. re-united	.70	2.00	4.00
201-208,219		.65	1.30
209-216,218,220,221-Byrne-a. 209-1st Herbie the Robot. 220-Brief origin			
	.25	.80	1.60
217-Dazzler app. by Byrne	.45	1.35	2.70
222-231		.65	1.30
232-Byrne-a begins	.50	1.55	3.10
233-235,237-249: All Byrne-a. 238-Origin Frankie Ray			
	.40	1.25	2.50
236-20th Anniversary issue(11/81, 64 pgs., $1.00)-Brief origin F.F.			
	.50	1.55	3.10
250,260: 250-Double size; Byrne-a; Skrulls impersonate New X-Men. 260-Alpha			
Flight app.	.50	1.55	3.10
251-259: Byrne-c/a. 252-Reads sideways; Annihilus app. 254-Contains skin			
"Tatooz" decals	.40	1.15	2.30
261-285: 261-Silver Surfer. 262-Origin Galactus; Byrne writes & draws himself			
into story. 264-Swipes-c of F.F. #1	.35	1.05	2.10
286-2nd app. X-Factor cont./Avengers #263	.60	.80	3.60
287-295: 292-Nick Fury app.		.50	1.00
296-($1.50)-Barry Smith-c/a; Thing rejoins	.35	1.05	2.10
297-305,307-318,320-330: 312-X-Factor x-over. 327-Mr. Fantastic & Invisible			
Girl return		.50	1.00
306-New team begins	.25	.75	1.50
319-Double size	.35	1.00	2.00
331-346,351-357: 334-Simonson-c/scripts begin. 337-Simonson-a begins. 342-			
Spider-Man cameo		.50	1.00
347-Ghost Rider, Wolverine, Spider-Man, Hulk-c/stories & Arthur Adams-c/a(p)			
in #347 thru 349	1.00	3.00	6.00
347-Gold 2nd printing	.35	1.00	2.00
348,349-Ghost Rider, Wolverine, Spidey, Hulk	.70	2.00	4.00
348-Gold 2nd printing		.50	1.00
350-($1.50, 52 pgs.)-Dr. Doom app.	.35	1.00	2.00
358-($2.25, 80 pgs., 30th Anniversary)	.40	1.15	2.30
Annual 1('63)-Origin F.F.; Ditko-i	28.00	86.00	200.00
Annual 2('64)-Dr. Doom origin & x-over	21.00	63.00	150.00
Annual 3('65)-Reed & Sue wed	10.00	30.00	70.00
Special 4(11/66)-G.A. Torch x-over & origin retold	5.00	15.00	35.00
Special 5(11/67)-New art; Intro. Psycho-Man; early Black Panther, Inhumans app.;			
1st solo Silver Surfer story	3.60	11.00	25.00

	Good	Fine	N-Mint
Special 6(11/68)-Intro. Annihilus; no reprints; birth of Franklin Richards			
	2.85	8.50	20.00
Special 7(11/69)-All reprints	2.30	7.00	15.00
Special 8(12/70), 9(12/71), 10('73)-All reprints	1.35	4.00	8.00
Annual 11-14: 11(6/76), 12(2/78), 13(10/78), 14(1/80)	.85	2.50	5.00
Annual 15-20: 15(10/80), 16(10/81), 17(9/83), 18(11/84), 19(11/85), 20(9/87)			
	.50	1.50	3.00
Annual 21(9/88)-Evolutionary War x-over	.55	1.70	3.40
Annual 22(1989, $2.00, 64pg.)-Atlantis Attacks x-over; Sub-Mariner & The Avengers app. Buckler-a	.35	1.00	2.00
Annual 23('90, $2.00, 68 pgs.)-Byrne-c, Guice-p	.35	1.00	2.00
Annual 24('91, $2.00, 68 pgs.)	.35	1.00	2.00
Special Edition 1 (5/84)-r/Annual #1; Byrne-c/a	.35	1.05	2.10

FANTASTIC FOUR ROAST
May, 1982 (One Shot, Direct Sale)
Marvel Comics Group

1-Celebrates 20th anniversary of F.F.#1; Golden, Miller, Buscema, Rogers, Byrne, Anderson, Austin-c(i)	.60	1.80	3.60

FANTASTIC FOUR VS. X-MEN
Feb, 1987-No. 4, June, 1987 (Mini-series)
Marvel Comics

1	.60	1.75	3.50
2-4: 4-Austin-a(i)	.40	1.25	2.50

FANTASY MASTERPIECES (Marvel Super Heroes No. 12 on)
Feb, 1966-No. 11, Oct, 1967; Dec, 1979-No. 14, Jan, 1981
Marvel Comics Group

1-Photo of Stan Lee (12 cent-c #1,2)	3.15	9.50	22.00
2	1.00	3.00	7.00
3-8: 3-G.A. Capt. America-r begin, end #6; 1st 25 cent Giant; Colan reprint. 7-Begin G.A. Sub-Mariner, Torch-r/M. Mystery. 8-Torch battles the Sub-Mariner r-/Marvel Mystery #9	1.50	4.50	10.00
9-Origin Human Torch r-/Marvel Comics #1	1.70	5.00	12.00
10,11: 10-R/origin & 1st app. All Winners Squad from All Winners #19. 11-R/origin of Toro(H.T. #1) & Black Knight	1.15	3.50	8.00
V2#1(12/79)-52 pgs.; 75 cents; r-/origin Silver Surfer from S. Surfer #1 with			

	Good	Fine	N-Mint
editing; J. Buscema-a	.70	2.00	4.00
2-14-Silver Surfer-r	.40	1.25	2.50

FAWCETT'S FUNNY ANIMALS (No. 1-26, 80-on titled Funny Animals)
12/42-#79, 4/53; #80, 6/53-#83, 12?/53; #84, 4/54-#91, 2/56
Fawcett Publications/Charlton Comics No. 84 on

	Good	Fine	N-Mint
1-Capt. Marvel on cover; intro. Hoppy The Captain Marvel Bunny, cloned from Capt. Marvel; Billy the Kid & Willie the Worm begin	29.00	85.00	200.00
2-Xmas-c	14.00	43.00	100.00
3-5	10.00	30.00	70.00
6,7,9,10	6.50	19.00	45.00
8-Flag-c	7.00	21.00	50.00
11-20	4.30	13.00	30.00
21-40: 25-Xmas-c. 26-St. Valentines Day-c	2.65	8.00	18.00
41-88,90,91	2.00	6.00	14.00
89-(2/55)-Merry Mailman ish (TV)-part photo-c	2.30	7.00	16.00

FEAR (Adventure into . . .)
Nov, 1970-No. 31, Dec, 1975 (No.1-6: Giant Size)
Marvel Comics Group

	Good	Fine	N-Mint
1-Fantasy & Sci-Fi reprints in early issues	.85	2.50	5.00
2-6	.40	1.25	2.50
7-9,11,12: 11-N. Adams-c. 12-Starlin/Buckler-a	.35	1.00	2.00
10-Man-Thing begins, ends #19; Morrow/Chaykin-c/a	1.00	3.00	6.00
13,14,16-18,20-31: 17-Origin/1st app. Wundarr. 20-Morbius, the Living Vampire begins, ends #31; Gulacy-a(p)	.25	.75	1.50
15-1st full-length Man-Thing story	.50	1.50	3.00
19-Intro. Howard the Duck; Val Mayerik-a	1.70	5.00	12.00

FEATURE COMICS (Formerly Feature Funnies)
No. 21, June, 1939-No. 144, May, 1950
Quality Comics Group

	Good	Fine	N-Mint
21-Strips continue from Feature Funnies	25.00	75.00	175.00
22-26: 23-Charlie Chan begins	19.00	58.00	135.00
26-(nn, nd)-c-in one color, (10 cents, 36 pgs.; issue No. blanked out. 2 variations exist, each contain half of the regular #26)	5.50	16.50	38.00
27-(Rare)-Origin/1st app. Dollman by Eisner	150.00	450.00	1050.00

	Good	Fine	N-Mint
28-1st Lou Fine Dollman	70.00	210.00	490.00
29,30	43.00	130.00	300.00
31-Last Clock & Charlie Chan issue	34.00	103.00	240.00
32-37: 32-Rusty Ryan & Samar begin. 34-Captain Fortune app. 37- Last Fine			
Dollman	27.00	80.00	185.00
38-41: 38-Origin the Ace of Space. 39-Origin The Destroying Demon, ends #40.			
40-Bruce Blackburn in costume	19.00	58.00	135.00
42,43,45-50: 42-USA, the Spirit of Old Glory begins. 46-Intro. Boyville Brigadiers			
in Rusty Ryan. 48-USA ends	13.00	40.00	90.00
44-Dollman by Crandall begins, ends #63; Crandall-a(2)			
	18.50	56.00	130.00
51-60: 56-Marijuana story in "Swing Session." 57-Spider Widow begins. 60-			
Raven begins, ends #71	11.00	32.00	75.00
61-68 (5/43)	10.00	30.00	70.00
69,70-Phantom Lady x-over in Spider Widow	11.00	32.00	75.00
71-80,100: 71-Phantom Lady x-over. 72-Spider Widow ends			
	7.00	21.00	50.00
81-99	6.00	18.00	42.00
101-144: 139-Last Dollman. 140-Intro. Stuntman Stetson			
	4.50	14.00	32.00

FEATURE FUNNIES (Feature Comics No. 21 on)
Oct, 1937-No. 20, May, 1939
Harry 'A' Chesler

	Good	Fine	N-Mint
1(V9#1-indicia)-Joe Palooka, Mickey Finn, The Bungles, Jane Arden, Dixie			
Dugan, Big Top, Ned Brant, Strange As It Seems, & Off the Record strip			
reprints begin	148.00	445.00	890.00
2-The Hawk app. (11/37); Goldberg-c	62.00	185.00	435.00
3-Hawks of Seas begins by Eisner, ends #12; The Clock begins; Christmas-c			
	43.00	130.00	300.00
4,5	31.00	92.00	215.00
6-12: 11-Archie O'Toole by Bud Thomas begins, ends #22			
	25.00	75.00	175.00
13-Espionage, Starring Black X begins by Eisner, ends #20			
	27.00	81.00	190.00
14-20	22.00	65.00	150.00

FELIX THE CAT (See The Funnies, New Funnies & Popular Comics)
2-3/48-No. 118, Nov, 1961; Sept-Nov, 1962-No. 12, July-Sept, 1965
Dell Publ. No. 1-19/Toby No. 20-61/Harvey No. 62-118/Dell

	Good	Fine	N-Mint
1(Dell)	16.00	48.00	110.00
2	8.00	24.00	55.00
3-5	6.00	18.00	42.00
6-19(2-3/51-Dell)	4.30	13.00	30.00
20-30(Toby): 28-(2/52)-Some copies have #29 on cover, #28 on inside			
	3.70	11.00	26.00
31,34,35-No Messmer-a	2.00	6.00	14.00
32,33,36-61(6/55-Toby)-Last Messmer issue	2.65	8.00	18.00
62(8/55)-100 (Harvey)	1.15	3.50	8.00
101-118(11/61)	1.00	3.00	7.00
12-269-211(#1, 9-11/62)(Dell)	1.70	5.00	12.00
212(7-9/65)(Dell, TV)	.85	2.60	6.00
3-D Comic Book 1(1953-One Shot)	22.00	65.00	150.00
Summer Annual 2('52)-Early 1930s Sunday strip-r (Exist?)			
	19.00	56.00	130.00
Summer Annual nn('53, 100 pgs., Toby)-1930s daily & Sunday-r			
	19.00	56.00	130.00
Winter Annual 2('54, 100 pgs., Toby)-1930s daily & Sunday-r			
	12.00	36.00	85.00
Summer Annual 3('55) (Exist?)	11.00	32.00	75.00

FIGHT COMICS

Jan, 1940-No. 83, 11/52; No. 84, Wint, 1952-53; No. 85, Spring, 1953;
    No. 86, Summer, 1954
Fiction House Magazines

1-Origin Spy Fighter, Starring Saber; Fine/Eisner-c; Eisner-a			
	100.00	300.00	700.00
2-Joe Louis life story	43.00	130.00	300.00
3-Rip Regan, the Power Man begins	40.00	120.00	280.00
4,5: 4-Fine-c	30.00	90.00	210.00
6-10: 6,7-Powell-c	25.00	75.00	175.00
11-14: Rip Regan ends	22.00	65.00	150.00
15-1st Super American	29.00	86.00	200.00
16-Captain Fight begins; Spy Fighter ends	29.00	86.00	200.00
17,18: Super American ends	25.00	75.00	175.00
19-Captain Fight ends; Senorita Rio begins (origin & 1st app.); Rip Carson, Chute			
Trooper begins	25.00	75.00	175.00
20	19.00	56.00	130.00
21-30	12.00	36.00	85.00
31,33-50: 31-Decapitation-c. 44-Capt. Flight returns. 48-Used in **Love and Death**			

	Good	Fine	N-Mint
by Legman	11.00	32.00	75.00
32-Tiger Girl begins	11.50	34.00	80.00
51-Origin Tiger Girl; Patsy Pin-Up app.	17.00	51.00	120.00
52-60	8.50	25.50	60.00
61-Origin Tiger Girl retold	11.00	32.00	75.00
62-65-Last Baker issue	8.50	25.50	60.00
66-78: 78-Used in POP, pg. 99	7.00	21.00	50.00
79-The Space Rangers app.	7.00	21.00	50.00
80-85	6.00	18.00	42.00
86-Two Tigerman stories by Evans; Moreira-a	7.00	21.00	50.00

FIGHTING AMERICAN
Apr-May, 1954-No. 7, Apr-May, 1955
Headline Publications/Prize

1-Origin Fighting American & Speedboy; S&K-c/a(3)			
	80.00	240.00	560.00
2-S&K-a(3)	39.00	116.00	270.00
3,4-S&K-a(3)	34.00	100.00	235.00
5-S&K-a(2); Kirby/?-a	34.00	100.00	235.00
6-Origin-r (4 pgs.) plus 2 pgs. by S&K	31.00	92.00	215.00
7-Kirby-a	29.00	86.00	200.00

FIGHTING YANK (See America's Best & Startling Comics)
Sept, 1942-No. 29, Aug, 1949
Nedor/Better Publ./Standard

1-The Fighting Yank begins; Mystico, the Wonder Man app; bondage-c			
	68.00	205.00	475.00
2	32.00	95.00	225.00
3	22.00	65.00	150.00
4	17.00	51.00	120.00
5-10: 7-The Grim Reaper app.	13.00	40.00	90.00
11-20: 11-The Oracle app. 12-Hirohito bondage-c. 18-The American Eagle app.			
	11.50	34.00	80.00
21,23,24: 21-Kara, Jungle Princess app. 24-Miss Masque app.			
	13.00	40.00	90.00
22-Miss Masque-c/story	16.00	48.00	110.00
25-Robinson/Meskin-a; strangulation, lingerie panel; The Cavalier app.			
	16.00	48.00	110.00
26-29: All-Robinson/Meskin-a. 28-One pg. Williamson-a			
	12.00	36.00	85.00

FIRESTAR
March, 1986-No. 4, June, 1986 (From Spider-Man TV series)
Marvel Comics Group

	Good	Fine	N-Mint
1-X-Men & New Mutants app.	.35	1.00	2.00
2-Wolverine-c by Art Adams (p)	.85	2.50	5.00
3,4	.25	.75	1.50

FLAME, THE (See Wonderworld Comics)
Summer, 1940-No. 8, Jan, 1942 (#1,2: 68 pgs; #3-8: 44 pgs.)
Fox Features Syndicate

1-Flame stories from Wonderworld #5-9; origin The Flame; Lou Fine-a, 36 pgs., r-/Wonderworld 3,10	150.00	450.00	900.00
2-Fine-a(2). Wing Turner by Tuska	61.00	182.00	425.00
3-8: 3-Powell-a	35.00	105.00	245.00

FLASH, THE (Formerly Flash Comics; see Adventure, The Brave and the Bold, Crisis On . . . , Green Lantern, Showcase & World's Finest)
No. 105, Feb-Mar, 1959-No. 350, Oct, 1985
National Periodical Publ./DC Comics

105-Origin Flash(retold), & Mirror Master	170.00	510.00	1200.00
106-Origin Grodd & Pied Piper; Flash's 1st visit to Gorilla City; begin Grodd the Super Gorilla trilogy, ends #108	65.00	195.00	450.00
107,108-Grodd trilogy ends	35.00	105.00	240.00
109	28.00	86.00	200.00
110-Intro/origin The Weather Wizard & Kid Flash who later becomes Flash in Crisis On Infinite Earths #12	52.00	156.00	360.00
111	16.50	50.00	115.00
112-Origin & 1st app. Elongated Man	17.00	51.00	120.00
113-Origin & 1st app. Trickster	18.00	54.00	125.00
114-Captain Cold app. (see Showcase #8)	14.00	42.00	99.00
115,116,118-120: 119-Elongated Man marries Sue Dearborn	11.50	34.00	80.00
117-Origin & 1st app. Capt. Boomerang	14.00	42.00	99.00
121,122: 122-Origin & 1st app. The Top	8.50	25.50	60.00
123-Re-intro. Golden Age Flash; origins of both Flashes; 1st mention of an Earth II where DC Golden Age heroes live	49.00	147.00	340.00
124-Last 10 cent issue	8.00	24.00	55.00

	Good	Fine	N-Mint
125-128,130-136,138,140: 128-Origin Abra Kadabra			
	5.30	16.00	38.00
129-G.A. Flash x-over; J.S.A. cameo in flashback	14.00	42.00	99.00
137-G.A. Flash x-over; J.S.A. cameo (1st real app. since 2-3/51); 1st Silver Age			
app. Vandall Savage	23.00	69.00	160.00
139-Origin/1st app. Prof. Zoom	6.50	19.00	45.00
141-150: 142-Trickster app.	3.60	11.00	25.00
151-G.A. Flash versus The Shade	4.30	13.00	30.00
152-159	2.30	7.00	16.00
160-80-Pg. Giant G-21-G.A.-r Flash & Johnny Quick			
	3.60	11.00	25.00
161-168,170: 165-Silver Age Flash weds Iris West. 167-New facts about Flash's			
origin. 170-Dr. Mid-Nite, Dr. Fate, G.A. Flash x-over			
	2.15	6.50	15.00
169-80-Pg. Giant G-34	3.60	11.00	25.00
171-174,176,177,179,180: 171-JLA, Green Lantern, Atom flashbacks. 173- G.A.			
Flash x-over. 174-Barry Allen reveals I.D. to wife			
	1.60	4.80	11.00
175-2nd Superman/Flash race; JLA cameo	2.85	8.50	20.00
178-80-Pg. Giant G-46	2.30	7.00	16.00
181-186,188-195,197-200: 186-Re-intro. Sargon	1.00	3.00	6.00
187,196: 68-Pg. Giants G-58, G-70	1.50	4.50	10.00
201-204,206-213,216,220: 201-New G.A. Flash story. 208-52 pg. begin, end			
#213,215,216. 206-Elongated Man begins	.50	1.50	3.00
205-68-Pg. Giant G-82	1.00	3.00	7.00
214-DC 100 Page Super Spectacluar DC-11; origin Metal Men-r/Showcase #37;			
never before pubbed G.A. Flash story	.85	2.50	5.00
215 (52 pgs.)-Flash-r/Showcase #4; G.A. Flash x-over, r-in #216			
	1.00	3.00	6.00
217-219: Neal Adams-a in all. 217-Green Lantern/Green Arrow series begins. 219-			
Last Green Arrow	1.00	3.00	7.00
221-225,227,228,230,231	.50	1.50	3.00
226-Neal Adams-a	.75	2.25	4.50
229,232,233-(All 100pgs.)-G.A. Flash-r & new-a	.60	1.75	3.00
234-274,277-288,290: 243-Death of The Top. 246-Last Green Lantern. 256-Death			
of The Top retold. 265-267-(44 pgs.). 267-Origin of Flash's uniform. 270-			
Intro The Clown. 286-Intro/origin Rainbow Raider	.35	1.00	2.00
275,276-Iris West Allen dies	.40	1.25	2.50
289-Perez 1st DC art; new Firestorm series begins, ends #304			
	.50	1.50	3.00

	Good	Fine	N-Mint
291-299,301-305: 298-Intro/origin new Shade	.35	1.00	2.00
300-(52 pgs.)-Origin Flash retold; 25th ann. ish	.50	1.50	3.00
306-Dr. Fate by Giffen begins, ends #313	.40	1.25	2.50
307-313-Giffen-a. 309-Origin Flash retold	.35	1.00	2.00
314-349: 344-Origin Kid Flash	.35	1.00	2.00
350-Double size ($1.25)	.75	2.25	4.50
Annual 1(10-12/63, 84 pgs.)-Origin Elongated Man & Kid Flash-r; origin Grod, G.A. Flash-r	27.00	81.00	190.00

FLASH
June, 1987-Present (75 cents, $1.00 #17 on)
DC Comics

	Good	Fine	N-Mint
1-Guice-c/a begins; New Teen Titans app.	1.50	4.50	9.00
2	1.00	3.00	6.00
3-Intro. Kilgore	.70	2.00	4.00
4-6: 5-Intro. Speed McGee	.50	1.50	3.00
7-10: 7-1st app. Blue Trinity. 8,9-Millennium tie-ins. 9-1st app. The Chunk	.40	1.25	2.50
11-20: 12-Free extra 16 pg. Dr. Light story. 19-Free extra 16 pg. Flash story	.35	1.00	2.00
21-30: 28-Capt. Cold app. 29-New Phantom Lady app.	.25	.75	1.50
31-49,51-56: 40-Dr. Alchemy app.		.50	1.00
50-($1.75, 52 pgs.)	.30	.90	1.80
Annual 1 (9/87, $1.25)	.60	1.75	3.50
Annual 2 (10/88, $1.50)	.50	1.50	3.00
Annual 3 (7/89, $1.75, 68 pgs.)-Gives history of G.A., Silver Age, & new Flash in text	.40	1.25	2.50
Special 1 (1990, $2.95, 84 pgs.)-50th anniversary issue; Kubert-c	.60	1.75	3.50

FLASH COMICS (The Flash No. 105 on) (Also see All-Flash)
Jan, 1940-No. 104, Feb, 1949
National Periodical Publications/All-American

	Good	Fine	VF-NM
1-Origin The Flash by Harry Lampert, Hawkman by Gardner Fox, The Whip, & Johnny Thunder by Stan Asch; Cliff Cornwall by Moldoff, Minute Movies begin; Moldoff (Shelly) cover; 1st app. Shiera Sanders who later becomes Hawkgirl, #24 (on sale 11/10/39)	1500.00	3750.00	9000.00

Flash Comics #42, © DC Comics

	Good	Fine	N-Mint
2-Rod Rian begins, ends #11	335.00	835.00	2000.00
3-The King begins, ends #41	258.00	645.00	1550.00
4-Moldoff (Shelly) Hawkman begins	225.00	560.00	1350.00
5	200.00	500.00	1200.00
6,7	158.00	395.00	950.00
8-10	120.00	302.00	725.00
11-20: 12-Les Watts begins; "Sparks" #16 on. 17-Last Cliff Cornwall			
	92.00	230.00	550.00
21-23	79.00	200.00	475.00
24-Shiera becomes Hawkgirl (12/41)	92.00	230.00	550.00
25-30: 28-Last Les Sparks. 29-Ghost Patrol begins (origin, 1st app.), ends #104			
	67.00	167.00	400.00
31-40: 33-Origin Shade	58.00	145.00	350.00
41-50	54.00	135.00	325.00
51-61: 59-Last Minute Movies. 61-Last Moldoff Hawkman			
	45.00	112.00	270.00
62-Hawkman by Kubert begins	57.00	142.00	340.00
63-70: 66-68-Hop Harrigan in all	45.00	112.00	270.00

	Good	Fine	N-Mint
71-85: 80-Atom begins, ends #104	45.00	112.00	270.00
86-Intro. The Black Canary in Johnny Thunder; rare in Mint due to black ink			
smearing on white cover	117.00	291.00	700.00
87-90: 88-Origin Ghost. 89-Intro villain Thorn	57.00	141.00	340.00
91,93-99: 98-Atom dons new costume	71.00	177.00	425.00
92-1st solo Black Canary	103.00	255.00	615.00
100 (10/48),103(Scarce)-52 pgs. each	117.00	291.00	700.00
101,102(Scarce)	92.00	230.00	550.00
104-Origin The Flash retold (Scarce)	217.00	541.00	1300.00

FLASH GORDON (See King Comics & The Phantom)
No. 10, 1943-No. 512, Nov, 1953
Dell Publishing Co.

	Good	Fine	N-Mint
4-Color 10(1943)-by Alex Raymond; reprints/ "The Ice Kingdom"			
	50.00	150.00	350.00
4-Color 84(1945)-by Alex Raymond; reprints/ "The Fiery Desert"			
	33.00	100.00	230.00
4-Color 173,190: 190-Bondage-c	11.50	34.00	80.00
4-Color 204,247	9.00	27.00	62.00
4-Color 424	6.50	19.50	45.00
2-(5-7/53-Dell)-Evans-a	3.50	10.50	24.00
4-Color 512	3.50	10.50	24.00

FLASH GORDON
9/66-#11, 12/67; #12, 2/69-#18, 1/70; #19, 10-11/78-#37, 3/82
(Painted covers No. 19-30, 34)
King #1-11/Charlton #12-18/Gold Key #19-23/Whitman #24 on

	Good	Fine	N-Mint
1-Williamson c/a(2); E.C. swipe/Incredible S.F. #32. Mandrake story			
	2.00	6.00	14.00
2-Bolle, Gil Kane-c; Mandrake story	1.50	4.50	10.00
3-Williamson-c	1.70	5.00	12.00
4-Secret Agent X-9 begins, Williamson-c/a(3)	1.70	5.00	12.00
5-Williamson-c/a(2)	1.70	5.00	12.00
6,8-Crandall-a. 8-Secret Agent X-9-r	2.30	7.00	16.00
7-Raboy-a	1.70	5.00	12.00
9,10-Raymond-r. 10-Buckler's 1st-a (11/67)	2.00	6.00	14.00
11-Crandall-a	1.50	4.50	10.00
12-Crandall-c/a	1.70	5.00	12.00
13-Jeff Jones-a (15 pgs.)	1.70	5.00	12.00

	Good	Fine	N-Mint
14-17: 17-Brick Bradford story	.85	2.60	6.00
18-Kaluta-a (1st pro work?)	1.00	3.00	7.00
19(9/78, G.K.), 20-30(10/80)	.35	1.00	2.00
30 (7/81; re-issue)		.30	.60
31-33: Movie adaptation; Williamson-a		.50	1.00
34-37: Movie adaptation		.40	.80

FLASH GORDON
June, 1988-No. 9, Holiday, 1988-'89 ($1.25, color, mini-series)
DC Comics

1-Painted-c	.35	1.00	2.00
2-9: 5-Painted-c	.25	.75	1.50

FLINTSTONES, THE (TV)
No. 2, Nov-Dec, 1961-No. 60, Sept, 1970 (Hanna-Barbera)
Dell Publ. Co./Gold Key No. 7 (10/62) on

2	4.50	14.00	32.00
3-6(7-8/62)	3.00	9.00	21.00
7 (10/62; 1st GK)	3.00	9.00	21.00
8-10: Mr. & Mrs. J. Evil Scientist begin?	2.65	8.00	18.00
11-1st app. Pebbles (6/63)	3.50	10.50	24.00
12-15,17-20	2.30	7.00	16.00
16-1st app. Bamm-Bamm (1/64)	2.65	8.00	18.00
21-30: 24-1st app. The Grusomes app.	2.00	6.00	14.00
31-33,35-40: 31-Xmas-c. 33-Meet Frankenstein & Dracula. 39-Reprints			
	1.70	5.00	12.00
34-1st app. The Great Gazoo	2.30	7.00	16.00
41-60: 45-Last 12 cent issue	1.50	4.50	10.00
At N. Y. World's Fair('64)-J.W. Books(25 cents)-1st printing; no date on-c			
(29 cent version exists, 2nd print?)	2.65	8.00	18.00
At N. Y. World's Fair (1965 on-c; re-issue). NOTE: Warehouse find in 1984			
	.70	2.00	4.00
Bigger & Boulder 1(#30013-211) (Gold Key Giant, 11/62, 25 cents, 84 pgs.)			
	4.30	13.00	30.00
Bigger & Boulder 2-(25 cents)(1966)-reprints B&B No. 1			
	3.60	11.00	25.00
... With Pebbles & Bamm Bamm(100 pgs., G.K.)-30028-511 (paper-c, 25 cents)			
(11/65)	3.60	11.00	25.00

FLINTSTONES, THE (TV)(. . . & Pebbles)
Nov, 1970-No. 50, Feb, 1977 (Hanna-Barbera)
Charlton Comics

	Good	Fine	N-Mint
1	2.15	6.50	15.00
2	1.15	3.50	8.00
3-7,9,10	.85	2.60	6.00
8-"Flintstones Summer Vacation," 52 pgs. (Summer, 1971)			
	1.00	3.00	7.00
11-20	.70	2.00	5.00
21-50: 37-Byrne text illos. 42-Byrne-a, 2pgs.	.70	2.00	4.00

FLY MAN (Formerly Adventures of The Fly)
No. 32, July, 1965-No. 39, Sept, 1966
Mighty Comics Group (Radio Comics) (Archie)

	Good	Fine	N-Mint
32,33-Comet, Shield, Black Hood, The Fly & Flygirl x-over; re-intro. Wizard, Hangman #33	2.85	8.50	20.00
34-36: 34-Shield begins. 35-Origin Black Hood. 36-Hangman x-over in Shield; re-intro. & origin of Web	1.70	5.00	12.00
37-39: 37-Hangman, Wizard x-over in Flyman; last Shield issue. 38-Web story. 39-Steel Sterling story	1.70	5.00	12.00

FOOLKILLER (Also see Defenders #73, Man-Thing #3 & Omega #8)
Oct, 1990-No. 10, July, 1991 ($1.75, color, limited series)
Marvel Comics

	Good	Fine	N-Mint
1-Origin 3rd Foolkiller; Greg Salinger app.	.35	1.00	2.00
2-10: DeZuniga-a(i) in 1-4	.30	.90	1.80

FORBIDDEN WORLDS
7-8/51-No. 34, 10-11/54; No. 35, 8/55-No. 145, 8/67
American Comics Group

	Good	Fine	N-Mint
1-Williamson/Frazetta-a (10 pgs.)	64.00	193.00	450.00
2	29.00	85.00	200.00
3-Williamson/Wood/Orlando-a (7 pgs.)	31.00	92.00	215.00
4	14.00	43.00	100.00
5-Williamson/Krenkel-a (8 pgs.)	25.00	75.00	175.00
6-Harrison/Williamson-a (8 pgs.)	22.00	65.00	155.00

	Good	Fine	N-Mint
7,8,10	11.00	32.00	75.00
9-A-Bomb explosion story	11.50	34.00	80.00
11-20	7.00	21.00	50.00
21-33: 24-E.C. swipe by Landau	5.00	15.00	35.00
34(10-11/54)(Becomes Young Heroes #35 on)-Last pre-code issue; A-Bomb			
explosion story	5.00	15.00	35.00
35(8/55)-62	2.85	8.50	20.00
63,69,76,78-Williamson-a in all; w/Krenkel #69	4.30	13.00	30.00
64,66-68,70-72,74,75,77,79-90: 86-Flying saucer-c	2.15	6.50	15.00
65-"There's a New Moon Tonight" listed in #114 as holding 1st record fan mail			
response	2.15	6.50	15.00
73-1st app. Herbie by Ogden Whitney	17.00	51.00	120.00
91-93,95-100	1.50	4.50	10.00
94-Herbie app.	4.30	13.00	30.00
101-109,111-113,115,117-120	1.15	3.50	8.00
110,114,116-Herbie app. 114-1st Herbie-c; contains list of editor's top 20 ACG			
stories. 116-Herbie goes to Hell	2.65	8.00	18.00
121-124: 124-Magic Agent app.	1.15	3.50	8.00
125-Magic Agent app.; intro. & origin Magicman series, ends #141			
	1.30	4.00	9.00
126-130	1.00	3.00	7.00
131-141: 133-Origin/1st app. Dragonia in Magicman (1-2/66); returns in #138.			
136-Nemesis x-over in Magicman. 140-Mark Midnight app. by Ditko			
	.85	2.60	6.00
142-145	.70	2.00	5.00

FOREVER PEOPLE, THE
Feb-Mar, 1971-No. 11, Oct-Nov, 1972
National Periodical Publications

1-Superman x-over; Kirby-c/a begins	1.70	5.00	12.00
2-5: 4-G.A. reprints begin, end #9	1.15	3.50	8.00
6-11: 9,10-Deadman app.	.85	2.60	6.00

FOUR MOST (. . . Boys No. 32-41)
Winter, 1941-42-V8#5(#36), 9-10/49; #37, 11-12/49-#41, 6-7/50
Novelty Publications/Star Publications No. 37-on

V1#1-The Target by Sid Greene, The Cadet & Dick Cole begin with origins retold;			
produced by Funnies Inc.	50.00	150.00	350.00
2-Last Target	24.00	72.00	165.00

	Good	Fine	N-Mint
3-Flag-c	21.00	62.00	145.00
4-1pg. Dr. Seuss(signed)	16.00	48.00	110.00
V2#1-4, V3#1-4	4.00	12.00	28.00
V4#1-4	3.00	9.00	21.00
V5#1-5: 1-The Target & Targeteers app.	2.65	8.00	18.00
V6#1-4,6: 1-White Rider & Super Horse begin	2.65	8.00	18.00
5-L. B. Cole-c	4.00	12.00	28.00
V7#1,3,5, V8#1	2.65	8.00	18.00
2,4,6-L. B. Cole-c. 6-Last Dick Cole	4.00	12.00	28.00
V8#2,3,5-L. B. Cole-c/a	5.30	16.00	38.00
4-L. B. Cole-a	3.50	10.50	24.00
37-41: 38-40-L.B. Cole-c. 38-Johnny Weismuller life story. 41-Exist?			
	3.50	10.50	24.00

FOX AND THE CROW (See Comic Cavalcade & Real Screen Comics)
Dec-Jan, 1951-52-No. 108, Feb-Mar, 1968
National Periodical Publications

1	54.00	160.00	375.00
2(Scarce)	27.00	80.00	185.00
3-5	16.00	48.00	110.00
6-10	11.00	32.00	75.00
11-20	7.00	21.00	50.00
21-40: 22-Last pre-code (2/55)	4.30	13.00	30.00
41-60	3.00	9.00	21.00
61-80	2.00	6.00	14.00
81-94	1.30	4.00	9.00
95-Stanley & His Monster begins (origin)	2.00	6.00	14.00
96-99,101-108	1.00	3.00	7.00
100	1.30	4.00	9.00

FRANKENSTEIN (The Monster of . . .)
Jan, 1973-No. 18, Sept, 1975
Marvel Comics Group

1-Ploog-c/a begins, ends #6	.70	2.00	4.00
2-18: 8,9-Dracula app.	.25	.75	1.50

FRANKENSTEIN COMICS (Also See Prize Comics)
Sum, 1945-V5#5(#33), Oct-Nov, 1954
Prize Publications (Crestwood/Feature)

	Good	Fine	N-Mint
1-Frankenstein begins by Dick Briefer (origin); Frank Sinatra parody			
	40.00	120.00	280.00
2	18.00	54.00	125.00
3-5	14.00	43.00	100.00
6-10: 7-S&K a(r)/Headline Comics. 8(7-8/47)-Superman satire			
	13.00	40.00	90.00
11-17(1-2/49)-11-Boris Karloff parody-c/story. 17-Last humor issue			
	10.00	30.00	70.00
18(3/52)-New origin, horror series begins	13.00	40.00	90.00
19,20(V3#4, 8-9/52)	7.00	21.00	50.00
21(V3#5), 22(V3#6)	7.00	21.00	50.00
23(V4#1)-#28(V4#6)	6.50	19.00	45.00
29(V5#1)-#33(V5#5)	6.50	19.00	45.00

FRIENDLY GHOST, CASPER, THE (Also see Casper . . .)
Aug, 1958-No. 224, Oct, 1982; No. 225, Oct, 1986-No. 253, 1989
Harvey Publications

	Good	Fine	N-Mint
1-Infinity-c	14.00	42.00	100.00
2	7.00	21.00	50.00
3-10: 6-X-Mas-c	4.00	12.00	28.00
11-20: 18-X-Mas-c	2.65	8.00	18.00
21-30	1.20	3.50	8.00
31-50	.70	2.00	5.00
51-100: 54-X-Mas-c	.55	1.60	3.20
101-159		.60	1.20
160-163: All 52 pg. Giants	.25	.75	1.50
164-237: 173,179,185-Cub Scout Specials		.35	.70
238-253: 238-Begin $1.00-c		.50	1.00

FRONTLINE COMBAT
July-Aug, 1951-No. 15, Jan, 1954
E. C. Comics

	Good	Fine	N-Mint
1	39.00	118.00	275.00
2	26.00	79.00	185.00
3	19.00	58.00	135.00
4-Used in **SOTI**, pg. 257; contains "Airburst" by Kurtzman which is his personal all-time favorite story	16.00	48.00	115.00
5	14.00	43.00	100.00
6-10	11.50	34.00	80.00

	Good	Fine	N-Mint
11-15	9.30	28.00	65.00

FUNNIES, THE (New Funnies No. 65 on)
Oct, 1936-No. 64, May, 1942
Dell Publishing Co.

	Good	Fine	N-Mint
1-Tailspin Tommy, Mutt & Jeff, Alley Oop (1st app?), Capt. Easy, Don Dixon begin	100.00	250.00	600.00
2-Scribbly by Mayer begins	43.00	130.00	300.00
3	38.00	115.00	265.00
4,5: 4-Christmas-c	31.00	92.00	215.00
6-10	24.00	73.00	170.00
11-20: 16-Christmas-c	22.00	65.00	150.00
21-29	18.00	54.00	125.00
30-John Carter of Mars (origin) begins by Edgar Rice Burroughs	54.00	160.00	375.00
31-44: 33-John Coleman Burroughs art begins on John Carter. 35-(9/39)-Mr. District Attorney begins-based on radio show	31.00	92.00	215.00
45-Origin/1st app. Phantasmo, the Master of the World (Dell's 1st super-hero) & his sidekick Whizzer McGee	24.00	73.00	170.00
46-50: 46-The Black Knight begins, ends #62	22.00	65.00	150.00
51-56-Last ERB John Carter of Mars	22.00	65.00	150.00
57-Intro. & origin Captain Midnight	54.00	160.00	375.00
58-60	22.00	65.00	150.00
61-Andy Panda begins by Walter Lantz	24.00	70.00	165.00
62,63: 63-Last Captain Midnight-c; bondage-c	22.00	65.00	150.00
64-Format change; Oswald the Rabbit, Felix the Cat, Li'l Eight Ball app.; origin & 1st app. Woody Woodpecker in Oswald; last Capt. Midnight	45.00	135.00	315.00

FUNNIES ON PARADE (Premium)
1933 (Probably the 1st comic book) (36 pgs.; slick cover)
No date or publisher listed
Eastern Color Printing Co.

	Good	Fine	VF-NM
nn-Contains Sunday page reprints of Mutt & Jeff, Joe Palooka, Hairbreadth Harry, Reg'lar Fellers, Skippy, & others (10,000 print run). This book was printed for Proctor & Gamble to be given away & came out before Famous Funnies or Century of Comics.	415.00	1040.00	2500.00

FUNNY PAGES (Formerly The Comics Magazine)
No. 6, Nov, 1936-No. 42, Oct, 1940
Comics Magazine Co./Ultem Publ.(Chesler)/Centaur Publications

	Good	Fine	N-Mint
V1#6 (nn, nd)-The Clock begins (2 pgs., 1st app.), ends #11			
	50.00	150.00	350.00
7-11	32.00	95.00	225.00
V2#1 (9/37)(V2#2 on-c; V2#1 in indicia)	25.00	75.00	175.00
V2#2 (10/37)(V2#3 on-c; V2#2 in indicia)	25.00	75.00	175.00
3(11/37)-5	25.00	75.00	175.00
6(1st Centaur, 3/38)	39.00	118.00	275.00
7-9	29.00	85.00	200.00
10(Scarce)-1st app. of The Arrow by Gustavson (Blue costume)			
	125.00	310.00	750.00
11,12	54.00	160.00	375.00
V3#1-6	54.00	160.00	375.00
7-1st Arrow-c (9/39)	68.00	205.00	475.00
8,9: 9-Tarpe Mills jungle-c	54.00	160.00	375.00
10-2nd Arrow-c	59.00	178.00	415.00
V4#1(1/40, Arrow-c)-(Rare)-The Owl & The Phantom Rider app.; origin Mantoka, Maker of Magic by Jack Cole. Mad Ming begins, ends #42. Tarpe Mills-a			
	64.00	193.00	450.00
35-38: 35-Arrow-c. 36-38-Mad Ming-c	47.00	140.00	325.00
39-42-Arrow-c. 42-Last Arrow	47.00	140.00	325.00

FUNNY STUFF
Summer, 1944-No. 79, July-Aug, 1954
All-American/National Periodical Publications No. 7 on

	Good	Fine	N-Mint
1-The Three Mouseketeers & The "Terrific Whatzit" begin-Sheldon Mayer-a			
	54.00	160.00	375.00
2-Sheldon Mayer-a	27.00	80.00	185.00
3-5	16.00	48.00	110.00
6-10 (6/46)	10.00	30.00	70.00
11-20: 18-The Dodo & the Frog begin?	7.00	21.00	50.00
21,23-30: 24-Infinity-c	5.00	15.00	35.00
22-Superman cameo	16.50	50.00	115.00
31-79: 75-Bo Bunny by Mayer	3.15	9.50	22.00

G

GABBY HAYES ADVENTURE COMICS
Dec, 1953
Toby Press

	Good	Fine	N-Mint
1-Photo-c	7.00	21.00	50.00

GABBY HAYES WESTERN (Movie star) (See Monte Hale, Real Western Hero
    & Western Hero)
Nov, 1948-No. 50, Jan, 1953; No. 51, Dec, 1954-No. 59, Jan, 1957
Fawcett/Toby Press/Charlton Comics No. 51 on

	Good	Fine	N-Mint
1-Gabby & his horse Corker begin; Photo front/back-c begin	27.00	80.00	185.00
2	12.00	36.00	85.00
3-5	9.30	28.00	65.00
6-10: 9-Young Falcon begins	8.00	24.00	56.00
11-20: 19-Last photo back-c	5.70	17.00	40.00
21-49: 20,22,24,26,28,29-(52 pgs.)	3.70	11.00	26.00
50-(1/53)-Last Fawcett issue; last photo-c?	4.00	12.00	28.00
51-(12/54)-1st Charlton issue; photo-c	4.00	12.00	28.00
52-59(Charlton '55-57): 53,55-Photo-c	2.30	7.00	16.00

GANG BUSTERS (Radio/TV)
Dec-Jan, 1947-48-No. 67, Dec-Jan, 1958-59 (No. 1-23: 52 pgs.)
National Periodical Publications

	Good	Fine	N-Mint
1	36.00	107.00	250.00
2	16.00	48.00	110.00
3-8	9.30	28.00	65.00
9,10-Photo-c	11.00	32.00	75.00
11-13-Photo-c	8.50	25.50	60.00
14,17-Frazetta-a, 8 pgs. each. 14-Photo-c	18.00	54.00	125.00
15,16,18-20	5.70	17.00	40.00
21-30: 26-Kirby-a	4.30	13.00	30.00
31-44: 44-Last Pre-code (2-3/55)	3.60	11.00	25.00
45-67	2.65	8.00	18.00

GENE AUTRY COMICS (Movie, Radio star; singing cowboy)
    (Dell takes over with No. 11)
1941 (On sale 12/31/41)-No. 10, 1943 (68 pgs.)
Fawcett Publications

	Good	Fine	N-Mint
1 (Rare)-Gene Autry & his horse Champion begin			
	156.00	390.00	935.00
2	52.00	156.00	365.00
3-5	40.00	120.00	280.00
6-10	35.00	105.00	245.00

GENE AUTRY COMICS (. . . & Champion No. 102 on)
No. 11, 1943-No. 121, Jan-Mar, 1959 (TV-later issues)
Dell Publishing Co.

11 (1943, 60 pgs.)-Continuation of Fawcett series; photo back-c			
	39.00	118.00	270.00
12 (2/44, 60 pgs.)	37.00	110.00	260.00
4-Color 47(1944, 60 pgs.)	36.00	107.00	250.00
4-Color 57(11/44),66('45)(52 pgs. each)	31.00	92.00	215.00
4-Color 75,83('45, 36 pgs. each)	25.00	75.00	175.00
4-Color 93,100('45-46, 36 pgs. each)	21.00	62.00	145.00
1(5-6/46, 52 pgs.)	36.00	107.00	250.00
2(7-8/46)-Photo-c begin, end #111	18.00	54.00	125.00
3-5: 4-Intro Flapjack Hobbs	14.00	43.00	100.00
6-10	10.00	30.00	70.00
11-20: 12-Line drawn-c. 20-Panhandle Pete begins	7.00	21.00	50.00
21-29(36 pgs.)	5.70	17.00	40.00
30-40(52 pgs.)	5.70	17.00	40.00
41-56(52 pgs.)	4.30	13.00	30.00
57-66(36 pgs.): 58-X-mas-c	2.85	8.50	20.00
67-80(52 pgs.)	3.50	10.50	24.00
81-90(52 pgs.): 82-X-mas-c. 87-Blank inside-c	2.65	8.00	18.00
91-99(36 pgs. No. 91-on). 94-X-mas-c	1.70	5.00	12.00
100	2.65	8.00	18.00
101-111-Last Gene Autry photo-c	1.70	5.00	12.00
112-121-All Champion painted-c	1.15	3.50	8.00

GEORGIE COMICS (. . . & Judy Comics #20-35?)
Spring, 1945-No. 39, Oct, 1952
Timely Comics/GPI No. 1-34

	Good	Fine	N-Mint
1-Dave Berg-a	9.30	28.00	65.00
2	4.50	14.00	32.00
3-5,7,8	3.00	9.00	21.00
6-Georgie visits Timely Comics	4.00	12.00	28.00
9,10-Kurtzman's "Hey Look" (1 & ?); Margie app.	4.00	12.00	28.00
11,12: 11-Margie, Millie app.	2.65	8.00	18.00
13-Kurtzman's "Hey Look," 3 pgs.	3.70	11.00	26.00
14-Wolverton art, 1 pg. & Kurtzman's "Hey Look"	4.00	12.00	28.00
15,16,18-20	2.00	6.00	14.00
17,29-Kurtzman's "Hey Look," 1 pg.	2.85	8.50	20.00
21-24,27,28,30-39: 21-Anti-Wertham editorial	1.50	4.50	10.00
25-Painted cover by classic pin-up artist Peter Driben			
	3.50	10.50	24.00
26-Logo design swipe from Archie Comics	1.50	4.50	10.00

GET SMART (TV)
June, 1966-No. 8, Sept, 1967 (All have Don Adams photo-c)
Dell Publishing Co.

	Good	Fine	N-Mint
1	5.70	17.00	40.00
2-Ditko-a	4.00	12.00	28.00
3-8: 3-Ditko-a(p)	3.50	10.50	24.00

GHOST RIDER (Also see Red Mask & Tim Holt)
1950-No. 14, 1954
Magazine Enterprises

	Good	Fine	N-Mint
1(A-1 #27)-Origin Ghost Rider	36.00	107.00	250.00
2-5: 2(A-1 #29), 3(A-1 #31), 4(A-1 #34), 5(A-1 #37)-All Frazetta-c only			
	36.00	107.00	250.00
6,7: 6(A-1 #44), 7(A-1 #51)	13.00	40.00	90.00
8,9: 8(A-1 #57)-Drug use story, 9(A-1 #69)-L.S.D. story			
	11.00	32.00	75.00
10(A-1 #71)-vs. Frankenstein	11.00	32.00	75.00
11-14: 11(A-1 #75), 12(A-1 #80, bondage-c), 13(A-1 #84), 14(A-1 #112)			
	8.50	25.50	60.00

GHOST RIDER, THE
Feb, 1967-No. 7, Nov, 1967 (Western hero)(All 12 cent-c)
Marvel Comics Group

Ghost Rider V2, #1, © Marvel Comics

	Good	Fine	N-Mint
1-Origin Ghost Rider; Kid Colt-r begin	3.50	10.50	24.00
2-7: 6-Last Kid Colt-r; All Ayers-c/a(p)	1.30	4.00	9.00

GHOST RIDER (See The Champions & Marvel Spotlight #5)
Sept, 1973-No. 81, June, 1983 (Super-hero)
Marvel Comics Group

	Good	Fine	N-Mint
1-Johnny Blaze, the Ghost Rider begins	5.50	16.50	39.00
2	3.15	9.50	22.00
3-5: 3-Ghost Rider gets new cycle; Son of Satan app.	2.65	8.00	18.00
6-10: 10-Reprints origin/1st app. from Marvel Spotlight #5; Ploog-a	1.60	4.80	11.00
11-19	1.50	4.50	10.00
20-Byrne-a	1.60	4.80	11.00
21-30: 30-Dr. Strange app.	1.10	3.30	6.60
31-50: 50-Double size	.75	2.20	4.40
51-67,69-76,78-80	.55	1.65	3.30

	Good	Fine	N-Mint
68,77-Origin retold	.75	2.25	4.50
81-Death of Ghost Rider	.90	2.75	5.50

GHOST RIDER (Also see Marvel Comics Presents)
V2#1, May, 1990-Present ($1.50, color)
Marvel Comics

	Good	Fine	N-Mint
V2#1-($1.95, 52 pgs.)-Origin; Kingpin app.	3.35	10.00	20.00
1-Gold 2nd printing	1.10	3.30	6.60
2	2.15	6.50	13.00
3,4: 3-Kingpin app.	1.30	4.00	8.00
5-Punisher app.	2.15	6.50	13.00
5-Gold 2nd printing	1.50	4.50	9.00
6-Punisher app.	1.30	4.00	8.00
7-10: 9-X-Factor app.	.60	1.75	3.50
11-14	.35	1.00	2.00
15-Glow in the Dark-c (Begin $1.75-c)	1.00	3.00	6.00
15-2nd printing ($1.75)	.35	1.00	2.00
16-20	.30	.90	1.80

G. I. COMBAT
Oct, 1952-No. 43, Dec, 1956
Quality Comics Group

	Good	Fine	N-Mint
1-Crandall-c	18.00	54.00	125.00
2	6.50	19.00	45.00
3-5,10-Crandall-c/a	6.50	19.00	45.00
6-Crandall-a	5.70	17.00	40.00
7-9	4.00	12.00	28.00
11-20	2.65	8.00	18.00
21-31,33,35-43	2.30	7.00	16.00
32-Nuclear attack-c	4.50	14.00	32.00
34-Crandall-a	4.00	12.00	28.00

G. I. COMBAT
No. 44, Jan, 1957-No. 288, Mar, 1987
National Periodical Publications/DC Comics

	Good	Fine	N-Mint
44	17.00	51.00	120.00
45	9.00	21.00	64.00
46-50	6.00	18.00	42.00

	Good	Fine	N-Mint
51-60	4.30	13.00	30.00
61-66,68-80	3.15	9.50	22.00
67-1st Tank Killer	5.00	15.00	35.00
81,82,84-86	2.30	7.00	16.00
83-1st Big Al, Little Al, & Charlie Cigar	3.85	9.50	20.00
87-1st Haunted Tank	5.00	15.00	35.00
88-90: Last 10 cent issue	1.60	4.50	11.00
91-113,115-120	1.15	3.50	8.00
114-Origin Haunted Tank	1.70	5.00	12.00
121-137,139,140	.85	2.50	5.00
138-Intro. The Losers (Capt. Storm, Gunner/Sarge, Johnny Cloud) in Haunted			
Tank (10-11/69)	.70	2.00	4.00
141-200: 151,153-Medal of Honor series by Maurer	.50	1.50	3.00
201-288	.35	1.00	2.00

GIGGLE COMICS (Also see Ha Ha Comics)
Oct, 1943-No. 99, Jan-Feb, 1955
Creston No.1-63/American Comics Group No. 64 on

1	17.00	50.00	115.00
2	7.00	21.00	50.00
3-5: Ken Hultgren-a begins?	5.00	15.00	35.00
6-10: 9-1st Superkatt	4.00	12.00	28.00
11-20	2.65	8.00	18.00
21-40: 32-Patriotic-c. 39-St. Valentine's Day-c	2.15	6.50	15.00
41-54,56-59,61-99: 95-Spencer Spook app.	1.70	5.00	12.00
55,60-Milt Gross-a	2.15	6.50	15.00

G. I. JOE AND THE TRANSFORMERS
Jan, 1987-No. 4, Apr, 1987 (Mini-series)
Marvel Comics Group

1	.35	1.00	2.00
2-4	.25	.75	1.50

G. I. JOE, A REAL AMERICAN HERO
June, 1982-Present
Marvel Comics Group

1-Printed on Baxter paper	2.30	7.00	14.00
2-Printed on reg. paper	3.00	9.00	18.00

	Good	Fine	N-Mint
2-10 (2nd printings)	.30	.90	1.80
3-5	1.35	4.00	8.00
6,8	1.50	4.50	9.00
7,9,10	1.35	4.00	8.00
11-Intro Airborne	1.00	3.00	6.00
12	1.50	4.50	9.00
13-15	1.35	4.00	8.00
14 (2nd printing)	.30	.90	1.80
16	1.15	3.50	7.00
17-20	.85	2.50	5.00
17-19 (2nd printings)	.25	.70	1.40
21,22	.85	2.50	5.00
23-25	.50	1.50	3.00
21,23,25 (2nd printings)	.25	.70	1.40
26,27-Origin Snake-Eyes parts 1 & 2	.75	2.25	4.50
26,27 (2nd printings)		.45	.90
28-30	.50	1.50	3.00
29,30 (2nd printings)		.45	.90
31-35: 33-New headquarters	.40	1.25	2.50
34-37 (2nd printings)		.45	.90
36-40	.35	1.00	2.00
41-49	.25	.75	1.50
50-Double size; intro Special Missions	.50	1.50	3.00
51-59: 59-$1.00 issues begin		.60	1.20
51 (2nd printing)		.35	.70
60-Todd McFarlane-a	.30	.90	1.80
61-99,101-120: 94-96,103-Snake-Eyes app.		.45	.90
100 ($1.50, 52 pgs.)	.25	.75	1.50
Special Treasury Edition (1982)-r/#1	1.20	3.60	7.20
... Yearbook 1 ('84)-r/#1	1.05	3.15	6.30
... Yearbook 2 ('85)	.60	1.80	3.60
... Yearbook 3 ('86, 68 pgs.)	.45	1.35	2.70
... Yearbook 4 (2/88)	.25	.80	1.60

G. I. JOE ORDER OF BATTLE, THE
Dec, 1986-No. 4, Mar, 1987 (Mini-series)
Marvel Comics Group

1	.50	1.50	3.00
2-4	.30	.90	1.80

G. I. JOE SPECIAL MISSIONS (Indicia title: Special Missions)
Oct, 1986-No. 28, Dec, 1989 ($1.00, color)
Marvel Comics Group

	Good	Fine	N-Mint
1	.50	1.50	3.00
2	.30	.90	1.80
3-10	.25	.75	1.50
11-28		.50	1.00

GODZILLA
August, 1977-No. 24, July, 1979 (Based on movie series)
Marvel Comics Group

1-Mooney-i	.70	2.00	4.00
2-10: 2-Tuska-i. 3-Champions app. 4,5-Sutton-a	.50	1.50	3.00
11-24: 20-F.F. app. 21,22-Devil Dinosaur app.	.35	1.00	2.00

GREEN ARROW (See Brave & the Bold, Green Lantern #76, Justice League
    of America #4, Leading, More Fun #73 & World's Finest)
May, 1983-No. 4, Aug, 1983 (Mini-series)
DC Comics

1-Origin; Speedy cameo	.70	2.00	4.00
2-4	.50	1.50	3.00

GREEN ARROW
Feb, 1988-Present ($1.00, mature readers)(Painted-c #1-3)
DC Comics

1-Mike Grell scripts in all	1.35	4.00	8.00
2	.70	2.00	4.00
3	.50	1.50	3.00
4,5	.40	1.25	2.50
6-12	.35	1.10	2.20
13-20	.30	.90	1.80
21-49,51-54	.25	.75	1.50
50-($2.50, 52 pgs.)	.40	1.25	2.50
Annual 1 ('88)-No Grell scripts	.35	1.00	2.00
Annual 2 ('89, $2.50, 68 pgs.)-No Grell scripts; recaps origin Green Arrow, Speedy, Black Canary & others	.40	1.25	2.50
Annual 3 ('90, $2.50, 68 pgs.)-Bill wray-a	.40	1.25	2.50

	Good	Fine	N-Mint
Annual 4 ('91, $2.00, 68 pgs.)-50th ann.; Grell-c	.35	1.00	2.00

GREEN ARROW: THE LONG BOW HUNTERS
Aug, 1987-No. 3, Oct, 1987 ($2.95, color, mature readers)
DC Comics

	Good	Fine	N-Mint
1-Grell-c/a in all	2.30	7.00	14.00
1,2-2nd printings	.50	1.50	3.00
2	1.35	4.00	8.00
3	.85	2.50	5.00

GREEN HORNET, THE
Nov, 1989-No. 14, Feb?, 1991 ($1.75-$1.95, color)
Now Comics

	Good	Fine	N-Mint
1 ($2.95, double-size)-Steranko painted-c; G.A. Green Hornet	3.35	10.00	20.00
1-2nd printing ('90, $3.95)-New Butler-c	.70	2.00	4.00
2	1.70	5.00	10.00
3,4	1.00	3.00	6.00
5-Death of original (1930s) Green Hornet	1.00	3.00	6.00
6-8	.50	1.50	3.00
9-14	.35	1.00	2.00

GREEN HORNET COMICS (. . . Racket Buster #44) (Radio, movies)
Dec, 1940-No. 47, Sept, 1949
Helnit Publ. Co.(Holyoke) No. 1-6/Family Comics(Harvey) No. 7-on

	Good	Fine	N-Mint
1-Green Hornet begins(1st app.); painted-c	140.00	420.00	980.00
2	64.00	193.00	420.00
3	50.00	150.00	350.00
4-6 (8/41)	39.00	118.00	275.00
7 (6/42)-Origin The Zebra; Robin Hood & Spirit of 76 begin	36.00	107.00	250.00
8-10	29.00	86.00	200.00
11,12-Mr. Q in both	25.00	75.00	175.00
13-20	22.00	65.00	150.00
21-30: 24-Sci-Fi-c	19.00	58.00	135.00
31-The Man in Black Called Fate begins	20.00	60.00	140.00
32-36: 36-Spanking panel	17.00	51.00	120.00

Green Hornet Comics #6, © Green Hornet, Inc.

	Good	Fine	N-Mint
37-Shock Gibson app. by Powell; S&K Kid Adonis reprinted from Stuntman #3			
	19.00	56.00	130.00
38-Shock Gibson, Kid Adonis app.	17.00	51.00	120.00
39-Stuntman story by S&K	22.00	65.00	150.00
40,41	11.50	34.00	80.00
42-45,47-Kerry Drake in all. 45-Boy Explorers on cover only			
	11.50	34.00	80.00
46-"Case of the Marijuana Racket" cover/story; Kerry Drake app.			
	11.50	34.00	80.00

GREEN LANTERN (1st Series) (See All-American, All Flash Quarterly,
    All Star Comics & Comic Cavalcade)
Fall, 1941-No. 38, May-June, 1949
National Periodical Publications/All-American

	Good	Fine	VF-NM
1-Origin retold	750.00	1875.00	4500.00

	Good	Fine	N-Mint
2-1st book-length story	300.00	750.00	1800.00
3	235.00	585.00	1400.00
4	158.00	395.00	950.00
5	125.00	312.00	750.00
6-8: 8-Hop Harrigan begins	108.00	270.00	650.00
9,10: 10-Origin Vandal Savage	95.00	240.00	570.00
11-17,19,20: 12-Origin Gambler	79.00	200.00	475.00
18-Christmas-c	90.00	225.00	540.00
21-30: 27-Origin Sky Pirate. 30-Origin/1st app. Streak the Wonder Dog by Toth			
	67.00	170.00	400.00
31-35	56.00	140.00	335.00
36-38: 37-Sargon the Sorcerer app.	67.00	170.00	400.00

Green Lantern #78 (2nd series), © DC Comics

GREEN LANTERN (2nd series) (See Adventure, Brave & the Bold,
    Flash, Justice League & Showcase; Green Lantern Corps #206 on)
78/60-No. 89, 4-5/72; No. 90, 8-9/76-No. 205, 10/86
National Periodical Publications/DC Comics

	Good	Fine	N-Mint
1-Origin retold; Gil Kane-a begins	125.00	375.00	865.00
2-1st Pieface	52.50	157.50	368.00
3	31.50	94.50	220.00
4,5: 5-Origin & 1st app. Hector Hammond; 1st 5700 A.D. story			
	26.00	78.00	180.00
6-10: 6-Intro Tomar-re the alien G.L. 7-Origin Sinestro. 9-1st Jordan Brothers;			
last 10 cent issue	15.00	45.00	105.00
11-15: 13-Flash x-over. 14-Origin Sonar	11.50	34.00	80.00
16-20: 16-Origin Star Sapphire. 20-Flash x-over	9.70	29.00	68.00
21-30: 21-Origin Dr. Polaris. 23-1st Tattooed Man. 24-Origin Shark.			
29-JLA cameo; 1st Blackhand	8.30	25.00	58.00
31-39	6.00	18.00	42.00
40-1st app. Crisis (10/65); 1st solo G.A. Green Lantern in Silver Age; origin The			
Guardians; Doiby Dickles app.	38.00	114.00	265.00
41-44,46-50: 42-Zatanna x-over. 43-Flash x-over	3.60	11.00	25.00
45-G.A. Green Lantern x-over (2nd S.A. app.)	4.85	14.50	34.00
51,53-58	2.15	6.50	15.00
52-G.A. Green Lantern x-over	3.00	9.00	21.00
59-1st app. Guy Gardner (3/68)	15.00	45.00	105.00
60,62-69: 69-Wood inks; last 12 cent issue	1.70	5.00	12.00
61-G.A. Green Lantern x-over	2.30	7.00	16.00
70-75	1.50	4.50	10.00
76-Begin Green Lantern/Green Arrow series (by Neal Adams #76-89) ends #122			
	9.50	28.50	66.00
77	3.50	10.50	24.00
78-80	2.85	8.50	20.00
81-84: 82-One pg. Wrightson inks. 83-G.L. reveals I.D. to Carol Ferris. 84-N.			
Adams/Wrightson-a, 22 pgs.	2.15	6.50	15.00
85,86(52 pgs.)-Drug propaganda books. 86-G.A. Green Lantern-r; Toth-a			
	3.15	9.50	22.00
87(52 pgs.): 2nd app. Guy Gardner (cameo); 1st app. John Stewart (becomes Green			
Lantern in #182)	2.00	6.00	14.00
88(52 pgs.,'72)-Unpubbed G.A. Green Lantern story; Green Lantern-r/ Showcase			
#23. N. Adams-a(1 pg.)	.50	1.50	3.00
89(4-5/72, 52 pgs.)-G.A. Green Lantern-r	1.15	3.50	7.00
90(8-9/76)-99	.35	1.00	2.00
100-(Giant)-1st app. new Air Wave	.50	1.50	3.00
101-111,113-115,117-119: 107-1st Tales of the G.L. Corps story. 108-110- (44pgs)-			
G.A. Green Lantern. 111-Origin retold; G.A. Green Lantern app.			
	.35	1.00	2.00
112-G.A. Green Lantern origin retold	.60	1.75	3.50

	Good	Fine	N-Mint
116-1st app. Guy Gardner as a Green Lantern	2.00	6.00	14.00

120,121,124-135,138-140,144-149: 123-Gr. Lantern back to solo action. 130-132-Tales of the G.L. Corps. 132-Adam Strange begins new series, ends 147. 144-Omega Men cameo. 148-Tales of the G.L. Corps begins, ends #173

	Good	Fine	N-Mint
		.60	1.20
122-Last Green Lantern/Green Arrow team-up	.25	.75	1.50
123-2nd Guy Gardner as Green Lantern	.70	2.00	4.00
136,137-1st app. Citadel; Space Ranger app.	.35	1.00	2.00
141-1st app. Omega Men	.50	1.50	3.00
142,143-The Omega Men app.; Perez-c	.35	1.00	2.00
150-Anniversary issue, 52 pgs.; no G.L. Corps	.35	1.00	2.00

151-194,196-199,201-205: 159-Origin Evil Star. 160,161-Omega Men app. 181-Hal Jordan resigns as G.L. 182-John Stewart becomes new G.L.; origin recap of Hal Jordan as G.L.

	Good	Fine	N-Mint
		.50	1.00
195-Guy Gardner becomes Green Lantern; Crisis x-over			
	1.15	3.50	7.00
200-Double-size	.35	1.00	2.00

GREEN LANTERN
June, 1990-Present ($1.00, color)
DC Comics

1-Hal Jordan, John Stewart & Guy Gardner return; Batman app.			
	.50	1.50	3.00
2,3	.25	.75	1.50
4-8		.50	1.00
9-12: Guy Gardner solo story	.25	.75	1.50
13-($1.75, 52 pgs.)	.30	.90	1.80
14-20		.50	1.00

GREEN LANTERN CORPS, THE (Formerly Green Lantern)
No. 206, Nov, 1986-No. 224, May, 1988
DC Comics

206-223: 220,221-Millennium tie-ins		.50	1.00
224-Double size last issue	.25	.75	1.50

GREEN LANTERN: EMERALD DAWN
Dec, 1989-No. 6, May, 1990 ($1.00, color, mini-series)
DC Comics

1-Origin retold; Giffen plots in all	2.00	6.00	12.00

	Good	Fine	N-Mint
2	1.00	3.00	6.00
3,4	.50	1.50	3.00
5,6	.35	1.00	2.00

GREEN MASK, THE (See Mystery Men)
Summer, 1940-No. 9, 2/42; No. 10, 8/44-No. 11, 11/44;
    V2#1, Spring, 1945-No. 6, 10-11/46
Fox Features Syndicate

V1#1-Origin The Green Mask & Domino; reprints/Mystery Men No. 1-3,5-7; Lou			
Fine-c	100.00	300.00	700.00
2-Zanzibar The Magician by Tuska	49.00	145.00	340.00
3-Powell-a; Marijuana story	30.00	90.00	210.00
4-Navy Jones begins, ends No. 6	24.00	72.00	165.00
5	21.00	62.00	145.00
6-The Nightbird begins, ends No. 9; bondage/torture-c			
	18.00	54.00	125.00
7-9	14.00	43.00	100.00
10,11: 10-Origin One Round Hogan & Rocket Kelly			
	12.00	36.00	85.00
V2#1	9.30	28.00	65.00
2-6	7.00	21.00	50.00

GUARDIANS OF THE GALAXY (Also see Marvel Super-Heroes #18,
    Marvel Presents & Marvel Two-In-One #5)
June, 1990-Present ($1.00, color)
Marvel Comics

1-Valentino-c/a(p); painted-c	.85	2.50	5.00
2,3	.60	1.75	3.50
4-6: 5-McFarlane-c(i)	.50	1.50	3.00
7-10: 7-Perez-c(i). 10-Jim Lee-c(i)	.35	1.00	2.00
11-12,15-18	.25	.75	1.50
13,14-Spirit of Vengeance app. (futuristic Ghost Rider)			
	.35	1.00	2.00
19-22		.50	1.00

GUNSMOKE (TV)
No. 679, 2/56-No. 27, 6-7/61; 2/69-No. 6, 2/70
Dell Publishing Co./Gold Key (All have James Arness photo-c)

4-Color 679(No. 1)	7.00	21.00	50.00

	Good	Fine	N-Mint
4-Color 720,769,797,844	4.50	14.00	32.00
6(11-1/57-58), 7	4.50	14.00	32.00
8,9,11,12-Williamson-a in all, 4 pgs. each	5.70	17.00	40.00
10-Williamson/Crandall-a, 4 pgs.	5.70	17.00	40.00
13-27	4.00	12.00	28.00
Gunsmoke Film Story (11/62-G.K. Giant) No. 30008-211			
	4.50	14.00	32.00
1 (Gold Key)	2.30	7.00	16.00
2-6('69-70)	1.30	4.00	9.00

H

HA HA COMICS (Also see Giggle Comics)
Oct, 1943-No. 99, Jan, 1955
Scope Mag.(Creston Publ.) No. 1-80/American Comics Group

	Good	Fine	N-Mint
1	17.00	50.00	115.00
2	7.00	21.00	50.00
3-5: Ken Hultgren-a begins?	5.00	15.00	35.00
6-10	4.00	12.00	28.00
11-20: 14-Infinity-c	2.65	8.00	18.00
21-40	2.15	6.50	15.00
41-94,96-99: 49-XMas-c	1.70	5.00	12.00
95-3-D effect-c	6.50	19.00	45.00

HAPPY COMICS
Aug, 1943-No. 40, Dec, 1950
Nedor Publ./Standard Comics (Animated Cartoons)

1	13.00	40.00	90.00
2	6.00	18.00	42.00
3-10	4.00	12.00	28.00
11-19	2.65	8.00	18.00
20-31,34-37-Frazetta text illos in all (2 in #34&35, 3 in #27,28,30). 27-Al Fago-a			
	3.50	10.50	24.00
32-Frazetta-a, 7 pgs. plus two text illos; Roussos-a	10.00	30.00	70.00
33-Frazetta-a(2), 6 pgs. each (Scarce)	16.00	48.00	110.00
38-40	1.70	5.00	12.00

HAUNT OF FEAR
No. 15, May-June, 1950-No. 28, Nov-Dec, 1954
E. C. Comics

15(#1, 1950)	135.00	405.00	950.00
16	68.00	205.00	475.00
17-Origin of Crypt of Terror, Vault of Horror, & Haunt of Fear; used in **SOTI**, pg. 43; last pg. Ingels-a used by N.Y. Legis. Comm.			
	68.00	205.00	475.00
4	50.00	150.00	350.00
5-Injury-to-eye panel, pg. 4	38.00	114.00	265.00

	Good	Fine	N-Mint
6-10: 8-Shrunken head cover	26.00	79.00	185.00
11-13,15-18	19.00	56.00	130.00
14-Origin Old Witch by Ingels	26.00	79.00	185.00
19-Used in **SOTI**, ill.-"A comic book baseball game" & Senate investigation on juvenile delinq. bondage/decapitation-c	25.00	75.00	175.00
20-Feldstein-r/Vault of Horror #12	17.00	51.00	120.00
21,22,25,27: 27-Cannibalism story	11.00	32.00	75.00
23-Used in **SOTI**, pg. 241	12.00	36.00	85.00
24-Used in Senate Investigative Report, pg.8	11.50	34.00	80.00
26-Contains anti-censorship editorial, 'Are you a Red Dupe?'	11.50	34.00	80.00
28-Low distribution	13.00	40.00	90.00

HAUNT OF FEAR, THE
May, 1991-No. 2, July, 1991 ($2.00, color 68 pgs.)
Gladstone Publishing

	Good	Fine	N-Mint
1,2: 1-Ghastly Ingels-c(r). 2-Craig-c(r)	.40	1.25	2.50

HAVOK AND WOLVERINE-MELTDOWN
Mar, 1989-No. 4, Oct, 1989 ($3.50, mini-series, squarebound)
Epic Comics (Marvel)

	Good	Fine	N-Mint
1-Mature readers, violent	1.00	3.00	6.00
2-4	.70	2.00	4.00

HAWK AND DOVE
Oct, 1988-No. 5, Feb, 1989 ($1.00, color, mini-series)
DC Comics

	Good	Fine	N-Mint
1-(1-4: Liefeld-a, early DC work)	.85	2.50	5.00
2-4	.50	1.50	3.00
5	.35	1.00	2.00

HAWK AND DOVE
June, 1989-No. 28, Sept., 1991 ($1.00, color)
DC Comics

	Good	Fine	N-Mint
1	.25	.75	1.50
2-24: 9-Copperhead app. 12-New Titans app. 18,19-The Creeper app.		.50	1.00
25,28: 25-($2.00, 52 pgs.). 28-($2.00, 68 pgs.)	.35	1.00	2.00
26,27 ($1.25)		.65	1.30

HAWK AND THE DOVE, THE (See Showcase #75 & Teen Titans)
Aug-Sept, 1968-No. 6, June-July, 1969
National Periodical Publications

	Good	Fine	N-Mint
1-Ditko-c/a	3.60	11.00	25.00
2-6: 5-Teen Titans cameo	2.30	7.00	16.00

HAWKMAN (See Atom & Hawkman, The Brave & the Bold, Detective, Flash
    Comics, Justice League of America #31 & Showcase)
Apr-May, 1964-No. 27, Aug-Sept, 1968
National Periodical Publications

1	28.00	86.00	200.00
2	11.00	32.00	75.00
3-5: 4-Origin & 1st app. Zatanna	7.00	21.00	50.00
6-10: 9-Atom cameo; Hawkman & Atom learn each other's I.D.; 2nd app.			
Shadow Thief	4.70	14.00	33.00
11-15	3.15	9.50	22.00
16-27: Adam Strange x-over #18, cameo #19. 25-G.A. Hawkman-r			
	2.15	6.50	15.00

Hawkman #2 (1st series), © *DC Comics*

HAWKMAN
Aug, 1986-No. 17, Dec, 1987
DC Comics

	Good	Fine	N-Mint
1	.30	.90	1.80
2-17: 10-Byrne-c		.50	1.00
Special #1 ('86, $1.25)	.25	.75	1.50

HEADLINE COMICS (. . . Crime No. 32-39)
Feb, 1943-No. 22, Nov-Dec, 1946; No. 23, 1947-No. 77, Oct, 1956
Prize Publications

	Good	Fine	N-Mint
1-Yank & Doodle x-over in Junior Rangers	20.00	60.00	140.00
2	8.50	25.50	60.00
3-Used in **POP**, pg. 84	7.00	21.00	50.00
4-7,9,10: 4,9,10-Hitler stories in each	5.70	17.00	50.00
8-Classic Hitler-c	10.00	30.00	70.00
11,12	4.00	12.00	28.00
13-15-Blue Streak in all	4.30	13.00	30.00
16-Origin Atomic Man	9.30	28.00	65.00
17,18,20,21: 21-Atomic Man ends (9-10/46)	5.00	15.00	35.00
19-S&K-a	11.00	32.00	75.00
22-Kiefer-c	2.65	8.00	18.00
23,24: (All S&K-a). 24-Dope-crazy killer story	11.00	32.00	75.00
25-35-S&K-c/a. 25-Powell-a	7.00	21.00	50.00
36-S&K-a	5.70	17.00	40.00
37-One pg. S&K, Severin-a	2.85	8.50	20.00
38,40-Meskin-a	2.30	7.00	16.00
39,41,42,45-48,50-55: 51-Kirby-c. 45-Kirby-a	1.50	4.50	10.00
43,49-Meskin-a	1.70	5.00	12.00
44-S&K-c; Severin/Elder, Meskin-a	3.50	10.50	24.00
56-S&K-a	2.85	8.50	20.00
57-77: 72-Meskin-c/a(i)	1.50	4.50	10.00

HELLBLAZER (John Constantine) (See Saga of Swamp Thing #37)
Jan, 1988-Present ($1.25-1.50, Adults)
DC Comics

1	1.70	5.00	10.00
2-5	1.00	3.00	6.00
6-10	.70	2.00	4.00

	Good	Fine	N-Mint
11-20	.50	1.50	3.00
21-30: 25,26-Grant Morrison scripts	.40	1.25	2.50
31-39,41,42-48: 36-Preview of World Without End	.30	.90	1.80
40-($2.25, 52 pgs.)-Preview of Kid Eternity	.40	1.25	2.50
Annual 1 (`89, $2.95, 68 pgs.)	.75	2.25	4.50

HERBIE (See Forbidden Worlds)
April-May, 1964-No. 23, Feb, 1967 (All 12 cents)
American Comics Group

1-Whitney-c/a in most issues	10.00	30.00	70.00
2-4	5.00	15.00	35.00
5-Beatles, Dean Martin, F. Sinatra app.	6.00	18.00	42.00
6,7,9,10	3.50	10.50	24.00
8-Origin The Fat Fury	5.00	15.00	35.00
11-23: 14-Nemesis & Magicman app. 17-R-2nd Herbie/Forbidden Worlds #94. 23-R-1st Herbie/F.W. #73	2.65	8.00	18.00

HERO FOR HIRE (Power Man No. 17 on)
June, 1972-No. 16, Dec, 1973
Marvel Comics Group

1-Origin Luke Cage retold; Tuska-a(p)	2.30	7.00	16.00
2-5: 2,3-Tuska-a(p). 3-1st app. Mace. 4-1st app. Phil Fox of the Bugle			
	1.15	3.50	8.00
6-10	.85	2.50	5.00
11-16: 14-Origin retold. 15-Everett Subby-r(`53). 16-Origin Stiletto; death of Rackham	.60	1.75	3.50

HEROIC COMICS (Reg'lar Fellers . . . #1-15; New Heroic #41 on)
Aug, 1940-No. 97, June, 1955
Eastern Color Printing Co./Famous Funnies(Funnies, Inc. No. 1)

1-Hydroman(origin) by Bill Everett, The Purple Zombie(origin) & Mann of India by Tarpe Mills begins	57.00	171.00	400.00
2	29.00	85.00	200.00
3,4	25.00	75.00	175.00
5,6	18.00	54.00	125.00
7-Origin Man O'Metal, 1 pg.	22.00	65.00	150.00
8-10: 10-Lingerie panels	12.00	36.00	85.00
11,13: 13-Crandall/Fine-a	11.00	32.00	75.00

	Good	Fine	N-Mint
12-Music Master(origin) begins by Everett, ends No. 31; last Purple Zombie & Mann of India	12.00	36.00	85.00
14,15-Hydroman x-over in Rainbow Boy. 14-Origin Rainbow Boy. 15-1st app. Downbeat	12.00	36.00	85.00
16-20: 17-Rainbow Boy x-over in Hydroman. 19-Rainbow Boy x-over in Hydroman & vice versa	8.50	25.50	60.00
21-30:25-Rainbow Boy x-over in Hydroman. 28-Last Man O'Metal. 29-Last Hydroman	5.70	17.00	40.00
31,34,38	1.70	5.00	12.00
32,36,37-Toth-a, 3-4 pgs.	3.15	9.50	22.00
33,35-Toth-a, 8 & 9 pgs.	3.50	10.50	24.00
39-42-Toth, Ingels-a	3.50	10.50	24.00
43,46,47,49-Toth-a, 2-4 pgs. 47-Ingels-a	2.30	7.00	16.00
44,45,50-Toth-a, 6-9 pgs.	2.85	8.50	20.00
48,53,54	1.30	4.00	9.00
51-Williamson-a	3.50	10.50	24.00
52-Williamson-a (3 pg. story)	2.00	6.00	14.00
55-Toth-c/a	2.65	8.00	18.00
56-60-Toth-c. 60-Everett-a	2.30	7.00	16.00
61-Everett-a	1.50	4.50	10.00
62,64-Everett-c/a	1.70	5.00	12.00
63-Everett-c	1.15	3.50	8.00
65-Williamson/Frazetta-a; Evans-a, 2 pgs.	5.00	15.00	35.00
66,75,94-Frazetta-a, 2 pgs. each	2.00	6.00	14.00
67,73-Frazetta-a, 4 pgs. each	2.85	8.50	20.00
68,74,76-80,84,85,88-93,95-97	1.00	3.00	7.00
69,72-Frazetta-a (6 & 8 pgs. each)	5.00	15.00	35.00
70,71,86,87-Frazetta, 3-4 pgs. each; 1 pg. ad by Frazetta in #70	2.65	8.00	18.00
81,82-One pg. Frazetta art	1.30	4.00	9.00
83-Frazetta-a, 1/2 pg.	1.30	4.00	9.00

HIT COMICS
July, 1940-No. 65, July, 1950
Quality Comics Group

	Good	Fine	N-Mint
1-Origin Neon, the Unknown & Hercules; intro. The Red Bee; Bob & Swab, Blaze Barton, the Strange Twins, X-5 Super Agent, Casey Jones & Jack & Jill (ends #7) begin	185.00	557.00	1300.00
2-The Old Witch begins, ends #14	87.00	261.00	610.00

	Good	Fine	N-Mint
3-Casey Jones ends; transvestism story-'Jack & Jill'			
	71.00	215.00	500.00
4-Super Agent (ends #17), & Betty Bates (ends #65) begin; X-5 ends			
	60.00	180.00	420.00
5-Classic cover	89.00	270.00	625.00
6-10: 10-Old Witch by Crandall, 4 pgs.-1st work in comics			
	50.00	150.00	350.00
11-17: 13-Blaze Barton ends. 17-Last Neon; Crandall Hercules in all			
	47.00	140.00	325.00
18-Origin Stormy Foster, the Great Defender; The Ghost of Flanders begins;			
Crandall-c	50.00	150.00	350.00
19,20	47.00	140.00	325.00
21-24: 21-Last Hercules. 24-Last Red Bee & Strange Twins			
	40.00	140.00	280.00
25-Origin Kid Eternity and begins by Moldoff	52.00	156.00	365.00
26-Blackhawk x-over in Kid Eternity	41.00	124.00	290.00
27-29	24.00	72.00	165.00
30,31-"Bill the Magnificent" by Kurtzman, 11 pgs. in each			
	20.00	60.00	140.00
32-40: 32-Plastic Man x-over. 34-Last Stormy Foster			
	10.00	30.00	70.00
41-50	7.00	21.00	50.00
51-60-Last Kid Eternity	6.00	18.00	42.00
61,63-Crandall-c/a; Jeb Rivers begins #61	7.00	21.00	50.00
62	5.30	16.00	38.00
64,65-Crandall-a	6.00	18.00	42.00

HOPALONG CASSIDY (Also see Bill Boyd Western, Master Comics,
　　Real Western Hero & Western Hero; Bill Boyd starred as Hopalong Cassidy
　　in the movies; H. Cassidy in movies, radio & TV)
Feb, 1943; No. 2, Summer, 1946-No. 85, Jan, 1954
Fawcett Publications

1 (1943, 68 pgs.)-H. Cassidy & his horse Topper begin (On sale 1/8/43)-Captain			
Marvel on-c	133.00	335.00	800.00
2-(Sum, '46)	43.00	130.00	300.00
3,4: 3-(Fall, '46, 52 pgs. begin)	22.00	65.00	150.00
5-"Mad Barber" story mentioned in **SOTI**, pgs. 308,309			
	20.00	60.00	140.00
6-10	16.00	48.00	110.00
11-19: 11,13-19-Photo-c	11.50	34.00	80.00

	Good	Fine	N-Mint
20-29 (52 pgs.)-Painted/photo-c	8.50	25.50	60.00
30,31,33,34,37-39,41 (52 pgs.)-Painted-c	5.50	16.50	38.00
32,40 (36 pgs.)-Painted-c	4.50	14.00	32.00
35,42,43,45 (52 pgs.)-Photo-c	5.50	16.50	38.00
36,44,48 (36 pgs.)-Photo-c	4.50	14.00	32.00
46,47,49-51,53,54,56 (52 pgs.)-Photo-c	5.00	15.00	35.00
52,55,57-70 (36 pgs.)-Photo-c	3.70	11.00	26.00
71-84-Photo-c	2.85	8.50	20.00
85-Last Fawcett issue; photo-c	3.50	10.50	24.00

HOPALONG CASSIDY (TV)
No. 86, Feb, 1954-No. 135, May-June, 1959 (All-36 pgs.)
National Periodical Publications

86-Photo covers continue	14.00	43.00	100.00
87	8.50	25.50	60.00
88-90	5.70	17.00	40.00
91-99 (98 has #93 on-c & is last pre-code issue, 2/55)			
	4.50	14.00	32.00
100	6.00	18.00	42.00
101-108-Last photo-c	4.00	12.00	28.00
109-135: 124-Painted-c	4.00	12.00	28.00

HOT STUFF, THE LITTLE DEVIL
10/57-No. 141, 7/77; No. 142, 2/78-No. 164, 8/82; No. 165, 10/86 - No. 171,
11/87; No. 172, 11/88; No. 173, Sept, 1990-No. 177, 1/91
Harvey Publications (Illustrated Humor)

1	14.00	43.00	100.00
2-1st app. Stumbo the Giant	9.00	27.00	62.00
3-5	6.50	19.00	45.00
6-10	3.15	9.50	22.00
11-20	1.70	5.00	12.00
21-40	.85	2.60	6.00
41-60	.55	1.60	3.20
61-105	.25	.80	1.60
106-112: All 52 pg. Giants	.35	1.00	2.00
113-177-Later issues $1.00-c		.40	.80

HOWARD THE DUCK (See Fear & Man-Thing)
Jan, 1976-No. 31, May, 1979; No. 32, Jan, 1986; No. 33, Sept, 1986
Marvel Comics Group

	Good	Fine	N-Mint
1-Brunner-c/a; Spider-Man x-over (low distr.)	1.35	4.00	8.00
2-Brunner-c/a (low distribution)	.25	.75	1.50
3-11: 3-Buscema-a	.25	.75	1.50
12-1st app. Kiss (cameo, 3/77)	.70	2.00	4.00
13-Kiss app. (1st full story)	.85	2.50	5.00
14-33: 16-Album issue; 3 pgs. comics		.50	1.00
Annual 1(9/77, 52 pgs.)		.50	1.00

HOWDY DOODY (TV)
1/50-No. 38, 7-9/56; No. 761, 1/57; No. 811, 7/57
Dell Publishing Co.

1-(Scarce)-Photo-c; 1st TV comic?	25.00	75.00	175.00
2-Photo-c	10.00	30.00	70.00
3-5: All photo-c	7.00	21.00	50.00
6-Used in **SOTI**, pg. 309; painted-c begin	6.50	19.00	45.00
7-10	5.70	17.00	40.00
11-20	4.30	13.00	30.00
21-38	3.50	10.50	24.00
4-Color 761,811	5.70	17.00	40.00

HUEY, DEWEY AND LOUIE JUNIOR WOODCHUCKS (Disney)
Aug, 1966-No. 81, 1984 (See Walt Disney's C&S #125)
Gold Key No. 1-61/Whitman No. 62 on

1	2.65	8.00	18.00
2,3(12/68)	1.70	5.00	12.00
4,5(4/70)-Barks-r	1.70	5.00	12.00
6-17-Written by Barks	1.15	3.50	8.00
18,27-30	.70	2.00	4.00
19-23,25-Written by Barks. 22,23,25-Barks-r	.85	2.50	5.00
24,26-Barks-r	.85	2.50	5.00
31-57,60-81: 41,70,80-Reprints	.25	.75	1.50
58,59-Barks-r	.35	1.00	2.00

HUMAN FLY, THE
Sept, 1977-No. 19, Mar, 1979
Marvel Comics Group

1-Origin; Spider-Man x-over	.50	1.50	3.00
2-Ghost Rider app.	.70	2.20	4.50
3-19: 9-Daredevil x-over		.50	1.00

The Human Torch #23, © Marvel Comics

HUMAN TORCH, THE (Red Raven #1)(See All-Select, All Winners,
   Marvel Mystery, Sub-Mariner & USA Comics)
No. 2, Fall, 1940-No. 15, Spring, 1944; No. 16, Fall, 1944-No. 35, Mar, 1949
   (Becomes Love Tales); No. 36, April, 1954-No. 38, Aug, 1954
Timely/Marvel Comics (TP 2,3/TCI 4-9/SePI 10/SnPC 11-25/CnPC 26-35/Atlas
   Comics (CPC 36-38))

	Good	Fine	VF-NM
2(#1)-Intro & Origin Toro; The Falcon, The Fiery Mask, Mantor the Magician, & Microman only app.; Human Torch by Burgos, Sub-Mariner by Everett begin (origin of each in text)	665.00	1665.00	4000.00

(Prices vary widely on this book)

	Good	Fine	N-Mint
3(#2)-40 pg. H.T. story; H.T. & S.M. battle over who is best artist in text-Everett or Burgos	250.00	625.00	1500.00
4(#3)-Origin The Patriot in text; last Everett Sub-Mariner; Sid Greene-a	192.00	480.00	1150.00
5(#4)-The Patriot app; Angel x-over in Sub-Mariner (Summer, 1941)	135.00	335.00	800.00

	Good	Fine	N-Mint
5-Human Torch battles Sub-Mariner (Fall, '41)	200.00	500.00	1200.00
6,7,9	87.00	220.00	525.00
8-Human Torch battles Sub-Mariner; Wolverton-a, 1 pg.			
	150.00	375.00	900.00
10-Human Torch battles Sub-Mariner; Wolverton-a, 1 pg.			
	108.00	270.00	650.00
11-15	68.00	170.00	410.00
16-20: 20-Last War issue	55.00	137.00	330.00
21-30: 23(Sum/46)-Becomes Junior Miss 24?	48.00	118.00	285.00
31-Namora x-over in Sub-Mariner (also #30); last Toro			
	39.00	98.00	235.00
32-Sungirl, Namora app.; Sungirl-c	39.00	98.00	235.00
33-Capt. America x-over	42.00	105.00	250.00
34-Sungirl solo	39.00	98.00	235.00
35-Captain America & Sungirl app. (1949)	42.00	105.00	250.00
36-38(1954)-Sub-Mariner in all	30.00	75.00	180.00

HUMAN TORCH, THE (See Fantastic Four & Strange Tales #101)
Sept, 1974-No. 8, Nov, 1975
Marvel Comics Group

1: 1-8-r/stories from Strange Tales #101-108	.85	2.50	5.00
2-8: 1st Human Torch title since G.A.	.50	1.50	3.00

I

IBIS, THE INVINCIBLE (Also see Whiz Comics)
1943 (Feb)-#2, 1943; #3, Wint, 1945-#5, Fall, 1946; #6, Spring, 1948
Fawcett Publications

	Good	Fine	N-Mint
1-Origin Ibis; Raboy-c; on sale 1/2/43	79.00	235.00	550.00
2-Bondage-c	39.00	118.00	275.00
3-Wolverton-a #3-6 (4 pgs. each)	32.00	95.00	225.00
4-6: 5-Bondage-c. 6-Beck-c	25.00	75.00	175.00

I LOVE LUCY COMICS (TV) (Also see The Lucy Show)
No. 535, Feb, 1954-No. 35, Apr-June, 1962 (All photo-c)
Dell Publishing Co.

4-Color 535(#1)	18.00	54.00	125.00
4-Color 559(#2, 5/54)	13.00	40.00	90.00
3 (8-10/54)-5	8.50	25.50	60.00
6-10	7.00	21.00	50.00
11-20	6.50	19.00	45.00
21-35	5.70	17.00	40.00

INCREDIBLE HULK, THE (See The Avengers #1 & The Defenders #1)
May, 1962-No. 6, Mar, 1963; No. 102, Apr, 1968-Present
Marvel Comics Group

1-Origin & 1st app. (skin is grey colored)	200.00	600.00	1400.00
2-1st green skinned Hulk	80.00	225.00	525.00
3-Origin retold	60.00	180.00	375.00
4-6: 4-Brief origin retold. 6-Intro. Teen Brigade	48.00	153.00	335.00
102-(Formerly Tales to Astonish)-Origin retold	18.00	54.00	125.00
103	7.00	21.00	50.00
104	6.50	19.00	45.00
105-108: 105-1st Missing Link	4.30	13.00	30.00
109,110: 109-Ka-Zar app.	2.85	8.50	20.00
111-117: 117-Last 12 cent issue	1.70	5.00	12.00
118-121,123-125	1.00	3.00	7.00
122-Hulk battles Thing (12/69)	1.30	4.00	9.00
126-140: 126-1st Barbara Norriss (Valkyrie). 131-1st Jim Wilson, Hulk's new sidekick. 136-1st Xeron, The Star-Slayer. 140-Written by Harlan Ellison; 1st Jarella, Hulk's love	1.00	3.00	6.00

	Good	Fine	N-Mint
141-1st app. Doc Samson	.85	2.50	5.00
142-144,146-161,163-171,173-175,179: 149-1st The Inheritor. 155-1st app. Shaper. 161-The Mimic dies; Beast app. 163-1st app. The Gremlin. 164-1st app. Capt. Omen & Colonel John D. Armbruster. 166-1st Zzzax. 168-1st The Harpy. 169-1st Bi-Beast	.70	2.00	4.00
145-(52 pgs.)-Origin retold	1.00	3.00	6.00
162-1st app. The Wendigo; Beast app.	.85	2.50	5.00
172-X-Men cameo; origin Juggernaut retold	.85	2.50	5.00
176-178-Warlock app.	.85	2.50	5.00
180-1st app. Wolverine (cameo on last page)	8.50	25.50	60.00
181-Wolverine app.	37.00	111.00	260.00
182-Wolverine cameo; 1st Crackajack Jackson	6.50	19.50	45.00
183-199: 185-Death of Col. Armbruster	.50	1.50	3.00
200-Silver Surfer app.; anniversary issue	2.25	8.00	15.00
201-240: 212-1st The Constrictor	.35	1.00	2.00
241-249,251-271: 271-Rocket Raccoon app.		.60	1.20
250-Giant size; Silver Surfer app.	.55	1.65	4.00
272-Alpha Flight app.	.50	1.50	3.00
273-299,301-313: 278,279-Most Marvel characters app.(Wolverine in both). 279-X-Men & Alpha Flight cameos. 282-She-Hulk app. 293-F.F. app. 312-Origin Hulk		.60	1.20
300-Double size	.35	1.00	2.00
314-Byrne-c/a begins, ends #319	.85	2.50	5.00
315-319: 319-Bruce Banner & Betty Talbot wed	.35	1.00	2.00
320-323,325,327-329		.60	1.20
324-1st app. Grey Hulk since earlier series	1.15	3.50	7.00
326-Grey vs. Green Hulk	.45	1.35	3.00
330-1st McFarlane issue	3.35	10.00	20.00
331-Grey Hulk series begins	2.30	7.00	140.00
332-334,336-339: 336,337-X-Factor app.	1.70	5.00	10.00
335-No McFarlane-a	.50	1.50	3.00
340-Hulk battles Wolverine by McFarlane	5.75	17.50	35.00
341-344	1.00	3.00	6.00
345-($1.50, 52 pgs.)	1.15	3.50	7.00
346-Last McFarlane issue	.85	2.50	5.00
347-349,351-358,360-366,368	.40	1.25	2.50
350-Double size	.50	1.50	3.00
359-Wolverine app. (illusion only)	.50	1.50	3.00
367-1st Dale Keown-a	1.35	4.00	8.00
369,370-Keown-a	.65	2.00	4.00
371,373-376:Keown-a	.40	1.25	2.50

	Good	Fine	N-Mint
372-Green Hulk	1.35	4.00	8.00
377-1st all new Hulk; flourescent-c	1.35	4.00	8.00
377-2nd printing	.30	1.00	2.00
378-380		.50	1.00
381-387-Keown-a		.50	1.00
Special 1(10/68, 68 pg.)-New-a; Steranko-c	4.30	13.00	30.00
Special 2(10/69, 25 cents, 68 pg.)-Origin retold	2.85	8.50	20.00
Special 3(1/71, 25 cents, 68 pg.)	1.00	3.00	6.00
Annual 4 (1/72)	.70	2.00	4.00
Annual 5(10/76)	.50	1.50	3.00
Annual 6 (11/77)	.25	.75	1.50
Annual 7(8/78)-Byrne/Layton-c/a; Iceman & Angel app.			
	.50	1.50	3.00
Annual 8-15: 8(11/79). 9(9/80). 10('81). 11(10/82)-Miller, Buckler-a(p).			
12(8/83). 13(11/84). 14(12/85). 15(10/86)	.35	1.00	2.00
Annual 16(1990, $2.00, 68 pgs.)-She-Hulk app.	.35	1.00	2.00
... Versus Quasimodo 1 (3/83, one-shot)-Based on Saturday morning cartoon			
		.50	1.00

INCREDIBLE HULK AND WOLVERINE, THE
Oct, 1986 (One shot, $2.50, color)
Marvel Comics Group

	Good	Fine	N-Mint
1-r-/1st app. Wolverine & Incred. Hulk from Incred. Hulk #180,181; Wolverine back-up by Austin(i); Byrne-c	1.75	5.50	11.00

INDIAN CHIEF (White Eagle ...)
No. 3, July-Sept, 1951-No. 33, Jan-Mar, 1959 (All painted-c)
Dell Publishing Co.

	Good	Fine	N-Mint
3	1.70	5.00	12.00
4-11: 6-White Eagle app.	1.15	3.50	8.00
12-1st White Eagle(10-12/53)-Not same as earlier character			
	1.70	5.00	12.00
13-29	1.00	3.00	7.00
30-33-Buscema-a	1.15	3.50	8.00

INFERIOR FIVE, THE (Inferior 5 #11, 12) (See Showcase #62, 63, 65)
3-4/67-No. 10, 9-10/68; No. 11, 8-9/72-No. 12, 10-11/72
National Periodical Publications (#1-10: 12 cents)

	Good	Fine	N-Mint
1-Sekowsky-a(p)	3.15	9.50	22.00

	Good	Fine	N-Mint
2-Plastic Man app.; Sekowsky-a(p)	1.50	4.50	10.00
3-12: 10-Superman x-over	1.15	3.50	8.00

INFINITY GAUNTLET
July, 1991-No. 6, Dec. 1991 ($2.50, color, mini-series, 52 pgs.)
Marvel Comics

1-Thanos-c/stories in all	.70	2.00	4.00
2-6	.40	1.25	2.50

INFINITY, INC. (See All-Star Squadron #25)
Mar, 1984-No. 53, Aug, 1988 ($1.25, Baxter paper, 36 pgs.)
DC Comics

1-Brainwave, Jr., Fury, The Huntress, Jade, Northwind, Nuklon, Obsidian, Power Girl, Silver Scarab & Star Spangled Kid begin	.50	1.50	3.00
2-5: 2-Dr. Midnite, G.A. Flash, W. Woman, Dr. Fate, Hourman, Green Lantern, Wildcat app. 5-Nudity panels	.35	1.00	2.00
6-13,38-49,51-53: 46,47-Millennium tie-ins	.25	.80	1.60
14-Todd McFarlane-a (5/85, 2nd full story)	.70	2.00	4.00
15-37-McFarlane-a (20,23,24: 5 pgs. only; 33: 2 pgs.); 18-24-Crisis x-over. 21-Intro new Hourman & Dr. Midnight. 26-New Wildcat app. 31-Star-Spangled Kid becomes Skyman. 32-Green Fury becomes Green Flame. 33-Origin Obsidian	.50	1.50	3.00
50 ($2.50, 52 pgs.)	.40	1.25	2.50
Annual 1,2: 1(12/85)-Crisis x-over. 2('88, $2.00)	.35	1.00	2.00
Special 1 ('87, $1.50)	.25	.75	1.50

IRON FIST (Also see Marvel Premiere & Power Man)
Nov, 1975-No. 15, Sept, 1977
Marvel Comics Group

1-McWilliams-a(i); Iron Man app.	2.85	8.50	20.00
2	1.50	4.50	10.00
3-5	1.35	4.00	8.00
6-10: 8-Origin retold	1.00	3.00	6.00
11-13: 12-Capt. America app.	.85	2.50	5.00
14-1st app. Sabretooth	7.00	21.00	50.00
15-New X-Men app., Byrne-a (.35 vers.)	3.15	9.50	22.00

Iron Man #2, © Marvel Comics

IRON MAN (Also see The Avengers #1 & Tales of Suspense #39)
May, 1968-Present
Marvel Comics Group

	Good	Fine	N-Mint
1-Origin; Colan-c/a(p); story continued from Iron Man & Sub-Mariner #1			
	43.00	130.00*	300.00
2	14.00	43.00	100.00
3	11.00	32.00	75.00
4,5	8.00	24.00	55.00
6-10	5.00	15.00	35.00
11-15: 15-Last 12 cent issue	4.00	12.00	28.00
16-20	2.65	8.00	18.00
21-42: 22-Death of Janice Cord. 27-Intro Fire Brand. 33-1st app. Spymaster. 42-Last 15 cent issue	1.70	5.00	12.00
43-Intro. The Guardsman; 25 cent giant	1.60	4.80	11.00
44-46,48-50: 46-The Guardsman dies. 50-Princess Python app.			
	1.30	4.00	9.00
47-Origin retold; Smith-a(p)	2.00	6.00	14.00

	Good	Fine	N-Mint
51-53	1.15	3.50	8.00
54-Iron Man battles Sub-Mariner	1.50	4.50	10.00
55-1st app. Thanos (2/73); Starlin-c/a (See Capt. Marvel)			
	10.00	30.00	70.00
56-Starlin-a	2.15	6.50	15.00
57-67,69,70: 59-Firebrand returns. 65-Origin Dr. Spectrum. 67-Last 20 cent issue			
	1.10	3.30	6.60
68-Starlin-c; origin retold	1.15	3.50	8.00
71-99: 76 r-/#9. 86-1st app. Blizzard. 87-Origin Blizzard. 89-Last 25 cent issue			
	.85	2.50	5.00
100-Starlin-c	1.50	4.50	10.00
101-117: 101-Intro DreadKnight. 109-1st app. new Crimson Dynamo. 110-Origin Jack of Hearts retold	.60	1.80	3.60
118-Byrne-a(p)	1.00	3.00	6.00
119,120,123-128-Tony Stark recovers from alcohol problem. 120,121-Sub-Mariner x-over. 125-Ant-Man app.	.75	2.20	4.40
121,122,129-149: 122-Origin. 131,132-Hulk x-over	.40	1.20	2.40
150-Double size	.55	1.65	3.30
151-168: 152-New armor. 161-Moon Knight app. 167-Tony Stark alcohol problem starts again	.35	1.00	2.00
169-New Iron Man (Jim Rhodes replaces Tony Stark)			
	1.45	4.40	8.80
170	.85	2.50	5.00
171	.40	1.20	2.40
172-199: 172-Captain America x-over. 186-Intro Vibro. 190-Scarlet Witch app. 191-198-Tony Stark returns as original Iron Man. 192- Both Iron Men battle	.35	1.00	2.00
200-Double size ($1.25)-Tony Stark returns as new Iron Man (red & white armor) thru #230	.75	2.20	4.40
201-224: 213-Intro new Dominic Fortune	.25	.75	1.50
225-Double size ($1.25)	.90	2.75	5.50
226-243,245-249: 228-Vs. Capt. America. 231-Intro new Iron Man. 233-Antman app. 243-Tony Stark looses use of legs. 247-Hulk x-over	.25	.75	1.50
244-($1.50, 52 pgs.)-New Armor makes him walk	.75	2.20	4.40
250 ($1.50, 52 pgs.)	.30	.85	1.70
251-272: 258-Byrne scripts begin		.50	1.00
Special 1(8/70)-Sub-Mariner x-over; Everett-c	1.70	5.00	12.00
Special 2(11/71)	1.00	3.00	6.00
Annual 3(6/76)-Man-Thing app.	.50	1.50	3.00
King Size 4(8/77)-Newton-a(i)	.50	1.50	3.00

	Good	Fine	N-Mint
Annual 5-9: 5(12/82). 6(11/83)-New Iron Man(J. Rhodes) app. 7(10/84). 8(10/86)-X-Factor app. 9(12/87)	.35	1.00	2.00
Annual 10(8/89, $2.00, 68 pgs.)-Atlantis Attacks x-over; P. Smith-a; Layton/Guice-a; Sub-Mariner app.	.40	1.25	2.50
Annual 11(1990, $2.00, 68 pgs.)-Origin of Mrs. Arbogast by Ditko (p&i)	.35	1.00	2.00

IRON MAN & SUB-MARINER
April, 1968 (One Shot) (Pre-dates Iron Man #1 & Sub-Mariner #1)
Marvel Comics Group

	Good	Fine	N-Mint
1-Iron Man story by Colan/Craig continued in Iron Man #1; Sub-Mariner story by Colan(p) continued in Sub-Mariner #1; Colan/Everett-c	20.00	60.00	140.00

J

JACE PEARSON OF THE TEXAS RANGERS (4-Color #396 is titled
   Tales of the Texas Rangers; . . . 's Tales of . . . #11-on)
No. 396, 5/52-No. 1021, 8-10/59 (No #10) (All-Photo-c)
Dell Publishing Co.

	Good	Fine	N-Mint
4-Color 396 (#1)	6.00	18.00	42.00
2(5-7/53)-9(2-4/55)	4.00	12.00	28.00
4-Color 648(9/55)	4.00	12.00	28.00
11(11-2/55/56)-14,17-20(6-8/58)	3.00	9.00	21.00
15,16-Toth-a	4.50	14.00	32.00
4-Color 961-Spiegle-a	3.50	10.50	24.00
4-Color 1021	3.00	9.00	21.00

JACKIE GLEASON AND THE HONEYMOONERS (TV)
June-July, 1956-No. 12, Apr-May, 1958
National Periodical Publications

1	45.00	135.00	315.00
2	32.00	95.00	225.00
3-11	25.00	75.00	175.00
12 (Scarce)	29.00	86.00	200.00

JACKIE ROBINSON (Famous Plays of . . .)
May, 1950-No. 6, 1952 (Baseball hero) (All photo-c)
Fawcett Publications

nn	36.00	107.00	250.00
2	23.00	70.00	160.00
3-6	20.00	60.00	140.00

JACKPOT COMICS
Spring, 1941-No. 9, Spring, 1943
MLJ Magazines

1-The Black Hood, Mr. Justice, Steel Sterling & Sgt. Boyle begin; Biro-c

	125.00	312.00	750.00
2	52.00	155.00	365.00
3	43.00	130.00	300.00

234

	Good	Fine	N-Mint
4-Archie begins (on sale 12/41)-(Also see Pep Comics No. 22); Montana-c			
	121.00	365.00	850.00
5-Hitler-c	54.00	160.00	375.00
6-9: 6,7-Bondage-c	47.00	140.00	325.00

JESSE JAMES
8/50-No. 9, 11/52; No. 15, 10/53-No. 29, 8-9/56
Avon Periodicals

	Good	Fine	N-Mint
1-Kubert Alabam r-/Cowpuncher #1	11.00	33.00	76.00
2-Kubert-a(3)	8.50	25.50	60.00
3-Kubert Alabam r-/Cowpuncher #2	7.00	21.00	50.00
4,9-No Kubert	2.85	8.50	20.00
5,6-Kubert Jesse James-a(3); 5-Wood-a(1pg.)	7.00	21.00	50.00
7-Kubert Jesse James-a(2)	6.00	18.00	42.00
8-Kinstler-a(3)	4.00	12.00	28.00
15-Kinstler r-/#3	2.15	6.50	15.00
16-Kinstler r-/#3 & Sheriff Bob Dixon's Chuck Wagon #1 with name changed to			
Sheriff Tom Wilson	2.65	8.00	18.00
17-19,21: 17-Jesse James r-/#4; Kinstler-c idea from Kubert splash in #6. 18-			
Kubert Jesse James r-/#5. 19-Kubert Jesse James-r. 21-Two Jesse James r-/#4,			
Kinstler r-/#4	1.70	5.00	12.00
20-Williamson/Frazetta-a; r-Chief Vic. Apache Massacre; Kubert Jesse James r-			
/#6	8.50	25.50	60.00
22,23-No Kubert	1.60	4.80	11.00
24-New McCarty strip by Kinstler; Kinstler-r	1.60	4.80	11.00
25-New McCarty Jesse James strip by Kinstler; Kinstler J. James r-/ #7,9			
	1.60	4.80	11.00
26,27-New McCarty J. James strip plus a Kinstler/McCann Jesse James-r			
	1.60	4.80	11.00
28,29: 28-Reprints most of Red Mountain, Featuring Quantrells Raiders			
	1.60	4.80	11.00
Annual(nn; 1952; 25 cents)-" . . . Brings Six-Gun Justice to the West" (100 pgs.)-3			
earlier issues rebound; Kubert, Kinstler-a(3)	17.00	51.00	120.00

JETSONS, THE (TV)
Jan, 1963-No. 36, Oct, 1970 (Hanna-Barbera)
Gold Key

	Good	Fine	N-Mint
1	13.00	40.00	90.00
2	8.00	24.00	55.00

	Good	Fine	N-Mint
3-10	5.70	17.00	40.00
11-20	4.50	14.00	32.00
21-36	3.60	11.00	25.00

JETSONS, THE (TV) (Hanna-Barbera)
Nov, 1970-No. 20, Dec, 1973
Charlton Comics

	Good	Fine	N-Mint
1	5.00	15.00	35.00
2	3.00	9.00	21.00
3-10	2.00	6.00	14.00
11-20	1.50	4.50	10.00

JIMMY WAKELY (Cowboy movie star)
Sept-Oct, 1949-No. 18, July-Aug, 1952 (1-13: 52 pgs.)
National Periodical Publications

	Good	Fine	N-Mint
1-Photo-c, 52 pgs. begin; Alex Toth-a; Kit Colby Girl Sheriff begins			
	39.00	118.00	275.00
2-Toth-a	25.00	75.00	175.00
3,6,7-Frazetta-a in all, 3 pgs. each; Toth-a in all. 7-Last photo-c?			
	27.00	81.00	190.00
4-Frazetta-a, 3 pgs.; Kurtzman "Pot-Shot Pete," 1 pg; Toth-a			
	27.00	81.00	190.00
5,8-15,18-Toth-a; 12,14-Kubert-a, 3 & 2 pgs.	20.00	60.00	140.00
16,17	14.00	43.00	100.00

JINGLE JANGLE COMICS
Feb, 1942-No. 42, Dec, 1949
Eastern Color Printing Co.

	Good	Fine	N-Mint
1-Pie-Face Prince of Old Pretzleburg, Jingle Jangle Tales by George Carlson, Hortense, & Benny Bear begin	25.00	75.00	175.00
2,3-No Pie-Face Prince	11.50	34.00	80.00
4-Pie-Face Prince cover	11.50	34.00	80.00
5	10.00	30.00	70.00
6-10: 8-No Pie-Face Prince	8.50	25.50	60.00
11-15	5.70	17.00	40.00
16-30: 17,18-No Pie-Face Prince. 30-XMas-c	4.30	13.00	30.00
31-42: 36,42-Xmas-c	3.00	9.00	21.00

JOE PALOOKA (1st Series) (Also see Big Shot & Feature Funnies)
1942-No. 4, 1944
Columbia Comic Corp. (Publication Enterprises)

	Good	Fine	N-Mint
1-1st to portray American president; gov't permission required			
	35.00	105.00	245.00
2 (1943)-Hitler-c	19.00	58.00	135.00
3,4	13.00	40.00	90.00

JOE PALOOKA (2nd Series) (Battle Adv. #68-74; . . . Advs. #75,77-81,
      83-85,87; Champ of the Comics #76,82,86,89-93) (See All-New)
Nov, 1945-No. 118, Mar, 1961
Harvey Publications

	Good	Fine	N-Mint
1	22.00	65.00	150.00
2	11.00	32.00	75.00
3,4,6	6.50	19.50	45.00
5-Boy Explorers by S&K (7-8/46)	9.50	28.00	65.00
7-1st Powell Flyin' Fool, ends #25	5.70	17.00	40.00
8-10	5.00	15.00	35.00
11-14,16-20: 19-Freedom Train-c	4.00	12.00	28.00
15-Origin Humphrey; Super heroine Atoma app. by Powell			
	5.00	15.00	35.00
21-30: 27-1st app. Little Max? (12/48). 30-Nude female painting			
	3.00	9.00	21.00
31-61: 44-Joe Palooka marries Ann Howe	2.30	7.00	16.00
62-S&K Boy Explorers-r	3.00	9.00	21.00
63-80: 66,67-'Commie' torture story	1.70	5.00	12.00
81-99,101-115	1.50	4.50	10.00
100	1.75	5.25	12.00
116-S&K Boy Explorers (r) (Giant, '60)	2.85	8.50	20.00
117,118-Giants	2.65	8.00	18.00

JOHNNY MACK BROWN (TV western star)
No. 269, Mar, 1950-No. 963, Feb, 1959 (All Photo-c)
Dell Publishing Co.

	Good	Fine	N-Mint
4-Color 269(#1)(3/50, 52 pgs.)-Johnny Mack Brown & his horse Rebel begin; photo front/back-c begin; Marsh-a begins, ends #9			
	13.00	40.00	90.00
2(10-12/50, 52 pgs.)	6.50	19.50	45.00

	Good	Fine	N-Mint
3(1-3/51, 52 pgs.)	4.30	13.00	30.00
4-10 (9-11/52)(36 pgs.)	3.50	10.50	24.00
4-Color 455,493,541,584,618	3.50	10.50	24.00
4-Color 645,685,722,776,834,963	3.50	10.50	24.00
4-Color 922-Manning-a	4.00	12.00	28.00

JOHN WAYNE ADVENTURE COMICS (Movie star)
Winter, 1949-50-No. 31, May, 1955 (Photo-c: 1-12,17,25-on)
Toby Press

	Good	Fine	N-Mint
1 (36 pgs.)-Photo-c begin	50.00	150.00	350.00
2 (36 pgs.)-Williamson/Frazetta-a(2) 6 & 2 pgs. (one r-/Billy the Kid #1); photo back-c	41.00	125.00	290.00
3 (36 pgs.)-Williamson/Frazetta-a(2), 16 pgs. total; photo back-c	41.00	125.00	290.00
4 (52 pgs.)-Williamson/Frazetta-a(2), 16 pgs. total	41.00	125.00	290.00
5 (52 pgs.)-Kurtzman-a-(Alfred "L" Newman in Potshot Pete)	28.50	85.00	200.00
6 (52 pgs.)-Williamson/Frazetta-a, 10 pgs; Kurtzman a-'Pot-Shot Pete,' 5 pgs.; & "Genius Jones," 1 pg.	39.00	120.00	275.00
7 (52 pgs.)-Williamson/Frazetta-a, 10 pgs.	32.00	95.00	225.00
8 (36 pgs.)-Williamson/Frazetta-a(2), 12 & 9 pgs.	39.00	120.00	275.00
9-11: Photo western-c	22.00	65.00	150.00
12-Photo war-c; Kurtzman-a, 2 pgs. "Genius"	22.00	65.00	150.00
13-15: 13-Line-drawn-c begin, end #24	18.00	54.00	125.00
16-Williamson/Frazetta r-/Billy the Kid #1	20.00	60.00	140.00
17-Photo-c	22.00	65.00	150.00
18-Williamson/Frazetta-a r-/#4 & 8, 19 pgs.	23.00	70.00	160.00
19-24: 23-Evans-a?	16.50	50.00	115.00
25-Photo-c return; end #31; Williamson/Frazetta-a r-/Billy the Kid #3	23.00	70.00	160.00
26-28,30-Photo-c	20.00	60.00	140.00
29,31-Williamson/Frazetta-a in each, r-/#4,2	22.00	65.00	150.00

JO-JO COMICS (. . . Congo King #7-29)
1945-No. 29, July, 1949 (two No.7's; no No. 13)
Fox Feature Syndicate

	Good	Fine	N-Mint
nn(1945)-Funny animal, humor	6.00	18.00	42.00

	Good	Fine	N-Mint
2(Sum,'46)-6: Funny animal; 2-Ten pg. Electro story			
	3.15	9.50	22.00
7(7/47)-Jo-Jo, Congo King begins	30.00	90.00	210.00
7(#8) (9/47)	23.00	70.00	160.00
8-10(#9-11): 8-Tanee begins	19.00	56.00	130.00
11,12(#12,13),14,16: 11,16-Kamen bondage-c	16.00	48.00	110.00
15-Cited by Dr. Wertham in 5/47 Saturday Review of Literature			
	17.00	51.00	120.00
17-Kamen bondage-c	17.00	51.00	120.00
18-20	16.00	48.00	110.00
21-29: 21-Hollingsworth-a(4 pgs.; 23-1 pg.)	14.00	43.00	100.00

JOKER, THE (See Batman, Batman: The Killing Joke, Brave & the Bold,
Detective & Justice League Annual #2)
May, 1975-No. 9, Sept-Oct, 1976
National Periodical Publications

1-Two-Face app.	3.60	11.00	25.00
2,3	2.00	6.00	14.00
4-6	1.70	5.00	12.00
7,8	1.30	4.00	9.00
9	1.50	4.50	10.00

JOKER COMICS
April, 1942-No. 42, August, 1950
Timely/Marvel Comics No. 36 on (TCI/CDS)

1-(Rare)-Powerhouse Pepper (1st app.) begins by Wolverton; Stuporman app.			
from Daring	90.00	270.00	630.00
2-Wolverton-a; 1st app. Tessie the Typist	38.00	115.00	265.00
3-5-Wolverton-a	25.00	75.00	175.00
6-10-Wolverton-a	17.00	51.00	120.00
11-20-Wolverton-a	14.00	43.00	100.00
21,22,24-27,29,30-Wolverton cont'd. & Kurtzman's "Hey Look" in #24-27			
	11.00	32.00	75.00
23-1st "Hey Look" by Kurtzman; Wolverton-a	13.00	40.00	90.00
28,32,34,37-41	2.30	7.00	16.00
31-Last Powerhouse Pepper; not in #28	8.50	25.50	60.00
33,35,36-Kurtzman's "Hey Look"	3.60	11.00	25.00
42-Only app. 'Patty Pinup,' a clone of Millie the Model			
	2.85	8.50	20.00

JONNY QUEST (TV)
December, 1964 (Hanna-Barbera)
Gold Key

	Good	Fine	N-Mint
1 (10139-412)	12.00	36.00	85.00

JONNY QUEST (TV)
June, 1986-No. 31, Dec, 1988 (Hanna-Barbera)
Comico

	Good	Fine	N-Mint
1	.70	2.00	4.00
2	.45	1.30	2.60
3,5-Dave Stevens-c	.50	1.50	3.00
4,6-10	.25	.75	1.50
11-31: #15 on, $1.75. 30-Adapts TV episode	.30	.90	1.80
Special 1(9/88, $1.75), 2(10/88, $1.75)	.25	.75	1.50

JOURNEY INTO MYSTERY (Thor No. 126 on)
6/52-No. 48, 8/57; No. 49, 11/58-No. 125, 2/66
Atlas(CPS No. 1-48/AMI No. 49-68/Marvel No. 69 (6/61) on)

	Good	Fine	N-Mint
1	70.00	210.00	490.00
2	33.00	100.00	232.00
3,4	27.00	80.00	195.00
5-11	16.00	48.00	113.00
12-20,22: 22-Davisesque-a; last pre-code issue (2/55)			
	13.00	40.00	93.00
21-Kubert-a; Tothish-a by Andru	15.00	45.00	103.00
23-32,35-38,40: 24-Torres?-a	7.50	22.50	52.00
33-Williamson-a	9.50	28.50	67.00
34,39: 34-Krigstein-a. 39-Wood-a	9.00	27.00	62.00
41-Crandall-a; Frazettaesque-a by Morrow	6.50	19.50	46.00
42,48-Torres-a	6.50	19.50	46.00
43,44-Williamson/Mayo-a in both	6.70	20.00	47.00
45,47,52,53	6.00	18.00	42.00
46-Torres & Krigstein-a	6.70	20.00	47.00
49-Matt Fox, Check-a	6.70	20.00	47.00
50,54: 50-Davis-a. 54-Williamson-a	6.00	18.00	42.00
51-Kirby/Wood-a	6.00	18.00	42.00
55-61,63-75: 66-Return of Xemnu. 75-Last 10 cent issue			
	5.30	16.00	37.00

	Good	Fine	N-Mint
62-1st app. Xemnu (Titan) called "The Hulk"	8.30	25.00	58.00
76,77,79-82-Fantasy content #74 on. 80-Anti-communist propaganda story			
	4.85	14.50	34.00
78-The Sorcerer app. (Dr. Strange prototype, 3/62)	6.00	18.00	42.00
83-Origin & 1st app. The Mighty Thor by Kirby (8/62) and begin series			
	140.00	430.00	1000.00
83-R-/from the Golden Record Comic Set	7.00	21.00	50.00
with the record (still sealed)	14.00	43.00	100.00
84-2nd app. Thor	37.00	111.00	260.00
85-1st app. Loki & Heimdall; Odin cameo (1 panel)			
	26.00	78.00	180.00
86-1st app. Odin	19.30	58.00	135.00
87-89: 89-Reprints origin Thor from #83	16.00	48.00	110.00
90-No Kirby-a	9.30	28.00	65.00
91,92,94-96-Sinnott-a	8.00	24.00	55.00
93,97-Kirby-a; Tales of Asgard series begins #97 (origin which concludes in #99)			
	11.00	32.00	75.00
98-100-Kirby/Heck-a. 98-Origin/1st app. The Human Cobra. 99-1st app. Surtur &			
Mr. Hyde	8.00	24.00	55.00
101-110: 102-Intro Sif. 105-109-Ten extra pages Kirby-a in each. 107-1st app.			
Grey Gargoyle	5.00	15.00	35.00
111,113,114,116-125: 119-Intro Hogun, Fandrall, Volstagg			
	4.00	12.00	28.00
112-Thor Vs. Hulk; origin Loki begins; ends #113			
	9.30	28.00	65.00
115-Detailed origin Loki	5.00	15.00	35.00
Annual 1('65)-1st app. Hercules; Kirby-c/a	10.00	30.00	70.00

JOURNEY INTO UNKNOWN WORLDS
No. 36, 9/50-No. 38, 2/51; No. 4, 4/51-No. 59, 8/57
Atlas Comics (WFP)

	Good	Fine	N-Mint
36(#1)-Science fiction/weird; 'End Of The Earth' c/story			
	46.00	138.00	325.00
37(#2)-Science fiction; 'When Worlds Collide' c/story; Everett-c/a; Hitler story			
	33.00	100.00	230.00
38(#3)-Science fiction	26.00	77.00	180.00
4-6,8,10-Science fiction/weird	17.00	51.00	120.00
7-Wolverton-a-"Planet of Terror," 6 pgs; electric chair c-inset/story			
	29.00	85.00	200.00
9-Giant eyeball story	17.00	51.00	120.00

	Good	Fine	N-Mint
11,12-Krigstein-a	12.00	36.00	85.00
13,16,17,20	8.50	25.50	60.00
14-Wolverton-a-"One of Our Graveyards Is Missing," 4 pgs; Tuska-a			
	26.00	77.00	180.00
15-Wolverton-a-"They Crawl By Night," 5 pgs.	26.00	77.00	180.00
18,19-Matt Fox-a	11.00	32.00	75.00
21-33: 21-Decapitation-c. 24-Sci/fic story. 26-Atom bomb panel. 27-Sid Check-a.			
33-Last pre-code (2/55)	5.70	17.00	40.00
34-Kubert, Torres-a	5.70	17.00	40.00
35-Torres-a	5.00	15.00	35.00
36-42	4.30	13.00	30.00
43,44: 43-Krigstein-a. 44-Davis-a	4.50	14.00	32.00
45,55,59-Williamson-a in all; with Mayo #55,59. Crandall-a, #55,59			
	5.70	17.00	40.00
46,47,49,52,56-58	3.50	10.50	24.00
48,53-Crandall-a; Check-a, #48	5.50	16.50	38.00
50-Davis, Crandall-a	5.00	15.00	35.00
51-Ditko, Wood-a	5.00	15.00	35.00
54-Torres-a	4.00	12.00	28.00

Jumbo Comics #58, © Fiction House

JUMBO COMICS (Created by S.M. Iger)
Sept, 1938-No. 167, Mar, 1953 (No. 1-3: 68 pgs.; No. 4-8: 52 pgs.)
    (No. 1-8 oversized-10"x14"; black & white)
Fiction House Magazines (Real Adv. Publ. Co.)

	Good	Fine	VF-NM
1-(Rare)-Sheena Queen of the Jungle by Meskin, The Hawk by Eisner, The Hunchback by Dick Briefer(ends #8) begin; 1st comic art by Jack Kirby (Count of Monte Cristo & Wilton of the West); Mickey Mouse appears (1 panel) with brief biography of Walt Disney. Note: Sheena was created by Iger for publication in England as a newspaper strip. The early issues of Jumbo contain Sheena strip-r	635.00	1585.00	3800.00
2-(Rare)-Origin Sheena. Diary of Dr. Hayward by Kirby (also #3) plus 2 other stories; contains strip from Universal Film featuring Edgar Bergen & Charlie McCarthy	300.00	750.00	1800.00
3-Last Kirby issue	233.00	585.00	1400.00
4-(Scarce)-Origin The Hawk by Eisner; Wilton of the West by Fine (ends #14) (1st comic work); Count of Monte Cristo by Fine (ends #15); The Diary of Dr. Hayward by Fine (cont'd. #8,9)	233.00	585.00	1400.00
5	150.00	375.00	900.00
6-8-Last B&W issue. #8 was a N. Y. World's Fair Special Edition	125.00	312.00	750.00
9-Stuart Taylor begins by Fine; Fine-c; 1st color issue(8-9/39)-8-1/4"x10-1/4"(oversized in width only)	133.00	335.00	800.00

	Good	Fine	N-Mint
10-14: 10-Regular size 68 pg. issues begin; Sheena dons new costume. 14-Lightning begins (Intro.)	67.00	165.00	400.00
15-20	34.00	103.00	240.00
21-30: 22-1st Tom, Dick & Harry; origin The Hawk retold	29.00	86.00	200.00
31-40: 35-Shows V2#11 (correct number does not appear)	25.00	75.00	175.00
41-50	22.00	65.00	150.00
51-60: 52-Last Tom, Dick & Harry	18.00	54.00	125.00
61-70: 68-Sky Girl begins, ends #130; not in #79	12.00	36.00	85.00
71-99: 89-ZX5 becomes a private eye. 94-Used in **Love and Death** by Legman	11.00	32.00	75.00
100	12.00	36.00	85.00
101-110: 103-Lingerie panel	9.30	28.00	65.00
111-140,150-158: 155-Used in **POP**, pg. 98	8.00	24.00	55.00

	Good	Fine	N-Mint
141-149-Two Sheena stories. 141-Long Bow, Indian Boy begins, ends #160			
	9.30	28.00	65.00
159-163: Space Scouts serial in all; 163-Suicide Smith app.			
	8.00	24.00	55.00
164-The Star Pirate begins, ends #165	8.00	24.00	55.00
165-167: 165,167-Space Rangers app.	8.00	24.00	55.00

JUNGLE COMICS
1/40-No. 157, 3/53; No. 158, Spr, 1953-No. 163, Summer, 1954
Fiction House Magazines

	Good	Fine	N-Mint
1-Origin The White Panther, Kaanga, Lord of the Jungle, Tabu, Wizard of the Jungle; Wambi, the Jungle Boy, Camilla & Capt. Terry Thunder begin			
	158.00	395.00	950.00
2-Fantomah, Mystery Woman of the Jungle begins			
	64.00	193.00	450.00
3,4	54.00	160.00	375.00
5	43.00	130.00	300.00
6-10: 7,8-Powell-c	37.00	110.00	255.00
11-20: 13-Tuska-c	26.00	79.00	185.00
21-30: 25-Shows V2#1 (correct number does not appear). #27-New origin Fantomah, Daughter of the Pharoahs; Camilla dons new costume			
	22.00	65.00	155.00
31-40	19.00	56.00	130.00
41,43-50	14.00	43.00	100.00
42-Kaanga by Crandall, 12 pgs.	17.00	51.00	120.00
51-60	12.00	36.00	85.00
61-70	11.00	32.00	75.00
71-80: 79-New origin Tabu	10.00	30.00	70.00
81-97,99,101-110	8.50	25.50	60.00
98-Used in **SOTI**, pg. 185 & illo-"In ordinary comic books, there are pictures within pictures for children who know how to look"; used by N.Y. Legis. Comm.			
	15.00	45.00	105.00
100	11.00	32.00	75.00
111-163: 118-Clyde Beatty app. 135-Desert Panther begins in Terry Thunder (origin), not in #137; ends (dies) #138. 143,145-Used in **POP**, pg. 99. 152-Tiger Girl begins. 158-Sheena app.			
	8.50	25.50	60.00

JUNGLE GIRL (Nyoka, Jungle Girl No. 2 on)
Fall, 1942 (One shot) (No month listed)
Fawcett Publications

	Good	Fine	N-Mint
1-Bondage-c; photo of Kay Aldridge who played Nyoka in movie serial app. on-c. Adaptation of the classic Republic movie serial Perils of Nyoka. 1st comic to devote entire contents to a movie adaptation			
	54.00	160.00	375.00

JUNGLE JIM (Also see Ace Comics)
No. 490, 8/53-No. 1020, 8-10/59 (Painted-c)
Dell Publishing Co.

	Good	Fine	N-Mint
4-Color 490(#1)	2.65	8.00	18.00
4-Color 565(#2, 6/54)	2.00	6.00	14.00
3(10-12/54)-5	1.70	5.00	12.00
6-19(1-3/59)	1.50	4.50	10.00
4-Color 1020(#20)	1.70	5.00	12.00

JUSTICE LEAGUE (. . . International #7-25; . . . America #26 on)
May, 1987-Present (Also see Legends #6)
DC Comics

	Good	Fine	N-Mint
1-Batman, Green Lantern(Guy Gardner), Blue Beetle, Mr. Miracle, Capt. Marvel & Martian Manhunter begin	1.50	4.50	9.00
2	.90	2.75	5.50
3-Regular cover (white background)	.75	2.25	4.50
3-Limited cover (yellow background, Superman logo)			
	13.00	40.00	90.00
4-Booster Gold joins	.70	2.00	4.00
5,6: 5-Origin Gray Man; Batman vs. Guy Gardner; Creeper app.			
	.40	1.25	2.50
7-Double size ($1.25); Capt. Marvel & Dr. Fate resign; Capt. Atom, Rocket Red join	.50	1.50	3.00
8-10: 9,10-Millennium x-over	.35	1.00	2.00
11-23: 16-Bruce Wayne-c/story. 18-21-Lobo app.		.60	1.20
24-($1.50)-1st app. Justice League Europe	.25	.75	1.50
25-49,51-56: 31,32-Justice League Europe x-over		.50	1.00
50-($1.75, 52 pgs.)	.30	.90	1.80
Annual 1 (9/87)	.50	1.50	3.00
Annual 2 ('88)-Joker-c/story	.70	2.00	4.00
Annual 3 ('89, $1.75, 68 pgs.)	.30	.90	1.75
Annual 4 ('90, $2.00, 68 pgs.)-Lobo story	.50	1.50	3.00
Special 1 ('90, $1.50, 52 pgs.)-Giffen plots	.25	.75	1.50
Special 2 ('91, $2.95)	.50	1.50	3.00

JUSTICE LEAGUE EUROPE
April, 1989-Present (75 cents; $1.00 #5 on)
DC Comics

	Good	Fine	N-Mint
1-Giffen plots in all; breakdowns in 1-8,13-24	.35	1.00	2.00
2-32: 7-9-Batman app. 7,8-JLA x-over		.50	1.00
Annual 1 (1990, $2.00, 68 pgs.)-Return of the Global Guardians; Giffen plots/			
breakdowns	.35	1.00	2.00

Justice League of America #9, © DC Comics

JUSTICE LEAGUE OF AMERICA (See Brave & the Bold #28-30 & Mystery In Space #75)
Oct-Nov, 1960-No. 261, Apr, 1987 (91-99,139-157: 52 pgs.)
National Periodical Publications/DC Comics

1-Origin Despero; Aquaman, Batman, Flash, Green Lantern, J'onn J'onzz, Superman & Wonder Woman continue from Brave and the Bold

| | 147.00 | 440.00 | 1025.00 |

	Good	Fine	N-Mint
2	52.00	156.00	360.00
3-Origin/1st app. Kanjar Ro	37.00	111.00	260.00
4-Green Arrow joins JLA	28.00	86.00	200.00
5-Origin Dr. Destiny	21.00	63.00	145.00
6-8,10: 6-Origin Prof. Amos Fortune. 7-Last 10 cent issue. 10-Origin Felix Faust;			
1st app. Time Lord	18.00	54.00	125.00
9-Origin J.L.A.	25.00	75.00	175.00
11-15: 12-Origin & 1st app. Dr. Light. 13-Speedy app. 14-Atom joins JLA			
	12.00	36.00	85.00
16-20: 17-Adam Strange flashback	9.30	28.00	65.00
21,22: 21-Re-intro. of JSA (1st S.A. app. Hourman & Dr. Fate). 22- JSA x-over			
	18.00	54.00	125.00
23-28: 24-Adam Strange app. 28-Robin app.	5.70	17.00	40.00
29,30-JSA x-over; 1st Silver Age app. Starman	5.70	17.00	40.00
31-Hawkman joins JLA, Hawkgirl cameo	3.15	9.50	22.00
32-Intro & Origin Brain Storm	2.65	8.00	18.00
33,35,36,40,41: 41-Intro & origin The Key	2.30	7.00	16.00
34-Joker-c/story	3.60	11.00	25.00
37,38-JSA x-over (1st S.A. app. Mr. Terrific #38)	5.30	16.00	38.00
39-Giant G-16	2.85	8.50	20.00
42-45: 42-Metamorpho app. 43-Intro. Royal Flush Gang			
	1.30	4.00	9.00
46-JSA x-over; 1st S.A. app. Sandman	3.60	11.00	25.00
47-JSA x-over	1.70	5.00	12.00
48-Giant G-29	1.70	5.00	12.00
49-54,56,57,59,60	1.15	3.50	8.00
55-1st Silver-Age app. G.A. Robin	2.30	7.00	16.00
58-Giant G-41	1.30	4.00	9.00
61-66,68-72: 64-Intro/origin Red Tornado. 69-Wonder Woman quits; 71-Man-			
hunter leaves. 72-Last 12 cent issue	.85	2.60	6.00
67-Giant G-53	1.00	3.00	7.00
73,74,77-80: 74-Black Canary joins. 78-Re-intro Vigilante			
	.70	2.00	4.00
75-2nd app. Green Arrow in new costume	1.00	3.00	6.00
76-Giant G-65	1.00	3.00	6.00
81-84,86-92: 83-Death of Spectre	.70	2.00	4.00
85,93-(Giant G-77,G-89; 68 pgs.)	1.00	3.00	6.00
94-Reprints 1st Sandman story (Adv. #40) & origin/1st app. Starman (Adv. #61);			
Deadman x-over; N. Adams-a(4 pgs.); begin 25 cent, 52 pg. issues, ends #99			
	2.30	7.00	16.00

	Good	Fine	N-Mint
95-Origin Dr. Fate & Dr. Midnight reprint (More Fun #67, All-American #25)			
	1.00	3.00	7.00
96-Origin Hourman (Adv. #48); Wildcat-r	1.00	3.00	7.00
97-Origin JLA retold; Sargon, Starman-r	.85	2.50	5.00
98,99: 98-G.A. Sargon, Starman-r. 99-G.A. Sandman, Starman, Atom-r; last 52 pg.			
issue	.85	2.50	5.00
100-102: 102-Red Tornado dies	.85	2.50	5.00
103-106: 103-Phantom Stranger joins. 105-Elongated Man joins 106-New Red			
Tornado joins	.50	1.50	3.00
107,108-G.A. Uncle Sam, Black Condor, The Ray, Dollman, Phantom Lady & The			
Human Bomb x-over	.85	2.50	5.00
109-116: 109-Hawkman resigns. 110-116: All 100 pg. issues. 111- Shining Knight,			
Green Arrow-r. 112-Crimson Avenger, Vigilante, origin Starman-r			
	.50	1.50	3.00
117-190: 117-Hawkman rejoins. 120,121,138-Adam Strange app. 128-Wonder			
Woman rejoins. 129-Death of Red Tornado. 135-137-G.A. Bulletman,			
Bulletgirl, Spy Smasher, Mr. Scarlet, Pinky & Ibis x-over. 137-Superman			
battles G.A. Capt. Marvel. 139-157-(52 pgs.). 144-Origin retold; origin J'onn			
J'onnz. 145-Red Tornado resur- rected. 158-160-(44 pgs.). 161-Zatanna joins			
& new costume. 171- Mr. Terrific murdered. 178-Cover similar to #1; J'onn			
J'onzz app. 179-Firestorm joins. 181-Gr. Arrow leaves			
	.35	1.00	2.00
191-199: 192,193-Real origin Red Tornado. 193-1st app. All-Star Squadron as free			
16 pg. insert	.25	.75	1.50
200-Anniversary issue (76pgs., $1.50); origin retold; Green Arrow rejoins			
	.50	1.50	3.00
201-220: 203-Intro/origin new Royal Flush Gang. 207,208-JSA, JLA, & All-Star			
Squadron team-up. 219,220-True origin Black Canary			
	.25	.75	1.50
221-250 (75 cents): 228-Re-intro Martian Manhunter. 233-New JLA begins. 243-			
Aquaman leaves. 244,245-Crisis x-over. 250-Batman rejoins			
	.25	.75	1.50
251-260: 253-1st time origin Despero. 258-Death of Vibe. 258-261-Legends x-over.			
260-Death of Steel	.50	1.00	
261-Last issue	.60	1.75	3.50
Annual 1 (1983)	.40	1.25	2.50
Annual 2 (1984)-Intro new J.L.A.	.25	.75	1.50
Annual 3 (1985)-Crisis x-over	.25	.75	1.50

K

KA'A'NGA COMICS (. . . Jungle King)(See Jungle Comics)
Spring, 1949-No. 20, Summer, 1954
Fiction House Magazines (Glen-Kel Publ. Co.)

	Good	Fine	N-Mint
1-Ka'a'nga, Lord of the Jungle begins	27.00	81.00	190.00
2 (Wint., `49-`50)	13.00	40.00	90.00
3,4	10.00	30.00	70.00
5-Camilla app.	7.00	21.00	50.00
6-10: 7-Tuska-a. 9-Tabu, Wizard of the Jungle app. 10-Used in **POP**, pg. 99			
	5.00	15.00	35.00
11-15	4.00	12.00	28.00
16-Sheena app.	4.30	13.00	30.00
17-20	3.50	10.50	24.00
I.W. Reprint #1 (r-/#18) Kinstler-c	.70	2.00	4.00

KAMANDI, THE LAST BOY ON EARTH
Oct-Nov, 1972-No. 59, Sept-Oct, 1978
National Periodical Publications/DC Comics

	Good	Fine	N-Mint
1-Origin	1.60	4.80	11.00
2-5: 4-Intro. Prince Tuftan of the Tigers	1.10	3.30	6.60
6-10	.75	2.20	4.40
11-20	.55	1.65	3.30
21-40: 29-Superman x-over. 31-Intro Pyra. 32-68 pgs.; r/origin from #1			
	.35	1.10	2.20
41-59	.30	.90	1.80

KATY KEENE (Also see Laugh Comics, Pep Comics & Wilbur)
1949-No. 4, 1951; No. 5, 3/52-No. 62, Oct, 1961
Archie Publ./Close-Up/Radio Comics

	Good	Fine	N-Mint
1-Bill Woggon-a begins	68.00	205.00	475.00
2	34.00	100.00	235.00
3-5	29.00	85.00	200.00
6-10	24.00	72.00	165.00
11,13-20	20.00	60.00	140.00
12-(Scarce)	22.00	65.00	155.00
21-40	14.00	43.00	100.00
41-62	11.00	32.00	75.00

	Good	Fine	N-Mint
Annual 1('54)	37.00	110.00	260.00
Annual 2-6('55-59)	19.00	57.00	135.00
3-D 1(1953-Large size)	30.00	90.00	210.00
Charm 1(9/58)	17.00	51.00	120.00
Glamour 1(1957)	17.00	51.00	120.00
Spectacular 1('56)	17.00	51.00	120.00

KEEN DETECTIVE FUNNIES
No. 8, July, 1938-No. 24, Sept, 1940
Centaur Publications

V1#8-The Clock continues-r/Funny Picture Stories #1			
	92.00	230.00	550.00
9-Tex Martin by Eisner	48.00	145.00	335.00
10,11: 11-Dean Denton story (begins?)	41.00	122.00	285.00
V2#1,2-The Eye Sees by Frank Thomas begins; ends #23 (Not in V2#3&5). 2-Jack			
Cole-a	36.00	107.00	250.00
3-6,9-11: 3-TNT Todd begins. 4-Gabby Flynn begins. 5-Dean Denton story			
	36.00	107.00	250.00
7-The Masked Marvel by Ben Thompson begins			
	71.00	215.00	500.00
8-Nudist ranch panel w/four girls	40.00	120.00	280.00
12(12/39)-Origin The Eye Sees by Frank Thomas; death of Masked Marvel's			
sidekick ZL	48.00	145.00	335.00
V3#1,2	41.00	122.00	285.00
18,19,21,22: 18-Bondage/torture-c	41.00	122.00	285.00
20-Classic Eye Sees-c by Thomas	48.00	145.00	335.00
23,24: 23-Air Man begins (intro). 24-Air Man-c	48.00	145.00	335.00

KERRY DRAKE DETECTIVE CASES (. . . Racket Buster No. 32,33)
1944-No. 5, 1944; No. 6, Jan, 1948-No. 33, Aug, 1952
Life's Romances/Compix/Magazine Ent. No.1-5/Harvey No.6 on

nn(1944)(A-1 Comics) (slightly over-size)	12.00	36.00	84.00
2	8.00	24.00	56.00
3-5(1944)	6.00	18.00	42.00
6,8(1948); 8-Bondage-c	3.50	10.50	24.00
7-Kubert-a; biog of Andriola (artist)	4.00	12.00	28.00
9,10-Two-part marijuana story; Kerry smokes marijuana in #10			
	6.75	20.00	47.00
11-15	3.00	9.00	21.00

	Good	Fine	N-Mint
16-33	2.35	7.00	16.00

KID KOMICS (. . . Movie Komics No. 11)
Feb, 1943-No. 10, Spring, 1946
Timely Comics (USA 1,2/FCI 3-10)

	Good	Fine	N-Mint
1-Origin Captain Wonder & sidekick Tim Mullrooney, & Subbie; intro the Sea-Going Lad, Pinto Pete, & Trixie Trouble; Knuckles & White-Wash Jones only app.; Wolverton art	138.00	345.00	825.00
2-The Young Allies, Red Hawk, & Tommy Tyme begin; last Captain Wonder & Subbie	78.00	195.00	470.00
3-The Vision & Daredevils app.	53.00	131.00	315.00
4-The Destroyer begins; Sub-Mariner app.; Red Hawk & Tommy Tyme end	46.00	115.00	275.00
5,6	35.00	88.00	210.00
7-10: The Whizzer app. 7; Destroyer not in #7,8; 10-Last Destroyer, Young Allies & Whizzer	35.00	88.00	210.00

KING COMICS (Strip reprints)
Apr, 1936-No. 159, Feb, 1952 (Winter on cover)
David McKay Publications/Standard #156-on

	Good	Fine	VF-NM
1-Flash Gordon by Alex Raymond; Brick Bradford, Mandrake the Magician, Popeye & Henry begin	367.00	915.00	2200.00
	Good	**Fine**	**N-Mint**
2	158.00	395.00	950.00
3	117.00	290.00	700.00
4	71.00	215.00	500.00
5	54.00	160.00	375.00
6-10: 9-X-Mas-c	36.00	107.00	250.00
11-20	29.00	85.00	200.00
21-30	23.00	70.00	160.00
31-40: 33-Last Segar Popeye	20.00	60.00	140.00
41-50: 46-Little Lulu, Alvin & Tubby app. as text illos by Marge Buell 50-The Lone Ranger begins	18.00	54.00	125.00
51-60: 52-Barney Baxter begins?	13.00	40.00	90.00
61-The Phantom begins	11.50	34.00	80.00
62-80: 76-Flag-c	9.30	28.00	65.00
81-99: 82-Blondie begins?	8.00	24.00	55.00
100	10.00	30.00	70.00

	Good	Fine	N-Mint
101-114: 114-Last Raymond issue (1 pg.); Flash Gordon by Austin Briggs begins,			
ends #155	7.00	21.00	50.00
115-145: 117-Phantom origin retold	5.30	16.00	38.00
146,147-Prince Valiant in both	4.00	12.00	28.00
148-155-Flash Gordon ends	4.00	12.00	28.00
156-159	3.15	9.50	22.00

KING OF THE ROYAL MOUNTED (Zane Grey's)
No. 207, Dec, 1948-No. 935, Sept-Nov, 1958
Dell Publishing Co.

4-Color 207(#1, 12/48)	11.50	34.00	80.00
4-Color 265,283	8.00	24.00	56.00
4-Color 310,340	5.00	15.00	35.00
4-Color 363,384	4.00	12.00	28.00
8(6-8/52)-10	4.00	12.00	28.00
11-20	3.50	10.50	24.00
21-28(3-5/58)	3.00	9.00	21.00
4-Color 935(9-11/58)	3.00	9.00	21.00

KITTY PRYDE AND WOLVERINE
Nov, 1984-No. 6, April, 1985 (6 issue mini-series)
Marvel Comics Group

1 (From X-Men)	1.15	3.50	7.00
2-6	.70	2.00	4.00

KORAK, SON OF TARZAN (Edgar Rice Burroughs)
Jan, 1964-No. 45, Jan, 1972 (Painted-c No. 1-?)
Gold Key

1-Russ Manning-a	4.00	12.00	28.00
2-11-Russ Manning-a	2.15	6.50	15.00
12-21: 14-Jon of the Kalahari ends. 15-Mabu, Jungle Boy begins. 21-Manning-a			
	1.50	4.50	10.00
22-30	1.00	3.00	7.00
31-45	.70	2.00	5.00

KRAZY KOMICS (1st Series)
July, 1942-No. 26, Spr, 1947 (Also see Ziggy Pig)
Timely Comics (USA No. 1-21/JPC No. 22-26)

	Good	Fine	N-Mint
1-Ziggy Pig & Silly Seal begins	22.00	65.00	150.00
2	11.00	32.00	75.00
3-10	6.50	19.00	45.00
11,13,14	4.50	14.00	32.00
12-Timely's entire art staff drew themselves into a Creeper story			
	7.00	21.00	50.00
15-(8-9/44)-Becomes Funny Tunes #16; has "Super Soldier" by Pfc. Stan Lee			
	4.50	14.00	32.00
16-24,26: 16-(10-11/44)	3.15	9.50	22.00
25-Kurtzman-a, 6 pgs.	5.00	15.00	35.00

KRAZY KOMICS (2nd Series)
Aug, 1948-No. 2, Nov, 1948
Timely/Marvel Comics

1-Wolverton (10 pgs.) & Kurtzman (8 pgs.)-a; Eustice Hayseed begins, Li'l Abner swipe	22.00	65.00	150.00
2-Wolverton-a, 10 pgs.; Powerhouse Pepper cameo			
	14.00	43.00	100.00

L

LADY LUCK (Formerly Smash #1-85)
No. 86, Dec, 1949-No. 90, Aug, 1950
Quality Comics Group

	Good	Fine	N-Mint
86(#1)	37.00	110.00	255.00
87-90	29.00	85.00	200.00

LASH LARUE WESTERN (Movie star; king of the bullwhip)
Sum, 1949-No. 46, Jan, 1954 (36 pgs., 1-7,9,13,16-on)
Fawcett Publications

	Good	Fine	N-Mint
1-Lash & his horse Black Diamond begin; photo front/back-c begin			
	61.00	182.00	425.00
2(11/49)	29.00	88.00	205.00
3-5	26.00	79.00	185.00
6,7,9: 6-Last photo back-c; intro. Frontier Phantom (Lash's twin brother)			
	19.00	58.00	135.00
8,10 (52 pgs.)	20.00	60.00	140.00
11,12,14,15 (52 pgs.)	12.00	36.00	85.00
13,16-20 (36 pgs.)	11.50	34.00	80.00
21-30: 21-The Frontier Phantom app.	10.00	30.00	70.00
31-45	8.50	25.50	60.00
46-Last Fawcett issue & photo-c	9.30	28.00	65.00

LASH LARUE WESTERN (Continues from Fawcett series)
No. 47, Mar-Apr, 1954-No. 84, June, 1961
Charlton Comics

	Good	Fine	N-Mint
47-Photo-c	8.00	24.00	55.00
48	6.50	19.00	45.00
49-60	5.00	15.00	35.00
61-66,69,70: 52-r/#8; 53-r/#22	4.30	13.00	30.00
67,68-(68 pgs.). 68-Check-a	4.50	14.00	32.00
71-83	2.85	8.50	20.00
84-Last issue	3.70	11.00	26.00

LASSIE (TV) (M-G-M's . . . No. 1-36)
June, 1950-No. 70, July, 1969
Dell Publishing Co./Gold Key No. 59 (10/62) on

	Good	Fine	N-Mint
1 (52 pgs.)-Photo-c; inside lists One Shot #282 in error			
	5.70	17.00	40.00
2-Painted-c begin	3.00	9.00	21.00
3-10	2.30	7.00	16.00
11-19: 12-Rocky Langford (Lassie's master) marries Gerry Lawrence.			
15-1st app. Timbu	1.70	5.00	12.00
20-22-Matt Baker-a	2.30	7.00	16.00
23-40: 33-Robinson-a. 39-1st app. Timmy as Lassie picks up her TV family			
	1.15	3.50	8.00
41-70: 63-Last Timmy. 64-r-/#19. 65-Forest Ranger Corey Stuart begins, ends #69.			
70-Forest Rangers Bob Ericson & Scott Turner app. (Lassie's new masters)			
	.85	2.50	5.00

LAUGH COMICS (Formerly Black Hood #1-19) (Laugh #226 on)
No. 20, Fall, 1946-No. 400, 1987
Archie Publications (Close-Up)

	Good	Fine	N-Mint
20-Archie begins; Katy Keene & Taffy begin by Woggon; Suzie & Wilbur also			
begin	41.00	122.00	285.00
21-25: 24-"Pipsy" by Kirby, 6 pgs.	19.00	57.00	135.00
26-30	11.00	32.00	75.00
31-40	8.00	24.00	55.00
41-60: 41,54-Debbi by Woggon	4.50	14.00	32.00
61-80: 67-Debbi by Woggon	2.85	8.50	20.00
81-99	2.00	6.00	14.00
100	3.00	9.00	21.00
101-126: 125-Debbi app.	1.35	4.00	9.00
127-144: Super-hero app. in all	1.70	5.00	12.00
145-160: 157-Josie app.	.85	2.50	5.00
161-165,167-200	.50	1.50	3.00
166-Beatles-c	1.30	4.00	9.00
201-240	.25	.75	1.50
241-280		.40	.80
281-400: 381-384-Katy Keene app.; by Woggon-381,382			
		.30	.60

LEADING COMICS (. . . Screen Comics No. 42 on)
Winter, 1941-42-No. 41, Feb-Mar, 1950
National Periodical Publications

1-Origin The Seven Soldiers of Victory; Crimson Avenger, Green Arrow &

Leading Comics #6, © DC Comics

	Good	Fine	N-Mint
Speedy, Shining Knight, The Vigilante, Star Spangled Kid & Stripesy begin.			
The Dummy (Vigilante villain) app.	192.00	480.00	1150.00
2-Meskin-a	68.00	205.00	475.00
3	54.00	160.00	375.00
4,5	46.00	140.00	325.00
6-10	39.00	118.00	275.00
11-14(Spring, 1945)	29.00	86.00	200.00
15-(Sum,'45)-Content change to funny animal	12.00	36.00	85.00
16-22,24-30	5.30	16.00	38.00
23-1st app. Peter Porkchops by Otto Feur	12.00	36.00	85.00
31,32,34-41	4.00	12.00	28.00
33-(Scarce)	6.00	18.00	42.00

LEADING SCREEN COMICS (Formerly Leading Comics)
No. 42, Apr-May, 1950-No. 77, Aug-Sept, 1955
National Periodical Publications

42	5.00	15.00	35.00

	Good	Fine	N-Mint
43-77	3.15	9.50	22.00

LEAVE IT TO BINKY (See Showcase #70) (No. 1-22: 52 pgs.)
2-3/48-#60, 10/58; #61, 6-7/68-#71, 2-3/70 (Teen-age humor)
National Periodical Publications

1-Lucy wears Superman costume	17.00	51.00	120.00
2	8.00	24.00	55.00
3-5: 5-Superman cameo	5.70	17.00	40.00
6-10	4.50	14.00	32.00
11-14,16-20	3.60	11.00	25.00
15-Scribbly story by Mayer	4.30	13.00	30.00
21-28,30-45: 45-Last pre-code (2/55)	2.30	7.00	16.00
29-Used in **POP**, pg. 78	2.30	7.00	16.00
46-60	1.30	4.00	9.00
61-71	.85	2.60	6.00

LEGENDS
Nov, 1986-No. 6, Apr, 1987 (Mini-series)
DC Comics

1-Byrne c/a(p) begins. 1st new Capt. Marvel	.35	1.10	2.20
2-5: 3-Intro new Suicide Squad; death of Blockbuster			
	.25	.70	1.40
6-Intro/1st app. New Justice League	1.00	3.00	6.00

LEGENDS OF THE DARK KNIGHT (Batman)
Nov, 1989-Present ($1.50, color)
DC Comics

1-"The Shaman of Gotham" begins, ends #5; outer cover has four different color			
variations, all worth same	.80	2.40	4.80
2	.50	1.50	3.00
3-5	.35	1.10	2.20
6-10-"Gothic" by Grant Morrison (scripts)	.50	1.50	3.00
11-18: 11-15-Gulacy/Austin-a. 14-Catwoman app.	.35	1.00	2.00
19-24: 19-Begin $1.75 cover	.30	.90	1.80

LEGION OF SUPER-HEROES (See Action, Adventure & Superboy)
Feb, 1973-No. 4, July-Aug, 1973
National Periodical Publications

	Good	Fine	N-Mint
1-Legion & Tommy Tomorrow reprints begin	1.00	3.00	6.00
2-4: 2-Forte-r. 3-r/Adv. #340. Action #240. 4-r/Adv. #341, Action #233; Mooney-r	.70	2.00	4.00

LEGION OF SUPER-HEROES
Aug, 1984-No. 63, Aug, 1989 ($1.25-$1.75, deluxe format)
DC Comics

	Good	Fine	N-Mint
1	.35	1.00	2.00
2-10: 4-Death of Karate Kid. 5-Death of Nemesis Kid	.25	.80	1.60
11-14: 12-Cosmic Boy, Lightning Lad, & Saturn Girl resign. 14-Intro new members: Tellus, Sensor Girl, Quislet		.60	1.20
15-18: 15-17-Crisis tie-ins. 18-Crisis x-over	.25	.80	1.60
19-25: 25-Sensor Girl I.D. revealed as Princess Projectra		.60	1.20
26-36,39-44: 35-Saturn Girl rejoins. 40-$1.75 cover price begins. 42,43-Millennium tie-ins. 44-Origin Quislet		.55	1.10
37,38-Death of Superboy	1.70	5.00	10.00
45 ($2.95, 68 pgs.)	.40	1.20	2.40
46-49,51-62		.55	1.10
50-Double size, $2.50	.35	1.00	2.00
63-Final issue	.25	.70	1.40
Annual 1 (10/85, 52 pgs.)-Crisis tie-in	.30	.90	1.80
Annual 2 (10/86, 52 pgs.). 3 (10/87, 52 pgs.)	.25	.80	1.60
Annual 4(11/88, $2.50, 52 pgs.)	.35	1.00	2.00

LEGION OF SUPER-HEROES
Nov, 1989-Present ($1.75, color)
DC Comics

	Good	Fine	N-Mint
1-Giffen-c/a(p) & scripts in all	.40	1.25	2.50
2-24: 8-Origin. 13-Free poster by Giffen showing new costumes	.30	.90	1.80
Annual 1 (1990, $3.50, 68 pgs.)	.60	1.75	3.50
Annual 2 (1991, $3.50, 68 pgs.)	.60	1.75	3.50

LITTLE ARCHIE (The Adventures of . . . #13-on)
1956-No. 180, Feb, 1983 (Giants No. 3-84)
Archie Publications

	Good	Fine	N-Mint
1-(Scarce)	29.00	86.00	200.00

	Good	Fine	N-Mint
2	14.00	43.00	100.00
3-5	9.30	28.00	65.00
6-10	6.00	18.00	42.00
11-20	3.70	11.00	26.00
21-30	2.30	7.00	16.00
31-40: Little Pureheart apps. #40-42,44	1.15	3.50	8.00
41-60: 42-Intro. The Little Archies. 59-Little Sabrina begins			
	.70	2.00	4.00
61-84: 84-Last Giant-Size	.35	1.00	2.00
85-100	.25	.75	1.50
101-180		.40	.80
...In Animal Land 1('57)	10.00	30.00	70.00
...In Animal Land 17(Winter, 1957-58)-19(Summer,'58)-Formerly Li'l Jinx			
	4.50	14.00	32.00

LITTLE DOT (See Sad Sack Comics)
Sept, 1953-No. 164, April, 1976
Harvey Publications

	Good	Fine	N-Mint
1-Intro./1st app. Richie Rich & Little Lotta	50.00	150.00	350.00
2-1st app. Freckles & Pee Wee (Richie Rich's poor friends)			
	25.00	75.00	175.00
3	16.00	48.00	110.00
4	11.50	34.00	80.00
5-Origin dots on Little Dot's dress	13.00	40.00	90.00
6-Richie Rich, Little Lotta, & Little Dot all on cover; 1st Richie Rich cover			
featured	13.00	40.00	90.00
7-10	5.70	17.00	40.00
11-20	4.00	12.00	28.00
21-40	2.00	6.00	14.00
41-60	1.00	3.00	7.00
61-80	.70	2.00	4.00
81-100	.50	1.50	3.00
101-141	.35	1.00	2.00
142-145: All 52 pg. Giants	.40	1.20	2.40
146-164		.50	1.00

LITTLE LOTTA
11/55-No. 110, 11/73; No. 111, 9/74-No. 121, 5/76
Harvey Publications

	Good	Fine	N-Mint
1-Richie Rich (r) & Little Dot begin	19.00	57.00	130.00
2,3	8.50	25.50	60.00
4,5	4.50	14.00	32.00
6-10	3.50	10.50	24.00
11-20	2.00	6.00	14.00
21-40	1.30	4.00	9.00
41-60	.85	2.50	6.00
61-80	.50	1.50	3.00
81-99	.35	1.00	2.00
100-103: All 52 pg. Giants	.40	1.20	2.40
104-121	.25	.75	1.50

LOBO (Also see Action #650, Advs. of Superman, Justice League,
    Mister Miracle, Omega Men #3 & Superman #41)
Nov, 1990-No. 4, Feb, 1991 ($1.50, color, mini-series)

1-(99 cents)-Giffen plots/Breakdowns in all	.50	1.50	3.00
2-Legion '89 spin-off	.40	1.25	2.50
3,4	.35	1.00	2.00

LOGAN'S RUN
Jan, 1977-No. 7, July, 1977
Marvel Comics Group

1: 1-5 are based on novel and movie	.35	1.00	2.00
2-5,7: 6,7-New stories based on novel		.60	1.20
6-Early Thanos app.	1.15	3.50	8.00

LONE RANGER, THE (Movie, radio & TV; Clayton Moore starred as L. Ranger
    in the movies; No. 1-37: strip reprints)
Jan-Feb, 1948-No. 145, May-July, 1962
Dell Publishing Co.

1 (36 pgs.)-The L. Ranger, his horse Silver, companion Tonto & his horse Scout			
begin	54.00	160.00	375.00
2 (52 pgs. begin, end #41)	26.00	77.00	180.00
3-5	20.00	60.00	140.00
6,7,9,10	17.00	51.00	120.00
8-Origin retold; Indian back-c begin, end #35	22.00	65.00	155.00

	Good	Fine	N-Mint
11-20: 11-"Young Hawk" Indian boy serial begins, ends #145			
	11.50	34.00	80.00
21,22,24-31: 51-Reprint. 31-1st Mask logo	9.30	28.00	65.00
23-Origin retold	13.00	40.00	90.00
32-37: 32-Painted-c begin. 36-Animal photo back-c begin, end #49. 37-Last			
newspaper-r issue; new outfit	7.00	21.00	50.00
38-41 (All 52 pgs.)	6.00	18.00	42.00
42-50 (36 pgs.)	5.00	15.00	35.00
51-74 (52 pgs.): 71-Blank inside-c	5.00	15.00	35.00
75-99: 76-Flag-c. 79-X-mas-c	4.00	12.00	28.00
100	5.70	17.00	40.00
101-111: Last painted-c	4.00	12.00	28.00
112-Clayton Moore photo-c begin, end #145	14.00	43.00	100.00
113-117	7.00	21.00	50.00
118-Origin Lone Ranger, Tonto, & Silver retold; Special anniversary issue			
	13.00	40.00	90.00
119-145: 139-Last issue by Fran Striker	6.50	19.00	45.00

LONE RANGER, THE
9/64-No. 16, 12/69; No. 17, 11/72; No. 18, 9/74-No. 28, 3/77
Gold Key (Reprints #13-20)

	Good	Fine	N-Mint
1-Retells origin	2.85	8.50	20.00
2	1.50	4.50	10.00
3-10: Small Bear-r in #6-10	1.00	3.00	7.00
11-17: Small Bear-r in #11,12	.85	2.50	6.00
18-28	.55	1.65	4.00
Golden West 1(30029-610)-Giant, 10/66-r/most Golden West #3-including			
Clayton Moore photo front/back-c	5.70	17.00	40.00

LONE WOLF AND CUB
May, 1987-Present ($1.95-$2.50-$2.95-$3.25, B&W, deluxe size)
First Comics

	Good	Fine	N-Mint
1	1.15	3.50	7.00
1-2nd print, 3rd print	.35	1.00	2.00
2	.85	2.50	5.00
2-2nd print	.35	1.00	2.00
3	.50	1.50	3.00
4-12: 6-72 pg. origin issue. 8-$2.50-c begins	.45	1.30	2.60
13-25	.40	1.25	2.50
26-30,33 ($2.95-c)	.50	1.50	3.00

	Good	Fine	N-Mint
31,32,34-38,40,42 ($3.25): 40,42-Ploog-c	.55	1.65	3.25
39-($5.95, 120 pgs.)-Ploog-c	1.00	3.00	6.00
41-($3.95, 84 pgs.)-Ploog-c	.70	2.00	4.00

LONGSHOT
Sept, 1985-No. 6, Feb, 1986 (Limited series)
Marvel Comics Group

	Good	Fine	N-Mint
1-Arthur Adams-c/a in all	3.70	11.00	22.00
2	3.00	9.00	18.00
3-5	2.30	7.00	14.00
6-Double size	3.00	9.00	18.00

Looney Tunes and Merrie Melodies Comics #29, © Warner Bros.

LOONEY TUNES AND MERRIE MELODIES COMICS
1941-No. 246, July-Sept, 1962
Dell Publishing Co.

	Good	Fine	VF-NM
1-Porky Pig, Bugs Bunny, Daffy Duck, Elmer Fudd, Mary Jane & Sniffles, Pat,			

	Good	Fine	VF-NM
Patsy and Pete begin (1st comic book app. of each). Bugs Bunny story by Win Smith (early Mickey Mouse artist)			
	136.00	405.00	950.00
	Good	**Fine**	**N-Mint**
2 (11/41)	60.00	180.00	420.00
3-Kandi the Cave Kid begins by Walt Kelly; also in #4-6,8,11,15			
	54.00	160.00	375.00
4-Kelly-a	47.00	140.00	330.00
5-Bugs Bunny The Super Rabbit app. (1st funny animal super hero?); Kelly-a			
	37.00	110.00	250.00
6,8-Kelly-a	26.00	77.00	180.00
7,9,10: 9-Painted-c. 10-Flag-c	21.00	62.00	145.00
11,15-Kelly-a; 15-X-Mas-c	21.00	62.00	145.00
12-14,16-19	17.00	51.00	120.00
20-25: Pat, Patsy & Pete by Walt Kelly in all	17.00	51.00	120.00
26-30	11.50	34.00	80.00
31-40	8.50	25.50	60.00
41-50	6.00	18.00	42.00
51-60	4.00	12.00	28.00
61-80	2.65	8.00	18.00
81-99: 87-X-Mas-c	2.00	6.00	14.00
100	2.15	7.00	16.00
101-120	1.60	4.80	11.00
121-150	1.30	4.00	9.00
151-200	1.00	3.00	7.00
201-246	.70	2.00	5.00

LORNA THE JUNGLE GIRL (. . . Jungle Queen #1-5)
July, 1953-No. 26, Aug, 1957
Atlas Comics (NPI 1/OMC 2-11/NPI 12-26)

1-Origin	12.00	36.00	85.00
2-Intro. & 1st app. Greg Knight	6.50	19.00	45.00
3-5	5.30	16.00	38.00
6-11: 11-Last pre-code (1/55)	4.00	12.00	28.00
12-17,19-26	3.00	9.00	21.00
18-Williamson/Colleta-c	4.30	13.00	30.00

LOVE CONFESSIONS
Oct, 1949-No. 54, Dec, 1956 (Photo-c: 6,11-18,21)
Quality Comics Group

	Good	Fine	N-Mint
1-Ward-c/a, 9 pgs; Gustavson-a	14.00	42.00	100.00
2-Gustavson-a	5.00	15.00	35.00
3	3.50	10.50	24.00
4-Crandall-a	4.65	14.00	32.00
5-Ward-a, 7 pgs.	5.50	16.50	38.00
6,7,9,11-13,15,16,18	1.70	5.00	12.00
8,10-Ward-a(2 stories in #10)	4.65	14.00	32.00
14,17,19,22-Ward-a; 17-Faith Domerque photo-c	3.85	11.50	27.00
20-Baker-a, Ward-a(2)	4.65	14.00	32.00
21,23-28,30-38,40-42: Last pre-code, 4/55	1.15	3.50	8.00
29-Ward-a	3.65	11.00	25.00
39-Matt Baker-a	1.70	5.00	12.00
43,44,46-48,50-54: 47-Ward-c?	1.00	3.00	7.00
45-Ward-a	2.15	6.50	15.00
49-Baker-c/a	2.65	8.00	18.00

LUCY SHOW, THE (TV) (Also see I Love Lucy)
June, 1963-No. 5, June, 1964 (Photo-c: 1,2)
Gold Key

	Good	Fine	N-Mint
1	6.50	19.00	45.00
2	4.30	13.00	30.00
3-5: Photo back-c,1,2,4,5	3.70	11.00	26.00

M

MAD
Oct-Nov, 1952-Present (No. 24 on are magazine format)
E. C. Comics

	Good	Fine	N-Mint
1-Wood, Davis, Elder start as regulars	107.00	321.00	750.00
2-Davis-c	47.00	140.00	325.00
3,4: 4-Reefer mention story "Flob Was a Slob" by Davis			
	30.00	90.00	210.00
5-Low distribution; Elder-c	52.00	155.00	365.00
6-11: 11-Wolverton-a	22.00	65.00	150.00
12-15	20.00	60.00	140.00
16-23(5/55): 21-1st app. Alfred E. Neuman on-c in fake ad. 22-all by Elder.			
23-Special cancel announcement	15.00	45.00	105.00
24(7/55)-1st magazine issue (25 cents); Kurtzman logo & border on-c			
	31.00	95.00	220.00
25-Jaffee starts as regular writer	16.00	48.00	110.00
26,27: 27-Davis-c; Jaffee starts as story artist; new logo			
	12.00	36.00	85.00
28-Elder-c; Heath back-c; last issue edited by Kurtzman; (three cover variations exist with different wording on contents banner on lower right of cover; value of each the same)	10.00	30.00	70.00
29-Wood-c; Kamen-a; Don Martin starts as regular; Feldstein editing begins			
	10.00	30.00	70.00
30-1st A. E. Neuman cover by Mingo; Crandall inside-c; last Elder-a; Bob Clarke starts as regular; Disneyland spoof	13.00	40.00	90.00
31-Freas starts as regular; last Davis art until #99	8.50	25.50	60.00
32,33: 32-Orlando, Drucker, Woodbridge start as regulars; Wood back-c.			
33-Orlando back-c	8.00	24.00	55.00
34-Berg starts as regular	7.00	21.00	50.00
35-Mingo wraparound-c; Crandall-a	7.00	21.00	50.00
36-40	5.00	15.00	35.00
41-50	3.50	10.50	24.00
51-60: 60-Two Clarke-c; Prohias starts as reg.	2.65	8.00	18.00
61-70: 64-Rickard starts as regular. 68-Martin-c	2.00	6.00	14.00
71-80: 76-Aragones starts as regular	1.70	5.00	12.00
81-90: 86-1st Fold-in. 89-One strip by Walt Kelly. 90-Frazetta back-c; Beatles app.			
	1.50	4.50	10.00

	Good	Fine	N-Mint
91-100: 91-Jaffee starts as story artist. 99-Davis-a resumes			
	1.15	3.50	8.00
101-120: 101-Infinity-c. 105-Batman TV show take-off. 106-Frazetta back-c			
	.85	2.60	6.00
121-140: 121-Beatles app. 122-Ronald Reagan photo inside; Drucker & Mingo-c. 128-Last Orlando. 130-Torres begins as reg. 131-Reagan photo back-c. 135,139-Davis-c	.70	2.00	4.00
141-170: 165-Martin-c. 169-Drucker-c	.40	1.25	2.50
171-200: 173,178-Davis-c. 176-Drucker-c. 182-Bob Jones starts as regular. 186-Star Trek take-off. 187-Harry North starts as regular. 196-Star Wars take-off	.35	1.00	2.00
201-300: 203-Star Wars take-off. 204-Hulk TV show take-off. 208- Superman movie take-off. 286-Drucker-c. 289-Batman movie parody. 291-TMNT parody	.25	.75	1.50

MAGIC COMICS
Aug, 1939-No. 123, Nov-Dec, 1949
David McKay Publications

	Good	Fine	N-Mint
1-Mandrake the Magician, Henry, Popeye (not by Segar), Blondie, Barney Baxter, Secret Agent X-9 (not by Raymond), Bunky by Billy DeBeck & Thornton Burgess text stories illustrated by Harrison Cady begin			
	117.00	291.00	700.00
2	47.00	141.00	330.00
3	36.00	107.00	250.00
4	30.00	90.00	210.00
5	24.00	73.00	170.00
6-10	19.00	58.00	135.00
11-16,18-20	16.00	48.00	110.00
17-The Lone Ranger begins	17.00	51.00	120.00
21-30	11.00	32.00	75.00
31-40	8.50	25.50	60.00
41-50	7.00	21.00	50.00
51-60	5.30	16.00	38.00
61-70	4.00	12.00	28.00
71-99	3.15	9.50	22.00
100	4.00	12.00	28.00
101-106,109-123	2.65	8.00	18.00
107,108-Flash Gordon app; not by Raymond	3.70	11.00	26.00

MAGNUS, ROBOT FIGHTER (. . . 4000 A.D.) (See Doctor Solar)
Feb, 1963-No. 46, Jan, 1977 (Painted-covers)
Gold Key

	Good	Fine	N-Mint
1-Origin Magnus; Aliens series begins	12.00	36.00	85.00
2,3	6.50	19.00	45.00
4-10	4.30	13.00	30.00
11-20	3.15	9.50	22.00
21,24-28: 22-Origin-r/#1. 28-Aliens ends	2.00	6.00	14.00
22,23-12 cent and 15 cent editions exist	2.00	6.00	14.00
29-46-Reprints	1.15	3.50	8.00

MAN-BAT (See Batman Family, Brave & the Bold, & Detective #400)
Dec-Jan, 1975-76-No. 2, Feb-Mar, 1976; Dec, 1984
National Periodical Publications/DC Comics

	Good	Fine	N-Mint
1-Ditko-a(p); Aparo-c; Batman, She-Bat app.	.85	2.50	5.00
2-Aparo-c	.50	1.50	3.00
1 (12/84)-N. Adams-r(3)/Det.(Vs. Batman on-c)	.70	2.00	4.00

MAN FROM U.N.C.L.E., THE (TV)
Feb, 1965-No. 22, April, 1969 (All photo covers)
Gold Key

	Good	Fine	N-Mint
1	10.00	30.00	70.00
2-Photo back c-2-8	6.85	20.50	48.00
3-10: 7-Jet Dream begins (all new stories)	4.30	13.00	30.00
11-22: 21,22-Reprint #10 & 7	3.50	10.50	24.00

MANHUNT! (Becomes Red Fox #15 on)
Oct, 1947-No. 14, 1953
Magazine Enterprises

1-Red Fox by L. B. Cole, Undercover Girl by Whitney, Space Ace begin;			
negligee panels	21.00	62.00	145.00
2-Electrocution-c	15.00	45.00	105.00
3-6	13.00	40.00	90.00
7-9: 7-Space Ace ends. 8-Trail Colt begins (intro/1st app.) by Guardineer			
	11.00	32.00	75.00
10-G. Ingels-a	11.00	32.00	75.00

	Good	Fine	N-Mint
11(8/48)-Frazetta-a, 7 pgs.; The Duke, Scotland Yard begin			
	19.00	57.00	132.00
12	8.00	24.00	55.00
13(A-1 #63)-Frazetta, r-/Trail Colt #1, 7 pgs.	17.00	51.00	120.00
14(A-1 #77)-Bondage/hypo-c; last L. B. Cole Red Fox; Ingels-a			
	11.50	34.00	80.00

MAN-THING (See Fear & Marvel Comics Presents)
Jan, 1974-No. 22, Oct, 1975; V2#1, Nov, 1979-V2#11, July, 1981
Marvel Comics Group

1-Howard the Duck(2nd app.) cont./Fear #19	1.60	4.80	11.00
2	.85	2.50	5.00
3-1st app. original Foolkiller	.85	2.50	5.00
4-Origin Foolkiller	.50	1.50	3.00
5-11-Ploog-a	.35	1.00	2.00
12-22: 19-1st app. Scavenger. 20-Spidey cameo. 21-Origin Scavenger, Man-Thing.			
22-Howard the Duck cameo	.25	.75	1.50
V2#1(1979)-11: 6-Golden-c		.50	1.00

MARC SPECTOR: MOON KNIGHT (Also see Moon Knight)
June, 1989-Present ($1.50, color, direct sale only)
Marvel Comics

1	.50	1.50	3.00
2-7: 4-Intro new Midnight	.30	.90	1.80
8,9-Punisher app.	1.00	3.00	6.00
10-18,22-24,26-32: 20-Guice-c. 21-23-Cowan-c(p)	.25	.75	1.50
19-21-Spider-Man & Punisher app.	.60	1.75	3.50
25-($2.50, 52 pgs.)-Ghost Rider app.	.40	1.25	2.50

MARGE'S LITTLE LULU (Little Lulu #207 on)
No. 74, 6/45-No. 164, 7-9/62; No. 165, 10/62-No. 206, 8/72
Dell Publishing Co./Gold Key #165-206

4-Color 74('45)-Intro Lulu, Tubby & Alvin	90.00	270.00	630.00
4-Color 97(2/46)	47.00	140.00	330.00
(Above two books are all John Stanley-cover, pencils, and inks.)			
4-Color 110('46)-1st Alvin Story Telling Time;	33.00	100.00	230.00
4-Color 115-1st app. Boys' Clubhouse	33.00	100.00	230.00

	Good	Fine	N-Mint
4-Color 120, 131: 120-1st app. Eddie	30.00	90.00	210.00
4-Color 139('47),146,158	27.00	81.00	190.00
4-Color 165 (10/47)-Smokes doll hair & has wild hallucinations. 1st Tubby detective story	27.00	81.00	190.00
1(1-2/48)-Lulu's Diary feat. begins	56.00	168.00	390.00
2-1st app. Gloria; 1st Tubby story in a L.L. comic; 1st app. Miss Feeny	29.00	87.00	200.00
3-5	25.00	75.00	175.00
6-10: 7-1st app. Annie; Xmas-c	18.00	54.00	125.00
11-20: 19-1st app. Wilbur. 20-1st app. Mr. McNabbem	15.00	45.00	105.00
21-30: 26-r/F.C. 110. 30-Xmas-c	11.50	34.00	80.00
31-38,40: 35-1st Mumday story	8.50	25.50	60.00
39-Intro. Witch Hazel in "That Awful Witch Hazel"	10.00	30.00	70.00
41-60: 42-Xmas-c. 45-2nd Witch Hazel app. 49-Gives Stanley & others credit	8.00	24.00	55.00
61-80: 63-1st app. Chubby (Tubby's cousin). 68-1st app. Prof. Cleff. 78-Xmas-c. 80-Intro. Little Itch (2/55)	5.70	17.00	40.00
81-99: 90-Xmas-c	4.00	12.00	30.00
100	4.60	14.00	35.00
101-130: 123-1st app. Fifi	3.00	9.00	21.00
131-164: 135-Last Stanley-p	2.65	8.00	18.00
165-Giant; ... In Paris ('62)	4.00	12.00	32.00
166-Giant; ... Christmas Diary ('62-'63)	4.00	12.00	32.00
167-169	1.70	5.00	12.00
170,172,175,176,178-196,198-200-Stanley-r. 182-1st app. Little Scarecrow Boy	1.30	4.00	9.00
171,173,174,177,197	.85	2.50	6.00
201,203,206-Last issue to carry Marge's name	.55	1.65	4.00
202,204,205-Stanley-r	1.00	3.00	7.00
... Tubby in Japan (12 cents)(5-7/62) 01476-207	5.70	17.00	40.00
... Summer Camp 1(8/67-G.K.-Giant) '57-58-r	4.65	14.00	32.00
... Trick `N' Treat 1(12-)(12/62-Gold Key)	5.00	15.00	35.00

MARGE'S TUBBY (Little Lulu)
No. 381, Aug, 1952-No. 49, Dec-Feb, 1961-62
Dell Publishing Co./Gold Key

4-Color 381(#1)-Stanley script; Irving Tripp-a	12.00	36.00	84.00
4-Color 430,444-Stanley-a	7.00	21.00	50.00

	Good	Fine	N-Mint
4-Color 461 (4/53)-1st Tubby & Men From Mars story; Stanley-a			
	6.50	19.50	45.00
5 (7-9/53)-Stanley-a	5.00	15.00	35.00
6-10	3.50	10.50	24.00
11-20	2.85	8.50	20.00
21-30	2.35	7.00	16.00
31-49	2.00	6.00	14.00
... & the Little Men From Mars No. 30020-410 (10/64-G.K.)-25 cents; 68 pgs.			
	5.00	15.00	40.00

MARVEL AND DC PRESENT (Featuring the Uncanny X-Men and the New Teen Titans)
Nov, 1982 (One Shot, $2.00, 68 pgs., printed on Baxter paper)
Marvel Comics Group/DC Comics

1-Simonson/Austin-c/a; Perez-a(p)	1.85	5.50	11.00

MARVEL BOY (Astonishing #3 on)
Dec, 1950-No. 2, Feb, 1951
Marvel Comics (MPC)

1-Origin Marvel Boy by Russ Heath	35.00	105.00	245.00
2-Everett-a	29.00	85.00	200.00

MARVEL COLLECTORS ITEM CLASSICS
Feb, 1965-No. 22, Aug, 1969 (68 pgs.)
Marvel Comics Group(ATF)

1-Fantastic Four, Spider-Man, Thor, Hulk, Iron Man-r begin; all are 25 cent cover price	4.50	14.00	32.00
2 (4/66)-4	2.65	8.00	18.00
5-22	1.15	3.50	8.00

MARVEL COMICS (Marvel Mystery Comics #2 on)
October, November, 1939
Timely Comics (Funnies, Inc.)

	Good	Fine	VF-NM
1-Origin Sub-Mariner by Bill Everett(1st newsstand app.); Human Torch by Carl Burgos, Kazar the Great (1st Tarzan clone), & Jungle Terror (only app.); intro.			

	Good	Fine	VF-NM
The Angel by Gustavson, The Masked Raider (ends #12)			
	5800.00	14,600.00	32,000.00

MARVEL COMICS PRESENTS
Early Sept, 1988-Present ($1.25, color, bi-weekly)
Marvel Comics

	Good	Fine	N-Mint
1-Wolverine by Buscema in #1-10	1.35	4.00	8.00
2-5	.70	2.00	4.00
6-10: 6-Sub-Mariner app. 10-Colossus begins	.50	1.50	3.00
11-24,26-37: 17-Cyclops begins. 19-1st app. Damage Control. 24-Havok begins. 26-Hulk begins by Rogers. 29-Quasar app. 31-Excalibur begins by Austin (i). 33-Capt. America. 37-Devil-Slayer app.		.60	1.25
25-Origin & 1st app. Nth Man	.35	1.00	2.00
38-Wolverine begins by Buscema; Hulk app.	.50	1.50	3.00
39-47,51-53: 39-Spider-Man app.	.35	1.00	2.00
48-50-Wolverine & Spider-Man team-up. 48-Wasp app. 50-Silver Surfer. 50-53-Comet Man; Bill Mumy scripts	.60	1.75	3.50
54-61-Wolverine/Hulk; 54-Werewolf by Night begins; The Shroud by Ditko. 58-Iron Man by Ditko. 59-Punisher	.70	2.00	4.00
62,63: 62-Deathlok story. 62,63-Wolverine stories	.35	1.00	2.00
64-71-Wolverine/Ghost Rider 8 part story	.35	1.00	2.00
72-Begin 13 part Weapon-X story(Wolverine) by B. Windsor-Smith (prologue)			
	.85	2.50	5.00
73-Part 1	.50	1.50	3.00
74-Part 2	.40	1.25	2.50
75-84-Weapon-X ends	.25	.75	1.50
85-90		.65	1.30

MARVEL FAMILY (Also see Captain Marvel Adventures No. 18)
Dec, 1945-No. 89, Jan, 1954
Fawcett Publications

	Good	Fine	N-Mint
1-Origin Captain Marvel, Captain Marvel Jr., Mary Marvel, & Uncle Marvel retold; Origin/1st app. Black Adam	70.00	210.00	490.00
2-The 3 Lt. Marvels & Uncle Marvel app.	35.00	105.00	245.00
3	25.00	75.00	175.00
4,5	22.00	65.00	150.00
6-10: 7-Shazam app.	17.00	51.00	120.00
11-20	12.00	36.00	85.00

The Marvel Family #41, © *Fawcett Publications*

	Good	**Fine**	**N-Mint**
21-30	9.30	28.00	65.00
31-40	8.00	24.00	55.00
41-46,48-50	6.50	19.00	45.00
47-Flying Saucer-c/story	8.00	24.00	55.00
51-76,79,80,82-89: 78,81-Used in **POP**, pgs. 92,93			
	5.70	17.00	40.00
77-Communist Threat-c	8.00	24.00	55.00

MARVEL FEATURE (See Marvel Two-In-One)
Dec, 1971-No. 12, Nov, 1973 (No. 1,2: 25 cents)(1-3: Quarterly)
Marvel Comics Group

1-Origin/1st app. The Defenders; Sub-Mariner, Hulk & Dr. Strange; '50s Sub-			
Mariner-r; Neal Adams-c	4.50	14.00	32.00
2-G.A. 1950s Sub-Mariner-r	2.15	6.50	15.00
3-Defender series ends	2.15	6.50	15.00
4-Re-intro Antman(1st app. since '60s), begin series; brief origin			
	1.00	3.00	7.00

	Good	Fine	N-Mint
5-10: 6-Wasp app. & begins team-ups. 8-Origin Antman & Wasp-r/ TTA #44. 9-Iron Man app. 10-Last Antman.	.70	2.00	4.00
11-Hulk battles Thing; origin Fantastic Four retold	1.00	3.00	6.00
12-Thing/Iron Man; Thanos app. (11/73)	.85	2.50	5.00

MARVEL MYSTERY COMICS (Formerly Marvel Comics) (Marvel Tales No. 93 on)
No. 2, Dec, 1939-No. 92, June, 1949
Timely /Marvel Comics (TP 2-17/TCI 18-54/MCI 55-92)

	Good	Fine	VF-NM
2-American Ace begins, ends #3; Human Torch (blue costume) by Burgos, Sub-Mariner by Everett continues; 2pg. origin recap of Human Torch	817.00	2040.00	4900.00
	Good	**Fine**	**N-Mint**
3-New logo from Marvel pulp begins	467.00	1165.00	2800.00
4-Intro. Electro, the Marvel of the Age (ends #19), The Ferret, Mystery Detective (ends #9)	383.00	960.00	2300.00
	Good	**Fine**	**VF-NM**
5 (Scarce)	567.00	1415.00	3400.00
	Good	**Fine**	**N-Mint**
6,7	233.00	585.00	1400.00
8-Human Torch & Sub-Mariner battle	300.00	750.00	1800.00
	Good	**Fine**	**VF-NM**
9-(Scarce)-Human Torch & Sub-Mariner battle	400.00	1000.00	2400.00
	Good	**Fine**	**N-Mint**
10-Human Torch & Sub-Mariner battle, conclusion; Terry Vance, the Schoolboy Sleuth begins, ends #57	207.00	515.00	1240.00
11	158.00	395.00	950.00
12-Classic Kirby-c	150.00	375.00	900.00
13-Intro. & 1st app. The Vision by S&K; Sub-Mariner dons new costume, ends #15	167.00	415.00	1000.00
14-16	107.00	265.00	640.00
17-Human Torch/Sub-Mariner team-up by Everett/Burgos; pin-up on back-c	121.00	300.00	725.00
18	100.00	250.00	600.00
19-Origin Toro in text	103.00	260.00	620.00
20-Origin The Angel in text	98.00	245.00	585.00
21-Intro. & 1st app. The Patriot; not in #46-48; pin-up on back-c	92.00	230.00	550.00

	Good	Fine	N-Mint

22-25: 23-Last Gustavson Angel; origin The Vision in text. 24-Injury- to-eye story
| | 77.00 | 190.00 | 460.00 |

26-30: 27-Ka-Zar ends; last S&K Vision who battles Satan. 28-Jimmy Jupiter in the Land of Nowhere begins, ends #48; Sub-Mariner vs. The Flying Dutchman
| | 70.00 | 175.00 | 420.00 |

31-Sub-Mariner by Everett ends, begins again #84
| | 67.00 | 170.00 | 400.00 |

| 32-1st app. The Boboes | 67.00 | 170.00 | 400.00 |
| 33,35-40: 40-Zeppelin-c | 67.00 | 170.00 | 400.00 |

34-Everett, Burgos, Martin Goodman, Funnies, Inc. office appear in story & battles Hitler; last Burgos Human Torch
| | 78.00 | 195.00 | 470.00 |

41-43,45-48: 46-Hitler-c. 48-Last Vision; flag-c	61.00	152.00	365.00
44-Classic Super Plane-c	61.00	152.00	365.00
49-Origin Miss America	78.00	195.00	470.00
50-Mary becomes Miss Patriot (origin)	61.00	152.00	365.00
51-60: 53-Bondage-c	57.00	141.00	340.00
61,62,64-Last German War-c	53.00	160.00	320.00

63-Classic Hitler War-c; The Villainess Cat-Woman only app.
| | 57.00 | 141.00 | 340.00 |

| 65,66-Last Japanese War-c | 53.00 | 160.00 | 320.00 |
| 67-75: 74-Last Patriot. 75-Young Allies begin | 48.00 | 120.00 | 290.00 |

76-78: 76-Ten Chapter Miss America serial begins, ends #85
| | 48.00 | 120.00 | 290.00 |

79-New cover format; Super Villains begin on cover; last Angel
| | 43.00 | 110.00 | 260.00 |

| 80-1st app. Capt. America in Marvel Comics | 58.00 | 145.00 | 350.00 |
| 81-Captain America app. | 46.00 | 115.00 | 275.00 |

82-Origin Namora; 1st Sub-Mariner/Namora team-up; Captain America app.
| | 79.00 | 200.00 | 475.00 |

83,85: 83-Last Young Allies. 85-Last Miss America; Blonde Phantom app.
| | 43.00 | 110.00 | 260.00 |

84-Blonde Phantom, Sub-Mariner by Everett begins; Captain America app.
| | 58.00 | 145.00 | 350.00 |

86-Blonde Phantom I.D. revealed; Captain America app.; last Bucky app.
| | 52.00 | 130.00 | 310.00 |

| 87-1st Capt. America/Golden Girl team-up | 57.00 | 141.00 | 340.00 |

88-Golden Girl, Namora, & Sun Girl (1st in Marvel Comics) x-over; Captain America, Blonde Phantom app.; last Toro
| | 50.00 | 125.00 | 300.00 |

89-1st Human Torch/Sun Girl team-up; 1st Captain America solo; Blonde Phantom app.
| | 52.00 | 130.00 | 310.00 |

	Good	Fine	N-Mint
90-Blonde Phantom un-masked; Captain America app.			
	53.00	132.00	320.00
91-Capt. America app.; intro Venus; Blonde Phantom & Sub-Mariner end			
	53.00	132.00	320.00
92-Feature story on the birth of the Human Torch and the death of Professor Horton (his creator); 1st app. The Witness in Marvel Comics; Captain America app.	83.00	210.00	500.00

MARVEL PREMIERE
April, 1972-No. 61, Aug, 1981 (A tryout book for new characters)
Marvel Comics Group

	Good	Fine	N-Mint
1-Origin Warlock (pre #1) by Gil Kane/Adkins; origin Counter-Earth			
	2.00	6.00	14.00
2-Warlock ends; Kirby Yellow Claw-r	1.30	4.00	9.00
3-Dr. Strange series begins (pre #1, 7/72), B. Smith-a(p); Smith-c?			
	2.00	6.00	14.00
4-Smith/Brunner-a	1.00	3.00	7.00
5-9	.70	2.00	4.00
10-Death of the Ancient One	.85	2.50	5.00
11-14: 11-Dr. Strange origin-r by Ditko. 14-Intro. God; last Dr. Strange (3/74), gets own title 3 months later	.50	1.50	3.00
15-Origin/1st app. Iron Fist (5/74), ends #25	2.00	6.00	14.00
16-20: Iron Fist in all. 16-Hama's 1st Marvel-a	.85	2.50	5.00
21-24,26,27: 26-Hercules. 27-Satana	.70	2.00	4.00
25-1st Byrne Iron Fist(moves to own title next)	1.30	4.00	9.00
28-Legion of Monsters (Ghost Rider, Man-Thing, Morbius & Werewolf)			
	1.15	3.50	8.00
29-49,51-56,61: 29,30-The Liberty Legion. 31-1st app. Woodgod. 32-1st app. Monark Starstalker. 33.34-1st color app. Solomon Kane. 35- Origin/1st app. 3-D Man. 38-1st Weirdworld. 41-1st Seeker 3001! 42-Tigra. 44-Jack of Hearts. 47-Origin new Ant-Man. 48-Ant-Man. 49-The Falcon(1st solo book, 8/79). 51,52-Black Panther. 54-1st Caleb Hammer. 56-1st color app. Dominic Fortune. 61-Star Lord		.50	1.00
50-1st comic book app. Alice Cooper	.70	2.00	4.00
57-Dr. Who (1st U.S. app.)	.35	1.00	2.00
58-60-Dr. Who	.25	.75	1.50

MARVEL PRESENTS
October, 1975-No. 12, Aug, 1977
Marvel Comics Group

	Good	**Fine**	**N-Mint**
1-Origin & 1st app. Bloodstone	.70	2.00	4.00
2-Origin Bloodstone continued; Kirby-c	.50	1.50	3.00
3-Guardians of the Galaxy (1st solo book) begins, ends #12			
	1.70	5.00	12.00
4-7,9-12: 9,10-Origin Starhawk	1.15	3.50	8.00
8-Reprints story from Silver Surfer #2	1.50	4.50	10.00

MARVEL SPOTLIGHT (A try-out book for new characters)
Nov, 1971-No. 33, Apr, 1977; V2#1, July, 1979-V2#11, Mar, 1981
Marvel Comics Group

1-Origin Red Wolf (1st solo book, pre #1); Wood inks, Neal Adams-c			
	1.30	4.00	9.00
2-(Giant, 52pgs.)-Venus-r by Everett; origin/1st app. Werewolf By Night (begins)			
by Ploog; N. Adams-c	1.50	4.50	10.00
3,4: 4-Werewolf By Night ends (2/72)	.70	2.00	4.00
5-Origin/1st app. Ghost Rider (8/72) & begins	10.00	30.00	70.00
6-8-Last Ploog issue	5.00	15.00	35.00
9-11-Last Ghost Rider(gets own title next mo.)	3.60	11.00	25.00
12-The Son of Satan begins (origin), ends #24	.70	2.00	4.00
13-21,23-27,30,31: 25-Sinbad. 26-1st app. Scarecrow. 27-Sub-Mariner. 30-The			
Warriors Three. 31-Nick Fury	.40	1.25	2.50
22-Ghost Rider app.	1.00	3.00	6.00
28,29: Moon Knight (28-1st solo app., 6/76)	.85	2.50	5.00
32-Intro/partial origin Spider-Woman(2/77); Nick Fury app.			
	.85	2.50	5.00
33-Deathlok	.85	2.50	5.00
V2#1-11: 1-4,8-Capt. Marvel. 5-Dragon Lord. 6,7-StarLord; origin #6. 9-11-Capt.			
Universe stories	.50	1.00	

MARVEL SUPER HEROES
October, 1966 (25 cents, 68 pgs.) (1st Marvel One-shot)
Marvel Comics Group

1-r-origin Daredevil from D.D. #1; r-Avengers #2; G.A. Sub-Mariner-r/ Marvel			
Mystery No. 8 (H. Torch app.)	7.00	21.00	50.00

MARVEL SUPER-HEROES (Formerly Fantasy Masterpieces #1-11)
No. 12, 12/67-No. 31, 11/71; No. 32, 9/72-No. 105, 1/82
Marvel Comics Group

	Good	Fine	N-Mint
12-Origin & 1st app. Capt. Marvel of the Kree; G.A. Human Torch, Destroyer, Capt. America, Black Knight, Sub-Mariner-r (#12-20 all have new stories and reprints)	8.50	25.50	60.00
13-2nd app. Capt. Marvel; G.A. Black Knight, Torch, Vision, Capt. America, Sub-Mariner-r	4.30	13.00	30.00
14-Amazing Spider-Man (new-a, 5/68); G.A. Sub-Mariner, Torch, Mercury, Black Knight, Capt. America reprints	8.00	24.00	55.00
15-Black Bolt cameo in Medusa; G.A. Black Knight, Sub-Mariner, Black Marvel, Capt. America-r	1.50	4.50	10.00
16-Origin & 1st app. Phantom Eagle; G.A. Torch, Capt. America, Black Knight, Patriot, Sub-Mariner-r	1.50	4.50	10.00
17-Origin Black Knight; G.A. Torch, Sub-Mariner-r; reprint from All-Winners Squad #21 (cover & story)	1.50	4.50	10.00
18-Origin/1st app. Guardians of the Galaxy; G.A. Sub-Mariner, All-Winners Squad-r	4.30	13.00	30.00
19-Ka-Zar; G.A. Torch, Marvel Boy, Black Knight, Sub-Mariner-r; Smith-c(p); Tuska-a(r)	1.50	4.50	10.00
20-Doctor Doom (5/69); r/Young Men #24 w/-c	1.50	4.50	10.00
21-31: All-r issues. 31-Last Giant issue	.85	2.50	5.00
32-105: 32-Hulk/Sub-Mariner-r begin from TTA. 56-r/origin Hulk/Inc. Hulk #102; Hulk-r begin		.50	1.00

MARVEL TALES (Formerly Marvel Mystery #1-92)
No. 93, Aug, 1949-No. 159, Aug, 1957
Marvel/Atlas Comics (MCI)

	Good	Fine	N-Mint
93	40.00	120.00	280.00
94-Everett-a	32.00	95.00	220.00
95,96,99,101,103,105	18.00	54.00	125.00
97-Sun Girl, 2 pgs; Kirbyish-a; one story used in N.Y. State Legislative document	25.00	75.00	175.00
98-Krigstein-a	19.00	56.00	130.00
100	19.00	56.00	130.00
102-Wolverton-a "The End of the World," 6 pgs.	32.00	95.00	225.00
104-Wolverton-a "Gateway to Horror," 6 pgs.	29.00	86.00	200.00
106,107-Krigstein-a. 106-Decapitation story	17.00	51.00	115.00
108-120: 118-Hypo-c/panels in End of World story. 120-Jack Katz-a	10.00	30.00	70.00
121,123-131: 128-Flying Saucer-c. 131-Last pre-code (2/55)	8.00	24.00	55.00
122-Kubert-a	8.50	25.50	60.00

	Good	Fine	N-Mint
132,133,135-141,143,145	4.50	14.00	32.00
134-Krigstein, Kubert-a; flying saucer-c	5.70	17.00	40.00
142-Krigstein-a	5.00	15.00	35.00
144-Williamson/Krenkel-a, 3 pgs.	5.70	17.00	40.00
146,148-151,154,155,158	3.60	11.00	25.00
147-Ditko-a	5.00	15.00	35.00
152-Wood, Morrow-a	5.00	15.00	35.00
153-Everett End of World c/story	5.70	17.00	40.00
156-Torres-a	3.70	11.00	26.00
157,159-Krigstein-a	5.00	15.00	35.00

Marvel Team-Up #54, © Marvel Comics

MARVEL TEAM-UP
March, 1972-No. 150, Feb, 1985
(Spider-Man team-ups most issues)
Marvel Comics Group

1-Human Torch	5.70	17.00	40.00

	Good	Fine	N-Mint
2,3-H-T	2.15	6.50	15.00
4-X-Men	3.60	11.00	25.00

5-10: 5-Vision. 6-Thing. 7-Thor. 8-The Cat. 9-Iron Man. 10-H-T

	1.15	3.50	8.00

11-14,16-20: 11-Inhumans. 12-Werewolf. 13-Capt. America. 14-Sub-Mariner. 16-Capt. Marvel. 17-Mr. Fantastic. 18-H-T/Hulk. 19-Ka-Zar. 20-Black Panther

	1.10	3.25	6.50
15-Early Ghost Rider app. (11/73)	1.50	4.50	10.00

21-30: 21-Dr. Strange. 22-Hawkeye. 23-H-T/Iceman (X-Men cameo). 24-Brother Voodoo. 25-Daredevil. 26-H-T/Thor. 27-Hulk. 28-Hercules. 29-H-T/Iron Man. 30-Falcon

	.85	2.50	5.00

31-45,47-50: 31-Iron Fist. 32-H-T/Son of Satan. 33-Nighthawk. 34-Valkyrie. 35-H-T/Dr. Strange. 36-Frankenstein. 37-Man-Wolf. 38-Beast. 39-H-T. 40-Sons of the Tiger/H-T. 41-Scarlet Witch. 42-The Vision. 43-Dr. Doom; retells origin. 44-Moondragon. 45-Killraven. 47-Thing. 48-Iron Man; last 25 cent issue. 49-Dr. Strange; Iron Man app. 50- Iron Man; Dr. Strange app.

	.70	2.00	4.00
46-Deathlok	1.25	3.75	7.50

51,52,56-57: 51-Iron Man; Dr. Strange app. 52-Capt. America. 56- Daredevil. 57-Black Widow.

	.35	1.10	2.20

53-Hulk; Woodgod & X-Men app., 1st by Byrne (1/77)

	1.70	5.00	10.00

54,55,59,60: 54-Hulk; Woodgod app. 55-Warlock. 59-Yellowjacket/The Wasp. 60-The Wasp (Byrne-a in all)

	.90	2.75	5.50
58-Ghost Rider app.	.70	2.00	4.00

61-70: All Byrne-a; 61-H-T. 62-Ms. Marvel. 63-Iron Fist. 64-Daughters of the Dragon. 65-Capt. Britain (1st U.S. app.). 66-Capt. Britain; 1st app. Arcade. 67-Tigra; Kraven the Hunter app. 68-Man-Thing. 69-Havok (from X-Men). 70-Thor

	.35	1.10	2.20

71-74,76-78,80: 71-Falcon. 72-Iron Man. 73-Daredevil. 74-Not Ready for Prime Time Players (Belushi). 76-Dr. Strange. 77-Ms. Marvel. 78-Wonder Man. 80-Dr. Strange/Clea

	.35	1.10	2.20

75,79: 75-Power Man. 79-Mary Jane Watson as Red Sonja. Both have Byrne-a(p)

	.55	1.65	3.30

81-85,87,88,89,90: 81-Satana. 82-Black Widow. 83-Nick Fury. 84-Shang-Chi. 85-Shang-Chi/Black Widow/Nick Fury. 86-Guardians of the Galaxy. 87- Black Panther. 88-Invisible Girl. 90-Beast

	.30	.85	1.70
86-Guardians of the Galaxy app.	.50	1.50	3.00
89-Nightcrawler	.35	1.10	2.20
91-Ghost Rider app.	.70	2.00	4.00

92-99: 92-Hawkeye. 93-Werewolf by Night. 94-SpM vs. The Shroud. 95-

	Good	Fine	N-Mint

Mockingbird (intro.); Nick Fury app. 96-Howard the Duck. 97-Spider-Woman/Hulk. 98-Black Widow. 99-Machine Man

	.30	.85	1.70

100-(Double-size)-Fantastic Four/Storm/Black Panther; origin/1st app. Karma, one of the New Mutants; origin Storm; X-Men x-over; Miller-a/c(p); Byrne-a (on X-Men app. only)

	1.30	3.85	7.70

101-116: 101-Nighthawk(Ditko-a). 102-Doc Samson. 103-Ant-Man. 104-Hulk/Ka-Zar. 105-Capt./Powerman/Iron Fist. 106-Capt. America. 107-She-Hulk. 108-Paladin; Dazzler cameo. 109-Dazzler; Paladin app. 110-Iron Man. 111-Devil-Slayer. 112-King Kull. 113-Quasar. 114-Falcon. 115-Thor. 116-Valkyrie

		.55	1.10
117-Wolverine	1.70	5.00	10.00

118-140,142-149: 118-Professor X; X-Men (Wolverine) cameo. 119-Gargoyle. 120-Dominic Fortune. 121-Human Torch. 122-Man-Thing. 123- Daredevil. 124-The Beast. 125-Tigra. 126-Hulk & Powerman/Son of Satan. 127-The Watcher. 128-Capt. America; Spider-Man/Capt. America photo-c. 129-The Vision. 130-Scarlet Witch. 131-Frogman. 132-Mr. Fantastic. 133-Fantastic-4. 134-Jack of Hearts. 135-Kitty Pryde; X-Men cameo. 136-Wonder Man. 137-Aunt May/Franklin Richards. 138-Sandman. 139-Nick Fury. 140-Black Widow. 142-Capt. Marvel. 143-Starfox. 144-Moon Knight. 145- Iron Man. 146-Nomad. 147-Human Torch; SpM old costume. 148- Thor. 149-Cannonball

		.45	.90

141-Same month as Amazing Spidey #252; ties for 1st black costume

	.35	1.00	2.00
150-X-Men ($1.00, double-size); B. Smith-c	.55	1.65	3.30
Annual 1(1976)-SpM/New X-Men (early app.)	1.85	5.50	11.00
Annuals 2 (12/79) -7 (10/84)	.30	.85	1.70

MARVEL TWO-IN-ONE (… Featuring …#82? on)
January, 1974-No. 100, June, 1983
Marvel Comics Group

1-Thing team-ups begin; Man-Thing	1.70	5.00	12.00

2-4: 2-Sub-Mariner; last 20 cent issue. 3-Daredevil. 4-Capt. America.

	1.00	3.00	6.00
5-Guardians of the Galaxy	1.60	4.80	11.00
6-Dr. Strange	1.30	4.00	9.00
7,9,10	.75	2.25	4.50
8-Early Ghost Rider app. (3/75)	1.00	3.00	6.00
11-20: 17-Spider-Man. 18-Last 25 cent issue	.50	1.50	3.00
21-26,28,30-40: 39-Vision	.35	1.00	2.00

	Good	Fine	N-Mint
27-Deathlok app.	.70	2.00	4.00
29-2nd app. Spider-Woman	.50	1.50	3.00
41,42,44-49: 42-Capt. America. 45-Capt. Marvel		.50	1.00
43,50,53,55-Byrne-a	.40	1.25	2.50
51-The Beast, Nick Fury, Ms. Marvel; Miller-p	.50	1.50	3.00
52-Moon Knight app.	.35	1.00	2.00
54-Death of Deathlok; Byrne-a	1.70	5.00	10.00
56-68,70-79,81,82: 60-Intro. Impossible Woman. 61-63-Warlock app. 76-Iceman		.50	1.00
69-Guardians of the Galaxy	.35	1.00	2.00
80-Ghost Rider	.70	2.00	4.00
83,84: 83-Sasquatch. 84-Alpha Flight app.	.50	1.50	3.00
85-99: 93-Jocasta dies. 96-X-Men-c & cameo		.40	.80
100-Double size, Byrne scripts	.25	.75	1.50
Annual 1(1976, 52 pgs.)-Thing/Liberty Legion	.25	.80	1.60
Annual 2(1977, 52 pgs.)-Thing/Spider-Man; Thanos dies; Starlin-c/a			
	2.15	6.50	15.00
Annual 3,4: 3(1978, 52 pgs.). 4(1979, 52 pgs.)		.50	1.00
Annual 5,6: 5(1980, 52 pgs.)-Hulk. 6(1981, 52 pgs.)-1st app. American Eagle			
		.50	1.00
Annual 7(1982, 52 pgs.)-The Thing/Champion; Sasquatch, Colossus app.			
		.50	1.00

MARY MARVEL COMICS (Monte Hale #29 on) (Also see Captain Marvel Adventures #18, Marvel Family & Wow Comics)
Dec, 1945-No. 28, Sept, 1948
Fawcett Publications

	Good	Fine	N-Mint
1-Captain Marvel intro. Mary on-c; intro/origin Georgia Sivana			
	65.00	195.00	455.00
2	32.00	95.00	225.00
3	22.00	65.00	155.00
4	17.00	51.00	120.00
5-8: 8-Bulletgirl x-over in Mary Marvel	14.00	43.00	100.00
9,10	11.00	32.00	75.00
11-20	8.50	25.50	60.00
21-28	7.00	21.00	50.00

MASTER COMICS
Mar, 1940-No. 133, Apr, 1953 (No. 1-6: oversized issues) (#1-3: 15 cents, 52 pgs.; #4-6: 10 cents, 36 pgs.)
Fawcett Publications

	Good	Fine	VF-NM
1-Origin Master Man; The Devil's Dagger, El Carim, Master of Magic, Rick O'Say, Morton Murch, White Rajah, Shipwreck Roberts, Frontier Marshal, Streak Sloan, Mr. Clue begin (all features end #6)			
	233.00	585.00	1400.00

	Good	Fine	N-Mint
2	115.00	290.00	690.00
3-5	75.00	190.00	450.00
6-Last Master Man	83.00	210.00	500.00

NOTE: *#1-6 rarely found in near mint to mint condition due to large-size format.*

	Good	Fine	N-Mint
7-(10/40)-Bulletman, Zoro, the Mystery Man (ends #22), Lee Granger, Jungle King, & Buck Jones begin; only app. The War Bird & Mark Swift & the Time Retarder	133.00	335.00	800.00
8-The Red Gaucho (ends #13), Captain Venture (ends #22) & The Planet Princess begin	57.00	170.00	400.00
9,10: 10-Lee Granger ends	50.00	150.00	350.00
11-Origin Minute-Man	117.00	300.00	700.00
12	57.00	170.00	400.00
13-Origin Bulletgirl	100.00	250.00	600.00
14-16: 14-Companions Three begins, ends #31	50.00	150.00	350.00
17-20: 17-Raboy-a on Bulletman begins. 20-Captain Marvel cameo app. in Bulletman	50.00	150.00	350.00

	Good	Fine	VF-NM
21-(12/41; Scarce)-Captain Marvel & Bulletman team up against Capt. Nazi; origin Captain Nazi; part I of trilogy origin of Capt. Marvel Jr. (see Whiz #25)	193.00	580.00	1350.00
22-(1/42)-Part III of trilogy origin of Capt. Marvel Jr. & his 1st cover and adventure	165.00	495.00	1150.00

	Good	Fine	N-Mint
23-Capt. Marvel Jr. c/stories begin; fights Capt. Nazi by himself	129.00	385.00	900.00
24,25,29: 29-r & Tojo-c	49.00	148.00	345.00
26-28,30-Captain Marvel Jr. vs. Capt. Nazi. 30-Flag-c	49.00	148.00	345.00
31,32: 32-Last El Carim & Buck Jones; Balbo, the Boy Magician intro. in El Carim	35.00	105.00	245.00
33-Balbo, the Boy Magician (ends #47), Hopalong Cassidy (ends #49) begins	35.00	105.00	245.00
34-Capt. Marvel Jr. vs. Capt. Nazi	35.00	105.00	245.00
35	35.00	105.00	245.00

	Good	Fine	N-Mint
36-40: 40-Flag-c	30.00	90.00	210.00
41-Bulletman, Capt. Marvel Jr. & Bulletgirl x-over in Minute-Man; only app. Crime Crusaders Club (Capt. Marvel Jr., Minute-Man, Bulletman & Bulletgirl)-only team in Fawcett Comics	34.00	100.00	235.00
42-47,49: 47-Hitler becomes Corpl. Hitler Jr. 49-Last Minute-Man	19.00	56.00	130.00
48-Intro. Bulletboy; Capt. Marvel cameo in Minute-Man	23.00	70.00	160.00
50-Radar, Nyoka the Jungle Girl begin; Capt. Marvel x-over in Radar; origin Radar	14.00	43.00	100.00
51-58	10.00	30.00	70.00
59-62: Nyoka serial "Terrible Tiara" in all; 61-Capt. Marvel Jr. 1st meets Uncle Marvel	11.50	34.00	80.00
63-80	8.00	24.00	55.00
81-92,94-99: 88-Hopalong Cassidy begins (ends #94). 95-Tom Mix begins (ends #133)	6.50	19.00	45.00
93-Krigstein-a	7.00	21.00	50.00
100	7.00	21.00	50.00
101-106-Last Bulletman	5.00	15.00	35.00
107-132: 132-B&W and color illus in POP	4.00	12.00	28.00
133-Bill Battle app.	5.70	17.00	40.00

MASTER OF KUNG FU (Formerly Special Marvel Edition)
No. 17, April, 1974-No. 125, June, 1983
Marvel Comics Group

17-Starlin-a; intro Black Jack Tarr	1.50	4.50	10.00
18-20: 19-Man-Thing app.	1.00	3.00	6.00
21-23,25-30	.70	2.00	4.00
24-Starlin, Simonson-a	.50	1.50	3.00
31-99: 33-1st Leiko Wu. 43-Last 25 cent issue		.60	1.20
100-Double size	.25	.75	1.50
101-125: 118,125-Double size		.60	1.20
Annual 1(4/76)-Iron Fist	.50	1.50	3.00

METAL MEN (See Brave and the Bold & Showcase)
4-5/63-No. 41, 12-1/69-70; No. 42, 2-3/73-No. 44, 7-8/73; No. 45, 4-5/76-No. 56, 2-3/78
National Periodical Publications/DC Comics

1	23.00	70.00	163.00

	Good	Fine	N-Mint
2	9.00	27.00	63.00
3-5	6.00	18.00	42.00
6-10	3.85	11.50	27.00
11-20	3.00	9.00	21.00
21-26,28-30	1.70	5.00	12.00
27-Origin Metal Men	4.15	12.50	29.00
31-41(1968-70): 38-Last 12 cent issue	1.60	4.80	11.00
42-44(1973)-Reprints	.70	2.00	4.00
45('76)-49-Simonson-a in all	.70	2.00	4.00
50-56: 50-Part-r. 54,55-Green Lantern x-over	.70	2.00	4.00

METAMORPHO (See Action, Brave and the Bold & World's Finest)
July-Aug, 1965-No. 17, Mar-Apr, 1968 (All 12 cent issues)
National Periodical Publications

1	8.00	24.00	55.00
2,3	3.70	11.00	26.00
4-6	2.15	6.50	15.00
7-9	1.50	4.50	10.00
10-Origin & 1st app. Element Girl (1-2/67)	2.65	8.00	18.00
11-17	1.00	3.00	7.00

MICKEY AND DONALD (Walt Disney's . . . #3 on)
Mar, 1988-No. 18, May, 1990 (95 cents, color)
Gladstone Publishing

1-Don Rosa-a; r-/1949 Firestone giveaway	1.00	3.00	6.00
2	.40	1.25	2.50
3-Infinity-c	.35	1.00	2.00
4-8: Barks-r		.60	1.20
9-15: 9-r/1948 Firestone giveaway; X-Mas-c		.50	1.00
16 ($1.50, 52 pgs.)-r/FC #157	.25	.75	1.50
17,18 ($1.95, 68 pgs.): 17-Barks M.M.-r/FC #79 plus Barks D.D.-r; Rosa-a; X-Mas-c. 18-Kelly-c(r); Barks-r	.35	1.00	2.00

MICKEY MOUSE (...Secret Agent #107-109; Walt Disney's...#148-205?) (See
  Mickey and Donald & Walt Disney's Comics and Stories)
No. 16, 1941-No. 84, 7-9/62; No. 85, 11/62-No. 218, 7/84; No. 219, 10/86-No.
  256, 4/90
Dell Publ. Co./Gold Key No. 85-204/Whitman No. 205-218/Gladstone No. 219 on

	Good	Fine	VF-NM
4-Color 16(1941)-1st M.M. comic book-"vs. the Phantom Blot" by Gottfredson			
	371.00	1115.00	2600.00
(Prices vary widely on this book)			

	Good	Fine	N-Mint
4-Color 27(1943)-"7 Colored Terror"	50.00	150.00	350.00
4-Color 79(1945)-By Carl Barks (1 story)	64.00	193.00	450.00
4-Color 116(1946)	17.00	51.00	120.00
4-Color 141,157(1947)	16.00	48.00	110.00
4-Color 170,181,194('48)	13.00	40.00	90.00
4-Color 214('49),231,248,261	10.00	30.00	70.00
4-Color 268-Reprints/WDC&S #22-24 by Gottfredson ("Surprise Visitor")			
	10.00	30.00	70.00
4-Color 279,286,296	8.50	25.50	60.00
4-Color 304,313(#1),325(#2),334	5.70	17.00	40.00
4-Color 343,352,362,371,387	4.30	13.00	30.00
4-Color 401,411,427(10-11/52)	3.50	10.50	24.00
4-Color 819-Mickey Mouse in Magicland	2.00	6.00	14.00
4-Color 1057,1151,1246(1959-61)-Album	1.70	5.00	12.00
28(12-1/52-53)-32,34	1.70	5.00	12.00
33-(Exists with 2 dates, 10-11/53 & 12-1/54)	1.70	5.00	12.00
35-50	1.15	3.50	8.00
51-73,75-80	.85	2.50	6.00
74-Story swipe-"The Rare Stamp Search"/4-Color 422-"The Gilded Man"			
	1.15	3.50	8.00
81-99: 93,95-titled "Mickey Mouse Club Album"	.85	2.50	6.00
100-105: Reprints 4-Color 427,194,279,170,343,214 in that order			
	1.00	3.00	7.00
106-120	.75	2.25	5.00
121-130	.70	2.00	4.00
131-146	.50	1.50	3.00
147,148: 147-Reprints "The Phantom Fires" from WDC&S 200-202. 148-Reprints "The Mystery of Lonely Valley" from WDC&S 208-210			
	.85	3.50	5.00
149-158	.35	1.00	2.00

	Good	Fine	N-Mint
159-Reprints "The Sunken City" from WDC&S 205-207			
	.70	2.00	4.00
160-170: 162-170-r	.35	1.00	2.00
171-178,180-199		.50	1.00
179-(52 pgs.)		.60	1.20
200-218: 200-r/Four Color #371		.40	.80
219-1st Gladstone issue; The Seven Ghosts serial-r begins by Gottfredson			
	.85	2.50	5.00
220,221	.50	1.50	3.00
222-225: 222-Editor-in Grief strip-r	.40	1.25	2.50
226-230	.25	.75	1.50
231-243,245-254: 240-r/March of Comics #27. 245-r/F.C. #279. 250-r/ F.C. #248			
		.50	1.00
244 (1/89, $2.95, 100 pgs.)-60th anniversary; gives history of Mickey			
	.60	1.75	3.50
255,256 ($1.95, 68 pgs.)	.35	1.00	2.00

MIGHTY MOUSE (1st.Series)
Fall, 1946-No. 4, Summer, 1947
Timely/Marvel Comics (20th Century Fox)

	Good	Fine	N-Mint
1	57.00	170.00	400.00
2	29.00	85.00	200.00
3,4	20.00	60.00	140.00

MIGHTY MOUSE (2nd Series) (Paul Terry's . . . #62-71)
Aug, 1947-No. 67, 11/55; No. 68, 3/56-No. 83, 6/59
St. John Publishing Co./Pines No. 68 (3/56) on (TV issues #72 on)

	Good	Fine	N-Mint
5(#1)	19.00	58.00	135.00
6-10	10.00	30.00	70.00
11-19	5.70	17.00	40.00
20 (11/50)-25-(52 pgs.)	4.30	13.00	30.00
20-25-(36 pg. editions)	4.00	12.00	28.00
26-37: 35-Flying saucer-c	3.15	9.50	22.00
38-45-(100 pgs.)	7.00	21.00	50.00
46-83: 62-64,67-Painted-c. 82-Infinity-c	2.30	7.00	16.00

MILITARY COMICS (Becomes Modern Comics #44 on)
Aug, 1941-No. 43, Oct, 1945
Quality Comics Group

Military Comics #37, © Quality Comics

	Good	Fine	VF-NM
1-Origin/1st app. Blackhawk by C. Cuidera (Eisner scripts); Miss America, The Death Patrol by Jack Cole (also #2-7,27-30), & The Blue Tracer by Guardineer; X of the Underground, The Yankee Eagle, Q-Boat & Shot & Shell, Archie Atkins, Loops & Banks by Bud Ernest (Bob Powell) (ends #13) begin	333.00	835.00	2000.00

	Good	Fine	N-Mint
2-Secret War News begins (by McWilliams #2-16); Cole-a	135.00	410.00	950.00
3-Origin/1st app. Chop Chop	107.00	320.00	750.00
4	93.00	280.00	650.00
5-The Sniper begins; Miss America in costume #4-7	75.00	225.00	525.00
6-9: 8-X of the Underground begins (ends #13). 9-The Phantom Clipper begins (ends #16)	63.00	190.00	440.00
10-Classic Eisner-c	67.00	200.00	470.00
11-Flag-c	50.00	150.00	350.00
12-Blackhawk by Crandall begins, ends #22	67.00	200.00	470.00
13-15: 14-Private Dogtag begins (ends #83)	45.00	135.00	315.00

	Good	Fine	N-Mint
16-20: 16-Blue Tracer ends. 17-P.T. Boat begins	40.00	120.00	275.00
21-31: 22-Last Crandall Blackhawk. 27-Death Patrol revived			
	36.00	107.00	250.00
32-43	30.00	90.00	210.00

MISS FURY COMICS (Newspaper strip reprints)
Winter, 1942-43-No. 8, Winter, 1946
Timely Comics (NPI 1/CmPI 2/MPC 3-8)

1-Origin Miss Fury by Tarpe' Mills (68 pgs.) in costume w/pin-ups			
	175.00	440.00	1050.00
2-(60 pgs.)-In costume w/pin-ups	69.00	205.00	480.00
3-(60 pgs.)-In costume w/pin-ups; Hitler-c	57.00	170.00	400.00
4-(52 pgs.)-In costume, 2 pgs. w/pin-ups	47.00	140.00	325.00
5-(52 pgs.)-In costume w/pin-ups	43.00	130.00	300.00
6-(52 pgs.)-Not in costume in inside stories, w/pin-ups			
	39.00	115.00	270.00
7,8-(36 pgs.)-In costume 1 pg. each, no pin-ups	39.00	115.00	270.00

MISSION IMPOSSIBLE (TV)
May, 1967-No. 4, Oct, 1968; No. 5, Oct, 1969 (All have photo-c)
Dell Publishing Co.

1	5.00	15.00	35.00
2-5: 5-reprints #1	3.50	10.50	24.00

MR. DISTRICT ATTORNEY (Radio/TV)
Jan-Feb, 1948-No. 67, Jan-Feb, 1959 (1-23: 52 pgs.)
National Periodical Publications

1	36.00	107.00	250.00
2	14.00	43.00	100.00
3-5	11.00	32.00	75.00
6-10	8.50	25.50	60.00
11-20	7.00	21.00	50.00
21-43: 43-Last pre-code (1-2/55)	5.00	15.00	35.00
44-67	3.60	11.00	25.00

MISTER MIRACLE
3-4/71-V4#18, 2-3/74; V5#19, 9/77-V6#25, 8-9/78; 1987
National Periodical Publications/DC Comics

	Good	Fine	N-Mint
1-(#1-3 are 15 cents)	1.15	3.50	8.00
2,3	.85	2.50	5.00
4-8: 4-Boy Commandos-r begin; all 52 pgs.	.75	2.20	4.40
9,10: 9-Origin Mr. Miracle	.60	1.75	3.50
11-18: 15-Intro/1st app. Shilo Norman. 18-Barda & Scott Free wed; New			
Gods app.	.50	1.50	3.00
19-25: (1977-1978)	.35	1.00	2.00
Special 1(1987, 52 pgs., $1.25)	.25	.75	1.50

MISTER MIRACLE
Jan, 1989-No. 28, June, 1991 (1.00, color)
DC Comics

1-Spin-off from Justice League International	.25	.75	1.50
2-28: 9-Intro Maxi-Man. 13,14-Lobo app. 22-1st new Mr. Miracle			
		.50	1.00

MISTER MYSTERY
Sept, 1951-No. 19, Oct, 1954
Mr. Publ. (Media Publ.) No. 1-3/SPM Publ./Stanmore (Aragon)

1-Kurtzmanesque horror story	23.00	70.00	160.00
2,3-Kurtzmanesque story	15.00	45.00	105.00
4,6: Bondage-c; 6-Torture	15.00	45.00	105.00
5,8,10	12.00	36.00	85.00
7-"The Brain Bats of Venus" by Wolverton; partially re-used in Weird Tales of Future #7			
	43.00	130.00	300.00
9-Nostrand-a	13.00	40.00	90.00
11-Wolverton "Robot Woman" story/Weird Mysteries #2, cut up, rewritten			
& partially redrawn	23.00	70.00	160.00
12-Classic injury to eye-c	35.00	105.00	245.00
13,14,17,19	9.30	28.00	65.00
15-"Living Dead" junkie story	11.00	32.00	75.00
16-Bondage-c	11.00	32.00	75.00
18-"Robot Woman" by Wolverton reprinted from Weird Mysteries #2;			
decapitation, bondage-c	20.00	60.00	140.00

MODERN COMICS (Formerly Military Comics #1-43)
No. 44, Nov, 1945-No. 102, Oct, 1950
Quality Comics Group

	Good	Fine	N-Mint
44-Blackhawk continues	30.00	90.00	210.00
45-52: 49-1st app. Fear, Lady Adventuress	18.00	54.00	125.00
53-Torchy by Ward begins (9/46)	23.00	70.00	160.00
54-60: 55-J. Cole-a	16.00	48.00	110.00
61-77,79,80: 73-J. Cole-a	14.00	43.00	100.00
78-1st app. Madame Butterfly	16.00	48.00	110.00
81-99,101: 82,83-One pg. J. Cole-a	14.00	43.00	100.00
100	14.00	43.00	100.00
102-(Scarce)-J. Cole-a; Spirit by Eisner app.	17.00	51.00	120.00

MONKEES, THE (TV)
March, 1967-No. 17, Oct, 1969 (#1-4,6,7,10 have photo-c)
Dell Publishing Co.

	Good	Fine	N-Mint
1	5.70	17.00	40.00
2-4,6,7,10: All photo-c	3.60	11.00	25.00
5,8,9,11-17: No photo-c; #17 reprints #1	2.65	8.00	18.00

MONTE HALE WESTERN (Movie star; Formerly Mary Marvel #1-28;
    also see Real Western Hero & Western Hero)
No. 29, Oct, 1948-No. 88, Jan, 1956
Fawcett Publications/Charlton No. 83 on

	Good	Fine	N-Mint
29-(#1, 52 pgs.)-Photo-c begin, end #82; Monte Hale & his horse Pardner begin			
	25.00	75.00	175.00
30-(52 pgs.)-Big Bow and Little Arrow begin, end #34; Captain Tootsie by Beck			
	14.00	43.00	100.00
31-36,38-40-(52 pgs.): 34-Gabby Hayes begins, ends #80. 39-Captain Tootsie by			
Beck	11.50	34.00	80.00
37,41,45,49-(36 pgs.)	7.00	21.00	50.00
42-44,46-48,50-(52 pgs.): 47-Big Bow & Little Arrow app.			
	8.00	24.00	55.00
51,52,54-56,58,59-(52 pgs.)	6.00	18.00	42.00
53,57-(36 pgs.): 53-Slim Pickens app.	4.50	14.00	32.00
60-81: 36 pgs. #60-on. 80-Gabby Hayes ends	4.50	14.00	32.00
82-Last Fawcett issue (6/53)	6.50	19.00	45.00
83-1st Charlton issue (2/55); B&W photo back-c begin. Gabby Hayes returns, ends			
#86	6.50	19.00	45.00
84 (4/55)	4.50	14.00	32.00
85-86	4.30	13.00	30.00
87-Wolverton-r, 1/2 pg.	4.50	14.00	32.00

	Good	Fine	N-Mint
88-Last issue	4.50	14.00	32.00

MOON KNIGHT (Also see Marc Spector . . . , Marvel Spotlight & Werewolf by
    Night #32)
November, 1980-No. 38, July, 1984 (Mando paper No. 33 on)
Marvel Comics Group

	Good	Fine	N-Mint
1-Origin resumed in #4; begin Sienkiewicz-c/a	.40	1.25	2.50
2-34,36-38: 4-Intro Midnight Man. 16-The Thing app. 25-Double size			
		.50	1.00
35-($1.00, 52 pgs.)-X-men app.; F.F. cameo	.25	.75	1.50

MORE FUN COMICS (Formerly New Fun Comics #1-6)
No. 7, Jan, 1936-No. 127, Nov-Dec, 1947 (No. 7,9-11: paper-c)
National Periodical Publications

	Good	Fine	VF-NM
7(1/36)-Oversized, paper-c; 1 pg. Kelly-a	333.00	835.00	2000.00
8(2/36)-Oversized (10x12"), slick-c; 1 pg. Kelly-a			
	300.00	750.00	1800.00
9(3-4/36)(Very rare, 1st comic-sized issue)-Last Henri Duval by Siegel & Shuster			
	300.00	750.00	1800.00
10,11(7/36): 11-1st 'Calling All Cars' by Siegel & Shuster			
	192.00	480.00	1150.00
12(8/36)-Slick-c begin	167.00	417.00	1000.00
V2#1(9/36, #13)	163.00	410.00	980.00
2(10/36, #14)-Dr. Occult in costume (Superman prototype) begins, ends #17;			
see The Comics Magazine	183.00	460.00	1100.00
V2#3(11/36, #15), 16(V2#4), 17(V2#5)-Cover numbering begins #16.			
16-Xmas-c	121.00	300.00	725.00
18-20(V2#8, 5/37)	92.00	230.00	550.00

	Good	Fine	N-Mint
21(V2#9)-24(V2#12, 9/37)	67.00	165.00	400.00
25(V3#1, 10/37)-27(V3#3, 12/37): 27-Xmas-c	67.00	165.00	400.00
28-30: 30-1st non-funny cover	67.00	165.00	400.00
31-35: 32-Last Dr. Occult	57.00	140.00	340.00
36-40: 36-The Masked Ranger begins, ends #41. 39-Xmas-c			
	53.00	130.00	315.00
41-50	47.00	115.00	280.00
51-The Spectre app. (in costume) in one panel ad at end of Buccaneer story			
	117.00	290.00	700.00

	Good	Fine	VF-NM
52-(2/40)-Origin/1st app. The Spectre (in costume splash panel only), Part 1 by Bernard Baily; last Wing Brady	1835.00	4580.00	11,000.00
53-Origin The Spectre (in costume at end of story), Part 2; Capt. Desmo begins	1250.00	3125.00	7500.00
54-The Spectre in costume; last King Carter	467.00	1170.00	2800.00
55-(Scarce)-Dr. Fate begins (Intro & 1st app.); last Bulldog Martin	500.00	1250.00	3000.00

	Good	Fine	N-Mint
56-60: 56-Congo Bill begins	205.00	510.00	1225.00
61-66: 63-Last St. Bob Neal. 64-Lance Larkin begins	150.00	375.00	900.00

	Good	Fine	VF-NM
67-Origin Dr. Fate; last Congo Bill & Biff Bronson	233.00	585.00	1400.00

	Good	Fine	N-Mint
68-70: 68-Clip Carson begins. 70-Last Lance Larkin	125.00	312.00	750.00

	Good	Fine	VF-NM
71-Origin & 1st app. Johnny Quick by Mort Wysinger	217.00	540.00	1300.00

	Good	Fine	N-Mint
72-Dr. Fate's new helmet; last Sgt. Carey, Sgt. O'Malley & Captain Desmo	108.00	270.00	650.00

	Good	Fine	VF-NM
73-Origin & 1st app. Aquaman (11/41); intro. Green Arrow & Speedy	333.00	835.00	2000.00

	Good	Fine	N-Mint
74-2nd Aquaman	125.00	312.00	750.00
75-80: 76-Last Clip Carson; Johnny Quick by Meskin begins, ends #97. 80-1st small logo	108.00	270.00	650.00
81-88: 87-Last Radio Squad	77.00	190.00	460.00
89-Origin Green Arrow & Speedy Team-up	92.00	230.00	550.00
90-99: 93-Dover & Clover begin. 97-Kubert-a. 98-Last Dr. Fate	50.00	125.00	300.00
100	67.00	165.00	400.00

	Good	Fine	VF-NM
101-Origin & 1st app. Superboy (3/44)(not by Siegel & Shuster); last Spectre issue	317.00	790.00	1900.00

	Good	Fine	N-Mint
102-2nd Superboy	83.00	210.00	500.00
103-3rd Superboy	63.00	155.00	375.00

	Good	Fine	N-Mint
104-107: 104-1st Superboy-c. 105-Superboy-c. 107-Last J. Quick & Superboy			
	52.00	130.00	310.00
108-120: 108-Genius Jones begins	8.00	24.00	55.00
121-124,126: 121-123,126-Post-c	6.50	19.00	45.00
125-Superman on cover	33.00	100.00	230.00
127-(Scarce)-Post c/a	14.00	42.00	100.00

MUNSTERS, THE (TV)
Jan, 1965-No. 16, Jan, 1968 (All have photo-c?)
Gold Key

	Good	Fine	N-Mint
1 (10134-501)-Photo-c	13.00	40.00	90.00
2	6.70	20.00	46.00
3-5: 4-Photo-c	5.85	17.50	41.00
6-16: 6,16-Photo-c	4.70	14.00	33.00

MURDER, INCORPORATED
1/48-No. 15, 12/49; (2 No.9's); 6/50-No. 3, 8/51
Fox Feature Syndicate

	Good	Fine	N-Mint
1 (1st Series)	18.00	54.00	125.00
2-Electrocution story; #1,2 have 'For Adults Only' on-c			
	13.00	40.00	90.00
3-7,9(4/49),10(5/49),11-15	6.50	19.00	45.00
8-Used in SOTI, pg. 160	9.30	28.00	65.00
9(3/49)-Possible use in SOTI, pg. 145; r-Blue Beetle #56('48)			
	7.00	21.00	50.00
5(#1, 6/50)(2nd Series)-Formerly My Desire	5.00	15.00	35.00
2(8/50)-Morisi-a	4.00	12.00	28.00
3(8/51)-Used in POP, pg. 81; Rico-a; lingerie-c/panels			
	5.00	15.00	35.00

MUTT AND JEFF (See All-American Comics, All-Flash #18, Comic Cavalcade,
  The Funnies & Popular Comics)
Summer, 1939 (nd)-No. 148, Nov, 1965
All American/National 1-103(6/58)/Dell 104(10/58)-115 (10-12/59)/ Harvey
  116(2/60)-148

	Good	Fine	N-Mint
1(nn)-Lost Wheels	86.00	257.00	600.00
2(nn)-Charging Bull (Summer 1940, nd; on sale 6/20/40)			
	48.00	145.00	335.00

	Good	Fine	N-Mint
3(nn)-Bucking Broncos (Summer 1941, nd)	34.00	100.00	235.00
4(Winter,'41), 5(Summer,'42)	25.00	75.00	175.00
6-10	14.00	43.00	100.00
11-20	10.00	30.00	70.00
21-30	7.00	21.00	50.00
31-50	4.00	12.00	28.00
51-75-Last Fisher issue. 53-Last 52 pgs.	2.65	8.00	18.00
76-99,101-103: 76-Last pre-code issue(1/55)	1.70	5.00	12.00
100	2.00	6.00	14.00
104-148: 117,118,120-131-Richie Rich app.	1.00	3.00	7.00

MY FAVORITE MARTIAN (TV)
1/64; No.2, 7/64-No. 9, 10/66 (No. 1,3-9 have photo-c)
Gold Key

	Good	Fine	N-Mint
1-Russ Manning-a	7.00	21.00	50.00
2	3.00	9.00	21.00
3-9	3.60	11.00	25.00

MY GREATEST ADVENTURE (Doom Patrol #86 on)
Jan-Feb, 1955-No. 85, Feb, 1964
National Periodical Publications

	Good	Fine	N-Mint
1-Before CCA	55.00	165.00	380.00
2	26.00	78.00	180.00
3-5	19.00	57.00	130.00
6-10	11.50	34.00	80.00
11-15,19	8.00	24.00	55.00
16-18,20,21,28-Kirby-a; 18-Kirby-c	7.00	21.00	50.00
22-27,29,30	4.30	13.00	30.00
31-40	3.15	9.50	22.00
41-57,59	2.00	6.00	14.00
58,60,61-Toth-a; Last 10 cent issue	2.65	8.00	18.00
62-76,78,79	1.30	4.00	9.00
77-Toth-a	1.50	4.50	10.00
80-(6/63)-Intro/origin Doom Patrol and begin series; origin Robotman, Negative Man, & Elasti-Girl	24.00	72.00	165.00
81-85: 81,85-Toth-a	9.30	28.00	65.00

MYSTERIES OF UNEXPLORED WORLDS
Aug, 1956 No. 6, Jan, 1957; No. 7, Feb, 1958-No. 48, Sept, 1965
Charlton Comics

	Good	Fine	N-Mint
1	14.00	43.00	100.00
2-No Ditko	5.70	17.00	40.00
3,4,8,9-Ditko-a	8.50	25.50	60.00
5,6-Ditko-c/a (all)	10.00	30.00	70.00
7-(2/58, 68 pgs.); Ditko-a(4)	10.00	30.00	70.00
10-Ditko-c/a(4)	10.00	30.00	70.00
11-Ditko-c/a(3)-signed J. Kotdi	10.00	30.00	70.00
12,19,21-24,26-Ditko-a	6.50	19.00	45.00
13-18,20	2.00	6.00	14.00
25,27-30	1.50	4.50	10.00
31-45	.70	2.00	5.00
46(5/65)-Son of Vulcan begins (origin)	1.30	4.00	9.00
47,48	.85	2.60	6.00

Mystery in Space #57, © DC Comics

MYSTERY IN SPACE
4-5/51-No. 110, 9/66; No. 111, 9/80-No. 117, 3/81 (#1-3: 52 pgs.)
National Periodical Publications

	Good	Fine	N-Mint
1-Frazetta-a, 8 pgs.; Knights of the Galaxy begins, ends #8			
	157.00	470.00	1100.00
2	62.00	185.00	435.00
3	50.00	150.00	350.00
4,5	36.00	107.00	250.00
6-10: 7-Toth-a	29.00	85.00	200.00
11-15: 13-Toth-a	20.00	60.00	140.00
16-18,20-25: Interplanetary Insurance feature by Infantino in all. 24-Last pre-code			
issue	17.00	51.00	120.00
19-Virgil Finlay-a	20.00	60.00	140.00
26-40: 26-Space Cabbie begins	12.00	36.00	85.00
41-52: 47-Space Cabbie feature ends	10.00	30.00	70.00
53-Adam Strange begins (8/59) (1st app. in Showcase)			
	70.00	210.00	485.00
54	26.00	78.00	180.00
55	16.00	48.00	110.00
56-60	12.00	36.00	85.00
61-71: 61-1st app. Adam Strange foe Ulthoon. 62-1st app. A.S. foe Mortan. 63-Origin Vandor. 66-Star Rovers begin. 68-Dust Devils app. 71-Last 10 cent			
issue	7.00	21.00	50.00
72-74,76-80	6.00	18.00	42.00
75-JLA x-over in Adam Strange (5/62)	6.70	20.00	47.00
81-86	3.15	9.50	22.00
87-Adam Strange & Hawkman stories (11/63); pre-dates Hawkman #1 (this is Hawkman's 3rd tryout series)	5.70	17.00	40.00
88-90-Adam Strange & Hawkman stories. 90-1st Adam Strange/Hawkman team-up; moves to own title next mo.	4.70	14.00	33.00
91-103: 91-End Infantino art on Adam Strange. 92-Space Ranger begins. 94,98-Adam Strange/Space Ranger team-up. 102-Adam Strange ends (no space Ranger). 103-Origin Ultra, the Multi-Alien; Space Ranger ends			
	1.50	4.50	10.00
104-110: 110-(9/66)-Last 10 cent issue	.70	2.00	4.00
V17#111(9/80)-117: 117-Newton-a(3 pgs.)		.65	1.30

MYSTERY MEN COMICS
Aug, 1939-No. 31, Feb, 1942
Fox Features Syndicate

1-Intro. & 1st app. The Blue Beetle, The Green Mask, Rex Dexter of Mars by Briefer, Zanzibar by Tuska, Lt. Drake, D-13-Secret Agent by Powell, Chen Chang, Wing Turner, & Captain Denny Scott

	Good	Fine	N-Mint
	175.00	440.00	1050.00
2	72.00	215.00	500.00
3 (10/39)	61.00	182.00	425.00
4-Capt. Savage begins	54.00	160.00	375.00
5	42.00	125.00	290.00
6-8	37.00	110.00	260.00
9-The Moth begins	31.00	92.00	215.00
10-Wing Turner by Kirby	31.00	92.00	215.00
11-Intro. Domino	24.00	73.00	170.00
12,14-18	22.00	65.00	155.00
13-Intro. Lynx & sidekick Blackie	24.00	73.00	170.00
19-Intro. & 1st app. Miss X (ends #21)	24.00	73.00	170.00
20-31: 26-The Wraith begins	20.00	60.00	140.00

MYSTERY TALES
March, 1952-No. 54, Aug, 1957
Atlas Comics (20CC)

	Good	Fine	N-Mint
1	22.00	65.00	150.00
2-Krigstein-a	11.00	32.00	75.00
3-9: 6-A-Bomb panel	7.00	21.00	50.00
10-Story similar to 'The Assassin' from Shock SuspenStories	8.00	24.00	55.00
11,13-17,19,20: 20-Electric chair issue	5.30	16.00	38.00
12-Matt Fox-a	6.50	19.00	45.00
18-Williamson-a	6.50	19.00	45.00
21-Matt Fox-a; decapitation story	6.00	18.00	42.00
22-Forte/Matt Fox c; a(i)	7.00	21.00	50.00
23-26 (2/55)-Last pre-code issue	4.50	14.00	32.00
27,29-32,34,35,37,38,41-43,48,49	3.00	9.00	21.00
28-Jack Katz-a	3.50	10.50	24.00
33-Crandall-a	4.30	13.00	30.00
36,39-Krigstein-a	4.30	13.00	30.00
40,45-Ditko-a	4.30	13.00	30.00
44,51-Williamson/Krenkel-a	5.00	15.00	35.00
46-Williamson/Krenkel-a; Crandall text illos	5.00	15.00	35.00
47-Crandall, Ditko, Powell-a	4.50	14.00	32.00
50-Torres, Morrow-a	4.30	13.00	30.00
52,53	2.30	7.00	16.00
54-Crandall, Check-a	3.50	10.50	24.00

MYSTIC COMICS (1st Series)
March, 1940-No. 10, Aug, 1942
Timely Comics (TPI 1-5/TCI 8-10)

	Good	Fine	VF-NM
1-Origin The Blue Blaze, The Dynamic Man, & Flexo the Rubber Man; Zephyr Jones, 3X's & Deep Sea Demon app.; The Magician begins; c-from Spider pulp V18#1, 6/39	500.00	1250.00	3000.00

	Good	Fine	N-Mint
2-The Invisible Man & Master Mind Excello begin; Space Rangers, Zara of the Jungle, Taxi Taylor app.	200.00	500.00	1200.00
3-Origin Hercules, who last appears in #4	154.00	385.00	925.00
4-Origin The Thin Man & The Black Widow; Merzak the Mystic app.; last Flexo, Dynamic Man, Invisible Man & Blue Blaze (some issues have date sticker on cover; others have July w/August overprint in silver color); Roosevelt assassination-c	180.00	450.00	1080.00
5-Origin The Black Marvel, The Blazing Skull, The Sub-Earth Man, Super Slave & The Terror; The Moon Man & Black Widow app.	173.00	435.00	1040.00
6-Origin The Challenger & The Destroyer	150.00	375.00	900.00
7-The Witness begins (origin); origin Davey & the Demon; last Black Widow; Simon & Kirby-c	125.00	312.00	750.00
8	100.00	250.00	600.00
9-Gary Gaunt app.; last Black Marvel, Mystic & Blazing Skull; Hitler-c	100.00	250.00	600.00
10-Father Time, World of Wonder, & Red Skeleton app.; last Challenger & Terror	100.00	250.00	600.00

MYSTIC COMICS (2nd Series)
Oct, 1944-No. 4, Winter, 1944-45
Timely Comics (ANC)

	Good	Fine	N-Mint
1-The Angel, The Destroyer, The Human Torch, Terry Vance the Schoolboy Sleuth, & Tommy Tyme begin	88.00	220.00	525.00
2-Last Human Torch & Terry Vance; bondage-hypo-c	54.00	135.00	325.00
3-Last Angel (two stories) & Tommy Tyme	50.00	125.00	300.00
4-The Young Allies app.	46.00	115.00	275.00

N

'NAM, THE
Dec, 1986-Present
Marvel Comics Group

	Good	Fine	N-Mint
1-Golden a(p)/c begins, ends #13	1.50	4.50	9.00
1 (2nd printing)	.35	1.00	2.00
2	.90	2.75	5.50
3,4	.70	2.00	4.00
5-7	.50	1.50	3.00
8-10	.35	1.00	2.00
11-20: 12-Severin-a	.25	.75	1.50
21-51: 25-begin $1.50-c. 32-Death R. Kennedy		.60	1.20
52-Frank Castle (The Punisher) app.	1.00	3.00	6.00
53-Frank Castle (The Punisher) app.	.70	2.00	4.00
52,53-Gold 2nd printings	.25	.75	1.50
54-62	.25	.75	1.50

NAMORA (See Marvel Mystery & Sub-Mariner Comics)
Fall, 1948-No. 3, Dec, 1948
Marvel Comics (PrPI)

	Good	Fine	N-Mint
1-Sub-Mariner x-over in Namora; Everett, Rico-a			
	81.00	245.00	485.00
2-The Blonde Phantom & Sub-Mariner story; Everett-a			
	67.00	200.00	400.00
3-(Scarce)-Sub-Mariner app.; Everett-a	60.00	150.00	360.00

NAMOR, THE SUB-MARINER (See The Sub-Mariner)
Apr, 1990-Present ($1.00, color)
Marvel Comics

	Good	Fine	N-Mint
1-Byrne-c/a/scripts in all	.60	1.75	3.50
2-5: 5-Iron Man app.	.35	1.00	2.00
6-11: 8,10-Re-intro. Iron Fist (#8 is cameo only)	.25	.75	1.50
12-($1.50, 52 pgs.)-Re-intro. The Invaders	.35	1.00	2.00
13-20		.50	1.00

NATIONAL COMICS
July, 1940-No. 75, Nov, 1949
Quality Comics Group

	Good	Fine	N-Mint
1-Uncle Sam begins; Origin sidekick Buddy by Eisner; origin Wonder Boy & Kid Dixon; Merlin the Magician (ends #45); Cyclone, Kid Patrol, Sally O'Neil Policewoman, Pen Miller (ends #22), Prop Powers (ends #26), & Paul Bunyan (ends #22) begin	178.00	535.00	1250.00
2	86.00	255.00	600.00
3-Last Eisner Uncle Sam	67.00	200.00	465.00
4-Last Cyclone	48.00	145.00	335.00
5-(11/40)-Quicksilver begins (3rd w/lightning speed?); origin Uncle Sam; bondage-c	61.00	182.00	425.00
6-11: 8-Jack & Jill begins (ends #22). 9-Flag-c	45.00	135.00	315.00
12	34.00	100.00	235.00
13-16-Lou Fine-a	42.00	125.00	290.00
17,19-22	30.00	90.00	210.00
18-(12/41)-Shows orientals attacking Pearl Harbor; on stands one month before actual event	37.00	110.00	255.00
23-The Unknown & Destroyer 171 begin	34.00	100.00	235.00
24-26,28,30: 26-Wonder Boy ends	24.00	71.00	165.00
27-G-2 the Unknown begins (ends #46)	24.00	71.00	165.00
29-Origin The Unknown	24.00	71.00	165.00
31-33: 33-Chic Carter begins (ends #47)	21.00	62.00	145.00
34-40: 35-Last Kid Patrol. 39-Hitler-c	12.00	36.00	85.00
41-50: 42-The Barker begins (1st app?). 48-Origin The Whistler	9.30	28.00	65.00
51-Sally O'Neil by Ward, 8 pgs. (12/45)	12.00	36.00	85.00
52-60	7.00	21.00	50.00
61-67: 67-Format change; Quicksilver app.	5.00	15.00	35.00
68-75: The Barker ends	3.50	10.50	24.00

NEW ADVENTURE COMICS (Formerly New Comics; becomes Adventure Comics #32 on)

V1#12, Jan, 1937-No. 31, Oct, 1938
National Periodical Publications

	Good	Fine	VF-NM
V1#12-Federal Men by Siegel & Shuster continues; Jor-L mentioned	154.00	385.00	925.00
V2#1(2/37, #13), V2#2 (#14)	113.00	285.00	680.00

	Good	Fine	N-Mint
15(V2#3)-20(V2#8): 15-1st Adventure logo. 16-1st Shuster-c; 1st non funny cover. 17-Nadir, Master of Magic begins, ends #30	113.00	285.00	680.00

	Good	Fine	N-Mint
21(V2#9),22(V2#10, 2/37): 22-X-Mas-c	92.00	230.00	550.00
23-31	75.00	190.00	450.00

NEW COMICS (New Adventure #12 on)
12/35-No. 11, 12/36 (No. 1-6: paper cover) (No. 1-5: 84 pgs.)
National Periodical Publ.

	Good	Fine	VF-NM
V1#1-Billy the Kid, Sagebrush 'n' Cactus, Jibby Jones, Needles, The Vikings, Sir Loin of Beef, Now-When I Was a Boy, & other 1-2 pg. strips; 2 pgs. Kelly art(1st)-(Gulliver's Travels); Sheldon Mayer-a(1st)	533.00	1335.00	3200.00
2-Federal Men by Siegel & Shuster begins (Also see The Comics Magazine #2); Sheldon Mayer, Kelly-a (Rare)	285.00	710.00	1700.00
3-6: 3,4-Sheldon Mayer-a which continues in The Comics Magazine #1. 5 Kiefer-a	167.00	415.00	1000.00
7-11: 11-Christmas-c	133.00	335.00	800.00

NEW FUN COMICS (More Fun #7 on; see Big Book of Fun Comics)
Feb, 1935-No. 6, Oct, 1935 (10x15", No. 1-4,6: slick covers) (No. 1-5: 36 pgs; 68 pgs. No. 6-on)
National Periodical Publications

	Good	Fine	V. Fine
V1#1 (1st DC comic); 1st app. Oswald The Rabbit. Jack Woods (cowboy) begins	1335.00	3335.00	8000.00
2(3/35)-(Very Rare)	917.00	2300.00	5500.00
3-5(8/35): 5-Soft-c	417.00	1040.00	2500.00
6(10/35)-1st Dr. Occult (Superman proto-type) by Siegel & Shuster (Leger & Reughts); last "New Fun" title. "New Comics #1 begins in Dec. which is reason for title change to More Fun; Henri Duval (ends #9) by Siegel & Shuster begins; paper-c	500.00	1250.00	3000.00

NEW FUNNIES
(The Funnies #1-64; Walter Lantz . . . #109 on; New TV . . . #259, 260, 272, 273; TV Funnies #261-271)
No. 65, July, 1942-No. 288, Mar-Apr, 1962
Dell Publishing Co.

	Good	Fine	N-Mint
65(#1)-Andy Panda in a world of real people, Raggedy Ann & Andy, Oswald the Rabbit (with Woody Woodpecker x-overs), Li'l Eight Ball & Peter Rabbit begin	42.00	125.00	290.00
66-70: 67-Billy & Bonnie Bee by Frank Thomas & Felix The Cat begin. 69-2 pg. Kelly-a; The Brownies begin (not by Kelly)	19.00	58.00	135.00
71-75: 72-Kelly illos. 75-Brownies by Kelly?	12.00	36.00	85.00
76-Andy Panda (Carl Barks & Pabian-a); Woody Woodpecker x-over in Oswald ends	57.00	171.00	400.00
77,78: 78-Andy Panda in a world with real people ends	12.00	36.00	85.00
79-81	8.50	25.50	60.00
82-Brownies by Kelly begins; Homer Pigeon begins	10.00	30.00	70.00
83-85-Brownies by Kelly in ea. 83-X-mas-c. 85-Woody Woodpecker, 1pg. strip begins	10.00	30.00	70.00
86-90: 87-Woody Woodpecker stories begin	5.00	15.00	35.00
91-99	3.15	9.50	22.00
100 (6/45)	3.70	11.00	26.00
101-110	2.15	6.50	15.00
111-120: 119-X-mas-c	1.60	4.80	11.00
121-150: 143-X-mas-c	1.15	3.50	8.00
151-200: 155-X-mas-c. 168-X-mas-c, 182-Origin & 1st app. Knothead & Splinter. 191-X-mas-c	.85	2.50	6.00
201-240	.70	2.00	5.00
241-288: 270,271-Walter Lantz c-app. 281-1st story swipe/WDC&S #100	.60	1.80	4.00

NEW GODS, THE (New Gods #12 on) (See Adventure #459)
2-3/71-V2#11, 10-11/72; V3#12, 7/77-V3#19, 7-8/78
National Periodical Publications/DC Comics

1-Intro/1st app. Orion (#1-3 are 15 cents)	1.85	5.50	13.00
2,3: 2-Darkseid app. 3-Last 15 cent issue	1.30	4.00	9.00
4-9: All 52 pg. giants, 25 cents. 4-Origin Manhunter. 7-Origin Orion. 9-1st app. Bug	1.15	3.50	8.00
10,11	1.10	3.30	6.60
12-19: 12-New costume Orion	.35	1.10	2.20

NEW GODS
Feb, 1989-No. 28, Aug. 1991 ($1.50, color)
DC Comics

	Good	Fine	N-Mint
1-Russell-i	.35	1.00	2.00
2-28: 2-4-Starlin scripts. 17-Darkseid app.	.25	.75	1.50

NEW MUTANTS, THE
March, 1983-No. 100, April, 1991
Marvel Comics Group

The New Mutants #90, © Marvel Comics

	Good	Fine	N-Mint
1	1.45	4.40	8.80
2,3	.75	2.20	4.40
4-10: 10-1st app. Magma	.55	1.65	3.30
11-20: 13-Kitty Pryde app. 18-Intro. Warlock	.45	1.40	2.80
21-Double size; new Warlock origin	.55	1.65	3.30
22-30: 23-25-Cloak & Dagger app.	.45	1.40	2.80
31-58: 50-Double size. 58-Contains pull-out mutant registration form			
	.35	1.10	2.20
59-Fall of The Mutants begins, ends #61	.70	2.00	4.00
60-Double size, $1.25	.45	1.40	2.80

	Good	Fine	N-Mint
61-Fall of The Mutants ends	.35	1.10	2.20
62,64-72,74-85: 68-Intro Spyder. 76-X-Factor & X-Terminator app.			
		.55	1.10
63-X-Men & Wolverine app.; begin $1.00-c	.55	1.65	3.30
73-($1.50, 52 pgs.)	.35	1.10	2.20
86-McFarlane-c(i) swiped from Ditko splash pg.; Liefeld-a begins			
	1.70	5.00	10.00
87-1st app. Cable; Liefeld covers begin	4.15	12.50	25.00
88-2nd app. Cable	2.00	6.00	12.00
89-3rd app. Cable	1.30	4.00	8.00
90,91- New costumes. 90,91-Sabertooth app.	1.15	3.50	7.00
92-Liefeld-c only	.50	1.50	3.00
93,94-Cable vs. Wolverine	1.00	3.00	6.00
95-97-X-Tinction Agenda x-over	.75	2.25	4.50
95-Gold 2nd printing		.50	1.00
98,99	.60	1.75	3.50
100-($1.50, 52 pgs.)-1st app. X-Force	.85	2.50	5.00
100-Gold 2nd printing ($1.50)	.25	.75	1.50
Annual 1 (1984)	.85	2.50	5.00
Annual 2 (1986; $1.25)	.35	1.00	2.00
Annual 3(1987, $1.25)	.25	.75	1.50
Annual 4('88, $1.75)-Evolutionary War x-over	.60	1.75	3.50
Annual 5('89, $2.00, 68 pgs.)-Atlantis Attacks x-over; 1st Liefeld-a on New Mutants	2.00	6.00	12.00
Annual 6('90, $2.00, 68 pgs.)-1st new costumes	.35	1.00	2.00
Annual 7('91, $2.00, 68 pgs.)-No Liefeld-a	.35	1.00	2.00
Special 1-Special Edition ('85, 68 pgs.)-ties in with X-Men Alpha Flight mini-series; Art Adams/Austin-a	1.00	3.00	6.00
Summer Special 1(Sum/90, $2.95, 84 pgs.)	.50	1.50	3.00

NEW TEEN TITANS, THE (See DC Comics Presents 26, Marvel and DC Present & Teen Titans; Tales of the Teen Titans #41 on)
November, 1980-No. 40, March, 1984
DC Comics

1-Robin, Kid Flash, Wonder Girl, The Changeling, Starfire, The Raven, Cyborg begin; partial origin	1.40	4.25	8.50
2-1st app. Deathstroke the Terminator	1.35	4.00	8.00
3-Origin Starfire; Intro The Fearsome 5	.70	2.00	4.00
4-Origin continues; J.L.A. app.	.70	2.00	4.00

	Good	Fine	N-Mint

5-9: 6-Origin Raven. 7-Cyborg origin. 8-Origin Kid Flash retold
| | .50 | 1.50 | 3.00 |

10-2nd app. Deathstroke; origin Changeling retold .85 2.50 5.00

11-20: 13-Return of Madame Rouge & Capt. Zahl; Robotman revived. 14-Return of Mento; origin Doom Patrol. 15-Death of Madame Rouge & Capt. Zahl; intro. new Brotherhood of Evil 16-1st app. Capt. Carrot (free 16 pg. preview). 18-Return of Starfire. 19-Hawkman teams-up .25 .75 1.50

21-30: 21-Intro Night Force in free 16 pg. insert; intro Brother Blood. 23-1st app. Vigilante (not in costume), & Blackfire. 24-Omega Men app. 25-Omega Men cameo; free 16 pg. preview Masters of the Universe. 26-1st Terra. 27-Free 16 pg. preview Atari Force. 29-The New Brotherhood of Evil & Speedy app. 30-Terra joins the Titans .60 1.20

31-33,35-38,40: 38-Origin Wonder Girl .40 .80

34-3rd app. Deathstroke the Terminator .50 1.50 3.00

39-Last Dick Grayson as Robin; Kid Flash quits .35 1.00 2.00

Annual 1(11/82)-Omega Men app. .25 .70 1.40

Annual 2(9/83)-1st app. Vigilante in costume .25 .75 1.50

Annual 3(1984)-Death of Terra .50 1.00

NEW TEEN TITANS, THE (The New Titans #50 on)
Aug, 1984-No. 49, Nov, 1988 ($1.25-$1.75; deluxe format)
DC Comics

1-New storyline; Perez-c/a begins .75 2.25 4.50

2,3: 2-Re-intro Lilith .45 1.40 2.80

4-10: 5-Death of Trigon. 7-9-Origin Lilith. 8-Intro Kole. 10-Kole joins
| | .30 | .90 | 1.80 |

11-19: 13,14-Crisis x-over .60 1.20

20-Robin (Jason Todd) joins; original Teen Titans return
| | .35 | 1.00 | 2.00 |

21-49: 37-Begin $1.75-c. 38-Infinity, Inc. x-over. 47-Origin all Titans. 48-1st app. Red Star .25 .70 1.40

Annual 1 (9/85)-Intro. Vanguard .35 1.00 2.00

Annual 2 (8/86; $2.50): Byrne c/a(p); origin Brother Blood; intro new Dr. Light
| | .40 | 1.25 | 2.50 |

Annual 3 (11/87)-Intro. Danny Chase .35 1.00 2.00

Annual 4 ('88, $2.50)-Perez-c .40 1.15 2.30

NEW TITANS, THE (Formerly The New Teen Titans)
No. 50, Dec, 1988-Present ($1.75, color)
DC Comics

	Good	Fine	N-Mint
50-Perez-c/a begins; new origin Wonder Girl	.75	2.25	4.50
51-59: 50-55-Painted-c. 55-Nightwing (Dick Grayson) forces Danny Chase to resign; Batman app. in flashback	.40	1.25	2.50
60-A Lonely Place of Dying Part 2 continues from Batman #440; new Robin tie-in	1.10	3.25	6.50
61-A Lonely Place of Dying Part 4	.70	2.00	4.00
62-82: 65-Timothy Drake (Robin) app. 71 (44 pgs.)-10th anniversary issue. 74-Intro. Pantha	.30	.90	1.80
Annual 5,6 (1989, 1990, $3.50, 68 pgs.)	.60	1.75	3.50

NEW WARRIORS, THE (See Thor #411,412)
July, 1990-Present ($1.00, color)
Marvel Comics

	Good	Fine	N-Mint
1-Williamson-i	1.25	3.75	7.50
1-Gold 2nd printing (7/91)		.50	1.00
2-Williamson-c/a(i)	.85	2.50	5.00
3-5: 3-Guice-c(i).	.60	1.75	3.50
6,7: 7-Punisher cameo (last pg.)	.35	1.00	2.00
8,9-Punisher app.	.50	1.50	3.00
10-18		.50	1.00
Annual 1 ('91, $2.00, 68 pgs.)-X-Force x-over (Cable); origins of all members of New Warriors	.35	1.00	2.00

NICKEL COMICS
May, 1940-No. 8, Aug, 1940 (36 pgs.; Bi-Weekly; 5 cents)
Fawcett Publications

	Good	Fine	N-Mint
1-Origin/1st app. Bulletman	110.00	330.00	770.00
2	50.00	150.00	350.00
3	43.00	130.00	300.00
4-The Red Gaucho begins	39.00	115.00	270.00
5-7	34.00	102.00	240.00
8-World's Fair-c; Bulletman moved to Master Comics #7 in Oct.	34.00	102.00	240.00

NICK FURY, AGENT OF SHIELD (See Marvel Spotlight #31, Shield & Strange Tales #135)
6/68-No. 15, 11/69; No. 16, 11/70-No. 18, 3/71
Marvel Comics Group

	Good	Fine	N-Mint
1	4.50	14.00	32.00
2-4: 4-Origin retold	2.30	7.00	16.00
5-Classic-c	2.85	8.50	20.00
6,7	1.50	4.50	10.00
8-11,13: 9-Hate Monger begins (ends #11). 11-Smith-c. 13-Last 12 cent issue			
	.85	2.50	5.00
12-Smith-c/a	1.00	3.00	6.00
14	.50	1.50	3.00
15-(15 cents)-1st app. & death of Bullseye(11/69)	2.15	6.50	15.00
16-18-(25 cents, 52 pgs.)-r/Str. Tales #135-143	.30	.90	1.80

NICK FURY VS. SHIELD
June, 1988-No. 6, Dec, 1988 ($3.50, 52 pgs, color, deluxe format)
Marvel Comics

1-Steranko-c	1.70	5.00	10.00
2	2.00	6.00	12.00
3	.85	2.50	5.00
4-6	.60	1.75	3.50

NIGHTCRAWLER
Nov, 1985-No. 4, Feb, 1986 (Mini-series from X-Men)
Marvel Comics Group

1-Cockrum-c/a	.50	1.50	3.00
2-4	.35	1.00	2.00

NOMAD (See Captain America #180)
Nov, 1990-No. 4, Feb., 1991 ($1.50, color)
Marvel Comics

1-Captain America app.	.40	1.25	2.50
2-2: 4-Captain America app.	.35	1.00	2.00

NOMAN (See Thunder Agents)
Nov, 1966-No. 2, March, 1967 (25 cents, 68 pgs.)
Tower Comics

1-Wood/Williamson-c; Lightning begins; Dynamo cameo; Kane-a(p); Whitney-a in both issues	3.60	11.00	25.00

	Good	Fine	N-Mint
2-Wood-c only; Dynamo x-over	2.15	6.50	15.00

NYOKA, THE JUNGLE GIRL (Formerly Jungle Girl; see Master #50)
No. 2, Winter, 1945-No. 77, June, 1953 (Movie serial)
Fawcett Publications

2	34.00	103.00	240.00
3	19.00	57.00	135.00
4,5	16.00	48.00	110.00
6-10	11.50	34.00	80.00
11,13,14,16-18-Krigstein-a	11.50	34.00	80.00
12,15,19,20	9.30	28.00	65.00
21-30: 25-Clayton Moore photo-c?	5.70	17.00	40.00
31-40	4.30	13.00	30.00
41-50	3.15	9.50	22.00
51-60	2.30	7.00	16.00
61-77	1.70	5.00	12.00

O

OFFICIAL HANDBOOK OF THE MARVEL UNIVERSE, THE
Jan, 1983-No. 15, May, 1984
Marvel Comics Group

	Good	Fine	N-Mint
1-Lists Marvel heroes & villains (letter A)	1.00	3.00	6.00
2 (B-C)	.85	2.50	5.00
3-5: 3-(C-D). 4-(D-G). 5-(H-J)	.70	2.00	4.00
6-9: 6-(K-L). 7-(M). 8-(N-P); Punisher-c. 9-(Q-S)	.50	1.50	3.00
10-15: 10-(S). 11-(S-U). 12-(V-Z); Wolverine-c. 13,14-Book of the Dead. 15-			
Weaponry catalogue	.40	1.25	2.50

OMEGA MEN, THE (See Green Lantern #141)
Dec, 1982-No. 38, May, 1986 ($1.00-$1.50; Baxter paper)
DC Comics

	Good	Fine	N-Mint
1	.25	.75	1.50
2,4,6-8,11-18,21-36,38: 2-Origin Broot. 7-Origin The Citadel. 26,27-Alan Moore			
scripts. 30-Intro new Primus. 31-Crisis x-over. 34,35-Teen Titans x-over			
		.50	1.00
3-1st app. Lobo (2/83)	1.50	4.50	10.00
5,9-2nd & 3rd app. Lobo (cameo, 2 pgs. each)	1.00	3.00	6.00
10-1st full Lobo story	1.50	4.50	10.00
19-Lobo cameo	.50	1.50	3.00
20-2nd full Lobo story	1.00	3.00	6.00
37-1st solo Lobo story (8 pgs.)	.70	2.00	4.00
Annual 1(11/84, 52 pgs.), 2(11/85)	.25	.75	1.50

OMEGA THE UNKNOWN
March, 1976-No. 10, Oct, 1977
Marvel Comics Group

	Good	Fine	N-Mint
1	.35	1.00	2.00
2-7,10: 2-Hulk app. 3-Electro app.		.50	1.00
8-1st app. 2nd Foolkiller (Greg Salinger), small cameos only			
	1.00	3.00	6.00
9-1st full app. Foolkiller	1.35	4.00	8.00

OUR ARMY AT WAR (Becomes Sgt. Rock #302 on)
Aug, 1952-No. 301, Feb, 1977
National Periodical Publications

	Good	Fine	N-Mint
1	50.00	150.00	350.00
2	24.00	70.00	165.00
3,4: 4-Krigstein-a	22.00	65.00	150.00
5-7	14.00	43.00	100.00
8-11,14-Krigstein-a	14.00	43.00	100.00
12,15-20	10.00	30.00	70.00
13-Krigstein c/a; flag-c	16.00	48.00	110.00
21-31: Last pre-code (2/55)	7.00	21.00	50.00
32-40	5.70	17.00	40.00
41-60	5.00	15.00	35.00
61-70	3.50	10.50	24.00
71-80	2.65	8.00	18.00
81-1st Sgt. Rock app. by Andru & Esposito in Easy Co. story			
	60.00	180.00	425.00
82-Sgt. Rock cameo in Easy Co. story (6 panels)	15.00	45.00	105.00
83-1st Kubert Sgt. Rock (6/59)	18.00	54.00	125.00
84,86-90	5.70	17.00	40.00
85-Origin & 1st app. Ice Cream Soldier	6.50	19.50	45.00
91-All Sgt. Rock issue	16.00	48.00	110.00
92-100: 92-1st app. Bulldozer. 95-1st app. Zack	3.60	11.00	25.00
101-120: 101-1st app. Buster. 111-1st app. Wee Willie & Sunny. 113-1st app. Jackie Johnson. 118-Sunny dies. 120-1st app. Wildman			
	1.50	4.50	10.00
121-127,129-150: 126-1st app. Canary. 139-1st app. Little Sure Shot			
	1.15	3.50	8.00
128-Training & origin Sgt. Rock	7.00	21.00	50.00
151-Intro. Enemy Ace by Kubert	5.70	17.00	40.00
152,154,156,157,159-163,165-170: 157-2 pg. pin-up. 162,163-Viking Prince x-over in Sgt. Rock	1.00	3.00	6.00
153-2nd app. Enemy Ace	3.60	11.00	25.00
155-3rd app. Enemy Ace	1.30	4.00	9.00
158-Origin & 1st app. Iron Major(1965), formerly Iron Captain			
	1.15	3.50	8.00
164-Giant G-19	1.15	3.50	8.00
171-176,178-181	.70	2.00	4.00
177-(80 pg. Giant G-32)	1.00	3.00	6.00

	Good	Fine	N-Mint
182,183,186-Neal Adams-a. 186-Origin retold	1.15	3.50	7.00
184,185,187-189,191-199: 184-Wee Willie dies. 189-Intro. The Teen-age Underground Fighters of Unit 3	.50	1.50	3.00
190-(80 pg. Giant G-44)	.70	2.00	4.00
200-12 pg. Rock story told in verse; Evans-a	.50	1.50	3.00
201-Krigstein-r/No. 14	.50	1.50	3.00
202,206-215	.35	1.05	2.10
203-(80 pg. Giant G-56)-All-r, no Sgt. Rock	.45	1.30	2.60
204,205-All reprints; no Sgt. Rock	.35	1.00	2.00
216,229-(80 pg. Giants G-68, G-80)	.45	1.30	2.60
217-228,230-239,241,243-301: 249-Wood-a	.35	1.05	2.10
240-Neal Adams-a	.45	1.30	2.60
242-(50 cent issue DC-9)-Kubert-c	.45	1.30	2.60

OUR GANG COMICS (Based on film characters)
Sept-Oct, 1942-No. 59, June, 1949
Dell Publishing Co.

	Good	Fine	N-Mint
1-Our Gang & Barney Bear by Kelly, Tom & Jerry, Pete Smith, Flip & Dip, The Milky Way begin	60.00	180.00	420.00
2	27.00	81.00	190.00
3-5: 3-Benny Burro begins	18.00	54.00	125.00
6-Bumbazine & Albert only app. by Kelly	31.00	92.00	220.00
7-No Kelly story	14.00	42.00	100.00
8-Benny Burro begins by Barks	31.00	92.00	215.00
9-Barks-a(2): Benny Burro & Happy Hound; no Kelly story	25.00	75.00	175.00
10-Benny Burro by Barks	20.00	60.00	140.00
11-1st Barney Bear & Benny Burro by Barks; Happy Hound by Barks	20.00	60.00	140.00
12-20	12.00	36.00	84.00
21-30: 30-X-Mas-c	9.00	27.00	63.00
31-36-Last Barks issue	6.50	19.50	45.00
37-40	2.65	8.00	18.00
41-50	2.00	6.00	14.00
51-57	1.70	5.00	12.00
58,59-No Kelly art or Our Gang stories	1.50	4.50	10.00

OUTLAW KID, THE (1st Series; see Wild Western)
Sept, 1954-No. 19, Sept, 1957
Atlas Comics (CCC No. 1-11/EPI No. 12-29)

	Good	Fine	N-Mint
1-Origin; The Outlaw Kid & his horse Thunder begin; Black Rider app.			
	10.00	30.00	70.00
2-Black Rider app.	5.00	15.00	35.00
3-Woodbridge/Williamson-a	5.00	15.00	35.00
4-7,9	3.50	10.50	24.00
8-Williamson/Woodbridge-a, 4 pgs.	4.30	13.00	30.00
10-Williamson-a	4.30	13.00	30.00
11-17,19	2.30	7.00	16.00
18-Williamson-a	4.00	12.00	28.00

OUTLAW KID, THE (2nd Series)
Aug, 1970-No. 30, Oct, 1975
Marvel Comics Group

	Good	Fine	N-Mint
1,2-Reprints; 1-Orlando-r, Wildey-r(3)	.50	1.50	3.00
3,9-Williamson-a(r)	.25	.75	1.50
4-8: 8-Crandall-r		.50	1.00
10-30: 10-Origin; new-a in #10-16. 27-Origin r-/#10		.35	.70

P

PARTRIDGE FAMILY, THE (TV)
March, 1971-No. 21, Dec, 1973
Charlton Comics

	Good	Fine	N-Mint
1	1.30	4.00	9.00
2-4,6-21	.70	2.00	5.00
5-Partridge Family Summer Special (52 pgs.); The Shadow, Lone Ranger, Charlie McCarthy, Flash Gordon, Hopalong Cassidy, Gene Autry & others app.			
	1.70	5.00	12.00

PEANUTS (Charlie Brown) (See Tip Top Comics)
No. 878, 2/58-No. 13, 5-7/62; 5/63-No. 4, 2/64
Dell Publishing Co./Gold Key

	Good	Fine	N-Mint
4-Color 878(#1)	7.00	21.00	50.00
4-Color 969,1015('59)	5.70	17.00	40.00
4(2-4/60)	4.00	12.00	28.00
5-13	2.65	8.00	18.00
1(Gold Key, 5/63)	3.50	10.50	24.00
2-4	2.30	7.00	16.00

PEP COMICS
Jan, 1940-No. 411?, 1987
MLJ Magazines/Archie Publications No. 56 (3/46) on

	Good	Fine	VF-NM
1-Intro. The Shield by Irving Novick (1st patriotic hero); origin The Comet by Jack Cole, The Queen of Diamonds & Kayo Ward; The Rocket, The Press Guardian (The Falcon #1 only), Sergeant Boyle, Fu Chang, & Bentley of Scotland Yard	233.00	585.00	1400.00

	Good	Fine	N-Mint
2-Origin The Rocket	77.00	230.00	540.00
3	62.00	185.00	435.00
4-Wizard cameo	54.00	160.00	375.00
5-Wizard cameo in Shield story	54.00	160.00	375.00
6-10: 8-Last Cole Comet; no Cole-a in #6,7	39.00	116.00	270.00
11-Dusty, Shield's sidekick begins; last Press Guardian, Fu Chang			
	40.00	120.00	280.00

Pep Comics #32, © Archie Publications

	Good	Fine	N-Mint
12-Origin Fireball; last Rocket & Queen of Diamonds			
	54.00	160.00	375.00
13-15	37.00	110.00	255.00
16-Origin Madam Satan; blood drainage-c	54.00	163.00	380.00
17-Origin The Hangman; death of The Comet	110.00	330.00	775.00
18-20-Last Fireball	36.00	107.00	250.00
21-Last Madam Satan	36.00	107.00	250.00

	Good	Fine	VF-NM
22-Intro. & 1st app. Archie, Betty, & Jughead(12/41); (also see Jackpot)			
	235.00	705.00	1650.00

	Good	Fine	N-Mint
23	63.00	190.00	440.00
24,25	53.00	160.00	370.00
26-1st app. Veronica Lodge	64.00	193.00	450.00
27-30: 30-Capt. Commando begins	42.00	125.00	295.00
31-35: 34-Bondage/Hypo-c	34.00	100.00	235.00
36-1st Archie-c	54.00	160.00	375.00

	Good	Fine	N-Mint
37-40	25.00	75.00	175.00

41-50: 41-Archie-c begin. 47-Last Hangman issue; infinity-c. 48-Black Hood
    begins (5/44); ends #51,59,60

	19.00	56.00	130.00

51-60: 52-Suzie begins. 56-Last Capt. Commando. 59-Black Hood not in costume;
    Archie dresses as his aunt; Suzie ends. 60-Katy Keene begins, ends #154

	13.00	40.00	90.00
61-65-Last Shield. 62-1st app. Li'l Jinx	9.30	28.00	65.00

66-80: 66-G-Man Club becomes Archie Club (2/48)

	6.50	19.50	45.00
81-99	4.35	13.00	30.00
100	5.00	15.00	35.00
101-130	2.00	6.00	14.00
131-149	1.00	3.00	7.00

150-160-Super-heroes app. in each (see note below). 150 (10/61?)-2nd or 3rd app.
    The Jaguar? 157-Li'l Jinx story

	1.15	3.50	8.00
161-167,169-200	.35	1.00	2.50
168-Jaguar app.	.85	2.60	6.00
201-260	.25	.75	1.50

261-411: 383-Marvelous Maureen begins (Sci/fi). 393-Thunderbunny begins

		.35	.70

*NOTE: The Fly app. in 151, 154, 160. Flygirl app. in 153, 155, 156, 158. Jaguar app. in 150,
152, 157, 159, 168. Katy Keene by Bill Woggon in many later issues.*

PETER PORKCHOPS (See Leading Comics #23)
11-12/49-No. 61, 9-11/59; No. 62, 10-12/60 (1-5: 52 pgs.)
National Periodical Publications

1	19.00	58.00	135.00
2	9.30	28.00	65.00
3-10	6.50	19.00	45.00
11-30	4.50	14.00	32.00
31-62	2.85	8.50	20.00

PHANTOM, THE (nn 29-Published overseas only) (See Ace Comics)
Nov, 1962-No. 17, July, 1966; No. 18, Sept, 1966-No. 28, Dec,
    1967; No. 30, Feb, 1969-No. 74, Jan, 1977
Gold Key (#1-17)/King (#18-28)/Charlton (#30 on)

1-Manning-a	5.70	17.00	40.00
2-King, Queen & Jack begins, ends #11	2.85	8.50	20.00
3-10	2.00	6.00	14.00

	Good	Fine	N-Mint
11-17: 12-Track Hunter begins	1.50	4.50	10.00
18-Flash Gordon begins; Wood-a	1.70	5.00	12.00
19,20-Flash Gordon ends (both by Gil Kane)	1.30	4.00	9.00
21-24,26,27: 21-Mandrake begins. 20,24-Girl Phantom app. 26-Brick Bradford			
app.	1.15	3.50	8.00
25-Jeff Jones-a(4 pgs.); 1 pg. Williamson ad	1.30	4.00	9.00
28(nn)-Brick Bradford app.	1.00	3.00	7.00
30-40: 36,39-Ditko-a	.70	2.00	5.00
41-66: 46-Intro. The Piranha. 62-Bolle-c	.50	1.50	3.00
67-71,73-Newton-c/a; 67-Origin retold	.35	1.00	2.00
72	.25	.75	1.50
74-Newton Flag-c; Newton-a	.35	1.00	2.00

PHANTOM, THE
May, 1988-No. 4, Aug, 1988 ($1.25, color)
DC Comics

	Good	Fine	N-Mint
1-Orlando-c/a in all	.35	1.00	2.00
2-4	.25	.75	1.50

PHANTOM, THE
Mar, 1989-No. 13, Mar, 1990 ($1.50, color)
DC Comics

	Good	Fine	N-Mint
1-Brief origin	.35	1.00	2.00
2-13	.25	.75	1.50

PHANTOM LADY (1st Series) (Also see All Top Comics)
No. 13, Aug, 1947-No. 23 April, 1949
Fox Features Syndicate

13(#1)-Phantom Lady by Matt Baker begins; The Blue Beetle app.

	Good	Fine	N-Mint
	121.00	365.00	850.00
14(#2)	79.00	235.00	550.00
15-P.L. injected with experimental drug	63.00	190.00	440.00
16-Negligee-c, panels	63.00	190.00	440.00
17-Classic bondage cover; used in **SOTI**, illo-"Sexual stimulation by combining 'headlights' with the sadist's dream of tying up a woman"			
	154.00	460.00	1075.00
18,19	57.00	171.00	400.00
20-23: 23-Bondage-c	49.00	146.00	340.00

	Good	Fine	N-Mint

PHANTOM STRANGER, THE (1st Series) (See Saga of Swamp Thing)
Aug-Sept, 1952-No. 6, June-July, 1953
National Periodical Publications

	Good	Fine	N-Mint
1 (Scarce)	65.00	195.00	455.00
2 (Scarce)	50.00	150.00	350.00
3-6 (Scarce)	40.00	120.00	280.00

PHANTOM STRANGER, THE (2nd Series) (See Showcase #80)
May-June, 1969-No. 41, Feb-Mar, 1976
National Periodical Publications

	Good	Fine	N-Mint
1-Only 12 cent issue	3.15	9.50	22.00
2,3: 2-? are 15 cents	1.50	4.50	10.00
4-Neal Adams-a	1.70	5.00	12.00
5-7	1.15	3.50	8.00
8-10	1.00	3.00	6.00
11-20	.50	1.50	3.00

21-41: 22-Dark Circle begins. 23-Spawn of Frankenstein begins by Kaluta; series
    ends #30. 31-The Black Orchid begins. 39-41-Deadman app.

	.35	1.00	2.00

PHANTOM STRANGER (See Justice League of America #103)
Oct, 1987-No. 4, Jan, 1988 (75 cents, color, mini-series)
DC Comics

	Good	Fine	N-Mint
1-Mignola/Russell-c/a in all	.25	.75	1.50
2-4		.50	1.00

PINK PANTHER, THE (TV)
April, 1971-No. 87, 1984 (Pink Panther began as a movie cartoon)
Gold Key

	Good	Fine	N-Mint
1-The Inspector begins	1.20	3.50	8.00
2-10	.70	2.00	4.00
11-30: Warren Tufts-a #16-on	.40	1.20	2.50
31-60	.25	.75	1.50
61-87		.50	1.00

PLANET COMICS
1/40-No. 62, 9/49; No. 63, Wint, 1949-50; No. 64, Spring, 1950; No. 65, 1951(nd);
    No. 66-68, 1952(nd); No. 69, Wint, 1952-53; No. 70-72, 1953(nd); No. 73,
    Winter, 1953-54
Fiction House Magazines

	Good	Fine	VF-NM
1-Origin Auro, Lord of Jupiter; Flint Baker & The Red Comet begin; Eisner/Fine-c			
	500.00	1250.00	3000.00
	Good	**Fine**	**N-Mint**
2-(Scarce)	233.00	585.00	1400.00
3-Eisner-c	192.00	480.00	1150.00
4-Gale Allen and the Girl Squadron begins	167.00	415.00	1000.00
5,6-(Scarce)	150.00	375.00	900.00
7-12: 12-The Star Pirate begins	107.00	320.00	750.00
13-14: 13-Reff Ryan begins	82.00	245.00	575.00
15-(Scarce)-Mars, God of War begins	86.00	257.00	600.00
16-20,22	79.00	235.00	550.00
21-The Lost World & Hunt Bowman begin	82.00	245.00	575.00
23-26: 26-The Space Rangers begin	79.00	235.00	505.00
27-30	57.00	170.00	400.00
31-35: 33-Origin Star Pirates Wonder Boots, reprinted in #52. 35- Mysta of the			
Moon begins	49.00	145.00	340.00
36-45: 41-New origin of "Auro, Lord of Jupiter." 42-Last Gale Allen. 43-Futura			
begins	43.00	130.00	300.00
46-60: 53-Used in **SOTI**, pg. 32	32.00	95.00	220.00
61-64	22.00	65.00	150.00
65-68,70: 65-70-All partial-r of earlier issues	22.00	65.00	150.00
69-Used in **POP**, pgs. 101,102	22.00	65.00	150.00
71-73-No series stories	17.00	51.00	120.00

PLASTIC MAN (Also see Police Comics & Smash Comics #17)
Sum, 1943-No. 64, Nov, 1956
Vital Publ. No. 1,2/Quality Comics No. 3 on

nn(#1)-'In The Game of Death;' Jack Cole-c/a begins; ends-#64?			
	143.00	430.00	1000.00
nn(#2, 2/44)-'The Gay Nineties Nightmare'	84.00	250.00	585.00
3 (Spr, '46)	55.00	165.00	385.00
4 (Sum, '46)	47.00	140.00	325.00
5 (Aut, '46)	40.00	120.00	280.00
6-10	29.00	88.00	205.00

	Good	Fine	N-Mint
11-20	25.00	75.00	175.00
21-30: 26-Last non-r issue?	21.00	62.00	145.00
31-40: 40-Used in **POP**, pg. 91	15.00	45.00	105.00
41-64: 53-Last pre-code issue	12.00	36.00	85.00

PLASTIC MAN
11-12/66-No. 10, 5-6/68; V4#11, 2-3/76-No. 20, 10-11/77
National Periodical Publications/DC Comics

	Good	Fine	N-Mint
1-Gil Kane-c/a; 12 cent issues begin	3.50	10.50	24.00
2-5: 4-Infantino-c; Mortimer-a	1.60	4.80	11.00
6-10('68): 10-Sparling-a; last 12 cent issue	.95	2.85	6.60
V4#11('76)-20: 11-20-Fraden-p. 17-Origin retold	.25	.75	1.50

POLICE COMICS
Aug, 1941-No. 127, Oct, 1953
Quality Comics Group (Comic Magazines)

	Good	Fine	N-Mint
1-Origin Plastic Man (1st app.) by Jack Cole, The Human Bomb by Gustavson, & No. 711; intro. Chic Carter by Eisner, The Firebrand by Reed Crandall, The Mouthpiece, Phantom Lady, & The Sword	350.00	875.00	2100.00
2-Plastic Man smuggles opium	143.00	430.00	1000.00
3	115.00	343.00	800.00
4	100.00	300.00	700.00
5-Plastic Man forced to smoke marijuana	100.00	300.00	700.00
6,7	90.00	270.00	630.00
8-Manhunter begins (origin)	105.00	315.00	735.00
9,10	82.00	245.00	575.00
11-The Spirit strip reprints begin by Eisner(Origin-strip #1)	134.00	400.00	935.00
12-Intro. Ebony	86.00	257.00	600.00
13-Intro. Woozy Winks; last Firebrand	86.00	257.00	600.00
14-19: 15-Last No. 711; Destiny begins	56.00	167.00	390.00
20-The Raven x-over in Phantom Lady; features Jack Cole himself	56.00	167.00	390.00
21,22-Raven & Spider Widow x-over in Phantom Lady #21; cameo in Phantom Lady #22	43.00	130.00	300.00
23-30: 23-Last Phantom Lady. 24-26-Flatfoot Burns by Kurtzman in all	37.00	110.00	260.00
31-41-Last Spirit-r by Eisner	27.00	80.00	185.00

	Good	Fine	N-Mint
42,43-Spirit-r by Eisner/Fine	23.00	70.00	160.00
44-Fine Spirit-r begin, end #88,90,92	19.00	58.00	135.00
45-50-(#50 on-c, #49 on inside)(1/46)	19.00	58.00	135.00
51-60: 58-Last Human Bomb	15.00	45.00	105.00
61-88: 63-(Some issues have #65 printed on cover, but #63 on inside) Kurtzman-a,			
6pgs.	13.00	40.00	90.00
89,91,93-No Spirit	11.50	34.00	80.00
90,92-Spirit by Fine	13.00	40.00	90.00
94-99,101,102: Spirit by Eisner in all; 101-Last Manhunter. 102-Last Spirit &			
Plastic Man by Jack Cole	17.00	51.00	120.00
100	20.00	60.00	140.00
103-Content change to crime-Ken Shannon begins (1st app.)			
	9.30	28.00	65.00
104-111,114-127-Crandall-a most issues	6.50	19.00	45.00
112-Crandall-a	6.50	19.00	45.00
113-Crandall-c/a(2), 9 pgs. each	7.00	21.00	50.00

POPEYE (See King Comics & Magic Comics)
24/48-#65, 7-9/62; #66, 10/62-#80, 5/66; #81, 8/66-#92, 12/67; #94, 2/69-#138, 1/77; #139, 5/78-#171, 7/84 (no #93,160,161)
Dell #1-65/Gold Key #66-80/King #81-92/Charlton #94-138/Gold Key #139-155/Whitman #156 on

1	24.00	71.00	165.00
2	12.00	36.00	85.00
3-10	10.00	30.00	70.00
11-20	8.00	24.00	55.00
21-40	5.70	17.00	40.00
41-45,47-50	4.00	12.00	28.00
46-Origin Swee' Pee	5.70	17.00	40.00
51-60	3.15	9.50	22.00
61-65 (Last Dell issue)	2.65	8.00	18.00
66,67-Both 84 pgs. (Gold Key)	4.00	12.00	32.00
68-80	2.00	6.00	14.00
81-92,94-100	1.15	3.50	8.00
101-130	.85	2.60	6.00
131-159,162-171: 144-50th Anniversary issue	.55	1.65	4.00

POPULAR COMICS
Feb, 1936-No. 145, July-Sept, 1948
Dell Publishing Co.

	Good	Fine	VF-NM
1-Dick Tracy (1st comic book app.), Little Orphan Annie, Terry & the Pirates, Gasoline Alley, Don Winslow, Harold Teen, Little Joe, Skippy, Moon Mullins, Mutt & Jeff, Tailspin Tommy, Smitty, Smokey Stover, Winnie Winkle & The Gumps begin (all strip-r)	183.00	460.00	1100.00
2	77.00	231.00	540.00
3	60.00	180.00	420.00
4,5: 5-Tom Mix begins	47.00	141.00	330.00
6-10: 8,9-Scribbly, Reglar Fellers app.	39.00	116.00	270.00

	Good	Fine	N-Mint
11-20: 12-Xmas-c	30.00	90.00	210.00
21-27-Last Terry & the Pirates, Little Orphan Annie, & Dick Tracy	22.00	65.00	150.00
28-37: 28-Gene Autry app. 31,32-Tim McCoy app. 35-Christmas-c; Tex Ritter app.	18.00	54.00	125.00
38-43-Tarzan in text only. 38-Gang Busters (radio) & Zane Grey's Tex Thorne begins? 43-1st non-funny-c?	21.00	62.00	145.00
44,45: 45-Tarzan-c	14.00	43.00	100.00
46-Origin Martan, the Marvel Man	19.00	57.00	135.00
47-50	13.00	40.00	90.00
51-Origin The Voice (The Invisible Detective) strip begins	14.00	43.00	100.00
52-59: 55-End of World story	11.50	34.00	80.00
60-Origin Professor Supermind and Son	12.00	36.00	85.00
61-71: 63-Smilin' Jack begins	10.00	30.00	70.00
72-The Owl & Terry & the Pirates begin; Smokey Stover reprints begin	16.00	48.00	110.00
73-75	12.00	36.00	85.00
76-78-Capt. Midnight in all	14.00	43.00	100.00
79-85-Last Owl	11.00	32.00	75.00
86-99: 98-Felix the Cat, Smokey Stover-r begin	8.50	25.50	60.00
100	10.00	30.00	70.00
101-130: 114-Last Dick Tracy-r?	5.30	16.00	38.00
131-145: 142-Last Terry & the Pirates	4.50	14.00	32.00

PORKY PIG (...& Bugs Bunny #40-69)
No. 16, 1942-No. 81, Mar-Apr, 1962; Jan, 1965-No. 109, July, 1984
Dell Publishing Co./Gold Key No. 1-93/Whitman No. 94 on

4-Color 16(#1, 1942)	40.00	120.00	280.00
4-Color 48(1944)-Carl Barks-a	70.00	210.00	490.00
4-Color 78(1945)	16.00	48.00	110.00

	Good	Fine	N-Mint
4-Color 112(7/46)	8.50	25.50	60.00
4-Color 156,182,191('49)	6.50	19.50	45.00
4-Color 226,241('49),260,271,277,284,295	4.30	13.00	30.00
4-Color 303,311,322,330	3.00	9.00	21.00
4-Color 342,351,360,370,385,399,410,426	2.30	7.00	16.00
25 (11-12/52)-30	1.30	4.00	9.00
31-50	.70	2.00	4.50
51-81(3-4/62)	.45	1.35	3.00
1(1/65-Gold Key)(2nd Series)	.75	2.25	5.00
2,4,5-R/4-Color 226,284 & 271 in that order	.45	1.35	3.00
3,6-10	.35	1.00	2.00
11-50		.50	1.00
51-109		.30	.60

POWERHOUSE PEPPER COMICS (See Joker Comics)
No. 1, 1943; No. 2, May, 1948-No. 5, Nov, 1948
Marvel Comics (20CC)

1-(60 pgs.)-Wolverton-c/a in all	63.00	190.00	440.00
2	39.00	116.00	270.00
3,4	36.00	107.00	250.00
5-(Scarce)	43.00	130.00	300.00

POWER MAN (Formerly Hero for Hire;...& Iron Fist #68 on)
No. 17, Feb, 1974-No. 125, Sept, 1986
Marvel Comics Group

17-Luke Cage continues; Iron Man app.	1.15	3.50	8.00
18-20: 18-Last 20 cent issue	.85	2.50	5.00
21-31: 31-Part Neal Adams-i. 34-Last 25 cents	.40	1.25	2.50
32-47: 36-r/Hero For Hire #12. 45-Starlin-c	.35	1.00	2.00
48-Byrne-a; Powerman/Iron Fist 1st meet	.50	1.50	3.00
49,50-Byrne-a(p); 50-Iron Fist joins Cage	.50	1.50	3.00
51-56,58-60: 58-Intro El Aguila		.60	1.25
57-Early New X-Men app.	.85	2.50	5.00
61-65,67-77,79-83,85-124: 75-Double size. 77-Daredevil app. 87-Moon Knight app. 90-Unus app. 109-The Reaper app. 100-Double size; origin K'un L'un		.50	1.00
66-2nd app. Sabretooth	2.50	7.50	17.00
78-3rd app. Sabretooth (under cloak)	1.15	3.50	7.00
84-4th app. Sabretooth	1.15	3.50	7.00

	Good	Fine	N-Mint
125-Double size; death of Iron Fist	.35	1.00	2.00
Annual 1(1976)-Punisher cameo in flashback	.50	1.50	3.00

POWER PACK
Aug, 1984-No. 62, Feb, 1991
Marvel Comics Group

	Good	Fine	N-Mint
1-($1.00, 52 pgs.)	.70	2.00	4.00
2-5	.45	1.35	2.70
6-8-Cloak & Dagger app. 6-Spider-man app.	.35	1.00	2.00
9-18	.25	.75	1.50
19-Dbl. size; Cloak & Dagger, Wolverine app.	1.70	5.00	10.00
20-24		.60	1.25
25-Double size	.30	.90	1.80
26-Begin direct sale; Cloak & Dagger app.		.60	1.25
27-Mutant massacre; Wolverine app.	2.00	6.00	12.00
28-43: 42-1st Inferno tie-in		.65	1.30
44,45,47-49,51-62: 44-Begin $1.50-c	.25	.75	1.50
46-Punisher app.	1.00	3.00	6.00
50-Double size ($1.95)	.35	1.00	2.00

PRIZE COMICS (...Western #69 on)
March, 1940-No. 68, Feb-Mar, 1948
Prize Publications

	Good	Fine	N-Mint
1-Origin Power Nelson, The Futureman & Jupiter, Master Magician; Ted O'Neil, Secret Agent M-11, Jaxon of the Jungle, Bucky Brady & Storm Curtis begin			
	84.00	250.00	585.00
2-The Black Owl begins	41.00	122.00	285.00
3,4	34.00	100.00	235.00
5,6: Dr. Dekkar, Master of Monsters app. in each			
	30.00	90.00	210.00
7-(Scarce)-Black Owl by S&K; origin/1st app. Dr. Frost & Frankenstein; The Green Lama, Capt. Gallant, The Great Voodini & Twist Turner begin; Kirby-c			
	68.00	205.00	475.00
8,9-Black Owl & Ted O'Neil by S&K	35.00	105.00	245.00
10-12,14-20: 11-Origin Bulldog Denny. 16-Spike Mason begins			
	30.00	90.00	210.00
13-Yank & Doodle begin (origin)	36.00	107.00	250.00
21-24	20.00	60.00	140.00
25-30	13.00	40.00	90.00

	Good	Fine	N-Mint
31-33	10.00	30.00	70.00

34-Origin Airmale, Yank & Doodle; The Black Owl joins army, Yank & Doodle's
   father assumes Black Owl's role

35-40: 35-Flying Fist & Bingo begin. 37-Intro. Stampy, Airmale's sidekick; Hitler-c

	8.50	25.50	60.00

41-50: 45-Yank & Doodle learn Black Owl's I.D. (their father). 48-Prince Ra
   begins

	6.50	19.00	45.00

51-62,64-68: 53-Transvestism story. 55-No Frankenstein. 57-X-Mas-c. 64-Black
   Owl retires. 65,66-Frankenstein-c by Briefer

	5.70	17.00	40.00
63-Simon & Kirby c/a	8.00	24.00	55.00

PRIZE COMICS WESTERN (Formerly Prize Comics #1-68)
No. 69(V7#2), Apr-May, 1948-No. 119, Nov-Dec, 1956
Prize Publications (Feature) (No. 69-84: 52 pgs.)

	Good	Fine	N-Mint
69(V7#2)	8.00	24.00	55.00
70-75	5.30	16.00	38.00

76-Randolph Scott photo-c; "Canadian Pacific" movie adaptation

	8.00	24.00	55.00

77-Photo-c; Severin, Mart Bailey-a; "Streets of Laredo" movie adapt.

	6.50	19.00	45.00

78-Photo-c; Kurtzman-a, 10 pgs.; Severin, Mart Bailey-a; "Bullet Code," &
   "Roughshod" movie adapt.

	9.30	28.00	65.00

79-Photo-c; Kurtzman-a, 8 pgs.; Severin & Elder, Severin, Mart Bailey-a; "Stage
   To Chino" movie adapt.

	9.30	28.00	65.00
80,81-Photo-c; Severin/Elder-a(2)	6.50	19.00	45.00

82-Photo-c; 1st app. The Preacher by Mart Bailey; Severin/Elder-a(3)

	6.50	19.00	45.00
83,84	5.00	15.00	35.00

85-American Eagle by John Severin begins (1-2/50)

	13.00	40.00	90.00
86,92,95,101-105	5.70	17.00	40.00

87-91,93,94,96-99,110,111-Severin/Elder a(2-3) each

	6.50	19.00	45.00
100	8.00	24.00	55.00
106-108,112	4.00	12.00	28.00
109-Severin/Williamson-a	6.50	19.00	45.00
113-Williamson/Severin-a(2)/Frazetta?	7.00	21.00	50.00

114-119: Drifter series in all; by Mort Meskin #114-118

	3.00	9.00	21.00

	Good	Fine	N-Mint

PUNISHER (See Amazing Spider-Man #129, Captain America #241, Daredevil #182-184, 257, Ghost Rider V2#5, 6, Marc Spector #8 & 9, Marvel Tales, Power Pack #46, Spectacular Spider-Man #81-83, 140, 141, 143 & new Strange Tales #13 & 14)
Jan, 1986-No. 5, May, 1986 (Mini-series)
Marvel Comics Group

	Good	Fine	N-Mint
1-Double size	6.70	20.00	47.00
2	3.60	11.00	25.00
3-Has 2 cover prices, 75 & 95(w/UPC) cents	2.50	7.50	15.00
4,5	2.00	6.00	12.00

PUNISHER
July, 1987-Present
Marvel Comics Group

	Good	Fine	N-Mint
V2#1	4.30	13.00	30.00
2	2.50	7.50	15.00
3-5	1.50	4.50	9.00
6-8	1.35	4.00	8.00
9	1.85	5.50	11.00
10-Daredevil app. (tie-in to Daredevil #257)	3.85	11.50	27.00
11-15: 13-18-Kingpin app.	1.15	3.50	7.00
16-20	.85	2.50	5.00
21-24,26-30: 24-1st app. Shadowmasters	.50	1.50	3.00
25-Double size ($1.50)-Shadowmasters app.	.70	2.00	4.00
31-40	.35	1.00	2.00
41-49		.65	1.25
50 ($1.50, 52 pgs.)	.25	.75	1.50
Annual 1(8/88)-Evolutionary War app.	2.00	6.00	12.00
Annual 2('89, $2.00, 68 pgs.)-Atlantis Attacks x-over; Moon Knight app.			
	1.00	3.00	6.00
Annual 3(1990, $2.00, 68 pgs.)	.50	1.50	3.00
Annual 4(1991, $2.00, 68 pgs.)-Golden-c(p)	.35	1.00	2.00
...and Wolverine in African Saga nn (1989, 52 pgs.)-Reprints Punisher War Journal #6,7; Jim Lee-c/a	1.00	3.00	6.00
...Movie Special 1(6/90, $5.95, 68 pgs.)	1.00	3.00	6.00
...No Escape nn (1990, $4.95, 52 pgs.)-New-a	1.00	3.00	6.00
...The Prize nn (1990, $4.95, 68 pgs.)-New-a	.85	2.50	5.00
...Summer Special 1 ($2.95, 52 pgs.)	.50	1.50	3.00

PUNISHER ARMORY, THE
July, 1990 ($1.50); No. 2, June, 1991 ($1.75)
Marvel Comics

	Good	Fine	N-Mint
1-r/weapons pgs. from War Journal; Jim Lee-c	.40	1.25	2.50
2-Jim Lee-c	.30	.90	1.75

The Punisher War Journal #15, © Marvel Comics

PUNISHER WAR JOURNAL, THE
Nov, 1988-Present ($1.50, color)
Marvel Comics

1-Origin The Punisher; Matt Murdock cameo; Jim Lee-c/a 1-13,17-19			
	2.85	8.50	17.00
2-Daredevil x-over	1.85	5.50	11.00
3-5: 3-Daredevil x-over	1.50	4.50	9.00
6-Two part Wolverine story begins	3.15	9.50	19.00
7-Wolverine story ends	1.50	4.50	9.00

	Good	Fine	N-Mint
8-10	1.00	3.00	6.00
11-13,17-19: 14,15-Jim Lee-c only	.70	2.00	4.00
14-16,20-22: No Jim Lee-a. 13-15-Heath-i. 14,15-Spider-Man x-over			
	.35	1.00	2.00
23-36: 23-Begin $1.75-c	.30	.90	1.80

Q

QUASAR (See Avengers #302 & Marvel Team-Up #113)
Oct, 1989-Present ($1.00, color) (Direct sale #17 on)
Marvel Comics

	Good	Fine	N-Mint
1-Origin; formerly Marvel Boy	.25	.75	1.50
2-5: 3-Human Torch app.		.60	1.20
8-15,18-24: 11-Excalibur x-over. 14-McFarlane-c. 20-Fantastic Four app.			
		.60	2.00
6,7: 6-Venom app. (2 pgs.). 7-Cosmic Spidey app.	.35	1.00	2.00
16 ($1.50, 52 pgs.)	.25	.75	1.50
17-Flash parody (Buried Alien)	.35	1.00	2.00
25 ($1.50, 52 pgs.)	.25	.75	1.50

QUEEN OF THE WEST, DALE EVANS (TV)
No. 479, 7/53-No. 22, 1-3/59 (All photo-c; photo back c-4-8, 15)
Dell Publishing Co.

	Good	Fine	N-Mint
4-Color 479(#1, '53)	8.00	24.00	55.00
4-Color 528(#2, '54)	5.70	17.00	40.00
3(4-6/54)-Toth-a	6.50	19.00	45.00
4-Toth, Manning-a	6.50	19.00	45.00
5-10-Manning-a. 5-Marsh-a	4.30	13.00	30.00
11,19,21-No Manning 21-Tufts-a	3.50	10.50	24.00
12-18,20,22-Manning-a	4.00	12.00	28.00

QUESTION, THE (Also see Crisis on Infinite Earths)
Feb, 1987-No. 36, Mar, 1990 ($1.50-$1.75, color, mature readers)
DC Comics

	Good	Fine	N-Mint
1-Sienkiewicz painted-c	.50	1.50	3.00
2-5	.35	1.00	2.00
6-36: 8-Intro. The Mikado. 16-Begin $1.75-c	.25	.75	1.50
Annual 1(1988)-Sienkiewicz-c(i)	.40	1.25	2.50
Annual 2('89, $3.50, 68 pgs.)-Green Arrow app.	.60	1.75	3.50

R

RAGGEDY ANN AND ANDY (Also see New Funnies)
No. 5, 1942-No. 533, 2/54; 10-12/64-No. 4, 3/66
Dell Publishing Co.

	Good	Fine	N-Mint
4-Color 5(1942)	37.00	110.00	255.00
4-Color 23(1943)	27.00	80.00	185.00
4-Color 45(1943)	22.00	65.00	155.00
4-Color 72(1945)	18.00	54.00	125.00
1(6/46)-Billy & Bonnie Bee by Frank Thomas	18.00	54.00	125.00
2,3: 3-Egbert Elephant by Dan Noonan begins	9.30	28.00	65.00
4-Kelly-a, 16 pgs.	10.00	30.00	70.00
5-10: 7-Little Black Sambo, Black Mumbo & Black Jumbo only app; Christmas-c			
	7.00	21.00	50.00
11-21: 21-Alice In Wonderland cover/story	5.70	17.00	40.00
22-27,29-39(8/49), 4-Color 262(1/50)	4.00	12.00	28.00
28-Kelly-c	4.30	13.00	30.00
4-Color 306,354,380,452,533	3.00	9.00	21.00
1(10-12/64-Dell)	1.15	3.50	8.00
2,3(10-12/65), 4(3/66)	.75	2.25	5.00

RANGERS COMICS (...of Freedom #1-7)
10/41-No. 67, 10/52; No. 68, Fall, 1952; No. 69, Winter, 1952-53
Fiction House Magazines (Flying stories)

	Good	Fine	N-Mint
1-Intro. Ranger Girl & The Rangers of Freedom; ends #7, cover app. only-#5			
	100.00	250.00	600.00
2	40.00	120.00	280.00
3	34.00	100.00	235.00
4,5	29.00	85.00	200.00
6-10: 8-U.S. Rangers begin	24.00	71.00	165.00
11,12-Commando Rangers app.	22.00	65.00	150.00
13-Commando Ranger begins-not same as Commando Rangers			
	22.00	65.00	150.00
14-20	16.00	48.00	110.00
21-Intro/origin Firehair (begins)	21.00	62.00	145.00
22-30: 23-Kazanda begins, ends #28. 28-Tiger Man begins (origin). 30-Crusoe Island begins, ends #40	14.00	43.00	100.00
31-40: 33-Hypodermic panels	12.00	36.00	84.00
41-46	9.30	28.00	65.00

	Good	Fine	N-Mint
47-56-"Eisnerish" Dr. Drew by Grandenetti	10.00	30.00	70.00
57-60-Straight Dr. Drew by Grandenetti	8.00	24.00	55.00
61,62,64-66: 64-Suicide Smith begins	7.00	21.00	50.00
63-Used in **POP**, pgs. 85, 99	7.00	21.00	50.00
67-69: 67-Space Rangers begin, end #69	7.00	21.00	50.00

RAWHIDE KID
3/55-No. 16, 9/57; No. 17, 8/60-No. 151, 5/79
Atlas/Marvel Comics (CnPC No. 1-16/AMI No. 17-30)

	Good	Fine	N-Mint
1-Rawhide Kid, his horse Apache & sidekick Randy begin; Wyatt Earp app.			
	30.00	90.00	210.00
2	13.50	41.00	95.00
3-5	8.30	25.00	58.00
6-10: 7-Williamson-a, 4 pgs.	6.00	18.00	42.00
11-16: 16-Torres-a	4.50	14.00	32.00
17-Origin by Jack Kirby	7.50	22.50	53.00
18-22,24-30	3.30	10.00	23.00
23-Origin retold by Jack Kirby	6.00	18.00	42.00
31,32,36-44: 40-Two-Gun Kid x-over. 42-1st Larry Lieber issue			
	2.70	8.00	19.00
33-35-Davis-a. 35-Intro & death of The Raven	3.15	9.50	22.00
45-Origin retold	3.15	9.50	22.00
46-Toth-a	3.00	9.00	21.00
47-70: 50-Kid Colt x-over. 64-Kid Colt story. 66-Two-Gun Kid story. 67-Kid Colt			
story	1.35	4.10	9.50
71-86: 79-Williamson-a(r). 86-Origin-r; Williamson-a r-/Ringo Kid #13 (4 pgs.)			
	.75	2.25	5.30
87-99,101-151: 115-Last new story	.55	1.60	3.20
100-Origin retold & expanded	.70	2.10	4.20
Special 1(9/71)-All Kirby/Ayers reprints	.55	1.60	3.20

REAL SCREEN COMICS (#1 titled Real Screen Funnies)
Spring, 1945-No. 128, May-June, 1959 (#1-40: 52 pgs.)
National Periodical Publications

	Good	Fine	N-Mint
1-The Fox & the Crow, Flippity & Flop, Tito & His Burro begin			
	61.00	182.00	425.00
2	29.00	86.00	200.00
3-5	16.00	48.00	110.00
6-10 (2-3/47)	11.00	32.00	75.00

	Good	Fine	N-Mint
11-20 (10-11/48): 13-The Crow x-over in Flippity & Flop			
	8.50	25.50	60.00
21-30 (6-7/50)	6.50	19.00	45.00
31-50	4.00	12.00	28.00
51-99	2.85	8.50	20.00
100	4.00	12.00	28.00
101-128	2.15	6.50	15.00

REAL WESTERN HERO (Formerly Wow #1-69; becomes Western
Hero #76 on)
No. 70, Sept, 1948-No. 75, Feb, 1949 (All 52 pgs.)
Fawcett Publications

	Good	Fine	N-Mint
70(#1)-Tom Mix, Monte Hale, Hopalong Cassidy, Young Falcon begin			
	21.00	62.00	145.00
71-Gabby Hayes begins; Captain Tootsie by Beck			
	13.00	40.00	90.00
72-75: 72-Captain Tootsie by Beck. 75-Big Bow and Little Arrow app.			
	13.00	40.00	90.00

RED MASK (Formerly Tim Holt)
No. 42, 6-7/1954-No. 53, 5/56; No. 54, 9/57
Magazine Enterprises No. 42-53/Sussex No. 54 (M.E. on-c)

	Good	Fine	N-Mint
42-Ghost Rider by Ayers continues, ends #50; Black Phantom continues; 3-D			
effect c/stories begin	11.50	34.00	80.00
43-3-D effect-c/stories	9.30	28.00	65.00
44-50: 47-Last pre-code. 3-D effect stories only. 50-Last Ghost Rider			
	8.50	25.50	60.00
51-The Presto Kid begins by Ayers (1st app.); Presto Kid-c begins, ends #54; last			
3-D effect story	8.50	25.50	60.00
52-Origin The Presto Kid	8.50	25.50	60.00
53,54-Last Black Phantom	6.50	19.00	45.00

RED RAVEN COMICS (Human Torch #2 on)
August, 1940 (Also see Sub-Mariner #26, 2nd series)
Timely Comics

	Good	Fine	VF-NM
1-Origin Red Raven; Comet Pierce & Mercury by Kirby, The Human Top & The			
Eternal Brain; intro. Magar, the Mystic & only app.; Kirby-c			
	583.00	1460.00	3500.00

(Prices vary widely on this book)

Red Ryder Comics #30, © Dell Publishing

RED RYDER COMICS (Hi Spot #2)(Movies, radio) (Also see Crackajack Funnies)
9/40; No. 3, 8/41-No. 5, 12/41; No. 6, 4/42-No. 151, 4-6/57
Hawley Publ. No. 1-5/Dell Publishing Co.(K.K.) No. 6 on

	Good	Fine	N-Mint
1-Red Ryder, his horse Thunder, Little Beaver & his horse Papoose strip reprints begin by Fred Harman; 1st meeting of Red & Little Beaver; Harman line-drawn-c #1-85	89.00	265.00	620.00
3-(Scarce)-Alley Oop, King of the Royal Mtd., Capt. Easy, Freckles & His Friends, Myra North & Dan Dunn strip-r begin	54.00	163.00	380.00
4,5	30.00	90.00	210.00
6-1st Dell issue	30.00	90.00	210.00
7-10	24.00	71.00	165.00
11-20	17.00	51.00	120.00
21-32-Last Alley Oop, Dan Dunn, Capt. Easy, Freckles	11.00	32.00	75.00
33-40 (52 pgs.)	7.00	21.00	50.00

	Good	Fine	N-Mint
41 (52 pgs.)-Rocky Lane photo back-c; photo back-c begin, end #57			
	8.00	24.00	55.00
42-46 (52 pgs.): 46-Last Red Ryder strip-r	6.00	18.00	42.00
47-53 (52 pgs.): 47-New stories on Red Ryder begin			
	4.50	14.00	32.00
54-57 (36 pgs.)	3.70	11.00	26.00
58-73 (36 pgs.): 73-Last King of the Royal Mtd; strip-r by Jim Gary			
	3.50	10.50	24.00
74-85,93 (52 pgs.)-Harman line-drawn-c	3.70	11.00	26.00
86-92 (52 pgs.)-Harman painted-c	3.70	11.00	26.00
94-96 (36 pgs.)-Harman painted-c	2.65	8.00	18.00
97,98,107,108 (36 pgs.)-Harman line-drawn-c	2.65	8.00	18.00
99,101-106 (36 pgs.)-Jim Bannon Photo-c	2.65	8.00	18.00
100 (36 pgs.)-Bannon photo-c	3.00	9.00	21.00
109-118 (52 pgs.)-Harman line-drawn-c	2.00	6.00	14.00
119-129 (52 pgs.): 119-Painted-c begin, not by Harman, end #151			
	1.70	5.00	12.00
130-144 (#130 on have 36 pgs.)	1.50	4.50	10.00
145-148: 145-Title change to Red Ryder Ranch Magazine with photos			
	1.30	4.00	9.00
149-151: 149-Title changed to Red Ryder Ranch Comics			
	1.30	4.00	9.00
4-Color 916 (7/58)	1.70	5.00	12.00

RED SONJA (Also see Conan #23)
1/77-No. 15, 5/79; V1#1, 2/83-V2#2, 3/83; V3#1, 8/83-V3#4, 2/84; V3#5, 1/85-
   V3#13, 1986
Marvel Comics Group

1-Created by Robert E. Howard	.50	1.50	3.00
2-5	.35	1.00	2.00
6-15, V1#1,2		.50	1.00
V3#1-4 ($1.00, 52 pgs.)		.60	1.20
5-13 (65-75 cents)		.50	1.00

REX ALLEN COMICS (Movie star)
No. 316, Feb, 1951-No. 31, Dec-Feb, 1958-59 (All-photo-c)
Dell Publishing Co.

4-Color 316(#1)(52 pgs.)-Rex Allen & his horse Koko begin; Marsh-a			
	12.00	36.00	85.00

	Good	Fine	N-Mint
2 (9-11/51, 36 pgs.)	6.00	18.00	42.00
3-10	4.65	14.00	32.00
11-20	3.70	11.00	26.00
21-23,25-31	3.50	10.50	24.00
24-Toth-a	4.30	13.00	30.00

RICHIE RICH (. . . the Poor Little Rich Boy) (See Little Dot)
Nov, 1960-#218, Oct, 1982; #219, Oct, 1986-#254, Jan, 1991
Harvey Publications

	Good	Fine	N-Mint
1-(See Little Dot for 1st app.)	90.00	250.00	440.00
2	40.00	100.00	180.00
3-5	20.00	60.00	120.00
6-10: 8-Christmas-c	12.50	37.50	75.00
11-20	5.35	16.00	32.00
21-40	3.00	9.00	18.00
41-60	2.00	6.00	12.00
61-80: 65-1st app. Dollar the Dog	1.20	3.50	7.00
81-100	.70	2.00	4.00
101-111,117-120	.50	1.50	3.00
112-116: All 52 pg. Giants	.60	1.80	3.60
121-140	.40	1.25	2.50
141-160: 145-Infinity-c	.35	1.00	2.00
161-180	.25	.75	1.50
181-254		.50	1.00

RIFLEMAN, THE (TV)
No. 1009, 7-9/59-No. 12, 7-9/62; No. 13, 11/62-No. 20, 10/64
Dell Publ. Co./Gold Key No. 13 on

	Good	Fine	N-Mint
4-Color 1009 (#1)	10.00	30.00	70.00
2 (1-3/60)	7.00	21.00	50.00
3-Toth-a, 4 pgs.	8.50	25.50	60.00
4,5,7-10	5.70	17.00	40.00
6-Toth-a, 4pgs.	7.00	21.00	50.00
11-20	5.00	15.00	35.00

RINGO KID WESTERN, THE (1st Series) (Also see Wild Western)
Aug, 1954-No. 21, Sept, 1957
Atlas Comics (HPC)/Marvel Comics

	Good	Fine	N-Mint
1-Origin; The Ringo Kid begins	11.00	32.00	75.00
2-Black Rider app.; origin/1st app. Ringo's Horse Arab			
	5.70	17.00	40.00
3-5	3.60	11.00	25.00
6-8-Severin-a(3) each	4.30	13.00	30.00
9,11,12,14-21: 12-Orlando-a, 4pgs.	2.65	8.00	18.00
10,13-Williamson-a, 4 pgs.	4.50	14.00	32.00

RIN TIN TIN (TV) (...& Rusty #21 on)
Nov, 1952-No. 38, May-July, 1961; Nov, 1963 (All Photo-c)
Dell Publishing Co./Gold Key

4-Color 434 (#1)	6.00	18.00	42.00
4-Color 476,523	4.30	13.00	30.00
4(3-5/54)-10	3.50	10.50	24.00
11-20	2.65	8.00	18.00
21-38	2.30	7.00	16.00
...& Rusty 1 (11/63-Gold Key)	2.30	7.00	16.00

RIP HUNTER TIME MASTER (See Showcase #20, 21, 25, 26)
Mar-Apr, 1961-No. 29, Nov-Dec, 1965
National Periodical Publications

1	26.00	78.00	182.00
2	13.30	40.00	93.00
3-5: 5-Last 10 cent issue	8.00	24.00	56.00
6,7-Toth-a in each	7.00	21.00	49.00
8-15	5.15	15.50	36.00
16-20	4.00	12.00	28.00
21-29: 29-G. Kane-c	3.60	11.00	25.00

ROBIN (See Batman, Detective Comics #38, New Teen Titans, Star Spangled Comics #65 & Teen Titans)
Jan, 1991-No. 5, May, 1991 ($1.00, color, mini-series)
DC Comics

1-Free poster by N. Adams; Bolland-c on all	2.00	6.00	12.00
1-2nd printing (without poster)	.70	2.00	4.00
1-3rd printing	.35	1.00	2.00
2	.85	2.50	5.00
2-2nd printing		.50	1.00

	Good	Fine	N-Mint
3-5	.40	1.25	2.50

ROBOCOP
March, 1990-Present ($1.50, color)
Marvel Comics

	Good	Fine	N-Mint
1-Based on movie	1.70	5.00	10.00
2	.85	2.50	5.00
3-6	.40	1.25	2.50
7-22	.25	.75	1.50

ROBOTECH MASTERS (TV)
July, 1985-No. 23, Apr, 1988 ($1.50, color)
Comico

	Good	Fine	N-Mint
1	.60	1.75	3.50
2,3	.40	1.25	2.50
4-23 (#23, $1.75)	.35	1.00	2.00

ROBOTECH: THE MACROSS SAGA (TV)
No. 2, Feb, 1985-No. 36, Feb, 1989 ($1.50, color)
Comico

	Good	Fine	N-Mint
2	.70	2.00	4.00
3-5	.50	1.50	3.00
6,7	.40	1.25	2.50
8-25: 12,17-Ken Steacy painted-c	.35	1.00	2.00
26-36: 26-34-$1.75. 35,36-$1.95-c	.30	.90	1.75

ROBOTECH: THE NEW GENERATION (TV)
July, 1985-No. 25, July, 1988 ($1.50, color)
Comico

	Good	Fine	N-Mint
1	.50	1.50	3.00
2-25: 9,13-Ken Steacy painted-c. 22-25 ($1.75)	.35	1.00	2.00

ROCKY LANE WESTERN (Movie star, TV)
May, 1949-No. 87, Nov, 1959
Fawcett Publications/Charlton No. 56 on

1 (36 pgs.)-Rocky, his stallion Black Jack, & Slim Pickens begin; photo-c begin,

	Good	Fine	N-Mint
end #57; photo back-c	49.00	145.00	340.00
2 (36 pgs.)-Last photo back-c	18.00	54.00	125.00
3-5 (52 pgs.): 4-Captain Tootsie by Beck	14.00	43.00	100.00
6,10 (36 pgs.)	11.00	32.00	75.00
7-9 (52 pgs.)	12.00	36.00	85.00
11-13,15-17 (52 pgs.): 15-Black Jack's Hitching Post begins, ends #25			
	9.30	28.00	65.00
14,18 (36 pgs.)	8.00	24.00	55.00
19-21,23,24 (52 pgs.): 20-Last Slim Pickens. 21-Dee Dickens begins, ends #55,57,65-68			
	8.00	24.00	55.00
22,25-28,30 (36 pgs. begin)	7.00	21.00	50.00
29-Classic complete novel "The Land of Missing Men,"-hidden land of ancient temple ruins (r-in #65)			
	8.50	25.50	60.00
31-40	6.50	19.00	45.00
41-54	5.30	16.00	38.00
55-Last Fawcett issue (1/54)	5.70	17.00	40.00
56-1st Charlton issue (2/54)-Photo-c	7.00	21.00	50.00
57,60-Photo-c	5.00	15.00	35.00
58,59,61-64: 59-61-Young Falcon app. 64-Slim Pickens app.			
	3.70	11.00	26.00
65-R-/#29, "The Land of Missing Men"	4.00	12.00	28.00
66-68: Reprints #30,31,32	3.00	9.00	21.00
69-78,80-86	3.00	9.00	21.00
79-Giant Edition, 68 pgs.	4.00	12.00	28.00
87-Last issue	3.70	11.00	26.00

ROD CAMERON WESTERN (Movie star)
Feb, 1950-No. 20, April, 1953
Fawcett Publications

1-Rod Cameron, his horse War Paint, & Sam The Sheriff begin; photo front/back-c begin	35.00	105.00	245.00
2	17.00	51.00	120.00
3-Novel length story "The Mystery of the Seven Cities of Cibola"			
	14.00	43.00	100.00
4-10: 9-Last photo back-c	11.50	34.00	80.00
11-19	10.00	30.00	70.00
20-Last issue & photo-c	11.00	32.00	75.00

ROMANTIC STORY
11/49-#22, Sum, 1953; #23, 5/54-#27, 12/54; #28, 8/55-#130, 11/73
Fawcett/Charlton Comics No. 23 on

	Good	Fine	N-Mint
1-Photo-c begin, end #22,24	7.00	21.00	50.00
2	3.15	9.50	22.00
3-5	2.65	8.00	18.00
6-14	2.30	7.00	16.00
15-Evans-a	3.50	10.50	24.00
16-22(Sum, '53; last Fawcett issue). 21-Toth-a?	1.70	5.00	12.00
23-39: 26,29-Wood swipes	1.70	5.00	12.00
40-(100 pgs.)	3.50	10.50	24.00
41-50	1.15	3.50	8.00
51-80: 57-Hypo needle story	.70	2.00	4.00
81-100	.35	1.00	2.00
101-130		.50	1.00

RONIN
July, 1983-No. 6, Apr, 1984 ($2.50, mini-series, 52 pgs.)
DC Comics

	Good	Fine	N-Mint
1-Miller script, c/a in all	1.00	3.00	6.00
2	.85	2.50	5.00
3-5	.70	2.00	4.00
6-Scarcer	1.35	4.00	8.00

ROY ROGERS COMICS (...& Trigger #92(8/55)-on) (Roy starred in Republic
movies, radio & TV) (Singing cowboy) (Also see Dale Evans)
Jan, 1948-No. 145, Sept-Oct, 1961 (#1-19: 36 pgs.)
Dell Publishing Co.

	Good	Fine	N-Mint
1-Roy, his horse Trigger, & Chuck Wagon Charley's Tales begin; photo-c begin, end #145	47.00	140.00	325.00
2	22.00	65.00	150.00
3-5	17.00	51.00	120.00
6-10	12.00	36.00	85.00
11-19: 19- ...Charley's Tales ends	8.50	25.50	60.00
20 (52 pgs.)-Trigger feature begins, ends #46	8.50	25.50	60.00
21-30 (52 pgs.)	7.00	21.00	50.00
31-46 (52 pgs.): 37-X-mas-c	5.30	16.00	38.00
47-56 (36 pgs.): 47-Chuck Wagon Charley's Tales returns, ends #133 49-X-mas-c. 55-Last photo back-c	4.30	13.00	30.00
57 (52 pgs.)-Heroin drug propaganda story	5.00	15.00	35.00
58-70 (52 pgs.): 61-X-mas-c	3.70	11.00	26.00
71-80 (52 pgs.): 73-X-mas-c	3.15	9.50	22.00

Roy Rogers Comics #3, © Roy Rogers

	Good	Fine	N-Mint
81-91 (36 pgs. #81-on): 85-X-mas-c	2.65	8.00	18.00
92-99,101-110,112-118: 92-Title changed to Roy Rogers and Trigger (8/55)			
	2.65	8.00	18.00
100-Trigger feature returns, ends #133?	4.00	12.00	28.00
111,119-124-Toth-a	4.35	13.00	30.00
125-131	3.00	9.00	21.00
132-144-Manning-a. 144-Dale Evans featured	3.50	10.50	24.00
145-Last issue	4.30	13.00	30.00

RULAH JUNGLE GODDESS (Formerly Zoot; also see All Top Comics)
No. 17, Aug, 1948-No. 27, June, 1949
Fox Features Syndicate

	Good	Fine	N-Mint
17	35.00	105.00	245.00
18-Classic girl-fight interior splash	29.00	86.00	200.00
19,20	27.00	80.00	185.00
21-Used in **SOTI**, pg. 388,389	29.00	86.00	200.00
22-Used in **SOTI**, pg. 22,23	27.00	80.00	185.00
23-27	19.00	57.00	130.00

S

SAD SACK COMICS
Sept, 1949-No. 287, Oct, 1982
Harvey Publications

	Good	Fine	N-Mint
1-Infinity-c; Little Dot begins (1st app.); civilian issues begin, end #21	22.00	65.00	150.00
2-Flying Fool by Powell	10.00	30.00	70.00
3	5.70	17.00	40.00
4-10	3.50	10.50	24.00
11-21	2.35	7.00	16.00
22-("Back In The Army Again" on covers #22-36). "The Specialist" story about Sad Sack's return to Army	1.35	4.00	8.00
23-50	.85	2.50	5.00
51-100	.50	1.50	3.00
101-150	.25	.75	1.50
151-222		.40	.80
223-228 (25 cent Giants, 52 pgs.)	.25	.75	1.50
229-287: 286,287 had limited distribution		.40	.80
3-D 1 (1/54-titled "Harvey 3-D Hits")	11.50	34.00	80.00

SAGA OF RA'S AL GHUL, THE (See Batman #232)
Jan, 1988-No. 4, Apr, 1988 ($2.50, color, mini-series)
DC Comics

	Good	Fine	N-Mint
1-Batman reprints; Neal Adams-a(r) in all	.75	2.25	4.50
2-4: 4-New N. Adams/Nebres-c	.65	1.90	3.75

SAGA OF SWAMP THING, THE (Swamp Thing #39-41,46 on)
May, 1982-Present (Later issues for mature readers; #86 on: $1.50)
DC Comics

	Good	Fine	N-Mint
1-Origin retold; Phantom Stranger series begins; ends #13; movie adaptation; Yeates-c/a begins	.25	.75	1.50
2-15: 2-Photo-c from movie		.50	1.00
16-19: Bissette-a. 13-Last Yeates-a	.35	1.00	2.00
20-1st Alan Moore issue	3.15	9.50	22.00
21-New origin	2.85	8.50	20.00
22-25: 24-JLA x-over; Last Yeates-c	1.30	4.00	8.00

	Good	Fine	N-Mint
26-30	.90	2.75	5.50
31-33: 33-Reprints 1st app./H.O.M. #92	.50	1.50	3.00
34	1.50	4.50	9.00
35,36	.35	1.10	2.25
37-1st app. John Constantine, apps. thru #40	1.25	3.75	7.50
38-40: John Constantine app.	.70	2.00	4.00
41-45: 44-Batman cameo	.30	.90	1.75
46-51: 46-Crisis x-over; Batman cameo & John Constantine app. 50- ($1.25, 52			
pgs.)-Deadman, Dr. Fate, Demon	.25	.75	1.50
52-Arkham Asylum-c/story; Joker-c/cameo	.50	1.50	3.00
53-($1.25, 52 pgs.)-Arkham Asylum; Batman-c/story			
	.70	2.00	4.00
54-64: 58-Spectre preview. 64-Last Moore issue	.60	1.25	
65-99,101-114: 65-Direct only begins. 79-Superman-c/story. 85-Jonah Hex app.			
102-Preview of World Without End	.30	.90	1.80
100 ($2.50, 52 pgs.)	.40	1.25	2.50
Annual 1(11/82)-Movie Adaptation		.50	1.00
Annual 2(1/85)-Alan Moore scripts, Bissette-a(p)	.50	1.50	3.00
Annual 3(10/87, $2.00)	.35	1.00	2.00
Annual 4(10/88)-Batman-c/story	.50	1.50	3.00
Annual 5('89, $2.95, 68 pgs.)-Batman cameo; re-intro Brother Power, 1st app.			
since 1968	.50	1.50	3.00
Annual 6('91, $2.95, 68 pgs.)	.50	1.50	3.00

SAGA OF THE ORIGINAL HUMAN TORCH
Apr, 1990-No. 4, July, 1990 ($1.50, color, limited-series)
Marvel Comics

1-Origin; Buckler-c/a(p) in all	.40	1.25	2.50
2-4: 3-Hitler-c	.25	.75	1.50

SAINT, THE (Also see Silver Streak Comics #18)
Aug, 1947-No. 12, Mar, 1952
Avon Periodicals

1-Kamen bondage-c/a	31.00	92.00	215.00
2	17.00	51.00	115.00
3,4: 4-Lingerie panels	13.00	40.00	90.00
5-Spanking panel	20.00	60.00	140.00
6-Miss Fury app., 14 pgs.	22.00	65.00	155.00
7-c-/Avon paperback #118	12.00	36.00	85.00

	Good	Fine	N-Mint
8,9(12/50): Saint strip-r in #8-12; 9-Kinstler-c	10.00	30.00	70.00
10-Wood-a, 1 pg; c-/Avon paperback #289	10.00	30.00	70.00
11	7.00	21.00	50.00
12-c-/Avon paperback #123	9.30	28.00	65.00

SAMSON (Also see Fantastic Comics)
Fall, 1940-No. 6, Sept, 1941
Fox Features Syndicate

	Good	Fine	N-Mint
1-Powell-a, signed 'Rensie;' Wing Turner by Tuska app; Fine-c?	65.00	195.00	455.00
2-Dr. Fung by Powell; Fine-c?	32.00	95.00	220.00
3-Navy Jones app.; Simon-c	25.00	75.00	175.00
4-Yarko the Great, Master Magician by Eisner begins; Fine-c?	22.00	65.00	150.00
5,6: 6-Origin The Topper	20.00	60.00	140.00

SANDMAN, THE (See Adventure Comics #40 & World's Finest #3)
Winter, 1974; No. 2, Apr-May, 1975-No. 6, Dec-Jan, 1975-76
National Periodical Publications

	Good	Fine	N-Mint
1-Kirby-a; Joe Simon scripts	.85	2.50	5.00
2-6: 6-Kirby/Wood-c/a	.60	1.75	3.50

SANDMAN
Jan, 1989-Present ($1.50, color, mature readers)
DC Comics

	Good	Fine	N-Mint
1 ($2.00, 52 pgs.)	3.70	11.00	22.00
2	2.50	7.50	15.00
3-5: 3-John Constantine app.	1.85	5.50	11.00
6-8: 8-Regular ed. has Jeanette Kahn publishorial & American Cancer Society ad w/no indicia on inside front-c	1.35	4.00	8.00
8-Limited ed. (600+ copies?); has Karen Berger editorial and next issue teaser (has indicia)	13.00	40.00	80.00
9-13	.85	2.50	5.00
14-($2.50, 52 pgs.)	1.00	3.00	6.00
15-20: 16-Photo-c	.40	1.25	2.50
21-32: 22-World w/out End preview. 24-Russell-i	.25	.75	1.50

SCOOBY DOO (TV) (...Where are you? #1-16,26)
March, 1970-No. 30, Feb, 1975 (Hanna-Barbera)
Gold Key

	Good	Fine	N-Mint
1	2.85	8.50	20.00
2-5	1.50	4.50	10.00
6-10	1.00	3.00	7.00
11-20: 11-Tufts-a	.70	2.00	5.00
21-30	.50	1.50	3.00

SCOOBY DOO (TV)
April, 1975-No. 11, Dec, 1976 (Hanna Barbera)
Charlton Comics

1	1.15	3.50	8.00
2-5	.70	2.00	4.00
6-11	.50	1.50	3.00

SCRIBBLY (See All-American Comics, The Funnies, & Popular)
8-9/48-No. 13, 8-9/50; No. 14, 10-11/51-No. 15, 12-1/51-52
National Periodical Publications

1-Sheldon Mayer-a in all; 52pgs. begin	55.00	165.00	385.00
2	35.00	105.00	245.00
3-5	29.00	86.00	200.00
6-10	20.00	60.00	140.00
11-15: 13-Last 52 pgs.	16.00	48.00	110.00

SEA DEVILS (See Showcase #27-29)
Sept-Oct, 1961-No. 35, May-June, 1967
National Periodical Publications

1	28.00	84.00	194.00
2-Last 10 cent issue	11.50	34.00	80.00
3-5: 3-Begin 12 cent issues thru #35	6.70	20.00	46.00
6-10	4.00	12.00	28.00
11,12,14-20	3.00	9.00	21.00
13-Kubert, Colan-a	3.30	10.00	23.00

Sea Devils #19, © DC Comics

	Good	Fine	N-Mint

21-35: 22-Intro. International Sea Devils; origin & 1st app. Capt. X & Man Fish

	2.00	6.00	14.00

SECRET ORIGINS (See 80 Page Giant #8)
Aug-Oct, 1961 (Annual) (Reprints)
National Periodical Publications

1('61)-Origin Adam Strange (Showcase #17), Green Lantern (G.L. #1),
   Challengers (partial/Showcase #6, 6 pgs. Kirby-a). J'onn J'onzz (Det. #225),
   The Flash (Showcase #4). Green Arrow (1pg. text). Superman-Batman team
   (W. Finest #94). Wonder Woman (Wonder Woman #105)

	20.00	60.00	140.00

SECRET ORIGINS
Feb-Mar, 1973-No. 6, Jan-Feb, 1974; No. 7, Oct-Nov, 1974
National Periodical Publications (All origin reprints)

1-Superman (Action #1, 1st time since G.A.), Batman (Batman #33), Ghost (Flash

	Good	Fine	N-Mint
#88), The Flash(Showcase #4)	1.00	3.00	7.00

2-4: 2-Green Lantern (Showcase #22), The Atom (Showcase #34), & Supergirl (Action #252). 3-Wonder Woman (W.W. #1), Wildcat (Sensation #1). 4-Vigilante (Action #42) by Meskin, Kid Eternity (Hit #25)

	.50	1.50	3.00

5-7: 5-The Spectre (More Fun?). 6-Blackhawk (Military #1) & Legion of Super-Heroes(Adv?). 7-Robin (Detective #38), Aquaman (More Fun #73?)

	.40	1.25	2.50

SECRET ORIGINS
4/86-No. 50, 8/90 (All origins)(52 pgs. #6 on)(#27 on: $1.50)
DC Comics

	Good	Fine	N-Mint
1-Origin Superman	.60	1.75	3.50
2-Blue Beetle	.50	1.50	3.00
3-5: 3-Shazam. 4-Firestorm. 5-Crimson Avenger/Shadow/Doll Man			
	.40	1.25	2.50
6-G.A. Batman	.70	2.00	4.00
7-10: 7-Green Lantern (Guy Gardner)	.40	1.15	2.25
11,12,14-26: 20-Batgirl/G.A. Dr. Mid-Nite	.35	1.00	2.00
13-Origin Nightwing; Johnny Thunder app.	.70	2.00	4.00
27-38,40-44: 38-Green Arrow/Speedy	.30	.90	1.80
39-Animal Man-c/story; Batman app.	.70	2.00	4.00
45-49: 46-JLA/LSH/New Titans. 47-LSH	.25	.75	1.50
50-($3.95, 100 pgs.)-Batman & Robin in text	.70	2.00	4.00
Annual 1 (8/87)-Capt. Comet/Doom Patrol	.35	1.00	2.00
Annual 2 ('88, $2.00)-Origin Flash II & Flash III	.35	1.00	2.00
Annual 3 ('89, $2.95, 84 pgs.)-Teen Titans; 1st app. new Flamebird who replaces original Bat-Girl	.50	1.50	3.00
Special 1 (10/89, $2.00)-Batman villains: Penguin, Riddler, & Two-Face; Bolland-c			
	.40	1.25	2.50

SENSATION COMICS
Jan, 1942-No. 109, May-June, 1952
National Periodical Publ./All-American

	Good	Fine	VF-NM
1-Origin Mr. Terrific, Wildcat, The Gay Ghost, & Little Boy Blue; Wonder Woman(cont'd from All Star #8), The Black Pirate begin; intro. Justice & Fair Play Club	417.00	1040.00	2500.00
	Good	Fine	N-Mint
2	150.00	450.00	1050.00

	Good	Fine	N-Mint
3-W. Woman gets secretary's job	87.00	260.00	610.00
4-1st app. Stretch Skinner in Wildcat	79.00	235.00	550.00
5-Intro. Justin, Black Pirate's son	59.00	175.00	410.00
6-Origin/1st app. Wonder Woman's magic lasso	52.00	155.00	360.00
7-10	48.00	145.00	335.00
11-20: 13-Hitler, Tojo, Mussolini-c	41.00	122.00	285.00
21-30	30.00	90.00	210.00
31-33	23.00	70.00	160.00
34-Sargon, the Sorcerer begins, ends #36; begins again #52			
	23.00	70.00	160.00
35-40: 38-Xmas-c	19.00	57.00	135.00
41-50: 43-The Whip app.	16.00	48.00	110.00
51-60: 51-Last Black Pirate. 56,57-Sargon by Kubert			
	14.00	43.00	100.00
61-80: 63-Last Mr. Terrific. 65,66-Wildcat by Kubert. 68-Origin Huntress			
	14.00	43.00	100.00
81-Used in SOTI, pg. 33,34; Krigstein-a	16.00	48.00	110.00
82-90: 83-Last Sargon. 86-The Atom app. 90-Last Wildcat			
	11.50	34.00	80.00
91-Streak begins by Alex Toth	11.50	34.00	80.00
92,93: 92-Toth-a, 2 pgs.	11.00	32.00	75.00
94-1st all girl issue	13.00	40.00	90.00
95-99,101-106: Wonder Woman ends. 99-1st app. Astra, Girl of the Future, ends 106. 105-Last 52 pgs.	13.00	40.00	90.00
100	18.00	54.00	125.00
107-(Scarce)-1st mystery issue; Toth-a	24.00	70.00	165.00
108-(Scarce)-Johnny Peril by Toth(p)	21.00	62.00	145.00
109-(Scarce)-Johnny Peril by Toth(p)	24.00	70.00	165.00

SERGEANT BILKO (Phil Silvers) (TV)
May-June, 1957-No. 18, Mar-Apr, 1960
National Periodical Publications

1	22.00	65.00	150.00
2	14.00	43.00	100.00
3-5	12.00	36.00	85.00
6-18: 11,12,15,17-Photo-c	10.00	30.00	70.00

SGT. BILKO'S PVT. DOBERMAN (TV)
June-July, 1958-No. 11, Feb-Mar, 1960
National Periodical Publications

	Good	Fine	N-Mint
1	16.00	48.00	110.00
2	10.00	30.00	70.00
3-5: 5-Photo-c	8.00	24.00	55.00
6-11: 6,9-Photo-c	5.70	17.00	40.00

SGT. FURY (& His Howling Commandos) (See Special Marvel Ed.)
May, 1963-No. 167, Dec, 1981
Marvel Comics Group (BPC earlier issues)

	Good	Fine	N-Mint
1-1st app. Sgt. Nick Fury; Kirby/Ayers-c/a	37.00	111.00	255.00
2-Kirby-a	13.50	41.00	94.00
3-5: 3-Reed Richards x-over. 4-Death of Junior Juniper. 5-1st Baron Strucker app.; Kirby-a	9.00	27.00	64.00
6-10: 8-Baron Zemo, 1st Percival Pinkerton app. 10-1st app. Capt. Savage (the Skipper)	6.85	20.50	48.00
11,12,14-20: 14-1st Blitz Squad. 18-Death of Pamela Hawley	3.50	10.50	24.00
13-Captain America & Bucky app.(12/64); 1st Capt. America x-over outside The Avengers; Kirby-a	11.00	32.00	75.00
21-30: 25-Red Skull app. 27-1st app. Eric Koenig; origin Fury's eye patch	1.85	5.50	13.00
31-50: 34-Origin Howling Commandos	1.50	4.50	10.00
51-100: 64-Capt. Savage & Raiders x-over. 98-Deadly Dozen x-over. 100-Captain America, Fantastic Four cameos	.85	2.60	6.00
101-167: 101-Origin retold. 167-reprints #1	.60	1.75	3.50
Annual 1('65, 25 cents, 72 pgs.)-r/#4,5 & new-a	5.00	15.00	35.00
Special 2('66)	1.50	4.50	10.00
Special 3('67)	1.15	3.50	8.00
Special 4('68)	1.00	3.00	7.00
Special 5-7('69-11/71)	.70	2.00	5.00

SERGEANT PRESTON OF THE YUKON (TV)
No. 344, Aug, 1951-No. 29, Nov-Jan, 1958-59
Dell Publishing Co.

	Good	Fine	N-Mint
4-Color 344(#1)-Sergeant Preston & his dog Yukon King begin; painted-c begin, end #18	6.50	19.00	45.00
4-Color 373,397,419('52)	4.00	12.00	28.00
5(11-1/52-53)-10(2-4/54)	3.00	9.00	21.00
11,12,14-17	2.30	7.00	16.00
13-Origin Sgt. Preston	3.00	9.00	21.00

	Good	Fine	N-Mint
18-Origin Yukon King; last painted-c	3.00	9.00	21.00
19-29: All photo-c	3.50	10.50	24.00

SGT. ROCK (Formerly Our Army at War; see Brave & the Bold #52)
No. 302, March, 1977-No. 422, July, 1988
National Periodical Publications/DC Comics

302	.85	2.60	6.00
303-320: 318-Reprints	.70	2.00	4.00
321-350	.50	1.50	3.00
351-422: 422-1st Joe, Adam, Andy Kubert-a team	.25	.75	1.50
Annual 2-4: 2(9/82), 3(8/83), 4(8/84)	.40	1.25	2.50

SHADOW, THE
Aug, 1964-No. 8, Sept, 1965 (All 12 cents)
Archie Comics (Radio Comics)

1	2.85	8.50	20.00
2-8-The Fly app. in some issues	1.70	5.00	12.00

SHADOW, THE
Oct-Nov, 1973-No. 12, Aug-Sept, 1975
National Periodical Publications

1-Kaluta-a begins	2.15	6.50	15.00
2	1.30	4.00	9.00
3-Kaluta/Wrightson-a	1.50	4.50	10.00
4,6-Kaluta-a ends	1.15	3.50	8.00
5,7-12: 11-The Avenger (pulp character) x-over	.70	2.00	4.00

SHADOW, THE
May, 1986-No. 4, Aug, 1986 (Mini-series, mature readers)
DC Comics

1-Chaykin-a in all	1.15	3.50	7.00
2-4	.75	2.25	4.50

SHADOW, THE
Aug, 1987-No. 19, Jan, 1989 ($1.50, mature readers)
DC Comics

	Good	Fine	N-Mint
1	.50	1.50	3.00
2-19: 13-Death of Shadow. 18-E.C.-c swipe	.35	1.00	2.00
Annual 1,2: 1(12/87, $2.25). 2(12/88, $2.50)	.40	1.25	2.50

SHADOW COMICS (Pulp, radio)
March, 1940-V9#5, Aug, 1949
Street & Smith Publications

	Good	Fine	N-Mint
V1#1-Shadow, Doc Savage, Bill Barnes, Nick Carter, Frank Merriwell, Iron Munro, the Astonishing Man begin	200.00	500.00	1200.00
2-The Avenger begins, ends #6; Capt. Fury only app.	72.00	215.00	500.00
3(nn-5/40)-Norgil the Magician app.	57.00	171.00	400.00
4,5: 4-The Three Musketeers begins, ends #8. 5-Doc Savage ends	50.00	150.00	350.00
6,8,9: 9-Norgil the Magician app.	40.00	120.00	280.00
7-Origin & 1st app. Hooded Wasp & Wasplet; series ends V3#8	45.00	135.00	315.00
10-Origin The Iron Ghost, ends #11; The Dead End Kids begins, ends #14	40.00	120.00	280.00
11-Origin The Hooded Wasp & Wasplet retold	40.00	120.00	280.00
12-Dead End Kids app.	34.00	103.00	240.00
V2#1,2(11/41): 2-Dead End Kids story	30.00	90.00	210.00
3-Origin & 1st app. Supersnipe; series begins; Little Nemo story	40.00	120.00	280.00
4, 5-Little Nemo story	29.00	85.00	200.00
6-9:-Blackstone the Magician app.	26.00	77.00	180.00
10-12: 10-Supersnipe app.	26.00	77.00	180.00
V3#1-12: 10-Doc Savage begins, not in V5#5, V6#10-12, V8#4	23.00	70.00	160.00
V4#1-12	21.00	62.00	145.00
V5#1-12	19.00	58.00	135.00
V6#1-11: 9-Intro. Shadow, Jr.	18.00	54.00	125.00
12-Powell-c/a; atom bomb panels	19.00	58.00	135.00
V7#1,2,5,7-9,12: 2,5-Shadow, Jr. app.; Powell-a	19.00	58.00	135.00
3,6,11-Powell-c/a	21.00	62.00	145.00
4-Powell-c/a; Atom bomb panels	23.00	70.00	160.00
10(1/48)-Flying Saucer issue; Powell-c/a (2nd of this theme; see The Spirit 9/28/47)	27.00	80.00	185.00
V8#1-12-Powell-a. 8-Powell Spider-c/a	21.00	62.00	145.00

	Good	Fine	N-Mint
V9#1,5-Powell-a	19.00	58.00	135.00
2-4-Powell-c/a	21.00	62.00	145.00

SHADOW OF THE BATMAN
Dec, 1985-No. 5, Apr, 1986 ($1.75 cover; mini-series)
DC Comics

1-Detective-r (all have wraparound-c)	1.70	5.00	10.00
2,3,5	1.15	3.50	7.00
4-Joker-c/story	1.50	4.50	9.00

SHEENA, QUEEN OF THE JUNGLE (See Jumbo Comics & 3-D....)
Spring, 1942; No. 2, Wint, 1942-43; No. 3, Spring, 1943; No. 4, Fall, 1948; No. 5,
   Sum, 1949; No. 6, Spring, 1950; No. 7-10, 1950(nd); No. 11, Spring, 1951-
   No. 18, Winter, 1952-53 (#1,2: 68 pgs.)
Fiction House Magazines

1-Sheena begins	118.00	355.00	825.00
2 (Winter, 1942/43)	61.00	182.00	425.00
3 (Spring, 1943)	40.00	120.00	280.00
4, 5 (Fall, 1948-Sum., `49)	25.00	75.00	175.00
6,7 (Spring, `50-`50, 52 pgs.)	22.00	65.00	150.00
8-10('50, 36 pgs.)	19.00	57.00	130.00
11-18: 18-Used in **POP**, pg. 98	16.00	48.00	110.00

SHIELD (Nick Fury & His Agents of . . .) (Also see Nick Fury)
Feb, 1973-No. 5, Oct, 1973 (All 20 cents)
Marvel Comics Group

1-Steranko-c	.70	2.00	4.00
2-Steranko flag-c	.35	1.00	2.00
3-5: 1-5 all contain-r from Strange Tales #146-155. 3-5-are cover-r; 3-Kirby/Steranko-c(r). 4-Steranko-c(r)	.35	1.00	2.00

SHIELD WIZARD COMICS (Also see Pep & Top-Notch Comics)
Summer, 1940-No. 13, Spring, 1944
MLJ Magazines

1-(V1#5 on inside)-Origin The Shield by Irving Novick & The Wizard by Ed Ashe, Jr; Flag-c	136.00	407.00	950.00

	Good	Fine	N-Mint
2-Origin The Shield retold; intro. Wizard's sidekick, Roy			
	62.00	185.00	435.00
3,4	42.00	125.00	290.00
5-Dusty, the Boy Detective begins	37.00	110.00	255.00
6-8: 6-Roy the Super Boy begins	32.00	95.00	225.00
9-13: 13-Bondage-c	27.00	81.00	190.00

SHOCK SUSPENSTORIES
Feb-Mar, 1952-No. 18, Dec-Jan, 1954-55
E. C. Comics

	Good	Fine	N-Mint
1-Classic Feldstein electrocution-c; Ray Bradbury adaptation			
	50.00	150.00	350.00
2	30.00	90.00	210.00
3	21.00	62.00	145.00
4-Used in SOTI, pg. 387,388	21.00	62.00	145.00
5-Hanging-c	19.00	58.00	135.00
6,7:6-Classic bondage-c. 7-Classic face melting-c			
	24.00	73.00	170.00
8-Williamson-a	21.00	62.00	145.00
9-11: 9-Injury to eye panel. 10-Junkie story	17.00	51.00	115.00
12-"The Monkey"-classic junkie cover/story; drug propaganda issue			
	20.00	60.00	140.00
13-Frazetta's only solo story for E.C., 7 pgs.	24.00	73.00	170.00
14-Used in Senate Investigation hearings	13.00	40.00	90.00
15-Used in 1954 Reader's Digest article, "For the Kiddies to Read"			
	13.00	40.00	90.00
16-"Red Dupe" editorial; rape story	12.00	36.00	85.00
17,18	12.00	36.00	85.00

SHOWCASE
3-4/56-No. 93, 9/70; No. 94, 8-9/77-No. 104, 9/78
National Periodical Publications/DC Comics

	Good	Fine	N-Mint
1-Fire Fighters	86.00	260.00	600.00
2-King of the Wild; Kubert-a (animal stories)	32.00	96.00	220.00
3-The Frogmen	28.00	84.00	195.00
	Good	Fine	VF-NM
4-Origin/1st app. The Flash (1st DC Silver Age hero, Sept-Oct, 1956) & The Turtle; Kubert-a; reprinted in Secret Origins #1 ('61 & '73)			
	472.00	1888.00	4775.00

	Good	Fine	N-Mint
5-Manhunters	40.00	120.00	275.00

6-Origin/1st app. Challengers of the Unknown by Kirby, partly r-/in Secret Origins #1 & Challengers #64,65 (1st DC Silver Age super- hero team)

	Good	Fine	N-Mint
	111.00	333.00	775.00

7-Challengers of the Unknown by Kirby r-in/Challengers of the Unknown #75

	Good	Fine	VF-NM
	60.00	180.00	415.00
8-The Flash; intro/origin Capt. Cold	222.00	666.00	1550.00

9,10-Lois Lane. 9-(Pre-#1, 7-8/57). 10-Jor-el cameo

	Good	Fine	N-Mint
	78.00	234.00	550.00
11,12-Challengers of the Unknown by Kirby	44.00	132.00	305.00
13-The Flash; origin Mr. Element	128.00	384.00	895.00

14-The Flash; origin Dr. Alchemy, former Mr. Element

	Good	Fine	N-Mint
	128.00	384.00	895.00
15-Space Ranger (1st app., 7-8/58)	45.00	135.00	315.00
16-Space Ranger	33.00	99.00	231.00

17-Adventures on Other Worlds; origin/1st app. Adam Strange (11-12/58)

	Good	Fine	N-Mint
	83.00	250.00	580.00
18-Adventures on Other Worlds(A. Strange)	38.00	114.00	265.00
19-Adam Strange	38.00	114.00	265.00

20-Origin & 1st app. Rip Hunter (5-6/59); Moriera-a

	Good	Fine	N-Mint
	35.00	105.00	242.00
21-Rip Hunter; Sekowsky-c/a	16.70	50.00	116.00

22-Origin & 1st app. Silver Age Green Lantern by Gil Kane (9-10/59); reprinted in Secret Origins #2

	Good	Fine	N-Mint
	165.00	495.00	1155.00
23,24-Green Lantern. 23-Nuclear explosion-c	63.00	190.00	440.00
25,26-Rip Hunter by Kubert	12.00	36.00	84.00
27-1st app. Sea Devils (7-8/60); Heath-c/a	32.00	96.00	220.00
28,29-Sea Devils; Heath-c/a	19.00	57.00	130.00
30-Origin Silver Age Aquaman	30.00	90.00	210.00
31-33-Aquaman	11.50	34.00	80.00

34-Origin & 1st app. Silver Age Atom by Kane & Anderson (9-10/61); reprinted in Secret Origins #2

	Good	Fine	N-Mint
	75.00	225.00	525.00
35-The Atom by Gil Kane; last 10 cent issue	24.00	72.00	168.00
36-The Atom by Gil Kane (1-2/61-62)	16.70	50.00	116.00
37-1st app. Metal Men (3-4/62)	32.00	96.00	220.00
38-40-Metal Men	12.70	38.00	89.00
41,42-Tommy Tomorrow (parts 1&2). 42-Origin	4.50	14.00	32.00

43-Dr. No (James Bond); Nodel-a; (1st DC Silver Age movie adaptation) (based on Ian Fleming novel, movie)

	Good	Fine	N-Mint
	27.00	81.00	185.00

	Good	Fine	N-Mint
44-Tommy Tomorrow	3.00	9.00	21.00
45-Sgt. Rock; origin retold; Heath-c	9.00	27.00	63.00
46,47-Tommy Tomorrow	1.70	5.00	12.00
48,49-Cave Carson	1.70	5.00	12.00
50,51-I Spy (Danger Trail-r by Infantino), King Farady story (#50 is not a reprint)			
	1.70	5.00	12.00
52-Cave Carson	1.70	5.00	12.00
53,54-G.I. Joe; Heath-a	1.70	5.00	12.00
55-Dr. Fate & Hourman. (3-4/65)-G.A. Green Lantern app. (early Silver Age app.)			
(pre-dates Gr. Lantern #40)	4.70	14.00	33.00
56-Dr. Fate & Hourman	1.70	5.00	12.00
57,58-Enemy Ace by Kubert	3.30	10.00	23.00
59-Teen Titans (3rd app., 11-12/65)	6.00	18.00	42.00
60-1st Silver Age app. The Spectre; Anderson-a (1-2/66); origin in text			
	9.00	27.00	63.00
61,64-The Spectre by Anderson	3.70	11.00	26.00
62-Origin & 1st app. Inferior Five (5-6/66)	3.70	11.00	26.00
63,65-Inferior Five	1.70	5.00	12.00
66,67-B'wana Beast	.75	2.25	5.30
68,69,71-Maniaks	.75	2.25	5.30
70-Binky	.75	2.25	5.30
72-Top Gun (Johnny Thunder-r)-Toth-a	.75	2.25	5.30
73-Origin/1st app. Creeper; Ditko-c/a (3-4/67)	4.30	13.00	30.00
74-Intro/1st app. Anthro; Post-c/a (5-6/67)	2.70	8.00	19.00
75-Origin/1st app. Hawk & the Dove; Ditko-c/a	4.50	14.00	32.00
76-1st app. Bat Lash (9-10/67)	1.40	4.20	9.50
77-1st app. Angel & The Ape	2.15	6.50	15.00
78-Jonny Double	.70	2.10	4.20
79-Dolphin; Aqualad origin-r	.90	1.80	6.30
80-Phantom Stranger-r; Neal Adams-c	.90	1.80	6.30
81-Windy & Willy	.70	2.10	4.20
82-1st app. Nightmaster by Grandenetti & Giordano; Kubert-c			
	3.30	10.00	23.00
83,84-Nightmaster by Wrightson w/Jones/Kaluta ink assist in each; Kubert-c. 84-			
Origin retold	3.30	10.00	23.00
85-87-Firehair; Kubert-a	.90	1.80	6.30
88-90-Jason's Quest: 90-Manhunter 2070 app.	.55	1.60	3.20
91-93-Manhunter 2070; origin-92	.55	1.60	3.20
94-Intro/origin new Doom Patrol & Robotman	.70	2.10	4.20
95,96-The Doom Patrol. 95-Origin Celsius	.35	1.05	2.10
97-99-Power Girl; origin-97,98; JSA cameos	.35	1.05	2.10

	Good	Fine	N-Mint
100-(52 pgs.)-Most Showcase characters feat.	.35	1.05	2.10
101-103-Hawkman; Adam Strange x-over	.35	1.05	2.10
104-(52 pgs.)-O.S.S. Spies at War	.35	1.05	2.10

SILVER STREAK COMICS (Crime Does Not Pay #22 on)
Dec, 1939-No. 21, May, 1942; No. 22-24, 1946 (Silver logo-#1-5)
Your Guide Publs. No. 1-7/New Friday Publs. No. 8-17/Comic House Publ./
  Newsbook Publ.

	Good	Fine	VF-NM
1-(Scarce)-Intro The Claw by Cole (r-/in Daredevil #21), Red Reeves, Boy Magician, & Captain Fearless; The Wasp, Mister Midnight begin; Spirit Man app. Silver metallic-c begin, end #5	400.00	1000.00	2400.00

	Good	Fine	N-Mint
2-The Claw by Cole; Simon c/a	157.00	470.00	1100.00
3-1st app. & origin Silver Streak (2nd with lightning speed); Dickie Dean the Boy Inventor, Lance Hale, Ace Powers, Bill Wayne, & The Planet Patrol begin	135.00	405.00	945.00
4-Sky Wolf begins; Silver Streak by Jack Cole (new costume); 1st app. Jackie, Lance Hale's sidekick	71.00	215.00	500.00
5-Jack Cole c/a(2)	82.00	245.00	575.00

	Good	Fine	VF-NM
6-(Scarce)-Origin & 1st app. Daredevil (blue & yellow costume) by Jack Binder; The Claw returns; classic Cole Claw-c	285.00	857.00	2000.00
7-Claw vs. Daredevil (new costume-blue & red) by Jack Cole & 3 other Cole stories (38 pgs.)	193.00	580.00	1350.00

	Good	Fine	N-Mint
8-Claw vs. Daredevil by Cole; last Cole Silver Streak	110.00	330.00	775.00
9-Claw vs. Daredevil by Cole	82.00	245.00	575.00
10-Origin Captain Battle; Claw vs. Daredevil by Cole	75.00	225.00	525.00
11-Intro. Mercury by Bob Wood, Silver Streak's sidekick; conclusion Claw vs. Daredevil by Rico; in 'Presto Martin,' 2nd pg., newspaper says 'Roussos does it again'	52.00	154.00	360.00
12-14: 13-Origin Thun-Dohr	43.00	130.00	300.00
15-17-Last Daredevil issue	40.00	120.00	280.00
18-The Saint begins; by Leslie Charteris	34.00	100.00	235.00
19-21(1942): 20,21-Wolverton's Scoop Scuttle	22.00	64.00	150.00

	Good	Fine	N-Mint
22,24(1946)-Reprints	13.00	40.00	90.00
23-Reprints?; bondage-c	13.00	40.00	90.00

The Silver Surfer #5 (1st series), © Marvel Comics

SILVER SURFER, THE (See Fantastic Four & Fantasy Masterpieces)
Aug, 1968-No. 18, Sept, 1970; June, 1982 (No. 1-7: 68 pgs.)
Marvel Comics Group

		Good	Fine	N-Mint
1-Origin by John Buscema (p); Watcher begins (origin), ends #7		26.00	78.00	180.00
2		8.50	25.50	60.00
3-1st app. Mephisto		7.00	21.00	50.00
4-Low distribution; Thor app.		26.00	78.00	180.00
5-7-Last giant size. 5-The Stranger app. 6-Brunner inks. 7-Brunner-c				
		5.30	16.00	38.00
8-10,14: 14-Spider-Man x-over		4.00	12.00	28.00
11-13,15-18: 18-Kirby-c/a		2.65	8.00	18.00
V2#1 (6/82, 52 pgs.)-Byrne-c/a		1.15	3.50	7.00

SILVER SURFER, THE
July, 1987-Present
Marvel Comics Group

	Good	Fine	N-Mint
1-Double size ($1.25)	.75	2.25	4.50
2	.50	1.50	3.00
3-10	.35	1.00	2.00
11-20	.25	.75	1.50
21-24,26-30,32,33,36,37,39-49,51-54: 35-Thanos app. 36-Capt. Marvel, Warlock app. 46,47-Warlock app.		.50	1.00
25,31 ($1.50, 52 pgs.): 25-Skrulls app.	.30	.90	1.80
34-Thanos returns; Starlin scripts begin	1.35	4.00	8.00
35,38-Thanos app.	.70	2.00	4.00
50-($1.50, 52 pgs.)-Silver Surfer battles Thanos	1.00	3.00	6.00
50-Gold 2nd printing	.25	.75	1.50
Annual 1 (8/88, $1.75)-Evolutionary War app.	.40	1.25	2.50
Annual 2 ('89, $2.00, 68 pgs.)-Atlantis Attacks	.35	1.00	2.00
Annual 3 ('90, $2.00, 68 pgs.)	.35	1.00	2.00
Annual 4 ('91, $2.00, 68 pgs.)-3 pg. origin; Silver Surfer battles Guardians of the Galaxy	.35	1.00	2.00

SILVER SURFER, THE
Dec, 1988-No. 2, Jan, 1989 ($1.00, limited series)
Epic Comics (Marvel)

1,2: By Stan Lee & Moebius	.35	1.00	2.00

SLAM BANG COMICS
March, 1940-No. 7, Sept, 1940 (Combined with Master Comics #7)
Fawcett Publications

1-Diamond Jack, Mark Swift & The Time Retarder, Lee Granger, Jungle King begin	65.00	195.00	455.00
2	30.00	90.00	210.00
3-Classic-c	40.00	120.00	280.00
4-7: 7-Bondage-c	25.00	75.00	175.00

SMASH COMICS (Lady Luck #86 on)
Aug, 1939-No. 85, Oct, 1949
Quality Comics Group

	Good	Fine	N-Mint
1-Origin Hugh Hazard & His Iron Man, Bozo the Robot, Espionage, Starring Black X by Eisner, & Invisible Justice; Chic Carter & Wings Wendall begin	79.00	235.00	550.00
2-The Lone Star Rider app; Invisible Hood gains power of invisibility	36.00	107.00	250.00
3-Captain Cook & John Law begin	24.00	73.00	170.00
4,5: 4-Flash Fulton begins	22.00	65.00	155.00
6-12: 12-One pg. Fine-a	18.00	54.00	125.00
13-Magno begins; last Eisner issue; The Ray app. in full page ad; The Purple Trio begins	18.00	54.00	125.00
14-Intro. The Ray by Lou Fine & others	110.00	330.00	770.00
15,16	55.00	165.00	385.00
17-Wun Cloo becomes plastic super-hero by Jack Cole (9-months before Plastic Man)	55.00	165.00	385.00
18-Midnight by Jack Cole begins (origin)	65.00	195.00	455.00
19-22: Last Fine Ray; The Jester begins-#22	38.00	115.00	265.00
23,24: 24-The Sword app.; last Chic Carter; Wings Wendall dons new costume #24,25	32.00	95.00	225.00
25-Origin Wildfire	38.00	115.00	265.00
26-30: 28-Midnight-c begin	29.00	85.00	200.00
31,32,34: Ray by Rudy Palais; also #33	22.00	65.00	150.00
33-Origin The Marksman	27.00	80.00	185.00
35-37	22.00	65.00	150.00
38-The Yankee Eagle begins; last Midnight by Jack Cole	22.00	65.00	150.00
39,40-Last Ray issue	17.00	51.00	120.00
41,43-50	8.00	24.00	55.00
42-Lady Luck begins by Klaus Nordling	9.50	28.50	65.00
51-60	6.50	19.00	45.00
61-70	5.30	16.00	38.00
71-85	5.00	15.00	35.00

SMILIN' JACK (See Popular Comics & Super Comics)
No. 5, 1940-No. 8, Oct-Dec, 1949
Dell Publishing Co.

	Good	Fine	N-Mint
4-Color 5	45.00	135.00	315.00
4-Color 10 (1940)	43.00	130.00	300.00
Large Feature Comic 12,14,25 (1941)	30.00	90.00	210.00
4-Color 4 (1942)	34.00	103.00	240.00
4-Color 14 (1943)	27.00	81.00	190.00

	Good	Fine	N-Mint
4-Color 36,58 (1943-44)	16.00	48.00	110.00
4-Color 80 (1945)	12.00	36.00	85.00
4-Color 149 (1947)	8.50	25.50	60.00
1 (1-3/48)	8.50	25.50	60.00
2	4.65	14.00	32.00
3-8 (10-12/49)	3.50	10.50	24.00

SMITTY (See Popular Comics & Super Comics)
No. 11, 1940-No. 7, Aug-Oct, 1949; Apr, 1958
Dell Publishing Co.

	Good	Fine	N-Mint
4-Color 11 (1940)	26.00	77.00	180.00
Large Feature Comic 26 (1941)	17.00	51.00	120.00
4-Color 6 (1942)	14.00	43.00	100.00
4-Color 32 (1943)	11.50	34.00	80.00
4-Color 65 (1945)	9.30	28.00	65.00
4-Color 99 (1946)	8.00	24.00	55.00
4-Color 138 (1947)	6.50	19.50	45.00
1 (11-1/47-48)	6.50	19.50	45.00
2	3.50	10.50	24.00
3 (8-10/48), 4 (1949)	2.30	7.00	16.00
5-7, 4-Color 909 (4/58)	1.70	5.00	12.00

SOLO AVENGERS (Becomes Avengers Spotlight #21 on)
Dec, 1987-No. 20, July, 1989 (75 cents-$1.00)
Marvel Comics

	Good	Fine	N-Mint
1	.35	1.10	2.20
2-5	.25	.70	1.40
6-20: 11-Intro Bobcat		.50	1.00

SPACE ADVENTURES
7/52-No. 21, 8/56; No. 23, 5/58-No. 59, 11/64; V3#60, 10/67; V1#2, 7/68-V1#8,
7/69; No. 9, 5/78-No. 13, 3/79
Capitol Stories/Charlton Comics

	Good	Fine	N-Mint
1	17.00	51.00	120.00
2	8.50	25.50	60.00
3-5	6.50	19.00	45.00
6-9: 7-Sex change story	5.70	17.00	40.00
10,11-Ditko-c/a; 11-Two Ditko stories	19.00	57.00	130.00

	Good	Fine	N-Mint
12-Ditko-c (classic)	22.00	65.00	150.00
13-(Fox-r, 10-11/54); Blue Beetle story	6.50	19.00	45.00
14-Blue Beetle story (Fox-r, 12-1/54-55)	5.30	16.00	38.00
15,17,18-Rocky Jones app.(TV); 15-Part photo-c	6.50	19.00	45.00
16-Krigstein-a; Rockey Jones app.	10.00	30.00	70.00
19	4.50	14.00	32.00
20-Reprints Fawcett's "Destination Moon"	12.00	36.00	85.00
21-(8/56) (no #22)	5.70	17.00	40.00
23-(5/58)-Reprints Faw. "Destination Moon"	10.00	30.00	70.00
24,25,31,32-Ditko-a	7.00	21.00	50.00
26,27-Ditko-a(4) each	9.00	27.00	62.00
28-30	2.65	8.00	18.00
33-Origin/1st app. Captain Atom by Ditko (3/60)	20.00	60.00	140.00
34-40,42-All Captain Atom by Ditko	8.00	24.00	55.00
41,43-59: 44,45-Mercury Man in each	1.00	3.00	7.00
V3#60(#1, 10/67)-Origin Paul Mann & The Saucers From the Future			
	1.15	3.50	8.00
2-8('68-'69)-2,5,6,8-Ditko-a; 2,4-Aparo-c/a	.70	2.00	4.00
9-13('78-'79)-Capt. Atom-r/Space Adventures by Ditko; 9-Reprints origin/1st app. from #33		.50	1.00

SPACE DETECTIVE
July, 1951-No. 4, July, 1952
Avon Periodicals

	Good	Fine	N-Mint
1-Rod Hathway, Space Det. begins, ends #4; Wood-c/a(3)-23 pgs.; "Opium Smugglers of Venus" drug story; Lucky Dale-r/Saint #4			
	65.00	195.00	455.00
2-Tales from the Shadow Squad story; Wood/Orlando-c; Wood inside layouts			
	32.00	95.00	225.00
3-Kinstler-c	20.00	60.00	140.00
4-Kinstler-a	20.00	60.00	140.00

SPACE FAMILY ROBINSON (TV) (...Lost in Space #15-36)
Dec, 1962-No. 36, Oct, 1969 (All painted covers)
Gold Key

	Good	Fine	N-Mint
1-(low distr.); Spiegle-a in all	11.00	32.00	75.00
2(3/63)-Family becomes lost in space	5.30	16.00	38.00
3-10: 6-Captain Venture begins	2.85	8.50	20.00

	Good	Fine	N-Mint
11-20	2.00	6.00	14.00
21-36	1.30	4.00	9.00

SPACE GHOST (TV)
March, 1967 (Hanna-Barbera) (TV debut was 9/10/66)
Gold Key

1 (10199-703)-Spiegle-a	15.00	45.00	105.00

SPACE GHOST (TV) (Graphic Novel)
Dec, 1987 (One Shot) (52 pgs.; deluxe format; $3.50) (Hanna-Barbera)
Comico

1-Steve Rude-c/a(p)	.85	2.50	5.00

SPACEMAN (Speed Carter...)
Sept, 1953-No. 6, July, 1954
Atlas Comics (CnPC)

1	26.00	77.00	180.00
2	17.00	51.00	120.00
3-6: 4-A-Bomb-c	14.00	43.00	100.00

SPACE MAN
No. 1253, 1-3/62-No. 8, 3-5/64; No. 9, 7/72-No. 10, 10/72
Dell Publishing Co.

4-Color 1253 (#1)(1-3/62)	4.00	12.00	28.00
2,3	2.00	6.00	14.00
4-8	1.30	4.00	9.00
9-Reprints #1253	.50	1.50	3.00
10-Reprints #2	.40	1.25	2.50

SPARKLER COMICS (Cover title is Nancy and Sluggo #101? on)
July, 1941-No. 120, Jan, 1955
United Features Syndicate

1-Origin Sparkman; Tarzan (by Hogarth in all issues), Captain & the Kids, Ella
Cinders, Danny Dingle, Dynamite Dunn, Nancy, Abbie & Slats, Frankie
Doodle, Broncho Bill begin; Sparkman c-#1-12

	79.00	235.00	550.00

	Good	Fine	N-Mint
2	35.00	105.00	245.00
3,4	30.00	90.00	210.00
5-10: 9-Sparkman's new costume	25.00	75.00	175.00
11-13,15-20: 12-Sparkman new costume-color change. 19-1st Race Riley			
	21.00	62.00	145.00
14-Tarzan-c by Hogarth	24.00	71.00	165.00
21-24,26,27,29,30: 22-Race Riley & the Commandos strips begin, ends #44			
	16.00	48.00	110.00
25,28,31,34,37,39-Tarzan-c by Hogarth	20.00	60.00	140.00
32,33,35,36,38,40	9.30	28.00	65.00
41,43,45,46,48,49	6.50	19.00	45.00
42,44,47,50-Tarzan-c	12.00	36.00	85.00
51,52,54-70: 57-Li'l Abner begins (not in #58); Fearless Fosdick app.-#58			
	4.50	14.00	32.00
53-Tarzan-c by Hogarth	11.00	32.00	75.00
71-80	3.70	11.00	26.00
81,82,84-90: 85-Li'l Abner ends	2.85	8.50	20.00
83-Tarzan-c	5.00	15.00	35.00
91-96,98-99	2.65	8.00	18.00
97-Origin Casey Ruggles by Warren Tufts	5.70	17.00	40.00
100	3.60	11.00	25.00
101-107,109-112,114-120	2.00	6.00	14.00
108,113-Toth-a	5.70	17.00	40.00

SPECIAL EDITION COMICS
1940 (August) (One Shot, 68 pgs.)
Fawcett Publications

	Good	Fine	VF-NM
1-1st book devoted entirely to Captain Marvel; C.C. Beck-c/a; only app. of Capt. Marvel with belt buckle; Capt. Marvel appears with button-down flap, 1st story (came out before Captain Marvel #1)	300.00	900.00	2100.00

SPECIAL EDITION X-MEN
Feb, 1983 (One Shot) (Baxter paper, $2.00)
Marvel Comics Group

	Good	Fine	N-Mint
1-R/Giant-Size X-Men #1 plus one new story	1.35	4.00	8.00

SPECIAL MARVEL EDITION (Master of Kung Fu #17 on)
Jan, 1971-No. 16, Feb, 1974
Marvel Comics Group

	Good	Fine	N-Mint
1-Thor-r by Kirby; 68 pgs.	.55	1.65	3.30
2-4: Thor-r by Kirby; 68 pg. Giant	.45	1.40	2.80
5-14: Sgt. Fury-r; 11-Reprints Sgt. Fury #13 (Captain America app.)			
	.35	1.10	2.20
15-Master of Kung Fu begins (1st app.); Starlin-a; origin & 1st app. Nayland Smith			
& Dr. Petric	2.65	8.00	18.00
16-1st app. Midnight; Starlin-a	1.70	5.00	12.00

SPECIAL MISSIONS (See G.I. Joe...)

SPECTACULAR SPIDER-MAN, THE (Peter Parker . . . #54-132,134)
Dec, 1976-Present
Marvel Comics Group

1-Origin retold; Tarantula app.	5.30	16.00	38.00
2-Kraven the Hunter app.	2.15	6.50	15.00
3-5: 4-Vulture app.	1.60	4.80	11.00
6-10: 6-8-Morbius app. 9,10-White Tiger app.	1.10	3.30	6.60
11-20: 17,18-Champions x-over	.90	2.75	5.50
21,24-26: 21-Scorpion app. 26-Daredevil app..	75	2.20	4.40
22,23-Moon Knight app.	1.10	3.30	6.60
27-Miller's 1st art on Daredevil (7/79); also see Captain America #235			
	2.30	7.00	16.00
28-Miller Daredevil (p)	1.85	5.50	13.00
29-57,59: 33-Origin Iguana. 38-Morbius app.	.60	1.80	3.60
58-Byrne-a(p)	.80	2.40	4.80
60-Double size; origin retold with new facts revealed			
	.60	1.80	3.60
61-63,65-68,71-74: 65-Kraven the Hunter app.	.50	1.50	3.00
64-1st app. Cloak & Dagger (3/82)	2.05	6.15	14.40
69,70-Cloak & Dagger app.	1.40	4.20	8.40
75-Double size	.60	1.80	3.60
76-80: 79-Punisher cameo	.40	1.20	2.40
81,82-Punisher, Cloak & Dagger app.	1.70	5.00	12.00
83-Origin Punisher retold	2.16	6.50	15.00
84,86-99: 90-Spider-man's new black costume, last panel(ties w/Amaz. Spider-			

	Good	Fine	N-Mint
Man #252). 94-96-Cloak & dagger app. 98-Intro The Spot			
	.35	1.00	2.00
85-1st told origin Hobgoblin; gains powers of original Green Goblin (see Amazing			
Spider-Man #238)	2.65	8.00	18.00
100-Double size	.70	2.00	4.00
101-115,117,118,121-129: 107-Death of Jean DeWolff. 111-Secret Wars II tie-in.			
128-Black Cat new costume	.40	1.25	2.50
116,119-Sabretooth app.	.50	1.50	3.00
130-Hobgoblin app.	.60	1.75	3.50
131-Six part Kraven tie-in	1.00	3.00	6.00
132-Kraven tie-in	.85	2.50	5.00
133-139: 139-Origin Tombstone	.35	1.00	2.00
140-Punisher cameo app.	.50	1.50	3.00
141-Punisher app.	1.10	3.25	6.50
142,143-Punisher app.	.75	2.25	4.50
144-157: 147-Hobgoblin app. 151-Tombstone returns			
	.35	1.00	2.00
158-Spider-Man gets new powers (1st Cosmic Spidey, continued in Web of Spider-			
Man #59)	1.00	3.00	6.00
159-Cosmic Spider-Man app.	.50	1.50	3.00
160-182: 161-163-Hobgoblin app. 168-170-Avengers x-over. 169-1st app. The			
Outlaws	.50	1.00	1.00
Annuals 1-7: 1(1979). 2(1980)-Origin/1st app. Rapier. 3(1981)-Last Manwolf.			
4(1984). 5(1985). 6(1985). 7(1987)	.50	1.50	3.00
Annual 8 ('88, $1.75)-Evolutionary War x-over	.70	2.00	4.00
Annual 9 ('89, $2.00, 68 pgs.)-Atlantis Attacks	.50	1.50	3.00
Annual 10 ('90, $2.00, 68 pgs.)-McFarlane-a	.40	1.25	2.50
Annual 11 ('91, $2.00, 68 pgs.)	.35	1.00	2.00

SPECTRE, THE (See Adventure Comics #431, More Fun & Showcase)
Nov-Dec, 1967-No. 10, May-June, 1969 (All 12 cents)
National Periodical Publications

	Good	Fine	N-Mint
1-Anderson-c/a	4.70	14.00	33.00
2-5-Neal Adams-c/a; 3-Wildcat x-over	3.00	9.00	21.00
6-8,10: 6-8-Anderson inks. 7-Hourman app.	1.35	4.10	9.50
9-Wrightson-a	1.50	4.50	10.50

SPECTRE, THE (See Saga of Swamp Thing #58)
Apr, 1987-No. 31, Oct, 1989 ($1.00, new format)
DC Comics

	Good	Fine	N-Mint
1-Colan-a(p) begins	.40	1.25	2.50
2-10: 9-Nudity panels. 10-Batman cameo.	.25	.75	1.50
11-31: 10,11-Millennium tie-ins		.60	1.25
Annual 1 (1988, $2.00)-Deadman app.	.35	1.00	2.00

Speed Comics #2, © Harvey Publications

SPEED COMICS
10/39-No. 11, 8/40; No. 12, 3/41-No. 44, 1-2/47
Brookwood Publ./Speed Publ./Harvey Publications No. 14 on

1-Origin Shock Gibson; Ted Parrish, the Man with 1000 Faces begins; Powell-a			
	86.00	257.00	600.00
2-Powell-a	43.00	130.00	300.00
3	26.00	77.00	180.00
4-Powell-a?	22.00	65.00	155.00
5	21.00	62.00	145.00
6-11: 7-Mars Mason begins, ends #11	18.00	54.00	125.00
12 (3/41; shows #11 in indicia)-The Wasp begins; Major Colt app. (Capt. Colt #12)			
	22.00	65.00	155.00

	Good	Fine	N-Mint
13-Intro. Captain Freedom & Young Defenders; Girl Commandos, Pat Parker, War Nurse begins; Major Colt app.	27.00	80.00	185.00
14-16 (100 pg. pocket size, 1941): 14-2nd Harvey comic. 15-Pat Parker dons costume, last in costume #23; no Girl Commandos	20.00	60.00	140.00
17-Black Cat begins (origin); not in #40,41	35.00	105.00	245.00
18-20	18.00	54.00	125.00
21,22,25-30: 26-Flag-c	16.00	48.00	110.00
23-Origin Girl Commandos	23.00	70.00	160.00
24-Pat Parker team-up with Girl Commandos	16.00	48.00	110.00
31-44: 38-Flag-c	13.00	40.00	90.00

SPIDER-MAN (See Amazing..., Marvel Tales, Marvel Team-Up, Spectacular..., & Web Of...)
Aug, 1990-Present ($1.75, color)
Marvel Comics

	Good	Fine	N-Mint
1-Silver edition, direct sale only (unbagged)	1.70	4.00	8.00
1-Silver bagged edition; direct sale, no price on comic, but $2.00 on plastic bag (still sealed) (125,000 print run)	3.35	10.00	20.00
1-Regular edition w/Spidey face in UPC area (unbagged); green-c	.85	2.50	5.00
1-Regular bagged edition w/Spidey face in UPC area (price is for still sealed only); green cover (125,000)	2.50	7.50	15.00
1-Newsstand bagged w/UPC code (sealed)	1.15	3.50	7.00
1-Gold edition, 2nd printing (unbagged) with Spider-Man in box (400,000-450,000)	1.15	3.50	7.00
1-Gold 2nd printing w/UPC code (2,000-5,000)	3.35	10.00	20.00
1-Platinum ed. mailed to retailers only (10,000 print run); has new McFarlane-a & editorial material instead of ads; stiff-c, no cover price	50.00	150.00	350.00
2-McFarlane-c/a/scripts continue	.85	2.50	5.00
3	.60	1.75	3.50
4,6,7: 6,7-Ghost Rider & Hobgoblin app.	.70	2.00	4.00
5,8: 8-Wolverine cameo	.50	1.50	3.00
9-12: 8-12-Five part Wolverine storyline	.35	1.00	2.00
13-16	.30	.90	1.80

SPIDER-MAN VS. WOLVERINE
Feb, 1987 (One-shot); V2#1, 1990 (Both have 68 pgs.)
Marvel Comics Group

	Good	Fine	N-Mint
1-Williamson-c(i); intro Charlemagne; death of Ned Leeds (old Hobgoblin)			
	3.00	9.00	18.00
V2#1 (1990, $4.95)-Reprints #1 (2/87)	.85	2.50	5.00

SPIRIT, THE (1st Series) (Also see Police Comics #11)
1944-No. 22, Aug, 1950
Quality Comics Group (Vital)

	Good	Fine	N-Mint
nn(#1)-"Wanted Dead or Alive"	43.00	130.00	300.00
nn(#2)-"Crime Doesn't Pay"	27.00	81.00	190.00
nn(#3)-"Murder Runs Wild"	21.00	62.00	145.00
4,5	15.00	45.00	105.00
6-10	14.00	41.00	95.00
11	12.00	36.00	85.00
12-17-Eisner-c	22.00	65.00	150.00
18-21-Strip-r by Eisner; Eisner-c	30.00	90.00	210.00
22-Used by N.Y. Legis. Comm; Classic Eisner-c	46.00	137.00	320.00

SPIRIT, THE (2nd Series)
Spring, 1952-No. 5, 1954
Fiction House Magazines

	Good	Fine	N-Mint
1-Not Eisner	21.00	62.00	145.00
2-Eisner-c/a(2)	23.00	70.00	160.00
3-Eisner/Grandenetti-c	15.00	45.00	105.00
4-Eisner/Grandenetti-c; Eisner-a	19.00	57.00	130.00
5-Eisner-c/a(4)	24.00	71.00	165.00

SPY SMASHER (See Whiz Comics)
Fall, 1941-No. 11, Feb, 1943
Fawcett Publications

	Good	Fine	N-Mint
1-Spy Smasher begins; silver metallic-c	130.00	390.00	910.00
2-Raboy-c	65.00	195.00	455.00
3,4: 3-Bondage-c	55.00	165.00	385.00
5-7: Raboy-a; 6-Raboy-c/a. 7-Part photo-c	47.00	140.00	325.00
8-11: 9-Hitler, Tojo, Mussolini-c. 10-Hitler-c	40.00	120.00	280.00

STAR SPANGLED COMICS (...War Stories #131 on)
Oct, 1941-No. 130, July, 1952
National Periodical Publications

	Good	Fine	N-Mint
1-Origin Tarantula; Captain X of the R.A.F., Star Spangled Kid (see Action #40) & Armstrong of the Army begin	175.00	440.00	1050.00
2	80.00	200.00	480.00
3-5	43.00	130.00	300.00
6-Last Armstrong of the Army	30.00	90.00	210.00

	Good	Fine	VF-NM
7-Origin/1st app. The Guardian by S&K, & Robotman by Paul Cassidy; The Newsboy Legion & TNT begin; last Captain X	217.00	540.00	1300.00

	Good	Fine	N-Mint
8-Origin TNT & Dan the Dyna-Mite	93.00	280.00	650.00
9,10	79.00	235.00	550.00
11-17	65.00	195.00	455.00
18-Origin Star Spangled Kid	80.00	240.00	560.00
19-Last Tarantula	65.00	195.00	455.00
20-Liberty Belle begins	65.00	195.00	455.00
21-29-Last S&K issue; 23-Last TNT. 25-Robotman by Jimmy Thompson begins	50.00	150.00	350.00
30-40: 31-S&K-c	23.00	70.00	160.00
41-50	20.00	60.00	140.00
51-64: Last Newsboy Legion & The Guardian; last Liberty Belle? #53 by S&K	20.00	60.00	140.00
65-Robin begins with cover app. (2/47); Batman cameo in 1 panel; Robin-c begin, end #95	47.00	140.00	325.00
66-Batman cameo in Robin story	25.00	75.00	175.00
67,68,70-80	22.00	65.00	150.00
69-Origin/1st app. Tomahawk by F. Ray	30.00	90.00	210.00
81-Origin Merry, Girl of 1000 Gimmicks in Star Spangled Kid story	19.00	56.00	130.00
82,85: 82-Last Robotman?	19.00	56.00	130.00
83-Tomahawk enters the lost valley, a land of dinosaurs; Capt. Compass begins, ends #130	19.00	56.00	130.00
84,87 (Rare): 87-Batman cameo in Robin	22.00	65.00	155.00
86-Batman cameo in Robin story; last Star Spangled Kid	22.00	65.00	150.00

88(1/49)-94: Batman-c/stories in all. 91-Federal Men begin, end #93. 94-

	Good	Fine	N-Mint
Manhunters Around the World begin, end #121			
	24.00	70.00	165.00
95-Batman story; last Robin-c	19.00	56.00	130.00
96,98-Batman cameo in Robin stories. 96-1st Tomahawk-c			
	16.00	48.00	110.00
97,99	14.00	43.00	100.00
100	19.00	58.00	135.00
101-109,118,119,121: 121-Last Tomahawk-c	11.50	34.00	80.00
110,111,120-Batman cameo in Robin stories. 120-Last 52 pgs.			
	14.00	43.00	100.00
112-Batman & Robin story	16.00	48.00	110.00
113-Frazetta-a (10 pgs.)	26.50	80.00	185.00
114-Retells Robin's origin (3/51); Batman & Robin story			
	19.00	58.00	135.00
115,117-Batman app. in Robin stories	13.00	40.00	90.00
116-Flag-c	12.00	36.00	85.00
122-(11/51)-Ghost Breaker-c/stories begin (origin), ends #130			
	12.00	36.00	85.00
123-126,128,129	8.50	25.50	60.00
127-Batman cameo	10.00	30.00	70.00
130-Batman cameo in Robin story	12.00	36.00	85.00

STAR SPANGLED WAR STORIES (Star Spangled Comics #1-130)
No. 131, 8/52-No. 133, 10/52; No. 3, 11/52-No. 204, 2-3/77
National Periodical Publications

	Good	Fine	N-Mint
131(#1)	30.00	90.00	210.00
132	19.00	57.00	131.00
133-Used in **POP**, Pg. 94	19.00	57.00	131.00
3-5: 4-Devil Dog Dugan app.	13.50	41.00	95.00
6-Evans-a	11.50	34.00	80.00
7-10	9.00	27.00	63.00
11-20	7.50	22.50	53.00
21-30: Last precode (2/55)	6.00	18.00	42.00
31-33,35-40	4.50	14.00	32.00
34-Krigstein-a	6.00	18.00	42.00
41-50	3.70	11.00	26.00
51-83: 67-Easy Co. story without Sgt. Rock	2.85	8.50	20.00
84-Origin Mlle. Marie	5.70	17.00	40.00
85-89-Mlle. Marie in all	3.60	11.00	25.00
90-1st dinosaur issue (4-5/60)	16.00	48.00	110.00

	Good	Fine	N-Mint
91,93-No dinosaur story	2.85	8.50	20.00
92,94-100: All dinosaur issues, ends #135	5.70	17.00	40.00
101-133,135-137-Last dinosaur story; Heath Birdman-#129,131			
	4.30	13.00	30.00
134-Neal Adams-a	5.00	15.00	35.00
138-Enemy Ace begins by Joe Kubert	2.15	6.50	15.00
139-143,145: 145-Last 12 cent issue (6-7/69)	2.65	8.00	8.00
144-Neal Adams & Kubert-a	1.50	4.50	10.00
146-148,152,153,155	.85	2.60	6.00
149,150-Viking Prince by Kubert	1.00	3.00	7.00
151-1st Unknown Soldier (6-7/70)	1.50	4.50	10.00
154-Origin Unknown Soldier	1.15	3.50	8.00
156-1st Battle Album	.70	2.00	4.00
157-161-Last Enemy Ace	.50	1.50	3.00
162-204: 181-183-Enemy Ace vs. Balloon Buster serial app.			
		.50	1.00

STARTLING COMICS
June, 1940-No. 53, May, 1948
Better Publications (Nedor)

1-Origin Captain Future-Man Of Tomorrow, Mystico (By Eisner/Fine), The Wonder Man; The Masked Rider begins; drug use story			
	77.00	230.00	540.00
2	32.00	95.00	220.00
3	24.00	73.00	170.00
4	19.00	57.00	130.00
5-9	14.00	43.00	100.00
10-The Fighting Yank begins (origin/1st app.)	61.00	182.00	425.00
11-15: 12-Hitler, Hirohito, Mussolini-c	18.00	54.00	125.00
16-Origin The Four Comrades; not in #32,35	21.00	62.00	145.00
17-Last Masked Rider & Mystico	13.00	40.00	90.00
18-Pyroman begins (origin)	35.00	105.00	245.00
19	14.00	43.00	100.00
20-The Oracle begins; not in #26,28,33,34	14.00	43.00	100.00
21-Origin The Ape, Oracle's enemy	13.00	40.00	90.00
22-33	11.50	34.00	80.00
34-Origin The Scarab & only app.	13.00	40.00	90.00
35-Hypodermic syringe attacks Fighting Yank in drug story			
	13.00	40.00	90.00

36-43: 36-Last Four Comrades. 38-Bondage/torture-c. 40-Last Capt. Future &

	Good	Fine	N-Mint
Oracle. 41-Front Page Peggy begins; A-Bomb-c. 43-Last Pyroman			
	11.50	34.00	80.00
44-Lance Lewis, Space Detective begins; Ingels-c			
	20.00	60.00	140.00
45-Tygra begins (Intro/origin)	20.00	60.00	140.00
46-Ingels-c/a	20.00	60.00	140.00
47-53: 49-Last Fighting Yank. 50,51-Sea-Eagle app.			
	14.00	43.00	100.00

STAR TREK (TV)
7/67; No. 2, 6/68; No. 3, 12/68; No. 4, 6/69-No. 61, 3/79
Gold Key

1-Photo-c begin, end #9	32.00	96.00	225.00
2-5	16.00	48.00	110.00
6-9	11.50	34.00	80.00
10-20	6.50	19.00	45.00
21-30	4.30	13.00	30.00
31-40	2.65	8.00	18.00
41-61: 52-Drug propaganda story	1.70	5.00	12.00

STAR TREK
April, 1980-No. 18, Feb, 1982
Marvel Comics Group

1-r/Marvel Super Special; movie adapt.	.70	2.00	4.00
2-18: 5-Miller-c	.40	1.25	2.50

STAR TREK
Feb, 1984-No. 56, Nov, 1988 (Mando paper, 75 cents)
DC Comics

1-Sutton-a(p) begin	1.30	4.00	8.00
2-5	.85	2.50	5.00
6-10: 7-Origin Saavik	.70	2.00	4.00
11-20	.40	1.25	2.50
21-32	.35	1.00	2.00
33-($1.25, 52 pgs.)-20th anniversary issue	.50	1.50	3.00
34-49: 37-Painted-c. 49-Begin $1.00-c	.25	.75	1.50
50-($1.50, 52 pgs.)	.40	1.25	2.50
51-56		.50	1.00

	Good	Fine	N-Mint
Annual 1-3: 1(1985). 2(1986). 3(1988, $1.50)	.40	1.25	2.50

STAR TREK
Oct, 1989-Present ($1.50, color)
DC Comics

1-Capt. Kirk and crew	.60	1.75	3.50
2,3	.35	1.00	2.00
4-26: 10-12-The Trial of James T. Kirk	.25	.75	1.50
Annual 1 (1990, $2.95, 68 pgs.)-Morrow-a	.50	1.50	3.00
Annual 2 (1991, $2.95, 68 pgs.)	.50	1.50	3.00

STAR TREK: THE NEXT GENERATION (TV)
Feb, 1988-No. 6, July, 1988 (Mini series, based on TV show)
DC Comics

1 (52 pgs.)-Sienkiewicz painted-c	1.15	3.50	7.00
2-6 ($1.00)	.70	2.00	4.00

STAR TREK: THE NEXT GENERATION (TV)
Oct, 1989-Present ($1.50, color)
DC Comics

1-Capt. Picard and crew from TV show	.75	2.20	4.40
2,3	.50	1.50	3.00
4-10	.35	1.10	2.20
11-24	.30	.90	1.80
Annual 1 (1990, $2.95, 68 pgs.)	.50	1.50	3.00

STAR WARS (Movie)
July, 1977-No. 107, Sept, 1986
Marvel Comics Group

1-(Regular 30 cent edition)-Price in square w/UPC code			
	2.50	7.50	15.00
1-(35 cent cover; limited distribution-1500 copies?)- Price in square w/UPC code			
	46.50	140.00	325.00
2-4: 4-Battle with Darth Vader	.85	2.50	5.00
5-10: 6-Dave Stevens inks	.50	1.50	3.00
11-20	.35	1.00	2.00
21-38	.25	.75	1.50

Star Wars #2, © *Lucasfilms*

	Good	Fine	N-Mint
39-44-The Empire Strikes Back-r by Al Williamson in all			
	.35	1.00	2.00
45-107: 92,100-($1.00, 52 pgs.)		.50	1.00
1-9-Reprints; has "reprint" in upper lefthand corner of cover or on inside or price and number inside a diamond with no date or UPC on cover; 30 cents and 35 cents issues published		.25	.50
Annual 1 (12/79)	.35	1.00	2.00
Annual 2 (11/82), 3(12/83)		.60	1.20

STRAIGHT ARROW (Radio)
Feb-Mar, 1950-No. 55, Mar, 1956 (All 36 pgs.)
Magazine Enterprises

1-Straight Arrow (alias Steve Adams) & his palomino Fury begin; 1st mention of Sundown Valley & the Secret Cave; Whitney-a			
	21.50	64.00	150.00
2-Red Hawk begins (1st app?) by Powell (Origin), ends #55			
	10.00	30.00	70.00

	Good	Fine	N-Mint
3-Frazetta-c	14.00	42.00	100.00
4,5: 4-Secret Cave-c	6.00	18.00	42.00
6-10	4.65	14.00	32.00
11-Classic story "The Valley of Time," with an ancient civilization made of gold			
	5.00	15.00	35.00
12-19	3.50	10.50	24.00
20-Origin Straight Arrow's Shield	5.00	15.00	35.00
21-Origin Fury	5.70	17.00	40.00
22-Frazetta-c	10.00	30.00	70.00
23,25-30: 25-Secret Cave-c. 28-Red Hawk meets The Vikings			
	3.00	9.00	21.00
24-Classic story "The Dragons of Doom!" with prehistoric pteradactyls			
	4.65	14.00	32.00
31-38	2.65	8.00	18.00
39-Classic story "The Canyon Beast," with a dinosaur egg hatching a Tyranosaurus Rex			
	3.50	10.50	24.00
40-Classic story "Secret of The Spanish Specters," with Conquistadors' lost treasure			
	3.50	10.50	24.00
41,42,44-54: 45-Secret Cave-c	2.15	6.50	15.00
43-1st app. Blaze, Straight Arrow's Warrior dog	2.65	8.00	18.00
55-Last issue	3.00	9.00	21.00

STRANGE ADVENTURES
Aug-Sept, 1950-No. 244, Oct-Nov, 1973 (No. 1-12: 52 pgs.)
National Periodical Publications

	Good	Fine	N-Mint
1-Adaptation of "Destination Moon;" Kris KL-99 & Darwin Jones begin; photo-c	130.00	390.00	910.00
2	59.00	175.00	410.00
3,4	39.00	116.00	270.00
5-8,10: 7-Origin Kris KL-99	34.00	100.00	240.00
9-Captain Comet begins (6/51, Intro/origin)	93.00	280.00	650.00
11,14,15	30.00	90.00	210.00
12,13,17,18-Toth-a	32.00	95.00	220.00
16,19,20	21.00	62.00	145.00
21-30	18.00	54.00	125.00
31,34-38	16.00	48.00	110.00
32,33-Krigstein-a	17.00	51.00	120.00
39-Ill. in SOTI-"Treating police contemptuously" (top right)			
	23.00	70.00	160.00
40-49-Last Capt. Comet; not in 45,47,48	14.00	41.00	95.00

	Good	Fine	N-Mint
50-53-Last pre-code issue (2/55)	10.00	30.00	70.00
54-70	5.70	17.00	40.00
71-99	4.30	13.00	30.00
100	6.50	19.00	45.00
101-110: 104-Space Museum begins	3.15	9.50	22.00
111-116: 114-Star Hawkins begins, ends #185; Heath-a in Wood E.C. style			
	2.85	8.50	20.00
117-Origin/1st app. Atomic Knights & begins (6/60)			
	22.00	66.00	150.00
118-120	5.70	17.00	40.00
121-134: 124-Origin Faceless Creature. 134-Last 10 cent issue			
	3.60	11.00	25.00
135-160: 159-Star Rovers app.; G. Kane/Anderson-a. 160-Last Atomic Knights			
	2.15	6.50	15.00
161-179: 161-Last Space Museum. 163-Star Rovers app. 170- Infinity-c. 177- Origin Immortal Man	.85	2.60	6.00
180-Origin/1st app. Animal Man	26.00	77.00	180.00
181-183,185-189,191-194,196-200,202-204: 187-Origin The Enchantress			
	.70	2.00	5.00
184-2nd app. Animal Man	14.00	43.00	100.00
190-1st app. Animal Man in costume	17.00	51.00	120.00
195-1st full length Animal Man story	10.00	30.00	70.00
201-Last Animal Man; 2nd full length story	5.00	15.00	35.00
205-Intro/origin Deadman by Infantino (10/67)	5.70	17.00	40.00
206-Neal Adams-a begins	3.15	9.50	22.00
207-210	2.15	6.50	15.00
211-216: 211-Space Museum-r. 216-Last Deadman			
	1.70	5.00	12.00
217-221,223-231: 217-Adam Strange & Atomic Knights-r begin. 218-Last 12 cent issue? 222-New Adam Strange story by Kane/Anderson. 226-236- (68-52 pgs.). 31-Last Atomic Knights-r	.50	1.50	3.00
222-New Adam Strange story by Kane/Anderson	.85	2.60	6.00
232-244	.25	.75	1.50

STRANGE STORIES OF SUSPENSE
No. 5, Oct, 1955-No. 16, Aug, 1957
Atlas Comics (CSI)

	Good	Fine	N-Mint
5(#1)	10.00	30.00	70.00
6,9	6.00	18.00	42.00
7-E. C. swipe cover/Vault of Horror #32	6.50	19.00	45.00

	Good	Fine	N-Mint
8-Williamson/Mayo-a; Pakula-a	7.00	21.00	50.00
10-Crandall, Torres, Meskin-a	7.00	21.00	50.00
11,13: 13-E.C. art swipes	3.60	11.00	25.00
12-Torres, Pakula-a	4.30	13.00	30.00
14,16: 14-Williamson-a. 16-Fox, Powell-a	5.00	15.00	35.00
15-Krigstein-a	4.50	14.00	32.00

STRANGE SUSPENSE STORIES (Lawbreakers Suspense Stories #10-15; This
   Is Suspense #23-26)
6/52-No. 5, 2/53; No. 16, 1/54-No. 22, 11/54; No. 27, 10/55-No. 77, 10/65; V3#1,
   10/67-V1#9, 9/69
Fawcett Publications/Charlton Comics No. 16 on

	Good	Fine	N-Mint
1-(Fawcett)-Powell, Sekowsky-a	25.00	75.00	175.00
2-George Evans horror story	17.00	51.00	120.00
3-5 (2/53)-George Evans horror stories	14.00	43.00	100.00
16(1-2/54)	7.00	21.00	50.00
17,21	5.70	17.00	40.00
18-E.C. swipe/HOF 7; Ditko-c/a(2)	12.00	36.00	85.00
19-Ditko electric chair-c; Ditko-a	14.00	43.00	100.00
20-Ditko-c/a(2)	12.00	36.00	85.00
22(11/54)-Ditko-c, Shuster-a; last pre-code issue; becomes This Is Suspense			
	10.00	30.00	70.00
27(10/55)-(Formerly This Is Suspense #26)	2.30	7.00	16.00
28-30,38	2.15	6.50	15.00
31-33,35,37,40,51-Ditko-c/a(2-3 each)	7.00	21.00	50.00
34-Story of ruthless business man, Wm. B. Gaines; Ditko-c/a			
	10.00	30.00	70.00
36-(68 pgs.); Ditko-a(4)	8.00	24.00	55.00
39,41,52,53-Ditko-a	5.70	17.00	40.00
42-44,46,49,54-60	1.70	5.00	12.00
45,47,48,50-Ditko-c/a	4.50	14.00	32.00
61-74	.70	2.00	4.00
75(6/65)-Reprints origin/1st app. Captain Atom by Ditko from Space Adventures #33 (75-77: 12 cent issues)	8.50	25.50	60.00
76,77-Captain Atom-r by Ditko/Space Advs.	3.50	10.50	24.00
V3#1(10/67)-4: All 12 cent issues	1.15	3.50	8.00
V1#2-9: 2-Ditko-a, atom bomb-c (all 12 cents)	.70	2.00	4.00

STRANGE TALES (Becomes Doctor Strange #169 on)
June, 1951-#168, May, 1968; #169, Sept, 1973-#188, Nov, 1976
Atlas (CCPC #1-67/ZPC #68-79/VPI #80-85)/Marvel #86(7/61) on

	Good	Fine	N-Mint
1	90.00	270.00	630.00
2	42.00	125.00	290.00
3,5: 3-Atom bomb panels	31.00	92.00	215.00
4-"The Evil Eye," cosmic eyeball story	33.00	100.00	230.00
6-9	22.00	64.00	150.00
10-Krigstein-a	23.00	70.00	160.00
11-14,16-20	11.50	34.00	80.00
15-Krigstein-a	12.00	36.00	85.00

21,23-27,29-32,34-Last pre-code issue(2/55): 27-Atom bomb panels

	Good	Fine	N-Mint
	9.30	28.00	65.00
22-Krigstein, Forte/Fox-a	10.00	30.00	70.00

28-Jack Katz story used in Senate Investigation report, pgs. 7 & 169

	Good	Fine	N-Mint
	10.00	30.00	70.00
33-Davis-a	9.30	28.00	65.00
35-41,43,44	6.50	19.00	45.00
42,45,59,61-Krigstein-a; #61 (2/58)	7.00	21.00	50.00
46-52,54,55,57,60: 60 (8/57)	5.70	17.00	40.00
53-Torres, Crandall-a	7.00	21.00	50.00
56-Crandall-a	6.00	18.00	42.00
58,64-Williamson-a in each, with Mayo-#58	7.00	21.00	50.00
62-Torres-a	5.70	17.00	40.00
63,65	5.30	16.00	38.00
66-Crandall-a	5.70	17.00	40.00
67-78,80-Ditko/Kirby-a	5.00	15.00	35.00
79-Dr. Strange proto-type (12/60); Ditko/Kirby-a	5.70	17.00	40.00
81-83,85-92-Last 10 cent issue. Ditko/Kirby-a	4.50	14.00	32.00
84-Magneto prototype (5/61)(See X-Men #1)	5.15	15.50	36.00
93-96,98-100-Kirby-a	4.30	13.00	30.00

97-Aunt May & Uncle Ben proto-type by Ditko, 3 months before Amazing Fantasy

	Good	Fine	N-Mint
#15. Kirby-a	8.50	25.50	60.00
101-Human Torch begins by Kirby (10/62)	47.00	140.00	325.00
102	18.00	54.00	125.00
103-105	15.00	45.00	105.00
106,108,109	10.00	30.00	70.00
107-Human Torch/Sub-Mariner battle	13.00	40.00	90.00

110-(7/63)-Intro Doctor Strange, Ancient One & Wong by Ditko

	Good	Fine	N-Mint
	46.00	138.00	320.00
111-2nd Dr. Strange	16.00	48.00	110.00
112,113	6.50	19.00	45.00

114-Acrobat disguised as Captain America, 1st app. since the G.A.; intro. & 1st

	Good	Fine	N-Mint
app. Victoria Bentley; 3rd Dr. Strange app. & begin series (11/63)			
	14.00	43.00	100.00
115-Origin Dr. Strange; Spider-Man & Sandman (Spidey villain) app. (early Spider-Man x-over, 12/63)	22.00	64.00	150.00
116-Human Torch battles Thing;1st Thing x-over	5.70	17.00	40.00
117,118,120: 120-1st Iceman x-over (from X-Men)	5.00	15.00	35.00
119-Spider-Man app.	5.70	17.00	40.00
121,122,124-129,131-134: Thing/Torch team-up in all; 126-Intro Clea. 134-Last H. Torch; Wood-a(i)	2.85	8.50	20.00
123-1st Thor x-over	3.15	9.50	22.00
130-The Beatles cameo	3.60	11.00	25.00
135-Origin/1st app. Nick Fury, Agent of Shield by Kirby (8/65); series begins, ends #168	5.00	15.00	35.00
136-147,149: 146-Last Ditko Dr. Strange who is in consecutive stories since #113			
	2.00	6.00	14.00
148-Origin Ancient One	2.30	7.00	16.00
150(11/66)-John Buscema's 1st work at Marvel	2.00	6.00	14.00
151-1st Marvel work by Steranko (w/Kirby)	2.30	7.00	16.00
152,153-Kirby/Steranko-a	2.00	6.00	14.00
154-158-Steranko-a/script	2.00	6.00	14.00
159-Origin Nick Fury retold; Intro Val; Captain America app; Steranko-a			
	2.30	7.00	16.00
160-162-Steranko-a/scripts; Capt. America app.	2.00	6.00	14.00
163-166,168-Steranko-a(p). 168-Last Nick Fury	2.00	6.00	14.00
167-Steranko pen/script; classic flag-c	2.65	8.00	18.00
169-177: 169,170-Brother Voodoo origin in each; series ends #173. 174-Origin Golem. 177-Brunner-c	.35	1.00	2.00
178-Warlock by Starlin with covers; origin Warlock & Him; Starlin scripts in 178-181	1.50	4.50	10.00
179-181-Warlock by Starlin with covers. 179-Intro/1st app. Pip the Troll. 180-Intro Gamora	.85	2.60	6.00
182-188	.35	1.00	2.00
Annual 1(1962)-Reprints from Strange Tales #73,76,78, Tales of Suspense #7,9, Tales to Astonish #1,6,7, & Journey Into Mystery #53, 55,59			
	24.00	71.00	165.00
Annual 2(7/63)-r-/from Strange Tales #67, Strange Worlds (Atlas) #1-3, World of Fantasy #16; new Human Torch vs. Spider-Man story by Kirby/Ditko (1st Spidey x-over); Kirby-c	29.00	86.00	200.00

STRANGE TALES
Apr, 1987-No. 19, Oct, 1988
Marvel Comics Group

	Good	Fine	N-Mint
V2#1		.50	1.00
2-12,15-19: 5,7-Defenders app. 18-X-Factor app.		.40	.80
13,14-Punisher app.	.35	1.00	2.00

STRANGE TERRORS
June, 1952-No. 7, Mar, 1953
St. John Publishing Co.

1-Bondage-c; Zombies spelled Zoombies on-c; Fineesque-a			
	16.00	48.00	110.00
2	8.50	25.50	60.00
3-Kubert-a; painted-c	11.50	34.00	80.00
4-Kubert-a(reprinted in Mystery Tales #18); Ekgren-c; Fineesque-a; Jerry Iger			
caricature	18.00	54.00	125.00
5-Kubert-a; painted-c	11.50	34.00	80.00
6-Giant, 100 pgs.(1/53); bondage-c	16.00	48.00	110.00
7-Giant, 100 pgs.; Kubert-c/a	18.50	56.00	130.00

STRANGE WORLDS (#18 continued from Avon's Eerie #1-17)
11/50-No. 9, 11/52; No. 18, 10-11/54-No. 22, 9-10/55 (No #11-17)
Avon Periodicals

1-Kenton of the Star Patrol by Kubert (r-/Eerie #1-'47); Crom the Barbarian by			
John Giunta	41.00	122.00	285.00
2-Wood-a; Crom the Barbarian by Giunta; Dara of the Vikings app.; used in			
SOTI, pg. 112; injury to eye panel	36.00	107.00	250.00
3-Wood/Orlando-a(Kenton), Wood/Williamson/Frazetta/Krenkel/Orlando-a			
(7 pgs.); Malu Slave Girl Princess app.; Kinstler-c			
	73.00	220.00	510.00
4-Wood-c/a (Kenton); Orlando-a; origin The Enchanted Daggar; Sultan-a			
	34.00	103.00	240.00
5-Orlando/Wood-a (Kenton); Wood-c	29.00	86.00	200.00
6-Kinstler-a(2); Orlando/Wood-c; Check-a	19.00	57.00	130.00
7-Kinstler, Fawcette & Becker/Alascia-a	14.00	43.00	100.00
8-Kubert, Kinstler, Hollingsworth & Lazarus-a; Lazarus-c			
	16.00	48.00	110.00
9-Kinstler, Fawcette, Alascia-a	14.00	43.00	100.00
18-(Formerly Eerie #17)-R/"Attack on Planet Mars" by Kubert			
	14.00	43.00	100.00
19-R/Avon's "Robotmen of the Lost Planet"	14.00	43.00	100.00
20-War stories; Wood-c(r)/U.S. Paratroops #1	3.65	11.00	25.00

	Good	Fine	N-Mint
21,22-War stories	3.35	10.00	23.00

STRANGE WORLDS
Dec, 1958-No. 5, Aug, 1959
Marvel Comics (MPI No. 1,2/Male No. 3,5)

	Good	Fine	N-Mint
1-Kirby & Ditko-a; flying saucer issue	24.00	72.00	170.00
2-Ditko-c/a	14.00	43.00	100.00
3-Kirby-a(2)	11.00	32.00	75.00
4-Williamson-a	12.00	36.00	85.00
5-Ditko-a	10.00	30.00	70.00

SUB-MARINER, THE (2nd Series) (Sub-Mariner #31 on)
May, 1968-No. 72, Sept, 1974 (No. 43: 52 pgs.)
Marvel Comics Group

1-Origin Sub-Mariner; story continued from Iron Man & Sub-Mariner #1

	Good	Fine	N-Mint
	13.50	41.00	95.00
2-Triton app.	4.30	13.00	30.00

3-10: 5-1st Tiger Shark. 7-Photo-c. 9-1st app. Serpent Crown (origin in #10
& 12)

	Good	Fine	N-Mint
	2.15	6.50	15.00
11-13	1.50	4.50	10.00

14-Sub-Mariner vs. G.A. Human Torch; death of Toro

	Good	Fine	N-Mint
	3.15	9.50	22.00

15-20: 19-1st Sting Ray

	Good	Fine	N-Mint
	1.00	3.00	7.00

21-40: 37-Death of Lady Dorma. 35-Ties into 1st Defenders story; 38-Origin

	Good	Fine	N-Mint
	.70	2.00	5.00

41-72: 44,45-Sub-Mariner vs. H. Torch. 50-1st app. Nita, Namor's niece. 61-Last
artwork by Everett; 1st 4 pgs. completed by Mortimer; pgs. 5-20 by Mooney.
62-1st Tales of Atlantis, ends #66

	Good	Fine	N-Mint
	.50	1.50	3.00
Special 1(1/71), Special 2(1/72)-Everett-a	.70	2.00	4.00

SUB-MARINER COMICS (1st Series) (The Sub-Mariner #1,2,33-42)
Spring, 1941-No. 23, Sum, `47; No. 24, Wint, `47-No. 31, 4/49; No. 32, 7/49; No.
33, 4/54-No. 42, 10/55
Timely/Marvel Comics (TCI 1-7/SePI 8/MPI 9-32/Atlas Comics (CCC 33-42)

	Good	Fine	VF-NM
1-The Sub-Mariner by Everett & The Angel begin			
	533.00	1335.00	3200.00

The Sub-Mariner #1 (5/68), © Marvel Comics

	Good	Fine	N-Mint
2-Everett-a	242.00	605.00	1450.00
3-Churchill assassination-c; 40 pg. Sub-Mariner story			
	167.00	415.00	1000.00
4-Everett-a, 40 pgs.; 1 pg. Wolverton-a	158.00	395.00	950.00
5	112.00	280.00	675.00
6-10: 9-Wolverton-a, 3 pgs.; flag-c	83.00	210.00	500.00
11-15	58.00	146.00	350.00
16-20	52.00	130.00	310.00
21-Last Angel; Everett-a	39.00	100.00	235.00
22-Young Allies app.	39.00	100.00	235.00
23-The Human Torch, Namora x-over	39.00	100.00	235.00
24-Namora x-over	39.00	100.00	235.00
25-The Blonde Phantom begins, ends No. 31; Kurtzman-a; Namora x-over			
	50.00	125.00	300.00
26,27	44.00	110.00	265.00
28-Namora cover; Everett-a	44.00	110.00	265.00
29-31 (4/49): 29-The Human Torch app. 31-Capt. America app.			
	44.00	110.00	265.00

	Good	Fine	N-Mint
32 (7/49, Scarce)-Origin Sub-Mariner	67.00	167.00	400.00
33 (4/54)-Origin Sub-Mariner; The Human Torch app.; Namora x-over in Sub-Mariner #33-42	39.00	100.00	235.00
34,35-Human Torch in each	28.00	70.00	165.00
36,37,39-41: 36,39-41-Namora app.	28.00	70.00	165.00
38-Origin Sub-Mariner's wings; Namora app. Last pre-code (2/55)	36.00	90.00	215.00
42-Last issue	32.00	80.00	190.00

SUGAR & SPIKE
Apr-May, 1956-No. 98, Oct-Nov, 1971
National Periodical Publications

	Good	Fine	N-Mint
1 (Scarce)	68.00	205.00	475.00
2	34.00	100.00	235.00
3-5	30.00	90.00	210.00
6-10	19.00	58.00	135.00
11-20	14.00	43.00	100.00
21-29,31-40: 26-XMas-c	8.00	24.00	55.00
30-Scribbly x-over	9.30	28.00	65.00
41-60	3.70	11.00	26.00
61-80: 72-Origin & 1st app. Bernie the Brain	2.65	8.00	18.00
81-98: 85-(68 pgs.); r-#72. #96-(68 pgs.). #97,98-(52 pgs.)	2.00	6.00	14.00

SUNSET CARSON
Feb, 1951-No. 4, 1951 (No month)
Charlton Comics

	Good	Fine	N-Mint
1-Photo/retouched-c (Scarce, all issues)	66.00	197.00	460.00
2	45.00	135.00	310.00
3,4	34.00	100.00	235.00

SUPERBOY (...& the Legion of Super-Heroes with #231) (Also see Adventure Comics, 80 Page Giant #10 & More Fun Comics #101)
Mar-Apr, 1949-No. 258, Dec, 1979 (#1-16: 52 pgs.)
National Periodical Publications/DC Comics

	Good	Fine	VF-NM
1-Superman cover	271.00	815.00	1900.00

	Good	Fine	N-Mint
2-Used in **SOTI**, pg. 35-36,226	101.00	305.00	710.00
3	74.00	220.00	515.00
4,5: 5-Pre-Supergirl tryout	62.00	185.00	435.00
6-10: 8-1st Superbaby. 10-1st Lana Lang	45.00	135.00	315.00
11-15	34.00	100.00	235.00
16-20	24.00	70.00	165.00
21-26,28-30	18.00	54.00	125.00
27-Low distribution	19.00	56.00	130.00
31-38: 38-Last pre-code issue	13.00	40.00	90.00
39-48,50 (7/56)	10.00	30.00	70.00
49 (6/56)-1st app. Metallo (Jor-El's robot)	11.50	34.00	80.00
51-60: 55-Spanking-c	7.00	21.00	50.00
61-67	5.70	17.00	40.00
68-Origin/1st app. original Bizarro (10-11/58)	23.00	70.00	160.00
69-77,79: 75-Spanking-c. 76-1st Supermonkey. 77-Pre-Pete Ross tryout			
	5.00	15.00	35.00
78-Origin Mr. Mxyzptlk & Superboy's costume	8.50	25.50	60.00
80-1st meeting Superboy/Supergirl (4/60)	5.70	17.00	40.00
81,83-85,87,88: 83-Origin & 1st app. Kryptonite Kid			
	3.60	11.00	25.00
82-1st Bizarro Krypto	4.30	13.00	30.00
86(1/61)-4th Legion app; Intro Pete Ross	9.70	29.00	68.00
89(6/61)-Mon-el 1st app.	14.00	43.00	100.00
90-92: 90-Pete Ross learns Superboy's I.D. 92-Last 10 cent issue			
	3.60	11.00	25.00
93(12/61)-10th Legion app; Chameleon Boy app.	3.60	11.00	25.00
94-97,99	1.85	5.50	13.00
98(7/62)-18th Legion app; Origin & intro. Ultra Boy; Pete Ross joins Legion			
	3.00	9.00	21.00
100(10/62)-Ultra Boy app; 1st app. Phantom Zone villains, Dr. Xadu & Erndine. 2 pg. map of Krypton; origin Superboy retold; r-cover of Superman #1; Pete Ross joins Legion	13.00	40.00	90.00
101-120: 104-Origin Phantom Zone. 115-Atomic bomb-c. 117-Legion app.			
	1.15	3.50	8.00
121-128: 124(10/65)-1st app. Insect Queen (Lana Lang). 125-Legion cameo. 126-Origin Krypto the Super Dog retold with new facts			
	.70	2.00	4.00
129- (80-pg. Giant G-22)-Reprints origin Mon-el	.85	2.60	6.00
130-137,139,140: 131-Legion statues cameo in Dog Legionnaires story. 132-1st app. Supremo			
	.50	1.50	3.00

	Good	Fine	N-Mint
138-(80-pg. Giant G-35)	.85	2.60	6.00

141-146,148-155,157-164,166-173,175,176: 145-Superboy's parents regain their youth. 172,173,176-Legion app.; 172-Origin Yango (Super Ape)

	.35	1.00	2.00

147(6/68)-Giant G-47; origin Saturn Girl, Lightning Lad, Cosmic Boy; origin Legion of Super-Pets-r/Adv. 293?

	.85	2.60	6.00
156,165,174 (Giants G-59,71,83)	.70	2.00	4.00

177-184,186,187 (All 52 pgs.): 184-Origin Dial H for Hero-r

		.50	1.00

185-DC 100 Pg. Super Spectacular #12; Legion-c/story; Teen Titans, Kid Eternity, Star Spangled Kid-r

	.25	.75	1.50

188-196: 191-Origin Sunboy retold; Legion app.

		.50	1.00

197-Legion series begins; Lightning Lad's new costume

	.75	2.25	4.50

198,199: 198-Element Lad & Princess Projectra get new costumes

	.35	1.00	2.00

200-Bouncing Boy & Duo Damsel marry; Jonn' Jonzz' cameo

	.75	2.25	4.50

201,204,206,207,209: 204-Supergirl resigns from Legion. 209-Karate Kid new costume

	.35	1.00	2.00

202,205-(100 pgs.): 202-Light Lass gets new costume

	.45	1.25	2.50
203-Invisible Kid dies	.50	1.50	3.00
208,210: 208-(68 pgs.). 210-Origin Karate Kid	.45	1.25	2.50

211-220: 212-Matter-Eater Lad resigns. 216-1st app. Tyroc who joins Legion in #218

	.30	.90	1.80

221-249: 226-Intro. Dawnstar. 228-Death of Chemical King. 240-Origin Dawnstar. 242-(52pgs.). 243-Legion of Substitute Heroes app. 243-245-(44 pgs.)

		.60	1.20

250-258: 253-Intro Blok. 257-Return of Bouncing Boy & Duo Damsel by Ditko

		.50	1.00
Annual 1(Sum/64, 84 pgs.)-Origin Krypto-r	7.00	21.00	50.00

SUPER COMICS
May, 1938-No. 121, Feb-Mar, 1949
Dell Publishing Co.

1-Terry & The Pirates, The Gumps, Dick Tracy, Little Orphan Annie, Gasoline Alley, Little Joe, Smilin' Jack, Smokey Stover, Smitty, Tiny Tim, Moon Mullins, Harold Teen, Winnie Winkle begin

	111.00	277.00	665.00

	Good	Fine	N-Mint
2	46.00	140.00	325.00
3	41.00	125.00	290.00
4,5	32.00	95.00	225.00
6-10	26.00	79.00	185.00
11-20	21.00	62.00	145.00
21-29: 21-Magic Morro begins (Origin, 2/40)	18.00	54.00	125.00
30-"Sea Hawk" movie adaptation-c/story with Errol Flynn			
	18.00	54.00	125.00
31-40	14.00	43.00	100.00
41-50: 43-Terry & The Pirates ends	11.50	34.00	80.00
51-60	8.50	25.50	60.00
61-70: 65-Brenda Starr-r begin? 67-X-mas-c	7.00	21.00	50.00
71-80	6.00	19.00	45.00
81-99	5.00	15.00	35.00
100	6.00	19.00	45.00
101-115-Last Dick Tracy (moves to own title)	4.00	12.00	28.00
116,118-All Smokey Stover	3.15	9.50	22.00
117-All Gasoline Alley	3.15	9.50	22.00
119-121-Terry & The Pirates app. in all	3.15	9.50	22.00

SUPER DUCK COMICS (The Cockeyed Wonder)
Fall, 1944-No. 94, Dec, 1960 (Also see Laugh #24)
MLJ Mag. No. 1-4(9/45)/Close-Up No. 5 on (Archie)

1-Origin	22.00	65.00	150.00
2	9.30	28.00	65.00
3-5: 3-1st Mr. Monster	7.00	21.00	50.00
6-10	5.00	15.00	35.00
11-20	3.15	9.50	22.00
21,23-40	2.65	8.00	18.00
22-Used in **SOTI**, pg. 35,307,308	3.50	10.50	24.00
41-60	1.70	5.00	12.00
61-94	1.30	4.00	9.00

SUPER MAGIC (Super Magician Comics #2 on)
May, 1941
Street & Smith Publications

V1#1-Blackstone the Magician app.; origin & 1st app. Rex King (Black Fury); not
    Eisner-c   42.00   125.00   290.00

SUPER MAGICIAN COMICS (Super Magic #1)
No. 2, Sept, 1941-V5#8, Feb-Mar, 1947
Street & Smith Publications

	Good	Fine	N-Mint
V1#2-Rex King, Man of Adventure app.	17.00	51.00	120.00
3-Tao-Anwar, Boy Magician begins	10.00	30.00	70.00
4-Origin Transo	9.30	28.00	65.00
5-7,9-12: 8-Abbott & Costello story. 11-Supersnipe app.			
	9.30	28.00	65.00
8-Abbott & Costello story	11.00	32.00	75.00
V2#1-The Shadow app.	14.00	43.00	100.00
2-12: 5-Origin Tigerman. 8-Red Dragon begins	5.00	15.00	35.00
V3#1-12: 5-Origin Mr. Twilight	5.00	15.00	35.00
V4#1-12: 11-Nigel Elliman begins	4.30	13.00	30.00
V5#1-6	4.30	13.00	30.00
7,8-Red Dragon by Cartier	13.00	40.00	90.00

SUPERMAN (Becomes Adventures Of . . . #424 on; see Action Comics &
    World's Finest Comics)
Summer, 1939-No. 423, Sept, 1986 (#1-5 are quarterly)
National Periodical Publications/DC Comics

	Good	Fine	VF-NM
1(nn)-1st four Action stories reprinted; origin Superman by Siegel & Shuster; has a new 2 pg. origin plus 4 pgs. omitted in Action story			
	4,300.00	11,800.00	28,000.00
	Good	**Fine**	**N-Mint**
2-All daily strip-r	600.00	1500.00	3600.00
3-2nd story-r from Action #5; 3rd story-r from Action #6			
	450.00	1125.00	2700.00
4-2nd mention of Daily Planet (Spr/40); also see Action #23; 2nd app. Luthor (1st Luthor-c & 1st bald Luthor; also see Action #23)			
	350.00	875.00	2100.00
5	258.00	645.00	1550.00
6,7: 7-1st Perry White?	200.00	500.00	1200.00
8-10: 10-Luthor app.	158.00	395.00	950.00
11-13,15: 13-Jimmy Olsen app.	119.00	300.00	715.00
14-Patriotic Shield-c by Fred Ray	142.00	355.00	850.00
16-20: 17-Hitler, Hirohito-c	100.00	250.00	600.00
21-23,25	79.00	200.00	475.00
24-Flag-c	92.00	230.00	550.00

Superman #5 (1st series), © DC Comics

	Good	Fine	N-Mint
26-29: 28-Lois Lane Girl Reporter series begins, ends #40,42			
	72.00	180.00	430.00
28-Overseas edition for Armed Forces; same as reg. #28			
	72.00	180.00	430.00
30-Origin/1st app. Mr. Mxyztplk (pronounced "Mix-it-plk"); name later became			
Mxyzptlk ("Mix-yez-pit-l-ick")	100.00	300.00	700.00
31-40: 33-(3-4/45)-3rd app. Mxyztplk	54.00	160.00	375.00
41-50: 45-Lois Lane as Superwoman (see Action #60 for 1st app.)			
	40.00	120.00	280.00
51,52	32.00	95.00	225.00
53-Origin Superman retold	79.00	235.00	550.00
54,56-60	33.00	100.00	230.00
55-Used in **SOTI**, pg. 33	36.00	107.00	250.00
61-Origin Superman retold; origin Green Kryptonite (1st Kryptonite story)			
	59.00	175.00	410.00
62-65,67-70: 62-Orson Welles app. 65-1st Krypton Foes: Mala, K120, & U-Ban			
	33.00	100.00	230.00
66-2nd Superbaby story	33.00	100.00	230.00

	Good	Fine	N-Mint
71-75: 75-Some have #74 on-c	30.00	90.00	210.00
72-Giveaway(9-10/51)-(Rare)-Price blackened out; came with banner wrapped			
around book	38.00	115.00	265.00
76-Batman x-over; Superman & Batman learn each other's I.D.			
	79.00	235.00	550.00
77-80: 78-Last 52 pgs.	27.00	80.00	185.00
81-Used in POP, pg. 88	27.00	80.00	185.00
82-90	24.00	73.00	170.00
91-95: 95-Last pre-code issue	23.00	70.00	160.00
96-99	19.00	58.00	135.00
100 (9-10/55)	69.00	207.00	480.00
101-110	16.00	48.00	110.00
111-120	14.00	41.00	95.00
121-130: 123-Pre-Supergirl tryout. 127-Origin/1st app. Titano. 128-Red Kryptonite			
used (4/59). 129-Intro/origin Lori Lemaris, The Mermaid			
	11.50	34.00	80.00
131-139: 139-Lori Lemaris app.	9.30	28.00	65.00
140-1st Blue Kryptonite & Bizarro Supergirl; origin Bizarro Jr. #1			
	9.30	28.00	65.00
141-145,148: 142-2nd Batman x-over	5.70	17.00	40.00
146-Superman's life story	7.00	21.00	50.00
147(8/61)-7th Legion app; 1st app. Legion of Super-Villains; 1st app. Adult Legion			
9.30		28.00	65.00
149(11/61)-9th Legion app. (cameo); last 10 cent issue			
	8.00	24.00	55.00
150-162: 152(4/62)-15th Legion app. 155(8/62)-19th Legion app; Lightning Man			
& Cosmic Man, & Adult Legion app. 156,162-Legion app. 157-Gold			
Kryptonite used (see Adv. 299); Mon-el app.; Lightning Lad cameo (11/62).			
158-1st app. Flamebird & Nightwing & Nor-Kan of Kandor. 161-1st told			
death of Ma and Pa Kent	3.60	11.00	25.00
163-166,168-180: 166-XMas-c. 168-All Luthor issue. 172,173-Legion cameos.			
174-Super-Mxyzptlk; Bizarro app.	2.65	8.00	18.00
167-New origin Brainiac & Brainiac 5; intro Tixarla (Later Luthor's wife)			
	5.00	15.00	35.00
181,182,184-186,188-192,194-196,198,200: 181-1st 2965 story/series 189-			
Origin/destruction of Krypton II.	1.50	4.50	10.00
183,187,193,197 (Giants G-18,G-23,G-31,G-36)	1.70	5.00	12.00
199-1st Superman/Flash race (8/67)	2.85	8.50	20.00
201,203-206,208-211,213-216,218-221,223-226,228-231,234-238: 213- Brainiac-5			
app.	1.00	3.00	7.00
202 (80-pg. Giant G-42)-All Bizarro issue	1.30	4.00	9.00

	Good	Fine	N-Mint
207,212,217,222,227,239 (Giants G-48,G-54,G-60,G-66,G-72,G-84): 207- Legion app.; 30th anniversary Superman	1.30	4.00	9.00
232(Giant, G-78)-All Krypton issue	1.30	4.00	9.00
233-2nd app. Morgan Edge; Clark Kent switch from newspaper reporter to TV newscaster	1.00	3.00	7.00
240-Kaluta-a	.70	2.00	4.00
241-244 (All 52 pgs.): 243-G.A.-r/#38	.50	1.50	3.00
245-DC 100 Pg. Super Spectacular #7; reprints	.70	2.00	4.00
246-248,250,251,253 (All 52 pgs.)	.35	1.00	2.00
249,254-Neal Adams-a. 249-(52 pgs.); origin & 1st app. Terra-Man by Neal Adams (inks)	1.00	3.00	6.00
252-DC 100 Pg. Super Spect. #13; N. Adams-c	.85	2.50	5.00
255-263: 263-Photo-c	.25	.75	1.50
264-1st app. Steve Lombard	.35	1.00	2.00
265-271,273-277,279-283,285-299: 276-Intro Capt. Thunder. 289-Photo-c. 292-Origin Lex Luthor retold	.25	.75	1.50
272,278,284-All 100 pgs. G.A.-r in all	.35	1.00	2.00
300-Retells origin	.70	2.00	4.00
301-399: 323-Intro. Atomic Skull. 353-Brief origin	.25	.75	1.50
400 (10/84, $1.50, 68 pgs.)-Many top artists featured; Chaykin painted cover, Miller back-c	.50	1.50	3.00
401-422: 405-Super-Batman story. 408-Nuclear Holocaust-c/story. 414, 415-Crisis x-over. 422-Horror-c	.25	.75	1.50
423-Alan Moore scripts; Perez-a(i)	1.00	3.00	7.00
Annual 1(10/60, 84 pgs.)-Reprints 1st Supergirl story/Action #252; r-/ Lois Lane #1 (1st Silver Age DC annual)	32.00	95.00	225.00
Annual 2(1960)-Brainiac, Titano, Metallo, Bizarro origin-r	19.00	58.00	135.00
Annual 3(1961)	14.00	43.00	100.00
Annual 4(1961)-11th Legion app; 1st Legion origins-text & pictures	12.00	36.00	85.00
Annual 5(Sum, '62)-All Krypton issue	8.50	25.50	60.00
Annual 6(Wint, '62-'63)-Legion-r/Adv. #247	7.00	21.00	50.00
Annual 7(Sum/'63)-Origin-r/Superman-Batman team/Adv. 275; r-1955 Superman dailies	5.70	17.00	40.00
Annual 8(Wint, '63-'64)-All origins issue	4.30	13.00	30.00
Annual 9(8/64)-Superman/Batman team-up	4.30	13.00	30.00
Annual 9(9/83)-Toth/Austin-a	.70	2.00	4.00
Annuals 10-12: 10(11/84, $1.25)-M. Anderson inks. 11(9/85)-Moore scripts. 12(8/86)	.50	1.50	3.00
Special 1(3/83)-G. Kane-c/a; contains German-r	.50	1.50	3.00

	Good	Fine	N-Mint
Special 2(3/84, 48 pgs.), 3(4/85, $1.25)	.50	1.50	3.00

SUPERMAN (2nd series)
Jan, 1987-Present (.75-$1.00, bi-weekly #19-?)
DC Comics

	Good	Fine	N-Mint
1-Byrne-c/a begins; intro Metallo	.35	1.00	2.00
2-8,10: 3-Legends x-over. 7-Origin/1st app. Rampage. 8-Legion app.			
		.60	1.20
9-Joker-c	.50	1.50	3.00
11-49,51,52,54-56,58-62: 11-1st app. Mr. Mxyzptlk. 12-Lori Lemaris revived. 13-			
1st app. Toyman. 13,14-Millennium x-over. 20-Supergirl revived in cameo.			
44-Batman story, part 1		.50	1.00
50-($1.50, 52 pgs.)-Clark Kent proposes to Lois	1.00	3.00	6.00
50-2nd printing		.50	1.00
53-Clark reveals I.D. to Lois cont'd from Action #662			
	.40	1.25	2.50
57 ($1.75, 52 pgs.)	.30	.90	1.80
Annual 1 (8/87)-No Byrne-a	.25	.75	1.50
Annual 2 ('88)-Byrne-a; Newsboy Legion	.25	.75	1.50
Annual 3 ('91, $2.00, 68 pgs.)Armaggedon x-over	.35	1.00	2.00

SUPERMAN'S GIRLFRIEND LOIS LANE (See Action Comics #1, 80 Page
   Giant #3,14, Showcase #9,10 & Superman #28)
Mar-Apr, 1958-No. 136, Jan-Feb, 1974; No. 137, Sept-Oct, 1974
National Periodical Publications

	Good	Fine	N-Mint
1	70.00	210.00	485.00
2	28.00	86.00	200.00
3-Spanking panel	21.00	63.00	145.00
4,5	17.00	51.00	120.00
6-10: 9-Pat Boone app.	11.50	34.00	80.00
11-20: 14-Supergirl x-over	6.70	20.00	47.00
21-29: 23-1st app. Lena Thorul, Lex Luthor's sister. 27-Bizarro-c/story. 29-Aqua-			
man, Batman, Green Arrow cameo; last 10 cent issue			
	4.15	12.50	29.00
30-32,34-49: 47-Legion app.	1.60	4.80	11.00
33(5/62)-Mon-el app.	2.15	6.50	15.00
50(7/64)-Triplicate Girl, Phantom Girl & Shrinking Violet app.			
	1.50	4.50	10.00

	Good	Fine	N-Mint
51-55,57-67,69: 59-Jor-el app.; Batman back-up story			
	.50	1.50	3.00
56-Saturn Girl app.	.85	2.50	5.00
68-(Giant G-26)	1.00	3.00	7.00
70-Penguin & Catwoman app. (1st S.A. Catwoman, 11/66); Batman & Robin			
cameo	4.30	13.00	30.00
71-76,78: 74-1st Bizarro Flash; JLA cameo	.50	1.50	3.00
77-(Giant G-39)	.70	2.00	4.00
79-Neal Adams-c begin, end #95,108	.40	1.25	2.50
80-85,87-94: 89-Batman x-over; all N. Adams-c	.35	1.00	2.00
86,95: 86-(Giant G-51). 95-(Giant G-63)-Wonder Woman x-over			
	.70	2.00	4.00
96-103,105-111: 105-Origin/1st app. The Rose & the Thorn. 108-Neal Adams-c.			
111-Morrow-a	.35	1.00	2.00
104,113-(Giants G-75,87)	.70	2.00	4.00
112,114-123 (52 pgs.): 122-G.A.-r/Superman #30. 123-G.A. Batman-r			
	.35	1.00	2.00
124-137: 130-Last Rose & the Thorn. 132-New Zatanna story. 136- Wonder			
Woman x-over	.35	1.00	2.00
Annual 1(Sum,'62)	6.50	19.00	45.00
Annual 2(Sum,'63)	3.60	11.00	25.00

SUPERMAN'S PAL JIMMY OLSEN (See Action #6 & 80 Page Giant)
Sept-Oct, 1954-No. 163, Feb-Mar, 1974
National Periodical Publications

1	100.00	300.00	700.00
2	43.00	130.00	300.00
3-Last pre-code issue	28.00	86.00	200.00
4,5	19.30	58.00	135.00
6-10	14.00	43.00	100.00
11-20	9.30	28.00	65.00
21-30: 29-1st app. Krypto in Jimmy Olsen	5.00	15.00	35.00
31-40: 31-Origin Elastic Lad. 33-One pg. biography of Jack Larson (TV Jimmy			
Olsen). 36-Intro Lucy Lane. 37-2nd app. Elastic Lad; 1st cover app.			
	3.15	9.50	22.00
41-50: 41-1st J.O. Robot. 48-Intro/origin Superman Emergency Squad			
	2.15	6.50	15.00
51-56: 56-Last 10 cent issue	1.30	4.00	9.00
57-62,64-70: 57-Olsen marries Supergirl. 70-Element Lad app.			
	.70	2.00	5.00

	Good	Fine	N-Mint
63(9/62)-Legion of Super-Villains app.	.85	2.50	6.00
71,74,75,78,80-84,86,89,90: 86-J.O. Robot becomes Congorilla			
	.50	1.50	3.00
72(10/63)-Legion app; Elastic Lad (Olsen) joins	.70	2.00	5.00
73-Ultra Boy app.	.70	2.00	5.00
76,85-Legion app.	.70	2.00	5.00
77-Olsen with Colossal Boy's powers & costume; origin Titano retold			
	.50	1.50	3.00
79(9/64)-Titled The Red-headed Beatle of 1000 B.C.			
	.50	1.50	3.00
87-Legion of Super-Villains app.	.70	2.00	5.00
88-Star Boy app.	.50	1.50	3.00
91-94,96-99,101-103,105-110: 99-Olsen w/powers & costumes of Lightning Lad,			
Sun Boy & Star Boy. 106-Legion app. 110-Infinity-c			
	.35	1.00	2.00
95,104 (Giants G-25,G-38)	.85	2.60	6.00
100-Legion cameo	.50	1.50	3.00
111,112,114-121,123-130,132	.35	1.00	2.00
113,122,131 (Giants G-50,G-62,G-74)	.35	1.00	2.00
133-Re-intro Newsboy Legion & begins by Kirby	.50	1.50	3.00
134-163: 134-1st app. Darkseid (cameo) & Morgan Edge. 135-G.A. Guardian app.			
136-Origin new Guardian. 139-Last 15 cent issue. 140-(Giant G-86). 141-			
Newsboy Legion reprints by S&K begin (52 pg. issues begin). 149,150-G.A.			
Plastic Man reprint in both; last 52 pg. issue. 150-Newsboy Legion app.			
	.35	1.00	2.00

SUPERMOUSE (...the Big Cheese; see Coo Coo Comics)
Dec, 1948-No. 34, Sept, 1955; No. 35, Apr, 1956-No. 45, Fall, 1958
Standard Comics/Pines No. 35 on (Literary Ent.)

	Good	Fine	N-Mint
1-Frazetta text illos (3)	17.00	51.00	120.00
2-Frazetta text illos	9.30	28.00	65.00
3,5,6-Text illos by Frazetta in all	7.00	21.00	50.00
4-Two pg. text illos by Frazetta	8.00	24.00	55.00
7-10	2.65	8.00	18.00
11-20: 13-Racist humor (Indians)	2.00	6.00	14.00
21-45	1.30	4.00	9.00
1-Summer Holiday issue (Summer,'56-Pines)-100 pgs.			
	5.70	17.00	40.00
2-Giant Summer issue (Summer,'58-Pines)-100 pgs.			
	4.50	14.00	32.00

SUPER-MYSTERY COMICS
July, 1940-V8#6, July, 1949
Ace Magazines (Periodical House)

	Good	Fine	N-Mint
V1#1-Magno, the Magnetic Man & Vulcan begin	79.00	235.00	550.00
2	38.00	115.00	265.00
3-The Black Spider begins	30.00	90.00	210.00
4-Origin Davy	27.00	81.00	190.00
5-Intro. The Clown; begin series	27.00	81.00	190.00
6(2/41)	23.00	70.00	160.00
V2#1(4/41)-Origin Buckskin	23.00	70.00	160.00
2-6(2/42)	21.00	62.00	145.00
V3#1(4/42),2: 1-Vulcan & Black Ace begin	19.00	56.00	130.00
3-Intro. The Lancer; Dr. Nemesis & The Sword begin; Kurtzman- c/a(2) (Mr. Risk & Paul Revere Jr.)	25.00	75.00	175.00
4-Kurtzman-a	21.00	62.00	145.00
5-Kurtzman-a(2); L.B. Cole-a; Mr. Risk app.	22.00	65.00	150.00
6(10/43)-Mr. Risk app.; Kurtzman's Paul Revere Jr.; L.B. Cole-a	22.00	65.00	150.00
V4#1(1/44)-L.B. Cole-a	16.00	48.00	110.00
2-6(4/45): 2,5,6-Mr. Risk app.	12.00	36.00	85.00
V5#1(7/45)-6	10.00	30.00	70.00
V6#1-6: 3-Torture story. 4-Last Magno. Mr. Risk app. in #2,4-6	8.50	25.50	60.00
V7#1-6, V8#1-4,6	8.50	25.50	60.00
V8#5-Meskin, Tuska, Sid Greene-a	10.00	30.00	70.00

SUPER RABBIT
Fall, 1944-No. 14, Nov, 1948
Timely Comics (CmPI)

	Good	Fine	N-Mint
1-Hitler-c	37.00	110.00	255.00
2	18.00	54.00	125.00
3-6: 6-Origin	10.00	30.00	70.00
7-10; 9-Infinity-c	6.00	18.00	42.00
11-Kurtzman's "Hey Look"	7.00	21.00	50.00
12-14	5.00	15.00	35.00

SUPERSNIPE COMICS (See Shadow Comics V2#3)
V1#6, Oct, 1942-V5#1, Aug-Sept, 1949
Street & Smith Publications

	Good	Fine	N-Mint
V1#6-Rex King Man of Adventure (costumed hero) by Jack Binder begins; Supersnipe by George Marcoux continues from Army & Navy #5; Bill Ward-a			
	39.00	115.00	270.00
7,8,10-12: 8-Hitler, Tojo, Mussolini-c. 11-Little Nemo app.			
	21.00	62.00	145.00
9-Doc Savage x-over in Supersnipe; Hitler-c	25.00	75.00	175.00
V2#1-12: 1-Huck Finn by Clare Dwiggins begins, ends V3#5			
	14.00	43.00	100.00
V3#1-12: 8-Bobby Crusoe by Dwiggins begins, ends V3#12. 9-Xmas-c			
	11.00	32.00	75.00
V4#1-12, V5#1: V4#10-Xmas-c	8.00	24.00	55.00

SUPER-VILLAIN TEAM-UP (See Fantastic Four #6)
8/75-No. 14, 10/77; No. 15, 11/78; No. 16, 5/79; No. 17, 6/80
Marvel Comics Group.

	Good	Fine	N-Mint
1-Sub-Mariner & Dr. Doom begin, end #10	.70	2.00	4.00
2-17: 5-1st Shroud. 6-F.F., Shroud app. 7-Origin The Shroud. 9-The Avengers. 11-15-Dr. Doom & Red Skull app.	.35	1.00	2.00

SUSPENSE (Radio/TV; Real Life Tales of ... #1-4)
Dec, 1949-No. 29, Apr, 1953 (#1-8,17-23: 52 pgs.)
Marvel/Atlas Comics (CnPC No. 1-10/BFP No. 11-29)

	Good	Fine	N-Mint
1-Powell-a; Peter Lorre, Sidney Greenstreet photo-c from Hammett's 'The Maltese Falcon'	22.00	65.00	150.00
2-Crime stories; Gale Storm & Dennis O'Keefe photo-c			
	11.00	32.00	75.00
3-Change to horror	11.00	32.00	75.00
4,7-10	7.00	21.00	50.00
5-Krigstein, Tuska, Everett-a	8.50	25.50	60.00
6-Tuska, Everett, Morisi-a	8.00	24.00	55.00
11-17,19,20: 14-Hypo-c; A-Bomb panels	6.00	18.00	42.00
18,22-Krigstein-a	7.00	21.00	50.00
21,23,26-29	4.50	14.00	32.00
24-Tuska-a	5.00	15.00	35.00
25-Electric chair-c/story	7.00	21.00	50.00

SWAMP THING (See Challengers of the Unk. #82, & The Saga of ...)
Oct-Nov, 1972-No. 24, Aug-Sept, 1976
National Periodical Publications/DC Comics

Swamp Thing #5, © Marvel Comics

	Good	Fine	N-Mint
1-Wrightson-c/a begins	3.85	11.50	27.00
2	2.00	6.00	14.00
3-Intro. Patchworkman	1.30	4.00	9.00
4-6,8-10: 10-Last Wrightson issue	1.05	3.15	7.50
7-Batman-c/story	1.30	4.00	9.00
11-24-Redondo-a; 23-Swamp Thing reverts back to Dr. Holland			
	.25	.75	1.50

T

TALES FROM THE CRYPT
No. 20, Oct-Nov, 1950-No. 46, Feb-Mar, 1955
E.C. Comics

	Good	Fine	N-Mint
20	68.00	205.00	480.00
21-Kurtzman-r/Haunt of Fear #15(#1)	56.00	170.00	395.00
22-Moon Girl costume at costume party, one panel			
	45.00	135.00	315.00
23-25	34.00	100.00	235.00
26-30	27.00	81.00	190.00
31-Williamson-a(1st at E.C.); B&W and color illos. in **POP**; Kamen draws himself, Gaines & Feldstein; Ingels, Craig & Davis draw themselves in his story	31.00	92.00	215.00
32,35-39	22.00	65.00	150.00
33-Origin The Crypt Keeper	38.00	115.00	265.00
34-Used in **POP**, pg. 83; lingerie panels	22.00	65.00	150.00
40-Used in Senate hearings & in Hartford Courant anti-comics editorials-1954			
	22.00	65.00	150.00
41-45: 45-2pgs. showing E.C. staff	20.00	60.00	140.00
46-Low distribution; pre-advertised cover for unpublished 4th horror title 'Crypt of Terror' used on this book	25.00	75.00	175.00

TALES FROM THE CRYPT
July, 1990-No. 6, May, 1991 ($1.95, color, 68 pgs.) (#4 on: $2.00)
Gladstone Publishing

1-r/TFTC #33 & Crime S.S. #17; Davis-c(r)	.70	2.00	4.00
2-Davis-c(r)	.50	1.50	3.00
3-6: 3,5,6-Davis-c(r). 4-Craig-c(r)	.40	1.25	2.50

TALES OF ASGARD
Oct, 1968 (25 cents, 68 pages); Feb, 1984 ($1.25, 52 pgs.)
Marvel Comics Group

1-Thor r-/from Journey into Mystery #97-106; new Kirby-c			
	2.65	8.00	18.00
V2#1 (2/84)-Thor-r; Simonson-c		.50	1.00

TALES OF SUSPENSE (Captain America #100 on)
Jan, 1959-No. 99, March, 1968
Atlas (WPI No. 1,2/Male No. 3-12/VPI No. 13-18)/Marvel No. 19 on

	Good	Fine	N-Mint
1-Williamson-a, 5 pgs.	55.00	165.00	385.00
2,3: 3-Flying saucer-c/story	25.00	75.00	175.00
4-Williamson-a, 4 pgs; Kirby/Everett c/a	26.00	77.00	180.00
5-10	16.00	48.00	110.00
11,13-15,17-20: 14-Intro. Colossus	11.00	32.00	75.00
12-Crandall-a	11.50	34.00	80.00
16-1st Metallo (Iron Man prototype, 7/61)	12.00	36.00	85.00
21-25: 25-Last 10 cent issue	8.00	24.00	55.00
26-38: 32-Sazzik The Sorcerer app. (Dr. Strange prototype)	6.50	19.00	45.00
39 (3/63)-Origin/1st app. Iron Man & begin series; 1st Iron Man story has Kirby layouts	130.00	520.00	1300.00
40-Iron Man in new armor	81.00	243.00	565.00
41	45.00	135.00	310.00
42-45: 45-Intro. & 1st app. Happy & Pepper	19.00	57.00	130.00
46,47	11.00	32.00	75.00
48-New Iron Man armor	13.00	40.00	90.00
49-1st X-Men x-over (same date as X-Men #3, 1/64); 1st Tales of the Watcher back-up story	8.50	25.50	60.00
50,51: 50-1st app. Mandarin	6.50	19.00	45.00
52-1st app. The Black Widow (4/64)	9.30	28.00	65.00
53-Origin & 2nd app. The Watcher (5/64); 2nd Black Widow app.	7.00	21.00	50.00
54-56	4.30	13.00	30.00
57-Origin/1st app. Hawkeye (9/64)	11.00	32.00	75.00
58-Captain America battles Iron Man (10/64)-Classic-c; 1st app. Cap in this title; 2nd Kraven app.	19.30	58.00	135.00
59-Iron Man plus Captain America double feature begins (11/64); 1st S.A. Captain America solo story; intro Jarvis, Avenger's butler; classic-c	16.00	48.00	110.00
60	5.70	17.00	40.00
61,62,64: 62-Origin Mandarin (2/65)	4.50	14.00	32.00
63-1st Silver Age origin Captain America(3/65)	11.50	34.00	80.00
65-1st Silver Age Red Skull (6/65)	6.50	19.00	45.00
66-Origin Red Skull	6.50	19.00	45.00

67-99: 69-1st app. Titanium Man. 75-1st app. Agent 13 later named Sharon Carter.
76-Intro Batroc & Sharon Carter, Agent 13 of Shield. 79-1st app. Cosmic

	Good	Fine	N-Mint
Cube. 92-1st Nick Fury x-over (as Agent of Shield, 8/67). 94-Intro Modok. 95-Capt. America's I.D. revealed. 99-Becomes Captain America with #100			
	2.85	8.50	20.00

TALES OF THE MYSTERIOUS TRAVELER
Aug, 1956-No. 13, June, 1959; V2#14, Oct, 1985-No. 15, Dec, 1985
Charlton Comics

	Good	Fine	N-Mint
1-No Ditko-a	17.00	51.00	120.00
2-Ditko-a(1)	14.00	40.00	95.00
3-Ditko-c/a(1)	12.00	36.00	85.00
4-6-Ditko-c/a(3-4 stories each)	19.00	56.00	130.00
7-9-Ditko-a(1-2 each)	12.00	36.00	85.00
10,11-Ditko-c/a(3-4 each)	15.00	45.00	105.00
12,13	5.30	16.00	38.00
V2#14,15 (1985)-Ditko-c/a		.40	.80

TALES OF THE TEEN TITANS (Formerly The New Teen Titans)
No. 41, April, 1984-No. 91, July, 1988 (75 cents)
DC Comics

	Good	Fine	N-Mint
41,45-59: 46-Aqualad & Aquagirl join. 50-Double size. 53-Intro Azrael. 56-Intro Jinx. 57-Neutron app. 59-r/DC Comics Presents #26			
		.40	.80
42-44:Deathstroke the Terminator app. (origin #44). 44-Dick Grayson becomes Nightwing (3rd to be Nightwing) & joins Titans; Jericho joins also.			
	1.00	3.00	6.00
60-91: r/New Teen Titans Baxter series. 68-B. Smith-c. 70-Origin Kole. #83-91 are $1.00 cover		.40	.80
Annual 3(`84; $1.25)-Death of Terra		.60	1.20
Annual 4(11/86, reprints), 5('87)		.60	1.20

TALES OF THE UNEXPECTED (The Unexpected #105 on)
Feb-Mar, 1956-No. 104, Dec-Jan, 1967-68
National Periodical Publications

	Good	Fine	N-Mint
1	43.00	130.00	300.00
2	19.00	56.00	130.00
3-5	11.50	34.00	80.00
6-10	8.50	25.50	60.00
11,14	5.00	15.00	35.00

	Good	Fine	N-Mint
12,13,15-18,21-24: All have Kirby-a. 16-Character named 'Thor' with a magic hammer (not like later Thor)	5.70	17.00	40.00
19,20,25-39	3.60	11.00	25.00
40-Space Ranger begins (8/59), ends #82 (1st app. in Showcase #15)	35.00	105.00	240.00
41,42-Space Ranger stories	11.50	34.00	80.00
43-1st Space Ranger cover & story	16.00	48.00	110.00
44-46	8.50	25.50	60.00
47-50	5.70	17.00	40.00
51-67: 67-Last 10 cent issue	4.00	12.00	28.00
68-82: 82-Last Space Ranger	2.15	6.50	15.00
83-100: 91-1st Automan (also in #94,97)	1.15	3.50	8.00
101-104	.85	2.60	6.00

TALES TO ASTONISH (Becomes The Incredible Hulk #102 on)
Jan, 1959-No. 101, March, 1968
Atlas (MAP No. 1/ZPC No. 2-14/VPI No. 15-21)/Marvel No. 22 on

	Good	Fine	N-Mint
1-Jack Davis-a	55.00	165.00	385.00
2-Ditko-c	25.00	75.00	175.00
3-5: 5-Williamson-a (4 pgs.)	19.00	58.00	135.00
6-10	16.00	48.00	110.00
11-20	9.30	28.00	65.00
21-26,28-34	5.70	17.00	40.00
27-1st Antman app. (1/62); last 10 cent issue	129.00	385.00	900.00
35-(9/62)-2nd app. Antman, 1st in costume; begin series	90.00	270.00	630.00
36	40.00	120.00	280.00
37-40	19.00	58.00	135.00
41-43	11.50	34.00	80.00
44-Origin & 1st app. The Wasp (6/63)	13.00	40.00	90.00
45-48	8.00	24.00	55.00
49-Antman becomes Giant Man	11.50	34.00	80.00
50-56,58: 50-Origin/1st app. Human Top. 52-Origin/1st app. Black Knight (2/64)	4.30	13.00	30.00
57-Early Spider-Man app. (7/64)	7.00	21.00	50.00
59-Giant Man vs. Hulk feature story	8.50	25.50	60.00
60-Giant Man/Hulk double feature begins	11.50	34.00	80.00
61-69: 62-1st app./origin The Leader; new Wasp costume. 65-New Giant Man costume. 68-New Human Top costume. 69-Last Giant Man	4.30	13.00	30.00

	Good	Fine	N-Mint
70-Sub-Mariner & Incredible Hulk begins	6.50	19.00	45.00
71-81,83-91,94-99,101: 90-1st app. The Abomination			
	3.15	9.50	22.00
82-1st Iron Man x-over (outside The Avengers)	4.30	13.00	30.00
92,93-1st Silver Surfer x-over outside of Fantastic Four (7/67 & 8/67)			
	4.30	13.00	30.00
100-Hulk battles Sub-Mariner	4.30	13.00	30.00

TARGET COMICS
Feb, 1940-V10#3 (#105), Aug-Sept, 1949
Funnies, Inc./Novelty Publications/Star Publications

	Good	Fine	N-Mint
V1#1-Origin & 1st app. Manowar, The White Streak by Burgos, & Bulls-Eye Bill by Everett; City Editor (ends #5), High Grass Twins by Jack Cole (ends #4), T-Men by Joe Simon (ends #9), Rip Rory (ends #4), Fantastic Feature Films by Tarpe Mills (ends #39, & Calling 2-R (ends #14) begin			
	182.00	550.00	1275.00
2	86.00	257.00	600.00
3,4	61.00	182.00	425.00
5-Origin The White Streak in text; Space Hawk by Wolverton begins (See Blue Bolt)	143.00	430.00	1000.00
6-The Chameleon by Everett begins; White Streak origin cont'd. in text			
	81.00	242.00	565.00
7-Wolverton Spacehawk-c (Scarce)	186.00	557.00	1300.00
8,9,12	59.00	175.00	410.00
10-Intro. & 1st app. The Target; Kirby-c	84.00	250.00	585.00
11-Origin The Target & The Targeteers	80.00	240.00	560.00
V2#1-Target by Bob Wood; flag-c	43.00	130.00	300.00
2-10-part Treasure Island serial begins; Harold Delay-a			
	41.00	122.00	285.00
3-5: 4-Kit Carter, The Cadet begins	30.00	90.00	210.00
6-9:Red Seal with White Streak in 6-10	30.00	90.00	210.00
10-Classic-c	36.00	107.00	250.00
11,12: 12-10-part Last of the Mohicans serial begins; Delay-a			
	30.00	90.00	210.00
V3#1-10-Last Wolverton issue. 8-Flag-c; 6-part Gulliver Travels serial begins; Delay-a	30.00	90.00	210.00
11,12	5.30	16.00	38.00
V4#1-5,7-12	3.15	9.50	22.00
6-Targetoons by Wolverton, 1 pg.	3.15	9.50	22.00
V5#1-8	2.65	8.00	18.00

	Good	Fine	N-Mint
V6#1-10, V7#1-12	2.30	7.00	16.00
V8#1,3-5,8,9,11,12	2.00	6.00	14.00
2,6,7-Krigstein-a	2.65	8.00	18.00
10-L.B. Cole-c	5.30	16.00	38.00
V9#1,3,6,8,10,12, V10#2-L.B. Cole-c	5.30	16.00	38.00
V9#2,4,5,7,9,11, V10#1,3	2.00	6.00	14.00

Tarzan #8, © Edgar Rice Burroughs

TARZAN (... of the Apes #138 on; also see Crackajack Funnies, Popular Comics, Sparkler Comics & Tip Top Comics)
1-2/48-No. 131, 7-8/62; No. 132, 11/62-No. 206, 2/72
Dell Publishing Co./Gold Key No. 132 on

1-Jesse Marsh-a begins	79.00	235.00	550.00
2	47.00	140.00	325.00
3-5	34.00	103.00	240.00
6-10: 6-1st Tantor the Elephant. 7-1st Valley of the Monsters			
	27.00	81.00	190.00

	Good	Fine	N-Mint
11-15: 11-Two Against the Jungle begins, ends #24. 13-Lex Barker photo-c begin			
	23.00	70.00	160.00
16-20	17.00	51.00	120.00
21-24,26-30	13.00	40.00	90.00
25-1st "Brothers of the Spear" episode; series ends #156,160,161,196-206			
	16.00	48.00	110.00
31-40	8.00	24.00	55.00
41-54: Last Barker photo-c	6.50	19.00	45.00
55-60: 56-Eight pg. Boy story	5.00	15.00	35.00
61,62,64-70	4.00	12.00	28.00
63-Two Tarzan stories, 1 by Manning	4.30	13.00	30.00
71-79	3.15	9.50	22.00
80-99: 80-Gordon Scott photo-c begin	3.50	10.50	24.00
100	4.30	13.00	30.00
101-109	2.85	8.50	20.00
110 (Scarce)-Last photo-c	3.15	9.50	22.00
111-120	2.30	7.00	16.00
121-131: Last Dell issue	1.70	5.00	12.00
132-154: 132-1st Gold Key issue	1.50	4.50	10.00
155-Origin Tarzan	1.70	5.00	12.00
156-161: 157-Banlu, Dog of the Arande begins, ends #159, 195. 169-Leopard Girl			
app.	1.00	3.00	7.00
162,165,168,171 (TV)-Ron Ely photo covers	1.30	4.00	9.00
163,164,166-167,169-170: 169-Leopard Girl app.	.85	2.60	6.00
172-199,201-206: 178-Tarzan origin r-/#155; Leopard Girl app, also in #179,190-			
193	.70	2.00	5.00
200 (Scarce)	.85	2.60	6.00
Story Digest 1(6/70)-G.K.	.85	2.60	6.00

TARZAN (Continuation of Gold Key series)
No. 207, April, 1972-No. 258, Feb, 1977
National Periodical Publications

	Good	Fine	N-Mint
207-Origin Tarzan by Joe Kubert, part 1; John Carter begins (origin); 52 pg. issues			
thru #209	.70	2.00	4.00
208,209: Origin, parts 2-4. 209-Last John Carter	.35	1.00	2.00
210,211: 210-Kubert-a. 211-Hogarth, Kubert-a	.25	.75	1.50
212-214: Adaptations from "Jungle Tales of Tarzan." 213-Beyond the Farthest Star			
begins, ends #218	.25	.75	1.50
215-218,224,225-All by Kubert. 215-part Foster-r	.25	.75	1.50

	Good	Fine	N-Mint
219-229: 219-223: Adapts "The Return of Tarzan" by Kubert. 226- Manning-a	.25	.75	1.50
230-100 pgs.; Kubert, Kaluta-a(p); Korak begins, ends #234; Carson of Venus app.	.35	1.00	2.00
231-234: Adapts "Tarzan and the Lion Man;" all 100 pgs.; Rex, the Wonder Dog r-#232, 233	.25	.75	1.50
235-Last Kubert issue; 100 pgs.	.25	.75	1.50
236-258: 238-(68 pgs.). 240-243 adapts "Tarzan & the Castaways." 250-256 adapts "Tarzan the Untamed." 252,253-r/#213	.25	.75	1.50

TEENAGE MUTANT NINJA TURTLES
1984-Present ($1.50-$1.75, B&W; all 44-52 pgs.)
Mirage Studios

	Good	Fine	N-Mint
1-1st printing (3000 copies)-Only printing to have ad for Gobbledygook #1 & 2	54.00	163.00	325.00
1-2nd printing (6/84) (15,000 copies)	11.70	35.00	70.00
1-3rd printing (2/85) (36,000 copies)	5.80	17.50	35.00
1-4th printing, new-c (50,000 copies)	3.35	10.00	20.00
1-5th printing, new-c (8/88-c, 11/88 inside)	.70	2.00	4.00
1-Counterfeit. Note: Most counterfeit copies have a ½-inch wide white streak or scratch marks across the center of back cover. Black part of cover is a bluish black instead of a deep black. Inside paper is very white & inside cover is bright white. These counterfeit the 1st printings.			
2-1st printing (15,000 copies)	17.00	50.00	100.00
2-2nd printing	2.50	7.50	15.00
2-3rd printing; new Corben-c/a (2/85)	1.00	3.00	6.00
2-Counterfeit with glossy cover stock.			
3-1st printing	7.50	22.50	45.00
3-Variant, 500 copies, given away in NYC. Has 'Laird's Photo' in white rather than light blue	13.30	40.00	80.00
3-2nd printing; contains new back-up story	1.00	3.00	6.00
4-1st printing	4.15	12.50	25.00
4-2nd printing (5/87)	.70	2.00	4.00
5-1st printing; Fugitoid begins, ends #7	3.00	9.00	18.00
5-2nd printing (11/87)	.70	2.00	4.00
6-1st printing (4/87-c, 5/87 inside)	2.50	7.50	15.00
6-2nd printing	.50	1.50	3.00
7-4pg. Corben color insert; 1st color TMNT	2.50	7.50	15.00
7-2nd printing (1/89)	.50	1.50	3.00
8-Cerebus guest stars	1.70	5.00	10.00

	Good	Fine	N-Mint
9,10: 9 (9/86)-Rip In Time by Corben	1.15	3.50	7.00
11-15	.85	2.50	5.00
16-18: 18-Mark Bode'-a	.70	2.00	4.00
18-2nd printing ($2.25, color, 44 pgs.)-New-c	.40	1.15	2.30
19-40: 19-Begin $1.75-c. 24-26-Veitch-c/a	.35	1.00	2.00
Book 1,2($1.50, B&W): 2-Corben-c	.25	.75	1.50

TEENAGE MUTANT NINJA TURTLES ADVENTURES (TV)
8/88-No. 3, 12/88; 3/89-Present ($1.00, color)
Archie Comics

	Good	Fine	N-Mint
1-Adapts TV cartoon; not by Eastman/Laird	.85	2.50	5.00
2,3 (Mini-series)	.50	1.50	3.00
1 (2nd on going series)	.50	1.50	3.00
2-5: 5-Begins original stories not based on TV	.35	1.00	2.00
6-24: 14-Donald Simpson-a(p)		.60	1.30
1-11: 2nd printings		.50	1.00
nn ($2.50, Spring, 1991, 68 pgs.)-(Meet Archie)	.40	1.25	2.50

NOTE: There are 2nd printings of #1-11 w/B&W inside covers. Originals are color.

TEEN TITANS (See Brave & the Bold, Marvel & DC Present, New Teen Titans
and Showcase)
12/66-No. 43, 1-2/73; No. 44, 11/76-No. 53, 2/78
National Periodical Publications/DC Comics

	Good	Fine	N-Mint
1-Titans join Peace Corps; Batman, Flash, Aquaman, Wonder Woman cameos			
	16.00	48.00	110.00
2	7.00	21.00	50.00
3-5: 4-Speedy app.	3.60	11.00	25.00
6-10: 6-Doom Patrol app.	2.65	8.00	18.00
11-19: 11-Speedy app. 18-1st app. Starfire (11-12/68). 19-Wood-i; Speedy begins			
as regular	2.00	6.00	14.00
20-22: All Neal Adams-a. 21-Hawk & Dove app. 22-Origin Wonder Girl			
	2.15	6.50	15.00
23-30: 23-Wonder Girl dons new costume. 25-Flash, Aquaman, Batman, Green Arrow, Green Lantern, Superman, & Hawk & Dove guests; 1st app. Lilith who joins T.T. West in #50. 29-Hawk & Dove & Ocean Master app. 30-Aquagirl app.	1.15	3.50	8.00
31-43: 31-Hawk & Dove app. 36,37-Superboy-r. 38-Green Arrow/ Speedy-r; Aquaman/Aqualad story. 39-Hawk & Dove-r. (36-39: 52 pgs.)	1.00	3.00	6.00

	Good	Fine	N-Mint
44,45,47,49,51,52: 44-Mal becomes the Guardian	.70	2.00	4.00
46-Joker's daughter begins	1.35	4.00	9.00
48-Intro Bumblebee; Joker's daughter becomes Harlequin			
	1.35	4.00	9.00
50-1st revival original Bat-Girl; intro. Teen Titans West			
	1.00	3.00	7.00
53-Origin retold	.85	2.50	5.00

TERMINATOR, THE
Sept, 1988-No. 17, 1989 ($1.75, color, Baxter paper)
Now Comics

	Good	Fine	N-Mint
1-Based on movie	3.35	10.00	20.00
2	1.70	5.00	10.00
3-5	1.00	3.00	6.00
6-10	.70	2.00	4.00
11,13-17	.40	1.25	2.50
12 ($1.75, 52 pgs.)-Intro. John Connor	.50	1.50	3.00

TERMINATOR, THE
Aug, 1990-No. 4, Nov, 1990 ($2.50, color, mini-series)
Dark Horse Comics

	Good	Fine	N-Mint
1-Set 39 years later than the movie	.60	1.75	3.50
2-4	.40	1.25	2.50

TERMINATOR: ALL MY FUTURES PAST, THE
V3#1, Aug, 1990-V3#2, Sept, 1990 ($1.75, color, mini-series)
Now Comics

	Good	Fine	N-Mint
V3#1,2	.40	1.25	2.50

TERMINATOR: THE BURNING EARTH, THE
V2#1, Mar, 1990-V2#5, July, 1990 ($1.75, color, mini-series)
Now Comics

	Good	Fine	N-Mint
V2#1	1.00	3.00	6.00
2	.70	2.00	4.00
3-5	.40	1.25	2.50

TERRY AND THE PIRATES (See Popular Comics & Super Comics)
No. 3, 4/47-No. 26, 4/51; No. 26, 6/55-No. 28, 10/55 (Daily strip-r)
Harvey Publications/Charlton No. 26-28 (Two #26's exist)

	Good	Fine	N-Mint
3(#1)-Boy Explorers by S&K; Terry & the Pirates begin by Caniff			
	22.00	65.00	150.00
4-S&K Boy Explorers	14.00	43.00	100.00
5-10	7.00	21.00	50.00
11-Man in Black app. by Powell	7.00	21.00	50.00
12-20: 16-Girl threatened with red hot poker	5.35	16.00	37.00
21-26(4/51)-Last Caniff issue	4.75	14.00	33.00
26-28('55)-Not by Caniff	3.70	11.00	26.00

TERRY-TOONS COMICS (Later issues titled "Paul Terry's...")
Oct, 1942-No. 86, May, 1951 (Two #60s exist)
Timely/Marvel No. 1-60 (8/47)/St. John No. 60 (9/47) on

1 (Scarce)-Features characters that 1st app. on movie screen; Gandy Goose begins			
	57.00	170.00	400.00
2	29.00	85.00	200.00
3-5	17.00	51.00	120.00
6-10: 7-Hitler, Hirohito, Mussolini-c	11.50	34.00	80.00
11-20	8.00	24.00	55.00
21-37	5.00	15.00	35.00
38-Mighty Mouse begins (1st app., 11/45)	43.00	130.00	300.00
39-2nd Mighty Mouse app.	14.00	43.00	100.00
40-49: 43-Infinity-c	6.50	19.00	45.00
50-1st app. Heckle & Jeckle	14.00	43.00	100.00
51-60(8/47): 55-Infinity-c. 60(9/47)-Atomic explosion panel			
	4.50	14.00	32.00
61-86	3.00	9.00	21.00

TEX RITTER WESTERN (Movie star; singing cowboy)
Oct, 1950-No. 46, May, 1959 (Photo-c: 1-21) (See Western Hero)
Fawcett No. 1-20 (1/54)/Charlton No. 21 on

1-Tex Ritter, his stallion White Flash & dog Fury begin; photo front/ back-c begin			
	33.00	100.00	230.00
2	18.00	54.00	125.00
3-5: 5-Last photo back-c	14.00	43.00	100.00
6-10	12.00	36.00	85.00

	Good	Fine	N-Mint
11-19	8.00	24.00	55.00
20-Last Fawcett issue (1/54)	9.30	28.00	65.00
21-1st Charlton issue; photo-c (3/54)	9.30	28.00	65.00
22-B&W photo back-c begin, end #32	5.00	15.00	35.00
23-30: 23-25-Young Falcon app.	3.70	11.00	26.00
31-38,40-45	3.15	9.50	22.00
39-Williamson-a; Whitman-c (1/58)	4.35	13.00	30.00
46-Last issue	3.50	10.50	24.00

THANOS QUEST, THE (See Captain Marvel #25, Iron Man #55, Logans's Run & Warlock #9)
1990-No. 2, 1990 ($4.95, color, squarebound, 52 pgs.)
Marvel Comics

1-Starlin scripts & covers	1.15	3.50	7.00
2	.85	2.50	5.00

THING!, THE
Feb, 1952-No. 17, Nov, 1954
Song Hits No. 1,2/Capitol Stories/Charlton

1	29.00	85.00	200.00
2,3	21.00	62.00	145.00
4-6,8,10: 5-Severed head-c; headlights	14.00	43.00	100.00
7-Injury to eye-c & inside panel. E.C. swipes from Vault of Horror #28	29.00	85.00	200.00
9-Used in **SOTI**, pg. 388 & illo-"Stomping on the face is a form of brutality which modern children learn early"	32.00	95.00	220.00
11-Necronomicon story; Hansel & Gretel parody; Injury-to-eye panel; Check-a	25.00	75.00	175.00
12-"Cinderella" parody; Ditko-c/a; lingerie panels	37.00	110.00	260.00
13,15-Ditko c/a(3 & 5); 13-Ditko E.C. swipe/Haunt of Fear #15(#1)-"House of Horror"	37.00	110.00	260.00
14-Extreme violence/torture; Rumpelstiltskin story; Ditko-c/a(4)	37.00	110.00	260.00
16-Injury to eye panel	19.00	58.00	135.00
17-Ditko-c; classic parody-"Through the Looking Glass;" Powell-a(r)	30.00	90.00	210.00

THIS MAGAZINE IS HAUNTED
Oct, 1951-No. 14, 12/53; No. 15, 2/54-V3#21, Nov, 1954
Fawcett Publications/Charlton No. 15(2/54) on

	Good	Fine	N-Mint
1-Evans-a(i?)	20.00	60.00	140.00
2,5-Evans-a	14.00	43.00	100.00
3,4	7.00	21.00	50.00
6-9,11,12	5.70	17.00	40.00
10-Severed head-c	9.30	28.00	65.00
13-Severed head-c/story	8.50	25.50	60.00
14,17-Ditko-c/a(3&4). 17-Blood drainage story	16.00	48.00	110.00
15,20	5.00	15.00	35.00
16,19-Ditko-c. 19-Injury-to-eye panel; story r-/#1	11.00	32.00	75.00
18-Ditko-c/a; E.C. swipe/Haunt of Fear 5; injury-to-eye panel			
	14.00	40.00	95.00
21-Ditko-c, Evans-a	10.00	30.00	70.00

THOR (Formerly Journey Into Mystery) (The Mighty Thor #? on)
March, 1966-Present (Also see The Avengers #1 & Tales of Asgard)
Marvel Comics Group

126	9.50	28.50	66.00
127-133,135-140	3.70	11.00	26.00
134-Intro High Evolutionary	5.30	16.00	37.00
141-157,159,160: 146-Inhumans begin, end #151. 146,147-Origin The Inhumans. 148,149-Origin Black Bolt in each; 149-Origin Medusa, Crystal, Maximus, Gorgon, Kornak	2.70	8.00	19.00
158-Origin-r/#83; 158,159-Origin Dr. Blake	6.70	20.00	47.00
161,163,164,167,170-179-Last Kirby issue	1.85	5.50	13.00
162,168,169-Origin Galactus	3.15	9.50	22.00
165,166-Warlock (Him) app.	2.00	6.00	14.00
180,181-Neal Adams-a	1.30	4.00	9.00
182-192,194-200	.70	2.00	4.00
193-(52 pgs.); Silver Surfer x-over	3.00	9.00	21.00
201-250: 225-Intro. Firelord	.50	1.50	3.00
251-280: 271-Iron Man x-over. 274-Death of Balder the Brave	.40	1.25	2.50
281-299: 294-Origin Asgard & Odin	.35	1.00	2.00
300-End of Asgard; origin of Odin & The Destroyer	.70	2.00	4.00

Thor #199, © Marvel Comics

	Good	Fine	N-Mint
301-336: 316-Iron Man x-over	.25	.75	1.50
337-Simonson-c/a begins, ends #382; Beta Ray Bill becomes new Thor			
	1.15	3.50	7.00
338	.50	1.50	3.00
339,340: 340-Donald Blake returns as Thor	.25	.75	1.50
341-373,375-381,383: 373-X-Factor tie-in		.50	1.00
374-Mutant massacre; X-Factor app.	1.35	4.00	8.00
382-($1.25)-Anniversary issue; last Simonson-a	.35	1.00	2.00
384-Intro. new Thor	.35	1.00	2.00
385-399,401-410,413-428: 395-Intro Earth Force. 427,428-Excalibur x-over			
		.50	1.00
400-($1.75, 68 pgs.)-Origin Loki	.40	1.25	2.50
411-Intro. New Warriors (cameo)	.50	1.50	3.00
412-1st full app. New Warriors	1.35	4.00	8.00
429,430-Ghost Rider app.	.40	1.25	2.50
431,433-440		.50	1.00
432 ($1.50, 52 pgs.)	.25	.75	1.50

	Good	Fine	N-Mint
Special 2(9/66)-See Journey Into Mystery for 1st annual			
	4.30	13.00	30.00
King Size Special 3(1/71)	.85	2.60	6.00
Special 4(12/71)	.85	2.60	6.00
Annual 5,7,8: 5(11/76). 7(1978). 8(1979)	.70	2.00	5.00
Annual 6 (10/77)-Guardians of the Galaxy app.	.70	2.00	5.00
Annual 9-12: 9(1981). 10(1982). 11(1983). 12(1984)	.50	1.50	3.00
Annual 13-16: 13(1985). 14(1989, $2.00, 68 pgs.)-Atlantis Attacks. 15(1990, $2.00, 68 pgs.). 16('91, $2.00, 68 pgs.)	.35	1.00	2.00

3-D BATMAN
1953, Reprinted in 1966
National Periodical Publications

	Good	Fine	N-Mint
1953-Reprints Batman #42 & 48; Tommy Tomorrow app. (25 cents)			
	79.00	235.00	550.00
1966-Tommy Tomorrow app.	25.00	75.00	175.00

3-D DOLLY
December, 1953 (2 pairs glasses included)
Harvey Publications

	Good	Fine	N-Mint
1-Richie Rich story redrawn from his 1st app. in Little Dot #1			
	13.00	40.00	90.00

3-D SHEENA, JUNGLE QUEEN
1953
Fiction House Magazines

	Good	Fine	N-Mint
1	40.00	120.00	280.00

THREE STOOGES
No. 1043, Oct-Dec, 1959-No. 55, June, 1972
Dell Publishing Co./Gold Key No. 10 (10/62) on

	Good	Fine	N-Mint
4-Color 1043 (#1)	8.50	25.50	60.00
4-Color 1078,1127,1170,1187	5.70	17.00	40.00
6(9-11/61)-10: 6-Professor Putter begins; ends #16			
	4.30	13.00	30.00
11-14,16-20: 17-The Little Monsters begin (5/64)(1st app.?)			
	4.00	12.00	28.00

	Good	Fine	N-Mint
15-Go Around the World in a Daze (movie scenes)	4.50	14.00	32.00
21,23-30	3.00	9.00	21.00
22-Movie scenes/'The Outlaws Is Coming'	4.30	13.00	30.00
31-55	2.30	7.00	16.00

THRILLING COMICS
Feb, 1940-No. 80, April, 1951
Better Publ./Nedor/Standard Comics

	Good	Fine	N-Mint
1-Origin Doc Strange (37 pgs.); Nickie Norton of the Secret Service begins			
	68.00	205.00	475.00
2-The Rio Kid, The Woman in Red, Pinocchio begins			
	30.00	90.00	210.00
3-The Ghost & Lone Eagle begin	27.00	81.00	190.00
4-10	18.00	54.00	125.00
11-18,20	14.00	41.00	95.00
19-Origin The American Crusader (1st app?), ends #39,41			
	19.50	58.00	135.00
21-30: 24-Intro. Mike, Doc Strange's sidekick. 29-Last Rio Kid			
	12.00	36.00	85.00
31-40: 36-Commando Cubs begin	10.00	30.00	70.00
41,44-Hittler-c	10.00	30.00	70.00
42,43,45-52: 52-The Ghost ends	8.00	24.00	55.00
53-The Phantom Detective begins; The Cavalier app.; no Commando Cubs			
	8.00	24.00	55.00
54-The Cavalier app.; no Commando Cubs	8.00	24.00	55.00
55-Lone Eagle ends	8.00	24.00	55.00
56-Princess Pantha begins	16.00	48.00	110.00
57-60	13.00	40.00	90.00
61-66: 61-Ingels-a; The Lone Eagle app. 65-Last Phantom Detective & Commando Cubs. 66-Frazetta text illo	13.00	40.00	90.00
67,70-73: Frazetta-a(5-7 pgs.) in each. 72-Sea Eagle app.			
	18.00	54.00	125.00
68,69-Frazetta-a(2), 8 & 6 pgs.; 9 & 7 pgs.	19.00	57.00	132.00
74-Last Princess Pantha; Tara app. Buck Ranger, Cowboy Detective begins			
	7.00	21.00	50.00
75-78: 75-Western format begins	4.00	12.00	28.00
79-Krigstein-a	5.30	16.00	38.00
80-Severin & Elder, Celardo, Moreira-a	5.30	16.00	38.00

THUNDER AGENTS (Also see Dynamo & Noman)
11/65-No. 17, 12/67; No. 18, 9/68, No. 19, 11/68, No. 20, 11/69 (No. 1-16: 68 pgs.;
    No. 17 on: 52 pgs.)(All are 25 cents)
Tower Comics

	Good	Fine	N-Mint
1-Origin & 1st app. Dynamo, Noman, Menthor, & The Thunder Squad; 1st app.			
The Iron Maiden	8.00	24.00	55.00
2-Death of Egghead	4.30	13.00	30.00
3-5: 4-Guy Gilbert becomes Lightning who joins Thunder Squad; Iron Maiden			
app.	3.15	9.50	22.00
6-10: 7-Death of Menthor. 8-Origin & 1st app. The Raven			
	2.00	6.00	14.00
11-15: 13-Undersea Agent app.; no Raven story	1.30	4.00	9.00
16-19	1.00	3.00	7.00
20-Special Collectors Edition; all reprints	.70	2.00	4.00

TIM HOLT (Movie star) (Red Mask #42 on; see Crack Western #72)
1948-No. 41, April-May, 1954 (All 36 pgs.)
Magazine Enterprises

	Good	Fine	N-Mint
1-(A-1 #14)-Photo-c begin, end No. 18, 29; Tim Holt, his horse Lightning &			
sidekick Chito begin	38.00	115.00	265.00
2-(A-1 #17)(9-10/48)	24.00	71.00	165.00
3-(A-1 #19)-Photo back-c	16.00	48.00	110.00
4(1-2/49),5: 5-Photo back-c	12.00	36.00	85.00
6-1st app. The Calico Kid (alias Rex Fury), his horse Ebony & sidekick Sing-			
Song (begin series); photo back-c	14.00	41.00	95.00
7-10: 7-Calico Kid by Ayers. 8-Calico Kid by Guardineer. 9-Map of Tim's Home			
Range	10.00	30.00	70.00
11-The Calico Kid becomes The Ghost Rider (Origin & 1st app.) by Dick Ayers;			
his horse Spectre & sidekick Sing-Song begin series			
	27.00	81.00	185.00
12-16,18-Last photo-c	7.00	21.00	50.00
17-Frazetta Ghost Rider-c	25.00	75.00	175.00
19,22,24: 19-Last Tim Holt-c; Bolle line-drawn-c begin			
	5.70	17.00	40.00
20-Tim Holt becomes Redmask (Origin); begin series; Redmask-c #20-on			
	9.50	28.50	65.00
21-Frazetta Ghost Rider/Redmask-c	21.50	65.00	150.00
23-Frazetta Redmask-c	17.00	51.00	120.00

	Good	Fine	N-Mint
25-1st app. Black Phantom	11.00	32.00	75.00
26-30: 28-Wild Bill Hickok, Bat Masterson team up with Redmask. 29-B&W			
photo-c	5.00	15.00	35.00
31-33-Ghost Rider ends	4.50	14.00	32.00
34-Tales of the Ghost Rider begins (horror)-Classic "The Flower Women" &			
"Hard Boiled Harry!"	5.70	17.00	40.00
35-Last Tales of the Ghost Rider	5.00	15.00	35.00
36-The Ghost Rider returns, ends #41; liquid hallucinogenic drug story			
	5.70	17.00	40.00
37-Ghost Rider classic "To Touch Is to Die!," about Inca treasure			
	5.70	17.00	40.00
38-The Black Phantom begins (not in #39); classic Ghost Rider "The Phantom			
Guns of Feather Gap!"	5.70	17.00	40.00
39-41: All 3-D effect c/stories	8.50	25.50	60.00

TIP TOP COMICS

4/36-No. 210, 1957; No. 211, 11-1/57-58-No. 225, 5-7/61
United Features #1-187/St. John #188-210/Dell Publishing Co. #211 on

	Good	Fine	VF-NM
1-Tarzan by Hal Foster, Li'l Abner, Broncho Bill, Fritzi Ritz, Ella Cinders, Capt.			
& The Kids begin; strip-r (1st comic book app. of each)			
	195.00	490.00	1175.00
2	90.00	225.00	540.00
3	61.00	182.00	425.00
4	46.00	137.00	320.00
5-10: 7-Photo & biography of Edgar Rice Burroughs. 8-Christmas-c			
	36.00	107.00	250.00
	Good	Fine	N-Mint
11-20: 20-Christmas-c	27.00	81.00	190.00
21-40: 36-Kurtzman panel (1st published comic work)			
	24.00	70.00	165.00
41-Has 1st Tarzan Sunday	24.00	70.00	165.00
42-50: 43-Mort Walker panel	20.00	60.00	140.00
51-53	17.00	51.00	120.00
54-Origin Mirror Man & Triple Terror, also featured on cover			
	22.00	65.00	150.00
55,56,58,60: Last Tarzan by Foster	14.00	43.00	100.00
57,59,61,62-Tarzan by Hogarth	19.00	57.00	130.00
63-80: 65,67-70,72-74,77,78-No Tarzan	9.30	28.00	65.00
81-90	8.50	25.50	60.00

	Good	Fine	N-Mint
91-99	6.00	18.00	42.00
100	7.00	21.00	50.00
101-140: 110-Gordo story. 111-Li'l Abner app. 118, 132-No Tarzan			
	4.00	12.00	28.00
141-170: 145,151-Gordo stories. 157-Last Li'l Abner; lingerie panels			
	2.85	8.50	20.00
171-188-Tarzan reprints by B. Lubbers in all. #177?-Peanuts by Schulz begins; no			
Peanuts in #178,179,181-183	3.15	9.50	22.00
189-225	1.85	5.50	13.00

T-MAN
Sept, 1951-No. 38, Dec, 1956
Quality Comics Group

	Good	Fine	N-Mint
1-Jack Cole-a	14.00	43.00	100.00
2-Crandall-c	8.50	25.50	60.00
3,6-8: All Crandall-c	7.00	21.00	50.00
4,5-Crandall-c/a each	8.00	24.00	55.00
9,10-Crandall-c	5.70	17.00	40.00
11-Used in POP, pg. 95 & color illo.	4.30	13.00	30.00
12-19,21,22,24,26: 24-Last pre-code (4/55)	2.85	8.50	20.00
20,23-H-Bomb explosion-c/stories	6.00	18.00	42.00
25-All Crandall-a	5.00	15.00	35.00
27-38	2.30	7.00	16.00

TOMAHAWK (Son of ...on-c of #131-140; see Star Spangled Comics #69 & World's Finest Comics #65)
Sept-Oct, 1950-No. 140, May-June, 1972
National Periodical Publications

	Good	Fine	N-Mint
1-Tomahawk begins by F. Ray	54.00	160.00	375.00
2-Frazetta/Williamson-a, 4 pgs.	27.00	81.00	190.00
3-5	16.00	48.00	110.00
6-10: 7-Last 52 pgs.	12.00	36.00	85.00
11-20	8.00	24.00	55.00
21-27,30: Last pre-code (2/55)	6.00	18.00	42.00
28-1st app. Lord Shilling (arch-foe)	8.00	24.00	55.00
29-Frazetta-r/Jimmy Wakely #3 (3 pgs.)	12.00	36.00	84.00
31-40	5.00	15.00	35.00
41-50	3.50	10.50	24.00
51-56,58-60	2.65	8.00	18.00

	Good	Fine	N-Mint
57-Frazetta-r/Jimmy Wakely #6 (3 pgs.)	6.50	19.50	45.00
61-77: 77-Last 10 cent issue	1.70	5.00	12.00
78-85: 81-1st app. Miss Liberty. 83-Origin Tomahawk's Rangers			
	1.00	3.00	7.00
86-100: 96-Origin/1st app. The Hood, alias Lady Shilling			
	.70	2.00	4.00
101-110: 107-Origin/1st app. Thunder-Man	.50	1.50	3.00
111-130,132-138,140	.35	1.00	2.00
131-Frazetta-r/Jimmy Wakely #7 (3 pgs.); origin Firehair retold			
	.40	1.25	2.50
139-Frazetta-r/Star Spangled #113	.25	.75	1.50

TOMB OF DRACULA
April, 1972-No. 70, Aug, 1979
Marvel Comics Group

1-Colan-p in all	2.85	8.50	20.00
2-5: 3-Intro. Dr. Rachel Van Helsing & Inspector Chelm			
	1.50	4.50	10.00
6-10: 10-1st app. Blade the Vampire Slayer	1.10	3.30	7.50
11-20: 12-Brunner-c(p). 13-Origin Blade	.85	2.50	5.00
21-70: 50-Silver Surfer app. 70-Double size	.50	1.50	3.00

TOM MIX WESTERN (Movie, radio star) (Also see Crackajack Funnies, Master
    Comics, Popular Comics, Real Western Hero & Western Hero)
Jan, 1948-No. 61, May, 1953 (1-17: 52 pgs.)
Fawcett Publications

1 (Photo-c, 52 pgs.)-Tom Mix & his horse Tony begin; Tumbleweed Jr begins,			
ends #52,54,55	50.00	150.00	350.00
2 (Photo-c)	26.00	77.00	180.00
3-5 (Painted/photo-c): 5-Billy the Kid & Oscar app.			
	21.00	62.00	145.00
6,7 (Painted/photo-c)	17.00	51.00	120.00
8-Kinstler tempera-c	17.00	51.00	120.00
9,10 (Painted/photo-c)-Used in **SOTI**, pgs. 323-325			
	16.00	48.00	110.00
11-Kinstler oil-c	14.00	43.00	100.00
12 (Painted/photo-c)	12.00	36.00	85.00
13-17 (Painted-c, 52 pgs.)	12.00	36.00	85.00
18,22 (Painted-c, 36 pgs.)	10.00	30.00	70.00

	Good	Fine	N-Mint
19 (Photo-c, 52 pgs.)	12.00	36.00	85.00
20,21,23 (Painted-c, 52 pgs.)	10.00	30.00	70.00
24,25,27-29 (52 pgs.): 24-Photo-c begin, end #61. 29-Slim Pickens app.			
	10.00	30.00	70.00
26,30 (36 pgs.)	9.30	28.00	65.00
31-33,35-37,39,40,42 (52 pgs.): 39-Red Eagle app.			
	8.50	25.50	60.00
34,38 (36 pgs. begin)	7.00	21.00	50.00
41,43-60	5.00	15.00	35.00
61-Last issue	6.00	18.00	42.00

TOP-NOTCH COMICS (...Laugh #28-45)
Dec, 1939-No. 45, June, 1944
MLJ Magazines

	Good	Fine	N-Mint
1-Origin The Wizard; Kardak the Mystic Magician, Swift of the Secret Service (ends #3), Air Patrol, The Westpointer, Manhunters (by J. Cole), Mystic (ends #2) & Scott Rand (ends #3) begin	107.00	321.00	750.00
2-Dick Storm (ends #8), Stacy Knight M.D. (ends #4) begin; Jack Cole-a	52.00	155.00	365.00
3-Bob Phantom, Scott Rand on Mars begin; J. Cole-a	41.00	122.00	285.00
4-Origin/1st app. Streak Chandler on Mars; Moore of the Mounted only app.; J. Cole-a	35.00	105.00	245.00
5-Flag-c; origin/1st app. Galahad; Shanghai Sheridan begins (ends #8); Shield cameo	30.00	90.00	210.00
6-Meskin-a	26.00	77.00	180.00
7-The Shield x-over in Wizard; The Wizard dons new costume	38.00	115.00	265.00
8-Origin The Firefly & Roy, the Super Boy	43.00	130.00	300.00
9-Origin & 1st app. The Black Hood; Fran Frazier begins	107.00	320.00	750.00
10	44.00	132.00	310.00
11-20	29.00	86.00	200.00
21-30: 23,24-No Wizard, Roy app. in each. 25-Last Bob Phantom, Roy app. 26-Roy app. 27-Last Firefly. 28-Suzie begins. 29-Last Kardak	23.00	70.00	160.00
31-44: 33-Dotty & Ditto by Woggon begins. 44-Black Hood series ends	13.00	40.00	90.00
45-Last issue	8.00	24.00	55.00

TRANSFORMERS, THE (TV) (Also see G.I. Joe and...)
Sept, 1984-No. 80, July, 1991 (.75-$1.00) (Prices are for 1st printings only)
Marvel Comics Group

	Good	Fine	N-Mint
1-Based on Hasbro toys	.50	1.50	3.00
2,3	.35	1.00	2.00
4-10,75: 75-($1.50, 52 pgs.)	.25	.75	1.50
11-74,76-80: 21-Intro. Aerialbots. 54-Intro. Micromasters			
		.50	1.00

TRUE CRIME COMICS
No. 2, May, 1947; No. 3, July-Aug, 1948-No. 6, June-July, 1949; V2#1, Aug-Sept,
1949 (52 pgs.)
Magazine Village

	Good	Fine	N-Mint
2-Jack Cole-c/a; used in **SOTI**, pg. 81,82 plus illo.-"A sample of the injury-to-eye motif" & illo.-"Dragging living people to death;" used in **POP**, pg. 105; "Murder, Morphine and Me" classic drug propaganda story used by N.Y. Legis. Comm.	75.00	225.00	525.00
3-Classic Cole-c/a; drug story with hypo, opium den & withdrawing addict	52.00	155.00	365.00
4-Jack Cole-c/a; c-taken from a story panel in #3; r-(2) **SOTI** & **POP** stories/#2	45.00	135.00	315.00
5-Jack Cole-c; Marijuana racket story	24.00	73.00	170.00
6	11.50	34.00	80.00
V2#1-Used in **SOTI**, pgs. 81,82 & illo.-"Dragging living people to death;" Toth, Wood (3 pgs.), Roussos-a; Cole-r from #2	35.00	105.00	245.00

TUROK, SON OF STONE
No. 596, 12/54-No. 29, 9/62; No. 30, 12/62-No. 91, 7/74; No. 92, 9/74-No. 125,
1/80; No. 126, 3/81-No. 130, 4/82
Dell Publ. Co. No. 1-29/Gold Key No. 30-91/Gold Key or Whitman No. 92-
125/Whitman No. 126 on

	Good	Fine	N-Mint
4-Color 596(#1)-1st app./origin Turok & Andar	28.00	86.00	200.00
4-Color 656 (10/55)(#2)-1st mention of Lanok	21.00	63.00	142.00
3(3-5/56)-5	14.00	43.00	100.00
6-10	9.30	28.00	65.00
11-20: 17-Prehistoric pygmies	4.85	14.50	34.00
21-30: 30-Back-c pin-ups begin. 30-33-Painted back-c pin-ups			
	2.65	8.00	18.00

	Good	Fine	N-Mint
31-50	1.50	4.50	10.00
51-60: 58-Flying Saucer c/story	.85	2.60	6.00
61-83: 62-12 & 15 cent-c. 63-Only line drawn-c	.50	1.50	3.00
84-Origin & 1st app. Hutec	.35	1.00	2.00
85-130: 114,115-(52 pgs.)		.50	1.00
Giant 1(30031-611) (11/66)	6.00	18.00	42.00

TWILIGHT ZONE, THE (TV)
No. 1173, 3-5/61-No. 91, 4/79; No. 92, 5/82
Dell Publishing Co./Gold Key/Whitman No. 92

	Good	Fine	N-Mint
4-Color 1173-Crandall/Evans-c/a	7.00	21.00	50.00
4-Color 1288-Crandall/Evans-c/a	5.70	17.00	40.00
01-860-207 (5-7/62-Dell, 15 cents)	4.50	14.00	32.00
12-860-210 on-c; 01-860-210 on inside(8-10/62-Dell)-Evans-c/a; Crandall/			
Frazetta-a(2)	4.50	14.00	32.00
1(11/62-Gold Key)-Crandall/Frazetta-a(10 & 11 pgs.); Evans-a			
	4.30	13.00	30.00
2	2.00	6.00	14.00
3,4,9-Toth-a, 11,10 & 15 pgs.	2.30	7.00	16.00
5-8,10,11	1.70	5.00	12.00
12,13,15: 12-Williamson-a. 13-Williamson/Crandall-a. 15-Crandall-a			
	2.00	6.00	14.00
14-Williamson/Orlando/Crandall/Torres-a	2.30	7.00	16.00
16-20	1.30	4.00	9.00
21-Crandall-a(r)	.85	2.60	6.00
22-27: 25-Evans/Crandall-a(r). 26-Crandall, Evans-a(r). 27-Evans-r(2)			
	.60	1.80	4.00
28-32: 32-Evans-a(r)	.35	1.00	2.00
33-42,44-50,52-70	.25	.75	1.50
43,51: 43-Crandall-a. 51-Williamson-a	.30	.90	1.80
71-92: 71-Reprint. 83,84-(52 pgs.)		.50	1.00

U

UNCANNY X-MEN, THE (See The X-Men)

UNCLE SAM QUARTERLY (Blackhawk #9 on; see National Comics)
Autumn, 1941-No. 8, Fall, 1943
Quality Comics Group

	Good	Fine	N-Mint
1-Origin Uncle Sam; Fine/Eisner-c, chapter headings, 2 pgs. by Eisner. (2 versions: dark cover, no price; light cover with price); Jack Cole-a			
	120.00	360.00	840.00
2-Cameos by The Ray, Black Condor, Quicksilver, The Red Bee, Alias the Spider, Hercules & Neon the Unknown; Eisner, Fine-c/a			
	57.00	170.00	400.00
3-Tuska-c/a	43.00	130.00	300.00
4	36.00	107.00	250.00
5-8	30.00	90.00	210.00

UNCLE SCROOGE (Disney)(See Walt Disney's Comics & Stories #98)
No. 386, 3/52-No. 39, 8-10/62; No. 40, 12/62-No. 209, 1984; No. 210, 10/86-No. 242, 4/90; No. 243, 5/90-Present
Dell #1-39/Gold Key #40-173/Whitman #174-209/Gladstone #210-242/ Disney Comics #243 on

	Good	Fine	N-Mint
4-Color 386(#1)-in "Only a Poor Old Man" by Carl Barks			
	60.00	180.00	450.00
4-Color 456(#2)-in "Back to the Klondike" by Carl Barks			
	29.00	86.00	215.00
4-Color 495(No.3)-r-in #105	26.00	77.00	190.00
4(12-2/53-54)	20.00	60.00	150.00
5	16.00	48.00	120.00
6-r-in U.S. #106,165,233	15.00	45.00	115.00
7-The Seven Cities of Cibola by Barks	11.50	34.00	85.00
8-10: 8-r-in #111,222. 9-r-in #104,214. 10-r-in #67			
	9.30	28.00	70.00
11-20: 11-r-in #237. 17-r-in #215. 20-r-in #213	8.00	24.00	60.00
21-30: 26-r-in #211	6.50	19.50	50.00
31-40: 34-r-in #228	5.50	16.50	42.00
41-50	4.00	12.00	32.00
51-60	3.70	11.00	28.00

Uncle Scrooge #28, © The Disney Co.

	Good	Fine	N-Mint
61-66,68-70: 70-Last Barks issue with original story			
	2.85	8.50	22.00
67,72,73-Barks-r	1.85	5.50	14.00
71-Written by Barks only	1.85	5.50	14.00
74-One pg. Barks-r	1.15	3.50	9.00
75-81,83-Not by Barks	1.15	3.50	9.00
82,84-Barks-r begin	1.15	3.50	9.00
85-100	1.00	3.00	7.00
101-110	.85	2.50	6.00
111-120	.70	2.00	5.00
121-141,143-152,154-157	.60	1.75	4.00
142-Reprints 4-Color #456 with-c	.70	2.00	5.00
153,158,162-164,166,168-170,178,180: No Barks	.25	.75	2.00
159-160,165,167,172-176-Barks-a	.25	.75	2.00
161(r-#14), 171(r-#11), 177(r-#16), 179(r-#9), 183(r-#6)-Barks-r			
	.25	.75	2.00
181(r-4-Color #495), 195(r-4-Color #386)	.25	.70	1.50
182,186,191-194,197-202,204-206: No Barks		.50	1.00

	Good	Fine	N-Mint
184,185,187,188-Barks-a		.50	1.00
189(r-#5), 190(r-#4), 196(r-#13), 203(r-#12), 207(r-#93,92), 208(r-U.S. #18), 209(r-U.S. #21)-Barks-r		.60	1.20
210-1st Gladstone issue; r-WDC&S #134 (1st Beagle Boys)	.85	2.50	5.00
211-218: 217-R-U.S. #7(Seven Cities of Cibola)	.40	1.25	2.50
219-Son Of The Sun by Rosa	1.70	5.00	10.00
220-Don Rosa story/art	.50	1.50	3.00
221-230: 224-Rosa-c/a. 226,227-Rosa-a	.25	.75	1.50
231-240: 235-Rosa story/art		.50	1.00
241-($1.95, 68 pgs.)-Rosa finishes over Barks-r	.35	1.00	2.00
242-($1.95, 68 pgs.)-Barks-r; Rosa-a(1 pg.)	.35	1.00	2.00
243-249,251-260 ($1.50)-Disney Comics; new-a begins	.25	.75	1.50
250-($2.25, 52 pgs.)-Barks-r; wraparound-c	.40	1.15	2.30
Uncle Scrooge & Money(G.K.)-Barks-r/from WDC&S #130 (3/67)	3.50	10.50	24.00

UNCLE SCROOGE ADVENTURES (Walt Disney's . . . #4 on)
Nov, 1987-No. 21, May, 1990
Gladstone Publishing

1-Barks-r begin	.70	2.00	4.00
2-5: 5-Rosa-c/a	.25	.75	1.50
6-19: 9,14-Rosa-a. 10-r/U.S. #18(all Barks)		.50	1.00
20,21 ($1.95, 68 pgs.) 20-Rosa-c/a. 21-Rosa-a	.35	1.00	2.00

UNDERDOG (TV)
July, 1970-No. 10, Jan, 1972; Mar, 1975-No. 23, Feb, 1979
Charlton Comics/Gold Key

1 (1st series)	3.00	9.00	21.00
2-10	1.15	3.50	8.00
1 (Gold Key)(2nd series)	1.70	5.00	12.00
2-10	.70	2.00	5.00
11-23: 13-1st app. Shack of Solitude	.60	1.80	4.00

UNEXPECTED, THE (Formerly Tales of the ...)
No. 105, Feb-Mar, 1968-No. 222, May, 1982
National Periodical Publications/DC Comics

	Good	Fine	N-Mint
105-Begin 12 cent cover price, ends ?	.85	2.60	6.00
106-115,117,118,120,122-127	.70	2.00	4.00
116,119,121,128-Wrightson-a	.70	2.00	5.00
129-162: 132-136-(52 pgs.). 157-162-(100 pgs.)	.35	1.00	2.00
163-188: 187,188-(44 pgs.)		.50	1.00
189,190,192-195 ($1.00, 68 pgs.)		.60	1.20
191-Rogers-a(p) ($1.00, 68 pgs.)	.25	.75	1.50
196-221: 200-Return of Johhny Peril by Tuska. 205-213-Johnny Peril app. 210-Time Warp story		.40	.80

UNTOLD LEGEND OF THE BATMAN, THE
July, 1980-No. 3, Sept, 1980 (Mini-series)
DC Comics

	Good	Fine	N-Mint
1-Origin; Joker-c; Byrne's 1st work at DC	.70	2.00	4.00
2,3	.50	1.50	3.00
1-3: Batman cereal premiums (28 pgs., 6x9"); 1st & 2nd printings known		.50	1.00

USA COMICS
Aug, 1941-No. 17, Fall, 1945
Timely Comics (USA)

	Good	Fine	VF-NM
1-Origin Major Liberty (called Mr. Liberty #1), Rockman by Wolverton, & The Whizzer by Avison; The Defender with sidekick Rusty & Jack Frost begin; The Young Avenger only app.; S&K-c plus 1 pg. art	383.00	960.00	2300.00

	Good	Fine	N-Mint
2-Origin Captain Terror & The Vagabond; last Wolverton Rockman	200.00	500.00	1200.00
3-No Whizzer	154.00	385.00	925.00
4-Last Rockman, Major Liberty, Defender, Jack Frost, & Capt. Terror; Corporal Dix app.	129.00	323.00	775.00
5-Origin American Avenger & Roko the Amazing; The Blue Blade, The Black Widow & Victory Boys, Gypo the Gypsy Giant & Hills of Horror only app.; Sergeant Dix begins; no Whizzer. Hitler-c	106.00	265.00	635.00
6-Captain America, The Destroyer, Jap Buster Johnson, Jeep Jones begin; Terror Squad only app.	125.00	312.00	750.00
7-Captain Daring, Disk-Eyes the Detective by Wolverton app.; origin & only app.			

	Good	Fine	N-Mint
Marvel Boy; Secret Stamp begins; no Whizzer, Sergeant Dix			
	108.00	270.00	650.00
8-10: 9-Last Secret Stamp. 10-The Thunderbird only app.			
	73.00	181.00	435.00
11,12: 11-No Jeep Jones	61.00	152.00	365.00
13-17: 13-No Whizzer; Jeep Jones ends. 15-No Destroyer; Jap Buster Johnson ends			
	46.00	115.00	275.00

U.S. AIR FORCE COMICS
Oct, 1958-No. 37, Mar-Apr, 1965
Charlton Comics

	Good	Fine	N-Mint
1	1.70	5.00	12.00
2	.85	2.60	6.00
3-10	.70	2.00	4.00
11-20	.50	1.50	3.00
21-37	.35	1.00	2.00

V

VAULT OF HORROR
No. 12, Apr-May, 1950-No. 40, Dec-Jan, 1954-55
E. C. Comics

	Good	Fine	N-Mint
12	150.00	450.00	1050.00
13-Morphine story	64.00	193.00	450.00
14	56.00	167.00	390.00
15	47.00	141.00	330.00
16	36.00	107.00	250.00
17-19	27.00	81.00	190.00
20-25: 23-Used in **POP**, pg. 84	21.00	62.00	145.00
26-B&W & color illos in **POP**	21.00	62.00	145.00
27-35: 35-X-Mas-c	16.00	48.00	110.00
36-"Pipe Dream"-classic opium addict story by Krigstein; "Twin Bill" cited in articles by T.E. Murphy, Wertham	16.00	48.00	110.00
37-Williamson-a	16.00	48.00	110.00
38-39: 39-Bondage-c	13.00	40.00	90.00
40-Low distribution	16.00	48.00	110.00

VAULT OF HORROR, THE
Aug, 1990-No. 6, June, 1991 ($1.95, color, 68 pgs.) (#4 on: $2.00)
Gladstone Publishing

1-Craig-c(r); all contain EC reprints	.70	2.00	4.00
2-Craig-c(r)	.50	1.50	3.00
3-6: 3-Ingels-c(r). 4-6-Craig-c(r)	.40	1.25	2.50

VENUS (See Marvel Mystery #91 & Marvel Spotlight #2)
August, 1948-No. 19, April, 1952
Marvel/Atlas Comics (CMC 1-9/LCC 10-19)

1-Venus & Hedy Devine begin; Kurtzman's "Hey Look"			
	46.00	139.00	325.00
2	27.00	81.00	190.00
3,5	24.00	71.00	165.00
4-Kurtzman's "Hey Look"	25.00	75.00	175.00
6-9: 6-Loki app. 7,8-Painted-c	22.00	65.00	155.00
10-S/F-horror issues begin (7/50)	24.00	71.00	165.00

	Good	Fine	N-Mint
11-S/F end of the world (11/50)	29.00	86.00	200.00
12-Colan-a	22.00	65.00	150.00
13-19-Venus by Everett, 2-3 stories each; covers-#13,15-19; 14-Everett part cover			
(Venus). 17-Bondage-c	32.00	95.00	220.00

V FOR VENDETTA
Sept, 1988-No. 10, May, 1989 ($2.00, maxi-series, mature readers)
DC Comics

1-Alan Moore scripts in all	.75	2.25	4.50
2-5	.40	1.25	2.50
6-10	.35	1.00	2.00

VIGILANTE, THE (Also see Action Comics #42 & Leading Comics)
Oct, 1983-No. 50, Feb, 1988 ($1.25; Baxter paper)
DC Comics

1-Origin	.85	2.50	5.00
2	.50	1.50	3.00
3-10: 3-Cyborg app. 4-1st app. The Exterminator; Newton-a(p). 6,7- Origin			
	.35	1.00	2.00
11-49: 17,18-Alan Moore scripts. 20,21-Nightwing app. 35-Origin Mad Bomber.			
47-Batman-c/story.	.30	.90	1.75
50-Death of Vigilante (suicide)	.35	1.00	2.00
Annual 1 (1985)	.40	1.25	2.50
Annual 2 (1986)	.35	1.10	2.25

W

WAGON TRAIN (1st Series) (TV)
No. 895, Mar, 1958-No. 13, Apr-June, 1962 (All photo-c)
Dell Publishing Co.

	Good	Fine	N-Mint
4-Color 895 (#1)	5.70	17.00	40.00
4-Color 971,1019	3.70	11.00	26.00
4(1-3/60),6-13	3.00	9.00	21.00
5-Toth-a	4.00	12.00	28.00

WAGON TRAIN (2nd Series) (TV)
Jan, 1964-No. 4, Oct, 1964 (All photo-c)
Gold Key

	Good	Fine	N-Mint
1	3.00	9.00	21.00
2-4-Tufts-a	2.00	6.00	14.00

WALT DISNEY'S COMICS AND STORIES (#1-30 contain Donald Duck
  newspaper reprints) (Titled 'Comics And Stories' #264 on)
10/40-#263, 8/62; #264, 10/62-#510, 1984; #511, 10/86-Present
Dell Publishing Co./Gold Key #264-473/Whitman #474-510/Gladstone #511-
  547(4/90)/Disney Comics #548(5/90) on
NOTE: *The whole number can always be found at the bottom of the title page in the
lower left-hand or right hand panel.*

	Good	Fine	VF-NM
1(V1#1-c; V2#1-indicia)-Donald Duck strip-r by Al Taliaferro & Gottfredson's Mickey Mouse begin	370.00	1480.00	3800.00

(Prices vary widely on this book)

	Good	Fine	N-Mint
2	220.00	660.00	1850.00
3	107.00	320.00	775.00
4-X-mas-c	77.00	231.00	575.00

4-Special promotional, complimentary issue; cover same except one corner was
  blanked out & boxed in to identify the giveaway (not a paste-over). This
  special pressing was probably sent out to former subscribers to Mickey Mouse

Walt Disney's Comics and Stories #73, © The Disney Co.

	Good	Fine	N-Mint
Mag. whose subscriptions had expired. (Very rare-5 known copies)			
	115.00	345.00	840.00
5	64.00	190.00	470.00
6-10	50.00	150.00	370.00
11-14	43.00	130.00	315.00
15-17: 15-The 3 Little Kittens (17 pgs.). 16-The 3 Little Pigs (29 pgs.); X-mas-c.			
17-The Ugly Duckling (4 pgs.)	38.00	115.00	285.00
18-21	30.00	90.00	235.00
22-30: 22-Flag-c	27.00	80.00	200.00
31-Donald Duck by Carl Barks begins; see Four Color #9 for first Barks Donald			
Duck	157.00	470.00	1150.00
32-Barks-a	90.00	270.00	650.00
33-Barks-a (infinity-c)	64.00	190.00	470.00
34-Gremlins by Walt Kelly begin, end #41; Barks-a			
	52.00	156.00	385.00
35,36-Barks-a	45.00	135.00	335.00
37-Donald Duck by Jack Hannah	21.00	64.00	160.00
38-40-Barks-a. 39-Christmas-c. 40-Gremlins by Kelly			
	32.00	95.00	235.00

	Good	Fine	N-Mint
41-50-Barks-a; 41-Gremlins by Kelly	26.00	77.00	190.00
51-60-Barks-a; 51-Christmas-c. 52-Li'l Bad Wolf begins, ends #203 (not in #55).			
58-Kelly flag-c	19.00	58.00	140.00
61-70: Barks-a. 61-Dumbo story. 63,64-Pinocchio stories. 63-c-swipe from New			
Funnies #94. 64-X-mas-c. 65-Pluto story. 66-Infinity-c.67,68-M. Mouse			
Sunday-r by Bill Wright	16.00	48.00	115.00
71-80: Barks-a. 75-77-Brer Rabbit stories, no Mickey Mouse. 76- X-Mas-c			
	11.50	34.00	80.00
81-87,89,90: Barks-a. 82-84-Bongo stories. 86-90-Goofy & Agnes app. 89-Chip			
'n' Dale story	9.50	28.50	65.00
88-1st app. Gladstone Gander by Barks	11.50	34.00	80.00
91-97,99: Barks-a. 95-1st WDC&S Barks-c. 96-No Mickey Mouse; Little Toot			
begins, ends #97. 99-X-Mas-c	7.50	22.50	52.00
98-1st Uncle Scrooge app. in WDC&S	16.00	48.00	110.00
100-Barks-a	8.50	25.50	60.00
101-106,108-110-Barks-a	6.50	19.50	45.00
107-Barks-a; Taliaferro-c. Donald acquires super powers			
	6.50	19.50	45.00
111,114,117-All Barks	5.00	15.00	35.00
112-Drug (ether) issue (Donald Duck)	5.50	16.50	38.00
113,115,116,118-123: Not by Barks. 116-Dumbo x-over. 121-Grandma Duck begins,			
ends in #135,142,146,15	2.15	6.50	15.00
124,126-130-All Barks. 124-X-Mas-c	4.35	13.00	30.00
125-1st app. Junior Woodchucks; Barks-a	7.00	21.00	50.00
131,133,135-139-All Barks	4.35	13.00	30.00
132-Barks-a(2) (D. Duck & Grandma Duck)	5.15	15.50	36.00
134-Intro. & 1st app. The Beagle Boys	8.50	25.50	60.00
140-1st app. Gyro Gearloose by Barks	8.50	25.50	60.00
141-150-All Barks. 143-Little Hiawatha begins, ends #151,159			
	2.65	8.00	18.00
151-170-All Barks	2.35	7.00	16.00
171-200-All Barks	2.00	6.00	14.00
201-240: All Barks. 204-Chip 'n' Dale & Scamp begin			
	1.70	5.00	12.00
241-283: Barks-a. 241-Dumbo x-over. 247-Gyro Gearloose begins, ends #274.			
256-Ludwig Von Drake begins, ends #274	1.50	4.50	9.00
284,285,287,290,295,296,309-311-Not by Barks	.85	2.50	5.00
286,288,289,291-294,297,298,308-All Barks stories; 293-Grandma Duck's Farm			
Friends. 297-Gyro Gearloose. 298-Daisy Duck's Diary-r			
	1.35	4.00	8.00

	Good	Fine	N-Mint
299-307-All contain early Barks-r (#43-117). 305-Gyro Gearloose			
	1.50	4.50	9.00
312-Last Barks issue with original story	1.35	4.00	8.00
313-315,317-327,329-334,336-341	.70	2.00	4.00
316-Last issue published during life of Walt Disney	.70	2.00	4.00
328,335,342-350-Barks-r	.85	2.50	5.00
351-360-w/posters inside; Barks reprints (2 versions of each with & without			
posters)-without posters . . .	.75	2.25	4.50
351-360-With posters	1.15	3.50	8.00
361-400-Barks-r	.75	2.25	4.50
401-429-Barks-r. 410-Annette Funicello photo-c	.50	1.50	3.00
430,433,437,438,441,444,445,466,506-No Barks		.35	.70
431,432,434-436,439,440,442,443-Barks-r	.25	.75	1.50
446-465,467-505,507-510: All Barks-r. 494-r/WDC&S #98 (1st Uncle Scrooge)			
		.50	1.00
511-Wuzzles by Disney studio	.85	2.50	5.00
512	.50	1.50	3.00
513-520: 518-Infinity-c	.30	.90	1.80
521-540: 522-r/1st app. Huey, Dewey & Louie from D. Duck Sunday page. 535-			
546-Barks-r	.25	.75	1.50
541-545: (All $1.50, 52 pgs.)	.25	.75	1.50
546,547-($1.95, 68 pgs.): 546-Kelly-r. 547-Rosa-a	.35	1.00	2.00
548,549,551-560 ($1.50): 548-New-a. 549-Barks-r begin. 556-r/Mickey Mouse			
Cheerios Premium by Dick Moores	.25	.75	1.50
550 ($2.25, 52 pgs.)-Donald Duck by Barks; previously only printed in The			
Netherlands (1st time in U.S.)	.40	1.15	2.30

WAMBI, JUNGLE BOY (Also see Jungle Comics)
Spring, 1942; No. 2, Wint, 1942-43; No. 3, Spring, 1943; No. 4, Fall, 1948; No. 5,
Sum, 1949; No. 6, Spring, 1950; No. 7-10, 1950(nd); No. 11, Spring, 1951-
No. 18, Winter, 1952-53 (#1-3: 68 pgs.)
Fiction House Magazines

	Good	Fine	N-Mint
1-Wambi, the Jungle Boy begins	34.00	100.00	235.00
2 (1942)-Kiefer-c	17.00	51.00	120.00
3 (1943)-Kiefer-c/a	12.00	36.00	85.00
4 (1948)-Origin in text	8.00	24.00	55.00
5 (Fall, '49, 36 pgs.)-Kiefer-c/a	7.00	21.00	50.00
6-10: 7-52 pgs.	5.70	17.00	40.00
11-18	4.00	12.00	28.00

WANTED, THE WORLD'S MOST DANGEROUS VILLAINS
July-Aug, 1972-No. 9, Aug-Sept, 1973 (All reprints)
National Periodical Publications

	Good	Fine	N-Mint
1-Batman, Green Lantern (story r-from G.L. #1), & Green Arrow			
	.50	1.50	3.00
2-Batman/Joker/Penguin-c/story r-from Batman #25; plus Flash story r-from			
Flash #121	.70	2.00	4.00
3-9: 3-Dr. Fate, Hawkman(r/Flash #100), & Vigilante. 4-Gr. Lantern & Kid			
Eternity. 5-Dollman/Green Lantern. 6-Burnley Starman; Wildcat/ Sargon. 7-			
Johnny Quick/Hawkman/Hourman by Baily. 8-Dr. Fate/ Flash(r/Flash #114).			
9-S&K Sandman/Superman	.25	.75	1.50

WAR COMICS
Dec, 1950-No. 49, Sept, 1957
Marvel/Atlas (USA No. 1-41/JPI No. 42-49)

	Good	Fine	N-Mint
1	8.00	24.00	55.00
2	4.00	12.00	28.00
3-10	3.00	9.00	21.00
11-20	1.70	5.00	12.00
21,23-32: Last pre-code (2/55). 26-Valley Forge story			
	1.50	4.50	10.00
22-Krigstein-a	3.70	11.00	26.00
33-37,39-42,44,45,47,48	1.50	4.50	10.00
38-Kubert/Moskowitz-a	2.65	8.00	18.00
43,49-Torres-a. 43-Davis E.C. swipe	2.30	7.00	16.00
46-Crandall-a	2.65	8.00	18.00

WARLOCK (The Power of . . .) (See Marvel Premiere & Strange Tales)
Aug, 1972-No. 8, Oct, 1973; No. 9, Oct, 1975-No. 15, Nov, 1976
Marvel Comics Group

	Good	Fine	N-Mint
1-Origin by Kane	1.50	4.50	10.00
2,3	.85	2.60	6.00
4-8: 4-Death of Eddie Roberts	.70	2.00	5.00
9-Thanos cameo app.; Starlin c/a	.85	2.50	5.00
10-Recap origin Thanos; Thanos-c; Starlin c/a	1.70	5.00	12.00
11-Thanos app.; Starlin c/a	1.70	5.00	12.00
12-14: No Thanos app.; Starlin c/a	.70	2.00	4.00
15-Thanos-c/story	2.15	6.50	15.00

WATCHMEN
Sept, 1986-No. 12, Oct, 1987 (12 issue maxi-series)
DC Comics

	Good	Fine	N-Mint
1-Alan Moore scripts in all	1.00	3.00	6.00
2,3	.70	2.00	4.00
4-10	.60	1.75	3.50
11,12	.50	1.50	3.00

WEB OF MYSTERY
Feb, 1951-No. 29, Sept, 1955
Ace Magazines (A. A. Wyn)

1	16.00	48.00	110.00
2-Bakerish-a	9.30	28.00	65.00
3-10	8.00	24.00	55.00
11-18,20-26: 13-Surrealistic-c	6.50	19.00	45.00
19-Reprints Challenge of the Unknown #6 used in N.Y. Legislative Committee			
	6.50	19.00	45.00
27-Bakerish-a(r); last pre-code issue	5.70	17.00	40.00
28,29: 28-All-r	3.70	11.00	26.00

WEB OF SPIDER-MAN, THE
Apr, 1985-Present
Marvel Comics Group

1-Painted-c (3rd app. black costume?)	2.00	6.00	12.00
2,3	.85	2.50	5.00
4-8: 7-Hulk x-over; Wolverine splash	.70	2.00	4.00
9-13: 10-Dominic Fortune guest stars; painted-c	.60	1.75	3.50
14-28: 19-Intro Humbug & Solo	.50	1.50	3.00
29-Wolverine app.	2.00	6.00	12.00
30-Origin The Rose & Hobgoblin; Punisher & Wolverine cameo in flashback			
	1.70	5.00	10.00
31,32-Six part Kraven storyline begins	1.15	3.50	7.00
33,34	.25	.75	1.50
35-37,39-47,49		.60	1.20
38-Hobgoblin app.; begin $1.00-c. 48-Hobgoblin, Kingpin app.			
	.40	1.25	2.50
48-Origin of New Hobgoblin	.70	2.00	4.00
50-($1.50, 52 pgs.)	.35	1.00	2.00
51-58		.55	1.10

The Web of Spider-Man #29, © *Marvel Comics*

	Good	Fine	N-Mint
59-Cosmic Spidey cont./Spect. Spider-Man	1.00	3.00	6.00
60-65,68-82: 69,70-Hulk x-over		.50	1.00
66,67-Green Goblin appears as a super-hero	.35	1.00	2.00
Annual 1 (9/85)	.45	1.30	2.60
Annual 2 (9/86)-New Mutants; Art Adams-a	1.15	3.50	7.00
Annual 3 (10/87)	.35	1.10	2.20
Annual 4 (10/88, $1.75)-Evolutionary War x-over	.55	1.65	3.30
Annual 5 (1989, $2.00, 68pgs.)-Atlantis Attacks; Captain Universe by Ditko (p) & Silver Sable stories; F.F. app.	.35	1.10	2.20
Annual 6 ('90, $2.00, 68 pgs.)-Punisher back-up plus Capt. Universe by Ditko; G. Kane-a	.35	1.00	2.00

WEIRD, THE
Apr, 1988-No. 4, July, 1988 ($1.50, color, mini-series)
DC Comics

	Good	Fine	N-Mint
1-Wrightson-c/a in all	.40	1.25	2.50
2-4	.35	1.00	2.00

WEIRD COMICS
April, 1940-No. 20, Jan, 1942
Fox Features Syndicate

	Good	Fine	N-Mint
1-The Birdman, Thor, God of Thunder (ends #5), The Sorceress of Zoom, Blast Bennett, Typhon, Voodoo Man, & Dr. Mortal begin; Fine bondage-c			
	118.00	355.00	825.00
2-Lou Fine-c	57.00	171.00	400.00
3,4: 3-Simon-c. 4-Torture-c	40.00	120.00	280.00
5-Intro. Dart & sidekick Ace (ends #20); bondage/hypo-c			
	43.00	130.00	300.00
6,7-Dynamite Thor app. in each	39.00	118.00	275.00
8-Dynamo, the Eagle (1st app.) & sidekick Buddy & Marga, the Panther Woman begin	39.00	118.00	275.00
9	32.00	95.00	225.00
10-Navy Jones app.	32.00	95.00	225.00
11-16: 16-Flag-c	26.00	77.00	180.00
17-Origin The Black Rider	26.00	77.00	180.00
18-20: 20-Origin The Rapier; Swoop Curtis app; Churchill, Hitler-c			
	26.00	77.00	180.00

WEIRD FANTASY (Becomes Weird Science-Fantasy #23 on)
No. 13, May-June, 1950-No. 22, Nov-Dec, 1953
E. C. Comics

13(#1) (1950)	93.00	280.00	650.00
14-Necronomicon story; atomic explosion-c	51.00	152.00	355.00
15,16: 16-Used in **SOTI**, pg. 144	42.00	125.00	290.00
17 (1951)	35.00	105.00	245.00
6-10	26.00	77.00	180.00
11-13 (1952)	19.00	58.00	135.00
14-Frazetta/Williamson(1st team-up at E.C.)/Krenkel-a, 7 pgs.; Orlando draws E.C. staff	34.00	100.00	235.00
15-Williamson/Evans-a(3), 4,3,&7 pgs.	22.00	65.00	150.00
16-19-Williamson/Krenkel-a in all. 18-Williamson/Feldstein-c			
	19.00	58.00	135.00
20-Frazetta/Williamson-a, 7 pgs.	22.00	65.00	150.00
21-Frazetta/Williamson-c & Williamson/Krenkel-a			
	34.00	100.00	235.00
22-Bradbury adaptation	14.00	43.00	100.00

WEIRD MYSTERIES
Oct, 1952-No. 12, Sept, 1954
Gillmore Publications

	Good	Fine	N-Mint
1-Partial Wolverton-c swiped from splash page "Flight to the Future" in Weird Tales of the Future #2; "Eternity" has an Ingels swipe			
	23.00	70.00	160.00
2-"Robot Woman" by Wolverton; Bernard Baily-c reprinted in Mister Mystery #18; acid in face panel			
	41.00	122.00	285.00
3,6: Both have decapitation-c	14.00	43.00	100.00
4-"The Man Who Never Smiled" (3 pgs.) by Wolverton; B. Baily skull-c			
	32.00	95.00	225.00
5-Wolverton story "Swamp Monster," 6 pgs.	36.00	107.00	250.00
7-Used in SOTI, illo-"Indeed" & illo-"Sex and blood"			
	24.00	73.00	170.00
8-Wolverton-c panel reprint/No. 5; used in a 1954 Readers Digest anti-comics article by T. E. Murphy entitled "For the Kiddies to Read"			
	14.00	43.00	100.00
9-Excessive violence, gore & torture	13.00	40.00	90.00
10-Silhouetted nudity panel	11.50	34.00	80.00
11,12	8.50	25.50	60.00

WEIRD SCIENCE (Becomes Weird Science-Fantasy #23 on)
No. 12, May-June, 1950-No. 22, Nov-Dec, 1953
E. C. Comics

	Good	Fine	N-Mint
12(#1) (1950)	97.00	290.00	675.00
13	54.00	163.00	380.00
14,15 (1950)	49.00	145.00	340.00
5-10: 5-Atomic explosion-c	30.00	90.00	210.00
11-14 (1952)	19.00	58.00	135.00
15-18-Williamson/Krenkel-a in each; 15-Williamson-a. 17-Used in POP, pgs. 81,82			
	22.00	65.00	155.00
19,20-Williamson/Frazetta-a, 7 pgs each. 19-Used in SOTI, illo-"A young girl on her wedding night stabs her sleeping husband to death with a hatpin …"			
	30.00	90.00	210.00
21-Williamson/Frazetta-a, 6 pgs.; Wood draws E.C. staff; Gaines & Feldstein app. in story			
	30.00	90.00	210.00
22-Williamson/Frazetta/Krenkel-a, 8 pgs.; Wood draws himself in his story-last pg. & panel			
	30.00	90.00	210.00

WEIRD SCIENCE
Sept, 1990-No. 4, Mar, 1991 ($1.95, color, 68 pgs.)(#3 on: $2.00)
Gladstone Publishing

	Good	Fine	N-Mint
1-Wood-c(r); all reprints in each	.50	1.50	3.00
2-4: 2-4-Wood-c(r)	.40	1.25	2.50

WEIRD SCIENCE-FANTASY (Formerly Weird Science & Weird Fantasy)
No. 23 Mar, 1954-No. 29, May-June, 1955
E. C. Comics

	Good	Fine	N-Mint
23-Williamson & Wood-a	22.00	65.00	150.00
24-Williamson & Wood-a; Harlan Ellison's 1st professional story, 'Upheaval!,' later adapted into a short story as 'Mealtime,' and then into a TV episode of Voyage to the Bottom of the Sea as 'The Price of Doom'			
	22.00	65.00	150.00
25-Williamson-c; Williamson/Torres/Krenkel-a plus Wood-a			
	26.00	77.00	180.00
26-Flying Saucer Report; Wood, Crandall, Orlando-a			
	21.00	62.00	145.00
27	22.00	65.00	150.00
28-Williamson/Krenkel/Torres-a; Wood-a	24.00	73.00	170.00
29-Frazetta-c; Williamson/Krenkel & Wood-a	44.00	133.00	310.00

WEIRD TALES OF THE FUTURE
March, 1952-No. 8, July, 1953
S.P.M. Publ. No. 1-4/Aragon Publ. No. 5-8

	Good	Fine	N-Mint
1-Andru-a(2)	29.00	85.00	200.00
2,3-Wolverton-c/a(3) each. 2-"Jumpin Jupiter" satire by Wolverton begins, ends #5			
	50.00	150.00	350.00
4-"Jumpin Jupiter" satire by Wolverton; partial Wolverton-c			
	27.00	80.00	185.00
5-Wolverton-c/a(2)	50.00	150.00	350.00
6-Bernard Baily-c	15.00	45.00	105.00
7-"The Mind Movers" from the art to Wolverton's "Brain Bats of Venus" from Mr. Mystery #7 which was cut apart, pasted up, partially redrawn, and rewritten by Harry Kantor, the editor; Bernard Baily-c			
	27.00	80.00	185.00
8-Reprints Weird Mysteries #1(10/52) minus cover; gory cover showing heart ripped out			
	15.00	45.00	105.00

WEIRD TERROR
Sept, 1952-No. 13, Sept, 1954
Allen Hardy Associates (Comic Media)

	Good	Fine	N-Mint
1-"Portrait of Death," adapted from Lovecraft's "Pickman's Model;" lingerie			
panels, Hitler story	14.00	43.00	100.00
2-Text on Marquis DeSade, Torture, Demonology, & St. Elmo's Fire			
	8.50	25.50	60.00
3-Extreme violence, whipping, torture; article on sin eating, dowsing			
	7.00	21.00	50.00
4-Dismemberment, decapitation, article on human flesh for sale, Devil, whipping			
	11.00	32.00	75.00
5-Article on body snatching, mutilation; cannibalism story			
	7.00	21.00	50.00
6-Dismemberment, decapitation, man hit by lightning			
	11.00	32.00	75.00
7,9,10	7.00	21.00	50.00
8-Decapitation story; Ambrose Bierce adapt.	9.30	28.00	65.00
11-End of the world story with atomic blast panels; Tothish-a by Bill Discount			
	9.30	28.00	65.00
12-Discount-a	5.70	17.00	40.00
13-Severed head panels	6.50	19.00	45.00

WEREWOLF BY NIGHT (See Marvel Spotlight #2-4)
Sept, 1972-No. 43, Mar, 1977
Marvel Comics Group

1-Ploog-a-cont'd. from Marvel Spotlight #4	1.50	4.50	10.00
2-31: 15-New origin Werewolf; Dracula app.	.35	1.00	2.00
32-Origin & 1st app. Moon Knight	2.85	8.50	20.00
33-2nd app. Moon Knight	1.70	5.00	12.00
34-36,38-43: 35-Starlin/Wrightson-c	.35	1.00	2.00
37-Moon Knight app; part Wrightson-c	.85	2.50	5.00

WEST COAST AVENGERS
Sept, 1984-No. 4, Dec, 1984 (Mini-series; Mando paper)
Marvel Comics Group

1-Hawkeye, Iron Man, Mockingbird, Tigra	1.15	3.50	7.00
2-4	.75	2.25	4.50

WEST COAST AVENGERS (Becomes Avengers West Coast #48 on)
Oct, 1985-No. 47, Aug, 1989 (On-going series)
Marvel Comics Group

	Good	Fine	N-Mint
V2#1	1.00	3.00	6.00
2,3	.70	2.00	4.00
4-6	.50	1.50	3.00
7-10	.40	1.25	2.50
11-20	.35	1.10	2.20
21-30	.25	.75	1.50
31-41		.60	1.20
42-Byrne-a(p)/scripts begin	.35	1.10	2.20
43-47: 46,46-Byrne-c. 46-1st app. Great Lakes Avengers			
		.55	1.10
Annual 1 (10/86)	.35	1.10	2.20
Annual 2 (9/87)	.35	1.00	2.00
Annual 3 (10/88, $1.75)-Evolutionary War app.	.45	1.40	2.80
Annual V2#4 ('89, $2.00, 68 pgs.)-Atlantis Attacks; Byrne/Austin-a			
	.35	1.10	2.20
Annual V2#5 ('90, $2.00, 68 pgs.)	.35	1.00	2.00

WESTERN COMICS
Jan-Feb, 1948-No. 85, Jan-Feb, 1961 (1-27: 52 pgs.)
National Periodical Publications

	Good	Fine	N-Mint
1-The Wyoming Kid & his horse Racer, The Vigilante (Meskin-a), The Cowboy Marshal, Rodeo Rick begin	36.00	107.00	250.00
2	20.00	60.00	140.00
3,4-Last Vigilante	16.00	48.00	110.00
5-Nighthawk & his horse Nightwind begin (not in #6); Captain Tootsie by Beck	14.00	43.00	100.00
6,7,9,10	11.00	32.00	75.00
8-Origin Wyoming Kid; 2 pg. pin-ups of rodeo queens	14.00	43.00	100.00
11-20	8.50	25.50	60.00
21-40: 24-Starr-a. 27-Last 52 pgs.	6.00	18.00	42.00
41-49: Last precode (2/55). 43-Pow Wow Smith begins, ends #85	5.00	15.00	35.00
50-60	5.00	15.00	35.00
61-85-Last Wyoming Kid. 77-Origin Matt Savage Trail Boss. 82-1st app. Fleetfoot, Pow Wow's girlfriend	3.00	9.00	21.00

WESTERN HERO (Wow Comics #1-69; Real Western Hero #70-75)
No. 76, Mar, 1949-No. 112, Mar, 1952
Fawcett Publications

	Good	Fine	N-Mint
76(#1, 52 pgs.)-Tom Mix, Hopalong Cassidy, Monte Hale, Gabby Hayes, Young Falcon (ends #78,80), & Big Bow and Little Arrow (ends #102,105) begin; painted-c begin	17.00	51.00	120.00
77 (52 pgs.)	11.50	34.00	80.00
78,80-82 (52 pgs.): 81-Capt. Tootsie by Beck	11.50	34.00	80.00
79,83 (36 pgs.): 83-Last painted-c	8.50	25.50	60.00
84-86,88-90 (52 pgs.): 84-Photo-c begin, end #112. 86-Last Hopalong Cassidy	9.30	28.00	65.00
87,91,95,99 (36 pgs.): 87-Bill Boyd begins, ends #95	8.00	24.00	55.00
92-94,96-98,101 (52 pgs.): 96-Tex Ritter begins. 101-Red Eagle app.	8.50	25.50	60.00
100 (52 pgs.)	9.30	28.00	65.00
102-111 (36 pgs. begin)	8.00	24.00	55.00
112-Last issue	8.50	25.50	60.00

WESTERN OUTLAWS
Feb, 1954-No. 21, Aug, 1957
Atlas Comics (ACI No. 1-14/WPI No. 15-21)

	Good	Fine	N-Mint
1-Heath, Powell-a; Maneely hanging-c	8.50	25.50	60.00
2	4.00	12.00	28.00
3-10: 7-Violent-a by R.Q. Sale	3.15	9.50	22.00
11,14-Williamson-a in both, 6 pgs. each	4.50	14.00	32.00
12,18,20,21: Severin covers	2.65	8.00	18.00
13-Baker-a	3.00	9.00	21.00
15-Torres-a	3.60	11.00	25.00
16-Williamson text illo	2.30	7.00	16.00
17-Crandall-a, Williamson text illo	3.50	10.50	24.00
19-Crandall-a	2.85	8.50	20.00

WESTERN WINNERS (Formerly All-West. Winners; Black Rider #8 on)
No. 5, June, 1949-No. 7, Dec, 1949
Marvel Comics (CDS)

	Good	Fine	N-Mint
5-Two-Gun Kid, Kid Colt, Black Rider	14.00	43.00	100.00

	Good	Fine	N-Mint

6-Two-Gun Kid, Black Rider, Heath Kid Colt story; Captain Tootsie by C.C.

Beck	12.00	36.00	85.00

7-Randolph Scott Photo-c w/true stories about the West

	12.00	36.00	85.00

WHAT IF . . . ? (1st series)
Feb, 1977-No. 47, Oct, 1985; June, 1988 (All 52 pgs.)
Marvel Comics Group

1-Brief origin Spider-Man, Fantastic Four	1.70	5.00	12.00
2-Origin The Hulk retold	1.00	3.00	7.00
3-5	.85	2.50	5.00
6-10: 9-Origins Venus, Marvel Boy, Human Robot, 3-D Man			
	.70	2.00	4.00
11,12	.50	1.50	3.00
13-Conan app.	.85	2.50	5.00
14-16,18-26,29,30: 22-Origin Dr. Doom retold	.40	1.25	2.50
17-Ghost Rider app.	.85	2.50	5.00
27-X-Men app.; Miller-c	1.15	3.50	8.00
28-Daredevil by Miller	1.15	3.50	8.00
31-X-Men app.; death of Hulk, Wolverine & Magneto			
	1.70	5.00	10.00

32-47: 32,36-Byrne-a. 34-Marvel crew each draw themselves. 35-What if Elektra
    had lived?; Miller/Austin-a. 37-Old X-Men & Silver Surfer app.

	.30	.85	1.70
Special 1 ($1.50, 6/88)-Iron Man, F.F., Thor app.	.35	1.00	2.00

WHAT IF . . . ? (2nd series)
July, 1989-Present ($1.25 color)
Marvel Comics

V2#1- ...The Avengers Had Lost the Evol. War	.50	1.50	3.00
2-5: 2-Daredevil, Punisher app.	.25	.70	1.40
6-X-Men app.	.40	1.25	2.50
7-Wolverine app.	.40	1.25	2.50
8,11	.25	.75	1.50
9-X-Men	.30	1.00	2.00
10-Punisher app.	.40	1.25	2.50
12-X-Men	.30	1.00	2.00

13-15,17-23,27,29,31: 13-Prof. X. 14-Capt. Marvel; Austin-c. 15-F.F. 17-Spider-

	Good	Fine	N-Mint
Man/Kraven. 18-F.F. 19-Vision. 20,21-Spider-Man. 22-Silver Surfer; Austin-i. 23-X-Men.		.60	1.30
16-Conan/Wolverine	.30	1.00	2.00
24-Wolverine; Punisher app.	.25	.75	1.50
25-Atlantis Attacks, Wolverine app.	.50	1.50	3.00
26-Punisher app.	.30	1.00	2.00
28 ($1.50, 52 pgs.)	.25	.75	1.50
30 ($1.75)	.25	.80	1.80

WHAT THE-?!
Aug, 1988-Present ($1.25-$1.50, semi-annually #5 on)
Marvel Comics

	Good	Fine	N-Mint
1-All contain parodies	.40	1.25	2.50
2,4,5: 5-Punisher/Wolverine parody	.25	.75	1.50
3-X-Men parody; Todd McFarlane-a	.50	1.50	3.00
6-15: 6-($1.00)-Acts of Vengeance (Punisher, Wolverine, Alpha Flight)-Byrne/Austin-a. 7-Avengers vs. Justice League parody; Patsy Walker story; begin $1.25-c. 9-Wolverine		.60	1.25

WHITE PRINCESS OF THE JUNGLE
July, 1951-No. 5, Nov, 1952
Avon Periodicals

	Good	Fine	N-Mint
1-Origin of White Princess (Taanda) & Capt'n Courage (r); Kinstler-c	23.00	70.00	160.00
2-Reprints origin of Malu, Slave Girl Princess from Avon's Slave Girl Comics #1 w/Malu changed to Zora; Kinstler-c/a(2)	17.00	51.00	120.00
3-Origin Blue Gorilla; Kinstler-c/a	13.00	40.00	90.00
4-Jack Barnum, White Hunter app.; r-/Sheena #9	11.00	32.00	75.00
5-Blue Gorilla by Kinstler	11.00	32.00	75.00

WHIZ COMICS
No. 2, Feb, 1940-No. 155, June, 1953
Fawcett Publications

	Good	Fine	VF-NM

1-(nn on cover, #2 inside)-Origin & 1st newsstand app. Captain Marvel by C. C. Beck (created by Bill Parker), Spy Smasher, Golden Arrow, Ibis the Invincible,

Whiz Comics #44, © Fawcett Publications

	Good	Fine	VF-NM
Dan Dare, Scoop Smith, Sivana, & Lance O'Casey begin	3,800.00	10,600.00	23,000.00

(The only Mint copy sold in 1990 for $74,000 cash/trade)

	Good	Fine	N-Mint
2-(nn on cover, #3 inside); Spy Smasher reveals I.D. to Eve	315.00	942.00	2200.00
3-(#3 on cover, #4 inside)-1st app. Beautia	195.00	590.00	1370.00
4-(#4 on cover, #5 inside)	160.00	480.00	1125.00
5-Captain Marvel wears button-down flap on splash page only	120.00	360.00	840.00
6-10: 7-Dr. Voodoo begins (by Raboy-#9-22)	98.00	295.00	685.00
11-14	64.00	193.00	450.00
15-Origin Sivana; Dr. Voodoo by Raboy	82.00	245.00	575.00
16-18-Spy Smasher battles Captain Marvel	82.00	245.00	575.00
19,20	45.00	135.00	315.00
21-Origin & 1st app. Lt. Marvels	47.00	141.00	330.00
22-24: 23-Only Dr. Voodoo by Tuska	37.00	110.00	260.00

	Good	Fine	N-Mint
25-(12/41)-1st app./origin Capt. Marvel Jr.(part 2 of origin; see Master); Capt. Nazi app.; origin Old Shazam in text	115.00	345.00	800.00
26-30	32.00	95.00	225.00
31,32: 32-1st app. The Trolls	25.00	75.00	175.00
33-Spy Smasher, Captain Marvel x-over	29.00	86.00	200.00
34,36-40: 37-The Trolls app. by Swayze	21.00	62.00	145.00
35-Captain Marvel & Spy Smasher-c	24.00	70.00	165.00
41-50: 43-Spy Smasher, Ibis, Golden Arrow x-over in Capt. Marvel. 44-Flag-c. 47-Origin recap (1 pg.)	13.00	40.00	90.00
51-60: 52-Capt. Marvel x-over in Ibis. 57-Spy Smasher, Golden Arrow, Ibis cameo	11.00	32.00	75.00
61-70	9.30	28.00	65.00
71,77-80	7.00	21.00	50.00
72-76-Two Captain Marvel stories in each; 76-Spy Smasher becomes Crime Smasher	8.00	24.00	55.00
81-99: 86-Captain Marvel battles Sivana Family. 91-Infinity-c	7.00	21.00	50.00
100	10.00	30.00	70.00
101-106: 102-Commando Yank app. 106-Bulletman app.	5.70	17.00	40.00
107-141,143-152: 107-White House photo-c. 108-Brooklyn Bridge photo-c. 112-photo-c. 139-Infinity-c	5.00	15.00	35.00
142-Used in **POP**, pg. 89	5.00	15.00	35.00
153-155-(Scarce)	10.00	30.00	70.00

WILBUR COMICS (Teen-age) (Also see Laugh Comics & Zip Comics)
Sum', 1944-No. 87, 11/59; No. 88, 9/63; No. 89, 10/64; No. 90, 10/65 (No. 1-46: 52 pgs.)
MLJ Magazines/Archie Publ. No. 8, Spring, 1946 on

1	27.00	80.00	185.00
2(Fall,'44)	13.00	40.00	90.00
3,4(Wint,'44-'45; Spr,'45)	11.00	32.00	75.00
5-1st app. Katy Keene (Sum, 1945) & begin series; Wilbur story same as Archie story in Archie #1 except that Wilbur replaces Archie	43.00	130.00	300.00
6-10(Fall,'46)	10.00	30.00	70.00
11-20	5.70	17.00	40.00
21-30(1949)	4.00	12.00	28.00
31-50	2.30	7.00	16.00
51-70	1.50	4.50	10.00

	Good	Fine	N-Mint
71-90: 88-Last 10 cent issue (9/63)	.85	2.60	6.00

WILD BOY OF THE CONGO
No. 10, Feb-Mar, 1951-No. 15, June, 1955
Ziff-Davis No. 10-12,4-6/St. John No. 7? on

	Good	Fine	N-Mint
10(#1)(2-3/51)-Origin; bondage-c by Saunders; used in **SOTI**, pg. 189	9.30	28.00	65.00
11(4-5/51),12(8-9/51)-Norman Saunders-c	5.00	15.00	35.00
4(10-11/51)-Saunders bondage-c	5.00	15.00	35.00
5(Winter,'51)-Saunders-c	4.00	12.00	28.00
6,8,9(10/53),10: 6-Saunders-c	4.00	12.00	28.00
7(8-9/52)-Baker-c; Kinstler-a	4.50	14.00	32.00
11-13-Baker-c(St. John)	4.50	14.00	32.00
14(4/55)-Baker-c; r-#12('51)	4.50	14.00	32.00
15(6/55)	3.00	9.00	21.00

WILD WEST (Wild Western #3 on) Spring, 1948-No. 2, July, 1948 Marvel Comics (WFP)

	Good	Fine	N-Mint
1-Two-Gun Kid, Arizona Annie, & Tex Taylor begin; Shores-c	11.50	34.00	80.00
2-Captain Tootsie by Beck; Shores-c	10.00	30.00	70.00

WILD WESTERN (Wild West #1,2)
No. 3, 9/48-No. 57, 9/57 (3-11: 52 pgs; 12-on: 36 pgs)
Marvel/Atlas Comics (WFP)

	Good	Fine	N-Mint
3(#1)-Tex Morgan begins; Two-Gun Kid, Tex Taylor, & Arizona Annie continue from Wild West	13.00	40.00	90.00
4-Last Arizona Annie; Captain Tootsie by Beck; Kid Colt app.	9.30	28.00	65.00
5-2nd app. Black Rider (1/49); Blaze Carson, Captain Tootsie by Beck app.	10.00	30.00	70.00
6-8: 6-Blaze Carson app; anti-Wertham editorial	7.00	21.00	50.00
9-Photo-c; Black Rider begins, ends #19	8.00	24.00	55.00
10-Charles Starrett photo-c	10.00	30.00	70.00
11-(Last 52 pg. issue)	6.50	19.00	45.00
12-14,16-19: All Black Rider-c/stories. 12-14-The Prairie Kid & his horse Fury app.	5.00	15.00	35.00

15-Red Larabee, Gunhawk (Origin), his horse Blaze, & Apache Kid begin, end

	Good	Fine	N-Mint
#22; Black Rider-c/story	6.50	19.00	45.00
20-29: 20-Kid Colt-c begin	4.50	14.00	32.00
30-Katz-a	5.00	15.00	35.00
31-40	3.15	9.50	22.00
41-47,49-51,53,57	2.15	6.50	15.00
48-Williamson/Torres-a (4 pgs); Drucker-a	4.30	13.00	30.00
52-Crandall-a	3.70	11.00	26.00
54,55-Williamson-a in both (5 & 4 pgs.), #54 with Mayo plus 2 text illos			
	4.00	12.00	28.00
56-Baker-a?	2.30	7.00	16.00

WINGS COMICS
9/40-No. 109, 9/49; No. 110, Wint, 1949-50; No. 111, Spring, 1950; No. 112, 1950(nd); No. 113-No. 115, 1950(nd); No. 116, 1952(nd); No. 117, Fall, 1952-No. 122, Wint, 1953-54; No. 123-No. 124, 1954(nd)
Fiction House Magazines

	Good	Fine	N-Mint
1-Skull Squad, Clipper Kirk, Suicide Smith, Jane Martin, War Nurse, Phantom Falcons, Greasemonkey Griffin, Parachute Patrol & Powder Burns begin			
	79.00	235.00	550.00
2	40.00	120.00	280.00
3-5	29.00	85.00	200.00
6-10	25.00	75.00	175.00
11-15	22.00	65.00	150.00
16-Origin Captain Wings	24.00	71.00	165.00
17-20	16.00	48.00	110.00
21-30	14.00	43.00	100.00
31-40	11.50	34.00	80.00
41-50	9.30	28.00	65.00
51-60: 60-Last Skull Squad	8.00	24.00	55.00
61-67: 66-Ghost Patrol begins (becomes Ghost Squadron #71 on)			
	8.00	24.00	55.00
68,69: 68-Clipper Kirk becomes The Phantom Falcon-origin, Part 1; part 2 in #69			
	8.00	24.00	55.00
70-72: 70-1st app. The Phantom Falcon in costume, origin-Part 3; Capt. Wings battles Col. Kamikaze in all			
	6.00	19.00	45.00
73-99	6.00	19.00	45.00
100	7.00	21.00	50.00
101-124: 111-Last Jane Martin. 112-Flying Saucer-c/story. 115-Used in **POP**, pg. 89			
	5.00	15.00	35.00

WITCHING HOUR (The...later issues)
Feb-Mar, 1969-No. 85, Oct, 1978
National Periodical Publications/DC Comics

	Good	Fine	N-Mint
1-Toth plus Neal Adams-a, 3 pgs.	.85	2.60	6.00
2,6: 2-Toth-a	.50	1.50	3.00
3,5-Wrightson-a; Toth-p. 3-Last 12 cent issue	.60	1.75	3.50
4,7,9-12: Toth-a in all	.35	1.00	2.00
8-Toth, Neal Adams-a	.50	1.50	3.00
13-Neal Adams-c/a, 2pgs.	.35	1.00	2.00
14-Williamson/Garzon, Jones-a; N. Adams-c	.35	1.00	2.00
15-20		.60	1.20
21-85: 38-(100 pgs.). 84-(44 pgs.)		.35	.70

WOLVERINE (See Alpha Flight, Daredevil #196, 249, Havok & ..., Incredible
  Hulk #180, Incredible Hulk & ..., Kitty Pryde And ...., Marvel Comics
  Presents, Power Pack, Punisher and ...., Spider-Man vs .... & X-Men #94)

Sept, 1982-No. 4, Dec, 1982 (Mini-series)
Marvel Comics Group

	Good	Fine	N-Mint
1-Frank Miller-c/a(p) in all	3.35	10.00	20.00
2,3	2.15	6.50	13.00
4	2.70	8.00	16.00

WOLVERINE
Nov, 1988-Present ($1.50-$1.75, color, Baxter paper)
Marvel Comics

	Good	Fine	N-Mint
1-Buscema a-1-16, c-1-10; Williamson i-1,4-8	3.35	10.00	20.00
2	1.70	5.00	10.00
3-5	1.15	3.50	7.00
6-9: 6-McFarlane back-c. 7,8-Hulk app.	1.00	3.00	6.00
10-1st battle with Sabertooth (before Claws)	3.70	11.00	22.00
11-16: 11-New costume	.50	1.50	3.00
17-20: 17-Byrne-c/a(p) begins, ends #23	.35	1.00	2.00
21-40,43-48: 26-Begin $1.75-c?	.30	.90	1.80
41-Sabretooth revealed as Wolverine's father	.85	2.50	5.00
42-Sabretooth & Cable app.	.35	1.00	2.00
Annual nn (1990, $4.50, squarebound, 52 pgs.)-The Jungle Adventure; Simonson scripts; Mignola-c/a	.75	2.25	4.50

	Good	Fine	N-Mint
Annual 2 (12/90, $4.95, squarebound, 52 pgs.)-Bloodlust			
	.85	2.50	5.00
... Battles the Incredible Hulk nn (1989, $4.95, squarebound, 52 pg.)- r/Incredible Hulk #180,181	1.15	3.50	7.00

WOLVERINE SAGA
Mid-Sept, 1989-No. 4, Dec, 1989 ($3.95, color, mini-series, 52 pgs.)
Marvel Comics

	Good	Fine	N-Mint
1-Gives history; Austin-c(i)	.85	2.50	5.00
2-4: 4-Kaluta-c	.70	2.00	4.00

WOMEN OUTLAWS
July, 1948-No. 8, Sept, 1949
Fox Features Syndicate

	Good	Fine	N-Mint
1-Used in **SOTI**, illo-"Giving children an image of American womanhood"; negligee panels	27.00	81.00	190.00
2-Spanking panel	23.00	70.00	160.00
3-Kamenish-a	20.00	60.00	140.00
4-8	14.00	42.00	100.00
nn(nd)-Contains Cody of the Pony Express; same cover as #7	11.00	32.00	75.00

WONDER COMICS (Wonderworld #3 on)
May, 1939-No. 2, June, 1939
Fox Features Syndicate

	Good	Fine	VF-NM
1-(Scarce)-Wonder Man only app. by Eisner; Dr. Fung (by Powell), K-51 begins; Bob Kane-a; Eisner-c	383.00	960.00	2300.00
	Good	**Fine**	**N-Mint**
2-(Scarce)-Yarko the Great, Master Magician by Eisner begins; 'Spark' Stevens by Bob Kane, Patty O'Day, Tex Mason app. Lou Fine's 1st-c; Fine-a (2 pgs.)	217.00	540.00	1300.00

WONDER COMICS
May, 1944-No. 20, Oct, 1948
Great/Nedor/Better Publications

	Good	Fine	N-Mint
1-The Grim Reaper & Spectro, the Mind Reader begin; Hitler/Hirohito bondage-c	36.00	107.00	250.00

	Good	Fine	N-Mint
2-Origin The Grim Reaper; Super Sleuths begins, end #8,17			
	22.00	65.00	150.00
3-5	19.00	56.00	130.00
6-10: 6-Flag-c. 8-Last Spectro. 9-Wonderman begins			
	16.00	48.00	110.00
11-14-Dick Devens, King of Futuria begins #11, ends #14			
	19.00	56.00	130.00
15-Tara begins (origin), ends #20	21.00	62.00	145.00
16,18: 16-Spectro app.; last Grim Reaper. 18-The Silver Knight begins			
	18.00	54.00	125.00
17-Wonderman with Frazetta panels; Jill Trent with all Frazetta inks			
	20.00	60.00	140.00
19-Frazetta panels	19.00	56.00	130.00
20-Most of Silver Knight by Frazetta	23.00	70.00	160.00

WONDER WOMAN (See All-Star, Sensation, & World's Finest #244)
Summer, 1942-No. 329, Feb, 1986
National Periodical Publications/All-American Publ./DC Comics

	Good	Fine	VF-NM
1-Origin Wonder Woman retold (see All-Star #8); H. G. Peter-a begins			
	417.00	1040.00	2500.00

	Good	Fine	N-Mint
2-Origin & 1st app. Mars; Duke of Deception app.			
	115.00	345.00	800.00
3	82.00	245.00	575.00
4,5: 5-1st Dr. Psycho app.	60.00	180.00	420.00
6-10: 6-1st Cheetah app.	47.00	140.00	330.00
11-20	36.00	107.00	250.00
21-30	27.00	81.00	190.00
31-40	20.00	60.00	140.00
41-44,46-48	16.00	48.00	110.00
45-Origin retold	27.00	81.00	190.00
49-Used in **SOTI**, pgs. 234,236; Last 52 pg. issue			
	16.00	48.00	110.00
50-(44 pgs.)-Used in **POP**, pg. 97	14.00	43.00	100.00
51-60	11.00	32.00	75.00
61-72: 62-Origin of W.W. I.D. 64-Story about 3-D movies. 70-1st Angle Man app.			
72-Last pre-code	9.30	28.00	65.00
73-90: 80-Origin The Invisible Plane. 89-Flying saucer-c/story			
	7.00	21.00	50.00

	Good	Fine	N-Mint

91-94,96-99: 97-Last H. G. Peter-a. 98-Orign W.W. I.D. with new facts

	5.00	15.00	35.00
95-A-Bomb-c	5.70	17.00	40.00
100	6.50	19.00	45.00

101-104,106-110: 107-1st advs. of Wonder Girl; 1st Merboy; tells how Wonder
    Woman won her costume   4.30   13.00   30.00

105-(Scarce)-Wonder Woman's secret origin; W. Woman appears as a girl (not
    Wonder Girl)   11.50   34.00   80.00

111-120	2.65	8.00	18.00

121-126: 122-1st app. Wonder Tot. 124-1st app. Wonder Woman Family. 126-Last
    10 cent issue   1.50   4.50   10.00

127-130: 128-Origin The Invisible Plane retold	1.30	4.00	9.00
131-150: 132-Flying saucer-c	.85	2.60	6.00
151-158,160-170 (1967)	.70	2.00	5.00
159-Origin retold	.85	2.60	6.00
171-178	.60	1.75	3.50

179-195: 179-Wears no costume to issue #203. 180-Death of Steve Trevor. 195-
    Wood inks?   .45   1.25   2.50

196 (52 pgs.)-Origin r-/All-Star 8	.50	1.50	3.00
197,198 (52 pgs.)-Reprints	.50	1.50	3.00
199,200 (5-6/72)-Jeff Jones-c; 52 pgs.	.85	2.50	5.00

201-210: 204-Return to old costume; death of I Ching. 202-Fafhrd & The Grey
    Mouser debut   .60   1.20

211-240: 211,214-(100 pgs.), 217-(68 pgs.). 220-N. Adams assist. 223- Steve
    Trevor revived as Steve Howard & learns W.W.'s I.D. 228- Both W. Women
    team up & new World War II stories begin, end #243. 237-Origin retold
             .50   1.00

241-266,269-280,284-286: 241-Intro Bouncer. 247-249-(44 pgs.). 248- Steve
    Trevor Howard dies. 249-Hawkgirl app. 250-Origin/1st app. Orana, the new
    W. Woman. 251-Orana dies. 269-Last Wood a(i) for DC? (7/80). 271-
    Huntress & 3rd Life of Steve Trevor begin   .50   1.00

267,268-Re-intro Animal Man (5/80 & 6/80)	2.85	8.50	20.00
281-283: Joker covers & stories	.50	1.50	3.00
287-New Teen Titans x-over	.25	.75	1.50

288-299,301-328: 288-New costume & logo. 291-293-Three part epic with Super-
    Heroines   .50   1.00

300-($1.50, 76 pgs.)-Anniversary issue; Giffen-a; New Teen Titans, JLA & G.A.
    Wonder Woman app.   .25   .75   1.50

329-Double size	.25	.75	1.50

WONDER WOMAN
Feb, 1987-Present
DC Comics

	Good	Fine	N-Mint
1-New origin; Perez-c/a begins	.50	1.50	3.00
2-20: 8-Origin Cheetah. 12,13-Millennium x-over. 18,26-Free 16 pg. story			
		.65	1.30
21-49,51-60: 24-Last Perez-a; c/scripts continue		.50	1.00
50-($1.50, 52 pgs.)-New Titans, Justice League	.25	.75	1.50
Annual 1 ('88, $1.50)-Art Adams-a(p&i)	.25	.75	1.50
Annual 2 ('89, $2.00, 68 pgs.)-All women artists issue; Perez-c(i)			
	.35	1.00	2.00

WONDERWORLD COMICS (Formerly Wonder Comics)
No. 3, July, 1939-No. 33, Jan, 1942
Fox Features Syndicate

	Good	Fine	N-Mint
3-Intro The Flame by Fine; Dr. Fung (Powell-a), K-51 (Powell-a?), & Yarko the Great, Master Magician (Eisner-a) continues; Eisner/ Fine-c			
	150.00	375.00	900.00
4	59.00	175.00	410.00
5-10	54.00	160.00	375.00
11-Origin The Flame	63.00	190.00	440.00
12-20: 13-Dr. Fung ends	34.00	100.00	235.00
21-Origin The Black Lion & Cub	30.00	90.00	210.00
22-27: 22,25-Dr. Fung app.	23.00	70.00	160.00
28-1st app/origin U.S. Jones; Lu-Nar, the Moon Man begins			
	29.00	85.00	200.00
29,31-33: 32-Hitler-c	18.00	54.00	125.00
30-Origin Flame Girl	34.00	100.00	235.00

WORLD'S BEST COMICS (World's Finest Comics #2 on)
Spring, 1941 (Cardboard-c)(DC's 6th annual format comic)
National Periodical Publications (100 pgs.)

	Good	Fine	VF-NM
1-The Batman, Superman, Crimson Avenger, Johnny Thunder, The King, Young Dr. Davis, Zatara, Lando, Man of Magic, & Red, White & Blue begin; Superman, Batman & Robin covers begin (inside-c blank)			
	500.00	1250.00	3000.00

World's Finest Comics #7, © DC Comics

WORLD'S FINEST COMICS (Formerly World's Best Comics #1)
No. 2, Sum, 1941-No. 323, Jan, 1986 (early issues have 100 pgs.)
National Periodical Publ./DC Comics (#1-17 have cardboard covers)

	Good	Fine	N-Mint
2 (100 pgs.)-Superman, Batman & Robin covers continue			
	225.00	562.00	1350.00
3-The Sandman begins; last Johnny Thunder; origin & 1st app. The Scarecrow			
	192.00	480.00	1150.00
4-Hop Harrigan app.; last Young Dr. Davis	133.00	335.00	800.00
5-Intro. TNT & Dan the Dyna-Mite; last King & Crimson Avenger			
	133.00	335.00	800.00
6-Star Spangled Kid begins; Aquaman app.; S&K Sandman with Sandy in new costume begins, ends #7	107.00	270.00	640.00
7-Green Arrow begins; last Lando, King, & Red, White & Blue; S&K art			
	107.00	270.00	640.00
8-Boy Commandos begin	96.00	240.00	575.00
9,10: S&K-a. 9-Batman cameo in Star Spangled Kid; last 100pg. issue; Hitler, Mussolini, Tojo-c	83.00	210.00	500.00

	Good	Fine	N-Mint
11-17-Last cardboard cover issue	75.00	190.00	450.00
18-20: 18-Paper covers begin; last Star Spangled Kid			
	67.00	167.00	400.00
21-30: 30-Johnny Peril app.	48.00	120.00	285.00
31-40: 33-35-Tomahawk app.	41.00	102.00	245.00
41-50: 41-Boy Commandos end. 42-Wyoming Kid begins, ends #63. 43-Full Steam Foley begins, ends #48. 48-Last square binding. 49-Tom Sparks, Boy Inventor begins	32.00	80.00	190.00
51-60: 51-Zatara ends. 59-Manhunters Around the World begins, ends #62			
	32.00	80.00	190.00
61-64: 63-Capt. Compass app.	28.00	70.00	165.00
65-Origin Superman; Tomahawk begins, ends #101			
	35.00	88.00	210.00
66-70-(15 cent issues)(Scarce)-Last 68 pg. issue	26.00	77.00	180.00
71-(10 cent issue)(Scarce)-Superman & Batman begin as team			
	32.00	95.00	220.00
72,73-(10 cent issues)(Scarce)	24.00	70.00	165.00
74-80: 74-Last pre-code issue	13.00	40.00	90.00
81-90: 88-1st Joker/Luthor team-up. 90-Batwoman's 1st app. in World's Finest	8.50	25.50	60.00
91-93,95-99: 96-99-Kirby Green Arrow	5.70	17.00	40.00
94-Origin Superman/Batman team retold	26.00	78.00	185.00
100 (3/59)	14.00	41.00	95.00
101-121: 102-Tommy Tomorrow begins, ends. #124. 113-Intro. Miss Arrowette in Green Arrow; 1st Bat-Mite/Mr. Mxyzptlk team-up. 121-Last 10 cent issue	4.30	13.00	30.00
122-128,130-142: 123-2nd Bat-Mite/Mr. Mxyzptlk team-up. 125-Aquaman begins, ends #139. 140-Last Green Arrow. 142-Origin The Composite Superman (villain); Legion app.	2.15	6.50	15.00
129-Joker-c/story	3.60	11.00	25.00
143-150: 143-1st Mailbag	1.30	4.00	9.00
151-155,157-160	1.00	3.00	7.00
156-1st Bizarro Batman; Joker-c/story	5.70	17.00	40.00
161,170 (80-Pg. Giants G-28,G-40)	1.30	4.00	9.00
162-165,167-169,171-174: 168,172-Adult Legion app.	.70	2.00	5.00
166-Joker-c/story	1.30	4.00	9.00
175,176-Neal Adams-a; both r-J'onn J'onzz origin/Detective #225,226	1.00	3.00	7.00
177-Joker-c/story	1.00	3.00	7.00

	Good	Fine	N-Mint
178,180-187: 182-Silent Knight-r/Brave & Bold #6. 186-Johnny Quick-r. 187-Green Arrow origin-r/Adv. #256	.50	1.50	3.00
179,188 (80-Pg. Giant G-52,G-64)	.70	2.00	4.00
189-196,200-204: 190-193-Robin-r	.35	1.00	2.00
197-(80-Pg. Giant G-76)	.50	1.50	3.00
198,199-3rd Superman/Flash race	1.50	4.50	9.00
205-6 pgs. Shining Knight by Frazetta/Adv. #153; 52 pgs.; Teen Titans x-over	.35	1.00	2.00
206 (80-Pg. Giant G-88)	.35	1.00	2.00
207-248: 207-212-(52 pgs.). 215-Intro. Batman Jr. & Superman Jr. 217-Metamorpho begins, ends #220; Batman/Superman team-ups begin. 223-228-(100 pgs.). 223-N. Adams-r. 223-Deadman origin. 226-N. Adams S&K, Toth-r; Manhunter part origin-r/Detective #225,226. 229-r/origin Superman-Batman team. 244-Green Arrow, Black Canary, Wonder Woman, Vigilante begin; $1.00, 84 pg. issues begin. 246-Death of Stuff in Vigilante; origin Vigilante retold. 248-Last Vigilante	.25	.75	1.50
249-The Creeper begins by Ditko, ends #255	.70	2.00	4.00
250-299: 250-The Creeper origin retold by Ditko. 252-Last 84 pg. issue. 253-Capt. Marvel begins; 68 pgs. begin, end #265. 255- Last Creeper. 256-Hawkman begins. 257-Black Lightning begins. 266-282-(52 pgs.). 268-Capt. Marvel Jr. origin retold. 271-Origin Superman/Batman team retold. 274-Zatanna begins. 279,280-Capt. Marvel Jr. & Kid Eternity learn they are brothers. 284-Legion app. 298-Begin 75 cent-c	.25	.75	1.50
300-($1.25, 52 pgs.)-Justice League of America, New Teen Titans & The Outsiders app.; Perez-a(3 pgs.)	.35	1.00	2.00
301-323: 304-Origin Null and Void. 309,319-Free 16 pg. story in each (309-Flash Force 2000, 319-Mask preview)	.25	.75	1.50

WOW COMICS (Real Western Hero #70 on)
Winter, 1940-41; No. 2, Summer, 1941-No. 69, Fall, 1948
Fawcett Publications

	Good	Fine	VF-NM
nn(#1)-Origin Mr. Scarlet by S&K; Atom Blake, Boy Wizard, Jim Dolan, & Rick O'Shay begin; Diamond Jack, The White Rajah & Shipwreck Roberts, only app.; the cover was printed on unstable paper stock & is rarely found in fine or mint condition; blank inside-c; bondage-c by Beck			
(Prices vary widely on this book)	650.00	1950.00	5200.00
	Good	**Fine**	**N-Mint**
2 (Scarce)-The Hunchback begins	75.00	225.00	525.00

	Good	Fine	N-Mint
3 (Fall, 1941)	46.00	137.00	320.00
4-Origin Pinky	50.00	150.00	350.00
5	36.00	107.00	250.00
6-Origin The Phantom Eagle; Commando Yank begins			
	30.00	90.00	210.00
7,8,10: 10-Swayze-c/a on Mary Marvel	27.00	81.00	190.00
9 (1/6/43)-Capt. Marvel, Capt. Marvel Jr., Shazam app.; Scarlet & Pinky x-over; Mary Marvel c/stories begin (cameo #9)			
	50.00	150.00	350.00
11-17,19,20: 15-Flag-c	18.00	54.00	125.00
18-1st app. Uncle Marvel (10/43); infinity-c	22.00	65.00	150.00
21-30: 28-Pinky x-over in Mary Marvel	11.00	32.00	75.00
31-40: 32-68-Phantom Eagle by Swayze	7.00	21.00	50.00
41-50	5.70	17.00	40.00
51-58: Last Mary Marvel	5.00	15.00	35.00
59-69: 59-Ozzie begins. 62-Flying Saucer gag-c (1/48). 65-69-Tom Mix stories			
	4.30	13.00	30.00

X

X-FACTOR (Also see The Avengers #263 & Fantastic Four #286)
Feb, 1986-Present
Marvel Comics Group

	Good	Fine	N-Mint
1-($1.25, 52 pgs)-Story recaps 1st app. from Avengers #263; original X-Men app.; Layton/Guice-a	1.35	4.00	8.00
2,3	.85	2.50	5.00
4,5	.75	2.25	4.50
6-10	.60	1.75	3.50
11-20	.50	1.50	3.00
21-23	.40	1.25	2.50
24-26: Fall Of The Mutants. 26-New outfits	.70	2.00	4.00
27-30	.35	1.00	2.00
31-37,39,41-49: 35-Origin Cyclops	.25	.75	1.50
38,50-Double size ($1.50)	.35	1.00	2.00
40-Rob Liefeld-c/a	.70	2.00	4.00
51-53-Sabretooth app.	.50	1.50	3.00
54-59,64-72: 54-Intro Crimson		.50	1.00
60-X-Tinction Agenda x-over	1.15	3.50	7.00
60-Gold 2nd print	.40	1.25	2.50
61,62-X-Tinction Agenda x-over. 62-Jim Lee-c	.75	2.25	4.50
63	.50	1.50	3.00
Annual 1 (10/86), 2 (10/87)	.40	1.25	2.50
Annual 3 ('88, $1.75)-Evolutionary War app.	.50	1.50	3.00
Annual 4 ('89, $2.00, 68 pgs.)-Atlantis Attacks; Byrne/Simonson-a, Byrne-c			
	.40	1.25	2.50
Annual 5 ('90, $2.00, 68 pgs.)-F.F., New Mutants x-over			
	.35	1.00	2.00
Annual 6 ('91, $2.00, 68 pgs.)	.35	1.00	2.00
...Prisoner of Love nn (1990, $4.95, 52 pgs.)-Starlin scripts; Guice-a			
	.85	2.50	5.00

X-FORCE (See New Mutants #100)
Aug. 1991-Present ($1.00, color)
Marvel Comics

1-($1.50, 52 pgs.)-Sealed in plastic bag with Marvel trading card inside; Liefeld-c/a begins	.35	1.00	2.00
2-4		.50	1.00

X-Men #51, © Marvel Comics

X-MEN, THE (X-Men #94-141; The Uncanny . . . #142 on; see Classic X-Men,
  Kitty Pryde and Wolverine, Marvel & DC Present, Marvel Team-up,
  Nightcrawler, Special Edition . . . , X-Factor & X-Terminators)
Sept, 1963-Present
Marvel Comics Group

	Good	Fine	N-Mint
1-Origin/1st app. X-Men; 1st app. Magneto	145.00	580.00	1300.00
2-1st app. The Vanisher	60.00	180.00	420.00
3-1st app. The Blob	31.00	95.00	220.00
4-1st Quick Silver & Scarlet Witch & Brotherhood of the Evil Mutants			
	27.00	80.00	185.00
5	21.00	62.00	145.00
6-10: 6-Sub-Mariner app. 8-1st Unus the Untouchable. 9-Early Avengers app. 10-			
1st S.A. app. Ka-Zar	16.00	48.00	110.00
11,13-15: 11-1st app. The Stranger. 14-1st app. Sentinels. 15-Origin Beast			
	10.00	30.00	70.00
12-Origin Prof. X	16.00	48.00	110.00
16-20: 19-1st app. The Mimic	7.00	21.00	50.00

	Good	Fine	N-Mint
21-27,29,30: 27-Re-enter The Mimic (r-in #75)	5.70	17.00	40.00
28-1st app. The Banshee (r-in #76)	6.50	19.00	45.00
31-34,36,37,39,40: 39-New costumes	4.00	12.00	28.00
35-Spider-Man x-over (8/67)(r-in #83)	6.50	19.00	45.00
38-Origins of the X-Men series begins, ends #57	5.00	15.00	35.00
41-49: 42-Death of Prof. X (Changeling disguised as). 44-Red Raven app. (G.A.). 49-Steranko-c; 1st Polaris	3.15	9.50	22.00
50,51-Steranko-c/a	4.00	12.00	28.00
52	2.65	8.00	18.00
53-Barry Smith-c/a (1st comic book work)	4.00	12.00	28.00
54,55-B. Smith-c. 54-1st app. Alex Summers	3.60	11.00	25.00
56-63,65-Neal Adams-a(p). 56-Intro. Havoc without costume. 65-Return of Professor X. 58-1st app. Havoil	4.30	13.00	30.00
64-1st Sunfire app.	3.15	9.50	22.00
66-Last new story w/original X-Men	2.15	6.50	15.00
67-70,72: All 52 pgs. 67-Reprints begin, end #93	1.85	5.50	13.00
71,73-93: 73-86 r-#25-38 w/new-c. 87-93 r-#39-45 with-c	1.70	5.00	12.00
94(8/75)-New X-Men begin; Colossus, Nightcrawler, Thunderbird, Storm, Wolverine, & Banshee join; Angel, Marvel Girl, & Iceman resign	20.00	60.00	140.00
95-Death Thunderbird	5.70	17.00	40.00
96-99 (regular 25 cent cover)	4.00	12.00	28.00
98,99 (30 cent cover)	4.00	12.00	28.00
100-Old vs. New X-Men; part origin Phoenix	4.30	13.00	30.00
101-Phoenix origin concludes	4.00	12.00	28.00
102-107: 102-Origin Storm. 104-Intro. Star Jammers. 106-Old vs. New X-Men	1.85	5.50	13.00
108-Byrne-a begins (See Marvel Team-Up 53)	4.35	13.00	30.00
109-1st Vindicator	3.70	11.00	25.00
110,111: 110-Phoenix joins	2.15	6.50	15.00
112-119: 117-Origin Professor X	1.70	5.00	12.00
120-1st app. Alpha Flight (cameo), story line begins	4.00	12.00	28.00
121-1st Alpha Flight (full story)	4.35	13.00	30.00
122-128: 124-Colossus becomes Proletarian	1.85	5.50	11.00
129-Intro Kitty Pryde	2.15	6.50	13.00
130-1st app. The Dazzler by Byrne	2.35	7.00	14.00
131-135: 131-Dazzler app. 133-Wolverine app. 134-Phoenix becomes Dark Phoenix	1.70	5.00	10.00

	Good	Fine	N-Mint
136,138: 138-Dazzler app.; Cyclops leaves	1.45	4.25	8.50
137-Giant; death of Phoenix	1.85	5.50	11.00
139-Alpha Flight app.; Kitty Pryde joins; new costume for Wolverine			
	2.50	7.50	15.00
140-Alpha Flight app.	3.00	9.00	18.00
141-Intro Future X-Men & The New Brotherhood of Evil Mutants; death of Frank Richards	2.00	6.00	12.00
142,143: 142-Deaths of Wolverine, Storm & Colossus. 143-Last Byrne issue			
	1.15	3.50	7.00
144-150: 144-Man-Thing app. 145-Old X-Men app. 148-Spider-Woman, Dazzler app. 150-Double size	1.00	3.00	6.00
151-157,159-161,163,164: 161-Origin Magneto. 163-Origin Binary. 164-1st app. Binary as Carol Danvers	.70	2.00	4.00
158-1st app. Rogue in X-Men (See Avengers Annual #10)			
	.85	2.50	5.00
162-Wolverine solo story	1.15	3.50	7.00
165-Paul Smith-a begins	1.00	3.00	6.00
166-Double size; Paul Smith-a	.85	2.50	5.00
167-170: 167-New Mutants x-over. 168-1st app. Madelyne Pryor in X-Men (See Avengers Annual #10)	.55	1.70	3.40
171-Rogue joins X-Men; Simonson-c/a	1.05	3.15	6.30
172-174: 172,173-Two part Wolverine solo story. 173-Two cover variations, blue & black. 174-Phoenix cameo	.55	1.70	3.40
175-Double size; anniversary issue; Phoenix returns. Last Paul Smith- c/a			
	.70	2.10	4.20
176-185: 181-Sunfire app. 182-Rogue solo story	.45	1.35	2.70
186-Double-size; Barry Smith/Austin-a	.60	1.85	3.70
187-192,194-199: 190,191-Spider-Man & Avengers x-over. 195-Power Pack x-over	.45	1.30	2.60
193-Double size; 100th app. New X-Men	.70	2.10	4.20
200-Double size	1.05	3.15	6.30
201-204,206-209: 204-Nightcrawler solo story. 207-Wolverine/Phoenix story	.70	2.10	4.20
205-Wolverine solo story by Barry Smith	1.00	3.00	6.00
210,211-Mutant Massacre in 210-213	2.15	6.50	15.00
212,213-Wolverine battles Sabretooth	3.15	9.50	22.00
214-221,223,224: 219-Havok joins	.50	1.50	3.00
222-Wolverine battles Sabretooth-c/story	1.35	4.00	9.00
225-227: Fall Of The Mutants. 226-Double size	1.00	3.00	7.00
228-239,241: 229-$1.00 begin	.40	1.25	2.50
240-Sabretooth app.	.70	2.00	4.00

	Good	Fine	N-Mint
242-Double size, X-Factor app., Inferno tie-in	.50	1.50	3.00
243-247: 245-Liefeld-a	.35	1.00	2.00
248-1st Jim Lee art on X-Men	2.70	8.00	16.00
249-252	.25	.75	1.50
253-255: 253-All new X-men begin	.35	1.00	2.00
256-Jim Lee-c/a begins	1.00	3.00	6.00
257-Jim Lee-a	.85	2.50	5.00
258-Wolverine solo story; Lee-a	.60	1.75	3.50
259-Jim Lee-a	.50	1.50	3.00
260-266: No Jim Lee-a	.35	1.00	2.00
267-Jim Lee-a resumes	1.35	4.00	8.00
268-Capt. America, Black Widow & Wolverine team-up			
	1.50	4.50	9.00
269-Lee-a	.85	2.50	5.00
270-X-Tinction Agenda x-over	.85	2.50	5.00
270-Gold 2nd printing	.25	.75	1.50
271,272-X-Tinction Agenda x-over	.70	2.00	4.00
273-New Mutants (Cable) & X-Factor app.	.50	1.50	3.00
274	.35	1.00	2.00
275-($1.50, 52 pgs.)	.50	1.50	3.00
276-282		.50	1.00
Special 1(12/70)-Kirby-c/a; origin The Stranger	3.60	11.00	25.00
Special 2(11/71)	3.60	11.00	25.00
Annual 3(1979)-New story	1.30	4.00	9.00
Annual 4(1980)-Dr. Strange app.	1.00	3.00	6.00
Annual 5(1981)	.70	2.10	4.25
Annual 6(1982)	.50	1.50	3.00
Annual 7(1983), 8(1984)	.40	1.25	2.50
Annual 9(1985)-New Mutants; Art Adams-a	1.50	4.50	10.00
Annual 10(1986)-Art Adams-a	1.50	4.50	10.00
Annual 11(1987)	.35	1.00	2.00
Annual 12(1988, $1.75)-Evolutionary War app.	.50	1.50	3.00
Annual 13(1989, $2.00, 68 pgs.)-Atlantis Attacks	.35	1.00	2.00
Annual 14(1990, $2.00, 68 pgs.) Fantastic Four, New Mutants & X-Factor x-over;			
Arthur Adams-a(p)	.35	1.00	2.00
Annual 15(1991, $2.00, 68 pgs.)-4 pg. origin; Wolverine solo back-up story;			
X-Force app.	.40	1.25	2.50

X-MEN/ALPHA FLIGHT
Jan, 1986-No. 2, Jan, 1986 ($1.50, mini-series)
Marvel Comics Group

	Good	Fine	N-Mint
1,2: 1-Intro. The Berserkers; Paul Smith-a	.60	1.75	3.50

X-MEN AND THE MICRONAUTS, THE
Jan, 1984-No. 4, April, 1984 (Mini-series)
Marvel Comics Group

1-4: Guice-c/a(p) in all	.25	.75	1.50

X-MEN CLASSIC (Formerly Classic X-Men)
No. 46, Apr, 1990-Present ($1.25, color)
Marvel Comics

46-60: Reprints from X-Men. 54-($1.25, 52 pgs.)		.65	1.30

X-MEN CLASSICS (Also see Classic X-Men)
Dec, 1983-No. 3, Feb, 1984 ($2.00; Baxter paper)
Marvel Comics Group

1-3: X-Men-r by Neal Adams	.50	1.50	3.00

X-MEN SPOTLIGHT ON . . . STARJAMMERS
1990-No. 2, 1990 ($4.50, squarebound, 52 pgs.)
Marvel Comics

1,2-Cockrum/Albrecht-a	.75	2.25	4.50

X-MEN VS. THE AVENGERS
Apr, 1987-No. 4, July, 1987 ($1.50, mini-series, Baxter paper)
Marvel Comics Group

1	.60	1.75	3.50
2-4	.40	1.25	2.50

X-TERMINATORS
Oct, 1988-No. 4, Jan, 1989 ($1.00, color, mini-series)
Marvel Comics

1-X-Men/X-Factor tie-in; Williamson-i	.50	1.50	3.00
2	.30	.90	1.75
3,4		.60	1.25

Y

YELLOW CLAW
Oct, 1956-No. 4, April, 1957
Atlas Comics (MjMC)

	Good	Fine	N-Mint
1-Origin by Joe Maneely	35.00	105.00	245.00
2-Kirby-a	26.00	77.00	180.00
3,4-Kirby-a; 4-Kirby/Severin-a	24.00	70.00	165.00

YOGI BEAR (TV) (Hanna-Barbera)
No. 1067, 12-2/59-60-No. 9, 7-9/62; No. 10, 10/62-No. 42, 10/70
Dell Publishing Co./Gold Key No. 10 on

	Good	Fine	N-Mint
4-Color 1067 (#1)	5.00	15.00	35.00
4-Color 1104,1162 (5-7/61)	3.50	10.50	24.00
4(8-9/61)-6(12-1/61-62)	2.65	8.00	18.00
4-Color 1271(11/61), 1349(1/62)	2.65	8.00	18.00
7(2-3/62)-9(7-9/62)-Last Dell	2.30	7.00	16.00
10(10/62-G.K.), 11(1/63)-titled "Yogi Bear Jellystone Jollies"-80 pgs.; 11-Xmas-c			
	2.50	7.50	20.00
12(4/63), 14-20	1.70	5.00	12.00
13(7/63)-Surprise Party, 68 pgs.	2.50	7.50	20.00
21-30	1.00	3.00	7.00
31-42	.60	1.80	4.00

YOGI BEAR (TV)
Nov, 1970-No. 35, Jan, 1976 (Hanna-Barbera)
Charlton Comics

	Good	Fine	N-Mint
1	1.00	3.00	7.00
2-6,8-35: 28-31-partial-r	.70	2.00	4.00
7-Summer Fun (Giant); 52 pgs.	.70	2.00	4.00

YOUNG ALLIES COMICS (All-Winners #21)
Summer, 1941-No. 20, Oct, 1946
Timely Comics (USA 1-7/NPI 8,9/YAI 10-20)

	Good	Fine	VF-NM
1-Origin/1st app. The Young Allies; 1st meeting of Captain America & Human			

	Good	Fine	VF-NM
Torch; Red Skull app.; S&K-c/splash; Hitler-c			
	283.00	710.00	1700.00

	Good	Fine	N-Mint
2-Captain America & Human Torch app.; Simon & Kirby-c			
	129.00	323.00	775.00
3-Fathertime, Captain America & Human Torch app.			
	100.00	250.00	600.00
4-The Vagabond & Red Skull, Capt. America, Human Torch app.			
	104.00	260.00	625.00
5-Captain America & Human Torch app.	57.00	140.00	340.00
6-10: 9-Hitler, Tojo, Mussolini-c. 10-Origin Tommy Tyme & Clock of Ages; ends #19	44.00	110.00	265.00
11-20: 12-Classic decapitation story	35.00	88.00	210.00

YOUNG ALL-STARS
June, 1987-No. 31, Nov, 1989 ($1.00, deluxe format, color)
DC Comics

	Good	Fine	N-Mint
1-1st app. Iron Munro & The Flying Fox	.50	1.50	3.00
2,3	.25	.80	1.60
4-31: 8,9-Millennium tie-ins	.25	.75	1.50
Annual 1 (1988, $2.00)	.30	.90	1.80

Z

ZANE GREY'S STORIES OF THE WEST
No. 197, 9/48-No. 996, 5-7/59; 11/64 (All painted-c)
Dell Publishing Co./Gold Key 11/64

	Good	Fine	N-Mint
4-Color 197(#1)(9/48)	7.00	21.00	50.00
4-Color 222,230,236(`49)	5.00	15.00	35.00
4-Color 246,255,270,301,314,333,346	3.70	11.00	26.00
4-Color 357,372,395,412,433,449,467,484	3.00	9.00	21.00
4-Color 511-Kinstler-a	3.50	10.50	24.00
4-Color 532,555,583,604,616,632(5/55)	3.00	9.00	21.00
27(9-11/55)-39(9-11/58)	2.30	7.00	16.00
4-Color 996(5-7/59)	2.30	7.00	16.00
10131-411-(11/64-G.K.)-Nevada; r-4-Color #996	1.30	4.00	9.00

ZIP COMICS
Feb, 1940-No. 47, Summer, 1944
MLJ Magazines

	Good	Fine	N-Mint
1-Origin Kalathar the Giant Man, The Scarlet Avenger, & Steel Sterling; Mr. Satan, Nevada Jones & Zambini, the Miracle Man, War Eagle, Captain Valor begins	125.00	312.00	750.00
2	54.00	160.00	375.00
3	42.00	125.00	290.00
4,5	36.00	107.00	250.00
6-9: 9-Last Kalathar & Mr. Satan	31.00	92.00	215.00
10-Inferno, the Flame Breather begins, ends #13	29.00	85.00	200.00
11,12: 11-Inferno without costume	27.00	80.00	185.00
13-17,19: 17-Last Scarlet Avenger	27.00	80.00	185.00
18-Wilbur begins (1st app.)	29.00	85.00	200.00
20-Origin Black Jack (1st app.)	40.00	120.00	280.00
21-26: 25-Last Nevada Jones. 26-Black Witch begins; last Captain Valor	26.00	77.00	180.00
27-Intro. Web	40.00	120.00	280.00
28-Origin Web	40.00	120.00	280.00
29,30	22.00	65.00	150.00

	Good	Fine	N-Mint
31-38: 34-1st Applejack app. 35-Last Zambini, Black Jack. 38-Last Web issue			
	16.00	48.00	110.00
39-Red Rube begins (origin, 8/43)	16.00	48.00	110.00
40-47: 45-Wilbur ends	11.50	34.00	80.00

ZOOT (Rulah Jungle Goddess #17 on)
nd (1946)-No. 16, July, 1948 (Two #13s & 14s)
Fox Features Syndicate

	Good	Fine	N-Mint
nn-Funny animal only	9.30	28.00	65.00
2-The Jaguar app.	8.00	24.00	55.00
3(Fall,'46)-6-Funny animals & teen-age	4.30	13.00	30.00
7-Rulah, Jungle Goddess begins (6/47); origin & 1st app.			
	36.00	107.00	250.00
8-10	27.00	80.00	185.00
11-Kamen bondage-c	29.00	85.00	200.00
12-Injury-to-eye panels	17.00	51.00	120.00
13(2/48)	17.00	51.00	120.00
14(3/48)-Used in **SOTI**, pg. 104, "One picture showing a girl nailed by her wrists to trees with blood flowing from the wounds, might be taken straight from an ill. ed. of the Marquis deSade"	22.00	65.00	150.00
13(4/48), 14(5/48)	17.00	51.00	120.00
15,16	17.00	51.00	120.00

ZORRO (Walt Disney with #882) (TV)
May, 1949-No. 15, Sept-Nov, 1961 (Photo-c 882 on)
Dell Publishing Co.

	Good	Fine	N-Mint
4-Color 228	18.00	54.00	125.00
4-Color 425,497,574,617,732	10.00	30.00	70.00
4-Color 538-Kinstler-a	11.00	32.00	75.00
4-Color 882-Photo-c begin; Toth-a	8.50	25.50	60.00
4-Color 920,933,960,976-Toth-a in all	8.50	25.50	60.00
4-Color 1003('59)	7.00	21.00	50.00
4-Color 1037-Annette Funicello photo-c	9.30	28.00	65.00
8(12-2/59-60)	4.50	14.00	32.00
9,12-Toth-a	5.70	17.00	40.00
10,11,13-15-Last photo-c	3.60	11.00	25.00

ZORRO (Walt Disney) (TV)	**Good**	**Fine**	**N-Mint**
Jan, 1966-No. 9, March, 1968 (All photo-c)			
Gold Key			
1-Toth-a	4.00	12.00	28.00
2,4,5,7-9-Toth-a	2.85	8.50	20.00
3,6-Tufts-a	2.30	7.00	16.00

Big Little
Books

INTRODUCTION

Big Little Books first appeared in 1933 in the heart of the depression, the same year that the first comic books were being tested. The idea for Big Little Books came about through a series of circumstances set in motion by a young Samuel Lowe, who headed the creative marketing and sales staff at Whitman. Sam frequently went into the shop to get a first-hand view of what the equipment could do. On one such trip through the bindery, he saw strips or blocks of paper falling from lifts of printed sheets on the cutter. It seemed to him that this paper was being wasted, and he picked up a handful. Holding it between thumb and middle finger, he walked around the office for several days asking people, "Don't you think this would make a nice book? It just fits a small hand. But what should go into it?"

The rest is history. They decided upon *Dick Tracy, Orphan Annie,* and *Mickey Mouse* for the first books. The first shipments went into nearby Milwaukee stores late in the year and before Christmas the phones were ringing like mad. Of course, the paper at the end of the sheets was not used except for the initial dummies—it was simply the source of the idea which created Big Little Books. Over the next three decades, after a title change to Better Little Books in 1938, hundreds of Big Little Books were produced.

Big Little Books all sold for 10 cents and were generally available at 10 cent stores such as Woolworths, Kresge, W.T. Grant, etc. They were displayed on shelves in a glass case with the spines facing front.

In the beginning, famous newspaper strips were adapted to the Big Little Book format, followed by popular movies, classic novels and some original material. The colorful covers and spines of these fat little books were eye-catching and caught on instantly. Other companies followed Whitman's lead and began their series of similarly formatted books. The largest of these was the Saalfield Publishing Co. who latched onto exclusive rights to publishing *Shirley Temple* books. Saalfield also published several collectible movie books as well as a few popular strip characters such as *Brick Bradford, Just Kids* and *Popeye.* However, most of their books were original western, crime and sport oriented themes. No other publisher ever came close to competing with the avalanche of

Whitman titles satisfying consumer demand. Whitman had all the best syndicated stars wrapped up early-on, including *Tarzan, Dick Tracy, Buck Rogers, Flash Gordon, Disney,* and a host of others, and never lost their hold on the market.

The public recognized from the beginning the uniqueness of these colorful children's books, and many collectors began saving them. Although the paper drives of the '40s consumed untold thousands, many survived and show up at flea markets, antique shows and comic book conventions for sale.

The name Big Little Book has now become a generic term in describing books of this type. It is believed that the name Big Little Book was changed to Better Little Book because the term had previously been used by another publisher. It is known that Little Big Book had been used in the late 1920s.

Today the collector's market for Big Little Books is very healthy and growing. These books are rare in mint condition and sell rapidly whenever they turn up in this grade.

Big Little Books are collected in many ways. Some collectors only want Whitman books. Others collect special characters or genres such as *Dick Tracy, Tarzan, Popeye,* westerns or Disney. Still others want them all.

The most popular titles, of course, correspond with the most popular characters. *Flash Gordon, Buck Rogers, Donald Duck, Mickey Mouse, Dick Tracy, Popeye, Tarzan, The Shadow, Captain Midnight, The Green Hornet,* etc. are high on everyone's list. Whatever your collecting interest, most Big Little Books are under $50.00, except for the highest grades, and are affordable to most budgets.

As supplies dry up with an ever-increasing demand, the future growth should continue to be good. No time is better than now to begin your collection. The following listing was completely compiled from several large private collections. It is not complete, but is nearly so, and will be expanded and improved with each new future edition.

Other variants of the Big Little Book are also listed, such as Big Big Books, Dime Action Books, Fast-Action Books, Nickel Books, Penny Books, Pop-Up Books, Top-Line Comics and Wee Little Books. The author would be grateful to know of any omissions or errors in the listings.

BIG LITTLE BOOK
GIVEAWAYS

Many popular titles were republished as giveaways or premiums and are listed alphabetically under the original version listing in most cases. Otherwise they will appear after the regular listings under each character.

The best known and most commonly found are the premiums issued by the Cocomalt Company (Cocomalt is a chocolate additive to milk). It was long known among collectors that the rarest and most sought after Cocomalt BLB was the Buck Rogers "City of Floating Globes." All Cocomalt BLBs were condensed versions of the same Whitman BLB of the same title. With the exception of one, all featured the same cover as their Whitman counterpart. All covers were soft. Cocomalt was the first company to give away BLBs as premiums.

All Whitman BLBs as well as the giveaway spin-offs were produced by Western Publishing Co. in Racine, Wis. Western also produced more Whitman condensed version premiums for American Gas Co., Kolynos Dental Cream and Phillips Tooth Paste.

A few special BLBs were prepared by Western to be given away by Santas in the toy department of large department stores such as Macy's, Stewart's, Mandel's (Chicago), Sears and others. Some of these premiums are very rare and difficult to obtain.

Soon after the Cocomalt BLBs appeared, several dairy companies contracted Western to produce premiums for them. The best known dairies were Tarzan Ice Cream and Buddy Ice Cream. Tarzan ice cream was purchased in cups and a BLB premium could be ordered through the mail only by sending in 12 cup lids. Buddy ice cream gave out coupons for each cone of ice cream purchased. A premium book of your choice would be sent for 12 coupons. More premiums were offered in the books by sending in 12 back covers. Since these books were not distributed to the stands and were so difficult to obtain, they are today among the rarest of the BLB premiums. And it is common for copies to turn up with the back cover missing.

There were many other companies that used BLB type premiums to promote their products. A few are: Poll Parrot shoes, Karmetz and Perkins.

In the late 1930s more premiums were offered to the public by gas companies such as Pan-Am and Gilmore. These were also produced by Western.

Many of these books are scarce and are very popular with BLB collectors who are lucky enough to find copies for their collections.

HOW TO USE THE
LISTINGS

All titles are listed alphabetically, regardless of publisher, with the following exception. When more than one book was published of a given character, they are listed numerically within that grouping. For instance, to look up a *Dick Tracy* book, you would go to the *Dick Tracy* listing first and then find the book listed numerically. If it is a giveaway with no number, you will usually find it listed under the original book and title it reprints. Generally, the earlier the date, the closer to the beginning of the listing the book will appear. The information is listed in this order: Issue number, title, date, publisher, page count (which includes covers and end sheets), special information, artists, etc.

GRADING

Before a Big Little Book's value can be assessed, its condition or state of pre-servation must be determined. A book in **Mint** condition will bring many times the price of the same book in **Poor** condition. Many variables influence the grading of a Big Little Book and all must be considered in the final evaluation. Due to the way they are constructed, damage occurs with very little use—usually to the spine, book edges and binding. Consequently, books in near mint to mint condition are scarce. More important defects that affect grading are: Split spines, pages missing, page browning or brittleness, writing, crayoning, loose pages, color fading, chunks missing, and rolling or out of square. The following grading guide is given to aid the novice.

Mint: Absolutely perfect in every way, regardless of age; white pages, original printing luster retained on covers and spine; no color fading; no wear on edges or corners of book; virtually an unread copy with binding still square and tight.

Near Mint: Almost perfect; full cover gloss and white pages with only very slight wear on book corners and edges; binding still square and tight with no pages missing.

Very Fine: Most of cover gloss retained with minor wear appearing at corners and around edges; paper quality still fresh from white to off-white; spine tight with no pages missing.

Fine: Slight wear beginning to show; cover gloss reduced but still clean; pages still relatively fresh and white; very minor splits and wear at spine and book edges. Relatively flat and square with no pages missing.

Very Good: Obviously a read copy with original printing luster almost gone; some fading and discoloration, but not soiled; some signs of wear such as minor corner splits, rolling and page yellowing with possibly one of the blank inside pages missing; no chunks missing.

472

Good: An average used copy complete with only minor pieces missing from spine which may be partially split; slightly soiled or marked with rolling, color flaking and wear around edges, but perfectly sound and legible; could have minor tape repairs or one or more of blank inside pages missing, but otherwise complete.

Fair: Very heavily read and soiled with small chunks missing from cover; most or all of spine could be missing; multiple splits in spine and loose pages, but still sound and legible, bringing 50 to 70 percent of good price.

Poor: Damaged, heavily weathered, soiled or otherwise unsuited for collecting purposes.

IMPORTANT

Most BLBs on the market today will fall in the very good to fine grade category. **Rarely** will very fine to near mint BLBs be offered for sale. When they are, they usually bring premium prices.

A WORD ON
PRICING

The prices are given for good, fine and near-mint condition. A book in fair would be 50-70% of the good price. Very good would be halfway between the good and fine price, and very fine would be halfway between the fine and near mint price. The prices listed were averaged from convention sales, dealers' lists, adzines, auctions, and by special contact with dealers and collectors from coast to coast. The prices and the spreads were determined from sales of copies in available condition or the highest grade known. Since most available copies are in the good to fine range, neither dealers nor collectors should let the near-mint column influence the prices they are willing to charge or pay for books in less than perfect condition.

In the past, the BLB market has lacked a point of focus due to the absence of an annual price guide that accurately reports sales and growth in the market. Due to this, current prices for BLBs still vary considerably from region to region. It is our hope that this book will contribute to the stability of the BLB market. The prices listed reflect a six times spread from good to near-mint (1 - 3 - 6). We feel this spread accurately reflects the current market, especially when you consider the scarcity of books in NM-Mint condition. When one or both end sheets are missing, the book's value would drop about a half grade.

Books with movie scenes are of double importance due to the high cross over demand by movie collectors.

Abbreviations: *a*-art; *c*-cover; *nn*-no number; *p*-pages; *r*-reprint.

Publisher Codes: *BRP*-Blue Ribbon Press; *ERB*-Edgar Rice Burroughs; *EVW*-Engel-van Wiseman; *FAW*-Fawcett Publishing Co.; *Gold*-Goldsmith Publishing Co.; *Lynn*-Lynn Publishing Co.; *McKay*-David McKay Co.; *Whit*-Whitman Publishing Co.; *World*-World Syndicate Publishing Co.

Terminology: *All Pictures Comics*-no text, all drawings; *Fast Action*-A special series of Dell books highly collected; *Flip Pictures*-upper right corner of interior pages contain drawings that are put into motion when riffled; *Movie Scenes*-book illustrated with scenes from the movie. *Soft Cover*-A thin single sheet of cardboard used in binding most of the giveaway versions.

"Big Little Book" is a registered trademark of Whitman Publishing Co.
"Pop-Up" is a registered trademark of Blue Ribbon Press.
"Little Big Book" is a registered trademark of the Saalfield Co.

BIG LITTLE BOOK
LISTINGS

	Good	Fine	N-Mint
1175-Abbie an' Slats, 1940, Sal, 400p	7.00	21.00	40.00
1182-Abbie an' Slats and Becky, 1940, Sal, 400p			
	7.00	21.00	40.00
1177-Ace Drummond, 1935, Whit, 432p	5.00	15.00	30.00
Admiral Byrd (See Paramount Newsreel . . .)			
nn-Adventures of Charlie McCarthy and Edgar Bergen, The, 1938, Dell, 194p, Fast-Action Story, soft-c	17.00	50.00	100.00
1422-Adventures of Huckleberry Finn, The, 1939, Whit, 432p, Henry E. Vallely-a	6.00	18.00	36.00
1648-Adventures of Jim Bowie (TV Series), 1958, Whit, 280p			
	3.00	9.00	18.00
1056-Adventures of Krazy Kat and Ignatz Mouse in Koko Land, 1934, Sal, 160p, oblong size, hard-c, Herriman c/a			
	46.00	140.00	280.00
1306-Adventures of Krazy Kat and Ignatz Mouse in Koko Land, 1934, Sal, 164p, oblong size, soft-c, Herriman c/a			
	46.00	140.00	280.00
1082-Adventures of Pete the Tramp, The, 1935, Sal, hard-c, by C. D. Russell	8.50	25.00	50.00
1312-Adventures of Pete the Tramp, The, 1935, Sal, soft-c, by C. D. Russell	8.50	25.00	50.00
1053-Adventures of Tim Tyler, 1934, Sal, hard-c, oblong-size, by Lyman Young	15.00	45.00	90.00
1303-Adventures of Tim Tyler, 1934, Sal, soft-c, oblong-size, by Lyman Young	15.00	45.00	90.00
1058-Adventures of Tom Sawyer, The, 1934, Sal, 160p, hard-c, Park Sumner-a	6.00	18.00	36.00
1308-Adventures of Tom Sawyer, The, 1934, Sal, 160p, soft-c, Park Sumner-a	6.00	18.00	36.00
1448-Air Fighters of America, 1941, Whit, 432p, flip pictures			
	5.50	16.50	33.00

	Good	Fine	N-Mint
Alexander Smart, ESQ. (See Top-Line Comics)			
759- Alice in Wonderland, 1933, Whit, 160p, hard photo-c, movie scenes			
	17.00	50.00	100.00
1481- Allen Pike of the Parachute Squad U.S.A., 1941, Whit, 432p			
	5.50	16.50	33.00
763- Alley Oop and Dinny, 1935, Whit, 384p, V. T. Hamlin-a			
	11.00	32.50	65.00

Alley Oop and Dinny in the Jungles of Moo #1473,
© NEA Service, 1938

	Good	Fine	N-Mint
1473- Alley Oop and Dinny in the Jungles of Moo, 1938, Whit, 432p, V. T. Hamlin-a	10.00	30.00	60.00
nn- Alley Oop and the Missing King of Moo, 1938, Whit, 36p, 2½ x 3½", Penny Book	5.00	15.00	30.00
nn- Alley Oop in the Kingdom of Foo, 1938, Whit, 68p, 3¼ x 3½", Pan-Am premium	11.00	32.50	65.00
nn- "Alley Oop the Invasion of Moo," 1935, Whit, 260p, Cocomalt premium, soft-c; V. T. Hamlin-a	12.50	37.50	75.00
Andy Burnette (See Walt Disney's . . .)			

	Good	Fine	N-Mint

Andy Panda (See Walter Lantz.)

531- **Andy Panda,** 1943, Whit. 3¾ x 8¾", Tall Comic Book, All Pictures
Comics .... 18.00 .... 55.00 ...... 110.00

1425- **Andy Panda and Tiny Tom,** 1944, Whit, All Pictures Comics
.... 8.00 .... 24.00 .... 48.00

1431- **Andy Panda and the Mad Dog Mystery,** 1947, Whit, 288p, by
Walter Lantz .... 6.00 .... 17.50 .... 35.00

1441- **Andy Panda in the City of Ice,** 1948, Whit, All Pictures Comics, by
Walter Lantz .... 7.50 .... 22.50 .... 45.00

1459- **Andy Panda and the Pirate Ghosts,** 1949, Whit, 288p, by Walter
Lantz .... 6.00 .... 17.50 .... 35.00

1485- **Andy Panda's Vacation,** 1946, Whit, All Pictures Comics, by Walter
Lantz .... 7.50 .... 22.50 .... 45.00

15- **Andy Panda (The Adventures of),** 1942, Dell, Fast-Action Story
.... 17.00 .... 50.00 ...... 100.00

707-10- **Andy Panda and Presto the Pup,** 1949, Whit
.... 5.00 .... 15.00 .... 30.00

1130- **Apple Mary and Dennie Foil the Swindlers,** 1936, Whit, 432p
(Forerunner to Mary Worth) .... 7.00 .... 21.00 .... 42.00

1403- **Apple Mary and Dennie's Lucky Apples,** 1939, Whit, 432p
.... 5.50 .... 16.50 .... 33.00

2017- (#17)- **Aquaman-Scourge of the Sea,** 1968, Whit, 260p, 39 cents,
hard-c, color illos .... 2.50 .... 7.50 .... 15.00

1192- **Arizona Kid on the Bandit Trail, The,** 1936, Whit, 432p
.... 5.00 .... 15.00 .... 30.00

1469- **Bambi (Walt Disney's),** 1942, Whit, 432p
.... 15.00 .... 45.00 .... 90.00

1497- **Bambi's Children (Disney),** 1943, Whit, 432p, Disney Studio-a
.... 15.00 .... 45.00 .... 90.00

1138- **Bandits at Bay,** 1938, Sal, 400p .... 5.00 .... 15.00 .... 30.00

1459- **Barney Baxter in the Air with the Eagle Squadron,** 1938, Whit,
432p .... 7.00 .... 21.00 .... 42.00

1083- **Barney Google,** 1935, Sal, hard-c .... 12.50 .... 37.50 .... 75.00

1313- **Barney Google,** 1935, Sal, soft-c .... 12.50 .... 37.50 .... 75.00

2031- **Batman and Robin in the Cheetah Caper,** 1969, Whit, 258p
.... 2.50 .... 7.50 .... 15.00

5771-2- **Batman and Robin in the Cheetah Caper,** 1975?, Whit, 258p
.... .50 .... 1.50 .... 3.00

nn- **Beauty and the Beast,** nd (1930s), np (Whit), 36p, 3 x 3½", Penny
Book .... 1.50 .... 4.50 .... 9.00

	Good	Fine	N-Mint
760- Believe It or Not!, 1931, Whit, 160p, by Ripley			
	7.50	22.50	45.00
Betty Bear's Lesson (See Wee Little Books)			
1119- Betty Boop in Snow White, 1934, Whit, 240p, hard-c; adapted from			
Max Fleischer Paramount Talkartoon	32.00	95.00	190.00
1158- Betty Boop in "Miss Gullivers Travels," 1935, Whit, 288p, hard-c			
	32.00	95.00	190.00
1432- Big Chief Wahoo and the Lost Pioneers, 1942, Whit, 432p, Elmer			
Woggon-a	6.00	18.00	36.00

Big Chief Wahoo and the Great Gusto #1443,
© Publishers Syndicate, 1938

1443- Big Chief Wahoo and the Great Gusto, 1938, Whit, 432p, Elmer			
Woggon-a	6.00	18.00	36.00
1483- Big Chief Wahoo and the Magic Lamp, 1940, Whit, 432p, flip			
pictures, Woggon-c/a	6.00	18.00	36.00
725- Big Little Mother Goose, The, 1934, Whit, 580p (Rare)			
	70.00	200.00	400.00
1006- Big Little Nickel Book, 1935, Whit, 144p, Blackie Bear stories, folk			

	Good	Fine	N-Mint
tales in primer style	5.00	15.00	30.00

1007- Big Little Nickel Book, 1935, Whit, 144p, Wee Wee Woman, etc.

	5.00	15.00	30.00

1008- Big Little Nickel Book, 1935, Whit, 144p, Peter Rabbit, etc.

	5.00	15.00	30.00

721- Big Little Paint Book, The, 1933, Whit, 336p, 3¾ x 8½", for crayoning (Rare)

	70.00	200.00	400.00

1178- Billy of Bar-Zero, 1940, Sal, 400p	5.00	15.00	30.00

773- Billy the Kid, 1935, Whit, 432p, Hal Arbo-a

	7.00	21.00	40.00

1159- Billy the Kid on Tall Butte, 1939, Sal, 400p

	5.00	15.00	30.00

1174- Billy the Kid's Pledge, 1940, Sal, 400p

	5.00	15.00	30.00

nn- Billy the Kid, Western Outlaw, 1935, Whit, 260p, Cocomalt premium, Hal Arbo-a, soft-c

	8.00	24.00	48.00

1057- Black Beauty, 1934, Sal, hard-c	5.00	15.00	30.00
1307- Black Beauty, 1934, Sal, soft-c	5.00	15.00	30.00

1414- Black Silver and His Pirate Crew, 1937, Whit, 300p

	5.50	16.50	33.00

1447- Blaze Brandon with the Foreign Legion, 1938, Whit, 432p

	5.50	16.50	33.00

1410- Blondie and Dagwood in Hot Water, 1946, Whit, 352p, by Chic Young

	6.00	18.00	36.00

1415- Blondie and Baby Dumpling, 1937, Whit, 432p, by Chic Young

	7.50	22.50	45.00

1419- Oh, Blondie the Bumsteads Carry On, 1941, Whit, 432p, flip pictures, by Young

	7.50	22.50	45.00

1423- Blondie Who's Boss?, 1942, Whit, 432p, flip pictures, by Chic Young

	7.50	22.50	45.00

1429- Blondie with Baby Dumpling and Daisy, 1939, Whit, 432p, by Chic Young

	7.50	22.50	45.00

1430- Blondie Count Cookie in Too!, 1947, Whit, 288p, by Chic Young

	6.00	18.00	36.00

1438- Blondie and Dagwood Everybody's Happy, 1948, Whit, 288p, by Chic Young

	6.00	18.00	36.00

1450- Blondie No Dull Moments, 1948, Whit, 288p, by Chic Young

	6.00	18.00	36.00

1463- Blondie Fun For All!, 1949, Whit, 288p, by Chic Young

	6.00	18.00	36.00

1466- Blondie or Life Among the Bumsteads, 1944, Whit, 352p, by Chic

	Good	Fine	N-Mint

Young   7.50   22.50   45.00
1476- **Blondie and Bouncing Baby Dumpling,** 1940, Whit, 432p, by Chic
   Young   7.50   22.50   45.00
1487- **Blondie Baby Dumpling and All!,** 1941, Whit, 432p, flip pictures,
   by Young   7.50   22.50   45.00
1490- **Blondie Papa Knows Best,** 1945, Whit, 352p, by Chic Young
                                                       6.00   18.00   36.00
1491- **Blondie-Cookie and Daisy's Pups,** 1943, Whit, 432p
                                                       7.50   22.50   45.00
703-10- **Blondie and Dagwood Some Fun!,** 1949, Whit, by Chic Young
                                                       5.00   15.00   30.00
   21- **Blondie and Dagwood,** 194?, Lynn, by Chic Young
                                                      12.00   35.00   70.00
1108- **Bobby Benson on the H-Bar-O Ranch,** 1934, Whit, 300p, based on
   radio serial   7.00   20.00   40.00
   Bobby Thatcher and the Samarang Emerald (See Top-Line Comics)
1432- **Bob Stone the Young Detective,** 1937, Whit, 240p, movie scenes
                                                       8.00   24.00   48.00
2002-(#2)- **Bonanza-The Bubble Gum Kid,** 1967, Whit, 260p, 39 cents, hard-c,
   color illos   3.00   9.00   18.00
1139- **Border Eagle, The,** 1938, Sal, 400p   5.00   15.00   30.00
1153- **Boss of the Chisholm Trail,** 1939, Sal, 400p
                                                       5.00   15.00   30.00
1425- **Brad Turner in Transatlantic Flight,** 1939, Whit, 432p
                                                       5.50   16.50   33.00
1058- **Brave Little Tailor, The** (Disney), 1939, Whit, 5 x 5¼", 68p, hard-c
   (Mickey Mouse)   7.50   22.50   45.00
1427- **Brenda Starr and the Masked Impostor,** 1943, Whit, 352p, Dale
   Messick-a   8.50   25.00   50.00
1426- **Brer Rabbit (Walt Disney's. . .),** 1947, Whit, All Pict, Comics, from
   Song Of The South Movie   13.00   40.00   80.00
704-10- **Brer Rabbit,** 1949?, Whit   12.00   35.00   70.00
1059- **Brick Bradford in the City Beneath the Sea,** 1934, Sal, hard-c, by
   William Ritt & Clarence Gray   12.00   35.00   70.00
1309- **Brick Bradford in the City Beneath the Sea,** 1934, Sal, soft-c, by
   Ritt & Gray   12.00   35.00   70.00
1468- **Brick Bradford with Brocco the Modern Buccaneer,** 1938, Whit,
   432p, by Wm. Ritt & Clarence Gray   7.00   21.00   42.00
1133- **Bringing Up Father,** 1936, Whit, 432p, by George McManus
                                                      11.00   32.50   65.00
1100- **Broadway Bill,** 1935, Sal, photo-c, 4½ x 5¼", movie scenes Colum-

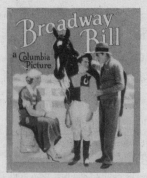

Broadway Bill #1100, © Columbia Pictures

	Good	Fine	N-Mint
bia Pictures, horse racing)	9.00	27.50	55.00
1580- Broadway Bill, 1935, Sal, soft-c, photo-c, movie scenes			
	9.00	27.50	55.00
1181- Broncho Bill, 1940, Sal, 400p	5.00	15.00	30.00
Broncho Bill in Suicide Canyon (See Top-Line Comics)			
1417- Bronc Peeler the Lone Cowboy, 1937, Whit, 432p, by Fred Harman,			
forerunner of Red Ryder	7.00	21.00	42.00
1470- Buccaneer, The, 1938, Whit, 240p, photo-c, movie scenes			
	8.50	25.00	50.00
1646- Buccaneers, The (TV Series), 1958, Whit, 4½ x 5¼", 280p, Russ			
Manning-a	2.50	7.50	15.00
1104- Buck Jones in the Fighting Code, 1934, Whit, 160p, hard-c, movie			
scenes	11.00	35.00	70.00
1116- Buck Jones in Ride 'Em Cowboy (Universal Presents), 1935, Whit,			
240p, photo-c, movie scenes	11.00	35.00	70.00
1174- Buck Jones in the Roaring West (Universal Presents), 1935, Whit,			
240p, movie scenes	11.00	35.00	70.00
1188- Buck Jones in the Fighting Rangers (Universal Presents), 1936,			

	Good	Fine	N-Mint
Whit, 240p, photo-c, movie scenes	11.00	35.00	70.00
1404- Buck Jones and the Two-Gun Kid, 1937, Whit, 432p	6.00	18.00	36.00
1451- Buck Jones and the Killers of Crooked Butte, 1940, Whit, 432p	6.00	18.00	36.00
1461- Buck Jones and the Rock Creek Cattle War, 1938, Whit, 432p	6.00	18.00	36.00
1486- Buck Jones and the Rough Riders in Forbidden Trails, 1943, Whit, flip pictures, based on movie; Tim McCoy app.	8.00	24.00	48.00
3- Buck Jones in the Red Ryder, 1934, EVW, 160p, movie scenes	13.00	40.00	80.00
15- Buck Jones in Rocky Rhodes, 1935, EVW, 160p, photo-c, movie scenes	13.00	40.00	80.00
4069- Buck Jones and the Night Riders, 1937, Whit, 7 x 9½", 320p, Big Big Book	32.00	95.00	190.00
nn- Buck Jones on the Six-Gun Trail, 1939, Whit, 36p, 2½ x 3½", Penny Book	4.50	14.00	28.00
742- Buck Rogers in the 25th Century A.D., 1933, Whit, 320p, Dick Calkins-a	30.00	90.00	180.00
nn- Buck Rogers in the 25th Century A.D., 1933, Whit, 204p, Cocomalt premium, Calkins-a	20.00	60.00	120.00
765- Buck Rogers in the City Below the Sea, 1934, Whit, 320p, Dick Calkins-a	18.00	55.00	110.00
765- Buck Rogers in the City Below the Sea, 1934, Whit, 324p, soft-c, Dick Calkins c/a	33.00	100.00	200.00
1143- Buck Rogers on the Moons of Saturn, 1934, Whit, 320p, Dick Calkins-a	18.00	55.00	110.00
nn- Buck Rogers on the Moons of Saturn, 1934, Whit, 324p, premium w/no ads, soft 3-color-c, Dick Calkins-a	33.00	100.00	200.00
1169- Buck Rogers and the Depth Men of Jupiter, 1935, Whit, 432p, Calkins-a	18.00	55.00	110.00
1178- Buck Rogers and the Doom Comet, 1935, Whit, 432p, Calkins-a	17.00	50.00	100.00
1197- Buck Rogers and the Planetoid Plot, 1936, Whit, 432p, Calkins-a	17.00	50.00	100.00
1409- Buck Rogers Vs. the Fiend of Space, 1940, Whit, 432p, Calkins-a	17.00	50.00	100.00
1437- Buck Rogers in the War with the Planet Venus, 1938, Whit, 432p, Calkins-a	17.00	50.00	100.00

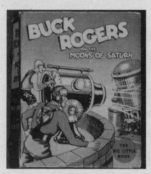

Buck Rogers on the Moons of Saturn, no #, © John F. Dille, 1934

	Good	Fine	N-Mint
1474- Buck Rogers and the Overturned World, 1941, Whit, 432p, flip pictures, Calkins-a	17.00	50.00	100.00
1490- Buck Rogers and the Super-Dwarf of Space, 1943, Whit, All Pictures Comics, Calkins-a	17.00	50.00	100.00
4057- Buck Rogers, The Adventures of, 1934, Whit, 7 x 9½", 320p, Big Big Book, "The Story of Buck Rogers on the Planet Eros;" Calkins-c/a	63.00	190.00	380.00
nn- Buck Rogers, 1935, Whit, 4 x 3½", Tarzan Ice Cream cup premium (Rare)	58.00	175.00	350.00
nn- Buck Rogers in the City of Floating Globes, 1935, Whit, 258p, Cocomalt premium, soft-c, Dick Calkins-a	43.00	130.00	260.00
1135- Buckskin and Bullets, 1938, Sal, 400p	5.00	15.00	30.00
Buffalo Bill (See Wild West Adventures of . . .)			
nn- Buffalo Bill, 1934, World, All pictures, by J. Carroll Mansfield	5.50	16.50	33.00
713- Buffalo Bill and the Pony Express, 1934, Whit, 384p, Hal Arbo-a	7.00	21.00	42.00

Buffalo Bill and the Pony Express #713,
© Whitman Publishing Co., 1934

	Good	Fine	N-Mint
1194- Buffalo Bill Plays a Lone Hand, 1936, Whit, 432p, Hal Arbo-a	5.50	16.50	33.00
530- Bugs Bunny, 1943, Whit, All Pictures Comics, Tall Comic Book, 3 ¾ x 8¾", reprints/Looney Tunes 1 & 5	18.00	55.00	110.00
1403- Bugs Bunny and the Pirate Loot, 1947, Whit, All Pictures Comics	7.00	21.00	42.00
1435- Bugs Bunny, 1944, Whit, All Pictures Comics	8.00	24.00	48.00
1440- Bugs Bunny in Risky Business, 1948, Whit, All Pictures Comics	7.00	21.00	42.00
1455- Bugs Bunny and Klondike Gold, 1948, Whit, 288p	7.00	21.00	42.00
1465- Bugs Bunny The Masked Marvel, 1949, Whit, 288p	7.00	21.00	42.00
1496- Bugs Bunny and His Pals, 1945, Whit, All Pictures Comics; r/4-Color 33	8.00	24.00	48.00

	Good	Fine	N-Mint
706-10- Bugs Bunny and the Giant Brothers, 1949, Whit			
	4.50	13.50	27.00
2007-(#7)- Bugs Bunny-Double Trouble on Diamond Fountain, 1967, Whit, 260p, 39 cents, hard-c, color illos	2.00	6.00	12.00
2952- Bugs Bunny's Mistake, 1949, Whit, 3¼ x 4", 24p, Tiny Tales, full color (5 cents)	4.00	12.00	24.00
5757-2- Bugs Bunny in Double Trouble on Diamond Island, 1967, (1980-reprints #2007), Whit, 260p, soft-c, 79 cents, B&W			
	.50	1.50	3.00
5772-2- Bugs Bunny the Last Crusader, 1975, Whit, 79 cents, flip-it book			
	.50	1.50	3.00
13- Bugs Bunny and the Secret of Storm Island, 1942, Dell, 194p, Fast-Action Story	17.00	50.00	100.00
1169- Bullet Benton, 1939, Sal, 400p	5.00	15.00	30.00
nn- Bulletman and the Return of Mr. Murder, 1941, Faw, 196p, Dime Action Book	25.00	75.00	150.00
1142- Bullets Across the Border (A Billy The Kid story), 1938, Sal, 400p	5.00	15.00	30.00
Bunky (See Top-Line Comics)			
837- Bunty (Punch and Judy), 1935, Whit, 28p, Magic-Action with 3 pop-ups	10.00	30.00	60.00
1091- Burn 'Em Up Barnes, 1935, Sal, Hard-c, movie scenes			
	8.50	25.00	50.00
1321- Burn 'Em Up Barnes, 1935, Sal, Soft-c, movie scenes			
	8.50	25.00	50.00
1415- Buz Sawyer and Bomber 13, 1946, Whit, 352p, Roy Crane-a			
	8.50	25.00	50.00
1412- Calling W-I-X-Y-Z, Jimmy Kean and the Radio Spies, 1939, Whit, 300p	7.00	21.00	42.00
Call of the Wild (See Jack London's . . .)			
1107- Camels are Coming, 1935, Sal, movie scenes			
	7.00	21.00	42.00
1587- Camels are Coming, 1935, Sal, movie scenes			
	7.00	21.00	42.00
nn- Captain and the Kids, Boys Will Be Boys, The, 1938, 68p, Pan-Am Oil premium, soft-c	8.50	25.00	50.00
1128- Captain Easy Soldier of Fortune, 1934, Whit, 432p, Roy Crane-a	10.00	30.00	60.00
nn- Captain Easy Soldier of Fortune, 1934, Whit, 436p, Premium-no ads, soft 3-color-c, Roy Crane-a	15.00	45.00	90.00

	Good	Fine	N-Mint
1474- Captain Easy Behind Enemy Lines, 1943, Whit, 352p, Roy Crane-a			
	9.00	27.50	55.00
nn- Captain Easy and Wash Tubbs, 1935, 260p, Cocomalt premium, Roy Crane-a			
	9.00	27.50	55.00
1444- Captain Frank Hawks Air Ace and the League of Twelve, 1938, Whit, 432p			
	6.00	18.00	36.00
nn- Captain Marvel, 1941, Faw, 196p, Dime Action Book			
	25.00	75.00	150.00
1402- Captain Midnight and Sheik Jomak Khan, 1946, Whit, 352p			
	12.50	37.50	75.00
1452- Captain Midnight and the Moon Woman, 1943, Whit, 352p			
	12.50	37.50	75.00

Captain Midnight vs. the Terror of the Orient #1458,
© The Wander Co., 1942

1458- Captain Midnight Vs. The Terror of the Orient, 1942, Whit, 432p, flip pictures, Hess-a 12.50   37.50   75.00
1488- Captain Midnight and the Secret Squadron, 1941, Whit, 432p
                             12.50   37.50   75.00

	Good	**Fine**	**N-Mint**

Captain Robb of . . . (See Dirigible ZR90 . . .)

L20- Ceiling Zero, 1936, Lynn, 128p, 7½ x 5", hard-c, James Cagney, Pat O'Brien photos on-c, movie scenes, Warner Bros. Pictures

	7.50	22.50	45.00

1093- Chandu the Magician, 1935, Sal, 5 x 5¼", 160p, hard-c, Bela Lugosi photo-c, movie scenes

	11.00	32.50	65.00

1323- Chandu the Magician, 1935, Sal, 5 x 5¼", 160p, soft-c, Bela Lugosi photo-c

	11.00	32.50	65.00

Charlie Chan (See Inspector . . .)

1459- Charlie Chan Solves a New Mystery (See Inspector . . .), 1940, Whit, 432p, Alfred Andriola-a

	10.00	30.00	60.00

1478- Charlie Chan of the Honolulu Police, Inspector, 1939, Whit, 432p, Andriola-a

	10.00	30.00	60.00

Charlie McCarthy (See Story Of . . .)

734- Chester Gump at Silver Creek Ranch, 1933, Whit, 320p, Sidney Smith-a

	10.00	30.00	60.00

nn- Chester Gump at Silver Creek Ranch, 1933, Whit, 204p, Cocomalt premium, soft-c, Sidney Smith-a

	12.00	35.00	70.00

nn- Chester Gump at Silver Creek Ranch, 1933, Whit, 52p, 4 x 5½", premium-no ads, soft-c, Sidney Smith-a

	15.00	45.00	90.00

766- Chester Gump Finds the Hidden Treasure, 1934, Whit, 320p, Sidney Smith-a

	10.00	30.00	60.00

nn- Chester Gump Finds the Hidden Treasure, 1934, Whit, 52p, 3½ x 5¾", premium-no ads, soft-c, Sidney Smith-a

	15.00	45.00	90.00

nn- Chester Gump Finds the Hidden Treasure, 1934, Whit, 52p, 4 x 5½", premium-no ads, Sidney Smith-a 15.00 45.00 90.00

1146- Chester Gump in the City Of Gold, 1935, Whit, 432p, Sidney Smith-a

	10.00	30.00	60.00

nn- Chester Gump in the City Of Gold, 1935, Whit, 436p, premium-no ads, 3-color, soft-c, Sidney Smith-a 17.00 50.00 100.00

1402- Chester Gump in the Pole to Pole Flight, 1937, Whit, 432p

	8.50	25.00	50.00

5- Chester Gump and His Friends, 1934, Whit, 132p, 3½ x 3½", soft-c, Tarzan Ice Cream cup lid premium 20.00 60.00 120.00

nn- Chester Gump at the North Pole, 1938, Whit, 68p, soft-c, 3¾ x 3½", Pan-Am giveaway

	11.00	32.50	65.00

nn- Chicken Greedy, nd(1930s), np(Whit), 36p, 3 x 2½", Penny Book

	1.50	4.50	9.00

	Good	Fine	N-Mint
nn- Chicken Licken, nd (1930s), np (Whit), 36p, 3 x 2½", Penny Book			
	1.50	4.50	9.00
1101- Chief of the Rangers, 1935, Sal, hard-c, Tom Mix photo-c, movie scenes from "The Miracle Rider"	12.50	37.50	75.00
1581- Chief of the Rangers, 1935, Sal, soft-c, Tom Mix photo-c, movie scenes	12.50	37.50	75.00
Child's Garden of Verses (See Wee Little Books)			
L14- Chip Collins' Adventures on Bat Island, 1935, Lynn, 192p			
	8.50	25.00	50.00
2025- Chitty Chitty Bang Bang, 1968, Whit, movie photos			
	2.50	7.50	15.00
Chubby Little Books, 1935, Whit, 3 x 2½", 200p			
W803 Golden Hours Story Book, The	4.00	12.00	24.00
W803 Story Hours Story Book, The	4.00	12.00	24.00
W804 Gay Book of Little Stories, The	4.00	12.00	24.00
W804 Glad Book of Little Stories, The			
	4.00	12.00	24.00
W804 Joy Book of Little Stories, The	4.00	12.00	24.00
W804 Sunny Book of Little Stories, The			
	4.00	12.00	24.00
1453- Chuck Malloy Railroad Detective on the Streamliner, 1938, Whit, 300p	5.50	16.50	33.00
Cinderella (See Walt Disney's . . .)			
Clyde Beatty (See The Steel Arena)			
1410- Clyde Beatty Daredevil Lion and Tiger Tamer, 1939, Whit, 300p	8.50	25.00	50.00
1480- Coach Bernie Bierman's Brick Barton and the Winning Eleven, 1938, 300p	5.50	16.50	33.00
1446- Convoy Patrol (A Thrilling U.S. Navy Story), 1942, Whit, 432p, flip pictures	5.50	16.50	33.00
1127- Corley of the Wilderness Trail, 1937, Sal, hard-c			
	6.00	18.00	36.00
1607- Corley of the Wilderness Trail, 1937, Sal, soft-c			
	6.00	18.00	36.00
1- Count of Monte Cristo, 1934, EVW, 160p, (Five Star Library), movie scenes, hard-c	12.00	35.00	70.00
1457- Cowboy Lingo Boys' Book of Western Facts, 1938, Whit, 300p, Fred Harman-a	6.00	18.00	36.00
1171- Cowboy Malloy, 1940, Sal, 400p	5.00	15.00	30.00
1106- Cowboy Millionaire, 1935, Sal, movie scenes with George O'Brien, photo-c, hard-c	10.00	30.00	60.00

	Good	Fine	N-Mint
1586-Cowboy Millionaire, 1935, Sal, movie scenes with George O'Brien, photo-c, soft-c	10.00	30.00	60.00
724-Cowboy Stories, 1933, Whit, 300p, Hal Arbo-a	9.00	27.00	54.00
nn-Cowboy Stories, 1933, Whit, 52p, soft-c, premium-no ads, 4 x 5½", Hal Arbo-a	10.00	30.00	60.00
1161-Crimson Cloak, The, 1939, Sal, 400p	5.00	15.00	30.00
L19-Curley Harper at Lakespur, 1935, Lynn, 192p	6.00	18.00	36.00
5785-2-Daffy Duck in Twice the Trouble, 1980, Whit, 260p, 79 cents, soft-c	.50	1.50	3.00
2018-(#18)-Daktari-Night of Terror, 1968, Whit, 260p, 39 cents, hard-c, color illos	2.50	7.50	15.00
1010-Dan Dunn And The Gangsters' Frame-Up, 1937, Whit, 7¼ x 5½", 64p, Nickle Book	7.50	22.50	45.00

Dan Dunn, "Crime Never Pays," #1116, © Publishers Syndicate, 1934

1116-Dan Dunn "Crime Never Pays," 1934, Whit, 320p, by Norman Marsh	8.50	25.00	50.00
1125-Dan Dunn on the Trail of the Counterfeiters, 1936, Whit, 432p, by Norman Marsh	8.50	25.00	50.00

	Good	Fine	N-Mint
1171-Dan Dunn and the Crime Master, 1937, Whit, 432p, by Norman Marsh	8.50	25.00	50.00
1417-Dan Dunn and the Underworld Gorillas, 1941, Whit, All Pictures Comics, flip pictures, by Norman Marsh	8.50	25.00	50.00
1454-Dan Dunn on the Trail of Wu Fang, 1938, Whit, 432p, by Norman Marsh	10.00	30.00	60.00
1481-Dan Dunn and the Border Smugglers, 1938, Whit, 432p, by Norman Marsh	8.50	25.00	50.00
1492-Dan Dunn and the Dope Ring, 1940, Whit, 432p, by Norman Marsh	8.50	25.00	50.00
nn-Dan Dunn and the Bank Hold-Up, 1938, Whit, 36p, 2½ x 3½", Penny Book	4.50	14.00	28.00
nn-Dan Dunn And The Zeppelin Of Doom, 1938, Dell, 196p, Fast-Action Story, soft-c	17.00	50.00	100.00
nn-Dan Dunn Meets Chang Loo, 1938, Whit, 66p, Pan-Am premium, by Norman Marsh	7.00	21.00	42.00
nn-Dan Dunn Plays a Lone Hand, 1938, Whit, 36p, 2½ x 3½", Penny Book	4.50	14.00	28.00
6-Dan Dunn and the Counterfeiter Ring, 1938, Whit, 132p, 3¾ x 3½", Buddy book	17.00	50.00	100.00
9-Dan Dunn's Mysterious Ruse, 1936, Whit, 132p, soft-c, 3½ x 3½", Tarzan Ice Cream cup lid premium	17.00	50.00	100.00
1177-Danger Trail North, 1940, Sal, 400p	5.00	15.00	30.00
1151-Danger Trails in Africa, 1935, Whit, 432p	6.00	18.00	42.00
nn-Daniel Boone, 1934, World, High Lights of History Series, hard-c, All in Pictures	5.50	16.50	33.00
1160-Dan of the Lazy L, 1939, Sal, 400p	5.00	15.00	30.00
1148-David Copperfield, 1934, Whit, hard-c, 160p, photo-c, movie scenes (W. C. Fields)	12.00	35.00	70.00
nn-David Copperfield, 1934, Whit, soft-c, 164p, movie scenes	12.00	35.00	70.00
1151-Death by Short Wave, 1938, Sal	8.00	24.00	48.00
1156-Denny the Ace Detective, 1938, Sal, 400p	5.00	15.00	30.00
1431-Desert Eagle and the Hidden Fortress, The, 1941, Whit, 432p, flip pictures	6.00	18.00	36.00
1458-Desert Eagle Rides Again, The, 1939, Whit, 300p	6.00	18.00	36.00
1136-Desert Justice, 1938, Sal, 400p	5.00	15.00	30.00

Detective Higgins of the Racket Squad #1484,
© Stephen Slesinger, 1938

	Good	Fine	N-Mint
1484- Detective Higgins of the Racket Squad, 1938, Whit, 432p			
	6.00	18.00	36.00
1124- Dickie Moore in the Little Red School House, 1936, Whit, 240p, photo-c, movie scenes (Chesterfield Motion Picts. Corp)			
	8.50	25.00	50.00
W-707- Dick Tracy the Detective, The Adventures Of, 1933, Whit, 320p (The 1st Big Little Book), by Chester Gould (Scarce)			
	85.00	250.00	500.00
nn- Dick Tracy Detective, The Adventures Of, 1933, Whit, 52p, 4 x 5½", premium-no ads, soft-c, by Chester Gould			
	38.00	115.00	230.00
710- Dick Tracy and Dick Tracy, Jr. (The Advs. of . . .), 1933, Whit, 320p, by Gould	33.00	100.00	200.00
nn- Dick Tracy and Dick Tracy, Jr. (The Advs. of . . .), 1933, Whit, 52p, premium-no ads, soft-c, 4 x 5½", by Chester Gould			
	33.00	100.00	200.00
nn- Dick Tracy the Detective and Dick Tracy, Jr., 1933, Whit, 52p,			

	Good	Fine	N-Mint
premium-no ads, 3½ x 5¼ ", soft-c, by Chester Gould			
	33.00	100.00	200.00
723- Dick Tracy Out West, 1933, Whit, 300p, by Chester Gould			
	27.00	80.00	160.00
749- Dick Tracy from Colorado to Nova Scotia, 1933, Whit, 320p, by Chester Gould			
	20.00	60.00	120.00
nn- Dick Tracy from Colorado to Nova Scotia, 1933, Whit, 204p, premium-no ads, soft-c, by Chester Gould	25.00	75.00	150.00
1105- Dick Tracy and the Stolen Bonds, 1934, Whit, 320p, by Chester Gould			
	17.00	50.00	100.00
1112- Dick Tracy and the Racketeer Gang, 1936, Whit, 432p, by Chester Gould			
	13.00	40.00	80.00
1137- Dick Tracy Solves the Penfield Mystery, 1934, Whit, 320p, by Chester Gould	17.00	50.00	100.00
nn- Dick Tracy Solves the Penfield Mystery, 1934, Whit, 324p, premium-no ads, 3-color, soft-c, by Chester Gould			
	25.00	75.00	150.00
1163- Dick Tracy and the Boris Arson Gang, 1935, Whit, 432p, by Chester Gould	12.50	37.50	75.00
1170- Dick Tracy on the Trail of Larceny Lu, 1935, Whit, 432p, by Chester Gould	12.50	37.50	75.00
1185- Dick Tracy in Chains of Crime, 1936, Whit, 432p, by Chester Gould			
	12.50	37.50	75.00
1412- Dick Tracy and Yogee Yamma, 1946, Whit, 352p, by Chester Gould			
	11.00	32.50	65.00
1420- Dick Tracy and the Hotel Murders, 1937, Whit, 432p, by Chester Gould	12.50	37.50	75.00
1434- Dick Tracy and the Phantom Ship, 1940, Whit, 432p, by Chester Gould	12.50	37.50	75.00
1436- Dick Tracy and the Mad Killer, 1947, Whit, 288p, by Chester Gould	11.00	32.50	65.00
1439- Dick Tracy and His G-Men, 1941, Whit, 432p, Flip pictures, by Chester Gould	12.50	37.50	75.00
1445- Dick Tracy and the Bicycle Gang, 1948, Whit, 288p, by Chester Gould	11.00	32.50	65.00
1446- Detective Dick Tracy and the Spider Gang, 1937, Whit, 240p, movie scenes from "Adventures of Dick Tracy" (Republic serial)			
	18.00	55.00	110.00
1449- Dick Tracy Special F.B.I. Operative, 1943, Whit, 432p, by Chester Gould	12.50	37.50	75.00

	Good	Fine	N-Mint
1454- Dick Tracy on the High Seas, 1939, Whit, 432p, by Chester Gould	12.50	37.50	75.00
1460- Dick Tracy and the Tiger Lilly Gang, 1949, Whit, 288p, by Chester Gould	11.00	32.50	65.00
1478- Dick Tracy on Voodoo Island, 1944, Whit, 352p, by Chester Gould	11.00	32.50	65.00
1479- Detective Dick Tracy VS. Crooks in Disguise, 1939, Whit, 432p, flip pictures, by Chester Gould	12.50	37.50	75.00
1482- Dick Tracy and the Wreath Kidnaping Case, 1945, Whit, 352p	11.00	32.50	65.00
1488- Dick Tracy the Super-Detective, 1939, Whit, 432p, by Chester Gould	12.50	37.50	75.00
1491- Dick Tracy the Man with No Face, 1938, Whit, 432p	12.50	37.50	75.00
1495- Dick Tracy Returns, 1939, Whit, 432p, based on Republic Motion Picture serial, Chester Gould-a	12.50	37.50	75.00
2001- (#1)-Dick Tracy-Encounters Facey, 1967, Whit, 260p, 39 cents, hard-c, color illos	2.50	7.50	15.00
4055- Dick Tracy, The Adventures Of, 1934, Whit, 7 x 9½", 320p, Big Big Book, by Chester Gould	53.00	160.00	320.00
4071- Dick Tracy and the Mystery of the Purple Cross, 1938, 7 x 9½", 320p, Big Big Book, by Chester Gould (Scarce)	83.00	250.00	500.00
nn- Dick Tracy and the Invisible Man, 1939, Whit, 3¼ x 3¾", 132p, stapled, soft-c, Quaker Oats premium; NBC radio play script, Chester Gould-a	18.00	55.00	110.00
Vol. 2- Dick Tracy's Ghost Ship, 1939, Whit, 3½ x 3½", 132p, soft-c, stapled, Quaker Oats premium; NBC radio play script episode from actual radio show; Gould-a	18.00	55.00	110.00
3- Dick Tracy Meets a New Gang, 1934, Whit, 3½ x 3½", 132p, soft-c, Tarzan Ice Cream cup lid premium	33.00	100.00	200.00
11- Dick Tracy in Smashing the Famon Racket, 1938, Whit, 3¾ x 3½", Buddy Book-ice cream premium, by Chester Gould	33.00	100.00	200.00
nn- Dick Tracy Gets His Man, 1938, Whit, 36p, 2x3", Penny Book	7.00	20.00	40.00
nn- Dick Tracy the Detective, 1938, Whit, 36p, 2x3", Penny Book	7.00	20.00	40.00
9- Dick Tracy and the Frozen Bullet Murders, 1941, Dell, 196p, Fast-Action Story, soft-c, by Gould	25.00	75.00	150.00

Dick Tracy and the Frozen Bullet Murders #9, © Chester Gould, 1941

	Good	Fine	N-Mint
6833- Dick Tracy Detective and Federal Agent, 1936, Dell, 244p, Cartoon Story Books, hard-c, by Chester Gould	27.00	80.00	160.00
nn-Dick Tracy Detective and Federal Agent, 1936, Dell, 244p, Fast-Action Story, soft-c, by Gould	25.00	75.00	150.00
nn-Dick Tracy and the Blackmailers, 1939, Dell, 196p, Fast-Action Story, soft-c, by Gould	25.00	75.00	150.00
nn-Dick Tracy and the Chain of Evidence, Detective, 1938, Whit, 196p, Fast-Action Story, soft-c, by Chester Gould	25.00	75.00	150.00
nn-Dick Tracy and the Crook Without a Face, 1938, Whit, 68p, 3¾ x 3½", Pan-Am giveaway, Gould c/a	15.00	45.00	90.00
nn-Dick Tracy and the Maroon Mask Gang, 1938, Dell, 196p, Fast-Action Story, soft-c, by Gould	25.00	75.00	150.00
nn-Dick Tracy Cross-Country Race, 1934, Whit, 8p, 2¹/₂ x 3", Big Thrill chewing gum premium	8.50	25.00	50.00
nn-Dick Whittington and his Cat, nd(1930s), np(Whit), 36p, Penny Book	1.50	4.50	9.00

	Good	Fine	N-Mint

Dinglehoofer und His Dog Adolph (See Top-Line Comics)

Dinky (See Jackie Cooper in . . .)

1464- Dirigible ZR90 and the Disappearing Zeppelin (Captain Robb Of . . .), 1941, Whit, 300p, Al Lewin-a

	13.00	40.00	80.00

1167- Dixie Dugan Among the Cowboys, 1939, Sal, 400p

	6.00	18.00	36.00

1188- Dixie Dugan and Cuddles, 1940, Sal, 400p, by Striebel & McEvoy

	6.00	18.00	36.00

Doctor Doom (See Foreign Spies . . . & International Spy.)

Dog of Flanders, A (See Frankie Thomas in . . .)

1114- Dog Stars of Hollywood, 1936, Sal, photo-c, photo-illos

	10.00	30.00	60.00

1594- Dog Stars of Hollywood, 1936, Sal, photo-c, soft-c, photo-illos

	10.00	30.00	60.00

Donald Duck (See Silly Symphony . . . & Walt Disney's . . .)

1404- Donald Duck (Says Such a Life) (Disney), 1939, Whit, 432p, Taliaferro-a

	12.00	35.00	70.00

1411- Donald Duck and Ghost Morgan's Treasure (Disney), 1946, Whit, All Pictures Comics, Barks-a; R/4-Color 9

	14.00	42.00	84.00

1422- Donald Duck Sees Stars (Disney), 1941, Whit, 432p, flip pictures, Taliaferro-a

	12.00	35.00	70.00

1424- Donald Duck Says Such Luck (Disney), 1941, Whit, 432p, flip pictures, Taliaferro-a

	12.00	35.00	70.00

1430- Donald Duck Headed For Trouble (Disney), 1942, Whit, 432p, flip pictures, Taliaferro-a

	12.00	35.00	70.00

1432- Donald Duck and the Green Serpent (Disney), 1947, Whit, All Pictures Comics, Barks-a; R/4-Color 108

	14.00	42.00	84.00

1434- Donald Duck Forgets To Duck (Disney), 1939, Whit, 432p, Taliaferro-a

	12.00	35.00	70.00

1438- Donald Duck Off the Beam (Disney), 1943, Whit, 352p, flip pictures, Taliaferro-a

	12.00	35.00	70.00

1438- Donald Duck Off the Beam (Disney), 1943, Whit, 432p, flip pictures, Taliaferro-a

	12.00	35.00	70.00

1449- Donald Duck Lays Down the Law, 1948, Whit, 288p, Barks-a

	14.00	42.00	84.00

1457- Donald Duck in Volcano Valley (Disney), 1949, Whit, 288p, Barks-a

	14.00	42.00	84.00

	Good	Fine	N-Mint
1462- Donald Duck Gets Fed Up (Disney), 1940, Whit, 432p, Taliaferro-a	12.00	35.00	70.00
1478- Donald Duck-Hunting For Trouble (Disney), 1938, Whit, 432p, Taliaferro-a	12.00	35.00	70.00
1484- Donald Duck is Here Again!, 1944, Whit, All Pictures Comics, Taliaferro-a	12.00	35.00	70.00
1486- Donald Duck Up in the Air (Disney), 1945, Whit, 352p, Barks-a	14.00	42.00	84.00
705-10- Donald Duck and the Mystery of the Double X (Disney), 1949, Whit, Barks-a	7.50	22.50	45.00
2009- (#9)-Donald Duck-The Fabulous Diamond Fountain (Walt Disney), 1967, Whit, 260p, 39 cents, hard-c, color illos	1.70	5.00	10.00
nn- Donald Duck and the Ducklings, 1938, Whit, 194p, Fast-Action Story, soft-c, Taliaferro-a	23.00	70.00	140.00
nn- Donald Duck Out of Luck (Disney), 1940, Dell, 196p, Fast-Action Story, has 4-Color No. 4 on back-c, Taliaferro-a	23.00	70.00	140.00
8- Donald Duck Takes It on the Chin (Disney), 1941, Dell, 196p, Fast-Action Story, soft-c, Taliaferro-a	23.00	70.00	140.00

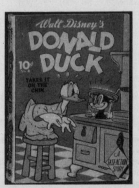

Donald Duck Takes It on the Chin #8, © The Disney Co., 1941

	Good	Fine	N-Mint
5760-2- Donald Duck in Volcano Valley (Disney), 1973, Whit, 79 cents, flip-it book	.50	1.50	3.00
L13- Donnie and the Pirates, 1935, Lynn, 192p	8.00	24.00	48.00
1438- Don O'Dare Finds War, 1940, Whit, 432p	5.50	16.50	33.00
1107- Don Winslow, U.S.N., 1935, Whit, 432p	10.00	30.00	60.00
nn- Don Winslow, U.S.N., 1935, Whit, 436p, premium-no ads, 3-color, soft-c	15.00	45.00	90.00
1408- Don Winslow and the Giant Girl Spy, 1946, Whit, 352p	7.50	22.50	45.00
1418- Don Winslow Navy Intelligence Ace, 1942, Whit, 432p, flip pictures	10.00	30.00	60.00
1419- Don Winslow of the Navy Vs. the Scorpion Gang, 1938, Whit, 432p	10.00	30.00	60.00
1453- Don Winslow of the Navy and the Secret Enemy Base, 1943, Whit, 352p	10.00	30.00	60.00
1489- Don Winslow of the Navy and the Great War Plot, 1940, Whit, 432p	10.00	30.00	60.00
nn- Don Winslow U.S. Navy and the Missing Admiral, 1938, Whit, 36p, 2½ x 3½", Penny Book	4.50	14.00	28.00
1137- Doomed To Die, 1938, Sal, 400p	5.00	15.00	30.00
1140- Down Cartridge Creek, 1938, Sal, 400p	5.00	15.00	30.00
1416- Draftie of the U.S. Army, 1943, Whit, All Pictures Comics	6.00	18.00	36.00
1100B- Dreams (Your dreams & what they mean), 1938, Whit, 36p, 2½ x 3½", Penny Book	2.00	6.00	12.00
L24- Dumb Dora and Bing Brown, 1936, Lynn	10.00	30.00	60.00
1400- Dumbo of the Circus-Only His Ears Grew! (Disney), 1941, Whit, 432p, based on Disney movie	13.00	40.00	80.00
10- Dumbo the Flying Elephant (Disney), 1944, Dell, 194p, Fast-Action Story, soft-c	18.00	55.00	110.00
nn- East O' the Sun and West O' the Moon, nd (1930s), np (Whit), 36p, 3 x 2½", Penny Book	1.50	4.50	9.00
774- Eddie Cantor in an Hour with You, 1934, Whit, 154p, 4¾ x 5¼", photo-c, movie scenes	11.00	32.50	65.00
nn- Eddie Cantor in Laughland, 1934, Gold, 132p, soft, photo-c, Vallely-a	10.00	30.00	60.00

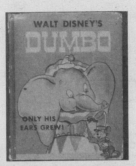

Dumbo of the Circus—Only His Ears Grew #1400,
© The Disney Co., 1941

	Good	Fine	N-Mint
1106- Ella Cinders and the Mysterious House, 1934, Whit, 432p			
	9.00	27.00	54.00
nn- Ella Cinders and the Mysterious House, 1934, Whit, 52p, premium- no ads, soft-c, 3½ x 5¼"	12.00	35.00	70.00
nn- Ella Cinders, 1935, Whit, 148p, 3³/₄ x 4", Tarzan Ice Cream cup lid premium	15.00	45.00	90.00
nn- Ella Cinders Plays Duchess, 1938, Whit, 68p, 3¾ x 3½", Pan-Am Oil premium	10.00	30.00	60.00
nn- Ella Cinders Solves a Mystery, 1938, Whit, 68p, Pan-Am Oil premium, soft-c	10.00	30.00	60.00
11- Ella Cinders' Exciting Experience, 1934, Whit, 3½ x 3½", 132p, Tarzan Ice Cream cup lid giveaway	15.00	45.00	90.00
1406- Ellery Queen the Adventure of the Last Man Club, 1940, Whit, 432p			
	8.50	25.00	50.00
1472- Ellery Queen the Master Detective, 1942, Whit, 432p, flip pictures			
	8.50	25.00	50.00
1081- Elmer and his Dog Spot, 1935, Sal, hard-c			
	6.00	18.00	36.00

	Good	Fine	N-Mint

1311- Elmer and his Dog Spot, 1935, Sal, soft-c

      6.00   18.00   36.00

722- Erik Noble and the Forty-Niners, 1934, Whit, 384p

      7.00   21.00   42.00

nn- Erik Noble and the Forty-Niners, 1934, Whit, 386p, 3-color, soft-c

     12.00   35.00   70.00

1058- Farmyard Symphony, The (Disney), 1939, 5 x 5½", 68p, hard-c

      7.50   22.50   45.00

1129- Felix the Cat, 1936, Whit, 432p, Messmer-a

     18.00   55.00   110.00

1439- Felix the Cat, 1943, Whit, All Pictures Comics, Messmer-a

     17.00   50.00   100.00

1465- Felix the Cat, 1945, Whit, All Pictures Comics, Messmer-a

     15.00   45.00   90.00

nn- Felix (Flip book), 1967, World Retrospective of Animation Cinema, 188p, 2½ x 4", by Otto Messmer   2.50   7.50   15.00

nn- Fighting Cowboy Of Nugget Gulch, The, 1939, Whit, 36p, 2½ x 3½", Penny Book   4.00   12.00   24.00

1401- Fighting Heroes Battle for Freedom, 1943, Whit, All Pictures Comics, from "Heroes of Democracy" strip, by Stookie Allen

      5.50   16.50   33.00

6- Fighting President, The, 1934, EVW (Five Star Library), 160p, photo-c, photo ill., F. D. Roosevelt   8.00   24.00   48.00

nn- Fire Chief Ed Wynn and "His Old Fire Horse," 1934, Gold, 132p, H. Vallely-a, photo, soft-c   8.00   24.00   48.00

1464- Flame Boy and the Indians' Secret, 1938, Whit, 300p, Sekakuku-a (Hopi Indian)   5.50   16.50   33.00

22- Flaming Guns, 1935, EVW, with Tom Mix, movie scenes

     12.00   35.00   70.00

1110- Flash Gordon on the Planet Mongo, 1934, Whit, 320p, by Alex Raymond   21.00   62.50   125.00

1166- Flash Gordon and the Monsters of Mongo, 1935, Whit, 432p, by Alex Raymond   17.00   50.00   100.00

nn- Flash Gordon and the Monsters of Mongo, 1935, Whit, 436p, premium-no ads, 3-color, soft-c, by Alex Raymond

     28.00   85.00   170.00

1171- Flash Gordon and the Tournaments of Mongo, 1935, Whit, 432p, by Alex Raymond   17.00   50.00   100.00

1190- Flash Gordon and the Witch Queen of Mongo, 1936, Whit, 432p, by Alex Raymond   15.00   45.00   90.00

Flash Gordon on the Planet Mongo #1110,
© King Features Syndicate, 1934

	Good	Fine	N-Mint
1407- Flash Gordon in the Water World of Mongo, 1937, Whit, 432p, by Alex Raymond	15.00	45.00	90.00
1423- Flash Gordon and the Perils of Mongo, 1940, Whit, 432p, by Alex Raymond	14.00	42.00	84.00
1424- Flash Gordon in the Jungles of Mongo, 1947, Whit., 352p, by Alex Raymond	12.50	37.50	75.00
1443- Flash Gordon in the Ice World of Mongo, 1942, Whit, 432p, flip pictures, by Alex Raymond	14.00	42.00	84.00
1447- Flash Gordon and the Fiery Desert of Mongo, 1948, Whit, 288p, Raymond-a	12.50	37.50	75.00
1469- Flash Gordon and the Power Men of Mongo, 1943, Whit, 352p, by Alex Raymond	14.00	42.00	84.00
1479- Flash Gordon and the Red Sword Invaders, 1945, Whit, 352p, by Alex Raymond	12.50	37.50	75.00
1484- Flash Gordon and the Tyrant of Mongo, 1941, Whit, 432p, flip pictures, by Alex Raymond	14.00	42.00	84.00
1492- Flash Gordon in the Forest Kingdom of Mongo, 1938, Whit, 432p, by Alex Raymond	15.00	45.00	90.00

	Good	Fine	N-Mint
12- Flash Gordon and the Ape Men of Mor, 1942, Dell, 196p, Fast-Action Story, by Raymond	28.00	85.00	170.00
6833- Flash Gordon Vs. the Emperor of Mongo, 1936, Dell, 244p, Cartoon Story Books, hard-c, Alex Raymond c/a	32.00	95.00	190.00
nn- Flash Gordon Vs. the Emperor of Mongo, 1936, Dell, 244p, Fast-Action Story, soft-c, Alex Raymond c/a	28.00	85.00	170.00
1467- Flint Roper and the Six-Gun Showdown, 1941, Whit, 300p	5.50	16.50	33.00
2014- (#14)-Flintstones-The Case of the Many Missing Things, 1968, Whit, 260p, 39 cents, hard-c, color illos	2.00	6.00	12.00
2003- (#3)-Flipper-Killer Whale Trouble, 1967, Whit, 260p, hard-c, 39 cents, color illos	1.70	5.00	10.00
1108- Flying the Sky Clipper with Winsie Atkins, 1936, Whit, 432p	5.50	16.50	33.00
1460- Foreign Spies Doctor Doom and the Ghost Submarine, 1939, Whit, 432p, Al McWilliams-a	7.50	22.50	45.00
1100B- Fortune Teller, 1938, Whit, 36p, 2½ x 3½" Penny Book	2.00	6.00	12.00
1175- Frank Buck Presents Ted Towers Animal Master, 1935, Whit, 432p	6.00	18.00	36.00
2015- (#15)-Frankenstein, Jr.-The Menace of the Heartless Monster, 1968, Whit, 260p, 39 cents, hard-c, color illos	2.00	6.00	12.00
16- Frankie Thomas in A Dog of Flanders, 1935, EVW, movie scenes	10.00	30.00	60.00
1121- Frank Merriwell at Yale, 1935, 432p	6.00	18.00	36.00
Freckles and His Friends in the North Woods (See TopLine Comics)			
nn- Freckles and his Friends Stage a Play, 1938, Whit, 36p, 2½ x 3½", Penny Book	4.50	14.00	28.00
1164- Freckles and the Lost Diamond Mine, 1937, Whit, 432p, Merrill Blosser-a	7.50	22.50	45.00
nn- Freckles and the Mystery Ship, 1935, Whit, 66p, Pan-Am premium	8.50	25.00	50.00
1100B- Fun, Puzzles, Riddles, 1938, Whit, 36p, 2½ x 3½", Penny Book	2.00	6.00	12.00
1433- Gang Busters Step In, 1939, Whit, 432p, Henry E. Vallely-a	7.00	21.00	42.00

	Good	Fine	N-Mint
1437- Gang Busters Smash Through, 1942, Whit, 432p			
	7.00	21.00	42.00
1451- Gang Busters in Action!, 1938, Whit, 432p			
	7.00	21.00	42.00
nn- Gangbusters and Guns of the Law, 1940, Dell, 4 x 5", 194p, Fast-Action Story, soft-c			
	17.00	50.00	100.00
nn- Gang Busters and the Radio Clues, 1938, Whit, 36p, 2½ x 3½", Penny Book			
	4.00	12.00	24.00
1409- Gene Autry and Raiders of the Range, 1946, Whit, 352p			
	8.00	24.00	48.00
1425- Gene Autry and the Mystery of Paint Rock Canyon, 1947, Whit, 288p			
	8.00	24.00	48.00
1428- Gene Autry Special Ranger, 1941, Whit, 432p, Erwin Hess-a			
	9.00	27.00	54.00
1430- Gene Autry and the Land Grab Mystery, 1948, Whit, 288p			
	7.00	21.00	42.00
1433- Gene Autry in Public Cowboy No. 1, 1938, Whit, 240p, photo-c, movie scenes (1st)			
	17.00	50.00	100.00
1434- Gene Autry and the Gun-Smoke Reckoning, 1943, Whit, 352p			
	9.00	27.00	54.00

Gene Autry and the Gun-Smoke Reckoning #1434, © Gene Autry, 1943

	Good	Fine	N-Mint
1456- Gene Autry in Special Ranger Rule, 1945, Whit, 352p, Henry E. Vallely-a	9.00	27.00	54.00
1461- Gene Autry and the Red Bandit's Ghost, 1949, Whit, 288p	7.00	21.00	42.00
1483- Gene Autry in Law of the Range, 1939, Whit, 432p	9.00	27.00	54.00
1493- Gene Autry and the Hawk of the Hills, 1942, Whit, 428p, flip pictures, Vallely-a	9.00	27.00	54.00
1494- Gene Autry Cowboy Detective, 1940, Whit, 432p, Erwin Hess-a	9.00	27.00	54.00
700-10- Gene Autry and the Bandits Of Silver Tip, 1949, Whit	5.00	15.00	30.00
714-10- Gene Autry and the Range War, 1950, Whit	5.00	15.00	30.00
nn- Gene Autry in Gun Smoke, 1938, Whit, 196p, Fast-Action Story, soft-c	18.00	55.00	110.00
1176- Gentleman Joe Palooka, 1940, Sal, 400p	10.00	30.00	60.00
George O'Brien (See The Cowboy Millionaire)			
1101- George O'Brien and the Arizona Badman, 1936?, Whit	10.00	30.00	60.00
1418- George O'Brien in Gun Law, 1938, Whit, 240p, photo-c, movie scenes, RKO Radio Pictures	10.00	30.00	60.00
1457- George O'Brien and the Hooded Riders, 1940, Whit, 432p, Erwin Hess-a	6.00	18.00	36.00
nn- George O'Brien and the Arizona Bad Man, 1939, Whit, 36p, 2½ x 3½", Penny Book	4.50	14.00	28.00
1462- Ghost Avenger, 1943, Whit, 432p, flip pictures, Henry Vallely-a	6.00	18.00	36.00
nn- Ghost Gun Gang meet Their Match, The, 1939, Whit, 36p, 2½ x 3½", Penny Book	4.00	12.00	24.00
nn- Gingerbread Boy, The, nd(1930s), np(Whit), 36p, Penny Book	1.50	4.50	9.00
1173- G-Man in Action, A, 1940, Sal, 400p, J.R. White-a	5.00	15.00	30.00
1118- G-Man on the Crime Trail, 1936, Whit, 432p	7.00	21.00	42.00
1147- G-Man Vs. the Red X, 1936, Whit, 432p	7.00	21.00	42.00
1162- G-Man Allen, 1939, Sal, 400p	5.00	15.00	30.00

	Good	Fine	N-Mint
1173- G-Man in Action, A, 1940, Sal, 400p	5.00	15.00	30.00
1434- G-Man and the Radio Bank Robberies, 1937, Whit, 432p	7.00	21.00	42.00
1469- G-Man and the Gun Runners, The, 1940, Whit, 432p	7.00	21.00	42.00
1470- G-Man Vs. the Fifth Column, 1941, Whit, 432p, flip pictures	7.00	21.00	42.00
1493- G-Man Breaking the Gambling Ring, 1938, Whit, 432p, James Gary-a	7.00	21.00	42.00
4- G-Men Foil the Kidnappers, 1936, Whit, 132p, 3½ x 3½", soft-c, Tarzan Ice Cream cup lid premium	15.00	45.00	90.00
nn- G-Man on Lightning Island, 1936, Dell, 244p, Fast-Action Story, soft-c, Henry E. Vallely-a	13.00	40.00	80.00
6833- G-Man on Lightning Island, 1936, Dell, 244p, Cartoon Story Book, hard-c, Henry E. Vallely-a	13.00	40.00	80.00
1157- G-Men on the Trail, 1938, Sal, 400p	5.00	15.00	30.00
1168- G Men on the Job, 1935, Whit, 432p	7.00	21.00	42.00
nn- G-Men on the Job Again, 1938, Whit, 36p, 2½ x 3½", Penny Book	4.00	12.00	24.00
nn- G-Men and Kidnap Justice, 1938, Whit, 68p, Pan-Am premium, soft-c	7.00	21.00	42.00
nn- G-Men and the Missing Clues, 1938, Whit, 36p, 2½ x 3½", Penny Book	4.00	12.00	24.00
1097- Go Into Your Dance, 1935, Sal, 160p, photo-c, movie scenes with Al Jolson & Ruby Keeler	10.00	30.00	60.00
1577- Go Into Your Dance, 1935, Sal, 160p, photo-c, movie scenes, soft-c	10.00	30.00	60.00
5751- Goofy in Giant Trouble (Walt Disney's . . .), 1968, Whit, 260p, 39 cents, soft-c, color illos	1.70	5.00	10.00
5751-2- Goofy in Giant Trouble, 1968 (1980-reprint of '67 version), Whit, 260p, 79 cents, soft-c, B&W	.50	1.50	3.00
8- Great Expectations, 1934, EVW, (Five Star Library), 160p, photo-c, movie scenes	12.00	35.00	70.00
1453- Green Hornet Strikes!, The, 1940, Whit, 432p, Robert Weisman-a	25.00	75.00	150.00
1480- Green Hornet Cracks Down, The, 1942, Whit, 432p, flip pictures, Henry Vallely-a	22.00	67.50	135.00
1496- Green Hornet Returns, The, 1941, Whit, 432p, flip pictures	22.00	67.50	135.00

The Green Hornet Returns #1496, © Green Hornet, Inc., 1941

	Good	Fine	N-Mint
1172- **Gullivers' Travels**, 1939, Sal, 320p, adapted from Paramount Pict. Cartoons	12.00	35.00	70.00
nn- **Gumps in Radio Land, The** (Andy Gump And The Chest of Gold), 1937, Lehn & Fink Prod. Corp., 100p, 3¼ x 5½", Pebeco Tooth Paste giveaway, by Gus Edson	14.00	42.00	84.00
nn- **Gunmen of Rustlers' Gulch, The**, 1939, Whit, 36p, 2½ x 3½", Penny Book	4.00	12.00	24.00
1426- **Guns in the Roaring West**, 1937, Whit, 300p	5.50	16.50	33.00
1647- **Gunsmoke** (TV Series), 1958, Whit, 280p, 4½ x 5¼"	4.50	13.50	27.00
1101- **Hairbreath Harry in Department QT**, 1935, Whit, 384p, by J. M. Alexander	7.50	22.50	45.00
1413- **Hal Hardy in the Lost Land of Giants**, 1938, Whit, 300p, "The World 1,000,000 Years Ago"	6.00	18.00	36.00
1159- **Hall of Fame of the Air**, 1936, Whit, 432p, by Capt. Eddie Rickenbacker	5.50	16.50	33.00

	Good	Fine	N-Mint
nn- **Hansel and Grethel, The Story of,** nd (1930s), no publ., 36p, Penny Book	1.50	4.50	9.00
1145- **Hap Lee's Selection of Movie Gags,** 1935, Whit, 160p, photos of stars	8.50	25.00	50.00
Happy Prince, The (See Wee Little Books)			
1111- **Hard Rock Harrigan-A Story of Boulder Dam,** 1935, Sal, photo-c, photo illus.	5.50	16.50	33.00
1591- **Hard Rock Harrigan-A Story of Boulder Dam,** 1935, Sal, photo-c, photo illus.	5.50	16.50	33.00
1418- **Harold Teen Swinging at the Sugar Bowl,** 1939, Whit, 432p, by Carl Ed	7.00	21.00	42.00
1100B- **Hobbies,** 1938, Whit, 36p, 2½ x 3½", Penny Book	2.00	6.00	12.00
1125- **Hockey Spare, The,** 1937, Sal, sports book	4.50	13.50	27.00
1605- **Hockey Spare, The,** 1937, Sal, soft-c	4.50	13.50	27.00
728- **Homeless Homer,** 1934, Whit, by Dee Dobbin, for young kids	2.00	6.00	12.00
17- **Hoosier Schoolmaster, The,** 1935, EVW, movie scenes	10.00	30.00	60.00
715- **Houdini's Big Little Book of Magic,** 1927 (1933), Whit, 300p	11.00	32.50	65.00
nn- **Houdini's Big Little Book of Magic,** 1927 (1933), Whit, 196p, American Oil Co. premium, soft-c	8.50	25.00	50.00
nn- **Houdini's Big Little Book of Magic,** 1927 (1933), Whit, 204p, Cocomalt premium, soft-c	8.50	25.00	50.00
Huckleberry Finn (See The Adventures of . . .)			
1644- **Hugh O'Brian TV's Wyatt Earp** (TV Series), 1958, Whit, 280p	4.00	12.00	24.00
1424- **Inspector Charlie Chan Villainy on the High Seas,** 1942, Whit, 432p, flip pictures	10.00	30.00	60.00
1186- **Inspector Wade of Scotland Yard,** 1940, Sal, 400p	6.00	18.00	36.00
1448- **Inspector Wade Solves the Mystery of the Red Aces,** 1937, Whit, 432p	6.00	18.00	36.00
1148- **International Spy Doctor Doom Faces Death at Dawn,** 1937, Whit, 432p, Arbo-a	7.50	22.50	45.00
1155- **In The Name of the Law,** 1937, Whit, 432p, Henry E. Vallely-a	7.00	21.00	42.00
2012- **(#12)-Invaders, The-Alien Missile Threat** (TV Series), 1967, Whit, 260p, hard-c, 39 cents, color illos	2.35	7.00	14.00

International Spy, Doctor Doom Faces Death at Dawn, #1148,
© Whitman Publishing Co., 1937

	Good	Fine	N-Mint
1403- Invisible Scarlet O'Neil, 1942, Whit, All Pictures Comics, flip pictures	7.00	21.00	42.00
1406- Invisible Scarlet O'Neil Versus the King of the Slums, 1946, Whit, 352p	6.00	18.00	36.00
1098- It Happened One Night, 1935, Sal, 160p, Little Big Book, Clark Gable, Claudette Colbert photo-c, movie scenes from Academy Award winner	13.00	40.00	80.00
1578- It Happened One Night, 1935, Sal, 160p, soft-c	13.00	40.00	80.00
Jack and Jill (See Wee Little Books)			
1432- Jack Armstrong and the Mystery of the Iron Key, 1939, Whit, 432p, Henry E. Vallely-a	7.50	22.50	45.00
1435- Jack Armstrong and the Ivory Treasure, 1937, Whit, 432p, Henry Vallely-a	7.50	22.50	45.00
Jackie Cooper (See Story Of . . .)			
1084- Jackie Cooper in Peck's Bad Boy, 1934, Sal, 160p, hard, photo-c, movie scenes	10.00	30.00	60.00

	Good	Fine	N-Mint
1314- Jackie Cooper in Peck's Bad Boy, 1934, Sal, 160p, soft, photo-c, movie scenes	10.00	30.00	60.00
1402- Jackie Cooper in "Gangster's Boy," 1939, Whit, 240p, photo-c, movie scenes	8.50	25.00	50.00
13- Jackie Cooper in Dinky, 1935, EVW, 160p, movie scenes	10.00	30.00	60.00
nn- Jack King of the Secret Service and the Counterfeiters, 1939, Whit, 36p, 2½ x 3½", Penny Book, by John G. Gray	4.00	12.00	24.00
L11- Jack London's Call of the Wild, 1935, Lynn, 20th Cent. Pic., movie scenes with Clark Gable	10.00	30.00	60.00
nn- Jack Pearl as Detective Baron Munchausen, 1934, Gold, 132p, soft-c	8.00	24.00	48.00
1102- Jack Swift and His Rocket Ship, 1934, Whit, 320p	12.00	35.00	70.00
1498- Jane Arden the Vanished Princess, Whit, 300p	7.00	21.00	42.00
1179- Jane Withers in This is the Life (20th Century-Fox Presents . . .), 1935, Whit, 240p, photo-c, movie scenes	9.00	27.00	54.00
1463- Jane Withers in Keep Smiling, 1938, Whit, 240p, photo-c, movie scenes	9.00	27.00	54.00
Jaragu of the Jungle (See Rex Beach's . . .)			
1447- Jerry Parker Police Reporter and the Candid Camera Clue, 1941, Whit, 300p	5.50	16.50	33.00
Jim Bowie (See Adventures of . . .)			
nn- Jim Bryant of the Highway Patrol and the Mysterious Accident, 1939, Whit, 36p, 2½ x 3½", Penny Book	4.50	14.00	28.00
1466- Jim Craig State Trooper and the Kidnapped Governor, 1938, Whit, 432p	5.50	16.50	33.00
nn- Jim Doyle Private Detective and the Train Hold-Up, 1939, Whit, 36p, 2½ x 3½", Penny Book	4.00	12.00	24.00
1180- Jim Hardy Ace Reporter, 1940, Sal, 400p, Dick Moores-a	6.00	18.00	36.00
1143- Jimmy Allen in the Air Mail Robbery, 1936, Whit, 432p	5.50	16.50	33.00
L15- Jimmy and the Tiger, 1935, Lynn, 192p	6.00	18.00	36.00
Jimmy Skunk's Justice (See Wee Little Books)			

	Good	Fine	N-Mint
1428- Jim Starr of the Border Patrol, 1937, Whit, 432p	5.50	16.50	33.00
Joan of Arc (See Wee Little Books)			
1105- Joe Louis the Brown Bomber, 1936, Whit, 240p, photo-c, photo-illus.	12.00	35.00	70.00
Joe Palooka (See Gentleman . . .)			
1123- Joe Palooka the Heavyweight Boxing Champ, 1934, Whit, 320p, Ham Fisher-a	10.00	30.00	60.00
1168- Joe Palooka's Greatest Adventure, 1939, Sal	10.00	30.00	60.00
nn- Joe Penner's Duck Farm, 1935, Gold, Henry Vallely-a	8.00	24.00	48.00

John Carter of Mars, no #, © Edgar Rice Burroughs, 1940

1402- John Carter of Mars, 1940, Whit, 432p, John Coleman Burroughs-a	33.00	100.00	200.00
nn- John Carter of Mars, 1940, Dell, 194p, Fast-Action Story, soft-c	33.00	100.00	200.00
1164- Johnny Forty Five, 1938, Sal, 400p	5.00	15.00	30.00
John Wayne (See Westward Ho!)			

	Good	Fine	N-Mint
1100B-Jokes (A book of laughs galore), 1938, Whit, 36p, 2½ x 3½", Penny Book	2.00	6.00	12.00
1100B-Jokes (A book of side-splitting funny stories), 1938, Whit, 36p, 2½ x 3½", Penny Book	2.00	6.00	12.00
2026-Journey to the Center of the Earth, The Fiery Foe, 1968, Whit	2.00	6.00	12.00

Jungle Jim (See Top-Line Comics)

	Good	Fine	N-Mint
1138-Jungle Jim, 1936, Whit, 432p, Alex Raymond-a	12.00	35.00	70.00
1139-Jungle Jim and the Vampire Woman, 1937, Whit, 432p, Alex Raymond-a	13.00	40.00	80.00
1442-Junior G-Men, 1937, Whit, 432p, Henry E. Vallely-a	6.00	18.00	36.00
nn-Junior G-Men Solve a Crime, 1939, Whit, 36p, 2½ x 3½", Penny Book	4.00	12.00	24.00
1422-Junior Nebb on the Diamond Bar Ranch, 1938, Whit, 300p, by Sol Hess	6.00	18.00	36.00
1470-Junior Nebb Joins the Circus, 1939, Whit, 300p, by Sol Hess	6.00	18.00	36.00
nn-Junior Nebb Elephant Trainer, 1939, Whit, 68p, Pan-Am Oil premium, soft-c	7.50	22.50	45.00
1052-"Just Kids" (Adventures of . . .), 1934, Sal, oblong size, by Ad Carter	15.00	45.00	90.00
1094-Just Kids and the Mysterious Stranger, 1935, Sal, 160p, by Ad Carter	9.00	27.00	54.00
1184-Just Kids and Deep-Sea Dan, 1940, Sal, 400p, by Ad Carter	7.00	21.00	42.00
1302-Just Kids, The Adventures of, 1934, Sal, oblong size, soft-c, by Ad Carter	15.00	45.00	90.00
1324-Just Kids and the Mysterious Stranger, 1935, Sal, 160p, soft-c, by Ad Carter	9.00	27.00	54.00
1401-Just Kids, 1937, Whit, 432p, by Ad Carter	8.00	24.00	48.00
1055-Katzenjammer Kids in the Mountains, 1934, Sal, Oblong, H. H. Knerr-a	14.00	42.00	84.00
14-Katzenjammer Kids, The, 1942, Dell, 194p, Fast-Action Story, H. H. Knerr-a	15.00	45.00	90.00
1411-Kay Darcy and the Mystery Hideout, 1937, Whit, 300p, Charles Mueller-a	7.00	21.00	42.00
1180-Kayo in the Land of Sunshine (With Moon Mullins), 1937, Whit, 432p, by Willard	8.00	24.00	48.00

	Good	Fine	N-Mint
1415- **Kayo and Moon Mullins and the One Man Gang,** 1939, Whit, 432p, by Frank Willard	8.00	24.00	48.00
7- **Kayo and Moon Mullins 'Way Down South,** 1938, Whit, 132p, 3½ x 3½", Buddy Book	17.00	50.00	100.00
1105- **Kazan in Revenge of the North** (James Oliver Curwood's . . .), 1937, Whit, 432p, Henry E. Vallely-a	5.50	16.50	33.00
1471- **Kazan, King of the Pack** (James Oliver Curwood's . . .), 1940, Whit, 432p	5.00	15.00	30.00
1420- **Keep 'Em Flying! U.S.A. for America's Defense,** 1943, Whit, 432p, Henry E. Vallely-a, flip pictures	5.50	16.50	33.00
1133- **Kelly King at Yale Hall,** 1937, Sal	5.00	15.00	30.00
Ken Maynard (See Strawberry Roan, Western Frontier & Wheels of Destiny)			
776- **Ken Maynard in "Gun Justice,"** 1934, Whit, 160p, movie scenes (Universal Pic.)	12.00	35.00	70.00
1430- **Ken Maynard in Western Justice,** 1938, Whit, 432p, Irwin Myers-a	7.00	21.00	42.00
1442- **Ken Maynard and the Gun Wolves of the Gila,** 1939, Whit, 432p	7.00	21.00	42.00
nn- **Ken Maynard in Six-Gun Law,** 1938, Whit, 36p, 2½ x 3½", Penny Book	6.00	17.50	35.00
1134- **King of Crime,** 1938, Sal, 400p	5.00	15.00	30.00
King of the Royal Mounted (See Zane Grey)			
1010- **King of the Royal Mounted in Arctic Law,** 1937, Whit, 7¼ x 5½", 64p, Nickle Book	8.50	25.50	50.00
nn- **Kit Carson,** 1933, World, by J. Carroll Mansfield, High Lights Of History Series, hard-c	5.50	16.50	33.00
nn- **Kit Carson,** 1933, World, same as hard-c above but with a black cloth-c	5.50	16.50	33.00
1105- **Kit Carson and the Mystery Riders,** 1935, Sal, hard-c, Johnny Mack Brown photo-c, movie scenes	12.00	35.00	70.00
1585- **Kit Carson and the Mystery Riders,** 1935, Sal, soft-c, Johnny Mack Brown photo-c, movie scenes	12.00	35.00	70.00
Krazy Kat (See Advs. of . . .)			
2004- (#4)-**Lassie-Adventure in Alaska** (TV Series), 1967, Whit, 260p, 39 cents, hard-c, color illos	2.00	6.00	12.00
2027- **Lassie and the Shabby Sheik** (TV Series), 1968, Whit	2.00	6.00	12.00
1132- **Last Days of Pompeii, The,** 1935, Whit, 5¼ x 6¼", 260p, photo-c, movie scenes	10.00	30.00	60.00

	Good	Fine	N-Mint

1128- Last Man Out (Baseball), 1937, Sal, hard-c

	4.50	13.50	27.00

L30- Last of the Mohicans, The, 1936, Lynn, 192p, movie scenes with Randolph Scott, United Artists Pictures

	10.00	30.00	60.00

The Laughing Dragon of Oz #1126, © Frank Baum, 1934

1126- Laughing Dragon of Oz, The, 1934, Whit, 432p, by Frank Baum

	43.00	130.00	260.00

1086- Laurel and Hardy, 1934, Sal, 160p, hard-c, photo-c, movie scenes

	12.00	35.00	70.00

1316- Laurel and Hardy, 1934, Sal, 160p, soft-c, photo-c, movie scenes

	12.00	35.00	70.00

1092- Law of the Wild, The, 1935, Sal, 160p, photo-c, movie scenes of Rex, The Wild Horse & Rin-Tin-Tin Jr.

	5.50	16.50	33.00

1322- Law of the Wild, The, 1935, Sal, 160p, photo-c, movie scenes, soft-c

	5.50	16.50	33.00

1100B- Learn to be a Ventriloquist, 1938, Whit, 36p, 2½ x 3½", Penny Book

	2.00	6.00	12.00

	Good	Fine	N-Mint
1149- Lee Brady Range Detective, 1938, Sal, 400p			
	5.00	15.00	30.00
L10- Les Miserables (Victor Hugo's . . .), 1935, Lynn, 192p, movie scenes			
	9.00	27.00	54.00
1441- Lightning Jim U.S. Marshal brings Law to the West, 1940, Whit, 432p, based on radio program			
	5.50	16.50	33.00
nn- Lightning Jim Whipple U.S. Marshal in Indian Territory, 1939, Whit, 36p, 2½ x 3½", Penny Book			
	4.00	12.00	24.00
653- Lions and Tigers (With Clyde Beatty), 1934, Whit, 160p, photo-c, movie scenes			
	10.00	30.00	60.00
1187- Li'l Abner and the Ratfields, 1940, Sal, 400p, by Al Capp			
	12.00	35.00	70.00
1193- Li'l Abner and Sadie Hawkins Day, 1940, Sal, 400p, by Al Capp			
	12.00	35.00	70.00

Li'l Abner in New York #1198, © United Features Syndicate, 1936

	Good	Fine	N-Mint
1198- Li'l Abner in New York, 1936, Whit, 432p, by Al Capp			
	12.00	35.00	70.00
1401- Li'l Abner among the Millionaires, 1939, Whit, 432p, by Al Capp			
	12.00	35.00	70.00

	Good	Fine	N-Mint
1054- Little Annie Rooney, 1934, Sal, Oblong-4 x 8", All Pictures Comics, hard-c	13.00	40.00	80.00
1304- Little Annie Rooney, 1934, Sal, Oblong-4 x 8", All Pictures, soft-c	13.00	40.00	80.00
1117- Little Annie Rooney and the Orphan House, 1936, Whit, 432p	7.00	21.00	42.00
1406- Little Annie Rooney on the Highway to Adventure, 1938, Whit, 432p	7.00	21.00	42.00
1149- Little Big Shot (With Sybil Jason), 1935, Whit, 240p, photo-c, movie scenes	7.00	21.00	42.00
nn- Little Black Sambo, nd (1930s), np (Whit), 36p, 3 x 2½", Penny Book	7.00	20.00	40.00
Little Bo-Peep (See Wee Little Books)			
Little Colonel, The (See Shirley Temple)			
1148- Little Green Door, The 1938, Sal, 400p	5.00	15.00	30.00
1112- Little Hollywood Stars, 1935, Sal, movie scenes (Little Rascals, etc.), hard-c	8.50	25.00	50.00
1592- Little Hollywood Stars, 1935, Sal, movie scenes, soft-c	8.50	25.00	50.00
1087- Little Jimmy's Gold Hunt, 1935, Sal, 160p, Hard-c, Little Big Book, by Swinnerton	7.50	22.50	45.00
1317- Little Jimmy's Gold Hunt, 1935, Sal, 160p, 4¼ x 5¾", soft-c, by Swinnerton	7.50	22.50	45.00
Little Joe and the City Gangsters (See Top-Line Comics)			
Little Joe Otter's Slide (See Wee Little Books)			
1118- Little Lord Fauntleroy, 1936, Sal, movie scenes, photo-c, 4½ x 5¼ ", starring Mickey Rooney & Freddie Bartholomew, hard-c	7.50	22.50	45.00
1598- Little Lord Fauntleroy, 1936, Sal, photo-c, movie scenes, soft-c	7.50	22.50	45.00
1192- Little Mary Mixup and the Grocery Robberies, 1940, Sal	6.00	18.00	36.00
8- Little Mary Mixup Wins A Prize, 1936, Whit, 132p, 3½ x 3½", soft-c, Tarzan Ice Cream cup lid premium	15.00	45.00	90.00
1150- Little Men, 1934, Whit, 4¼ x 5¼", movie scenes (Mascot Prod.), photo-c, hard-c	7.50	22.50	45.00
9- Little Minister, The-Katharine Hepburn, 1935, 160p, 4¼ x 5½", EVW (Five Star Library), movie scenes (RKO)	10.00	30.00	60.00

	Good	Fine	N-Mint
1120- Little Miss Muffet, 1936, Whit, 432p, by Fanny Y. Cory			
	7.00	21.00	42.00
708- Little Orphan Annie, 1933, Whit, 320p, by Harold Gray, the 2nd Big Little Book			
	33.00	100.00	200.00
nn- Little Orphan Annie, 1928 ('33), Whit, 52p, 4 x 5½", premium~no ads, soft-c, by Harold Gray			
	20.00	60.00	120.00
716- Little Orphan Annie and Sandy, 1933, Whit, 320p, by Harold Gray			
	17.00	50.00	100.00
716- Little Orphan Annie and Sandy, 1933, Whit, 300p, by Harold Gray			
	17.00	50.00	100.00
nn- Little Orphan Annie and Sandy, 1933, Whit, 52p, premium~no ads, 4 x 5½", soft-c, by Harold Gray			
	20.00	60.00	120.00
748- Little Orphan Annie and Chizzler, 1933, Whit, 320p, by Harold Gray			
	14.00	42.00	84.00
1010- Little Orphan Annie and the Big Town Gunmen, 1937, 7¼ x 5½", 64p, Nickle Book			
	8.50	25.00	50.00
1103- Little Orphan Annie with the Circus, 1934, Whit, 320p, by Harold Gray			
	12.00	35.00	70.00
1140- Little Orphan Annie and the Big Train Robbery, 1934, Whit, 300p, by Gray			
	12.00	35.00	70.00
1140- Little Orphan Annie and the Big Train Robbery, 1934, Whit, 300p, premium-no ads, soft-c, by Harold Gray			
	17.00	50.00	100.00
1154- Little Orphan Annie and the Ghost Gang, 1935, Whit, 432p, by Harold Gray			
	12.00	32.50	65.00
nn- Little Orphan Annie and the Ghost Gang, 1935, Whit, 436p, premium-no ads, 3-color, soft-c, by Harold Gray			
	17.00	50.00	100.00
1162- Little Orphan Annie and Punjab the Wizard, 1935, Whit, 432p, by Harold Gray			
	12.00	32.50	65.00
1186- Little Orphan Annie and the $1,000,000 Formula, 1936, Whit, 432p, by Gray			
	10.00	30.00	60.00
1414- Little Orphan Annie and the Ancient Treasure of Am, 1939, Whit, 432p, by Gray			
	8.50	25.00	50.00
1416- Little Orphan Annie in the Movies, 1937, Whit, 432p, by Harold Gray			
	8.50	25.00	50.00
1417- Little Orphan Annie and the Secret of the Well, 1947, Whit, 352p, by Gray			
	7.50	22.50	45.00
1435- Little Orphan Annie and the Gooneyville Mystery, 1947, Whit, 288p, by Gray			
	7.50	22.50	45.00

Little Orphan Annie in the Movies #1416, © Harold Gray, 1937

	Good	Fine	N-Mint
1446- Little Orphan Annie in the Thieves' Den, 1948, Whit, 288p, by			
Harold Gray	7.50	22.50	45.00
1449- Little Orphan Annie and the Mysterious Shoemaker, 1938, Whit,			
432p, by Harold Gray	8.50	25.00	50.00
1457- Little Orphan Annie and Her Junior Commandos, 1943, Whit,			
352p, by H. Gray	7.50	22.50	45.00
1461- Little Orphan Annie and the Underground Hide-Out, 1945, Whit,			
352p, by Gray	7.50	22.50	45.00
1468- Little Orphan Annie and the Ancient Treasure of Am, 1949			
(Misdated 1939), 288p, by Gray	8.00	24.00	48.00
1482- Little Orphan Annie and the Haunted Mansion, 1941, Whit, 432p,			
flip pictures, by Harold Gray	8.50	25.00	50.00
4054- Little Orphan Annie, The Story Of, 1934, 7 x 9½", 320p, Big Big			
Book, Harold Gray c/a	43.00	130.00	260.00
nn- Little Orphan Annie gets into Trouble, 1938, Whit, 36p, 2½ x 3½",			
Penny Book	4.50	14.00	28.00
nn- Little Orphan Annie in Hollywood, 1937, Whit, 3½ x 3¾", Pan-Am			
premium, soft-c	10.00	30.00	60.00

	Good	Fine	N-Mint
nn- **Little Orphan Annie in Rags to Riches**, 1938, Dell, 194p, Fast-Action Story, soft-c	18.00	55.00	110.00
nn- **Little Orphan Annie Saves Sandy**, 1938, Whit, 36p, 2½ x 3½", Penny Book	4.50	14.00	28.00
nn- **Little Orphan Annie Under the Big Top**, 1938, Dell, 194p, Fast-Action Story, soft-c	18.00	55.00	110.00
nn- **Little Orphan Annie Wee Little Books** (In open box) nn, 1934, Whit, 44p, by H. Gray			
L.O.A. And Daddy Warbucks	5.00	15.00	30.00
L.O.A. And Her Dog Sandy	5.00	15.00	30.00
L.O.A. And The Lucky Knife	5.00	15.00	30.00
L.O.A. And The Pinch-Pennys	5.00	15.00	30.00
L.O.A. At Happy Home	5.00	15.00	30.00
L.O.A. Finds Mickey	5.00	15.00	30.00
Complete set with box	40.00	120.00	240.00
nn- **Little Polly Flinders, The Story of,** nd (1930s), no publ., 36p, 2½ x 3", Penny Book	1.50	4.50	9.00
nn- **Little Red Hen, The**, nd(1930s), np(Whit), 36p, Penny Book	1.50	4.50	9.00
nn- **Little Red Riding Hood,** nd (1930s), np (Whit), 36p, 3 x 2½", Penny Book	1.50	4.50	9.00
nn- **Little Red Riding Hood And The Big Bad Wolf** (Disney), 1934, McKay, 36p, stiff-c, Disney Studio-a	18.00	55.00	110.00
757- **Little Women**, 1934, Whit, 4¼ x 5¼", 160p, photo-c, movie scenes, starring Katharine Hepburn	11.00	32.50	65.00
Littlest Rebel, The (See Shirley Temple)			
1181- **Lone Ranger and his Horse Silver**, 1935, Whit, 432p, Hal Arbo-a	15.00	45.00	90.00
1196- **Lone Ranger and the Vanishing Herd**, 1936, Whit, 432p	12.00	35.00	70.00
1407- **Lone Ranger and Dead Men's Mine, The**, 1939, Whit, 432p	11.00	32.50	65.00
1421- **Lone Ranger on the Barbary Coast, The**, 1944, Whit, 352p, Henry Vallely-a	9.00	27.00	54.00
1428- **Lone Ranger and the Secret Weapon, The**, 1943, Whit, 352p	9.00	27.00	54.00
1431- **Lone Ranger and the Secret Killer, The**, 1937, Whit, 432p, H. Anderson-a	11.00	35.00	70.00
1450- **Lone Ranger and the Black Shirt Highwayman, The**, 1939, Whit, 432p	11.00	32.50	65.00

The Lone Ranger and the Menace of Murder Valley #1465,
© The Lone Ranger, Inc., 1938

	Good	Fine	N-Mint
1465- Lone Ranger and the Menace of Murder Valley, The, 1938, Whit, 432p, Robert Wiseman-a	11.00	32.50	65.00
1468- Lone Ranger Follows Through, The, 1941, Whit, 432p, H. E. Vallely-a	11.00	32.50	65.00
1477- Lone Ranger and the Great Western Span, The, 1942, Whit, 424p, H.E. Vallely-a	9.00	27.00	54.00
1489- Lone Ranger and the Red Renegades, The, 1939, Whit, 432p	11.00	32.50	65.00
1498- Lone Ranger and the Silver Bullets, 1946, Whit, 352p, Henry E. Vallely-a	9.00	27.00	54.00
712-10- Lone Ranger and the Secret of Somber Cavern, The, 1950, Whit	5.00	15.00	30.00
2013- (#13)-Lone Ranger Outwits Crazy Cougar, The, 1968, Whit, 260p, 39 cents, hard-c, color illos	2.00	6.00	12.00
nn- Lone Ranger and the Lost Valley, The, 1938, Dell, 196p, Fast-Action Story, soft-c	18.00	55.00	110.00
1405- Lone Star Martin of the Texas Rangers, 1939, Whit, 432p	5.00	15.00	30.00

	Good	**Fine**	**N-Mint**
19- Lost City, The, 1935, EVW, movie scenes	10.00	30.00	60.00
1103- Lost Jungle, The (With Clyde Beatty), 1936, Sal, movie scenes, hard-c	10.00	30.00	60.00
1583- Lost Jungle, The (With Clyde Beatty), 1936, Sal, movie scenes, soft-c	9.00	27.00	54.00
753- Lost Patrol, The, 1934, Whit, 160p, photo-c, movie scenes with Boris Karloff	9.00	27.00	54.00
1189- Mac of the Marines in Africa, 1936, Whit, 432p	7.00	21.00	42.00
1400- Mac of the Marines in China, 1938, Whit, 432p	7.00	21.00	42.00
1100B- Magic Tricks (With explanations), 1938, Whit, 36p, 2½ x 3½", Penny Book	2.00	6.00	12.00
1100B- Magic Tricks (How to do them), 1938, Whit, 36p, 2½ x 3½", Penny Book	2.00	6.00	12.00
Major Hoople (See Our Boarding House)			
1167- Mandrake the Magician, 1935, Whit, 432p, by Lee Falk & Phil Davis	12.00	35.00	70.00
1418- Mandrake the Magician and the Flame Pearls, 1946, Whit, 352p, by Lee Falk & Phil Davis	8.00	24.00	48.00
1431- Mandrake the Magician and the Midnight Monster, 1939, Whit, 432p, by Lee Falk & Phil Davis	9.00	27.00	54.00
1454- Mandrake the Magician Mighty Solver of Mysteries, 1941, Whit, 432p, by Lee Falk & Phil Davis, flip pictures	9.00	27.00	54.00
2011- (#11)-Man From U.N.C.L.E., The-The Calcutta Affair (TV Series), 1967, Whit, 260p, 39 cents, hard-c, color illos	2.50	8.00	16.00
1429- Marge's Little Lulu Alvin and Tubby, 1947, Whit, All Pictures Comics, Stanley-a	13.00	40.00	80.00
1438- Mary Lee and the Mystery of the Indian Beads, 1937, Whit, 300p	5.50	16.50	33.00
1165- Masked Man of the Mesa, The, 1939, Sal, 400p	5.00	15.00	30.00
1436- Maximo the Amazing Superman, 1940, Whit, 432p, Henry E. Vallely-a	8.50	25.00	50.00
1444- Maximo the Amazing Superman and the Crystals of Doom, 1941, Whit, 432p, Henry E. Vallely-a	8.50	25.00	50.00

Maximo the Amazing Superman and the Supermachine #1445,
© Whitman Publishing Co., 1941

	Good	Fine	N-Mint
1445- Maximo the Amazing Superman and the Supermachine, 1941, Whit, 432p	8.50	25.00	50.00
755- Men of the Mounted, 1934, Whit, 320p	8.50	25.00	50.00
nn- Men of the Mounted, 1933, Whit, 52p, 3½ x 5¼", premium~no ads; another versions with Poll Parrot & Perkins ad; soft-c	12.00	35.00	70.00
nn- Men of the Mounted, 1934, Whit, Cocomalt premium, soft-c, by Ted McCall	7.50	22.50	45.00
1475- Men With Wings, 1938, Whit, 240p, photo-c, movie scenes (Paramount Pics.)	7.00	21.00	42.00
1170- Mickey Finn, 1940, Sal, 400p, by Frank Leonard	7.00	21.00	42.00
717- Mickey Mouse (Disney), 1933, Whit, 320p, Gottfredson-a (Two diff. covers printed)	80.00	240.00	480.00
726- Mickey Mouse in Blaggard Castle (Disney), 1934, Whit, 320p, Gottfredson-a	17.00	50.00	100.00
731- Mickey Mouse the Mail Pilot (Disney), 1933, Whit, 300p, Gottfredson-a	18.00	55.00	110.00

	Good	Fine	N-Mint

nn- Mickey Mouse the Mail Pilot (Disney), 1933, Whit, 292p, American Oil Co. premium, soft-c, Gottfredson-a; another version 3½ x 4¼"

	17.00	50.00	100.00

750- Mickey Mouse Sails for Treasure Island (Disney), 1933, Whit, 320p, Gottfredson-a

	18.00	55.00	110.00

nn- Mickey Mouse Sails for Treasure Island (Disney), 1935, Whit, 196p, premium-no ads, soft-c, Gottfredson-a (Scarce)

	20.00	60.00	120.00

nn- Mickey Mouse Sails for Treasure Island (Disney), 1935, Whit, 196p, Kolynos Dental Cream premium (Scarce)

	20.00	60.00	120.00

756- Mickey Mouse Presents a Walt Disney Silly Symphony (Disney), 1934, Whit, 240p, Bucky Bug app.   16.00   48.00   96.00

1111- Mickey Mouse Presents Walt Disney's Silly Symphonies Stories, 1936, Whit, 432p, Donald Duck, Bucky Bug app.

	16.00	48.00	96.00

1128- Mickey Mouse and Pluto the Racer (Disney), 1936, Whit, 432p, Gottfredson-a   14.00   42.00   84.00

1139- Mickey Mouse the Detective (Disney), 1934, Whit, 300p, Gottfredson-a   16.00   48.00   96.00

1139- Mickey Mouse the Detective (Disney), 1934, Whit, 304p, premium-no ads, soft-c, Gottfredson-a (Scarce) 23.00   70.00   140.00

1153- Mickey Mouse and the Bat Bandit (Disney), 1935, Whit, 432p, Gottfredson-a   15.00   45.00   90.00

nn- Mickey Mouse and the Bat Bandit (Disney), 1935, Whit, 436p, premium-no ads, 3-color, soft-c, Gottfredson-a (Scarce)

	23.00	70.00	140.00

1160- Mickey Mouse and Bobo the Elephant (Disney), 1935, Whit, 432p, Gottfredson-a   15.00   45.00   90.00

1187- Mickey Mouse and the Sacred Jewel (Disney), 1936, Whit, 432p, Gottfredson-a   13.00   40.00   80.00

1401- Mickey Mouse in the Treasure Hunt (Disney), 1941, Whit, 430p, flip pictures with Pluto, Gottfredson-a

	12.00	35.00	70.00

1409- Mickey Mouse Runs His Own Newspaper (Disney), 1937, Whit, 432p, Gottfredson-a   12.00   35.00   70.00

1413- Mickey Mouse and the 'Lectro Box (Disney), 1946, Whit, 352p, Gottfredson-a   10.00   30.00   60.00

1417- Mickey Mouse on Sky Island (Disney), 1941, Whit, 432p, flip

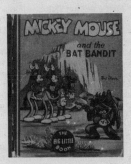

Mickey Mouse and the Bat Bandit #1153, © The Disney Co., 1935

	Good	Fine	N-Mint
pictures, Gottfredson-a; considered by Gottfredson to be his best Mickey story	12.00	35.00	70.00
1428-Mickey Mouse in the Foreign Legion (Disney), 1940, Whit, 432p, Gottfredson-a	12.00	35.00	70.00
1429-Mickey Mouse and the Magic Lamp (Disney), 1942, Whit, 432p, flip pictures	12.00	35.00	70.00
1433-Mickey Mouse and the Lazy Daisy Mystery (Disney), 1947, Whit, 288p	10.00	30.00	60.00
1444-Mickey Mouse in the World of Tomorrow (Disney), 1948, Whit, 288p, Gottfredson-a	13.00	40.00	80.00
1451-Mickey Mouse and the Desert Palace (Disney),1948, Whit, 288p	10.00	30.00	60.00
1463-Mickey Mouse and the Pirate Submarine (Disney), 1939, Whit, 432p, Gottfredson-a	12.00	35.00	70.00
1464-Mickey Mouse and the Stolen Jewels (Disney), 1949, Whit, 288p	11.00	32.50	65.00
1471-Mickey Mouse and the Dude Ranch Bandit (Disney), 1943, Whit, 432p, flip pictures	12.00	35.00	70.00

	Good	Fine	N-Mint

1475-Mickey Mouse and the 7 Ghosts (Disney), 1940, Whit, 432p,
Gottfredson-a   12.00   35.00   70.00

1476-Mickey Mouse in the Race for Riches (Disney), 1938, Whit, 432p,
Gottfredson-a   12.00   35.00   70.00

1483-Mickey Mouse Bell Boy Detective (Disney), 1945, Whit, 352p
                                   11.00   32.50   65.00

1499-Mickey Mouse on the Cave-Man Island (Disney), 1944, Whit, 352p
                                   11.00   32.50   65.00

4062-Mickey Mouse, The Story Of, 1935, Whit, 7 x 9½", 320p, Big Big
Book, Gottfredson-a   53.00   160.00   320.00

4062-Mickey Mouse and the Smugglers, The Story Of, (Scarce), 1935,
Whit, 7 x 9½", 320p, Big Big Book, same contents as above version;
Gottfredson-a   75.00   225.00   450.00

708-10-Mickey Mouse on the Haunted Island (Disney), 1950, Whit,
Gottfredson-a   7.00   20.00   40.00

nn-Mickey Mouse and Minnie at Macy's, 1934, Whit, 148p, 3¼ x 3½",
soft-c, R. H. Macy & Co. Xmas giveaway
                                   60.00   175.00   350.00

nn-Mickey Mouse and Minnie March to Macy's, 1935, Whit, 148p,
3½ x 3½", soft-c, R. H. Macy & Co. Xmas giveaway
                                   60.00   175.00   350.00

nn-Mickey Mouse and the Magic Carpet, 1935, Whit, 148p, 3½ x 4",
soft-c, giveaway, Gottfredson-a, Donald Duck app.
                                   47.00   140.00   280.00

nn-Mickey Mouse Silly Symphonies, 1934, Dean & Son, Ltd (England),
48p, with 4 pop-ups, Babes In The Woods, King Neptune, with dust
jacket   58.00   175.00   350.00
Without dust jacket   42.00   125.00   250.00

3061-Mickey Mouse to Draw and Color (The Big Little Set), nd (early
1930s), Whit, with crayons; box contains 320 loose pages to color,
reprinted from early Mickey Mouse BLBs
                                   58.00   175.00   350.00

16-Mickey Mouse and Pluto (Disney), Dell, 196p, Fast-Action Story
                                   25.00   75.00   150.00

nn-Mickey Mouse the Sheriff of Nugget Gulch (Disney), 1938, Dell,
196p, Fast-Action Story, soft-c, Gottfredson-a
                                   25.00   75.00   150.00

nn-Mickey Mouse with Goofy and Mickey's Nephews, 1938, Dell,
196p, Fast-Action Story, Gottfredson-a
                                   25.00   75.00   150.00

Series A-Mickey Mouse (In actual Motion Pictures), nd (1932?), Moviescope

	Good	Fine	N-Mint
Corp., 50p, stapled, 1 x 2½" flip book. Earliest known M. Mouse flip book	7.00	20.00	40.00

512- Mickey Mouse Wee Little Books (In open box), nn, 1934, 44p, small size, soft-c

	Good	Fine	N-Mint
M. Mouse And Tanglefoot	6.00	18.00	36.00
M. Mouse At The Carnival	6.00	18.00	36.00
M. Mouse Will Not Quit!	6.00	18.00	36.00
M. Mouse Wins The Race!	6.00	18.00	36.00
M. Mouse's Misfortune	6.00	18.00	36.00
M. Mouse's Uphill Fight	6.00	18.00	36.00
Complete set with box	43.00	130.00	260.00

Mickey Rooney and Judy Garland and How They Got Into the Movies #1493,
© Metro-Goldwyn-Mayer, 1941

1493- Mickey Rooney And Judy Garland And How They Got Into The Movies, 1941, Whit, 432p, photo-c 8.50 25.00 50.00
1427- Mickey Rooney Himself, 1939, Whit, 240p, photo-c, movie scenes, life story 8.50 25.00 50.00
532- Mickey's Dog Pluto (Disney), 1943, Whit, All Picture Comics, A Tall Comic Book, 3¼ x 8¾" 18.00 55.00 110.00

	Good	Fine	N-Mint

2113- **Midget Jumbo Coloring Book,** 1935, Sal

    20.00   60.00   120.00

21- **Midsummer Night's Dream,** 1935, EVW, movie scenes

    10.00   30.00   60.00

nn- **Minute-Man** (Mystery of the Spy Ring), 1941, Faw, Dime Action Book   25.00   75.00   150.00

710- **Moby Dick the Great White Whale, The Story Of,** 1934, Whit, 160p, photo-c, movie scenes from "The Sea Beast"

    8.50   25.00   50.00

746- **Moon Mullins and Kayo** (Kayo and Moon Mullins-inside), 1933, Whit, 320p, Frank Willard c/a   11.00   32.50   65.00

nn- **Moon Mullins and Kayo,** 1933, Whit, Cocomalt premium, soft-c, by Willard   11.00   32.50   65.00

1134- **Moon Mullins and the Plushbottom Twins,** 1935, Whit, 432p, Willard c/a   10.00   30.00   60.00

nn- **Moon Mullins and the Plushbottom Twins,** 1935, Whit, 436p, premium-no ads, 3-color, soft-c, by Frank Willard

    17.00   50.00   100.00

1058- **Mother Pluto** (Disney), 1939, Whit, 68p, hard-c

    7.50   22.50   45.00

1100B- **Movie Jokes** (From the talkies), 1938, Whit, 36p, 2½ x 3½", Penny Book   2.00   6.00   12.00

1408- **Mr. District Attorney on the Job,** 1941, Whit, 432p, flip pictures

    5.50   16.50   33.00

nn- **Musicians of Bremen, The,** nd (1930s), np (Whit), 36p, 3 x 2½", Penny Book   1.50   4.50   9.00

1113- **Mutt and Jeff,** 1936, Whit, 300p, by Bud Fisher

    12.00   35.00   70.00

1116- **My Life and Times** (By Shirley Temple), 1936, Sal, Little Big Book, hard-c, photo-c/illos   10.00   30.00   60.00

1596- **My Life and Times** (By Shirley Temple), 1936, Sal, Little Big Book, soft-c, photo-c/illos   10.00   30.00   60.00

1497- **Myra North Special Nurse and Foreign Spies,** 1938, Whit, 432p

    7.00   20.00   40.00

1400- **Nancy and Sluggo,** 1946, Whit, All Pictures Comics, Ernie Bushmiller-a   7.00   21.00   42.00

1487- **Nancy has Fun,** 1944, Whit, All Pictures Comics

    7.00   21.00   42.00

1150- **Napoleon and Uncle Elby,** 1938, Sal, 400p, by Clifford McBride

    7.00   21.00   42.00

Nancy Has Fun #1487, © United Features Syndicate, 1944

		Good	Fine	N-Mint
1166-	**Napoleon, Uncle Elby And Little Mary**, 1939, Sal, 400p, by Clifford McBride	7.00	21.00	42.00
1179-	**Ned Brant Adventure Bound**, 1940, Sal, 400p	6.00	18.00	36.00
1146-	**Nevada Rides The Danger Trail**, 1938, Sal, 400p, J. R. White-a	5.00	15.00	30.00
1147-	**Nevada Whalen, Avenger**, 1938, Sal, 400p	5.00	15.00	30.00
	Nicodemus O'Malley (See Top-Line Comics)			
1115-	**Og Son of Fire**, 1936, Whit, 432p	5.00	15.00	30.00
1419-	**Oh, Blondie the Bumsteads** (See Blondie)			
11-	**Oliver Twist**, 1935, EVW (Five Star Library), movie scenes, starring Dickie Moore (Monogram Pictures)	10.00	30.00	60.00
718-	**"Once Upon a Time. . .,"** 1933, Whit, 364p, soft-c	10.00	30.00	60.00
712-	**100 Fairy Tales for Children, The**, 1933, Whit, 288p, Circle Library	4.50	14.00	28.00
1099-	**One Night of Love**, 1935, Sal, 160p, hard-c, photo-c, movie scenes,			

	Good	Fine	N-Mint

Columbia Pictures, starring Grace Moore

| | 8.50 | 25.00 | 50.00 |

1579- **One Night of Love,** 1935, Sal, 160p, soft-c, photo-c, movie scenes, Columbia Pictures, starring Grace Moore

| | 8.50 | 25.00 | 50.00 |

1155- **$1000 Reward,** 1938, Sal, 400p

| | 5.00 | 15.00 | 30.00 |

Orphan Annie (See Little Orphan . . .)

L17- **O'Shaughnessy's Boy,** 1935, Lynn, 192p, movie scenes, w/Wallace Beery & Jackie Cooper (Metro-Goldwyn-Mayer)

| | 7.50 | 22.50 | 45.00 |

1109- **Oswald the Lucky Rabbit,** 1934, Whit, 288p

| | 11.00 | 32.50 | 65.00 |

1403- **Oswald Rabbit Plays G Man,** 1937, Whit, 240p, movie scenes by Walter Lantz

| | 12.00 | 35.00 | 70.00 |

1190- **Our Boarding House, Major Hoople and his Horse,** 1940, Sal, 400p

| | 8.00 | 24.00 | 48.00 |

1085- **Our Gang,** 1934, Sal, 160p, photo-c movie scenes, hard-c

| | 8.50 | 25.00 | 50.00 |

1315- **Our Gang,** 1934, Sal, 160p, photo-c movie scenes, soft-c

| | 8.50 | 25.00 | 50.00 |

1451- **"Our Gang" on the March,** 1942, Whit, 432p, flip pictures, Vallely-a

| | 8.50 | 25.00 | 50.00 |

1456- **Our Gang Adventures,** 1948, Whit, 288p

| | 7.00 | 21.00 | 42.00 |

nn- **Paramount Newsreel Men with Admiral Byrd in Little America,** 1934, Whit, 96p, 6¼ x 6¼", photo-c, photo ill.

| | 7.00 | 21.00 | 42.00 |

nn- **Patch,** nd (1930s), np (Whit), 36p, 3x2", Penny Book

| | 1.50 | 4.50 | 9.00 |

1445- **Pat Nelson Ace of Test Pilots,** 1937, Whit, 432p

| | 5.00 | 15.00 | 30.00 |

1411- **Peggy Brown and the Mystery Basket,** 1941, Whit, 432p, flip pictures, Henry E. Vallely-a

| | 6.00 | 18.00 | 36.00 |

1423- **Peggy Brown and the Secret Treasure,** 1947, Whit, 288p, Henry E. Vallely-a

| | 6.00 | 18.00 | 36.00 |

1427- **Peggy Brown and the Runaway Auto Trailer,** 1937, Whit, 300p, Henry E. Vallely-a

| | 6.00 | 18.00 | 36.00 |

1463- **Peggy Brown and the Jewel of Fire,** 1943, Whit, 352p, Henry E. Vallely-a

| | 6.00 | 18.00 | 36.00 |

1491- **Peggy Brown in the Big Haunted House,** 1940, Whit, 432p, Vallely-a

| | 6.00 | 18.00 | 36.00 |

	Good	Fine	N-Mint
1143-Peril Afloat, 1938, Sal, 400p	5.00	15.00	30.00
1199-Perry Winkle and the Rinkeydinks, 1937, Whit, 432p, by Martin Branner	8.50	25.00	50.00
1487-Perry Winkle and the Rinkeydinks get a Horse, 1938, Whit, 432p, by Martin Branner	8.50	25.00	50.00
Peter Pan (See Wee Little Books)			
nn-Peter Rabbit, nd(1930s), np(Whit), 36p, Penny Book, 3 x 2½"	2.00	6.00	12.00
Peter Rabbit's Carrots (See Wee Little Books)			
1100-Phantom, The, 1936, Whit, 432p, by Lee Falk & Ray Moore	20.00	60.00	120.00
1416-Phantom and the Girl of Mystery, The, 1947, Whit, 352p, by Falk & Moore	10.00	30.00	60.00

The Phantom and Desert Justice #1421,
© King Features Syndicate, 1941

	Good	Fine	N-Mint
1421-Phantom and Desert Justice, The, 1941, Whit, 432p, flip pictures, by Falk & Moore	12.50	37.50	75.00
1468-Phantom and the Sky Pirates, The, 1945, Whit, 352p, by Falk & Moore	10.00	30.00	60.00

	Good	Fine	N-Mint
1474- Phantom and the Sign of the Skull, The, 1939, Whit, 432p, by Falk & Moore	14.00	42.00	84.00
1489- Phantom, Return of the . . . , 1942, Whit, 432p, flip pictures, by Falk & Moore	12.50	37.50	75.00
1130- Phil Barton, Sleuth (Scout Book), 1937, Sal, hard-c	4.50	13.50	27.00
Pied Piper of Hamlin (See Wee Little Books)			
1466- Pilot Pete Dive Bomber, 1941, Whit, 432p, flip pictures	5.50	16.50	33.00
5783-2- Pink Panther at Castle Kreep, The, 1980, Whit, 260p, soft-c, 79 cents, B&W	.50	1.50	3.00
Pinocchio and Jiminy Cricket (See Walt Disney's . . .)			
nn- Pioneers of the Wild West (Blue-c), 1933, World, High Lights Of History Series	5.50	16.50	33.00
nn- Pioneers of the Wild West (Red-c), 1933, World, High Lights Of History Series	5.50	16.50	33.00
1123- Plainsman, The, 1936, Whit, 240p, photo-c, movie scenes (Paramount Pics.)	7.00	21.00	42.00
Pluto (See Mickey's Dog . . . & Walt Disney's . . .)			
2114- Pocket Coloring Book, 1935, Sal	20.00	60.00	120.00
1060- Polly and Her Pals on the Farm, 1934, Sal, 164p, hard-c, by Cliff Sterrett	10.00	30.00	60.00
1310- Polly and Her Pals on the Farm, 1934, Sal, soft-c	10.00	30.00	60.00
1051- Popeye, Adventures of . . . , 1934, Sal, oblong-size, E. C. Segar-a, hard-c	25.00	75.00	150.00
1088- Popeye in Puddleburg, 1934, Sal, 160p, hard-c, E. C. Segar-a	12.00	35.00	70.00
1113- Popeye Starring in Choose Your Weppins, 1936, Sal, 160p, hard-c, Segar-a	12.00	35.00	70.00
1117- Popeye's Ark, 1936, Sal, 4½ x 5½", hard-c, Segar-a	12.00	35.00	70.00
1163- Popeye Sees the Sea, 1936, Whit, 432p, Segar-a	13.00	40.00	80.00
1301- Popeye, Adventures of . . . , 1934, Sal, oblong-size, Segar-a	25.00	75.00	150.00
1318- Popeye in Puddleburg, 1934, Sal, 160p, soft-c, Segar-a	12.00	35.00	70.00
1405- Popeye and the Jeep, 1937, Whit, 432p, Segar-a	13.00	40.00	80.00

Popeye Sees the Sea #1163, © King Features Syndicate, 1936

	Good	Fine	N-Mint
1406- Popeye the Super-Fighter, 1939, Whit, All Pictures Comics, flip pictures, Segar-a	12.50	37.50	75.00
1422- Popeye the Sailor Man, 1947, Whit, All Pictures Comics	9.00	27.00	54.00
1450- Popeye in Quest of His Poopdeck Pappy, 1937, Whit, 432p, Segar c/a	13.00	40.00	80.00
1458- Popeye and Queen Olive Oyl, 1949, Whit, 288p, Sagendorf-a	8.50	25.00	50.00
1459- Popeye and the Quest for the Rainbird, 1943, Whit, Winner & Zaboly-a	10.00	30.00	60.00
1480- Popeye the Spinach Eater, 1945, Whit, All Pictures Comics	9.00	27.00	54.00
1485- Popeye in a Sock for Susan's Sake, 1940, Whit, 432p, flip pictures	10.00	30.00	60.00
1497- Popeye and Caster Oyl the Detective, 1941, Whit, 432p, flip pictures, Segar-a	12.00	35.00	70.00
1499- Popeye and the Deep Sea Mystery, 1939, Whit, 432p, Segar c/a	12.00	35.00	70.00

	Good	Fine	N-Mint

1593- **Popeye Starring in Choose Your Weppins**, 1936, Sal, 160p, soft-c,
Segar-a   12.00   35.00   70.00

1597- **Popeye's Ark**, 1936, Sal, 4½ x 5½", soft-c, Segar-a
                                                           12.00   35.00   70.00

2008- (#8)-**Popeye-Ghost Ship to Treasure Island**, 1967, Whit, 260p, 39
cents, hard-c, color illos   2.00   6.00   12.00

4063- **Popeye, Thimble Theatre Starring**, 1935, Whit, 7 x 9½", 320p, Big
Big Book, Segar c/a; (Cactus cover w/yellow logo)
                                                           38.00   115.00   230.00

4063- **Popeye, Thimble Theatre Starring**, 1935, Whit, 7 x 9½", 320p, Big
Big Book, Segar c/a; (Big Balloon-c w/red logo), (2nd printing
w/same contents as above)   43.00   130.00   260.00

5761-2- **Popeye and Queen Olive Oyl**, 1973 (1980-reprint of 1973 version),
260p, 79 cents, B&W, soft-c   .50   1.50   3.00

103- **"Pop-Up" Buck Rogers in the Dangerous Mission** (with Pop-Up
picture), 1934, BRP, 62p, The Midget Pop-Up Book w/Pop-Up in
center of book, Calkins-a   47.00   140.00   280.00

206- **"Pop-Up" Buck Rogers-Strange Adventures in the Spider-Ship,
The**, 1935, BRP, 24p, 8x9", 3 Pop-Ups, hard-c, by Dick Calkins
                                                           68.00   205.00   410.00

nn- **"Pop-Up" Cinderella**, 1933, BRP, 7½ x 9¾", 4 Pop-Ups, hard-c
w/dust jacket ($2.00)   57.00   170.00   340.00
        Without dust jacket   47.00   140.00   280.00

207- **"Pop-Up" Dick Tracy-Capture of Boris Arson**, 1935, BRP, 24p, 8 x
9", 3 Pop-Ups, hard-c, by Gould   58.00   175.00   350.00

210- **"Pop-Up" Flash Gordon Tournament of Death, The**, 1935, BRP,
24p, 8 x 9", 3 Pop-Ups, hard-c, by Alex Raymond
                                                           58.00   175.00   350.00

202- **"Pop-Up" Goldilocks and the Three Bears, The**, 1934, BRP, 24p, 8 x
9", 3 Pop-Ups, hard-c   18.00   55.00   110.00

nn- **"Pop-Up" Jack and the Beanstalk**, 1933, BRP, hard-c (50 cents), 1
Pop-Up   12.50   37.50   75.00

nn- **"Pop-Up" Jack the Giant Killer**, 1933, BRP, hard-c (50 cents), 1
Pop-Up   12.50   37.50   75.00

nn- **"Pop-Up" Jack the Giant Killer**, 1933, BRP, 4 Pop-Ups, hard-c
w/dust jacket ($2.00)   57.00   170.00   340.00
        Without dust jacket   47.00   140.00   280.00

nn- **"Pop-Up" Little Black Sambo** (with Pop-Up picture), 1934, BRP,
62p, The Midget Pop-Up Book, one Pop-Up in center of book
                                                           33.00   100.00   200.00

	Good	Fine	N-Mint

208-"Pop-Up" Little Orphan Annie and Jumbo the Circus Elephant, 1935, BRP, 24p, 8 x 9", 3 Pop-Ups, hard-c, by H. Gray

	43.00	130.00	260.00

nn-"Pop-Up" Little Red Ridinghood, 1933, BRP, hard-c (50 cents), 1 Pop-Up

	12.50	37.50	75.00

nn-"Pop-Up" Mickey Mouse, The, 1933, BRP, 34p, 6½ x 9", 3 Pop-Ups, hard-c, Gottfredson-a (75 cents) 68.00   205.00   410.00

nn-"Pop-Up" Mickey Mouse in King Arthur's Court, The, 1933, BRP, 56p, 7½ x 9¾", 4 Pop-Ups, hard-c, w/dust jacket, Gottfredson-a ($2.00)

	88.00	265.00	530.00
Without dust jacket	70.00	200.00	400.00

101-"Pop-Up" Mickey Mouse in "Ye Olden Days" (with Pop-Up picture), 1934, 62p, BRP, The Midget Pop-Up Book, one Pop-Up in center of book, Gottfredson-a   47.00   140.00   280.00

nn-"Pop-Up" Minnie Mouse, The, 1933, BRP, 36p, 6½ x 9", 3 Pop-Ups, hard-c (75 cents), Gottfredson-a   68.00   205.00   410.00

203-"Pop-Up" Mother Goose, The, 1934, BRP, 24p, 8 x 9¾", 3 Pop-Ups, hard-c   33.00   100.00   200.00

nn-"Pop-Up" Mother Goose Rhymes, The, 1933, BRP, 96p, 7½ x 9¾", 4 Pop-Ups, hard-c w/dust jacket ($2.00)

	57.00	170.00	340.00
Without dust jacket	47.00	140.00	280.00

209-"Pop-Up" New Adventures of Tarzan, 1935, BRP, 24p, 8 x 9", 3 Pop-Ups, hard-c   57.00   170.00   340.00

104-"Pop-Up" Peter Rabbit, The (with Pop-Up picture), 1934, BRP, 62p, The Midget Pop-Up Book, one Pop-Up in center of book

	27.00	80.00	160.00

nn-"Pop-Up" Pinocchio, 1933, BRP, 7½ x 9¾", 4 Pop-Ups, hard-c w/dust jacket ($2.00)

	73.00	220.00	440.00
Without dust jacket	62.00	185.00	370.00

102-"Pop-Up" Popeye among the White Savages (with Pop-Up picture), 1934, BRP, 62p, The Midget Pop-Up Book, one Pop-Up in center of book, E. C. Segar-a   43.00   130.00   260.00

205-"Pop-Up" Popeye with the Hag of the Seven Seas, The, 1935, BRP, 24p, 8 x 9", 3 Pop-Ups, hard-c, Segar-a

	43.00	130.00	260.00

201-"Pop-Up" Puss In-Boots, The, 1934, BRP, 24p, 3 Pop-Ups, hard-c

	18.00	55.00	110.00

nn-"Pop-Up" Silly Symphonies, The (Mickey Mouse Presents His . . .), 1933, BRP, 56p, 9¾ x 7½", 4 Pop-Ups, hard-c w/dust jacket ($2.00)

	83.00	250.00	500.00

The "Pop-Up" Peter Rabbit #104, © Blue Ribbon Press, 1934.

	Good	Fine	N-Mint
Without dust jacket	70.00	200.00	400.00

nn- "Pop-Up" Sleeping Beauty, 1933, BRP, hard-c (50 cents), 1 Pop-Up

	26.00	77.50	155.00

212- "Pop-Up" Terry and the Pirates in Shipwrecked, The, 1935, BRP, 24p, 8 x 9", 3 Pop-Ups, hard-c

	43.00	130.00	260.00

211- "Pop-Up" Tim Tyler in the Jungle, The, 1935, BRP, 24p, 8 x 9", 3 Pop-Ups, hard-c

	26.00	77.50	155.00

1404- Porky Pig and His Gang, 1946, Whit, All Pictures Comics, Barks-a r/4-Color 48

	13.00	40.00	80.00

1408- Porky Pig and Petunia, 1942, Whit, All Pictures Comics, flip pictures, r/4-Color 16 & Famous Gang Book of Comics

	8.50	25.00	50.00

1176- Powder Smoke Range, 1935, Whit, 240p, photo-c, movie scenes, Hoot Gibson, Harey Carey app. (RKO Radio Pict.)

	8.50	25.00	50.00

1058- Practical Pig!, The (Disney), 1939, Whit, 68p, 5 x 5½", hard-c

	7.50	22.50	45.00

758- Prairie Bill and the Covered Wagon, 1934, Whit, 384p, Hal Arbo-a

	7.00	21.00	42.00

	Good	Fine	N-Mint
nn- Prairie Bill and the Covered Wagon, 1934, Whit, 390p, premium-no ads, 3-color, soft-c, Hal Arbo-a	12.00	35.00	70.00
1440- Punch Davis of the U.S. Aircraft Carrier, 1945, Whit, 352p	5.00	15.00	30.00
nn- Puss in Boots, nd(1930s), np(Whit), 36p, Penny Book	1.50	4.50	9.00
1100B- Puzzle Book, 1938, Whit, 36p, 2½ x 3½", Penny Book	2.00	6.00	12.00
1100B- Puzzles, 1938, Whit, 36p, 2½ x 3½", Penny Book	2.00	6.00	12.00
1100B- Quiz Book, The, 1938, Whit, 36p, 2½ x 3½", Penny Book	2.00	6.00	12.00
1142- Radio Patrol, 1935, Whit, 432p, by Eddie Sullivan & Charlie Schmidt (#1)	7.50	22.50	45.00
1173- Radio Patrol Trailing the Safeblowers, 1937, Whit, 432p	6.00	18.00	36.00
1496- Radio Patrol Outwitting the Gang Chief, 1939, Whit, 432p	6.00	18.00	36.00
1498- Radio Patrol and Big Dan's Mobsters, 1937, Whit, 432p	6.00	18.00	36.00
1441- Range Busters, The, 1942, Whit, 432p, Henry E. Vallely-a	6.00	18.00	36.00
1163- Ranger and the Cowboy, The, 1939, Sal, 400p	5.00	15.00	30.00
1154- Rangers on the Rio Grande, 1938, Sal, 400p	5.00	15.00	30.00
1447- Ray Land of the Tank Corps, U.S.A., 1942, Whit, 432p, flip pictures, Hess-a	5.00	15.00	30.00
1157- Red Barry Ace-Detective, 1935, Whit, 432p, by Will Gould	7.00	21.00	42.00
1426- Red Barry Undercover Man, 1939, Whit, 432p, by Will Gould	6.00	18.00	36.00
20- Red Davis, 1935, EVW, 160p	8.00	24.00	48.00
1449- Red Death on the Range, The, 1940, Whit, 432p, Fred Harman-a (Bronc Peeler)	7.00	21.00	42.00
nn- Red Hen and the Fox, The, nd(1930s), np(Whit), 36p, 3 x 2½", Penny Book	1.50	4.50	9.00
1145- Red Hot Holsters, 1938, Sal, 400p	5.00	15.00	30.00
1400- Red Ryder and Little Beaver on Hoofs of Thunder, 1939, Whit, 432p, Harman c/a	10.00	30.00	60.00

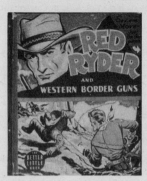

Red Ryder and Western Border Guns #1450, © NEA Service, 1942

	Good	Fine	N-Mint
1414- Red Ryder and the Squaw-Tooth Rustlers, 1946, Whit, 352p, Fred Harman-a	7.00	21.00	42.00
1427- Red Ryder and the Code of the West, 1941, Whit, 432p, flip pictures, by Harman	9.00	27.00	54.00
1440- Red Ryder the Fighting Westerner, 1940, Whit, Harman-a	9.00	27.00	54.00
1443- Red Ryder and the Rimrock Killer, 1948, Whit, 288p, Harman-a	6.00	18.00	36.00
1450- Red Ryder and Western Border Guns, 1942, Whit, 432p, flip pictures, by Harman	9.00	27.00	54.00
1454- Red Ryder and the Secret Canyon, 1948, Whit, 288p, Harman-a	6.00	18.00	36.00
1466- Red Ryder and Circus Luck, 1947, Whit, 288p, by Fred Harman	6.00	18.00	36.00
1473- Red Ryder in War on the Range, 1945, Whit, 352p, by Fred Harman	7.00	21.00	42.00
1475- Red Ryder and the Outlaws of Painted Valley, 1943, Whit, 352p, by Harman	7.50	22.50	45.00

	Good	Fine	N-Mint
702-10- Red Ryder acting Sheriff, 1949, Whit, by Fred Harman	5.00	15.00	30.00
nn- Red Ryder Brings Law to Devil's Hole, 1939, Dell, 196p, Fast-Action Story, Harman c/a	17.00	50.00	100.00
nn- Red Ryder and the Highway Robbers, 1938, Whit, 36p, 2½ x 3½", Penny Book	5.00	15.00	30.00
754- Reg'lar Fellers, 1933, Whit, 320p, by Gene Byrnes	9.00	27.00	54.00
nn- Reg'lar Fellers, 1933, Whit, 202p, Cocomalt premium, by Gene Byrnes	10.00	30.00	60.00
1424- Rex Beach's Jaragu of the Jungle, 1937, Whit, 432p	5.50	16.50	33.00
12- Rex, King of Wild Horses in "Stampede," 1935, EVW, 160p, movie scenes, Columbia Pictures	7.00	21.00	42.00
1100B- Riddles for Fun, 1938, Whit, 36p, 2½ x 3½", Penny Book	2.00	6.00	12.00
1100B- Riddles to Guess, 1938, Whit, 36p, 2½ x 3½", Penny Book	2.00	6.00	12.00
1425- Riders of Lone Trails, 1937, Whit, 300p	5.00	15.00	30.00
1141- Rio Raiders (A Billy The Kid Story), 1938, Sal, 400p	5.00	15.00	30.00
5767-2- Road Runner, The Lost Road Runner Mine, The, 1974 (1980), 260p, 79 cents, B&W, soft-c	.50	1.50	3.00
Robin Hood (See Wee Little Books)			
10- Robin Hood, 1935, EVW, 160p, movie scenes w/Douglas Fairbanks (United Artists), hard-c	12.00	35.00	70.00
719- Robinson Crusoe (The Story Of . . .), nd (1933), Whit, 364p, soft-c	9.00	27.00	54.00
1421- Roy Rogers and the Dwarf-Cattle Ranch, 1947, Whit, 352p, Henry E. Vallely-a	8.00	24.00	48.00
1437- Roy Rogers and the Deadly Treasure, 1947, Whit, 288p	7.00	21.00	42.00
1448- Roy Rogers and the Mystery of the Howling Mesa, 1948, Whit, 288p	7.00	21.00	42.00
1452- Roy Rogers in Robbers' Roost, 1948, Whit, 288p	7.00	21.00	42.00
1460- Roy Rogers Robinhood of the Range, 1942, Whit, 432p, Hess-a (1st)	8.00	24.00	48.00
1462- Roy Rogers and the Mystery of the Lazy M, 1949, Whit	6.00	18.00	36.00

Roy Rogers and the Mystery of the Lazy M #1462, © Roy Rogers, 1949

	Good	Fine	N-Mint
1476- Roy Rogers King of the Cowboys, 1943, Whit, 352p, Irwin Myers-a, based on movie	9.00	27.00	54.00
1494- Roy Rogers at Crossed Feathers Ranch, 1945, Whit, 320p, Erwin Hess-a	7.00	21.00	42.00
701-10- Roy Rogers and the Snowbound Outlaws, 1949, 3¼ x 5½"	4.50	14.00	28.00
715-10- Roy Rogers Range Detective, 1950, Whit, 2½ x 5"	4.50	14.00	28.00
nn- Sandy Gregg Federal Agent on Special Assignment, 1939, Whit, 36p, 2½ x 3½", Penny Book	4.00	12.00	24.00
Sappo (See Top-Line Comics)			
1122- Scrappy, 1934, Whit, 288p	12.00	35.00	70.00
L12- Scrappy (The Adventures Of . . .), 1935, Lynn, 192p, movie scenes	12.00	35.00	70.00
1191- Secret Agent K-7, 1940, Sal, 400p, based on radio show	5.00	15.00	30.00
1144- Secret Agent X-9, 1936, Whit, 432p, Charles Flanders-a	9.00	27.00	54.00

	Good	Fine	N-Mint
1472- Secret Agent X-9 and the Mad Assassin, 1938, Whit, 432p, Charles Flanders-a	9.00	27.00	54.00
1161- Sequoia, 1935, Whit, 160p, photo-c, movie scenes	8.50	25.00	50.00

The Shadow and the Living Death #1430,
© Condé Nast Publishing, 1940

1430- Shadow and the Living Death, The, 1940, Whit, 432p, Erwin Hess-a	30.00	90.00	180.00
1443- Shadow and the Master of Evil, The, 1941, Whit, 432p, flip pictures, Hess-a	30.00	90.00	180.00
1495- Shadow and the Ghost Makers, The, 1942, Whit, 432p, John Coleman Burroughs-c	30.00	90.00	180.00
2024- Shazzan, The Glass Princess, 1968, Whit	2.00	6.00	12.00
Shirley Temple (See My Life & Times & Story of . . .)			
1095- Shirley Temple and Lionel Barrymore Starring in "The Little Colonel," 1935, Sal, photo-c, movie scenes	10.00	30.00	60.00

	Good	Fine	N-Mint
1115- Shirley Temple in the Littlest Rebel, 1935, Sal, photo-c, movie scenes, hard-c	10.00	30.00	60.00
1595- Shirley Temple in the Littlest Rebel, 1935, Sal, photo-c, movie scenes, soft-c	10.00	30.00	60.00
1195- Shooting Sheriffs of the Wild West, 1936, Whit, 432p	5.50	16.50	33.00
1169- Silly Smyphony Featuring Donald Duck (Disney), 1937, Whit, 432p, Taliaferro-a	14.00	42.00	84.00
1441- Silly Symphony Featuring Donald Duck and His (Mis-) Adventures (Disney), 1937, Whit, 432p, Taliaferro-a	14.00	42.00	84.00
1155- Silver Streak, The, 1935, Whit, 160p, photo-c, movie scenes (RKO Radio Pict.)	7.00	21.00	42.00
Simple Simon (See Wee Little Books)			
1649- Sir Lancelot (TV Series), 1958, Whit, 280p	3.00	9.00	18.00
1112- Skeezix in Africa, 1934, Whit, 300p, Frank King-a	7.50	22.50	45.00
1408- Skeezix at the Military Academy, 1938, Whit, 432p, Frank King-a	6.00	18.00	36.00
1414- Skeezix goes to War, 1944, Whit, 352p, Frank King-a	6.00	18.00	36.00
1419- Skeezix on His Own in the Big City, 1941, Whit, All Pictures Comics, flip pictures, Frank King-a	7.00	21.00	42.00
761- Skippy, 1934, Whit. 320p, by Percy Crosby	10.00	30.00	60.00
4056- Skippy, The Story Of, 1934, Whit, 320p, 7 x 9½", Big Big Book, Percy Crosby-a	33.00	100.00	200.00
nn- Skippy, The Story Of, 1934, Whit, Phillips Dental Magnesia premium, soft-c, by Percy Crosby	8.50	25.00	50.00
1439- Skyroads with Clipper Williams of the Flying Legion, 1938, Whit, 432p, by Lt. Dick Calkins, Russell Keaton-a	6.00	18.00	36.00
1127- Skyroads with Hurricane Hawk, 1936, Whit, 432p, by Lt. Dick Calkins, Russell Keaton-a	6.00	18.00	36.00
Smilin' Jack and his Flivver Plane (See Top-Line Comics)			
1152- Smilin' Jack and the Stratosphere Ascent, 1937, Whit, 432p, Zack Mosley-a	10.00	30.00	60.00
1412- Smilin' Jack Flying High with "Downwind," 1942, Whit, 432p, Zack Mosley-a	9.00	27.00	54.00

Smilin' Jack and the Stratosphere Ascent #1152,
© New York News Syndicate, 1937

	Good	Fine	N-Mint
1416- Smilin' Jack in Wings over the Pacific, 1939, Whit, 432p, Zack			
Mosley-a	9.00	27.00	54.00
1419- Smilin' Jack and the Jungle Pipe Line, 1947, Whit, 352p, Zack			
Mosley-a	8.00	24.00	48.00
1445- Smilin' Jack and the Escape from Death Rock, 1943, Whit, 352p,			
Mosley-a	8.00	24.00	48.00
1464- Smilin' Jack and the Coral Princess, 1945, Whit, 352p, Zack			
Mosley-a	8.00	24.00	48.00
1473- Smilin' Jack Speed Pilot, 1941, Whit, 432p, Zack Mosley-a			
	9.00	27.00	54.00
2- Smilin' Jack and his Stratosphere Plane, 1938, Whit, 132p, Buddy			
Book, soft-c, Zack Mosley-a	17.00	50.00	100.00
nn- Smilin' Jack Grounded on a Tropical Shore, 1938, Whit, 36p, 2½ x			
3½", Penny Book	4.50	14.00	28.00
11- Smilin' Jack and the Border Bandits, 1941, Dell, 196p, Fast-Action			
Story, soft-c, Zack Mosley-a	18.00	55.00	110.00
745- Smitty Golden Gloves Tournament, 1934, Whit, 320p, Walter			
Berndt-a	9.00	27.00	54.00

	Good	Fine	N-Mint
nn- Smitty Golden Gloves Tournament, 1934, Whit, 204p, Cocomalt premium, soft-c, Walter Berndt-a	11.00	32.50	65.00
1404- Smitty and Herbie Lost Among the Indians, 1941, Whit, All Pictures Comics	6.00	18.00	36.00
1477- Smitty in Going Native, 1938, Whit, 300p, Walter Berndt-a	6.00	18.00	36.00
2- Smitty and Herby, 1936, Whit, 132p, 3½ x 3½", soft-c, Tarzan Ice Cream cup lid premium	17.00	50.00	100.00
9- Smitty's Brother Herby and the Police Horse, 1938, Whit, 132p, 3¾ x 3½", Buddy Book-ice cream premium, by Walter Berndt	17.00	50.00	100.00
1010- Smokey Stover Firefighter of Foo, 1937, Whit, 7¼ x 5½", 64p, Nickle Book, Bill Holman-a	8.50	25.00	50.00
1413- Smokey Stover, 1942, Whit, All Pictures Comics, flip pictures, Bill Holman-a	7.00	21.00	42.00
1421- Smokey Stover the Foo Fighter, 1938, Whit, 432p, Bill Holman-a	7.00	21.00	42.00
1481- Smokey Stover the Foolish Foo Fighter, 1942, Whit, All Pictures Comics	7.00	21.00	42.00
1- Smokey Stover the Fireman of Foo, 1938, Whit, 3¼ x 3½", 132p, Buddy Book-ice cream premium, by Bill Holman	17.00	50.00	100.00
1100A- Smokey Stover, 1938, Whit, 36p, 2½ x 3½", Penny Book	4.50	14.00	28.00
nn- Smokey Stover and the Fire Chief of Foo, 1938, Whit, 36p, 2½ x 3½", Penny Book, yellow shirt on-c	4.50	14.00	28.00
nn- Smokey Stover and the Fire Chief of Foo, 1938, Whit, 36p, Penny Book, Green shirt on-c	5.50	16.00	32.00
1460- Snow White and the Seven Dwarfs (The Story of Walt Disney's . . .), 1938, Whit, 288p	15.00	45.00	90.00
1136- Sombrero Pete, 1936, Whit, 432p	5.50	16.50	33.00
1152- Son of Mystery, 1939, Sal, 400p	5.00	15.00	30.00
1191- SOS Coast Guard, 1936, Whit, 432p, Henry E. Vallely-a	5.00	15.00	30.00
2016- (#16)-Space Ghost-The Sorceress of Cyba-3 (TV Cartoon), 1968, Whit, 260p, 39 cents, hard-c, color illos	4.50	14.00	28.00
1455- Speed Douglas and the Mole Gang-The Great Sabotage Plot, 1941, Whit, 432p, flip pictures	5.00	15.00	30.00
5779-2- Spider-Man Zaps Mr. Zodiac, 1976 (1980), 260p, 79 cents, soft-c, B&W	.50	1.50	3.00

	Good	Fine	N-Mint
1467-Spike Kelly of the Commandos, 1943, Whit, 352p			
	5.00	15.00	30.00
1144-Spook Riders on the Overland, 1938, Sal, 400p			
	5.00	15.00	30.00
768-Spy, The, 1936, Whit, 300p	7.00	21.00	42.00
nn-Spy Smasher and the Red Death, 1941, Faw, 4 x 5½", Dime Action Book	25.00	75.00	150.00
1120-Stan Kent Freshman Fullback, 1936, Sal, 148p, hard-c			
	4.50	13.50	27.00
1132-Stan Kent, Captain, 1937, Sal	4.50	13.50	27.00
1600-Stan Kent Freshman Fullback, 1936, Sal, 148p, soft-c			
	4.50	13.50	27.00
1123-Stan Kent Varsity Man, 1936, Sal, 160p, hard-c			
	4.50	13.50	27.00
1603-Stan Kent Varsity Man, 1936, Sal, 160p, soft-c			
	4.50	13.50	27.00
1104-Steel Arena, The (With Clyde Beatty), 1936, Sal, hard-c, movie scenes adapted from *The Lost Jungle*	8.00	24.00	48.00
1584-Steel Arena, The (With Clyde Beatty), 1936, Sal, soft-c, movie scenes	8.00	24.00	48.00
1426-Steve Hunter of the U.S. Coast Guard Under Secret Orders, 1942, Whit, 432p	5.00	15.00	30.00
1456-Story of Charlie McCarthy and Edgar Bergen, The, 1938, Whit, 288p	7.00	21.00	42.00
Story of Daniel, The (See Wee Little Books)			
Story of David, The (See Wee Little Books)			
1110-Story of Freddie Bartholemew, The, 1935, Sal, 4½ x 5¼", hard-c, movie scenes (MGM)	7.00	21.00	42.00
1590-Story of Freddie Bartholemew, The, 1935, Sal, 4½ x 5¼", soft-c, movie scenes (MGM)	7.00	21.00	42.00
Story of Gideon, The (See Wee Little Books)			
W714-Story of Jackie Cooper, The, 1933, Whit, 240p, photo-c, movie scenes, "Skippy" & "Sooky" movie	9.00	27.00	54.00
Story of Joseph, The (See Wee Little Books)			
Story of Moses, The (See Wee Little Books)			
Story of Ruth and Naomi (See Wee Little Books)			
1089-Story of Shirley Temple, The, 1934, Sal, 160p, hard photo-c, movie scenes	10.00	30.00	60.00
1319-Story of Shirley Temple, The, 1934, Sal, 160p, soft photo-c, movie scenes	10.00	30.00	60.00

	Good	Fine	N-Mint
1090- **Strawberry-Roan,** 1934, Sal, 160p, hard-c, Ken Maynard photo-c, movie scenes	10.00	30.00	60.00
1320- **Strawberry-Roan,** 1934, Sal, 160p, soft-c, Ken Maynard photo-c, movie scenes	10.00	30.00	60.00
Streaky and the Football Signals (See Top-Line Comics)			
5780-2- **Superman in the Phantom Zone Connection,** 1980, 260p, 79 cents, soft-c, B&W	.50	1.50	3.00

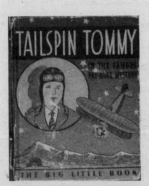

Tailspin Tommy in the Famous Pay-Roll Mystery #747,
© Stephen Slesinger, 1933

	Good	Fine	N-Mint
747- **Tailspin Tommy in the Famous Pay-Roll Mystery,** 1933, Whit, 320p, Hal Forrest-a (#1)	10.00	30.00	60.00
nn- **Tailspin Tommy the Pay-Roll Mystery,** 1934, Whit, 52p, 3½ x 5¼", premium-no ads, soft-c; another version with Perkins ad, Hal Forrest-a	13.00	40.00	80.00
1110- **Tailspin Tommy and the Island in the Sky,** 1936, Whit, 432p, Hal Forrest-a	8.00	24.00	48.00
1124- **Tailspin Tommy the Dirigible Flight to the North Pole,** 1934, Whit, 432p, H. Forrest-a	9.00	27.00	54.00

	Good	Fine	N-Mint
nn-Tailspin Tommy the Dirigible Flight to the North Pole, 1934, Whit, 436p, 3-color, soft-c, premium-no ads, Hal Forrest-a	17.00	50.00	100.00
1172-Tailspin Tommy Hunting for Pirate Gold, 1935, Whit, 432p, Hal Forrest-a	8.00	24.00	48.00
1183-Tailspin Tommy Air Racer, 1940, Sal, 400p, hard-c	8.00	24.00	48.00
1184-Tailspin Tommy in the Great Air Mystery, 1936, Whit, 240p, photo-c, movie scenes	10.00	30.00	60.00
1410-Tailspin Tommy the Weasel and His "Skywaymen," 1941, Whit, All Pictures Comics, flip pictures	7.00	21.00	42.00
1413-Tailspin Tommy and the Lost Transport, 1940, Whit, 432p, Hal Forrest-a	7.00	21.00	42.00
1423-Tailspin Tommy and the Hooded Flyer, 1937, Whit, 432p, Hal Forrest-a	8.00	24.00	48.00
1494-Tailspin Tommy and the Sky Bandits, 1938, Whit, 432p, Hal Forrest-a	8.00	24.00	48.00
nn-Tailspin Tommy and the Airliner Mystery, 1938, Whit, 196p, Fast-Action Story, soft-c, Hal Forrest-a	20.00	60.00	120.00
nn-Tailspin Tommy in Flying Aces, 1938, Dell, 196p, Fast-Action Story, soft-c, Hal Forrest-a	20.00	60.00	120.00
nn-Tailspin Tommy in Wings Over the Arctic, 1934, Whit, Cocomalt premium, Forrest-a	11.00	32.50	65.00
3-Tailspin Tommy on the Mountain of Human Sacrifice, 1938, Whit, soft-c, Buddy Book	17.00	50.00	100.00
7-Tailspin Tommy's Perilous Adventure, 1934, Whit, 132p, 3½ x 3½", soft-c, Tarzan Ice Cream cup premium	17.00	50.00	100.00
L16-Tale of Two Cities, A, 1935, Lynn, movie scenes	10.00	30.00	60.00
744-Tarzan of the Apes, 1933, Whit, 320p, by Edgar Rice Burroughs (1st)	18.00	55.00	110.00
nn-Tarzan of the Apes, 1935, Whit, 52p, 3½ x 5¼", soft-c, stapled, premium, no ad; another version with a Perkins ad	25.00	75.00	150.00
769-Tarzan the Fearless, 1934, Whit, 240p, Buster Crabbe photo-c, movie scenes, ERB	15.00	45.00	90.00
770-Tarzan Twins, The, 1934, Whit, 432p, ERB	42.00	125.00	250.00
770-Tarzan Twins, The, 1935, Whit, 432p, ERB	27.00	80.00	160.00

Tarzan, no # (Tarzan Ice Cream Cup premium),
© Edgar Rice Burroughs, 1935

	Good	Fine	N-Mint
nn- **Tarzan Twins, The,** 1935, Whit, 52p, 3½ x 5¼", premium-no ads, soft-c, ERB	28.00	85.00	170.00
nn- **Tarzan Twins, The,** 1935, Whit, 436p, 3-color, soft-c, premium-no ads, ERB	30.00	90.00	180.00
778- **Tarzan of the Screen** (The Story of Johnny Weissmuller), 1934, Whit, 240p, photo-c, movie scenes, ERB	17.00	50.00	100.00
1102- **Tarzan, The Return of,** 1936, Whit, 432p, Edgar Rice Burroughs	12.50	37.50	75.00
1180- **Tarzan, The New Adventures of,** 1935, Whit, 160p, Herman Brix photo-c, movie scenes, ERB	12.50	37.50	75.00
1182- **Tarzan Escapes,** 1936, Whit, 240p, Johnny Weissmuller photo-c, movie scenes, ERB	17.00	50.00	100.00
1407- **Tarzan Lord of the Jungle,** 1946, Whit, 352p, ERB	10.00	30.00	60.00
1410- **Tarzan, The Beasts of,** 1937, Whit, 432p, Edgar Rice Burroughs	12.00	35.00	70.00

	Good	Fine	N-Mint
1442- Tarzan and the Lost Empire, 1948, Whit, 288p, ERB	11.00	32.50	65.00
1444- Tarzan and the Ant Men, 1945, Whit, 352p, ERB	11.00	32.50	65.00
1448- Tarzan and the Golden Lion, 1943, Whit, 432p, ERB	12.00	35.00	70.00
1452- Tarzan the Untamed, 1941, Whit, 432p, flip pictures, ERB	12.00	35.00	70.00
1453- Tarzan the Terrible, 1942, Whit, 432p, flip pictures, ERB	12.00	35.00	70.00
1467- Tarzan in the Land of the Giant Apes, 1949, Whit, ERB	11.00	32.50	65.00
1477- Tarzan, The Son of, 1939, Whit, 432p, ERB	12.50	37.50	75.00
1488- Tarzan's Revenge, 1938, Whit, 432p, ERB	12.50	37.50	75.00
1495- Tarzan and the Jewels of Opar, 1940, Whit, 432p	12.50	37.50	75.00
4056- Tarzan and the Tarzan Twins with Jad-Bal-Ja the Golden Lion, 1936, Whit, 7 x 9½", 320p, Big Big Book	70.00	200.00	400.00
709-10- Tarzan and the Journey of Terror, 1950, Whit, 2½ x 5", ERB, Marsh-a	6.00	18.00	36.00
2005- (#5)-Tarzan: The Mark of the Red Hyena, 1967, Whit, 260p, 39 cents, hard-c, color illos	2.50	7.50	15.00
nn- Tarzan, 1935, Whit, 148p, soft-c, 3½ x 4", Tarzan Ice Cream cup premium, ERB (Scarce)	52.00	155.00	310.00
nn- Tarzan and a Daring Rescue, 1938, Whit, 68p, Pan-Am premium, soft-c, ERB	17.00	50.00	100.00
nn- Tarzan and his Jungle Friends, 1936, Whit, 132p, soft-c, 3½ x 3½", Tarzan Ice Cream cup premium, ERB (Scarce)	50.00	150.00	300.00
nn- Tarzan in the Golden City, 1938, Whit, 68p, Pan-Am premium, soft-c, ERB	17.00	50.00	100.00
nn- Tarzan The Avenger, 1939, Dell, 194p, Fast-Action Story, ERB, soft-c	27.00	80.00	160.00
nn- Tarzan with the Tarzan Twins in the Jungle, 1938, Dell, 194p, Fast-Action Story, ERB	27.00	80.00	160.00
1100B- Tell Your Fortune, 1938, Whit, 36p, 2½x 3½", Penny Book	2.30	7.00	14.00

	Good	Fine	N-Mint
1156-Terry and the Pirates, 1935, Whit, 432p, Milton Caniff-a (#1)			
	12.00	35.00	70.00
nn-Terry and the Pirates, 1935, Whit, 52p, 3½ x 5¾", soft-c, prem-ium, Milton Caniff-a; 3 versions: No ad, Sears ad & Perkins ad			
	15.00	45.00	90.00
1412-Terry and the Pirates Shipwrecked on a Desert Island, 1938, Whit, 432p, Milton Caniff-a	9.00	27.00	54.00
1420-Terry and War in the Jungle, 1946, Whit, 352p, Milton Caniff-a			
	8.00	24.00	48.00
1436-Terry and the Pirates the Plantation Mystery, 1942, Whit, 432p, flip pictures, Milton Caniff-a	9.00	27.00	54.00
1446-Terry and the Pirates and the Giant's Vengeance, 1939, Whit, 432p, Caniff-a	9.00	27.00	54.00
1499-Terry and the Pirates in the Mountain Stronghold, 1941, Whit, 432p, Caniff-a	9.00	27.00	54.00
4073-Terry and the Pirates, The Adventures of, 1938, Whit, 7 x 9½", 320p, Big Big Book, Milton Caniff-a	53.00	160.00	320.00
10-Terry and the Pirates Meet Again, 1936, Whit, 132p, 3½ x 3½", soft-c, Tarzan Ice Cream cup lid premium			
	23.00	70.00	140.00
nn-Terry and the Pirates, Adventures of, 1938, 36p, 2½ x 3½", Penny Book, Caniff-a	7.00	20.00	40.00
nn-Terry and the Pirates and the Island Rescue, 1938, Whit, 68p, 3¾ x 3½", Pan-Am premium	12.00	35.00	70.00
nn-Terry and the Pirates on Their Travels, 1938, 36p, 2½ x 3½", Penny Book, Caniff-a	7.00	20.00	40.00
nn-Terry and the Pirates and the Mystery Ship, 1938, Dell, 194p, Fast-Action Story, soft-c	23.00	70.00	140.00
1492-Terry Lee Flight Officer U.S.A., 1944, Whit, 352p, Milton Caniff-a			
	8.00	24.00	48.00
7-Texas Bad Man, The (Tom Mix), 1934, EVW, 160p, (Five Star Library), movie scenes	14.00	42.00	84.00
1429-Texas Kid, The, 1937, Whit, 432p	5.50	16.50	33.00
1135-Texas Ranger, The, 1936, Whit, 432p, Hal Arbo-a			
	5.50	16.50	33.00
nn-Texas Ranger, The, 1935, Whit, 260p, Cocomalt premium, soft-c, Hal Arbo-a	7.00	20.00	40.00
nn-Texas Ranger in the West, The, 1938, Whit, 36p, 2½ x 3½", Penny Book	4.00	12.00	24.00
nn-Texas Ranger to the Rescue, The, 1938, Whit, 36p, 2½ x 3½", Penny Book	4.00	12.00	24.00

	Good	Fine	N-Mint

12- Texas Rangers in Rustler Strategy, The, 1936, Whit, 132p, 3½ x
3½", soft-c, Tarzan Ice Cream cup lid premium

	15.00	45.00	90.00

Tex Thorne (See Zane Grey)

Thimble Theatre (See Popeye)

L26- 13 Hours By Air, 1936, Lynn, 128p, 5 x 7½", photo-c, movie scenes
(Paramount Pictures)

	10.00	30.00	60.00

nn- Three Bears, The, nd (1930s), np (Whit), 36p, 3 x 2½", Penny Book

	1.50	4.50	9.00

1129- Three Finger Joe (Baseball), 1937, Sal, Robert A. Graef-a

	5.00	15.00	30.00

nn- Three Little Pigs, The, nd(1930s), np(Whit), 36p, 3 x 2½", Penny
Book

	1.50	4.50	9.00

1131- Three Musketeers, 1935, Whit, 182p, 5¼ x 6¼", photo-c, movie
scenes

	10.00	30.00	60.00

1409- Thumper and the Seven Dwarfs (Disney), 1944, Whit, All Pictures
Comics

	11.00	32.50	65.00

1108- Tiger Lady, The (The life of Mabel Stark, animal trainer), 1935, Sal,
photo-c, movie scenes, hard-c

	7.00	21.00	42.00

1588- Tiger Lady, The, 1935, Sal, photo-c, movie scenes, soft-c

	7.00	21.00	42.00

1442- Tillie the Toiler and the Wild Man of Desert Island, 1941, Whit,
432p, Russ Westover-a

	8.00	24.00	48.00

1058- "Timid Elmer" (Disney), 1939, Whit, 5 x 5½", 68p, hard-c

	7.50	22.50	45.00

1152- Tim McCoy in the Prescott Kid, 1935, Whit, 160p, hard photo-c,
movie scenes

	13.00	40.00	80.00

1193- Tim McCoy in the Westerner, 1936, Whit, 240p, photo-c, movie
scenes

	12.50	37.50	75.00

1436- Tim McCoy on the Tomahawk Trail, 1937, Whit, 432p, Robert
Weisman-a

	7.00	21.00	42.00

1490- Tim McCoy and the Sandy Gulch Stampede, 1939, Whit, 424p

	7.00	21.00	42.00

2- Tim McCoy in Beyond the Law, 1934, EVW, Five Star Library,
photo-c, movie scenes (Columbia Pictures)

	14.00	42.00	84.00

10- Tim McCoy in Fighting the Redskins, 1938, Whit, 130p, Buddy
Book, soft-c

	17.00	50.00	100.00

14- Tim McCoy in Speedwings, 1935, EVW, Five Star Library, 160p,
photo-c, movie scenes (Columbia Pictures)

	14.00	42.00	84.00

Tim McCoy in Beyond the Law #2, © Engel-Van Wiseman, Inc., 1934

	Good	Fine	N-Mint
nn- Tim the Builder, nd (1930s), np (Whit), 36p, 3 x 2½", Penny Book			
	1.50	4.50	9.00
Tim Tyler (See Adventures of . . .)			
1140- Tim Tyler's Luck Adventures in the Ivory Patrol, 1937, Whit,			
432p, by Lyman Young	7.00	21.00	42.00
1479- Tim Tyler's Luck and the Plot of the Exiled King, 1939, Whit,			
432p, by Lyman Young	6.00	18.00	36.00
767- Tiny Tim, The Adventures of, 1935, Whit, 384p, by Stanley Link			
	9.00	27.00	54.00
1172- Tiny Tim and the Mechanical Men, 1937, Whit, 432p, by Stanley			
Link	8.00	24.00	48.00
1472- Tiny Tim in the Big, Big World, 1945, Whit, 352p, by Stanley Link			
	7.00	21.00	42.00
2006- (#6)-Tom and Jerry Meet Mr. Fingers, 1967, Whit, 39 cents, 260p,			
hard-c, color illos	2.00	6.00	12.00
5787-2- Tom and Jerry Under the Big Top, 1980, Whit, 79 cents, 260p,			
soft-c, B&W	.50	1.50	3.00
723- Tom Beatty Ace of the Service, 1934, Whit, 256p, George Taylor-a			
	8.00	24.00	48.00

	Good	Fine	N-Mint
nn-Tom Beatty Ace of the Service, 1934, Whit, 260p, soft-c			
	8.00	24.00	48.00
1165-Tom Beatty Ace of the Service Scores Again, 1937, Whit, 432p, Weisman-a	7.00	21.00	42.00
1420-Tom Beatty Ace of the Service and the Big Brain Gang, 1939, Whit, 432p	7.00	21.00	42.00
nn-Tom Beatty Ace Detective and the Gorgon Gang, 1938?, Whit, 36p, 2½ x 3½", Penny Book	4.00	12.00	24.00
nn-Tom Beatty Ace of the Service and the Kidnapers, 1938? Whit, 36p, 2½ x 3½", Penny Book	4.00	12.00	24.00
1102-Tom Mason on Top, 1935, Sal, 160p, Tom Mix photo-c, from Mascot serial "The Miracle Rider," movie scenes, hard-c			
	12.00	35.00	70.00
1582-Tom Mason on Top, 1935, Sal, 160p, Tom Mix photo-c, movie scenes, soft-c	12.00	35.00	70.00
Tom Mix (See Chief of the Rangers, Flaming Guns & Texas Bad Man)			
762-Tom Mix and Tony Jr. in "Terror Trail," 1934, Whit, 160p, movie scenes	12.00	35.00	70.00
1144-Tom Mix in the Fighting Cowboy, 1935, Whit, 432p, Hal Arbo-a			
	8.50	25.00	50.00
nn-Tom Mix in the Fighting Cowboy, 1935, Whit, 436p, premium-no ads, 3 color, soft-c, Hal Arbo-a	15.00	45.00	90.00
1166-Tom Mix in the Range War, 1937, Whit, 432p, Hal Arbo-a			
	8.00	24.00	48.00
1173-Tom Mix Plays a Lone Hand, 1935, Whit, 288p, hard-c, Hal Arbo-a			
	8.00	24.00	48.00
1183-Tom Mix and the Stranger from the South, 1936, Whit, 432p			
	8.00	24.00	48.00
1462-Tom Mix and the Hoard of Montezuma, 1937, Whit, 432p, H. E. Vallely-a	8.00	24.00	48.00
1482-Tom Mix and His Circus on the Barbary Coast, 1940, Whit, 432p, James Gary-a	8.00	24.00	48.00
4068-Tom Mix and the Scourge of Paradise Valley, 1937, Whit, 7 x 9½", 320p, Big Big Book, Vallely-a	32.00	95.00	190.00
nn-Tom Mix Riders to the Rescue, 1939, 36p, 2½ x 3½", Penny Book			
	4.50	14.00	28.00
6833-Tom Mix in the Riding Avenger, 1936, Dell, 244p, Cartoon Story Book, hard-c	17.00	50.00	100.00
nn-Tom Mix Avenges the Dry Gulched Range King, 1939, Dell, 196p, Fast-Action Story, soft-c	17.00	50.00	100.00

	Good	Fine	N-Mint
nn- Tom Mix in the Riding Avenger, 1936, Dell, 244p, Fast-Action Story	17.00	50.00	100.00
4- Tom Mix and Tony in the Rider of Death Valley, 1934, EVW, Five Star Library, 160p, movie scenes (Universal Pictures), hard-c	14.00	42.00	84.00
7- Tom Mix in the Texas Bad Man, 1934, EVW, Five Star Library, 160p, movie scenes	14.00	42.00	84.00
10- Tom Mix in the Tepee Ranch Mystery, 1938, Whit, 132p, Buddy Book, soft-c	17.00	50.00	100.00
nn- Tom Mix the Trail of the Terrible 6, 1935, Ralston Purina Co., 84p, 3 x 3½", premium	12.50	37.50	75.00
1126- Tommy of Troop Six (Scout Book), 1937, Sal, hard-c	4.50	13.50	27.00
1606- Tommy of Troop Six (Scout Book), 1937, Sal, soft-c	4.50	13.50	27.00
Tom Sawyer (See Adventures of . . .)			
1437- Tom Swift and His Magnetic Silencer, 1941, Whit, 432p, flip pictures	10.00	30.00	60.00
1485- Tom Swift and His Giant Telescope, 1939, Whit, 432p, James Gary-a	10.00	30.00	60.00
540- Top-Line Comics (In Open Box), 1935, Whit, 164p, 3½ x 3½", 3 books in set, all soft-c:			
Bobby Thatcher and the Samarang Emerald	12.00	35.00	70.00
Broncho Bill in Suicide Canyon	12.00	35.00	70.00
Freckles and His Friends in the North Woods	12.00	35.00	70.00
Complete set with box	44.00	132.50	265.00
541- Top-Line Comics (In Open Box), 1935, Whit, 164p, 3½ x 3½", 3 books in set; all soft-c:			
Little Joe and the City Gangsters	12.00	35.00	70.00
Smilin' Jack and His Flivver Plane	12.00	35.00	70.00
Streaky and the Football Signals	12.00	35.00	70.00
Complete set with box	44.00	132.50	265.00
542- Top-Line Comics (In Open Box), 1935, Whit, 164p, 3½ x 3½", 3 books in set; all soft-c:			
Dinglehoofer Und His Dog Adolph by Knerr	12.00	35.00	70.00
Jungle Jim by Alex Raymond	17.00	50.00	100.00
Sappo by Segar	17.00	50.00	100.00
Complete set with box	53.00	160.00	320.00

	Good	Fine	N-Mint
543- Top-Line Comics (In Open Box), 1935, Whit, 164p, 3½ x 3½", 3 books in set; all soft-c:			
Alexander Smart, ESQ by Winner	12.00	35.00	70.00
Bunky by Billy de Beck	12.00	35.00	70.00
Nicodemus O'Malley by Carter	12.00	35.00	70.00
Complete set with box	44.00	132.50	265.00
1158- Tracked by a G-Man, 1939, Sal, 400p			
	5.00	15.00	30.00
L25- Trail of the Lonesome Pine, The, 1936, Lynn, movie scenes			
	10.00	30.00	60.00
nn- Trail of the Terrible 6 (See Tom Mix . . .)			
1185- Trail to Squaw Gulch, The, 1940, Sal, 400p			
	5.00	15.00	30.00

Treasure Island #720, © Whitman Publishing Co., 1933

	Good	Fine	N-Mint
720- Treasure Island, 1933, Whit. 362p	10.00	30.00	60.00
1141- Treasure Island, 1934, Whit, 160p, 4¼ x 5¼", Jackie Cooper photo-c, movie scenes	8.00	24.00	48.00
1100B- Tricks Easy to Do (Slight of hand & magic), 1938, Whit, 36p, 2½ x 3½", Penny Book	2.00	6.00	12.00

	Good	**Fine**	**N-Mint**

1100B- Tricks You can Do, 1938, Whit, 36p, 2½ x 3½", Penny Book
| | 2.00 | 6.00 | 12.00 |

1104- Two-Gun Montana, 1936, Whit, 432p, Henry E. Vallely-a
| | 5.50 | 16.50 | 33.00 |

nn- Two-Gun Montana Shoots it Out, 1939, Whit, 36p, 2½ x 3½", Penny Book
| | 4.00 | 12.00 | 24.00 |

1058- Ugly Duckling, The (Disney), 1939, Whit, 68p, 5 x 5½", hard-c
| | 7.50 | 22.50 | 45.00 |

nn- Ugly Duckling, The, nd(1930s), np(Whit), 36p, 3 x 2½", Penny Book
| | 1.50 | 4.50 | 9.00 |

Unc' Billy Gets Even (See Wee Little Books)

1114- Uncle Don's Strange Adventures, 1935, Whit, 300p, radio star-Uncle Don Carney
| | 6.00 | 18.00 | 36.00 |

722- Uncle Ray's Story of the United States, 1934, Whit, 300p
| | 7.00 | 21.00 | 42.00 |

1461- Uncle Sam's Sky Defenders, 1941, Whit, 432p, flip pictures
| | 5.50 | 16.50 | 33.00 |

1405- Uncle Wiggily's Adventures, 1946, Whit, All Pictures Comics
| | 8.00 | 24.00 | 48.00 |

1411- Union Pacific, 1939, Whit, 240p, photo-c, movie scenes
| | 8.00 | 24.00 | 48.00 |

1189- Up Dead Horse Canyon, 1940, Sal, 400p
| | 5.00 | 15.00 | 30.00 |

1455- Vic Sands of the U.S. Flying Fortress Bomber Squadron, 1944, Whit, 352p
| | 5.00 | 15.00 | 30.00 |

1645- Walt Disney's Andy Burnett on the Trail (TV Series), 1958, Whit, 280p
| | 3.00 | 9.00 | 18.00 |

711-10- Walt Disney's Cinderella and the Magic Wand, 1950, Whit, 2½ x 5", based on Disney movie
| | 6.00 | 18.00 | 36.00 |

845- Walt Disney's Donald Duck and his Cat Troubles (Disney), 1948, Whit, 100p, 5 x 5½", hard-c
| | 7.00 | 21.00 | 42.00 |

845- Walt Disney's Donald Duck and the Boys, 1948, Whit, 100p, 5 x 5½", hard-c, Barks-a
| | 20.00 | 60.00 | 120.00 |

2952- Walt Disney's Donald Duck in the Great Kite Maker, 1949, Whit, 24p, 3¼ x 4", Tiny Tales, full color (5 cents)
| | 4.50 | 14.00 | 28.00 |

804- Walt Disney's Mickey and the Beanstalk, 1948, Whit, hard-c
| | 7.00 | 21.00 | 42.00 |

2952- Walt Disney's Mickey Mouse and the Night Prowlers, Whit, 1949, 24p, 3¼ x 4", Tiny Tales, full color (5 cents)
| | 4.50 | 14.00 | 28.00 |

	Good	Fine	N-Mint
845- **Walt Disney's Mickey Mouse and the Boy Thursday,** 1948, Whit, 5 x 5½", 100p	7.00	21.00	42.00
845- **Walt Disney's Mickey Mouse the Miracle Maker,** 1948, Whit, 5 x 5½", 100p	7.00	21.00	42.00

Walt Disney's Minnie Mouse and the Antique Chair #845,
© The Disney Co., 1948

	Good	Fine	N-Mint
845- **Walt Disney's Minnie Mouse and the Antique Chair,** 1948, Whit, 5 x 5½", 100p	7.00	21.00	42.00
1435- **Walt Disney's Pinocchio and Jiminy Cricket,** 1940, Whit, 432p	11.50	35.00	70.00
1467- **Walt Disney's Pluto the Pup** (Disney), 1938, Whit, 432p, Gottfredson-a	12.50	37.50	75.00
845- **Walt Disney's Poor Pluto,** 1948, Whit, 5 x 5½", 100p, hard-c	7.00	21.00	42.00
1066- **Walt Disney's Story of Clarabelle Cow** (Disney), 1938, Whit, 100p	7.00	21.00	42.00
1066- **Walt Disney's Story of Dippy the Goof** (Disney), 1938, Whit, 100p	7.00	21.00	42.00

	Good	Fine	N-Mint
1066-Walt Disney's Story of Donald Duck (Disney), 1938, Whit, 100p, hard-c, Taliaferro-a	7.00	21.00	42.00
1066-Walt Disney's Story of Mickey Mouse (Disney), 1938, Whit, 100p, hard-c, Gottfredson-a, Donald Duck app.	7.00	21.00	42.00
1066-Walt Disney's Story of Minnie Mouse (Disney), 1938, Whit, 100p, hard-c	7.00	21.00	42.00
1066-Walt Disney's Story of Pluto the Pup, (Disney), 1938, Whit, 100p, hard-c	7.00	21.00	42.00
2952-Walter Lantz Presents Andy Panda's Rescue, 1949, Whit, Tiny Tales, full color (5 cents)	4.50	14.00	28.00
751-Wash Tubbs in Pandemonia, 1934, Whit, 320p, Roy Crane-a	8.00	24.00	48.00
1455-Wash Tubbs and Captain Easy Hunting For Whales, 1938, Whit, 432p, Roy Crane-a	7.00	21.00	42.00
6-Wash Tubbs in Foreign Travel, 1934, Whit, soft-c, 3½ x 3½", Tarzan Ice Cream cup premium	15.00	45.00	90.00
nn-Wash Tubbs, 1934, Whit, 52p, 4 x 5½", premium-no ads, soft-c, Roy Crane-a	11.00	32.50	65.00
513-Wee Little Books (In Open Box), 1934, Whit, 44p, small size, 6 books in set			
Child's Garden of Verses	2.00	6.00	12.00
The Happy Prince (The Story Of)	2.00	6.00	12.00
Joan Of Arc (The Story Of)	2.00	6.00	12.00
Peter Pan (The Story Of)	2.50	7.50	15.00
Pied Piper Of Hamlin	2.00	6.00	12.00
Robin Hood (A Story Of . . .)	2.00	6.00	12.00
Complete set with box	17.00	50.00	100.00
514-Wee Little Books (In Open Box), 1934, Whit, 44p, small size, 6 books in set			
Jack And Jill	2.00	6.00	12.00
Little Bo-Peep	2.00	6.00	12.00
Little Tommy Tucker	2.00	6.00	12.00
Mother Goose	2.00	6.00	12.00
Simple Simon	2.00	6.00	12.00
Complete set with box	17.00	50.00	100.00
518-Wee Little Books (In Open Box), 1933, Whit, 44p, small size, 6 books in set, written by Thornton Burgess			
Betty Bear's Lesson-1930	3.00	9.00	18.00
Jimmy Skunk's Justice-1933	3.00	9.00	18.00
Little Joe Otter's Slide-1929	3.00	9.00	18.00

	Good	Fine	N-Mint
Peter Rabbit's Carrots-1933	3.50	10.00	20.00
Unc' Billy Gets Even-1930	3.00	9.00	18.00
Whitefoot's Secret-1933	3.00	9.00	18.00
Complete set with box	23.00	70.00	140.00

519- Wee Little Books (In Open Box) (Bible Stories), 1934, Whit, 44p, small size, 6 books in set, Helen Janes-a

The Story of David	1.35	5.00	10.00
The Story of Gideon	1.35	5.00	10.00
The Story of Daniel	1.35	5.00	10.00
The Story of Joseph	1.35	5.00	10.00
The Story of Ruth and Naomi	1.35	5.00	10.00
The Story of Moses	1.35	5.00	10.00
Complete set with box	13.00	40.00	80.00

1471- Wells Fargo, 1938, Whit, 240p, photo-c, movie scenes

	8.50	25.00	50.00

L18- Western Frontier, 1935, Lynn, 192p, starring Ken Maynard, movie scenes

	14.00	42.00	84.00

1121- West Pointers on the Gridiron, 1936, Sal, 148p, hard-c, sports book

	4.50	13.50	27.00

1601- West Pointers on the Gridiron, 1936, Sal, 148p, soft-c, sports book

	4.50	13.50	27.00

1124- West Point Five, The, 1937, Sal, 4¼ x 5¼", sports book, hard-c

	4.50	13.50	27.00

1604- West Point Five, The, 1937, Sal, 4¼ x 5¼", sports book, soft-c

	4.50	13.50	27.00

1164- West Point of the Air, 1935, Whit, 160p, photo-c, movie scenes

	7.00	21.00	42.00

18- Westward Ho!, 1935, EVW, 160p, movie scenes, starring John Wayne (Scarce)

	30.00	90.00	180.00

1109- We Three, 1935, Sal, 160p, photo-c, movie scenes, by John Barrymore, hard-c

	6.00	18.00	36.00

1589- We Three, 1935, Sal, 160p, photo-c, movie scenes, by John Barrymore, soft-c

	6.00	18.00	36.00

5- Wheels of Destiny, 1934, EVW, 160p, movie scenes, starring Ken Maynard

	14.00	42.00	84.00

Whitefoot's Secret (See Wee Little Books)

nn- Who's Afraid of the Big Bad Wolf, "Three Little Pigs" (Disney), 1933, McKay, 36p, 6 x 8½", stiff-c, Disney studio-a

	22.00	65.00	130.00

nn- Wild West Adventures of Buffalo Bill, 1935, Whit, 260p, Cocomalt premium, soft-c, Hal Arbo-a

	8.50	25.00	50.00

	Good	Fine	N-Mint
1096- Will Rogers, The Story of, 1935, Sal, photo-hard-c			
	7.00	21.00	42.00
1576- Will Rogers, The Story of, 1935, Sal, photo-soft-c			
	7.00	21.00	42.00

Wimpy the Hamburger Eater #1458, © King Features Syndicate, 1938

	Good	Fine	N-Mint
1458- Wimpy the Hamburger Eater, 1938, Whit, 432p, E.C. Segar-a			
	12.00	35.00	70.00
1433- Windy Wayne and His Flying Wing, 1942, Whit, 432p, flip pictures			
	5.00	15.00	30.00
1131- Winged Four, The, 1937, Sal, sports book, hard-c			
	5.00	15.00	30.00
1407- Wings of the U.S.A., 1940, Whit, 432p, Thomas Hickey-a			
	5.00	15.00	30.00
nn- Winning of the Old Northwest, The, 1934, World, High Lights of History Series			
	5.50	16.50	33.00
1122- Winning Point, The, 1936, Sal, (Football), hard-c			
	4.50	13.50	27.00
1602- Winning Point, The, 1936, Sal, soft-c	4.50	13.50	27.00

	Good	Fine	N-Mint
710-10- Woody Woodpecker Big Game Hunter, 1950, Whit, by Walter Lantz	4.50	13.50	27.00
2010- (#10)-Woody Woodpecker-The Meteor Menace, 1967, Whit, 260p, 39 cents, hard-c, color illos	2.00	6.00	12.00
2028- Woody Woodpecker-The Sinister Signal, 1969, Whit	2.00	6.00	12.00
23- World of Monsters, The, 1935, EVW, Five Star Library, movie scenes	10.00	30.00	60.00
779- World War in Photographs, The, 1934, photo-c, photo illus.	5.50	16.50	33.00

Wyatt Earp (See Hugh O'Brian . . .)

Zane Grey's King of the Royal Mounted, the Long Arm of the Law #1405,
© King Features Syndicate, 1938

	Good	Fine	N-Mint
nn- Zane Grey's Cowboys of the West, 1935, Whit, 148p, 3¾ x 4", Tarzan Ice Cream Cup premium, soft-c, Arbo-a	17.00	50.00	100.00
Zane Grey's King of the Royal Mounted (See Men Of The Mounted)			
1103- Zane Grey's King of the Royal Mounted, 1936, Whit, 432p	9.00	27.00	54.00

	Good	Fine	N-Mint
nn- Zane Grey's King of the Royal Mounted, 1935, Whit, 260p, Cocomalt premium, soft-c	12.00	35.00	70.00
1179- Zane Grey's King of the Royal Mounted and the Northern Treasure, 1937, Whit, 432p	8.50	25.00	50.00
1405- Zane Grey's King of the Royal Mounted the Long Arm of the Law, 1942, Whit, All Pictures Comics	8.50	25.00	50.00
1452- Zane Grey's King of the Royal Mounted Gets His Man, 1938, Whit, 432p	8.50	25.00	50.00
1486- Zane Grey's King of the Royal Mounted and the Great Jewel Mystery, 1939, Whit, 432p	8.50	25.00	50.00
5- Zane Grey's King of the Royal Mounted in the Far North, 1938, Whit, 132p, Buddy Book, soft-c	17.00	50.00	100.00
nn- Zane Grey's King of the Royal Mounted in Law of the North, 1939, Whit, 36p, 2½ x 3½", Penny Book	4.50	14.00	28.00
nn- Zane Grey's King of the Royal Mounted Policing the Frozen North, 1938, Dell, 196p, Fast-Action Story, soft-c	14.00	42.00	84.00
1440- Zane Grey's Tex Thorne Comes Out of the West, 1937, Whit, 432p	5.00	15.00	30.00
1465- Zip Saunders King of the Speedway, 1939, 432p, Weisman-a	5.00	15.00	30.00

ABOUT THE COVER ARTIST

Mark Bagley

Mark has been working full time in comics for four years. His first break came when he won the Marvel Try-Out Contest. Soon after he was working on some of the New Universe titles and doing numerous fill-ins as well as some annuals.

His first regular monthly assignment was on *Strikeforce: Morituri*. Next came the *New Warriors* and he has recently taken over the pencilling chores on *The Amazing Spider-Man*.

Mark makes his home in Georgia with his wife, daughter, and pick-up truck.

Cover character: Spider-Man, originally created by Steve Ditko in 1962, will be celebrating his 30th anniversary in 1992. One of today's most popular superheroes, Spider-Man appears in many different comic book titles as well as on TV.